A
DESCRIPTIVE CATALOGUE
OF
RARE AND UNEDITED
ROMAN COINS

A
DESCRIPTIVE CATALOGUE
OF
RARE AND UNEDITED
ROMAN COINS:

FROM
THE EARLIEST PERIOD OF THE ROMAN COINAGE,
TO THE EXTINCTION OF THE EMPIRE UNDER
CONSTANTINUS PALEOLOGOS.

BY
J. Y. AKERMAN, F. S. A.

IN TWO VOLUMES
VOL. II.

GYAN
. I .

Published by

Gyan Publishing House
5, Ansari Road
Daryaganj, New Delhi-110002
Phone: 011-47034999, 9811692060
E-mail: books@gyanbooks.com

Distribution Network
gyanbooks.com
India, USA, Canada, UK, Australia, France

ISBN: 978-81-212-7113-4 (Set)
978-81-212-7111-0 (PB)
First Published, 1834

2nd Impression 2024

Printed at: Gyan Press, Delhi.

**A DESCRIPTIVE CATALOGUE OF RARE
AND UNEDITED ROMAN COINS (VOL. II)**
Author: J. Y. AKERMAN

A

DESCRIPTIVE CATALOGUE

OF

RARE AND UNEDITED

ROMAN COINS:

FROM

THE EARLIEST PERIOD OF THE ROMAN COINAGE,
TO THE EXTINCTION OF THE EMPIRE UNDER
CONSTANTINUS PALEOLOGOS.

WITH NUMEROUS PLATES FROM THE ORIGINALS.

BY

J. Y. AKERMAN, F. S. A.

IN TWO VOLUMES.—VOL. II.

LONDON:

EFFINGHAM WILSON, ROYAL EXCHANGE.

M.DCCC.XXXIV.

ROMAN COINS.

TREBONIANUS GALLUS.

[Caius Vibius Trebonianus Gallus, was born at Meninx, an island on the coast of Africa, about the year of Rome 960 (A. D. 207). He was General of the Roman army under Trajan Decius, whom he caused to be assassinated, when the soldiers proclaimed him emperor, in 1004 (A. D. 251). Gallus was murdered by his soldiers at Interamna in Umbria, when about to march from that city to suppress the revolt of the army in Maesia, which had proclaimed Aemilian emperor, in the year of Rome 1007 (A. D. 254)].

STYLE:——IMP. GALLVS. AVG.——IMP. VIB. TREB. GALLVS. AVG.——IMP. C. GALLVS. AVG.——IMP. CAES. TREBONIANVS. AVG. [On reverse, P. P.]——IMP. C. TREB. GALLVS. AVG.——IMP. C. VIB. GALLVS. AVG.——IMP. C. VIB. TREB. GALLVS. AVG.——IMP. C. (*or* CAE. *or* CAES.) C. VIB. (*or* VIBIVS.) TREB. (*or* TREBONIANVS.) GALLVS. AVG. [On reverse, sometimes, P. P. *or* PRINCEPS. IVVENTVTIS.] ——IMP. C. GALLVS. P. FELIX. AVG.——IMP. C. C. VIB. TREB. GALLVS. P. F. AVG.

Gold -	R 6
Silver medallions - - - - - - - - - - - - - - -	R 8
Silver - - - - - - - - - - - - - - - - - - -	C
,, with the name of Gallus only - - - - - - - - -	R 6
,, quinarii - - - - - - - - - - - - - - - -	R 6
Brass medallions - - - - - - - - - - - - - - -	R 6
,, with the heads of Gallus and Volusian - - -	R 8
First brass - - - - - - - - - - - - - - - - -	S
Second brass - - - - - - - - - - - - - - - -	S

SILVER MEDALLIONS.

1.

MONETA. AVG.   The three Monetæ, standing.

2.

MONETA. AVGG.   A similar type.

No. 2 is rather larger than the other, and is therefore more valuable. It equals in circumference the first brass of this period, and is of fine fabric.

GOLD AND SILVER, USUAL SIZE, WITH RARE REVERSES.

1.

ADVENTVS. AVG.   The emperor on horseback. - - - - - AR

2.

AETERNITAS. AVGG.   A woman standing, holding a bird on a globe. - - - - - - - - - - - - - - - - AU & AR

3.

ARMONA. AVGG. A woman standing, holding a javelin inverted. AU

4.

Same legend.   A woman standing, with the skin of an elephant on her head. (See *Khell*). - - - - - - - - - - - - - AU

5.

CONCORDIA. AVGG.   Concord, standing. - - - - - AU & AR

6.

Same legend.   Concord seated, holding a patera and a double cornucopia. - - - - - - - - - - - - - - - - AU

7.

FELICITAS. PVBLICA.   Felicity, standing. - - - - - - AU

8.

Same legend.   A similar type.   (A *quinarius*).   (*Plate ix, No. 1.*)   AR

9.

IVNO. MARTIALIS.   Statue of Juno, seated, within a temple.   AR

10.

LIBERALITAS. AVGG.   Liberality, standing. - - - - - AR

11.

LIBERTAS. AVGG.   Liberty, standing. - - - - - - - AU

12.

Same legend.   A similar type.   (Very small size). - - - - - AU

13.

PAX. AETERNA.   Peace, standing. - - - - - - - AU & AR

14.

PIETAS. AVGG. Piety standing, her arms extended. (*Plate ix, No.2*). AU

15.

Same legend.   A similar type.   (Very small size). - - - - - AU

16.

PROVIDENTIA. AVGG.   Providence, standing. - - - - - AR

17.

ROMAE. AETERNAE.   Rome, seated. - - ⁻ - - - - - AR

18.

SAECVLVM. NOVVM.   A statue, within a temple. - - - - AR

19.

SALVS. AVGG.   Hygeia standing, feeding a serpent.   - - - AU

20.

VIRTVS. AVGG.   A military figure standing, holding a spear and a
buckler. - - - - - - - - - - - - - - - - - AU

21.

VOTIS. DECENNALIBVS. within a garland. - - - - - - AR

In gold, Nos. 5, 6, 7, are the rarest.   In silver, the quinarius No. 8 is
much the rarest; and No. 9 is rarer than the remaining numbers.

BRASS MEDALLIONS.

1.

ADVENTVS. AVGG.   Trebonianus and Volusian, on horseback;
preceded by Victory, and followed by two soldiers, bearing standards.

2

ARN. ASI.   Apollo standing, with radiated head, holding a laurel
branch and a bow.

3.

FORTVNAE. REDVCI.   The two emperors in the toga, sacrificing
before a temple: five figures assisting.

4.

IVNONI. MARTIALI.   Statue of Juno, seated within a temple; a
peacock at her feet.

5.

P. M. TR. P. IIII. COS. II. P. P. S. C.   The emperor sacrificing on an
altar.

6.

SAECVLI. FELICITAS.   The four Seasons, with their attributes.

7.

SALVS. AVGG. S. C.   Hygeia standing, feeding a serpent out of a
patera.

8.

SECVRITAS. AVGG.   Security, leaning on a column.

9.

VOTIS. DECENNALIBVS. within a laurel garland.

No. 4 is the rarest.   The next in rarity are Nos. 2, 3, and 6; then
No. 1.

[TREBONIANUS AND VOLUSIANUS].

1.

IMP. GALLVS. AVG. IMP. VOLVSIANVS. AVG. The laureated heads of Trebonianus and Volusian, face to face.—*Rev.* ADVENTVS. AVGG. The two emperors, on horseback; preceded by Victory, and followed by two soldiers, bearing standards.

2.

Same legend. The two emperors on horseback.

3.

FORTVNAE. REDVCI. The two emperors in the toga, sacrificing before a temple, in which is a statue of Fortune seated: five other figures assisting.

4.

IVNONI. MARTIALI. Statue of Juno, seated, within a circular temple; a peacock at her feet. (*Tanini*, page 28.)

5.

PONTIF. MAX. TR. P. II. COS. II. ET. COS. The two emperors in a quadriga, crowned by Victory: on each side of the horses, a foot soldier; several figures following, bearing palm branches.

6.

CONCORDIA. AVGVSTORVM. The heads of Trebonianus and Volusianus, face to face.—*Rev.* VOTA. PVBLICA. The two emperors sacrificing before a temple, in which is a statue of Jupiter seated; several figures assisting: a bull at the foot of the altar.

No. 2 is the least rare. The other numbers are valued by Mionnet at 200 francs each.

FIRST BRASS, WITH RARE REVERSES.

1.

ADVENTVS. AVG. The emperor on horseback.

2.

IVNONI. MARTIALI. Juno, seated.

3.

Same legend. Statue of Jupiter, seated, within a circular temple.

4.

LIBERALITAS. AVGG. Liberality, standing.

5.

LIBERTAS. AVGG. Liberty, standing.

6.

MARTI. PACIFERO. Mars, standing.

7.

PAX. AVGG. Peace, standing.

8.

P. M. TR. P. IIII. COS. II. P. P. The emperor in the toga, sacrificing.

9.

PRINC. IVVENTVTIS.   A woman seated, holding a laurel branch.

10.

VOTIS. DECENNALIBVS. within a laurel garland.

Nos. 1, 7, and 8, are the rarest.   No. 2 is the least rare.

SECOND BRASS, WITH RARE REVERSES.

1.

PAX. AVGG.   Peace, standing.

2.

PRINCIPI. IVVENTVTIS. A woman seated, holding a laurel branch;
her left elbow resting on a lyre.

3.

VOTIS. DECENNALIBVS. within a laurel garland.

No. 2 is the rarest.

VOLUSIANUS.

[Caius Vibius Afinius Trebonianus Gallus Veldumnianus Volusianus,
the son of Trebonianus, was born in the year of Rome ——.   He was
created Caesar by his father in 1004 (A. D. 251); and after the death
of Hostilian in the following year, was made Augustus, and associated
with Trebonianus in the empire.   Volusian was assassinated by the
soldiers, at the same time as his father, in the year 1007 (A. D. 254)].

STYLE:——C. VIBIVS. VOLVSIANVS. CAES. [On reverse, some-
times, PRINCEPS. IVVENTVTIS.]——C. VIB. VOLVSIANVS. NOB.
C.——IMP. VOLVSIANVS. AVG.——IMP. GALLVS. VO-
LVSIANVS. AVG.——IMP. C. VIB. VOLVSIANVS.——IMP.
C. VIB. GALL. VOLVSIANVS.——IMP. C. VOLVSIANVS.
AVG.——IMP. CAE. VIB. VOLVSIANVS. AVG. [On re-
verse, sometimes, PRINCEPS. IVVENTVTIS.]——IMP. C. (or CAE. or
CAES.) C. VIB. VOLVSIANVS. AVG. [On reverse, sometimes,
P. P. or PRINCEPS. IVVENTVTIS.]——IM. (or IMP.) C. V. AF. GAL.
VEND.   [In the place of VELDvmnianvs, as in inscriptions.]
——VOLVSIANVS. AVG.——IMP. C. VOLVSIANVS. P. F.
AVG.——IMP. C. C. VOLVSIANVS. P. F. AVG.

The name TREBONIANVS is found only on Greek coins of this prince.
All those which bear the titles PIVS. FELIX. are colonial.

Gold - - - - - - - - - - - - - - - - - - R 6

Silver medallions, of small size - - - - - - - - - - R 1

Silver, of the usual size   - - - - - - - - - - - - - S
  „ with the names, c. v. af. gal. vend. - - - - - - - R 4
Brass medallions   - - - - - - - - - - - - - - - R 8
First brass   - - - - - - - - - - - - - - - - - S
Second brass - - - - - - - - - - - - - - - - - S

SILVER MEDALLION.

FELICITAS. PVBLICA.   Felicity standing, leaning on a column,
  holding a caduceus and a spear transversely.

GOLD AND SILVER, USUAL SIZE, WITH RARE REVERSES.

[The coins marked with a (*) bear the name, c. v. af. gal. vend.]

1.
AETERNITAS. AVGG.   A woman standing, holding in her right
  hand a bird on a globe. - - - - - - - - - - - - AU
  There is a modern fabrication of this coin.

2.
ADVENTVS. AVGG.   The emperor, on horseback. - - - - AR

3.
APOLL. SALVTARI.   Apollo, standing. - - - - - AU & AR

4.
CONCORDIA. AVGG.   Concord, standing.   - - - - - - AU

5.
Same legend.   Concord, seated. - - - - - - - - - - AU

6.
FELICITAS. PVBLICA.   A woman standing, holding a caduceus and
  a cornucopia. - - - - - - - - - - - - - - AU & AR

7.
IVNONI. MARTIALI.   A statue within a temple. - - AU & AR

8.
LIBERALITAS. AVGG.   Liberality, standing. - - - - - AR

9.
MARTI. PACIFERO.   Mars, standing. - - - - - - - *AR

10.
MARTEM. PROPVGNATOREM.   Mars, marching. - - - AR

11.
MONETA. AVGG.   The three Monetæ, standing. - - - - - AU

12.
PAX. AVG.   Peace, standing. - - - - - - - - - - *AR

13.
PIETAS. AVGG.   Piety standing before an altar, her hands raised.
  (*Plate ix, No.3*). - - - - - - - - - - - - - - - AU

14.

PIETAS. AVGG. A similar type; and a star. - - - - - - AU

15.

Same legend. A similar type; but without the star. (Small size). AU

16.

PVDICITIA. AVG. Pudicitia, seated. - - - - - - - - AR

17.

ROMAE. AETERNAE. AVG. Rome, seated. - - - - - AR

18.

SAECVLVM. NOVVM. A statue seated, within a temple. - - AU

19.

SALVS. AVGG. Hygeia standing, feeding a serpent. - - - AU

20.

VBERITAS. A woman, standing. - - - - - - - - - *AR

21.

VOTIS. DECENNALIBVS. within a garland. - - - - - - AR

In gold, No. 11 is much rarer than the other types; and No. 15 is the least rare. In silver, Nos. 2 and 10 are the rarest; excepting those marked with a star, which are valued by Mionnet at twenty francs each.

BRASS MEDALLIONS.

1.

ADVENTVS. AVGG. Trebonianus and Volusianus on horseback, preceded by Victory, and followed by two soldiers, bearing standards.

2.

FORTVNAE. REDVCI. The two emperors sacrificing before a temple, within which is the statue of Fortune: several figures assisting.

3.

LIBERALITAS. AVGVSTORVM. S. C. Liberality, standing.

4.

MONETA. AVGG. The three Monetæ, standing, with their attributes.

5.

VIRTVS. AVGVSTORVM. The emperor standing between two ensigns, sacrificing on an altar : behind, a soldier placing a garland on his head; a figure playing on the flute, and a victim.

6.

VIRTVS. AVGVSTORVM. Volusian, sacrificing; a soldier placing a garland on his head; another soldier and a flute player: below, a tripod and Victory.

Nos. 2, 5, and 6, are the rarest: the next in rarity is No. 1.

FIRST BRASS, WITH RARE REVERSES.

1.

CONCORDIA. AVGG.   Concord, seated.

2.

IVNONI. MARTIALI. Statue of Juno, seated, within a circular temple.

3.

LIBERALITAS. AVGG.   Liberality, standing.

4.

P. M. TR. P. IIII. COS. II. P. P.   The emperor in the toga, sacrificing.

5.

PIETAS. AVGG.   Piety standing, with her arms extended.

6.

C. VIB. VOLVSIANO. NOB. C.   Bare head of Volusianus.—*Rev.*
PRINCIPI. IVVENTVT. (*or* IVVENTVTIS.).   A military
figure, standing.

7.

Another, of a similar description, but with C. VIBIO. VOLVSIANO.
CAES.

8.

IMP. CAE. (*or* CAES.) C. VIB. VOLVSIANO. AVG.   Laureated
head of Volusianus.—*Rev.* PRINCIPI. IVVENTVTIS. A military
figure, standing.

9.

VOTIS. DECENNALIBVS. within a garland.

Nos. 2, 3, 6, 7, 8, 9, are the rarest types; and of these, Nos. 6 and 8
are the rarest.

FIRST BRASS, WITH RARE REVERSES.

1.

IVNONI. MARTIALI.   Statue of Juno, seated, within a temple.

2.

VOTIS. DECENNALIBVS. within a laurel garland.

No. 2 is the rarest.

AEMILIANUS.

[Marcus (or Caius) Julius Aemilius Aemilianus was born in Mauretania,
of obscure parents, about the year of Rome 961 (A. D. 208). This
usurper was governor of Maesia and Pannonia under Trebonianus,
and was proclaimed emperor by the legions of those provinces in 1006
(A. D. 253). He was murdered by his troops near Spoletta in Umbria,
when about to contest the empire with Valerian, who had been
elected by the legions of Rhetia and Noricum, in the year of Rome
1007 (A. D. 254)].

STYLE:——IMP. M. AEM. AEMILIANVS.——IMP. CAES. AE-
MILIANVS. AVG.——IMP. C. AEMIL. AEMILIANVS. AVG.
——IMP. C. M. AEMIL. AEMILIANVS. AVG.——IMP. CAES.
C. IVL. AEMILIANVS. PIVS. AVG.——IMP. AEMILIANVS.
PIVS. FEL. AVG. [On reverse, sometimes, P. P.]——IMP. M.
AEMIL. AEMILIANVS. P. F. AVG.——IMP. C. (or CAES.)
AEMILIANVS. P. (or PIVS.) F. (or FEL.) AVG.—— IMP.
CAES. C. IVL. AEMILIANVS. PIVS. FEL. AVG.

Gold -	R 8
Silver -	R 1
First brass - - - - - - - - - - - - - - - - - - -	R 5
Second brass - - - - - - - - - - - - - - - - - - -	R 6
Third brass (?) - - - - - - - - - - - - - - - - - -	R 6

GOLD AND SILVER, WITH RARE REVERSES.

1.
APOLLO. CONSERVAT. Apollo naked, standing. - - AU & AR
There are modern fabrications of this type in both metals.

2.
CONCORDIA. AVGG. Two hands, joined. - - - - - - AR

3.
DIANAE. VICTRICI. Diana, standing. - - - - - AU & AR

4.
ERCVL. (or ERCVLI.) *sic.* VICTORI. Hercules, standing. - AR

5.
Same legend. A similar type. - - - - - - - - - - - AU
Doubts have been entertained as to the authenticity of this type in
gold.

6.
IOVI. CONSERVAT. Jupiter presenting a globe to the emperor. AR

7.
Same legend. Jupiter, and the emperor, standing; the latter in the
toga. - - - - - - - - - - - - - - - - - - - AR.

8.
MARTI. PACIF. Mars, standing. - - - - - - - - - AR

9.
MARTI. PROPVGNAT. Mars, marching. - - - - - - AR

10.
PAX. AVG. Peace, marching. - - - - - - - - - - - AR

11.
PACI. AVG. Peace, leaning on a column. - - - - - - - AR

12.

P. M. TR. P. I. P. P.   The emperor in a military habit, standing, holding an ensign and a spear. - - - - - - - - - - AR

13.

ROMAE. AETERN.   Rome, standing. - - - - - - - - AR

14.

SALVS. AVG.   Hygeia, standing, feeding a serpent. - - - - AR

15.

SPES. PVBLICA.   Hope, marching. - - - - - - - - - AR

16.

VICTORIA. AVG.   Victory, marching. - - - - - - - - AR

17.

VIRTVS. AVG.   A military figure, standing. - - - - - - AR

18.

VOTIS. DECENNALIBVS. within a garland. - - - - - - AR

The above types, in gold, are valued by Mionnet at 1000 francs each. In silver, No. 6 is the rarest; No. 2 is the next in rarity; then Nos. 1, 7, 13, 14, and 18.

FIRST BRASS, WITH RARE REVERSES.

1.

AETERNITAS. AVGG.   A woman standing, holding a globe surmounted by a phoenix.

2.

APOLL. CONSERVAT.   Apollo standing, holding a laurel branch in his right hand; his left resting on a lyre.

3.

FIDES. EXERCIT.   A similar type.

4.

IOVI. CONSERVAT.   Jupiter, standing.

5.

IOVI. CONSERVATORI.   Jupiter and the emperor, standing.

6.

PACI. AVG.   Peace, holding an olive branch and the hasta, and leaning on a column.

7.

P. M. TR. POT.   The emperor, in a military habit, standing at an altar: an ensign in the field.

8.

ROMA. AETERNA.   Rome standing, holding a bird on her right hand.

9.

ROMAE. AETERN.   Rome standing, holding a globe surmounted by a phoenix.

10.

SPES. PVBLICA. Hope, marching.

11.

VICTORIA. AVG. Victory, marching.

12.

VIRTVS. AVGVSTI. A military figure, standing.

13.

VIRTVS. AVG. A similar type.

14.

VOTIS. DECENNALIBVS. within a laurel garland.

Nos. 5 and 11 are much the rarest; they are valued by Mionnet at 100 francs each, and the remaining types at eighty francs each. No. 14 is least rare.

SECOND BRASS, WITH RARE REVERSES.

1.

P. M. TR. POT. A veiled figure, sacrificing.

2.

P. M. TR. POT. A military figure, sacrificing; an ensign on one side.

3.

P. M. TR. P. P. P. A similar type.

4.

SPES. PVBLICA. Hope, marching.

5.

VOTIS. DECENNALIBVS. within a garland.

These types are valued by Mionnet at fifty francs each.

THIRD BRASS, WITH RARE REVERSES.

1.

AEQVITAS. AVG. Equity, standing.

2.

MART. PROPVGT. (*sic*). Mars, with spear and shield.

These types are equally rare; but query if they be really third brass?

CORNELIA SUPERA.

[Caia (or Cnea) Cornelia Supera, the wife of Aemilianus, is known only by her coins. Some authors have supposed this lady to have been the wife of the younger Valerian, while others have assigned her to Trebonianus. Eckhel, however, has proved that she was the wife of Aemilianus. As to the prenomen, most writers agree that the C. which occurs on her Latin coins, and the Γ. which is generally found on those bearing Greek legends, signifies Caia: indeed some of the latter bear the letters ΓΑΙ. Vaillant and Sestini have each published a coin of Supera, with the letters ΓΝ. which in all probability signifies Cnea].

Silver - R 8
Third brass - - - - - - - - - - - - - - - - - - - R 8

SILVER.

1.
CONCORDIA. AVG.   Concord, seated.   *(Musei Theupoli)*.

2.
IVNO. REGINA.   Juno standing: on some, a peacock at her feet. *(Plate ix, No. 4.)*

3.
VENVS. VICTRIX.   Venus, standing.   *(Mus. Theup.)*

4.
VESTA.   Vesta standing, holding the palladium and the hasta.

5.
Same legend.   Vesta standing, holding a patera and the hasta.

Nos. 1, 2, and 3, are much the rarest.   One of the other numbers ("Vesta") brought 13*l.* 15*s.* at the sale of the Henderson collection in 1830.

THIRD BRASS.

1.
CONCORDIA. AVG.   Concord, seated.   *(Mus. Theup.)*

2.
VENVS. VICTRIX.   Venus-Victrix, standing.   *(Ibid)*.

These are valued by Mionnet at seventy-two francs each.

VALERIANUS.

[Publius Licinius Valerianus was born of an illustrious family, in the year of Rome 943 (A.D. 190).   Having been directed by Trebonianus to march against Aemilianus, he was saluted emperor by the army he commanded.   The deaths of Aemilianus and Trebonianus secured to him the possession of the empire in 1007 (A. D. 254).   Valerian was taken prisoner by the Persians in 1013 (A. D. 260), by whom he was most barbarously treated.   He died, as is supposed, about three years afterwards].

STYLE:——IMP. VALERIVS. AVG.   [On reverse, sometimes, P. P.]
—— IMP. (*or* IMPERATOR.) LICINIVS. VALERIANVS. AVG.——IMP. P. LIC. VALERIANVS. AVG.——IMP. C. (*or*

CAES.) P. LIC. VALERIANVS. AVG. [On reverse, often, p. p.]——IMP. VALERIANVS. P. (*or* PIVS.) AVG.——IMP. C. VALERIANVS. P. AV.——VALERIANVS. P. F. AVG. ——IMP. VALERIANVS. P. F. AVG.——IMP. LIC. VALE-RIANVS. PI. FE. AVG.——IMP. C. P. VALERIANVS. P. F. AVG.——IMP. C. P. LIC. (*or* LICI. *or* LICINIVS.) VALERIA-NVS. P. F. AVG. [On reverse, sometimes, p. p. *or* GERMANICVS. MAX. *or* RESTITVT. GENER. HVMANI. *or* RESTITVTOR. ORBIS. *or* RESTITVT. ORIENTIS].

Gold - R 6
„ quinarii - - - - - - - - - - - - - - - - R 7
Silver medallions - - - - - - - - - - - - - R 8
„ of the usual size - - - - - - - - - - - - C
„ quinarii - - - - - - - - - - - - - - - R 3
Brass medallions - - - - - - - - - - - - - R 1
First brass - - - - - - - - - - - - - - - - R 1
Second brass - - - - - - - - - - - - - - - - S
Third brass - - - - - - - - - - - - - - - - C

SILVER MEDALLIONS.
1.
AEQVITAS. AVGG. The three Monetæ, standing.
2.
ADLOCVTIO. AVGVSTORVM. The usual type. (Large size).
3.
MONETA. AVGG. The three Monetæ, standing.

Mionnet values No. 1 at 200 francs; No. 2 at 300 francs; and No. 3 at from 60 to 100 francs, according to the diameter.

GOLD AND SILVER, OF THE USUAL SIZE.
1.
AETERNITAS. AVGG. The Sun, naked, standing. - - - - AU
2.
AETERNITATI. AVGG. Saturn veiled, standing, holding the harpa. AU
3.
ANNONA. AVGG. Annona, standing. - - - - - - AU & AR
4.
APOLLINI. CONSERVA. Apollo standing, with laurel branch and lyre. - - - - - - - - - - - - - AU & AR

5.

APOLLINI. PROPVG.   Apollo standing, fitting an arrow to his bow.
                                                            AR
6.

BONAE. FORTVNAE.   Fortune, standing.   - - - - - - AR
7.

CONCOR. LEGG.   Concord, seated. - - - - - - - - - AR
8.

CONCORD. AVGG.   Concord, seated. - - - - - - - - AR
9.

CONCORDIA. AVGG.   Valerian and Gallienus, standing. - - AR
10.

Same legend.   Concord, standing. - - - - - - - - - AR
11.

CONCORDIA. MILITVM.   A woman, holding two standards. - AR
12.

CONSERVAT. AVGG.   Apollo and Diana, standing.   - - - AR
13.

Same legend.   Apollo, standing.   - - - - - - - - - AR
14.

DEO. VOLKOAN.   A statue of Vulcan, within a temple.   - - AR
15.

DIANA. LVCIFERA.   Diana standing, holding a torch. - - - AR
16.

FELICITAS. AVGG.   Felicity standing, with her attributes.   - AU
17.

FELICITAS. SAECVLI.   Diana Lucifera, walking. - - - - AR
18.

FORTVNA. REDVX.   Mercury, standing. - - - - - - - AR
19.

GALLIENVS. CVM. EXER. SVO.   Statue of Jupiter-Victor on a
    cippus, on which is inscribed IOVI. VICTORI.   - - - - AR
20.

GERMANICVS. MAX. TER.   A trophy, and two captives. - - AR
21.

IOVI. CONSERVAT.   Jupiter, standing. (A *quinarius*).   - - AR
22.

IOVI. CONSERVATORI.   A similar type. - - - - - - - AU
23.

Same legend.   A similar type. (A *quinarius*).   - - - - - AR
24.

IOVI. PACATORI. ORBIS.   Jupiter seated, an eagle at his feet. AR

25.

IOVI. STATORI. Jupiter-Stator, standing. - - - - - - AR

26.

LIBERALITAS. AVGG. Liberality, standing. - - - AU & AR

27.

Same legend. The two emperors seated, and a figure standing. - AR

28.

Same legend. Liberality, seated. *(Mionnet)*. - - - - - - AR

29.

LIBERALITAS. AVG. (*or* AVGG. III.) Liberality, standing.
AU & AR

30.

ORIENS. AVGG. The Sun, standing. - - - - . - - AU & AR

31.

Same legend. A similar type. (A *quinarius*). - - - - - - AU

32.

PACATORI. ORBIS. Jupiter seated, holding a patera; an eagle at his feet. - - - - - - - - - - - - - - - - - - - AR

33.

PIETAS. AVG. (*or* AVGG.) The two emperors, sacrificing. - AR

34.

Same legend. A female seated, and three children standing. *(Mion.)* AR

35.

PIETATI. AVGG. A woman leaning on a column, and holding the hasta pura. - - - - - - - - - - - - - - - - AR

36.

P. M. TR. P. V. COS. IIII. P. P. Two figures, standing. - - AR

37.

Same legend. The emperor seated, holding a globe and a staff. - AR

38.

RELIGIO. AVGG. Diana in her hunting habit, standing. - - AR

39.

RESTITVT. (*or* RESTITVTI.) (*sic*) GENER. HVMANI. The Sun, standing. - - - - - - - - - - - - - - - AR

40.

RESTITVT. ORIENTIS. A woman crowning the emperor. - AR

41.

RESTITVTOR. ORBIS. The emperor raising up a female. AU & AR

42.

ROMAE. AETERNAE. Roma-Victrix seated on a shield. - AU & AR

43.

SAECVLI. FELICITAS. Felicity, standing. - - - - - - AR

44.

SECVRIT. PERPET. Security, leaning on a column. - - - AR

45.

TEMPORVM. FELICITAS. Felicity, standing. - - - - - AR

46.

VENVS. VICTRIX. Venus-Victrix, standing. - - - - - AR

47.

VICTORIA. AVGG. Victory standing, with palm-branch and garland.
AU

48.

VICTORIA. AVGG. Victory, standing: her right hand on a buckler;
her left, holding a palm-branch. - - - - - - - - - AU

49.

Same legend. Victory, marching. - - - - - - - - - AU

50.

VICTORIAE. AVGG. Victory in a biga. - - - - - - - AR

51.

Same legend. A military figure, standing. - - - - - - AR

52.

VICT. PART. Victory standing: a captive on the ground. - - AR

53.

VICTORIA. GERMANICA. Victory, standing. - - - - - AR

54.

VICTORIA. PARTHICA. Victory placing a garland on the head of
the emperor. - - - - - - - - - - - - - - - AR

55.

Same legend. Victory trampling on a captive. - - - - - AR

56.

VIRTVS. AVGG. Two military figures. - - - - - - - AR

57.

Same legend. A military figure standing, holding a Victory and a
spear. - - - - - - - - - - - - - - - - - - AU

58.

Same legend. A military figure standing; his right hand resting on a
buckler, his left holding a javelin inverted. - - - - - - AU

59.

VOTA. ORBIS. Two Victories: a buckler suspended from a tree:
above, S. C. - - - - - - - - - - - - - - - AR

60.

VOTIS. DECENNALIBVS. within a garland. - - - - - - AR

In gold, Nos. 4, 57, and 58, are the rarest. In silver, Nos. 2, 9, 15,
18, 20, 21, 23, 28, 34, 38, 50, and 60, are the rarest.

BRASS MEDALLIONS.

1.

ADLOCVTIO. AVGVSTORVM. The usual type.

2.

FELICITAS. TEMPORVM. Valerian crowned by Victory, in a quadriga, between his two sons: a foot soldier on each side.

3.

LIBERALITAS. AVG. Valerian and Gallienus seated on an estrade, and three figures standing; a third figure ascending the estrade.

4.

MONETA. AVGG. The three Monetæ, standing.

5.

ORIENS. AVGG. S. C. The Sun, standing.

6.

PONTIFEX. MAX. TR. P. P. P. A quadriga, driven by a child: two figures behind, supporting a Victory, holding an amphora; below, two captives.

7.

VICTORIA. AVGVSTORVM. The two emperors standing, supporting a globe surmounted by a figure of Victory; on each side a soldier, holding a standard.

8.

VICTORIA. AVGG. Victory standing, holding a garland and a palm branch.

Nos. 4, 5, and 8, are much less rare than the others.

[VALERIANUS AND GALLIENUS].

1.

CONCORDIA. AVGG. The heads of the emperors, face to face.—*Rev.* ADLOCVTIO. AVGVSTORVM. The usual type.

2.

CONCORDIA. AVGVSTORVM. The heads of the emperors, face to face.—*Rev.* ADVENTVS. AVGVSTORVM. The two emperors on horseback, preceded by Victory and a soldier; four standards.

3.

PIETAS. AVGG. (*or* AVGVSTORVM.) The heads of the emperors. —*Rev.* ADVENTVS. AVGG. The emperors on horseback, preceded by Victory, and followed by two standard bearers.

The first of these is much the rarest.

FIRST BRASS, WITH RARE REVERSES.

1.

APOLLONI. CONSERVA.   Apollo, standing, with laurel branch and lyre.

2.

APOLLINI. PROPVG.   Apollo bending his bow.

3.

CONCORDIAE. AVGG.   Concord standing, holding a patera and a double cornucopia.

4.

CONCORDIAE. EXERCITVS.   A similar type.

5.

FELICIT. AVGVSTORVM.   The emperor and two other figures, in a triumphal car, attended by soldiers.

6.

FELICITAS. AVGG.   Felicity, standing.

7.

FELICITAS. SAECVLI.   A similar type.

8.

FIDES. MILITVM.   A woman, holding two standards.

9.

IOVI. CONSERVATORI.   Jupiter, standing.

10.

LIBERALITAS. AVGG.   Liberality, standing.

11.

LIBERALITAS. AVG. III.   A similar type.   (*Vaillant*).

12.

MARTI. PACIF.   Mars, marching.

13.

ORIENS. AVGG.   The Sun, standing.

14.

P. M. TR. P. V. COS. IIII. P. P.   The emperor, seated on a curule chair, holding a sceptre and a globe.

15.

RESTITVTOR. ORBIS.   The emperor, raising up a figure.

16.

SALVS. AVGG.   Salus, standing before an altar from which a serpent is rising.

17.

VICTORIA. AVGG.   Victory, standing; her right hand on a buckler, and a palm branch in her left.

18.

VICTORIA. AVGG. Victory standing, holding a palm branch and a garland.

19.

Same legend. Victory, marching.

20.

VICTORIA. GERMANICA. Victory standing, holding in her right hand a palm branch; a captive at her feet.

21.

VESTA. Vesta standing, holding a patera and the hasta, transversely.

22.

VIRTVS. AVGG. A military figure, standing.

23.

VOTIS. DECENNALIBVS. within a garland.

No. 5 is an extremely rare type. Nos. 7, 12, and 16, are very rare; and Nos. 2, 3, 6, 11, 13, 14, 15, 20, and 21, are rarer than the other numbers.

SECOND BRASS, WITH RARE REVERSES.

1.

FELICITAS. AVGG. Felicity, standing.

2.

LIBERALITAS. AVGG. Liberality, standing.

3.

ORIENS. AVGG. The Sun, standing.

4.

P. M. TR. P. V. COS. II. P. P. The emperor, seated, holding a globe and a sceptre.

5.

VENVS. VICTRIX. Venus-Victrix, standing.

6.

VICTORIA. GERM. Victory, standing: a captive on the ground.

7.

VIRTVS. AVGG. A military figure, standing.

8.

VOTIS. DECENNALIBVS. within a laurel garland.

No. 5 is much rarer than the others.

[VALERIANUS AND GALLIENUS].

1.

CONCORDIA. AVGVSTOR. The laureated heads of Valerianus and Gallienus, face to face.—*Rev.* ADLOCVTIO. AVGVSTORUM. The usual type.

2.

ADVENTVS. AVGG. Valerianus and Gallienus on horseback, preceded by Victory, and followed by a soldier.

3.

LIBERALITAS. AVGVSTOR. (*or* AVGG. I.) The emperors, seated on an estrade, distributing the congiarium to several figures below.

The first number is the rarest.

THIRD BRASS, WITH RARE REVERSES.

1.

P. M. TR. P. V. COS. IIII. P. P. Two figures standing, in the toga; between them, two spears and two bucklers.

2.

RELIGIO. AVGG. Diana, standing: in the field, Q.

3.

VENVS. VICTRIX. Venus, standing.

4.

VICTORIA. AVGGIT. *(sic)* GERM. Victory, standing; a captive on the ground.

No. 1 is the rarest; and No. 4 is rarer than the other numbers.

[VALERIANUS AND GALLIENUS].

1.

CONCORDIA. AVGVSTORVM. The heads of Gallienus and Valerianus, face to face.—*Rev.* LIBERALITAS. AVGVSTOR. Liberality standing, with her attributes.

MARINIANA.

[This lady, the supposed wife of Valerianus, is known only by her coins, from the types of which, it is supposed that she died in the beginning of the reign of Valerianus, and that she was consecrated. Vaillant and Beauvais say, that she was taken prisoner with Valerianus, and that she died in captivity, but without any authority: indeed this is disproved by her coins struck at Viminacium, a city of Mæsia. On these coins she is styled DIVA. MARINIANA, as on those struck at Rome, and they bear the date xv., that of the city, which corresponds with the 1007th year of Rome. Mionnet remarks, that it is not certain that Mariniana was the wife of Valerianus: the coins described below may belong to his mother, his daughter, or his sister. The discovery of some colonial coin may perhaps, at a future time, decide this question].

STYLE:——DIVA. MARINIANA.

Silver (base) - - - - - - - - - - - - - - - - - - - R 1
" quinarii - - - - - - - - - - - - - - - - - R 3
First brass - - - - - - - - - - - - - - - - - - - R 4
Second brass - - - - - - - - - - - - - - - - - - - R 2
Third brass - - - - - - - - - - - - - - - - - - - R 2

BASE SILVER, WITH RARE REVERSES.
1.
CONSECRATIO. A peacock, with its tail spread.
2.
Same legend. Mariniana, borne by a peacock in full flight.
3.
Same legend. A similar type. (A *quinarius*).
4.
FELICITAS. DEORVM. Felicity, standing. *(Mionnet)*.

FIRST BRASS.
1.
CONSECRATIO. A peacock, with its tail spread.
2.
Same legend. Mariniana, borne by a peacock, as on the silver.
No. 2 is much the rarest.

SECOND BRASS.
1.
CONSECRATIO. A peacock, as on the first brass.
2.
Same legend. Mariniana, borne by a peacock, as on the first brass.
No. 2 is the rarest.

THIRD BRASS.
1.
CONSECRATIO. A peacock.
2.
Same legend. A peacock, bearing the empress.
No. 2 is the rarest.

GALLIENUS.

[Publius Licinius Gallienus, the son of the emperor Valerianus, was born in the year of Rome 971 (A. D. 218), and associated in the empire with his father, with the titles of Caesar and Augustus, in 1006 (A. D. 253). After the capture of Valerian by the Persians, he reigned alone until the year 1021 (A. D. 268), when he was murdered by his officers near Milan, whither he had gone to quell the insurrection under Aureolus, the commander of his cavalry].

STYLE:——IMP. LICIN. GALLIEN. (*or* GALLIENVS.)——IMP. C. LIC. GALLIENVS.——GALLIENVS. AVG. [On reverse, sometimes, P. P. *or* CONSERVAT. PIETAT. *or* INVICTVS.]——IMP. GALLIENVS. AVG. [On reverse, sometimes, P. P. RESTIT. (*or* RESTITVTOR.) GALLIAR.] —— IMP. LICI. GALLIENVS. AVG. —— IMP. C. GALLIENVS. AVG. —— IMP. C. LICI. (*or* LICIN.) GALLIENVS. AVG.——IMP. C. (*or* CAES.) P. LIC. GALLIENVS. AVG. [On reverse, sometimes, P. P. *or* RESTITV. GENER. HVMANI. *or* RESTITVT. ORIENTIS.] —— GALLIENVS. P. AVG.——IMP. GALLIENVS. P. (*or* PIVS.) AVG. [On reverse P. P. (*or* RESTIT. *or* RESTITVTOR.) GALLIAR.]——GALLIENVS. P. F. AVG. [On reverse, often, P. P. and sometimes, GERMANICVS. MAX. (*or* OPTIMVS. PRINCEPS. *or* RESTIT. *or* RESTITVTOR.) GALLIAR.] —— IMP. GALLIENVS. P. (*or* PIVS.) F. (*or* FEL. *or* FELIX.) AVG. [On reverse, sometimes, P. P. (*or* GERMANICVS. MAXIMVS. *or* RESTIT. GALLIAR.)]——IMP. P. LIC. GALLIENVS. P. F. AVG. [On reverse, GERMANICVS. MAX.]——IMP. C. P. LIC. GALLIENVS. P. F. AVG. [On reverse, sometimes, P. P. (*or* OPTIMVS. PRINCEPS.)] —— GALLIENVS. AVG. GERM. —— IMP. GALLIENVS. AVG. GERM. [On reverse, P. P. (*or* GERMANICVS. MAX. *or* RESTITVTOR. GALLIAR.]——IMP. GALLIENVS. P. F. AVG. GER. (*or* GERM.) [On reverse P. P.]——IMP. C. GALLIENVS. P. F. AVG. GERM.——GALLIENA. AVGVSTA.

The coin which has this last title is somewhat puzzling. It does not bear the head of a female, but that of Gallienus, with a wheaten garland.

Gold medallions - - - - - - - - - - - - - - - - - R 6
  ,, of the usual size - - - - - - - - - - - - - R 2
  ,, with the legend GALLIENAE. AVGVSTAE. - - - - - - - R 6
  ,, quinarii   - - - - - - - - - - - - - - - - R 3

Silver medallions - - - - - - - - - - - - - R 6
Base silver, of usual size - - - - - - - - - - - -- - - C
Restored coins - - -' - - - - - - - - - - - - - R 1
Quinarii - - - - - - - - - - - - - - - - - R 2
Brass medallions (washed) - - - - - - - - - - - - R 2
First brass - - - - - - - - - - - - - - - - - R 1
Second brass - - - - - - - - - - - - - - - - - S
Third brass - - - - - - - - - - - - - - - - - - VC

GOLD AND SILVER MEDALLIONS.

1.

CHORS. (sic) TERTIA. PRETORIA. (sic). The emperor in a military dress, holding the hasta pura, standing in the midst of four ensigns. - - - - - - - - - - - - - - - - - AU

2.

FIDES. MILITVM. A woman, holding two ensigns. - - - AU

3.

IOVIS. STATOR. Jupiter-Stator, standing. In the field, ς. - AR

4.

LIBERALITAS. AVG. III. Three figures, seated. - - - - AR

5.

OB. CONSERVATOREM. PATRIAE. Hygeia, feeding a serpent. AR

6.

OB. CONSERVATOREM. SALVTIS. A similar type. - - - AR

7.

OB. REDDIT. LIBERT. A woman, standing. - - - - - AR

8.

MONETA. AVG. The three Monetæ, standing. - - - - - AR

9.

Another, of a smaller size. - - - - - - - - - - - AR

10.

Another, still smaller. - - - - - - - - - - - - - AR

11.

P. M. TR. P. IMP. VI. COS. V. P. P. The emperor on horseback, holding a spear, preceded by a soldier, and followed by Victory, who places a garland on his head. - - - - - - - - - AU

12.

VIRTVS. AVGVSTORVM. The emperor, seated on a coat of mail, Victory placing a garland on his head : before, a military figure ; behind, two standards. (Tanini). - - - - - - - - - AR

13.

VIRTVS. GALLIENI. AVGVSTI. The emperor in the paludamentum, marching, with a labarum in each hand. *(Tanini),* - - - AU

In gold, Nos. 2 and 12 are valued at 200 francs; Nos. 10 at 400; and No. 1 at 300 francs, by Mionnet. In silver, No. 8 is much the rarest; and Nos. 3 and 4 are much less rare than the remainder.

[GALLIENUS AND VALERIANUS].

PIETAS. AVGVSTORVM. The laureated heads of Gallienus and Valerianus; each with the paludamentum, and face to face.—*Rev.* MONETA. AVGG. The three Monetæ, standing. - - - AR

Mionnet values this medallion at 200 francs.

[GALLIENUS AND SALONINA].

CONCORDIA. AVGG. Heads of the emperor and empress.—*Rev.* PIETAS. FALERI. A tree, a goat, and two children. - - AR

Mionnet values this rare medallion at 300 francs.

[GALLIENUS AND SALONINUS].

CONCORDIA. AVGVSTORVM. The heads of Gallienus and Saloninus, face to face; the first laureated, the other bare.—*Rev.* ADVENTVS. AVGG. Three helmed figures on horseback, their right hands raised: Victory preceding them, and several foot soldiers bearing standards: two captives on the ground. - - - - - - - AR

Valued at the same price as the preceding.

GOLD AND BILLON, USUAL SIZE, WITH RARE REVERSES.

1.

ABVNDANTIA. AVG. A river-god seated on the ground; S. P. Q. R. - B

2.

ADVENTVS. AVG. The emperor on horseback. - - - AU & B

3.

AETERNITAS. AVG. Remus and Romulus, suckled by the wolf. B

4.

Same legend. The Sun, standing. - - - - - - - - - - AU

5.

AETERNITATI. AVG. Two hands joined. - - - - - - - - B

6.

APOLLINI. CONS. AVG. A centaur. - - - - - - - - - B

7.

Same legend. A griffin. - - - - - - - - - - - - - - B

8.

APOLLINI. PROPVG. Apollo bending his bow. - - - - - - B

9.

BONAE. FORTVNAE. Fortune, standing. - - - - - - - B

10.

BON. EVENTVS. Bonus-Eventus, standing. - - - - - - - B

11.

COHH. *(sic)* PRAET. VI. *(or* VII.) P. VI. F. A lion walking. - B

12.

CONCORDIA. AVG. Concord, standing. - - - - - - - AU

13.

CONCORDIA. AVGG. Two hands joined. - - - - - - - B

14.

Same legend. Concord, seated. - - - - - - - - - - - B

15.

CONCORDIA. EXERCIT. Concord, standing. - - - - - - B

16.

CONSECRATIO. An eagle. *(Tanini)*. - - - - - - - - B

17.

CONSERVATOR. AVG. Æsculapius, standing. - - - - - B

18.

CONSERVAT. PIETAT. The emperor raising up a child. In the
exergue, XII. - - - - - - - - - - - - - - - - B

19.

COS. IIII. P. P. The emperor in a quadriga. - - - - - - - B

20.

DEO. AVGVSTO. Laureated head of Augustus. - - - - - AU

21.

DEO. MARTI. Statue of Mars within a temple. - - - - - - B

22.

DIANAE. CONS. AVG. Diana standing, and a stag. - - - - B

23.

DONA. AVG. Mercury standing, and a ram. - - - - - - B

24.

FELICITAS. AVG. *(or* AVGG.) Felicity, standing. - - - - AU

25.

FELICITAS. SAECVLI. Felicity, standing. - - - - - AU

26.

FIDES. AVG. Mercury, standing. In the exergue, P X V. - - B

27.

FIDES. MILITVM. A woman, holding two standards. - - - AU

28.

Same legend. A woman, holding a standard and a spear. (A *quina-rius*). - AU

29.

FIDEI. MILITVM. (*or* EQVITVM.) within a garland. - - AU & B

30.

FIDEI. PRAET. Three Prætorian standards. - - - - AU & B

31.

Same legend. A figure standing, and an ensign. - - - - - AU

32.

FID. PRAETORIANORVM. A woman standing, holding a patera and a cornucopia: behind, a legionary eagle. - - - - - - B

33.

FORTVNA. REDVX. Fortune, standing. - - - - - - - AU

34.

Same legend. Fortune, standing. (A *quinarius*). - - - - - AU

35.

Same legend. Mercury, standing. - - - - - - - - - - AU

36.

HERCVLI. CONS. AVG. A boar. In the exergue, Є. - - - B

37.

IANO. PATRI. Janus standing, holding a patera and the hasta pura.
AU

38.

INVICTVS. The Sun standing: a star in the field. - - - - - B

39.

IO. CANTAB. Jupiter, standing. - - - - - - - - - - B

40.

IOVI. CONSERVA. Jupiter, standing. - - - - - - - AU

41.

IOVI. CONSERV. AVG. A goat. - - - - - - - - - - B

42.

IOVI. CONSERVATORI. Jupiter and the emperor, standing. - B

43.

IOVI. CONSERVATORI. Jupiter, standing. (A *quinarius*). - B

44.

IOVI. CRESCENTI. The infant Jupiter riding on a goat. - - - B

45.

IOVIS. STATOR. Jupiter-Stator, standing. - - - - - AU & B

46.

IOVI. VLTORI. Jupiter, hurling a thunderbolt. - - - AU & B

47.

IVBENTVS. *(sic)* AVG. Jupiter, standing. - - - - - - - B

48.

LAETITIA. AVGG. Laetitia, standing. - - - - - - - AU

49.

LEG. I. ADI. VI. P. VI. F. Capricorn. - - - - - - - B

50.

Same legend. A pegasus. - - - - - - - - - - - - - B

51.

LEG. I. AVG. VI. P. VI. F. Mars, standing. - - - - - - B

52.

LEG. I. ITAL. VI. P. VI. F. A boar. - - - - - - - - - B

53.

LEG. I. ITAL. VII. P. VII. F. Capricorn. - - - - - - - B

54.

LEG. I. MIN. VI. P. VI. F. Minerva, standing. - - - - - B

55.

LEG. II. ADI. VI. P. VI. F. A pegasus. - - - - - - - - B

56.

LEG. II. ITAL. VI. P. VI. F. Romulus and Remus suckled by the
wolf. - - - - - - - - - - - - - - - - - - - B

57.

LEG. II. PART. V. P. V. F. A centaur. - - - - - - - - B

58.

LEG. II. PART. VI. P. VI. F. A centaur. - - - - - - - B

59.

LEG. III. ITAL. VII. P. VII. F. A stork. - - - - - - - B

60.

LEG. IIII. FL. VI. P. VI. F. A lion. - - - - - - - - - B

61.

LEG. V. MAC. VI. (*or* VII.) P. VI. (*or* VII.) F. Victory: an eagle. B

62.
LEG. VII. CL. VII. P. VII. F.   An ox.   - - - - - - - - B

63.
LEG. VIII. AVG. VI. P. VI. F.   A similar type.   - - - - - B

64.
LEG. X. GERM. VI. P. VI. F.   A bull.   - - - - - - - - B

65.
LEG. XI. CL. VI. P. VI. F.   Neptune, standing.   - - - - - B

66.
LEG. XIII. GEM. VI. P. VI. F.   Victory, and a lion.   - - - - B

67.
LEG. XIIII. GEM. VI. P. VI. F.   Capricorn.   - - - - - - B

68.
LEG. IIXX. VI. (or VII.) P. VI. (or VII.) F.   Capricorn.   - - B

69.
LEG. XX. VI. P. VI. F.   Capricorn.   - - - - - - - - B

70.
Same legend.   Neptune, standing. - - - - - - - - - - B

71.
LEG. XXII. VI. P. VI. F.   Capricorn.   - - - - - - - B

72.
LEG. XXX. VLP. VI. P. VI. F.   Capricorn. - - - - - - - B

73.
Same legend.   Neptune, standing.   - - - - - - - - - B

74.
LIB. AVG. T.   A woman, standing.   - - - - - - - AU & B

75.
LIBERAL. AVGG.   A similar type: P. or T. in the exergue.   - AU

76.
LIBERALITAS. AVG.   A woman standing : in the field, S. C.
(Large size).   See *Vaillant.* - - - - - - - - - - B

77.
Same legend.   A woman standing, with tessera and cornucopia.   - AU

78.
LIBERALITAS. AVG. IIII.   A similar type.   *(Mediobarba).*   AU

79.
LIBERO. P. CONS. AVG.   A panther.   - - - - - - - B

80.
LIBERTAS. AVGG.   Liberty, standing.   - - - - - - AU & B

81.

MARTI. PROPVGNATORI.   Mars, and a captive.   - - AU & B

82.

MONETA. AVG.   Moneta, standing.   - - - - - - - - - B

83.

NEPTVNO. CONS. AVG.   A sea-horse.   - - - - - - - - B

84.

OB. LIBERTAT. REC.   A woman, standing.   - - - - - - AU

85.

ORIENS. AVG.   The emperor and a woman, standing: a garland.   B

86.

ORIENS. AVGG.   The Sun, standing.   - - - - - - - - AU

87.

PACATORI. ORBIS.   Jupiter seated, and an eagle.   - - - - - B

88.

PAX. AVGG.   Peace, standing.   (A *quinarius*).   - - - - - AU

89.

PAX. FUNDATA.   A trophy, and two captives.   - - - - - - B

90.

PERPETVITATI. AVG.   A woman, standing.   - - - - - - B

91.

PIETAS. AVG.   Piety, standing before an altar: P. in the exergue.   AU

92.

PIETAS. AVGG.   A male and female figure, standing: a tripod.   B

93.

PIETAS. SAECVLI.   A similar type.   *(Mionnet)*.   - - - - - B

94.

P. M. TR. COS. P. P.   The emperor, standing: two river-gods.
(Vaillant).   - - - - - - - - - - - - - - - - - - B

95.

P. M. TR. P. V. COS. IIII. P. P.   Two figures, standing; between
them, two bucklers and two spears.   - - - - - - - - - B

96.

P. M. TR. P. VII. COS. P. P.   The emperor standing, and two river-
gods. - AU

97.

P. M. TR. P. VII. COS. IIII. P. P.   Mars marching, with a trophy
and a spear.   - - - - - - - - - - - - - - - - - B

98.

P. M. TR. P. X. COS. IIII. P. P.   The emperor, in a quadriga.   - B

99.
P. M. TR. P. XII. COS. VI. P. P.   The emperor, on horseback.   -   B

100.
PRINCIPI. IVVENT.   The emperor standing, in a military habit, holding a globe and a spear.   - - - - - - - - - - B

101.
PROVIDENTIA. AVG.   Mercury, standing. - - - - - - - B

102.
PROVIDENTIA. AVGG.   Providence, standing. - - - - - AU

103.
Same legend.   A woman, holding a standard.   - - - - - - AU

104.
RESTITVTOR. GALLIARVM.   The emperor, raising up a woman.   B

105.
RESTITVT. GENER. HVMANI.   A figure, with radiated head, standing.   - - - - - - - - - - - - - - - - - B

106.
RESTITVTOR. ORBIS.   The emperor standing, raising up a woman kneeling before him.   - - - - - - - - - - - - B

107.
RESTITVT. ORIENTIS.   A woman, crowning the emperor. - - B

108.
SAECVLARES. AVG.   A goat. - - - - - - - - - - - B

109.
SALVS. AVG.   Hygeia and the emperor, standing - - - - - B

110.
SECVRIT. (or SECVRITAS.) ORBIS.   Security, seated.   - - AU

111.
SECVRIT. PERPET.   Security, standing.   - - - - - AU & B

112.
SECVRIT. PERPET. S. P. Q. R.   A lion, within a garland.   - AU

113.
SISCIA. AVG.   A female seated, and a river-god seated on the ground.   - - - - - - - - - - - - - - - - B

114.
SOLI. CONS. AVG.   A bull: in the exergue, XI.   - - - - - B

115.
SOLI. INVICTO.   The Sun, standing. - - - - - - - - AU

116.
SPES. PVBLICA.   Hope. - - - - - - - - - - - - - B

117.

S. P. Q. R. A lion walking; an eagle on his back; the whole within a garland. *(Khell).* - - - - - - - - - - - - - AU

118.

S. P. Q. R. OPTIMO. PRINCIPI. within a garland. - - - - - B

119.

TRIB. POT. COS. P. P. Mars standing, and Venus reclining. - AU

120.

TRIB. POT. VIII. COS. III. A similar type. - - - - - - B

121.

VBERITAS. AVG. A woman, standing. (A *quinarius*). - - AU

122.

VBIQVE. PAX. Victory, in a biga. - - - - - - - - - AU

123.

GALLIENAE. AVGVSTAE. The head of Gallienus, with a wheaten garland.—*Rev.* VBIQVE. PAX. Victory, in a biga. - - AU

124.

VENVS. VICTRIX. Venus-Victrix, standing. - - - - - - AU

125.

VICT. GAL. AVG. Three Victories, standing. - - - - - - B

126.

VICT. GAL. AVG. III. A similar type. - - - - - - - B

127.

Same legend. Victory, marching. - - - - - - - - - - B

128.

VICT. GALLIENI. AVG. A soldier, trampling on a captive. - B

129.

VICT. (*or* VICTORIA.) GERMANICA. Victory on a globe: a captive seated on each side. - - - - - - - - - - - - B

130.

Same legend. Victory, trampling on a captive. - - - - - - AU

131.

VICTOR. AVG. Victory, inscribing III. - - - - - - - - B

132.

VICTORIA. AVG. Victory crowning the emperor, who holds the hasta and a globe. *(Plate ix, No. 5).* - - - - - - AU & B

133.

Same legend. Victory, standing. - - - - - - - - - - AU

134.

VICTORIA. AVG. III. Three Victories, standing. - - - - - B

135.

VICTORIA. AVG. III. (*or* IIII.) Victory, marching. - - - AU

136.

VICTORIA. AVG. III. (or IIII.) with T. in the field. - - - AU

137.

VICTORIA. AVGG. Victory standing, her right hand resting on a buckler, and her left holding a palm-branch. - - - - - AU

138.

Same legend. A similar type. (A *quinarius*). - - - - - - - B

139.

Same legend. Victory flying, full-faced. - - - - - - - - AU

140.

VICTORIA. GALL. AVG. III. Victory, marching. - - AU & B

141.

VICTORIA. GERM. (or G. M.) Victory, standing: a captive on the ground. (A *quinarius*). - - - - - - - - - - - B

142.

VICTORIA. GERMAN. Victory crowning the emperor. - - - B

143.

VICTORIA. NEPT. A similar type. - - - - - - - - - B

144.

VICTORIA. PART. Victory, presenting a garland to the emperor. B

145.

VICTORIAE. AVGG. Two Victories holding a globe, surmounted by a figure of Victory. - - - - - - - - - - - - - AU

146.

Same legend. Victory, in a biga. - - - - - - - - - AU

147.

VICTORIAE. AVGG. II. GERM. Victory, marching: a captive. B

148.

VIRT. GALLIENI. AVG. Hercules, standing. - - - - - AU

149.

VIRTVS. AVG. A youthful head, helmeted. - - - - AU & B

150.

VIRTVS. AVGG. (or AVG.) Virtue, standing. - - - - - AU

151.

Same legend. A military figure, bearing a trophy and a spear. - AU

152.

VIRTVS. AVGVSTI. Hercules, standing. - - - - - - - AU

153.

VIRTVS. VALERI. A trophy. - - - - - - - - - - - B

154.

VOTA. DECENNALIA. Victory, inscribing. - - - - - - B

155.

VOTIS. DECENNALIB. (*or* DECENNALIBVS.) within a garland.

AU & B

156.

VOT. (*or* VOTIS.) X. ET. XX. within a garland. - - - - - AU

In gold, No. 123 is by far the rarest. The next in rarity are Nos. 96, 117, and 119; then Nos. 2, 12, 15, 20, 24, 25, 27, 30, 37, 84, 112, 148, 149, and 155. Nos. 4, 28, 33 to 35, 40, 45, 46, 48, 80, 88, 91, 102, 111, 115, 121, 122, 124, 130, 132, 135 to 137, 139, 145, 146, 150, and 151, are the least rare. In silver, Nos. 38 and 76 are extremely rare. Nos. 1, 98, 113, and 149, are next in rarity. Nos. 5, 16, 18, 19, 39, 44, 56, 61, 65, 72, 73, 85, 87, 93, 94, 118, 120, 125, 126, 132, 134, 143, and 144, are much rarer than the remaining numbers.

[COINS IN BILLON, RESTORED BY GALLIENUS].

AUGUSTUS. 1.

DIVO. AVGVSTO. Head of Augustus, with radiated crown.—*Rev.* CONSECRATIO. An eagle with expanded wings.

2.

Same legends. An altar with the fire kindled.

3.

DIVO. AVGVSTO. The head of Augustus, with radiated crown.— *Rev.* IVNONI. MARTIALI. A statue of Juno, within a temple.

No. 3 is extremely rare, and valued by Mionnet at 100 francs.

VESPASIANUS.

DIVO. VESPASIANO. Head of Vespasian, with radiated crown.— *Rev.* CONSECRATIO. An eagle; or an altar, as above.

TITUS.

DIVO. TITO. Head of Titus, with radiated crown.—*Rev.* CONSE-CRATIO. An eagle; or an altar.

NERVA.

DIVO. NERVAE. The same types as the preceding.

These are rather more rare than those of Vespasian and Titus.

TRAJANUS. 1.

DIVO. TRAIANO. Head of Trajan, with radiated crown.—*Rev.* CON-SECRATIO. An eagle; or an altar, with the fire kindled.

2.

IMP. TRAIANO. PIO. FEL. AVG. P. P. Head of Trajan.—*Rev.* VIA. TRAIANO. A woman seated on the ground, leaning on a wheel, and holding a whip.

This coin, supposed unique, is at present in the cabinet of Mons. Gosselin of Paris. It was originally in the collection of d'Ennery and in his catalogue is stated to be of a fabric similar to those of the time of Trajanus Decius or Gallienus. Mionnet, however, is of opinion that it belongs to an earlier reign than Gallienus, the fabric being superior to the other coins supposed to have been restored by that emperor, here described.

HADRIANUS.

DIVO. HADRIANO. Head of Hadrianus, with radiated crown.—*Rev.* CONSECRATIO. An eagle; or an altar, with the fire kindled.

ANTONINUS PIUS.

DIVO. PIO. Head of Antoninus Pius, with radiated crown.—*Rev.* CONSECRATIO. An eagle; or an altar, with the fire kindled.

MARCUS AURELIUS. 1.

DIVO. MARCO. Head of Marcus Aurelius, with radiated crown.— *Rev.* CONSECRATIO. An eagle; or an altar, with the fire kindled.

2.

DIVO. MARCO. ANTONINO.—*Rev.* CONSECRATIO. Same types.

The coins with this last legend are much rarer than those with DIVO. MARCO. only.

COMMODUS.

DIVO. COMMODO. Head of Commodus, with radiated crown.—*Rev.* CONSECRATIO. An eagle; or an altar, with the fire kindled.

SEPTIMIUS SEVERUS.

DIVO. SEVERO. Head of Severus, with radiated crown.—*Rev.* CONSECRATIO. An eagle; or an altar, with the fire kindled.

SEVERUS ALEXANDER.

DIVO. ALEXANDRO. Head of Severus Alexander, with radiated crown.—*Rev.* CONSECRATIO. An altar, with the fire kindled; or an eagle.

BRASS MEDALLIONS.

1.

ADVENTVS. AVGG. The two emperors on horseback, preceded by Victory, with standards, and followed by a soldier.

2.

ADLOCVTIO. AVGG. (*or* AVGVSTORVM.) The usual type.

3.

AEQVITAS. PVBLICA. The three Monetæ, standing.

4.

APOLLONI. CONSERVATORI. Apollo, standing.

5.

CORNELIA. SALONINA. AVGVSTA. Head of Salonina.

6.

FIDES. EXERCITVS. Valerian and Gallienus standing, joining hands; the first crowned by Victory: a river-god seated at the feet of each.

7.

FORTVNA. REDVX. Fortune, with her attributes, standing.

8.

LIBERALITAS. AVG. S. C. Liberality, standing.

9.

MONETA. AVG. (*or* AVGG.). The three Monetæ, standing.

10.

P. M. TRI. P. X. P. P. COS. II. (*or* V.). The emperor in a quadriga.

11.

VBERITAS. AVG. A woman standing, holding a cornucopia and a purse.

12.

VICT. GAL. AVG. III. Victory in a biga.

13.

VICTORIA. GERMANICA. Victory, crowning the emperor, standing : a child kneeling on one side, and on the other an aged figure seated on the ground.

14.

VOTIS. DECENNALIBVS. S. C. within an oak garland.

No. 6 is extremely rare: the next in rarity are Nos. 1, 2, and 5 ; then Nos. 10 and 13 ; the least rare are Nos. 8 and 9.

[GALLIENUS AND SALONINA].

1.

IMP. GALLIENUS. P. F. AVG. Bust of Gallienus, with spear and shield.—*Rev.* CORNELIA. SALONINA. AVGVSTA. The head of Salonina.

2.

IMP. CAES. P. LICINIVS. GALLIENVS. AVG. CORNELIA. SALONINA. GALLIENI. AVG. The heads of Gallienus and Salonina, face to face.—*Rev.* LIBERALITAS. AVGVSTORVM. The same type.

3.

CONCORDIA. AVGG. The same heads.—*Rev.* ADVENTVS. AVGG. The two emperors on horseback; their right hands raised; preceded by Victory, and followed by two foot soldiers bearing standards.

4.

CONCORDIA. AVGG. Same heads.—*Rev.* AEQVITAS. PVBLICA. The three Monetæ, standing.

5.

CONCORDIA. AVGVSTORVM. Same heads—*Rev.* LIBERALI-TAS. AVG. Gallienus and Salonina seated on an estrade, between the Praetorian praefect and Liberality.

6.

CONCORDIA. AVGVSTORVM. Same heads.—*Rev.* MONETA. AVG. The three Monetæ, standing.

Nos. 2, 3, and 5, are far more rare than the other numbers.

[GALLIENUS AND SALONINUS].

CONCORDIA. AVGVSTORVM. The heads of Gallienus and Saloninus, face to face.—*Rev.* VICTORIA. AVGVSTORVM. Two emperors standing, holding a globe surmounted by a Victory: on each side a standard bearer.

Mionnet values this rare medallion at 100 francs.

FIRST BRASS, WITH RARE REVERSES.

1.

ANNONA. AVGG. A woman standing, holding ears of corn and a cornucopia: the modius at her feet.

2.

APOLLONI. CONSERVA. Apollo, standing.

3.

COHORT. PRAEF. PRINCIPI. SVO. within a garland.

4.

CONCORDIA. AVGG. Two hands joined.

5.

CONCORDIA. EXERCIT. Concord, standing.

6.

DIANA. FELIX. Diana in her hunting habit, attended by a dog.

7.

FELICITAS. AVGG. Felicity, standing.

8.

FIDES. MILITVM. A woman, holding two standards.

9.

GENIVS. AVG. A naked male figure standing, with the modius on his head: a patera in his right hand, and a cornucopia on his left arm: a standard on one side.

10.

IOVI. CONSERVA. (or CONSERVATORI.). Jupiter, standing.

11.

LIBERALITAS. AVGG. Liberality, standing.

12.

MARTI. PACIF. Mars, marching.

13.

MONETA. AVGG. The three Monetæ, standing.

14.

Another, with IMP. GALLIENVS. AVG. COS. V. on the head side.

15.

ORIENS. AVGG. The Sun, standing.

16.

PAX. AVG. Peace, standing.

17.

RESTIT. GALLIAR. The emperor raising up a prostrate woman.

18.

RESTITVTOR. ORBIS. A similar type.

19.

SECVRITAS. AVGG. Security leaning on a column.

20.
SERAPIDI. COMITI. AVG. Serapis standing: an ibis by his side.
21.
S. P. Q. R. OPTIMO. PRINCIPI. within a garland.
22.
VESTA. Vesta, standing.
23.
VICTORIA. AVGG. Victory, marching.
24.
VICTORIA. GERM. Victory, standing; a captive on the ground.
25.
VIRTVS. AVGG. A military figure, standing.
26.
VOTIS. DECENNALIBVS. within a garland.
27.
GENIVS. P. R. The head of Gallienus, with radiated crown, surmounted by the modius.—*Rev.* S. C. within a garland.
28.
Same legend. The same heads.—*Rev.* INT. VRB. S. C. within a garland.

Nos. 3, 14, 18, and 21, are very rare. The next in rarity are Nos. 12, and 22. The least rare are Nos. 2, 5, 7, 8, 10, 15, 16, 19, and 25.

[GALLIENUS AND SALONINA].

CONCORDIA. AVGVSTORVM. The heads of Gallienus and Salonina, face to face.—*Rev.* ADVENTVS. AVGG. Two emperors on horseback, preceded by Victory, and followed by a soldier.

Mionnet values this very rare type at 50 francs.

SECOND BRASS, WITH RARE REVERSES.

1.
ADVENTVS. AVGG. Two emperors on horseback, preceded by Victory, and followed by a foot soldier.
2.
ALACRITATI. A pegasus.
3.
APOLLINI. CONSERVA. Apollo, standing.
4.
CONCORDIA. AVGG. Two hands, joined.
5.
CONCORDIA. EXERCIT. Concord, seated.

6.

FELICITAS. AVGG.   Felicity, standing.

7.

FIDES. MILITVM.   A woman, holding two standards.

8.

GENIVS. P. R.   The head of Gallienus, laureated, or with a radiated crown.—*Rev.* INT. VRB. S. C. within a garland.

9.

LIBERALITAS. AVGG.   Liberality, standing.

10.

P. M. TR. P. II. COS. III. P. P.   The emperor in the toga, sacrificing on a tripod; a figure slaying a bull.

11.

VICTORIA. GERM.   Victory, standing; a captive on the ground.

12.

GALLIENVM. AVG. P. R.   Bust of Gallienus, with spear and buckler. —*Rev.* OB. CONSERVATIONEM. SALVTIS.   Hygeia, standing.

13.

GALLIENVM. AVG. SENATVS.   Head of Gallienus.—*Rev.* OB. LIBERTATEM. RECEPTAM.   A woman, standing.

Nos. 1, 2, and 10, are the rarest.   The next in rarity are Nos. 12 and 13.

[GALLIENUS AND SALONINA].

1.

CONCORDIA. AVGVSTORVM.   The heads of Gallienus and Salonina, face to face.—*Rev.* ADVENTVS. AVGG.   Two horsemen, preceded by Victory, and followed by a foot soldier, bearing a standard.

2.

VIRTVS. AVGVSTI.   Helmed head of Gallienus.—*Rev.* SALONINA. AVG.   Head of Salonina.

Mionnet values No. 1 at thirty, and No. 2 at fifteen francs.

[GALLIENUS AND VALERIANUS].

1.

CONCORDIA. AVGVSTORVM.   The laureated heads of Gallienus and Valerian, face to face.—*Rev.* ADVENTVS. AVGG.   Two horsemen, &c.

2.

Same legend.   Same heads.—*Rev.* LIBERALITAS. AVGG. I.   Two figures, male and female, seated on an estrade, attended by two figures, standing; a third figure ascending the steps of the estrade.

3.

CONCORDIA. AVGVSTORVM. The laureated heads of Gallienus and Valerian, face to face.—*Rev.* LIBERALITAS. AVGVSTOR. Liberality, standing.

Mionnet values the two first at fifteen francs each; and the third at eight francs.

THIRD BRASS, WITH RARE REVERSES.

1.

AETERNITAS. AVG. Saturn standing, holding the harpa; PXV.

2.

Same legend. Romulus and Remus, suckled by the wolf. In the exergue, a palm branch (*or* S. P. Q. R.)

3.

APOLLI. PAL. S. P. Q. R. Apollo standing, wearing the pallium, holding a patera and a staff, terminating in a cross.

4.

CONSECRATIO. An eagle with wings expanded.

5.

CONSERVATOR. AVG, Æsculapius, standing.

6.

FECVNDITAS. AVG. A woman standing, holding a cornucopia; a child by her side.

7.

FIDES. MILITVM. within a laurel garland.

8.

GENIVS. EXERCIT. Bonus Eventus, standing.

9.

INDVLGENT. AVG. A woman, seated.

10.

IOVI. CONSERVATORI. Jupiter and the emperor, standing.

11.

IVBENTVS. *(sic)* AVG. The emperor, standing. In the exergue, VIIC.

12.

MERCVRIO. CONS. AVG. Capricorn.

13.

OB. REDDIT. LIBERT. Liberty, standing. (*Mus. Theupoli.*)

14.

PAX. FVNDATA. A trophy and two captives.

15.

PIETAS. AVGG. Two emperors standing, joining hands over a tripod standing between them.

16.

P. M. TR. P. IIII. COS. The emperor in a quadriga, crowned by Victory.

17.

P. M. TR. P. X. COS. III. P. P. The emperor in a quadriga.

18.

RESTITVTOR. ORBIS. The emperor standing, raising up a woman.

19.

SECVRIT. ORBIS. A woman, seated.

20.

VESTA. The goddess, standing.

21.

VICTO. GAL. AVG. (or VICT. GAL. AVG. III.) Three Victories, standing.

22.

VICTORIA. GERMA. The emperor and Victory, standing.

23.

VOTIS. X. within a garland.

24.

VOTIS. DECENNALIBVS. within a garland.

No. 13 is extremely rare. Nos. 3, 6, 11, 18, and 21 are rarer than the other numbers.

SALONINA.

[Cornelia Salonina, the wife of Gallienus, was married to the emperor about ten years before his succession to the empire. It is supposed that she was assassinated with her husband before Milan, in the year of Rome 1021 (A. D. 268)].

STYLE:——SALONINA. AVG. [On reverse, sometimes, AVG. (or AVGVST. or AVGVSTA.) IN. PACE.]——COR. (or CORN. or CORNE. or CORNELIA.) SALONINA. AVG. [On reverse, sometimes, as before].

Gold - - - - - - - - - - - - - - - - - - - R 6
Silver medallions - - - - - - - - - - - - - - - R 6
Base silver, of the usual size - - - - - - - - - - - - C
„ quinarii - - - - - - - - - - - - - - - R 2
Brass medallions - - - - - - - - - - - - - - - R 3
First brass - - - - - - - - - - - - - - - - - R 2
Second brass - - - - - - - - - - - - - - - - - R 1
Third brass - - - - - - - - - - - - - - - - - C

SILVER MEDALLIONS.

1.

AEQVITAS. PVBLICA.　The three Monetæ, standing.

2.

IVNO. REGINA.　Juno standing, veiled, holding a patera and the hasta pura.

This medallion is larger in circumference than the first brass.

3.

PIETAS. AVGG.　A woman seated, holding the hasta pura; before, two naked figures, standing.

4.

PVDICITIA. AVGVSTAE.　The empress seated, between two females standing.

The above are valued according to their diameter. No. 2, which is the largest, is valued by Mionnet at 200 francs; the others at from 50 to 72 francs.

GOLD AND BASE SILVER, OF THE USUAL SIZE.

1.

AEQVITAS. AVG.　A woman, standing. - - - - - - - - B

2.

ANNONA. AVG.　A woman, standing.　- - - - - - - - B

3.

AVG. (*or* AVGVST. IN. PACE.)　A woman, seated.　- - - - B

4.

BENERI. *(sic)* GENETRICI.　Venus, standing - - - - - - B

5.

CONCORDIA. AVGG.　Gallienus snd Salonina, standing.　- - B

6.

Same legend.　Three hands, joined. - - - - - - - - - - B

7.

Same legend.　The heads of Salonina and Gallienus, face to face. (*Tanini*). - - - - - - - - - - - - - - - AU

8.

DEAE. SEGETIAE.　Statue of the goddess, seated within a temple.
　　　　　　　　　　　　　　　　　　　　　　AU & B

Segetia was a deity, supposed by the Romans to preside over harvests. *

---

* Some authors are of opinion that she was the same as Fortune, called also Sejana, to whom as Pliny informs us, Nero built a temple of transparent marble.

9.

FELICITAS. PVBLICA. A woman, seated. - - - - - AU & B

10.

IVNO. REGINA. Juno, standing. - - - - - - - - - AU

11.

Same legend. A similar type. (A *quinarius*). - - - - - - B

12.

IVNONI. CONS. AVG. A hind. - - - - - - - - - - B

13.

PIETAS. AVGG. A woman seated, and two children. - - - - B

14.

Same legend. A similar type. (A *quinarius*). - - - - - - B

15.

ROMAE. AETERNAE. Rome seated, and the emperor standing. AU

16.

SECVRITAS. PERPET. Security, leaning on a column. - - - B

17.

VENEREM. GENETRICEM. Venus, standing. *(Khell)*. - - B

18.

SALONINA. AVG. Head of the empress to the right.—*Rev.* VENUS.
FELIX. Venus seated, clad in the stola, and holding the hasta
pura. - - - - - - - - - - - - - - - - - - - AU

Mionnet quotes this coin as being in the collection of the library at
Autun.

19.

VENVS. GENETRIX. Venus and a child, standing. - - - AU

20.

VENVS. VICTRIX. Venus, leaning on a column. - - - - AU

21.

Same legend. Venus, standing. - - - - - - - - - - - AU

22.

VESTA. Vesta, standing. *(Khell)*. - - - - - - - - - AU

23.

VESTA. AETERNAE. Vesta, seated. - - - - - - - - - B

24.

VESTA. FELIX. Vesta, standing. - - - - - - - - - - B

25.

O. V. X. X. V. X. *(sic)*. A female standing, her right hand raised,
and her left holding the hasta pura. - - - - - - - - B

In gold, Nos. 7; 8, 10, 15, 18, and 22, are the rarest. In silver, No. 17
is much the rarest. Nos. 6, 11, 14, are the next in rarity.

BRASS MEDALLIONS, WITH RARE REVERSES.

1.

ABVNDANTIA. TEMPORVM. A woman seated, holding a cornucopia, which she holds towards five children; a woman on each side, standing.

2.

AEQVITAS. PVBLICA. The three Monetæ, standing.

3.

IMP. GALLIENVS. P. F. AVG. Bust of Gallienus, with coat of mail and spear.

4.

IVVO. REGINA. S. C. Same type.

Mionnet values the first at 100 francs; the second at 24; the third at 72, and the fourth at 30 francs.

FIRST BRASS, WITH RARE REVERSES.

1.

AEQVITAS. PVBLICA. The three Monetæ, standing.

2.

FECVNDITAS. AVG. A woman standing, holding by the right hand a small figure, and an infant with her left.

3.

IVNO. REGINA. Juno standing, veiled, holding a patera in her right hand, and the hasta in her left.

4.

PIETAS. AVGG. A woman seated; before her, two naked children.

5.

PVDICITIA. Pudicitia, seated.

6.

VENVS. GENETRIX. Venus standing, holding a figure and the hasta; a child by her side. (*Vaillant*).

7.

VESTA. Vesta, seated.

No. 1 is a very rare type. No. 7 is the next in rarity, but by no means so rare. Nos. 2 and 5 are rarer than the remaining numbers.

SECOND BRASS.

1.

FECVNDITAS. AVG. A woman standing, holding a child; another child by her side.

2.

FELICITAS. AVGG. A female seated; before her, two children.

3.

IVNO. REGINA. Juno, standing.

4.

PIETAS. AVGVST. A woman standing, and two small figures.

5.

PVDICITIA. A woman, seated.

6.

VENVS. GENETRIX. Venus standing, and a child.

Nos. 3, 4, and 6 are the least rare.

THIRD BRASS, WITH RARE REVERSES.

1.

IVNO. AVG. Juno-Lucina seated, with two children.

2.

VESTA. FELIX. Vesta, standing.

SALONINUS.

[Publius Licinius Cornelius Saloninus Valerianus Gallienus, the son of
Gallienus and Salonina, was born in the year of Rome 995 (A. D. 242),
and invested with the title of Caesar by Valerian, at the same time that
his father was associated with that emperor in the empire, 1006 (A. D.
253). Saloninus was put to death by Postumus, governor of Gaul, in
the year of Rome 1012 (A. D. 259)].

STYLE:——VALERIANVS. CAES. [On reverse, sometimes, PRINC. (or
PRINCEPS.) IVVENT. or IVVENTVT. or IVVENTVTIS.]——LIC. VALE-
RIANVS. CAES. [On reverse, sometimes, PRINC. (or PRINCEPS.)
IVVENT. (or IVVENTVT. or IVVENTVTIS.)]——P. LIC. VALERIANVS.
CAES. (or CAESAR.)——P. LIC. COR. VALERIANVS. CAES.
——SAL. (or SALON.) VALERIANVS. CAES.——[On reverse,
sometimes, PRINC. (or PRINCEPS. IVVENT. or IVVENTVT. or IVVEN-
TVTIS.)]——P. COR. SAL. VALERIANVS. CAES. ——VA-
LERIANVS. NOBIL. CAES. [On reverse, sometimes, PRINC.
(or PRINCEPS.) IVVENT. (or IVVENTVT. or IVVENTVTIS.)]——P. C. L:
VALERIANVS. NOB. CAES. [On reverse, sometimes, PRINC.
(or PRINCEPS.) IVVENT. (or IVVENTVT. or IVVENTVTIS.)]——SALON.
VALERIANVS. NOB. CAES.——LIC. COR. SAL. VALERIA-
NVS. N. (or NOB.) C. (or CAES.) [On reverse, as before.]——P.
C. S. VALERIANVS. NOB. CAES.——IMP. C. L. VALERIA-

NVS. NOB. CAES.——IMP. CAES. P. LIC. CORN. GALLIE-
NVS.——P. LIC. VALERIANVS. AVG.——IMP. VALERIA-
NVS. AVG.——IMP. SALON. VALERIANVS. AVG.——
VALERIANVS. P. F. AVG.——IMP. VALERIANVS. P. F.
AVG.——IMP. C. P. LIC. VALERIANVS. P. F. AVG. [On
reverse, as above.]——DIVVS. VALERIANVS.——DIVVS.
VALERIANVS. CAES. —— DIVVS. CAES. (or CAESAR.)
VALERIANVS.——DIVVS. CORN. SAL. VALERIANVS.

It appears, by Eckhel, that the coins hitherto assigned to Valerian
junior, in reality belong to this prince. This author shews that Valerian
the younger never had the titles of Caesar and Augustus conferred upon
him, and, consequently, that no coins were struck in his honour.

With regard to the titles on the coins of Saloninus, Eckhel is of
opinion that the reason why some of them, struck during the lifetime of
this prince, bear the style of Augustus, although those struck after his
death, bear that of Caesar only, is as follows :—When Gallienus quitted
Gaul, and passed into Pannonia, to quell the revolt in that country, he
invested Saloninus with the title of Imperator, with a view to give more
authority to the young prince ; and it is probable that the moneyers of
Rome and the provinces, considered that this title comprised also that of
Augustus, both being generally borne together. That the title of
Imperator was conferred upon Saloninus, is proved by several ancient
monuments cited by Eckhel, in which it is coupled with that of Caesar,
or Nobilissimus Caesar.

Gold - - - - - - - - - - - - - - - - - -	R 6
„ quinarii - - - - - - - - - - - - - - -	R 8
Silver medallions - - - - - - - - - - - - - -	R 8
Base siver, of the usual size - - - - - - - - - - -	C
„ with the title of Augustus - - - - - - - -	R 4
„ quinarii - - - - - - - - - - - - - -	R 4
Brass medallions - - - - - - - - - - - - - - -	R 8
First brass - - - - - - - - - - - - - - - -	R 6
Second brass - - - - - - - - - - - - - - - -	R 2
Third brass - - - - - - - - - - - - - - - -	S

SILVER MEDALLION.

CONCORDIA. AVGVSTORVM. The heads of Gallienus and Saloninus, face to face ; the first laureated, the other bare : each with
the paludamentum.—*Rev.* ADVENTVS. AVGG. Three emperors

on horseback, preceded by Victory, and followed by several foot-soldiers, bearing standards; two captives on the ground.

Mionnet values this medallion at 300 francs. It is of large diameter.

GOLD AND BASE SILVER, WITH RARE REVERSES.

1.

CONSECRATIO. A funeral pile. - - - - - - - - - - B

2.

Same legend. An eagle, bearing Saloninus. - - - ˙ - - - - - B

This type, as well as Nos. 5, 6, 8, and 11, were formerly ascribed to Valerian the younger.

3.

DEO. MARTI. Statue of Mars, within a temple. - - - - - - B

4.

DII. NVTRITORES. Jupiter and a figure, standing. - - - - B

5.

FIDES. MILITVM. Three standards. - - - - - - - - - B

6.

IOVI. CRESCENTI. The infant Jupiter, riding on a goat. AU & B

7.

LIBERALITAS. AVGG. Liberality, standing. (*Cabinet of Vienna*). B

8.

ORIENS. Saloninus, crowning a trophy. - - - - - - - - B

9.

ORIENS. AVGG. The Sun, standing. - - - - - - - - - B

10.

SALON. VALERIANVS. CAES. Bare head of Saloninus to the right, with the paludamentum.—*Rev.* PIETAS. Sacrificial instruments. (A *quinarius*). - - - - - - - - - - - - - - - AU

11.

PIETAS. AVGG. Two figures sacrificing: a star in the field. - B

12.

Same legend. Sacrificial instruments. - - - - - - - - - AU

13.

PRINC. IVVENTVTIS. A military figure crowning a trophy. - B

14.

PRINCEPS. IVVENTVTIS. A figure standing, with an ensign. B

15.

PRINCIPI. IVVENTVTIS. A figure standing, holding a globe and a spear. - - - - - - - - - - - - - - - - - AU & B

16.

PRINCIPI. IVVENTVTIS.   A military figure, holding two standards.

AU

17.

Same legend. A similar type. *(A quinarius).* - - - - - - - B

18.

SPES. PVBLICA.   Hope and the emperor, standing.   - - - - B

19.

Another, with the titles of Imperator and Augustus on the obverse.   B

20.

VICTORIA. GERMANICA.   Victory crowning a figure. - - - B

21.

VICTORIA, PART.   Victory crowning the emperor.   - - - - B

22.

VIRTVS. AVGG. Rome, seated. - - - - - - - - - - B

   In gold, Nos. 6, 12, and 15, are much the rarest.   In silver, Nos. 2,
7, and 17, are much the rarest; the next in rarity are Nos. 4, 5, 8 and 21.

BRASS MEDALLIONS.

1.

CONSECRATIO.   A funeral pile. *(Mus. Pisanum).*

2.

MONETA. AVGG.   The three Monetæ, standing.

3.

PRINÇIPI. IVVENTVTIS.   Saloninus standing, holding a globe and
   the hasta: a captive at his feet.

   Mionnet values the first at 200, the second at 100, and the third at
200 francs.

FIRST BRASS.

1.

CONSECRATI.   A funeral pile.

   The diameter of this coin varies.

2.

PIETAS. SAECVLI.   Bare head of Saloninus.—*Rev.* IOVI. CRES-
   CENTI.   A child riding on a goat.

3.

PRINCIPI. IVVENT.   Saloninus standing, holding an ensign and a
   spear.

   No. 2 is by far the rarest, and No. 1 is much rarer than No. 3.

SECOND BRASS.

1.

CONSECRATIO. A funeral pile.

2.

Same legend. Saloninus borne by an eagle in full flight.

3.

PIETAS. AVGG. Sacrificial instruments.

4.

PRINC. IVVENT. (*or* PRINCIPI. IVVENT. *or* PRINCIPI. IVVEN-
TVTIS.) Saloninus standing, holding a globe and an ensign.

Nos. 2 and 3 are the rarest: the next in rarity is No. 1.

THIRD BRASS.

1.

DII. NVTRITORES. Jupiter and Saloninus standing; the latter
receiving a small figure from Jupiter.

2.

IOVI. CRESCENTI. A child riding on a goat.

3.

PRINC. IVVENTVTIS. The prince standing, crowning a trophy.

4.

SPES. PVBLICA. The emperor and Hope, standing.

No. 1 is the rarest, and No. 4 is rarer than the others.

JULIUS GALLIENUS.

[Quintus Julius Gallienus, son of Gallienus and Salonina, was declared
Caesar by his father after the death of his brother, in the year of Rome
1012 (A. D. 259). The time of his death is not known. Historians
have spoken of him but slightly, and Zonaras is the only one who
mentions his death. This writer says that he was put to death,
together with his uncle Valerian the younger, by order of the senate;
while Pollio and Eutropius say that the younger Valerian perished
with his brother, the emperor Gallienus, at the siege of Milan].

The coins attributed to this prince are uncertain. If they may be
considered authentic, Julius Gallienus died before his father, who had
him placed among the gods.

VALERIANUS THE YOUNGER.

[Valerianus, the son, as is supposed, of Valerian the elder and his wife Mariniana, was, according to the authors above mentioned, assassinated at the siege of Milan in the year of Rome 1021 (A.D. 268)].

LICINIA GALLIENA.

[Licina Galliena is supposed to have been the cousin of the emperor].

The coins of the emperor Gallienus with the legend GALLIENAE. AVGVSTAE. were attributed by Goltzius to this lady, but Eckhel restores them to the emperor. No others are known.

POSTUMUS.

[Marcus Cassianus Latinius Postumus, was born in Gaul, of an obscure family. He was governor of that country under Valerian, when he assumed the purple, in the year of Rome 1011 (A.D. 258). Postumus and his son were murdered by their soldiers after the taking of Mayence, in which the usurper Lollian, or Lælian, had sought refuge].

STYLE:——POSTVMVS. AVG. [On reverse, sometimes, P. P.]—— IMP. POSTVMVS. AVG.——POSTVMVS. PIVS. AVG. [On reverse, sometimes, P. P. (or IMP. P. P.)]——POSTVMVS. PIVS. FEL. (or FELIX.) AVG.——IMP. C. (or CAES.) POSTVMVS. P. F. AVG. [On reverse, sometimes, P. P. (or IMP. or RESTITVTOR. GALLIAR. or REST. ORBIS. or PACATOR. ORBIS.] —— IMP. C. (or CAES.) M. CASS. LAT. POSTVMVS. P. F. AVG. [On reverse, sometimes, P. P. (or GERMANICVS. MAX. or RESTITVTOR. GALLIAR.)].

Gold medallions, with four heads - - - - - - - - - - R 8
„ of the usual size - - - - - - - - - - - - - - R 4
„ with the supposed head of his son - - - - - - - *unique*
„ quinarii - - - - - - - - - - - - - - - - R 6
Base silver - - - - - - - - - - - - - - - - - C
„ with the supposed head of his son - - - - - - *unique*
„ with the head of Postumus, accompanied by the attributes of Hercules - - - - - - - - - - - - - - R 2
„ with the heads of Postumus and Hercules - - - - R 4
Brass medallions - - - - - - - - - - - - - - - R 2

First brass - - - - - - - - - - - - - - - - C
Second brass - - - - - - - - - - - - - - - - S
Third brass - - - - - - - - - - - - - - - - VC
   ,,   with the head of Postumus, accompanied by the attributes
of Hercules - - - - - - - - - - - - - - - - R 2

GOLD MEDALLION.

IMP. POSTVMVS. P. F. AVG. The heads of Postumus and Hercules,
side by side, both laureated. — *Rev.* FELICITAS. AVG. The
busts of Victory and Peace, side by side.

There are modern fabrications of this very beautiful medallion, which
is larger than the second brass of this period. Mionnet values it at 1200
francs.

GOLD AND BASE SILVER OR BILLON, WITH RARE REVERSES.

[Those types marked with an (*) have on the obverse the laureated
heads of Postumus and Hercules, side by side: legend, POSTVMVS. PIVS.
FELIX. AVG. Those marked thus (+) have on the obverse the helmed
head of Postumus: legend, POSTVMVS. AVG.].

1.
AETERNITAS. AVG. Three radiated heads; the centre one full-
faced. - - - - - - - - - - - - - - - - - AU

2.
CASTOR. Castor standing by his horse, which he holds by the rein.
AU & B

3.
CLARITAS. AVG. The heads of the Sun and the Moon. - - *AU

4.
COMITI. AVG. The heads of Postumus and Hercules, as on the
obverse. - - - - - - - - - - - - - - - *AU

5.
CONCORDIA. EQVIT. (*or* EQVITVM.) Concord, standing. - B

6.
CONSERVATORI. AVG. The heads of Postumus and Hercules, as
on the obverse. - - - - - - - - - - - - - - *AU

7.
Same legend. Jupiter-Victor, seated. - - - - - - - - AU

8.

CONSERVATORES. AVG. The heads of Apollo and Diana, side by
side. - - - - - - - - - - - - - - - - - •AU & B

9.

Same legend. The heads of Mars and Victory. - - - - •AU & B

10.

COS. IIII. Victory standing, holding a long palm branch. - - - B

11.

DIANAE. REDVCI. Diana marching, guiding a stag. - - - B

12.

FELICITAS. AVG. The laureated heads of Postumus and Hercules,
face to face. - - - - - - - - - - - - - - - - AU

13.

Same legend. The heads of Peace and Victory, side by side. (*Plate
ix, No. 7*). - - - - - - - - - - - - - - - - •AU

Brought, in fine preservation, 11*l.* 5*s.* at the Trattle sale.

14.

FELICITAS. TEMP. (*or* TEMPORVM.) A galley, with the labarum.
•B

15.

FORTVNA. REDVX. Statue of Fortune, seated within a temple. B

16.

HERC. DEVSONIENSI. Statue of Hercules, within a temple. - B

17.

HERCVLI. CRETENSI. Hercules, struggling with a bull. - •AU

18.

HERCVLI. ERYMANTINO. Hercules, carrying the carcass of a
boar on his shoulders; Eurystheus, concealing himself in his tub. •B

A similar type occurs on the Greek coins of Gordian, Geta, and
Probus. The story of Eurystheus, and his fright at beholding the carcass
of the huge boar, must be well known.

19.

HERCVLI. IMMORTALI. Hercules, chaining Cerberus. - - B

20.

HERCVLI. INVICTO. Hercules, standing; his foot resting on a
monster - - - - - - - - - - - - - - - - - - B

21.

Same legend. Hercules, strangling the Nemæan lion. - - - †AU

22.

HERCVLI. LIBYCO. Hercules, vanquishing Antaeus. - - *AU

23.

HERCVLI. MAGVSANO. Hercules, standing. - - - - - - B

24.

HERCVLI. NEMAEO. Hercules, strangling the Nemæan lion. *AU

25.

HERCVLI. PACIFERO. Hercules standing, holding a branch.
AU & B

26.

HERCVLI. ROMANO. AVG. A bow, club, etc. - - - - - B

27.

HERCVLI. THRACIO. Hercules, subduing a horse. - - - - B

28.

Same legend. Same type. - - - - - - - - - - - - AU

The obverse of this coin has the radiated head of Postumus, with the portrait three-quarter faced.

29.

INDVL. PIA. POSTVMI. AVG. Postumus seated; a woman kneeling before him. - - - - - - - - - - - - - - - - - AU

30.

Another, with the head of Postumus full-faced. - - - - - - AU

31.

IMP. C. POSTVMVS. P. F. AVG. Radiated head of Postumus, as on the other side. - - - - - - - - - - - - - - - B

32.

IMP. X. COS. V. Victory standing, holding a long palm branch. B

33.

INVICTO. AVG. Radiated bust of Postumus the younger (?), holding a sceptre or staff resting on his shoulder. - - - - - AU & B

34.

IOVI. STATORI. Jupiter-Stator, standing. - - - - - - - B

The obverse of this coin has the head of Postumus, with the attributes of Hercules.

35.

IOVI. VICTORI. Jupiter marching, with the hasta and thunderbolt. B

36.

LIBERALITAS. AVG. The emperor seated on an estrade, and three figures standing. - - - - - - - - - - - - - - AU

37.

MARS. VICTOR. Mars, standing. - - - - - - - - - - B

38.

MERCVRIO. FELICI. Mercury, standing. - - - - - - - B

39.

MINER. FAVT. Minerva, marching. - - - - - - - - - B

40.

NEPT. COMITI. Neptune standing, holding a trident and a dolphin; his right foot resting on the prow of a vessel. - - - - - AU

41.

PACATOR. ORBIS. Radiated head of the Sun.—" Représenté, (says Mionnet), " sous les traits de Postume le fils." - - - - - B

42.

PAX. EQVITVM. Peace, standing; T. - - - - - - - - B

43.

PIETAS. AVG. A woman standing, and four children. - AU & B

44.

P. M. TR. P. COS. P. P. A lion, with radiated head, walking. AU & B

45.

P. M. T. P. IMP. COS. III. P. P. Five figures, sacrificing at an altar, standing before the the temple of Vesta. - - - - - - - AU

46.

P. M. G. M. T. P. COS. III. P. P. (sic). Two captives, seated at the foot of a trophy. - - - - - - - - - - - - - - -. †AU

47.

P. M. TR. P. IIII. COS. III. P. P. Mars naked, marching. - †AU

48.

P. M. TR. P. IMP. V. COS. III. P. P. The emperor, seated in the curule chair, holding a globe and a wand. - - - - - - AU

49.

P. M. T. P. COS. IIII. P. P. The emperor, in a quadriga. - - AU

50.

P. M. TR. P. X. COS. V. P. P. The emperor, standing. - - - B

51.

Same legend. Victory standing, her foot resting on a globe; holding a buckler inscribed VO. XX. - - - - - - - - - - - B

52.

POSTVMVS. AVG. Bare head of Postumus (or Hercules) full-faced. †AU

53,

PROVIDENTIA. AVG. A woman, leaning on a column. - - - B

54.

PROVIDENTIA. AVG. A woman, standing near a column; a globe
at her feet. - - - - - - - - - - - - - - - - †AU

55.

Same legend. Providence, standing. (A *quinarius*) - - - - AU

56.

PROVID. DEOR. COS. III. A similar type. (A *quinarius*). - AU

57.

QVINQVENNALES. POSTVMI. AVG. Victory standing, inscribing
on a buckler, VOT. X. - - - - - - - - - - - - - †AU

58.

Same legend. Victory standing, inscribing X., *or* VOT. X. on a
buckler. - - - - - - - - - - - - - - - - - AU

59.

QVINQVENNALES. AVG. A similar type. (A *quinarius*). AU

60.

RESTIT. GALLIARVM. (*or* RESTITVTOR. GALLIAR.) Postumus,
standing; Gaul personified, kneeling before him. - - - - - B

61.

REST. ORBIS. The emperor raising up a woman, who kneels before
him. - - - - - - - - - - - - - - - - - AU & B

62.

ROMAE. AETERNAE. Rome seated, holding the palladium. - AU

Brought, fine, 3*l.* at the sale of the Trattle collection.

63.

SAECVLI. FELICITAS. The emperor in a military habit, holding a
globe and the hasta, transversely. - - - - - - - - - B

64.

POSTVMVS. AVG. The heads of Postumus and Hercules, side by side.
—*Rev.* SALVS. AVG. Æsculapius, standing. (A *quinarius*). AU

65.

SALVS. EXERCITI. Æsculapius, standing. - - - - - - AU

On the last two types, the head of Postumus is both laureated and
radiated.

66.

SALVS. POSTVMI. AVG. Æsculapius and Hygeia, standing. AU

67.

Same legend. Hygeia, standing. - - - - - - - - - - B

68.

SALVS. PROVINCIARVM.   The Rhine personified, seated : her left
arm resting on a vase; her right hand holding an anchor.   AU & B

This coin is given by Banduri and others to Postumus the younger;
but without proof of its really belonging to that prince.

69.

VICTORIA. AVG.   Victory seated on spoils, before a trophy, inscribing
on a buckler, VO. X. - - - - - - - - - - - - - - AU

70.

Same legend.   Victory, in a biga.   - - - - - - - - - - AU

71.

Same legend.   Victory, trampling on a captive.   - - - - AU & B

72.

VIC. GERM. P. M. TR. P. V. COS. III. P. P.   Victory, crowning the
emperor. - - - - - - - - - - - - - - - - AU & B

73.

VIRTVS. AVG.   Hercules, standing.   - - - - - - - - - B

74.

VIRTVTI. AVG.   The heads of Postumus and Mars. - - - - AU

In gold, Nos. 12, 24, 28, 30, and 74, are much the rarest, excepting
No. 33, which is supposed unique.   Nos. 3, 4, 6, 8, 9, 13, 17, 21, 22, 45,
52, and 64, are the next in rarity ; and Nos. 2, 7, 29, 36, 40, 49, 68, and
72, are much rarer than the remaining numbers.   In billon, No. 33 is
supposed unique.   No. 18 is an extremely rare type.   The next in rarity
is No. 14; then Nos. 19, 20, and 27, though much less rare; then
Nos. 8 and 9.   Nos. 2, 15, 23, 26, 31, and 72, are much rarer than the
remainder.

BRASS MEDALLIONS.

[Those marked with an (*) are of a very large diameter, and have on
their obverse, the heads of Postumus and Hercules, side by side].

1.

ADLOCVTIO.   The usual type.

2.

FELICITAS. POSTVMI. AVG.   The emperor, sacrificing before a
woman; on the left, an attendant and an ox.*

A very large medallion, composed of brass and copper.

3.

FELICITAS. PVBLICA. Felicity, with radiated head, holding a long caduceus and a cornucopia.

4.

FIDES. MILITVM. A woman standing, holding two military standards.

5.

HERCVLI. COMITI. AVG. COS. III. Hercules naked, standing between the emperor, sacrificing, and a figure holding a victim, and bearing a pole-axe on his shoulder.*

6.

LAETITIA. AVG. A galley with rowers.

7.

P. M. TR. P. COS. III. P. P. S. C. The emperor standing, holding the hasta and a globe.

8.

RESTITVTOR. GALLIAR. (or GALLIARVM.) The emperor standing, raising up a woman.

9.

SALVS. AVG. Hygeia standing, feeding a serpent, entwined around an altar.

10.

VICTORIA. AVG. Victory, marching; a captive at her feet.

11.

VICTORIA. AVG. (or VICTORIAE. AVG. S. C.) Two Victories, suspending a buckler from a tree; at the foot of which, are two captives.

12.

VIRTVS. AVG. S. C. A military figure, standing.

13.

Without legend. The emperor addressing his soldiers.*

This medallion is of a very large size, and is formed of copper and brass.

Nos. 2, 5, and 13, are by far the rarest. Mionnet values the first two of these at 150, and the other at 124 francs. No. 1 is much rarer than the remainder.

FIRST BRASS, WITH RARE REVERSES.

1.

ADVENTVS. AVG. The emperor, on horseback.

2.

EXERCITVS. AVG.   The emperor on horseback, addressing his soldiers.   (The size varies).*

3.

EXERCITVS. VAC. (*or* V.)   The emperor on horseback, addressing his soldiers.

4.

FELICITAS. inscribed on the frieze of a triumphal arch ; above, a trophy and two captives.   In the exergue, AVG.

5.

FECICITAS. PVBLICA.   Felicity, standing.

6.

HERC. PACIFER. (*or* PACIFERO.)   A similar type.

7.

HERCVLI. DEVSONIENSI.   Hercules, standing.

8.

Same legend.   Statue of Hercules, standing, within a temple.

9.

HERCVLI. DEVSONIENSI. AVG.   Hercules, standing.

10.

HERCVLI. MAGVSANO.   A similar type.

11.

IMP. C. M. CASS. LAT. POSTVMVS. P. F. AVG.   Head of Postumus with radiated crown, on both sides of the coin.

12.

IOVI. PROPVGNATORI.   Jupiter bearing an eagle, and launching a thunderbolt.

13.

LAETITIA. AVG.   The prow of a vessel.—*Obverse.* VIRTVS. POS-TVMI. AVG.   Helmed head of Postumus.

14.

MERCVRIO. PACIFERO.   Mercury, standing.

15.

MINERVE. *(sic)* . . . . TR.   Minerva, marching with spear and buckler, holding an olive branch.

16.

MONITA. *(sic).* AVGG.   ("ut videtur," says Mionnet).   Moneta standing, with her attributes.

---

* The value of the coins of Postumus must depend upon their fabric, as well as their size, both of which are very unequal.

17.

PAX. AVG. Victory, marching.

18.

VIRTVS. POSTVMI. AVG. Helmed head of Postumus.—*Rev.* P. M. TR. P. COS. II. P. P. A military figure, standing.

19.

PROVIDENTIA. AVG. Providence, standing.

20.

RESTITVTOR. GALLIAR. (*or* GALLIARVM.) The emperor, standing, raising up the province personified, kneeling before him.

21.

SALVS. AVG. Hygeia seated, feeding a serpent on an altar.

22.

VICTORIA. AVG. Victory, bearing a palm branch, marching over a buckler : two captives on the ground.

23.

VICTORIA. GERMANICA. Victory, marching.

24.

VICTORIAE. AVG. Two Victories, suspending a buckler from a palm tree ; two captives seated on the ground.

25.

VIRTVS. AVG. Bearded helmed head of Postumus, with spear and buckler.

26.

VIRTVS. POSTVMI. AVG. Victory standing, crowning the emperor ; a prisoner on the ground.

The rarest types are Nos. 2, 3, 8, and 25. The next in rarity are Nos. 1, 5. 9, 11, 14, 17, 18, and 19.

SECOND BRASS, WITH RARE REVERSES.

1.

ADVENTVS. AVG. The emperor, on horseback.

2.

EXERCITVS. VSC. (*sic*). The emperor on horseback, addressing his soldiers.

3.

FELICITAS. inscribed on a triumphal arch ; above, a trophy and two captives. In the exergue, AVG.

4.

FIDES. EXERC. A woman standing, holding two ensigns.

5.

GERMANICVS. MAX. Two captives, at the foot of a trophy.

6.

HERCVLI. DEVSONIENSI. Head of Hercules.

7.

Same legend. Hercules, standing.

8.

Same legend. Statue of Hercules, standing, within a temple.

9.

HERCVLI. INVICTO. Hercules overpowering a bull.

10.

HERCVLO. PACIFERO. Hercules, standing.

11.

I. IMP. O. POSTV. . . . Head of Postumus, with radiated crown.

12.

I. O. M. SPONSORI. SAECVLI. AVG. The emperor, sacrificing.

13.

MINERV. FAVTR. Minerva, standing.

14.

NEPTVNO. REDVCI. Neptune, standing.

15.

PROVIDENTIO. AVG. Providence, standing.

16.

RESTITVTOR. GALLIAR. The emperor raising up the province personified.

17.

SAECVLI. FELICITAS. The emperor, standing, holding a globe and a javelin, reversed.

18.

SAECVLO. FRVGIFERO. A winged caduceus.

19.

SPEI. PERPETVAE. Hope.

20.

VICT. COMES. AVG. The emperor on horseback, preceded by Victory on foot.

21.

VIRTVS. POSTVMI. AVG. Hercules, overpowering a stag.

Nos. 6 and 12 are the rarest types. The next in rarity are Nos. 2, 9, 11. Nos. 3, 7, 8, 10, 15, and 19, are much less rare.

THIRD BRASS, WITH RARE REVERSES.

1.

COS. IIII. (*or* V.) Victory, standing.

2.

DIANAE. LVCIFERAE. Diana with her quiver, holding a torch.

3.

FELICITAS. AVG. Felicity, standing.

4.

FIDES. EXERCITVS. Four standards.

5.

IOVI. CONSERVAT. Jupiter standing; at his feet, a small figure.

6.

HERCVLI. ROMANO. AVG. A bow, club, and quiver.

7.

PACATOR. ORBIS. Radiated head of the sun.

8.

PAX. AVG. Peace, standing.

The obverse has the radiated bust of Postumus, with the attributes of Hercules.

9.

PAX. EQVITVM. Peace, standing.

10.

P. M. TR. P. VIIII. COS. IIII. P. P. A bow, quiver, and club.

Same obverse as No. 8.

11.

P. M. TR. P. X. COS. II. P. P. The emperor, in the toga, standing.

12.

RESTITVTOR. GALLIAR. The emperor, raising up the province.

Nos. 1, 4, 5, 9, and 11 are the least rare.

JUNIA DONATA.

[Junia Donata, the alleged wife of Postumus, is mentioned by no historian. The coins published by Goltzius and others are suspected; and the existence of such a princess is not authenticated].

POSTUMUS THE YOUNGER. (?)

[Postumus, the son of the usurper, was declared Caesar, and shortly afterwards Augustus, by his father, in the year of Rome 1011 (A. D. 258). He was put to death at the same time as his father, in the year 1020 (A. D. 267) by the soldiers under their command].

Gold - *unique.*
Base silver - - - - - - - - - - - - - - - - - - *unique.*

IMP. C. POSTVMVS. P. F. AVG.   The laureated head of Postumus to the right.—*Rev.* INVICTO. AVG.   Bust of Postumus, the younger (?) to the left, with radiated crown and a sceptre, or baton, resting on the shoulder.

The only historian who makes mention of Postumus the younger is Trebellius Pollio, an author considered by some as of doubtful authority. Eckhel is of opinion that no such person existed as Postumus the younger. Banduri has assigned several coins to this supposed prince, but they have long since been restored to the elder Postumus.   The type described above is thought by M. Mionnet to belong to the son; but although the experience of this indefatigable numismatist merits attention, it must nevertheless be allowed that the supposed youth of the bust on the reverse is but a slight authority for such an hypothesis.   Mionnet, in speaking of this coin, says, " La tête du revers est sensiblement plus jèune que celle qui est de l'autre côté ; ce ne peut donc être celle d'une divinité, telle qu' Hercule ou Mars ; ce n'est point non plus celle de Victorin que Postume prit pour collègue ; car Victorin étoit un général consommé lorsqu'il fut associé à Postume, et devoit être d'un âge peu différent de celui de ce denier : ce ne peut donc être que la tête du fils de Postume."   That the bust in question is not that of Victorinus, no one the least acquainted with the portraits of that usurper will deny. The nose of Victorinus is, on all his coins, decidedly acquiline ; but that of Postumus is always of a different form.   With respect to the supposed youth of the bust, M. Prosper Dupre* very justly observes that this might not have been intentional, but merely owing to the smallness of the object upon which the engraver had to exercise his skill.   This writer remarks that many persons consider the length and size of the beard as furnishing a distinction between the Emperor and the Caesar ; whilst the absurdity of these opinions is shewn by the coins of some emperors, Macrinus especially, upon which the bust appears sometimes with a very ample, and at others with a short, curled beard.   A perusal of the very ingenious and learned tract of M. Dupré, will satisfy the reader that there are very slight grounds for M. Mionnet's attribution.

---

* Dissertation sur les Médailles attribuées au fils de l'Empereur Postume, par M. Prosper Dupré.   Paris, Renouard.   1825.   8vo.

LAELIANUS.

[Ulpius Cornelius Laelianus, an usurper in the reign of Gallienus, was killed by his troops at the instigation of Victorinus].

Style:——IMP. C. VLP. COR. LAELIANVS.——IMP. C. LAELIANVS. P. F. AVG.

The names of Laelianus, Lollianus, and Aelianus, are used indiscriminately by historians, who appear to apply them to the same personage; namely, the usurper who assumed the purple in Gaul, during the reign of Postumus, in that country; but, according to some coins, upon which the prenomen is different, the above names belong to three different persons. The coins of Laelianus are fully authenticated. Those of Lollianus are given by Tanini as existing in the cabinet of the Prince de Waldeck; and Eckhel has expressed his belief in their authenticity, as well as in those of Aelianus, published in the *Museum Theupoli.* Those published by Goltzius and Chifflet are spurious.

Gold - R 8
Base silver - - - - - - - - - - - - - - - - - R 2
Third brass - - - - - - - - - - - - - - - - - R 2
   ,,   or base silver, with the legend VLP. COR. LAELIANVS. - R 5

GOLD AND BASE SILVER.

1.

TEMPORVM. FELICITAS. Spain personified, seated on the ground; holding a branch in her right hand; a rabbit near her left elbow. (*Plate ix, No. 8*). - - - - - - - - - - - - - - - AU

2.

VICTORIA. AVG. Victory, marching to the right, or to the left; holding a palm-branch and a garland.

At the sale of the Trattle collection, No. 1, in fine preservation, brought forty-three pounds. This type is valued by Mionnet at 300 francs only.

LOLLIANUS.

The coins assigned to this usurper, in the reign of Gallienus, are doubted. Tanini thus describes a coin in third brass :—

IMP. C. LOLLIANVS. P. F. AVG. Head of Lollianus.—*Rev.* ARA. PACIS. The temple of Janus, shut; before it, an altar, with the fire kindled.

AELIANUS.

A coin of this usurper is described in the Museum Theupoli thus:—

THIRD BRASS.

IMP. C. Q. VALENS. AELIANUS. P. AVG.   Head of Aelianus.
—*Rev.* IOVI. CONSER. AVGG.   Jupiter standing, holding the hasta and thunderbolt: in the exergue, S. M. I.

The authenticity of this coin is doubted; but Eckhel bears testimony to the general accuracy of the coins described in the collection above mentioned.   The letters in the exergue create a doubt as to the time of this usurper's revolt; and it has been by some supposed that he is the same personage who is styled by Eutropius, Aemilianus, and who usurped the purple in Gaul in the reign of Diocletian, in whose reign the practice of placing letters in the exergue became common.

VICTORINUS THE ELDER.

[Marcus Piauvonius Victorinus, General of the legions under Postumus, was associated with that usurper in the government of Gaul, about the year of Rome 1018 (A. D. 265).   Victorinus was murdered by his soldiers at Cologne in 1020 (A. D. 267)].

STYLE:——VICTORINVS. AVG.   [On reverse, sometimes, P. P.]—— IMP. VICTORINVS. AVG.——IMP. C. PIAV. VICTORINVS. AVG.——IMP. VICTORINVS. PIVS. AVG.——IMP. VICTO- RINVS. P. F. AVG.——IMP. C. (*or* CAES.) VICTORINVS. P. F. AVG.   [On reverse, sometimes, P. P. *or* INVICTVS.]——IMP. C. PI. (*or* PIAV.) VICTORINVS. P. F. AVG.——IMP. C. M. PI- AVVONIVS. VICTORINVS. P. F. AVG.——DIVVS. VICTO- RINVS. PIVS.

The coins described by Mediobarba and Banduri, with the legends, MARCVS. AVRELIVS. VICTORINVS, are doubted.

Gold - - - - - - - - - - - - - - - - - -	R 6
,, quinarii - - - - - - - - - - - - - - -	R 8
Base silver or billon - - - - - - - - - - - - -	R 1
,, with type of consecration - - - - - - -	R 3
Brass medallion - - - - - - - - - - - - - - - -	*unique.*
Third brass - - - - - - - - - - - - - - - -	VC

Those which appear to be of fine silver are plated on the small brass.

GOLD AND BASE SILVER, WITH RARE REVERSES.

1.

ADIVTRIX. AVG. A woman standing; at her feet, a bow and a quiver. - - - - - - - - - - - - - - - - - AU

2.

ADVENTVS. AVG. The emperor, on horseback. - - - - - AU

3.

AEQVITAS. AVG. Equity, standing. - - - - - - - - - B

4.

COMES. AVG. Victory, standing. - - - - - - - - - - AU

5.

COMES. AVG. Bust of Mars, with coat of mail and helmet. The obverse has the laureated head of Victorinus to the right: legend, IMP. VICTORINVS. P. F. AVG. (*Plate ix, No. 9*). - - AU (Unique and unpublished, in the cabinet of *T. Thomas, Esq.*)

6.

DIVO. VICTORINO. PIO. Head of Victorinus, with radiated crown. —*Rev.* CONSECRATIO. An eagle, with expanded wings. - - B

7.

INVICTVS. The sun: a star in the field. - - - - - - - - B

8.

Same legend. Radiated head of the sun. - - - - - - - - AU

9.

IOVI. STATORI. Jupiter-Stator, standing. - - - - - - - B

10.

LEG. IIII. FLAVIA. P. F. A helmed head and two lions. - - AU

11.

LEG. X. FRETENSIS. An ox: P. F. in the exergue. - - - AU

12.

LEG. XX. VAL. VICTRIX. A boar, running: P. F. in the exergue. AU

13.

LEG. XXX. VLPIA. PIA. F. Jupiter, standing; Capricorn. - AU

14.

PAX. AVG. Peace, standing. - - - - - - - - - AU & B

15.

P. M. TR. P. III. COS. II. P. P. The emperor, sacrificing. (A *quinarius*). - - - - - - - - - - - - - - - - AU

The obverse has the bust of Victorinus with coat of mail, and holding a spear and buckler.

16.

SAECVLI. FELICITAS. A woman standing, holding a child; at her feet, the prow of a vessel and a rudder. - - - - - - - AU

17.

VICTORIA. AVG. Victory, marching. - - - - - - - - B

18.

IMP. VICTORINVS. PIVS. AVG. The heads of Victorinus and a Divinity.—*Rev.* VICTORIA. AVG. The winged bust of Victory. (*Mionnet*). - - - - - - - - - - - - - - - - - AU

19.

Same legend. Victory standing, holding a palm branch and a garland.
AU

20.

VIRTVS. AVG. A military figure, standing. - - - - - - B.

21.

VOTA. AVGVSTI. The heads of Mars and Diana, side by side. AU

22.

Same legend. The heads of Apollo and Diana, face to face. - - AU

In gold, Nos. 18 and 19 are much the rarest; excepting, of course, No. 5. The next in rarity are Nos. 15, 21, and 22. Then Nos. 1, 2, 7, 10, 11, 12. No. 14 is the least rare. In base silver, No. 20 is a very rare type: the next in rarity is No. 17. No. 5 is much rarer than the remaining numbers.

BRASS MEDALLION.

IMP. CAES. VICTORINVS. PIVS. FELIX. AVG. Laureated bust of Victorinus to the right.—*Rev.* RESTITVTOR. GALLIARVM. The emperor standing, holding the parazonium, and extending his right hand to the Province kneeling before him : behind the emperor, Victory placing a garland on his head; before, Abundance, holding the hasta and a cornucopia: in the exergue, VICTORIA. AVG.

This very fine medallion has, unfortunately, sustained some injury on the reverse. It belongs to the collection of the Bibliothéque du Roi at Paris, and is supposed unique.

THIRD BRASS, WITH RARE REVERSES.

1.

AEQVITAS. AVG. Equity, standing.

2.

COMES. AVG.   Victory, marching.

3.

CONSECRATIO.   An eagle, on a globe.

4.

FORT. REDVX.   Fortune, seated.

5.

INDVLGENTIA. . . . . . .   The emperor, in a military habit, raising up a woman kneeling before him.

(Unpublished, in the cabinet of *F. Douce, Esq.*)

6.

INVICTVS.   The Sun, marching.

7.

LEG. XXII. PRIMIGENIE.   Hercules, standing: Capricorn.

8.

ORIENS. AVG.   The Sun, standing; his right hand raised, his left holding a whip: in the field, P.

9.

P. M. TR. P. COS. II. P. P.   The emperor, bearing a trophy.

10.

SAECVLI. FELICITAS.   Victorinus standing, holding a javelin and a globe.

11.

SALVS. AVG.   Hygeia standing, holding a patera and serpent.

12.

SECVRITAS. AVGG.   Security, seated.

13.

VICTORIA. AVG.   Victory, sacrificing.

14.

VIRTVS. AVG.   A military figure, standing.

Of the above, Nos. 4, 6, and 14, are the least rare.

VICTORINUS THE YOUNGER.

[The younger Victorinus was created Caesar by his father when dying, and shortly after, fell by the hands of the soldiers who had assassinated that usurper. The coins hitherto given to this prince, belong to the elder Victorinus, as is shewn by Eckhel].

VICTORINA.

[Victorina, or Victoria, the mother of the elder Victorinus, was styled by the legions of Gaul, AVGVSTA. and MATER. CASTRORVM. (Mother of Armies). Through the influence of this celebrated woman, Victorinus was associated with Postumus. Marius and Tetricus successively owed their election to her. She died some months after the elevation of the latter, not without suspicion of having been poisoned by his order, in the year of Rome 1021 (A. D. 268). Some authors say positively that she died a natural death].

STYLE:——IMP. VICTORINA. AVG.——IMP. VICTORIA. AVG.

Third brass (if authentic) - - - - - - - - - - - - - - - R 8

IMP. VICTORIA. *(sic). or* VICTORINA. AVG. A helmed head.—
    Rev. CONSECRATIO. An eagle with expanded wings, holding
    a thunderbolt in its talons. In the exergue, JL. (*Catalogue
    d'Ennery*, p. 616).

Beauvais quotes this coin from d'Ennery's cabinet.

MARIUS.

[Marcus Aurelius Marius, an usurper in the reign of Gallienus, was a man of obscure origin. The legions of Gaul proclaimed him emperor, after the death of Victorinus, in the year of Rome 1020 (A. D. 267). History savs that he was assassinated three days after his election, but Eckhel is of opinion that his reign was not so short, and that it probably extended to one or two months].

STYLE:——IMP. C. M. AVR. MARIVS. AVG.——IMP. C. MARIVS.
    P. F. AVG. [On reverse, sometimes, PACATOR. ORBIS.]——IMP.
    C. M. AVR. MARIVS. P. F. AVG.

Gold - R 8
Base silver - - - - - - - - - - - - - - - - - - R 3
Third brass - - - - - - - - - - - - - - - - - - R 1

The coins which appear to be of fine silver, are casts from the third brass.

GOLD AND BASE SILVER.
1.

AEQVITAS. Equity, standing. - - - - - - - - - - - B

2.

CONCORDIA. MILITVM. Two hands joined. - - - - AU & B

3.

FELICITAS. AVG. Felicity, standing. - - - - - - - - - B

4.

FIDES. MILITVM. A woman, holding two standards. (*Catalogue d'Ennery*, p. 224). - - - - - - - - - - - - - AU & B

5.

SAECVLI. FELICITAS. Felicity, standing. - - - - - AU & B

6.

VICTORIA. AVG. Victory, marching. - - - - - - - - - B

7.

Same legend. Victory standing, her right hand on a shield resting on the ground; her left holding a palm branch. The obverse has the laureated head of Marius to the right: legend, IMP. C. M. AVR. MARIVS. P. F. AVG. - - - - - - - - - - - - - AU

(Unpublished: in the cabinet of *Berne, Switzerland.*)

8.

VIRTVS. AVG. A military figure, standing. - - - - - - - B

In gold, No. 7 is the rarest. In base silver, Nos. 1 and 7 are rarer than the others.

THIRD BRASS.

1.

CONCORD. MILIT. *or* CONCORDIA. MILITVM. Two hands joined.

2.

PACATOR. ORBIS. Radiated head of the Sun.

Mionnet, in describing this type, says, "I am supposing this type given by Vaillant, genuine; but I have before me this reverse, which belongs to Postumus, *encasted* in a coin of Marius."

3.

SAEC. FELICITAS. Felicity, standing.

4.

VICTORIA. AVG. Victory marching, or standing.

5.

VIRTVS. AVG. Usual type.

No. 2 is a very rare type. No. 5 is rarer than the remaining numbers.

TETRICUS THE ELDER.

[Caius Pesuvius Tetricus, an usurper in the reign of Gallienus, descended
from a senatorial family, was governor of Aquitaine under the emperors
Valerian and Gallienus. The legions of Gaul elected him emperor in
the year of Rome 1020 (A. D. 267), just previous to the death of
Gallienus. Tetricus held the sovereignty he had seized, during the
whole of the reign of Claudius Gothicus, and part of that of his successor Aurelian, when he voluntarily gave up the provinces to that
emperor, and retired to private life, in the year of Rome 1025 (A.
D. 272). The time of his death is not known.]

STYLE, ASSOCIATED WITH HIS SON :——IMPP. TETRICI. AVGG. [On
reverse, sometimes, P. P.]——IMPP. TETRICI. PII. AVGG.——
IMP. INVICTI. PII. AVGG.

TETRICUS THE ELDER, ALONE :——IMP. TETRICVS. AVG.——IMP. C.
TETRICVS. AVG.——IMP. C. C. PESV. TETRICVS. AVG.
——IMP. TETRICVS. PIVS. AVG. [On reverse, sometimes, P
P.]——IMP. TETRICVS. P. F. AVG. [On reverse, sometimes,
P. P.]——IMP. C. TETRICVS. P. F. AVG. [On reverse, some-
times, P. P. (or PRINC. IVVENT.)].

Gold medallion - - - - - - - - - - - - - - - *unique*
  ,, of the usual size - - - - - - - - - - - - - - R 6
Quinarii - - - - - - - - - - - - - - - - - - R 8
Base silver, or billon - - - - - - - - - - - - - - R 4
Brass medallion (see Beauvais, Histoire Abr. des Empereurs Romaines)?
Third brass - - - - - - - - - - - - - - - - - VC

GOLD MEDALLION.

IMP. TETRICVS. AVG. The half-length figure of Tetricus in the
imperial habit, to the left; in his right hand an olive branch, in his
left a sceptre surmounted by an eagle.

This medallion is composed of two thin leaves of gold stamped together: it has a large ornamented border with two loops. (See the paper
of M. de Boze: Memoirs of the Academy of Inscriptions, &c. Vol. xxvi.
page 504).

GOLD AND BASE SILVER, WITH RARE REVERSES.

1.

ADVENTVS. AVG. The emperor, on horseback. - - - - - AU

2.

COMES. AVG. A figure standing, winged (sometimes not winged). AU

3.

Same legend. Victory standing, holding a garland and a palm branch. - B

4.

FELICITAS. PVBLICA. Felicity, standing near a column. - AU

5.

HILARITAS. AVGG. A woman standing, holding a palm branch and a cornucopia. - - - - - - - - - - - - - - B

6.

HILARITAS. AVGG. A similar type, but with two children at the feet of the woman. - - - - - - - - - - - - - AU & B

7.

IOVI. VICTORI. Jupiter-Victor, seated. - - - - - - - AU

8.

LAETITIA. AVGG. N. Laetitia, standing. - - - - - - AU

9.

NOBILITAS. A woman standing, holding a globe and the hasta. AU

10.

PAX. AETERNA. Peace, standing. - - - - - - - AU & B

11.

P. M. TR. P. COS. P. P. The emperor standing, in the toga. - AU

12.

Same legend. The emperor, seated in a curule chair. - - - - AU

13.

P. M. TR. P. II. COS. P. P. The emperor standing, in the toga, holding a branch and the parazonium. (*Plate ix, No.* 10). - - - AU

14.

P. M. TR. P. III. COS. P. P. A woman standing, holding an ensign and the hasta pura. - - - - - - - - - - - - - - AU

15.

Same legend. A military figure standing, holding the hasta and a branch; his foot resting on a globe. - - - - - - - - AU

16.

SALVS. AVGG. Hygeia standing, sacrificing. - - - - - - B

17.

SPES. PVBLICA. Hope, marching. - - - - - - - - - AU

18.

VBERITAS. AVGG. A woman standing, holding a cornucopia and a purse. - - - - - - - - - - - - - - - - - - AU

19.

VICTORIA. AVGG.   Victory, marching. - - - - - - - AU

20.

VICTORIA. AVGG.   Victory, bearing a trophy. - - - - - AU

21.

VIRTVS. AVG.   A military figure standing, holding a globe and the
parazonium : a captive at his feet. - - - - - - - - - AU

22.

Same legend.   A military figure, seated on a coat of mail, holding a
laurel branch and the hasta pura. - - - - - - - - - AU

23.

IMP. C. TETRICVS. AVG.   Head of Tetricus, full faced, with the
paludamentum.—*Rev.* VOTIS. DECENNALIBVS. Victory standing, her left foot on a globe, inscribing on a buckler, X. (A *quinarius*). - - - - - - - - - - - - - - - - - - - AU

In gold, No. 12 is the rarest type.   The next in rarity are Nos. 1, 20,
and 23.   Then Nos. 2, 11, 13, 19, 21, 22.   In base silver, the types
described are equally rare.   Mionnet values them at ten francs each.

[TETRICUS, AND HIS SON TETRICUS].

GOLD.

1.

IMP. C. TETRICVS. P. F. AVG.   The heads of Tetricus and his son,
side by side.—*Rev.* AETERNITAS. AVGG.   A woman standing,
holding a phoenix on a globe. - - - - - - - - - - - AU

2.

IMPP. INVICTI. PII. AVGG.   Heads as before.—*Rev.* HILARITAS.
AVGG.   A woman standing, with two children at her feet. - AU

3.

IMPP. TETRICII. PII. AVGG.   Heads as before.—*Rev.* IOVI.
VICTORI.   Jupiter-Victor, seated. - - - - - - - - AU

4.

Same legend.   Same heads.—*Rev.* VICTORIA. AVGG.   Victory,
seated before a trophy, inscribing VOT. X. on a buckler.   - AU

The above are valued by Mionnet at 200 francs each.

THIRD BRASS, WITH RARE REVERSES.

[The many barbarous coins of Victorinus, with unintelligible legends,
are not noticed here].

1.

ABVNDANTIA. AVG.   A woman, standing, with a cornucopia reversed.

2.

COMES. AVG. (or COMES. AVG. N.)   Victory standing, holding a palm branch and a garland.

3.

CONSACRATIO. (sic).   A woman, standing before an altar.

4.

FELICITAS. AVG.   Felicity, standing.

5.

HILARITAS.   A woman standing, holding the hasta and a garland.

6.

HILARITAS. AC. (sic).   A woman standing, holding a flower and a cornucopia.

7.

HILARITAS. AVG.   Pontifical vases.

8.

IMP. C. CLAVDIVS. AVG.   Head of Claudius, with radiated crown.

9.

INVICTVS.   The Sun standing, with his attributes.

10.

IOVI. VICTORI.   Jupiter-Victor, seated.

11.

LAETITIA. AVG. N.   Laetitia standing, holding an anchor and a garland.

12.

MARS. VIC.   Mars marching, with a trophy and a spear.

13.

MONETA. AVG.   Moneta, standing.

14.

NEPTVNO. CONS. AVG.   A sea-horse.

15.

PIETAS. ACV. (sic).   Pontifical vases.

16.

Same legend.   A woman, standing before an altar.

17.

PRO. AVG. (or PROVID. AVG. or PROVIDENTIA. AVG.).   Providence, standing.

18.

P. TETRICI.   A woman standing, holding a palm and a cornucopia.

19.

SALVS. AVGG.   A woman standing, holding a palm-branch; her left
hand resting on an anchor.

20.

SPES. AVG.   Hope.

21.

VICTORIA. AVG.   Victory, marching.

22.

VOTA. PVBLICA.   An altar.

The rarest types are Nos. 2, 7, 8, 13, 14, and 22.   The next in rarity
are Nos. 1, 3, 9, 12, 15, 16, 18, and 19.

[TETRICUS, AND HIS SON TETRICUS].

1.

IMPP. TETRICI. AVGG.   The heads of the Tetrici, face to face : the
first, laureated; the other, bare.—*Rev.* P. M. TR. P. COS. III. P.
P. VOTA.   Tetricus and his son, sacrificing : one of them crowned
by Victory.

2.

Another, with the Tetrici, sacrificing : one of them crowned by Victory;
the other by a military figure.

3.

IMPP. TETRICI. AVGG.   The heads of Tetricus and his son, side by
side : the first, laureated; the other, bare. — *Rev.* PAX. AVG.
Peace, standing, with hasta pura and olive branch.

4.

IMP. TETRICVS. AVG. (*or* P. F. AVG.).   Bearded head of the elder
Tetricus, with radiated crown.—*Rev.* PIVESV. (*or* C. PIVESV.
TETRICVS. CAES. *or* PIVESV. TETRICVS. C.).   Beardless
head of the younger Tetricus, with radiated crown.

These four types are of great rarity : the second is the rarest, and the
last is the least rare.

TETRICUS THE YOUNGER.

[Caius Pesuvius Pivesus Tetricus, the son of the elder Tetricus, was
declared Caesar by his father in the year of Rome 1020 (A. D. 276);
and retired with him to private life, about the year 1026 (A. D. 272)].

PLATE 10.

Style:——PIVESVS. TETRICVS. CAES.——C. TETRICVS. CAES.
——C. PES. TETRICVS. CAES.——C. PEVESV. TETRICVS.
CAES. [On reverse, sometimes, PRINC. IVVENT.]——IMPE. TET.
PIVES.——IMP. C. TETRICVS. C.——. . . .TETRICVS. AVG.
——C. PIV. TETRICVS. A.——C.PIVESV.TETRICVS. C. AVG.
——IMP. C. TETRICVS. A.——IMP. TETRICVS. P. F. AVG.

The sixth legend is remarkable for the repetition of the title CAESAR.
This also occurs on the coins of Carinus and Numerianus. The last
three legends are found on coins of this prince in the cabinet of the French
king. One of these is in gold; the others in third brass. The coins
with the legends TETRICVS. AVG., and C. PIV. TETRICVS. A. are in third
brass, and have been published by Banduri and Eckhel, both of whom
have offered their comments on the title of Augustus given to Tetricus
the younger. Treb. Pollio and Victor speak of this prince as Caesar
only, and never style him Augustus; but Banduri maintains that he bore
this title; while Eckhel is of a contrary opinion, and supposes that the
legend in question is an error, found only on the brass coins of this
prince, the striking of which was confided to illiterate moneyers. Since
this learned antiquary wrote, a gold coin of Tetricus with the title of
Augustus has been published by M. Mionnet, who nevertheless thinks it
probable that the engraver of the dye has by mistake put CAVG. instead
of CAES. and considers the question as still undecided.

Gold - - - - - - - - - - - - - - - - - - - R 6
„ quinarii - - - - - - - - - - - - - - - R 8
Base silver - - - - - - - - - - - - - - - - R 7
Third brass - - - - - - - - - - - - - - - - V C

GOLD AND BASE SILVER, WITH RARE REVERSES.

1.
COMES. AVG. Victory standing, with garland and palm branch. B

2.
PAX. AVG. A woman standing: in the field, V. and a star. - - B

3.
PIETAS. AVGVSTOR. Sacrificial instruments. - - - - - - B

4.
SPES. AVG. Hope. (*Plate x, No.* 1). - - - - - - - - - B

5.
SPES. AVGG. Hope. - - - - - - - - - - - - - AU & B

6.

C. PEVESV. TETRICVS. C. AVG.   Head of the younger Tetricus to
the right, with radiated crown, and the paludamentum. — *Rev.*
SPES. AVGG.   Hope.   (A *quinarius*). - - - - - - - AU

This is the only gold coin known with the title of AVGVSTVS.   (See the
note following the style).

7.

SPES. PVBLICA.   Hope. - - - - - - - - - - - AU & B

In gold, No. 7 is much the rarest type.   The base silver are all equally
rare.

THIRD BRASS, WITH RARE REVERSES.

1.

ABVNDANT. AVG.   The praefericulum.

2.

COM. IMP. AVG.   Minerva standing, holding her shield and a branch.

3.

IMP. TETRICVS. AVG. (*or* P. F. AVG.).   The head of the elder
Tetricus.

4.

INVICTVS.   The Sun, naked, standing.

5.

LAETITIA. AVG. N.   A woman standing: a garland in her right
hand; her left resting on an anchor.

6.

NOBILITAS. AVGG.   A woman, standing, with hasta and globe.

7.

PIETAS. AVGG.   Pontifical vases.

8.

PRINC. IVVENT.   The younger Tetricus standing, in a military habit,
holding an ensign and a truncheon.

9.

ℳ within a temple.   (Of the size of the *quinarius*).

10.

SALVS. AVG.   A woman, sacrificing.

11.

Same legend.   Victory, standing.

12.

Same legend.   A woman, standing; her right hand raised, her left
resting on an anchor.

13.

SECVLVM. *(sic).*   An altar, with the fire kindled.

14.

SOLI. CONSER.   A centaur, bending a bow.

15.

SPES. AVGG.   Hope, marching.

16.

VBERITAS. AVG.   A woman standing, holding ears of corn and a cornucopia.

No. 3 is an extremely rare type.   Nos. 1, 2, 4, 5, 13 are rarer than the remaining numbers.

CYRIADES.

[The writer in the Augustan history says, that Cyriades caused himself to be proclaimed emperor in the East, in the year of Rome 1010 (A. D. 257), and was killed by his own soldiers upon the news of the approach of Valerianus: Gibbon, however, supposes that this is an error, and that Cyriades was probably set up by Sapor, after the capture of Valerian.   See *chap. x.*]

Goltzius and others have published coins of Cyriades, but they are not authenticated.

MACRIANUS THE ELDER.

[Another usurper during the distracted reign of Gallienus.   He was defeated by Aureolus, in Illyria, and shortly after murdered by his own soldiers, in the year of Rome 1015 (A. D. 262)].

The coins quoted by Beauvais in his history belong to the younger Macrianus.

MACRIANUS THE YOUNGER.

[Marcus (or Titus) Fulvius Macrianus was declared Augustus at the same time as his father, by the legions of the East, in the year of Rome 1013 (A. D. 260).   He shared the fate of his parent, after their defeat by Aureolus].

Style :——MACRIANVS. NOBIL. CAES.——IMP. C. FVL. MA-CRIANVS. P. F. AVG.

It would appear from the first of these titles, that, contrary to the testimony of historians, Macrianus the younger was first declared Caesar, and that that of Augustus was conferred upon him subsequently.   The Latin coins of the younger Macrianus do not bear the prenomen.

His Greek coins differ in the name : some have MARCVS., others TITVS. If any of the coins with these names bore an old head, instead of the youthful portrait always found on them, it might reasonably be supposed that either Titus or Marcus belonged to the elder Macrianus. Nevertheless, it is certain that many of the imperial Greek coins have portraits but little resembling those on the Latin coins of the same emperors. Sestini has published a Greek coin,* which if authentic, might solve this question; but its genuineness is doubted.

Base silver (often described as third brass). - - - - - - - R 4

BASE SILVER.
1.
AEQVTVS. (*sic*.) AVGG.   Equity, standing : a star in the field.
2.
APOLINI. (*sic*) CONSERVA.   Apollo standing, with lyre and laurel branch.
3.
FIDES. MILITVM.   Three standards. *(Haym).*
4.
FORTVNA. REDVX.   Fortune, seated : a star.
5.
INDVLGENTIAE. AVG.   A woman, seated.
6.
IOVI. CONSERVATORI.   Jupiter, seated : an eagle at his feet.
7.
ROMAE. AETERNAE.   Rome, seated.
8.
SOL. (*or* SOLI.) INVICTO.   The Sun, standing, naked.
9.
SPES. PVBLICA.   Hope.
10.
VICTORIA. AVGG.   Victory, marching.

Nos. 3, 7, and 10, are the rarest.

QUIETUS.

[Caius Fulvius Quietus, another son of Macrianus the elder, was invested with the title of Augustus at the same time as his father and brother, in the year of Rome 1013 (A. D. 260). These having been destroyed, Quietus sought refuge in Emesa; but Odenathus, prince of Palmyra, having taken that city, he was put to death, in the year of Rome 1015 (A.D. 262)].

---

* Lett. tom. iv. p. 132.

S<small>TYLE</small>:——IMP. C. FVL. QVIETVS. P. F. AVG.

Gold - - - - - - - - - - - - - - - *unique, if antique*
Base silver - - - - - - - - - - - - - - - - - R 4
Second brass - - - - - - - - - - - - - - - - R 8

GOLD, AND BASE SILVER.

1.
AEQVTAS. *(sic)* AVGG.   Equity, standing. - - - - - - - B

2.
APOLLINI. CONSERVA.   Apollo, standing: a star. - - - - B

3.
FORT. (*or* FORTVN.) REDVX.   A woman, seated: a star. - - B

4.
INDVLGENTIA. AVG.   A woman, seated. - - - - - - - B

5.
IOVI. CONSERVATORI.   Jupiter, seated: an eagle at his feet. - B

6.
IMP. C. FVL. QVIETVS. P. F. AVG.   Radiated head of Quietus.—
   Rev. MARTI. PROPVGNATORI.   Mars, marching. - - - B

7.
ROMAE. AETERNAE.   Rome, seated. - - - - - - - - B

8.
SOL. INVICTO.   The Sun standing, with his attributes: a star in the
   field. - - - - - - - - - - - - - - - - - AU & B

9.
SPES. PVBLICA.   Hope: a star in the field. - - - - - - B

10.
VICTORIA. AVGG.   Victory, marching. - - - - - - - - B

In base silver, No. 6 is by far the rarest. Of the other numbers, 4
and 8 are the least rare.

SECOND BRASS.

AEQVITAS. AVGG.   Equity standing, with her attributes. (*Mus.
Vindob*).

BALISTA.

[Another tyrant in the east, in the reign of Gallienus. Killed, as is
supposed, by one of the soldiers of Odenathus].

No authentic coins.

INGENUUS.

[A tyrant in Pannonia and Moesia, who assumed the purple, upon the capture of Valerian. Ingenuus was defeated by Gallienus, and shortly afterwards murdered by his own soldiers, in the year of Rome 1014 (A. D. 261)].

No authentic coins.

REGALIANUS.

[Regalianus was a Dacian, and general of the army of Gallienus in Illyria, in the year of Rome 1014. He defeated the legions who had proclaimed Ingenuus, and was in his turn saluted emperor by the army of Mœsia; but he died, as is supposed, by the hands of those who had raised him to the empire].

STYLE:——IMP. C. P. REGALIANVS. AVG.

Silver - R 8

The coins of this usurper, if really antique, are of the first rarity; beside the types described below, there is another quoted by Mionnet. It is in the cabinet of Vienna, and appears to have been struck on a coin of Caracalla. The obverse bears the legend, ... c. p. c. REGALIANV-TORI. with the radiated head of Regalianus: on the reverse, ... CON. . . . . . . ANTONINVS. PIV. . . . . . A woman standing, and the remains of the laureated head of Caracalla. The coin originally bore on the obverse, ANTONINVS. PIVS. AVG. BRIT.—and on the reverse, MARTI. PACATORI.

SILVER.

1.

IMP. C. P. REGALIANVS. AVG.   Radiated head of Regalianus.—
   Rev. LIBERALITAS. AVGG.   Liberality, standing, holding a purse and the hasta, transversely.   *(Cabinet of Vienna).*

2.

ORIENS. AVG.   The Sun standing, with his attributes.

DRYANTILLA.

[Sulpicia Dryantilla, the supposed wife of Regalianus, is not mentioned by any Historian. She is assigned by Eckhel to this usurper. (*Tom.*

vii, p. 463). The same author cites two types struck on coins of an earlier date. One has SA. AVG. YANTILLA.—reverse, PVVNONI. REDIN. The other bears PIETASTNIL . . . .—reverse, IVLIAN. IREDIN. The first of these was originally a Julia Maesa; and the other, one of the Julias, with PIETAS. on the reverse].

STYLE:——SVLP. DRYANTILLA. AVG.

The coins of this lady are not authenticated (see the preceding note). I have seen a modern forgery, among a parcel of common antique coins recently brought from Alexandria.

VALENS.

[Valens was proconsul of Achaia, under Gallienus. He assumed the purple upon hearing that Macrianus sought his life, but was killed by his own soldiers at the end of six months, a few days after the murder of Piso, in the year of Rome 1014 (A. D. 261)].

No authentic coins.

PISO FRUGI.

[Piso Frugi was a senator, and descended from the illustrious family of the Pisos. He attended Valerian in his war against the Persians, and subsequently entered into the service of Macrianus, who sent him against Valens. Piso failed in his mission, and, passing into Thessaly, assumed the purple. He was shortly after assassinated, by order of Valens].

No coins.

A. AEMILIANUS.

[Alexander Aemilianus was praefect of Egypt in the reigns of Valerian and Gallienus, and caused himself to be nominated emperor by the troops under his command, about the year of Rome 1015. He was soon defeated and captured; and, being sent prisoner to Gallienus, was strangled in his dungeon].

No authentic coins.

SATURNINUS I.

[A general under Valerian and Gallienus; killed by the same soldiers who had invested him with the purple].

No authentic coins.

TREBELLIANUS.

['Trebellianus was a famous pirate, who assumed the purple in Isauria. He
perished in a battle with the army sent out against him by Gallienus.
No coins known].

CELSUS.

[Celsus cultivated a farm in Africa, and was, against his wish, elected
emperor about the year of Rome 1018.   He was killed, after a reign
of seven days, by Galliena, a cousin of Gallienus the emperor].

The authenticity of the coins published by Goltzius and others is
doubted.

AUREOLUS.

[Marcus Acilius Aureolus was born of an obscure family in Dacia.   He
was governor of Illyria, under Gallienus, and, after quelling the revolt
of the Macriani, he caused himself to be proclaimed emperor, in the
year of Rome 1020 (A. D. 267).   Gallienus defeated him near Milan,
and Aureolus fled to that city for refuge.   Milan was invested, but
during the siege Gallienus was assassinated.   Aureolus surrendered
himself in the following year to Claudius Gothicus, whose soldiers
immediately put him to death].

STYLE:——IMP. AVREOLVS. AVG.——IMP. C. AVREOLVS.
    AVG.——IMP. M. ACIL. AVREOLVS. P. F. AVG.

Gold (if antique) - - - - - - - - - - - - - - - R 8
Third brass - - - - - - - - - - - - - - - - - - R 8

GOLD.

PROVIDENTIA. AVG.   Providence standing, with the usual attributes.

THIRD BRASS.
1.
CONCORDIA. EQVIT.   A woman, standing; her right foot on the
prow of a vessel, her left holding a rudder.
2.
CONCORD. IIMC. (sic). or CONCORDIA. MIL.   Two hands, joined.
3.
L. I. MIN. RESTITVTA.   Minerva and Aureolus joining hands.
(Dubious).

S. ANTONINUS.

[Sulpicius Antoninus is supposed by Zosimus to have assumed the purple about the same time as Aureolus, and to have met the usual fate of the usurpers of that period; but a date on one of the coins quoted below indicates that it was in the year of Rome 1006 (A. D. 253), at the commencement of the reign of Valerian. The scene of the revolt of Antoninus appears from these coins to have been Emesa, in Syria].

Potin, or bell-metal, - - - - - - - - - - - - - - - R 8
Second brass - - - - - - - - - - - - - - - - - - R 8

Both Syrian, with Greek characters. No Latin coins are known.

CLAUDIUS GOTHICUS.

[Marcus Aurelius Claudius was born in Illyria, of an obscure family, in the year of Rome 967 or 968 (A. D. 214 or 215). He was governor of that province, under Valerian and Gallienus. The latter summoned him to Italy, for the purpose of guarding Turin, while Gallienus besieged Aureolus. Upon the death of the emperor, Claudius was saluted Augustus by the army and senate. The victory which he gained over the Goths in Moesia, in the year 1022 (A. D. 269), procured for him the surname of Gothicus. He died of the plague, near Sirmium in Pannonia, in the year of Rome 1023 (A. D. 270)].

STYLE:——IMP. CLAVDIVS. A. (or AVG.)——IMP. CLAVDIVS. CAES. AVG.——IMP. C. CLAVDIVS. AVG. [On reverse, P. P. (or CONSERVAT. PIETAT.)]——IMP. C. M. AVR. CLAVDIVS. AVG.——IMP. CLAVDIVS. P. AVG.——IMP. CLAVDIVS. P. F. AVG.——IMP. C. (or CAES.) CLAVDIVS. P. (or PIVS.) F. (or FELIX. AVG.)——IMP. C. M. AVR. CLAVDIVS. GER. GOTHICVS.——IMP. C. M. AVR. CLAVDIVS. P. F. AVG. GERM. GOTHICVS. —— DIVVS. CLAVDIVS. —— DIVVS. CLAVDIVS. GOTHICVS. —— DIVVS. CLAVD. (or CLAV-DIVS.) OPT. (or OPTIMVS.) IMP.

Gold - - - - - - - - - - - - - - - - - - R 8
  ,, quinarii - - - - - - - - - - - - - - - - - R 8

Silver (none) *
Brass medallions - - - - - - - - - - - - - - - R 2
First brass - - - - - - - - - - - - - - - - R 4
Second brass - - - - - - - - - - - - - - - R 1
Third brass - - - - - - - - - - - - - - - - VC

GOLD.

1.

AEQVITAS. AVG.   Equity, standing.

2.

CONCOR. EXERC.   A woman, standing between two ensigns.   (*Dr. Mead's Catalogue*).

3.

DIANA. LVCIF.   Diana, walking.

4.

INVICTVS. AVG.   The helmed head of Claudius.

5.

MEMORIAE. AETERNAE.   An eagle, with expanded wings.   In the exergue, P. S.

6.

ROMAE. AETERNAE.   Statue of Rome, seated within a temple.

7.

SPES. PVBLICA.   A woman, standing.   (*Khell*).

8.

VICTORIA. AVG.   Victory, standing between two captives.

9.

Same legend.   A similar type.   (A *quinarius*).

10.

VIRTVS. CLAVDII.   The emperor on horseback, bare headed, armed with a spear, and riding over several prostrate figures.   (*Plate x, No. 2.*)

Unpublished: in the cabinet of *T. Thomas, Esq.*

Nos. 2, 4, and 10, are the rarest.

BRASS MEDALLIONS.

1.

ADVENTVS. AVG.   The emperor on horseback, preceded by Victory and a soldier, and followed by two other soldiers.

---

* Mionnet says that the coins described by Vaillant and Tanini are, in all probability, neither silver nor billon, but third brass washed with silver or tin. Such, says this author, were the coins of Claudius Gothicus, described as silver in d'Ennery's Catalogue. Fine silver appears again in the reign of Diocletianus.

2.

CONSECRATIO. An altar with the fire kindled.

3.

MARS. VLTOR. Mars, marching with a trophy.

4.

MARTI. PACIFERO. Mars, marching with an olive branch and the hasta.

5.

MONETA. AVG. The three Monetæ, standing.

6.

P. M. TR. P. . . II. COS. P. P. Hercules, leaning on his club.

No. 1 is the rarest type. No. 5 is much less rare than the other numbers.

FIRST BRASS, WITH RARE REVERSES.

1.

CONSECRATIO. An eagle with expanded wings.

Struck from the dye of the third brass on the size of first brass.

2.

Same legend. An altar.

3.

IOVI. VICTORI. Jupiter, standing.

The last two are much the rarest.

SECOND BRASS, WITH RARE REVERSES.

1.

IOVI. VICTORI. Jupiter standing, wearing the pallium, holding the thunderbolt and hasta pura.

2.

MARS. VLTOR. Mars, marching with a trophy and a lance.

3.

Same legend. Mars, marching with spear and buckler.

4.

VICTORIA. AVG. Victory, standing.

5.

VIRTVS. AVG. A military figure standing, holding a branch and a spear. In the exergue, E.

No. 5 is the rarest. The next in rarity is No. 3.

THIRD BRASS, WITH RARE REVERSES.

1.

ADVENTVS. AVG. The emperor, on horseback.

2.

AETER. AVG. A woman, and the Sun, standing.

3.

CLAVSECRATIO. *(sic)*. An eagle with expanded wings. In the exergue, ω.

4.

CONCOR. AVG. Two veiled women, each holding a torch and ears of corn.

5.

CONCOR. EXERCI. A woman standing, holding an ensign and the hasta transversely.

6.

CONCORD. LEGI. A similar type.

7.

CONSECRATIO. An altar with the fire kindled.

8.

Same legend. A funeral pile.

9.

CONSECR. AVG. Jupiter and Juno, standing.

10.

CONSER. AVG. Serapis, standing. In the exergue, T.

11.

CONSERVAT. AVG. Æsculapius, standing. In the exergue, S. P. Q. R.

12.

CONSERVAT. PIETAT. A military figure raising up a woman kneeling before him.

13.

DEO. CABIRO. One of the Cabiri, standing.

14.

DIANA. LVCIF. Diana-Lucifera, standing.

15.

DIANAE. VICTR. Diana, standing: a stag by her side.

16.

FELIC. AVG. A woman and Fortune, standing.'

17.

FIDES. AVG. Mercury, standing.

18.

FORTVNA. REDVX. Fortune, standing. In the exergue, S. P. Q. R.

19.

HILARITAS. AVGG. A woman standing, holding a palm branch and a cornucopia.

20.

IVNO. REGINA. Juno, standing; a peacock at her side.

21.

IVVENTAS. *(sic)*. AVG. Hercules, standing.

22.

IVVENTVS. AVG. A similar type.

23.

LIBERITAS. *(sic)*. AVG. Mercury, standing.

24.

LIBERO. CONS. AVG. A panther, walking.

25.

MARS. VLTOR. Mars, marching.

26.

MARS. VICTOR. A similar type.

27.

MEMORIAE. AETERNAE. An eagle with expanded wings.

28.

Same legend. A lion, walking; above, a club.

29.

MONETA. AVG. Moneta, standing.

30.

NEPTVN. (*or* NEPTVNO.) AVG. Neptune, standing.

31.

ORIENS. AVG. The Sun, standing.

32.

PAX. EXERC. (*or* EXERCIT.) Peace, standing.

33.

PIETAS. AVG. Mercury standing, with his attributes.

34.

P. M. TR. P. II. COS. P. P. The emperor standing, with the paludamentum, holding a globe and the hasta transversely.

35.

REGI. ARTIS.   Vulcan, standing.

36.

REQVIES. OPTIMOR. MERIT.   The emperor veiled, seated.

37.

SALVS. AVG.   Isis, standing; Є.

38.

Same legend.   Apollo standing, with his lyre ; his right hand holding ears of corn.

39.

Same legend.   Æsculapius, standing.

40.

SOL. AVG.   The Sun, standing.

41.

SOLVS. AVG.   *(sic)*.   The Sun, standing.

42.

SPES. PVBLIC.   Æsculapius and Hygeia, standing.

43.

TEMPORVM. FELIC.   Felicity standing, holding a long caduceus and a cornucopia.

44.

VENVS. AVG.   Venus, standing.

45.

VICTORIA. AVG.   Victory, marching : two captives on the ground.

46.

VICTORIA. GERMAN.   Two captives at the foot of a trophy.

47.

VICTORIAE. GOTHIC.   A similar type.

48.

VIR. AVG.   Minerva and one of the Cabiri, standing.

49.

VIRTVS. AVGVSTI.   A military figure, standing.

50.

VOTA. ORBIS.   Two Victories, standing on each side of a palm-tree, to the trunk of which is attached a buckler, inscribed S. C.

No. 35 is much the rarest type.   Nos. 13, 41, 42, and 48, are rarer than the remaining numbers.

CENSORINUS.

[Censorinus was proclaimed emperor against his consent by the legions in Italy, during the absence of Claudius, who was engaged in the war with the Goths, in the year of Rome 1023 (A. D. 270). He perished by the hands of those who had invested him with the purple, seven days afterwards].

Goltzius and others have published coins of Censorinus, but they have not been authenticated.

QUINTILLUS.

[Marcus Aurelius Claudius Quintillus, brother of Claudius Gothicus, was invested with the purple by the army under his command, near Aquileia, upon the news of the death of Claudius, in the year of Rome 1023 (A. D. 270). But the soldiers having received intelligence of the election of Aurelian by the legions of Pannonia, abandoned Quintillus, who caused his veins to be opened, and expired, according to most historians, after a short reign of seventeen days. Zosimus, however, says he reigned some months; and Eckhel, remarking on the variety of the types of the coins of Quintillus, is of opinion that his reign was not so short as has been represented].

STYLE: —— IMP. QVINTILLVS. AVG. —— IMP. C. M. AVR. QVINTILLVS. AVG.——IMP. C. M. AVR. CL. QVINTILLVS. AVG. [On reverse, sometimes, p. p.]——IMP. C. M. AVR. CL. QVINTILLVS. P. F. AVG.

Gold - R 8
Base silver (none). See the note to Claudius.
Brass medallion - - - - - - - - - - - - - - - R 8
Third brass - - - - - - - - - - - - - - - - - S

GOLD.

1.

FIDES. MILITVM. A woman, holding two standards.

2.

TEMP. FELICITAS. within a laurel garland.

Mionnet values these types at 700 francs each.

BRASS MEDALLION.

APOLLINI. CONSERVATORI. A temple, with the statue of Apollo. (*Mus. Theupoli*).

THIRD BRASS.

1.

APOLLINI. AVG.   Apollo, standing before an altar.

2.

CONCO. EXER.   A woman standing, holding an ensign and a cornu-copia.   In the exergue, T.

3.

FIDES. MILITVM.   A woman standing, holding an ensign and the hasta.   In the field, Є.

4.

GENIVS. AVG.   The Genius, standing before an altar.

5.

P. M. TR. P. COS. P. P.   The emperor, standing.

No. 2 is the least rare. The coins of Quintillus, in third brass, are less common in England than in France and Italy, although they are some-times discovered in this country with those of other emperors of about the same period. None of the types are remarkable.

AURELIANUS.

[Lucius Claudius Domitius Aurelianus was born at Sirmium in Pan-nonia, of an obscure family, about the year of Rome 960 (A. D. 207). He was general of cavalry in the reign of Claudius Gothicus; and after the death of that emperor, was proclaimed by the legions of Pan-nonia, in the year of Rome 1023 (A. D. 270). Aurelianus was assassinated between Byzantium and Heraclea, when about to march against the Persians, in the year of Rome 1028 (A. D. 275)].

STYLE : —— IMP. C. L. D. AVRELIANVS. —— AVRELIANVS. AVG.——IMP. AVRELIANVS. AVG.   [On reverse, sometimes P. P. (or RESTITVTOR. EXERCITI. or RESTITVTOR. ORBIS. or RESTITVTOR. ORIENTIS. or RESTIT. SAECVLI.]—— IMP. C. AVRELIANVS. AVG. [On reverse, sometimes, P. P. (or PACATOR. ORBIS.)]—— IMP. C. DOM. AVRELIANVS. AVG. —— IMP. C. L. AVRE-LIALVS. AVG. ——IMP. C. L. D. (or DOM.) AVRELIANVS. AVG.——IMP. CAE. (or CAES.) CL. DOM. AVRELIANVS. AVG.——IMP. CL. DOM. AVRELIANVS. P. F. AVG.   [On reverse, sometimes, P. P.]—— IMP. C. AVRELIANVS. IN-VICTVS. AVG. —— DEVS. ET. DOMINVS. NATVS. AVRE-LIANVS. AVG.   [On reverse, sometimes, RESTITVT. ORBIS.]—— DEVS. ET. DOMINVS. NOSTER. AVRELIANVS. AVG.   [On reverse, sometimes, RESTITVT. ORBIS.]

P. 91

AURELIANUS.

P. 228

CONSTANTINUS MAGNUS.

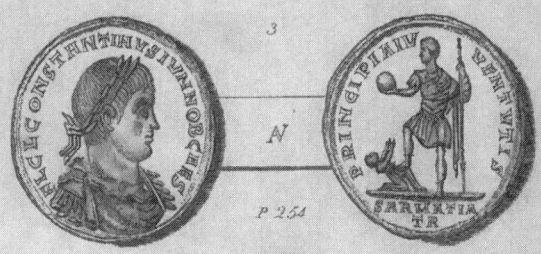

P. 254

CONSTANTINUS II.

P. 251

CONSTANTINUS II.

P. 272

CONSTANTIUS II.

Engraved by Harp & Cog

London, Published by Effingham Wilson, 1 Jan. 1834.

Gold, small medallions - - - - - - - - - - - - - -	R 4
„ of the usual size - - - - - - - - - - - - -	R 4
Base silver - - - - - - - - - - - - - - - - -	R 4
Brass medallions - - - - - - - - - - - - - -	R 2
Second brass - - - - - - - - - - - - - - - -	S
Third brass - - - - - - - - - - - - - - - -	VC

GOLD MEDALLIONS.

1.

ADVENTVS. AVG. The emperor on horseback. *(Plate F, No. 1.)*
Valued by Mionnet at 200 francs. This type, well preserved, brought
7*l.* 2*s.* 6*d.* at the sale of the Trattle collection: another, very fine, brought
12*l.* 12*s.* Mr. Trattle purchased a medallion of this type, at the sale of
the Tyssen collection in 1802, for 8*l.* 18*s.* 6*d.* It was in very fine preservation.

2.

IMP. AVRELIANVS. AVG. The laureated bust of Aurelianus, with
   coat of mail, to the right.—*Rev.* VIRTVS. AVG. Mars marching
   to the right, with a trophy on his shoulder, and a spear in his right
   hand.

This is also valued at 200 francs by Mionnet.

GOLD AND BILLON, OF THE USUAL SIZE.

(Many of the coins described by Banduri and Tanini, are supposed to
be third brass washed with silver).

1.

APOLLINI. CONS. Apollo, seated. - - - - - - - - - AU

2.

CONCORD. LEGI. A woman standing, holding two ensigns. - AU

3.

CONCORDIA. MILI: A woman seated, holding two ensigns. In the
   exergue, P. - - - - - - - - - - - - - - AU

4.

Same legend. Two women standing, and three military standards. AU

5.

CONS. PRINC. AVG. The emperor crowning a trophy, at the foot of
   which are two captives. - - - - - - - - - - - - B

6.

FIDES. MILITVM. A woman, holding two standards. - - - AU

7.

GENIVS. ILLYR. Genius, standing: an ensign. - - - - AU

8.

ORIENS. AVG. The Sun, standing: two captives on the ground. AU

9.

P. M. TR. P. COS. P. P. A lion, walking: a star. - - - - - AU

10.

P. M. TR. P. IIII. COS. III. P. P. Mars marching, with a trophy.
AU

11.

P. M. TR. P. VI. COS. II. The Sun, standing. - - - - - AU

12.

P. M. TR. P. VII. COS. II. P. P. Mars, marching. - - - - AU

This type, extremely fine, brought 7*l.* 12*s.* 6*d.*, in 1802, at the sale of the Tyssen collection.

13.

PROVIDENTIA. DEOR. Providence and the Sun, standing. In the
exergue, SXXT. - - - - - - - - - - - - - - - AU

14.

RESTITVTOR. ORIENTIS. The Sun, standing. - - - - - AU

15.

ROMAE. AETER. Rome, seated. - - - - - - - - AU

16.

VICTORIA. AVG. Victory, marching: in the field, P. and a star. AU

17.

VIRTVS. AVG. An armed figure, marching: a captive. - - AU

18.

Same legend. Mars, marching. - - - - - - - - - - AU

19.

VIRTVS. ILLYRICI. A military figure, standing: a captive on the
ground. - - - - - - - - - - - - - - - - - AU

In gold, Nos. 1, 3, 4, 6, 7, 8, 9, 10, 13, 15, and 19, are the rarest.

BRASS MEDALLION.

SEVERINA. AVG. Bust of the empress, with the stola, and a crescent
on the shoulders.

SECOND BRASS.

1.

AVRELIANVS. AVG. CONS. The emperor in a military habit, sacrificing.

2.

Same legend. The emperor in the toga, sacrificing.

3.

CONCORDIA. AVG. Two figures joining hands: the head of the Sun.

4.

DEO. ET. DOMINO. NATO. AVRELIANO. AVG. Head of the emperor.—*Rev.* RESTITVT. ORBIS. A woman crowning the emperor.

5.

ROMAE. AETER. Rome, seated.

6.

SEVERINA. AVG. Head of Severina.

7.

SOL. DOM. IMP. ROMANI. Radiated head of the Sun: before, four horses.

8.

SOL. DOMINVS. IMPERI. ROMANI. Head of the Sun.

The last two types are much the rarest. The next in rarity is No. 5; then Nos. 1 and 2.

THIRD BRASS, WITH RARE REVERSES.

1.

AETERNIT. AVG. The Sun, holding a globe in his left hand, his right raised aloft.

2.

CONCORD. LEGI. A woman, holding two standards. In the exergue, P. *or* T.

3.

CONCORDIA. MILI. A woman seated, holding two ensigns. In the exergue, T.

4.

FELICIT. TEMP. Felicity standing, with her attributes.

5.

FIDES. MILITVM. Two military figures standing, supporting a globe, surmounted by a figure of Victory. In the exergue, T.

6.

MARS. INVICTVS.   Two figures, standing.

7.

PACATOR. ORBIS.   The Sun, standing.   In the exergue, AL. (*or* CL.)

8.

PACATOR. ORIENTIS.   The emperor, raising up a woman kneeling before him.

9.

PANNONIA.   A woman, holding two standards.

10.

PIETAS. AVG.   Two figures, sacrificing.   In the exergue, S.

11.

P. M. TR. P. COS.   Neptune standing, with his attributes.

12.

P. M. TR. P. T. P. *(sic)*. COS.   A lion, passant.

13.

PROVIDENTIA. AVG.   A woman standing, holding the head of Minerva in her right hand, and in her left the hasta, transversely; a buckler on the ground.

14.

RESTITVTOR. EXERCITI. *(sic)*. Є.   The emperor and a soldier standing, supporting between them, a globe; one holding the hasta pura, the other a spear.   In the exergue, XXI.

15.

RESTITVTOR. ORBIS.   The emperor crowned by a woman, both standing: a star in the field.   In the exergue, KAГ.

The obverse has the title INVICTVS.

16.

DEO. ET. DOMINO. NATO. AVRELIANO. AVG.   The head of Aurelianus.—*Rev.* RESTITVT. ORBIS.   A woman crowning the emperor.

17.

VABALATHVS. VCRIMDR.   Laureated head of Vabalathus.

18.

VICTORIA. AVG.   Victory marching, with palm-branch and garland: a captive on the ground.   In the exergue, A. or B.

19.

VICTORIA. GOTHIC.   A trophy, between two captives.

No. 10 is the rarest type.   Nos. 15 and 16 are the next in rarity; then No. 17.

SEVERINA.

[Ulpia Severina, the wife of the emperor Aurelian, is not mentioned by any historian ; but from her Greek coins struck at Alexandria, it appears that she survived her husband.   On these she has the name of Ulpia, from which Eckhel thinks it probable that she was daughter of Ulpius Crinitus, a descendant of Trajan, who adopted Aurelian].

STYLE :——SEVERINA. AVG.——SEVERINA, P. F. AVG.

Gold, small medallion - - - - - - - - - - - - - - R 8
,, of the usual size   - - - - - - - - - - - - - - R 6
Base silver (or third brass washed with silver)   - - - - - - C
,, with the titles of PIA. FELIX. - - - - - - - - - R 1
Small brass medallions - - - - - - - - - - - - - - R 1
Second brass - - - - - - - - - - - - - - - - - - S
Third brass - - - - - - - - - - - - - - - - - - C

GOLD MEDALLION.

VENVS. FELIX.   Venus, standing.   In the exergue, ϵ.

GOLD, OF THE USUAL SIZE.
1.
CONCORDIA. MILITVM.   A woman standing, holding two ensigns.
2.
CONCORDIAE. MILITUM.   A similar type.   In the exergue, R. (*Plate x, No.* 3).

BRASS MEDALLION.

IMP. AVRELIANVS. AVG.   Head of Aurelian, with radiated crown.

SECOND BRASS, WITH RARE REVERSES.
1.
IMP. AVRELIANVS. AVG.   Laureated bust of Aurelian, with coat of mail.
2.
IVNO. REGINA.   Juno, standing.   In the exergue, C. or Z.

No. 1 is much the rarest.

THIRD BRASS, WITH RARE REVERSE.

CONCORD. MILIT.   Concord, seated.   In the exergue, B. or BL.

PRINCES OF PALMYRA.

ODENATHUS.

[Septimius Odenathus was born at Palmyra; according to some writers, of an obscure family, but according to others, he traced his descent from princes. Odenathus took the title of king, after his defeat of the Persian army, in the year of Rome 1014 (A. D. 261). He was associated with Gallienus in the empire, and invested with the title of Augustus in 1017 (A. D. 264), in reward for his services against Sapor, after the capture of Valerian. This brave prince was assassinated by his cousin Maeonius, in the year of Rome 1019 or 1020 (A. D. 266, or 267)].

The coins published of this prince are not authenticated. The name of Septimius occurs on an inscription found at Palmyra. (See *Eckhel*, *tom. vii.*).

ZENOBIA.

[Septimia Zenobia, the wife of Odenathus, was created queen by her husband in the year of Rome 1014 (A. D. 261). After his death she took upon herself the titles of Augusta and Queen of the East, which she governed in the name of her infant children, who were created Caesars. As soon as Aurelian was proclaimed emperor, he resolved to curb Zenobia. After two battles, he overthrew her army, and subsequently took her prisoner. She ended her days on an estate near Tibur, which had been presented to her by the conqueror, in the year of Rome 1026 (A. D. 273)].

THIRD BRASS.

ZENOBIA. AVG. The head of Zenobia on a crescent.—*Rev.* PIETAS. AVGG. A woman standing, extending her hand towards a child by her side. (*Tanini. Sup. ad Bandl.*).

This is the only Latin coin of Zenobia, but it is not accredited. Her other coins are Greek, and struck at Alexandria. They are extremely rare.

HERODES, HERENNIANUS, AND TIMOLAUS.

[Of the first of these princes (the son of Odenathus by his first wife), and of the other two (his sons by Zenobia), there are no authentic coins. Pinkerton has described a unique Greek coin of Timolaus, in the cabinet of Doctor Hunter].

VABALATHUS.

[Vabalathus Athenodorus, the son of Zenobia by, as is supposed, an Arab prince, her first husband, was raised by his mother to the Imperial dignity at the same time as his brothers, in the year of Rome 1019 or 1020 (A. D. 266 or 267). He was made prisoner with Zenobia in 1026 (A. D. 273). The time of his death is not known].

STYLE : —— VABALATHVS. VCRIMDR. —— IMP. C. VABALA-THVS. AVG.

Base silver, or third brass, without the head of Aurelian - - - R 6
    ,,   with the head of Aurelian - - - - - - - - R 2

The names of Vabalathus Athenodorus have been given to two different princes, but in reality one of them is a translation of the other. Vabalathus, or Vhabalathus, is a Syriac word, and Athenodorus is its Greek interpretation; namely, *Given of Minerva.* *(Mionnet, tom. ii, p.* 109*).* Froelich and Corsini have endeavoured to interpret the meaning of the letters, VCRIMDR. but they are not satisfactory.

BASE SILVER, OR THIRD BRASS.

1.

AEQVITAS. AVG. Equity standing, with her attributes.

2.

AETERNITAS. AVG. The Sun, standing : a star.

3.

IOVI. STATORI, Jupiter standing, holding a globe and the hasta; an eagle at his feet : a star in the field.

4.

VENVS. AVG. Venus standing, holding a helmet in her right hand and a spear in her left, transversely : a buckler on the ground.

5.

VICTORIA. AVG. Victory, marching : a star.

6.

VIRTVS. AVG.   Hercules, standing.

7.

Same legend.   An armed figure, standing : a star.

No. 1 is the least rare.

[VABALATHUS AND AURELIANUS].

VABALATHVS. VCRIMDR.   Laureated head of Vabalathus—*Rev.*
IMP. C. AVRELIANVS. AVG.   Head of Aurelianus, with
radiated crown : below, B. *or* Γ. *or* Δ. *or* E. *or* ϛ. *or* Z. *or* H.

MAEONIUS.

[Maeonius assumed the purple after he had assassinated his cousin
  Odenathus and his son Herodes, in the year of Rome 1019 or 1020.
  He was shortly after put to death by order of Zenobia].

FIRMUS.

[Marcus Firmus, a rich merchant of Egypt, assumed the Imperial purple
  in the city of Alexandria ,in the year of Rome 1026 (A. D. 273).   He
  was shortly after defeated by Aurelian, taken prisoner, tortured and
  put to death].

Goltzius produces a coin of this usurper, but it has not been authenticated.   According to Vopiscus, he coined money at Alexandria.   A
piece is described in the Pembroke collection, which is considered
dubious.   I am, however, informed by an eminent numismatist, that he
has seen what he considers to be an undoubted coin of Firmus.

TACITUS.

[Marcus Claudius Tacitus was a senator, and traced his descent from the
  great historian of that name.   The senate elected him emperor in the
  year of Rome 1028 (A. D. 275).   He reigned but six months and
  about twenty days, and died at Tarsus in Cilicia, or, as some say, at

Tyana in Cappadocia, in the year of Rome 1029 (A. D. 276). Eutropius and the Victors say he died a natural death, but Zosimus and Zonarus tell us that he was killed by his soldiers].

STYLE :——IMP. CL. TACITVS. AVG.   [On reverse, sometimes, RESTITVTOR. ORBIS.]——IMP. C. CL. TACITVS. AVG.——IMP. C. M. CL. (or CLA.) TACITVS. AVG.   [On reverse, sometimes, CONSERVAT. (or CONSERVATOR.) MILIT. (or MILITVM.]——IMP. C. M. CL. TACITVS. P. AVG.——IMP. CL. TACITVS, P. F. AVG.——IMP. C. M. CL. TACITVS. P. (or PIVS.) F. (or FEL.) AVG.——IMP. C. TACITVS. INVICTVS. AVG.

Gold - R 4
Base silver (none). They are in all probability third brass, washed.
Brass medallions - - - - - - - - - - - - - - - - R 6
Second brass - - - - - - - - - - - - - - - - - - R 6
Third brass - - - - - - - - - - - - - - - - - - C

GOLD.

1.

CONSERVATOR. AVG.   One of the Dioscuri standing, with his horse.

2.

PAX. PVBLICA.   Peace, standing.

3.

P. M. TR. P. CONSVL.   The emperor seated; holding in his right hand a globe, and in his left the hasta. *(Cabinet of Vienna).*

4.

P. M. TR. POT. COS. DES. II.   A woman standing, holding a cornucopia and ears of corn: the modius on the ground.

5.

PROVIDENTIA. DEORVM.   Providence standing, with her attributes.

6.

ROMAE. AETERNAE.   Rome, seated.   *(Plate x, No. 4).*

At the sale of the Trattle collection this type, fine, brought 5*l.* 18*s.*

7.

Same legend.   Rome-Nicephore, seated: S. C. in the exergue.

8.

SECVRIT. PVBLIC.   A woman standing, holding the hasta and leaning on a column.

9.

VICTORIA. AVG. Victory, standing.

10.

VICTORIA. GOTHICA. COS. II. Victory, marching: a prisoner on the ground.

No. 3 is much the rarest type. The next in rarity are Nos. 1, 4, and 10. Nos. 6, 7, and 9, are the least rare.

BRASS MEDALLIONS.

1.

ADLOCVTIO. AVG. The emperor, in the paludamentum, on an estrade, attended by the Praetorian praefect, addressing his troops.

2.

ADLOCVTIO. TACITI. AVG. A similar type.

3.

ADVENTVS. AVG. The emperor on horseback, preceded by Victory, and followed by several soldiers bearing standards.

4.

AEQVITAS. AVG. Equity, standing.

5.

MONETA. AVGVSTI. The three Monetæ, standing.

6.

RESTITVT. REIPVBLICAE. The emperor raising up a woman.

7.

TEMPORVM. FELICITAS. Rome seated, presenting a globe to the emperor, standing before her: Felicity and Victory attending; the latter placing a garland on the head of Tacitus.

8.

VIRTVS. AVGVSTI. Hercules naked, standing; his right hand on a trophy; his left holding his club and the lion's skin.

The rarest type is No. 2; the next in rarity is No. 1; then Nos. 3 and 7; the others are much less rare.

SECOND BRASS.

1.

AETERNITAS. AVG. The emperor crowned by Victory, standing.

2.

FIDES. MILITVM. A woman, holding two ensigns.

3.

VOTIS. X. ET. XX. The emperor in a military habit, standing between an armed figure who places a garland on his head, and Victory seated on a coat of mail, holding a buckler inscribed VOT. X. ET. XX.

The last is the rarest. No. 2 is the least rare.

THIRD BRASS, WITH RARE REVERSES.

1.

ANNONA. AVGVSTI. A woman standing, holding ears of corn and a cornucopia; the modius on the ground. In the exergue. T.

2.

MARTI. PACIF. Mars, marching. In the exergue, ϛ.

3.

RESTITVTOR. ORBIS. Victory and the emperor, standing. In the exergue, B. A.

4.

ROMAE. AETERNAE. Rome, seated. In the exergue, XXIII. or XXVI. or XXLVI. *(sic)*.

5.

SPES. PVBLICA. Victory and the emperor, standing. In the exergue, I. K. (*or* P.)

6.

TRANQVILLITAS. AVG. Tranquillity standing, holding in her right hand a dragon, and in her left the hasta.

7.

VBERITAS. A woman standing, holding a purse and a cornucopia. In the exergue, XXIϵ.

8.

VICTORIA. GOTTHI. Victory, standing. In the exergue, P.

9.

VICTORIA. PONTICA. Victory standing, presenting a garland to the emperor in the paludamentum, also standing: in the field, a star. In the exergue, KAΔ. *(Mionnet:* from the cabinet of the *Prince of Waldeck).*

10.

VIRTVS. AVG. A military figure, standing.

Mionnet values No. 9 at fifty francs. Of the others, Nos. 6, 7, and 8, are the rarest.

FLORIANUS.

[Marcus Annius Florianus, the brother of Tacitus, was praefect of the
Praetorians, during the brief reign of that prince, and after his death
was proclaimed emperor by the legions of Cilicia. Syria, however,
favoured the cause of Probus. The claims of either party were about
to be settled by a battle, when Florianus was murdered by his own
soldiers, at Tarsus, three months after he had assumed the purple,
1029 (A. D. 276)].

STYLE:——FLORIANVS. AVG.——IMP. FLORIANVS. AVG.——
IMP. M. ANNIVS. FLORIANVS. AVG. [On reverse, some-
times, PRINCEPS. IVVENTVT.]——IMP. C. FLORIANVS. AVG.——
IMP. C. M. AN. (or ANN. or ANNIVS.) FLORIANVS. AVG.
[On reverse, sometimes, PACATOR. ORBIS. or PRINCEPS. IVVENTVT.]
——IMP. C. M. AN. FLORIANVS. P. AVG. [On reverse,
sometimes, PRINCEPS. IVVENTVT.]——IMP. C. M. AN. (or ANN.)
FLORIANVS. P. F. AVG. [On reverse, sometimes, PACATOR. ORBIS.
(or PRINCEPS. IVVENTVT.)].

Gold - - - - - - - - - - - - - - - - - - - R 6
Base silver (doubtful if any)
Brass medallions - - - - - - - - - - - - - - - R 2
Second brass - - - - - - - - - - - - - - - - - R 2
Third brass - - - - - - - - - - - - - - - - - R 1

GOLD.

1.
CONCORD. MILIT.   Two figures joining hands.

2.
CONSERVATOR. AVG.   The Sun, in a quadriga.

3.
IOVI. VICTORI.   Jupiter-Nicephore, standing; an eagle at his feet.

4.
PERPETVITATE. *(sic)*. AVG.   A woman standing, leaning on a
column, and holding a globe.

5.
ROMAE. AETERNAE.   Rome-Nicephore, seated.

6.
VIRTVS. AVGVSTI.   Mars marching, and a captive.

Nos. 1, 2, and 4, are the rarest types.

BRASS MEDALLION.

MONETA. AVG.   The three Monetæ standing, with their attributes.

SECOND BRASS.
1.
AEQVITAS AVG.   Equity, standing.
2.
FELICITAS. AVG.   A woman, before an altar.
3.
INDVLGENTIA. AVG.   Hope, walking.
4.
IOVI. STATORI.   Jupiter-Stator, standing.
5.
LAETITIA. FVND.   Laetitia, standing.
6.
PACATOR. ORBIS.   The Sun, standing.
7.
PAX. AETERNA.   Peace, marching.
8.
Same legend.   The Sun, marching.
9.
PERPETVIT. AVG.   A woman, standing.
10.
PROVIDENTIA. AVG.   Providence standing, with her attributes.
11.
PROVIDENTIA. DEOR.   Two figures, standing.
12.
SALVS. AVG.   Hygeia, standing.
13.
SECVRITAS. AVG.   Security, standing.
14.
TEMPORVM. FELICITAS.   Felicity standing, with her attributes.
15.
VIRTVS. AVG.   The emperor, on horseback: a captive.
16.
Same legend.   The emperor standing, holding a globe and a spear.

Of the above types, Nos. 3, 6, 7, 8, 9, are the rarest.   Nos. 13 and 16 are the least rare.

THIRD BRASS, WITH RARE REVERSES.

1.

AEQVITAS. AVG. Equity, standing. In the exergue, XXI. *or* XXIΓ.

2.

AETERNITAS. AVG. A woman, standing. In the exergue, IIII.

3.

CLEMENTIA. TEMP. A woman leaning on a column, and holding the hasta. In the exergue. XXIA. *or* XXIΓ. *or* XXIZ.

4.

CONCORDIA. EXERCI. A woman, holding two ensigns. In the exergue, VITI.

5.

CONCORD. MILITVM. Two figures, standing; one in the stola, the other in the toga, joining hands. In the exergue, T.

6.

FELICITAS. AVG. A woman before an altar. In the field, Q. In the exergue, XXI.

7.

Another, with similar type; without the letter in the field, but with P. or Q. or ç or T. in the exergue.

8.

FELICITAS. SAECVLI. A similar type; with P. in the exergue.

9.

FIDES. MILIT. A woman, holding a standard and the hasta. In the exergue, XXXIЄ

10.

INDVLGENTIA. AVG. Hope.

11.

IOVI. CONSERVAT. Jupiter, standing. In the exergue, TTI.

12.

IOVI. STATORI. Jupiter, standing. In the exergue, XXIZ.

13.

LAETITIA. FVND. A woman, standing. In the exergue, XI. or XXIB.

14.

MARTI. PACIFERO. Mars, standing.

15.

PACATOR. ORBIS. The Sun, marching. In the exergue, II. or III.

16.

PAX. AETERNA. Peace, walking.

17. ·

PAX. AVGVSTI. Peace, standing.

18.

PERPETVIT. AVG. (*or* PERPETVITATE.) *(sic)* AVG. A similar type. In the exergue, Q. TI.

19.

PRINCIPI. IVVENTVT. The emperor, standing. In the exergue, PTI.

20.

PROVIDENTIA. AVG. Providence, standing. In the exergue, III. or XXIII. or XXIA.

21.

PROVIDEN. DEOR. Two figures, standing. In the field, a star. In the exergue, various letters.

22.

REDITVS. AVG. Rome seated, presenting a globe to the emperor, standing before her.

This curious type is given by *Tanini.*

23.

SALVS. AVG. Hygeia, feeding a serpent on an altar. In the exergue, XXIΔ.

24.

SECVRITAS. AVG. Security, standing. In the field, R. I.

This type is published by Pere Khell as in silver, but it does not exist in that metal. Many of the washed third brass of this period were once supposed to be silver.

25.

SECVRITAS. SAECVLI. A woman seated, holding a sceptre.

26.

TEMPORVM. FELICITAS. A woman, standing. In the exergue, I.

27.

VIRTVS. AVG. The emperor, on horseback: a prisoner.

28.

Same legend. The emperor standing, holding a spear and a globe. (Size of the *quinarius*).

The scarce types are Nos. 2, 3, 7, 8, 11, 13, 14, 16, 17, 18, 19, 24, and 28, except No. 22, which is much scarcer than the other numbers.

PROBUS.

[Marcus Aurelius Probus, was born at Sirmium in Pannonia, in the year of Rome 985 (A. D. 232), and held the office of praefect of the East under his predecessors. After the death of Tacitus, the legions of the East proclaimed him emperor; and his title was confirmed by the Roman senate, upon the murder of Florian. Probus was assassinated by his soldiers at the place of his birth, in the year of Rome 1035 (A. D. 282)].

STYLE:——PROBVS.——PROBVS. AVG.——IMP. PROBVS. AVG. [On reverse, sometimes, PRINCEPS. IVVENTVTIS. (or VICTORIOSVS. SEMPER.]——IMP. C. PROBVS. AVG. [On reverse, sometimes, P. P. (or RESTITVT. SAECVLI.)]——IMP. C. M. AVR. PROBVS. AVG. [On reverse, sometimes, P. P. (or RESTITVTOR. SAEC.)]—— PROBVS. P. AVG.——IMP. C. PROBVS. PIVS. AVG.—— IMP. C. M. AVR. PROBVS. P. (or PIVS.) AVG.——IMP. CAES. M. AVR. PROBVS. P. F.——PROBVS. P. F. AVG.—— IMP. PROBVS. P. F. AVG.——IMP. C. PROBVS. P. F. AVG. [On reverse, sometimes, RESTITVTOR. ORBIS.] —— IMP. C. (or CAES.) M. AVR. PROBVS. P. F. AVG. [On reverse, sometimes, P. P. (or RESTITVTOR. EXERCITI.] ——PERPETVVS. IMP. PROBVS. AVG. —— PROBVS. INVICTVS. AVG. —— IMP. PROBVS. INV: (or INVIC. or INVICT.) AVG. —— INVIC-TVS. PROBVS. P. F. AVG.——IMP. C. PROBVS. INVIC. (or INVICT.) P. F. AVG. —— IMP. C. M. AVR. PRO-BVS. INVICT. (or INVICTVS.) AVG. —— PERPETVVS. IMP. C. PROBVS. INVICT. AVG. [On reverse, RESTITVTOR. ORBIS.]——BONVS. IMP. C. M. AVR. PROBVS. AVG.—— BONVS. IMP. PROBVS. INVICT. AVG.——BONVS. IMP. C. PROBVS. P. F. INVICT. AVG.

Gold medallions, of small size - - - - - - - - - - -	R 6
„ of the usual size - - - - - - - - - - - - -	R 4
Silver medallions, of small size - - - - - - - - - -	R 8
„ (if really of that metal) - - - - - - - - -	R 8
„ quinarii (none known)	
Brass medallions - - - - - - - - - - - - - - -	R 4
Second brass - - - - - - - - - - - - - - -	R 4
Third brass - - - - - - - - - - - - - - - -	VC
„ with the Consulate on the obverse - - - - - -	R 2
Brass, of the size of the quinarius - - - - - - - - -	R 1

GOLD AND SILVER MEDALLIONS.

1.

GLORIA. ORBIS. COS. V. The emperor, in a car drawn by six horses, crowned by Victory: two foot-soldiers. - - - - - AR

2.

SOLI. INVICTO. COMITI. AVG. Radiated head of the Sun. - AU

3.

TEMP. FELICITAS. A youthful figure holding a circle, within which are represented several women, presenting him with fruits: before, a genius, holding a cornucopia? In the exergue, SIS. AU

4.

VICTORIAE. AVGVSTI. Two Victories, attaching a buckler to the trunk of a palm-tree, at the foot of which are two captives: VOT. X. inscribed on the buckler. SIS. in the exergue. - - - - - AU

In gold, No. 3 is much the rarest; the next in rarity is No. 4. The silver medallion is valued by Mionnet at 150 francs.

GOLD, OF THE USUAL SIZE.

1.

ADLOCVTIO. AVG. The usual type.

2.

ADVENTVS. AVG. The emperor on horseback, preceded by Victory, and followed by a soldier.

3.

ADVENTVS. PROBI. AVG. The emperor on horseback, and two figures.

4.

Same legend. The emperor on horseback: a captive on the ground.

5.

AETERNITAS. AVG. The Sun, standing.

6.

CONSERVAT. AVG. A similar type.

7.

HERCVLI. ERYMANTHIO. Hercules, bearing the carcass of the Erymanthean boar.

8.

HERCVLI. ROMANO. AVG. Hercules standing, crowning a trophy.

There were two of this type in the Trattle sale: one, in fine preservation, brought 3*l.* 3*s.*; another, 4*l.*

9.

MARS. VICTOR. Mars marching, with a trophy and a spear.

10.

ORIENS. AVG. The Sun, standing.

11.

ORIENS. AVGVST. (*or* AVGVSTI.) A similar type. SIS. in the exergue.

This type, fine, brought 3*l*. 7*s*. at the Trattle sale.

12.

P. M. TRI. P. COS. III. The emperor, in a quadriga.

The obverse has the radiated or helmed head of Probus, with the legend, VIRTVS. PROBI. AVG.

13.

PAX. AETERNA. Peace, standing.

14.

PRINCIPIS. IVVENTVTI. *(sic)*. The emperor, standing.

15.

ROMAE. AETERNAE. Rome, seated.

16.

SECVRITAS. SAECVLI. A woman, seated. Sometimes, in the exergue, SIS.

This type, fine, brought 2*l*. 11*s*. at the Trattle sale.

17.

SOLI. INVICTO. The Sun, driving a quadriga.

18.

VICTORIA. AVG. Two Victories supporting a buckler, inscribed, VOTIS. XXX. MVLTIS. XXXX.

19.

Same legend. Victory, on a globe, between two captives seated on the ground.

20.

VICTORIA. GERM. A trophy, between two captives. *(Khell)*.

21.

VICTORIA. GOTHIC. Victory, marching: a captive.

22.

VICTORIA. PROBI. AVG. Victory, crowning a trophy, at the foot of which are two captives.

23.

VICTORIAE. AVG.   Victory, in a quadriga.   (*Plate x, No. 5*).

24.

VICTORIAE. AVGG.   Victory, in a biga.

25.

VICTORIOSO. SEMPER.   The emperor standing, holding the parazonium: two figures kneeling; two others standing.

26.

VIRTVS. AVG.   Probus, seated between Rome, Victory, and another
figure, standing.   In the exergue, a garland.

27.

Same legend.   The emperor on horseback, attended by several figures.

The obverse has the heads of Probus and Jupiter: legend, IOVI. CON-
SERVATORI. PROBI. AVG.

28.

VIRTVS. AVGVSTI.   The emperor in the paludamentum, standing:
a trophy; and two captives seated on the ground.

29.

VIRTVS. PROBI. AVG.   The emperor on horseback: and a captive.

The rarest types are Nos. 25 and 27.   The next in rarity are Nos. 1,
2, 12, 17, and 26; then, Nos. 1, 2, 17, and 24.   Nos. 3, 4, 7, 20, and 22,
are rarer than the remaining numbers.

BRASS MEDALLIONS.

1.

ADLOCVTIO. AVG.   The usual type.

2.

ADLOCVTIO. MILITVM.   The usual type.

3.

ADVENTVS. AVG.   The emperor on horseback, preceded by Victory,
and followed by foot soldiers bearing standards.

4.

Same legend.   The emperor on horseback, preceded by Victory, and
followed by foot soldiers.   (Large size).

5.

EXERCITVS. PERS.   The emperor in the paludamentum, standing on
an estrade, and addressing his soldiers: behind, several figures standing; one of them holding a horse by the bridle.

6.

FIDES. MAXIMA.   Fortune standing, holding a rudder, and presenting a globe to the emperor: between them, an altar.

7.

GLORIA. ORBIS. COS. V.   The emperor, crowned by Victory, in a
car drawn by six horses: on each side, foot soldiers, bearing palm
branches.

8.

MONETA. AVG.   The three Monetæ, standing.

"There are," says Mionnet, "many varieties of this type: the most
remarkable is that with the head of Probus covered with the lion's skin."
This medallion is much rarer than any of the others with the same
reverse.

9.

PROBVS. P. F. AVG. COS. IIII.   The emperor crowned by Victory,
in a quadriga, preceded by a woman, and attended by three soldiers
bearing palm branches.

10.

ROMAE. AETERNAE.   Rome, seated on a buckler.

11.

SAECVLI. FELICITAS.   Four children, representing the four Seasons.

12.

SOLI. INVICTO.   The Sun, in a quadriga.

13.

SOLI. INVIC. COMITI. AVG. COS. IIII.   The Sun in a quadriga,
preceded by a woman.

14.

TEMPORVM. FELICITAS.   The emperor, standing between Victory
and Felicity, presenting a globe to Rome, seated.

15.

VIRT. AVGVT. *(sic)* NOSTRI.   The emperor on horseback, preceded
by a soldier, and followed by another: SIS.

16.

VIRTVS. AVGVSTI.   The emperor on horseback, casting a javelin :
prostrate figures below.

17.

VOT. SOLVTA. X.   Victory in a biga.   *(Tanini)*.

The rarest are Nos. 7 and 11.   The next in rarity are Nos. 5, 9, 13, 14,
and 17: then Nos. 1, 2, 6, 12.   The least rare are Nos. 8 and 10.

[PROBUS AND HIS WIFE].

1.

IMP. C. PROBVS. INVIC. P. F. AVG. The heads of the emperor and empress, side by side.—*Rev.* MONETA. AVG. The three Monetæ standing, with their attributes,

This medallion, in fine preservation, brought 9*l.* 10*s.* at the Trattle sale.

2.

FIDES. MAXIMA. Fortune standing, holding a rudder and presenting a globe to the emperor: between them an altar. (Very large size).

Mionnet values the first at 200, and the other at 250 francs.

SECOND BRASS.

VICTORIA. GERM, A trophy, and two captives.

THIRD BRASS, WITH RARE REVERSES.

1.

ABVNDANTIA. AVG. A woman standing, holding a cornucopia. In the exergue, IIII. *or* IIIΓ.

2.

ADLOCVTIO. AVG. The usual type.

3.

CALLIOPE. AVG. Calliope playing on a lyre, resting on a column. (*Tanini*).

4.

COMES. AVG. Minerva standing, holding an olive branch and the hasta. In the field, A.

5.

COMITI. PROBI. AVG. A similar type. In the exergue, I.

6.

CONCORDIA. AVG. The Sun, standing, and a woman holding two ensigns. In the field of some, SXXT.

7.

FELICIA. TEMPORA. Four children, representing the four Seasons. (Size of the quinarius).

8.

INDVLGENTIA. AVG. Hope. In the exergue, VTI.

9.

IOVI. CONSERVAT. Jupiter and Probus supporting a globe. In the exergue, VXXT.

10.

IOVI. CONS. PROB. AVG. Jupiter standing, with hasta and thunder-bolt. In the exergue, a thunderbolt; between the letters P. B. or R. B.

11.

MARS. VICTOR. Mars, standing: a captive.

12.

MARS. VLTOR. Mars marching, with spear and shield. (Size of the quinarius).

13.

IMP. PROBVS. AVG. Head of Probus with radiated crown, to the right.—*Rev.* ORIENS. AVG. A diota. (Cabinet of *M. Welzel de Wellenheim, of Vienna—Mionnet*, p. 123).

14.

ORIGINI. AVG. Romulus and Remus suckled by the wolf. In the exergue, XXIT.

15.

P. M. TR. P. COS. P. P. The emperor in the paludamentum, holding a spear, and standing between two ensigns. In the exergue, XXIII. or XXIΔ.

16.

P. M. TRI. P. COS. II. P. P. A lion, walking: the head of a bull, full-faced, in the field. In the exergue, XXIS.

17.

PROV. PROBI. AVG. NOSTRI. Providence, standing, with her attributes. In the exergue, XXI.

18.

RESTITVTOR. EXERCITI. Mars and the emperor standing, sup-porting a globe.

19.

RESTITVT. SEC. The emperor standing, holding a globe and the hasta; and a Victory also standing, holding a palm-branch. In the exergue, VIXXT.

20.

RESTITVTOR. SECV. The emperor standing, holding a globe and the hasta; his right foot on a captive: the Sun, standing. In the exergue, XXIQ.

21.

SECVRITAS. ORBIS. (*or* PERPETVA.) Security standing, holding the hasta.

22.

SISCIA. PROBI. AVG. A figure seated, and two river-gods. In the exergue, XIQ.

23.

SOLI. INVICTO.   Statue of the Sun, within a temple.   In the exergue,
SXXT.

24.

SPES. AVG.   Hope.

25.

VICTORIAE. AVG.   Victory, driving a biga.

26.

Same legend.   Victory, standing between two captives.   (Size of the
quinarius).

27.

VICTOR. GERM.   Victory, marching; two captives seated on the
ground.   (Size of the quinarius).

28.

VICTORIA. GERM.   Two captives at the foot of a trophy.   (Size of
the quinarius).

29.

VIRTVS. INVICTI. AVG.   The emperor on horseback, striking down
an enemy; Victory preceding him.

30.

VOTIS. X. ET. XX. FEL. within a garland.

31.

VOTIS. X. PROBI. AVG. ET. XX.   *(Beger—Mionnet)*.

No. 7 is very rare, as are also Nos. 2 and 3.   Of the remaining numbers,
12, 13, 16, 20, 21, are the rarest.

BONOSUS.—SATURNINUS II.—PROCULUS.

[Bonosus was defeated and slain by Probus, near Cologne: Saturninus
was put to death in the east, where he had revolted; and Proculus met
the same fate, after the suppression of his revolt at Cologne].

Coins of these usurpers have been published by Goltzius, Mediobarba
and others; but they are not authenticated.

CARUS.

[Marcus Aurelius Carus was born at Narbonne in Illyricum,* about the
year of Rome 983 (A. D. 230).   He was Praetorian praefect under

---

* Eutropius says, Narbonne in Gaul, but this is an error.   (See *Scaliger*,
Animad. ad Euseb. Chron. p. 241).

Probus, and after the death of that prince, was elected emperor by the legions of Pannonia, his title, according to most authors, being ratified by the senate. Carus was killed by thunder, after the taking of Ctesiphon, in Assyria; but some say he died a natural death, and that his attendants fired his tent in an excess of grief, and consumed the body of their master, in the year of Rome 1036 (A. D. 283), the year after his election].

STYLE :——IMP. C. M. AVR. CARVS.——CARVS. AVG.——IMP. CARVS. AVG.——IMP. C. M. AVR. CARVS. (or KARVS.) AVG.——IMP. CARVS. P. F. AVG.——IMP. C. KARVS. P. F. AVG.——IMP. C. M. AVR. CARVS. P. F. AVG.——CARVS. INVICTVS. AVG.——DEVS. ET. DOMINVS. CARVS. AVG. ——DEVS. ET. DOMINVS. CARVS. INVIC. AVG.——DIVVS. CARVS.——DIVVS. CARVS. AVG.——DIVVS. CARVS. PIVS. ——DIVVS. CARVS. PARTHICVS.——DIVVS. CARVS. PERS.

CARUS AND HIS SON :——CARVS. ET. CARINVS. AVGG.

Gold - - - - - - - - - - - - - - - - - - - R 6
Silver (very doubtful if any).
Brass medallions - - - - - - - - - - - - - R 4
    „   with his head, and that of Carinus - - - - - R 8
Second brass - - - - - - - - - - - - - - - - R 4
Third brass - - - - - - - - - - - - - - - - - C
Brass, of the size of the quinarius - - - - - - - - - - R 1

GOLD.

1.

ADVENTVS. AVG. The emperor on horseback, holding the hasta, his right hand elevated.

2.

CONSECRATIO. An eagle with expanded wings, on a globe.

3.

FORTVNA. AVG. Fortune, standing.

4.

PAX. AETERNAE. A similar type.

5.

PAX. AVG. Peace, marching.

6.

PROVIDENT. AVG. Providence, standing.

7.

SPES. PVBLICA. Hope. *(Plate x, No. 6).*

This type, fine, brought 6*l.* 15*s.* at the Trattle sale. Another, not so fine, 4*l.* 4*s.*

8.

VICTORI. AVG. Victory, in a biga.

9.

VICTORIA. AVG. A similar type. In the exergue, O. *or* K.

10.

DEO. ET. DOMINO. CARO. AVG. Head of Carus.—*Rev.* VICTO-
RIA. AVG. Victory, on a globe.

11.

Same legend. Victory, on a globe.

12.

VICTORIA. AVG. (*or* AVGG. FEL.) Victory, holding a garland : a
buckler on a pedestal.

13.

VIRTVS. AVGG. Mars, marching : a captive.

14.

VIRTVS.CARI. INVICTI. AVG. Hercules, standing. In the exergue, K.

No. 10 is much the rarest. The next in rarity are Nos. 1, 12, and 14.
Nos. 2, 8, 9, and 13, are rarer than the remaining numbers.

[CARUS AND CARINUS].

IMP. C. M. AVR. KARVS. AVG. (*or* P. F. AVG.) Laureated head
of Carus to the right, with the paludamentum.—*Rev.* KARINVS.
NOBIL.* CAES. Laureated head of Carinus, with the paludamentum.

Valued by Mionnet at 200 francs.

BRASS MEDALLIONS.

MONETA. AVG. The three Monetæ standing, with their attributes.

Valued by Mionnet at twenty-four francs.

---

* " Under the predecessors of Constantine," says Gibbon, chapter xviii.
" Nobilissimus was a vague epithet, rather than a legal and determined title."
This is not proved ; and there is some reason for supposing that the title was not
vague and unimportant ; but I leave this to the decision of the learned.

[CARUS AND CARINUS].

IMP. CARO. AVG. ET. CARINO. N. CAES. Laureated head of Carus and Carinus, face to face.—*Rev.* SAECVLI. FELICITAS. Four children, representing the four Seasons.

Valued by Mionnet at 200 francs.

SECOND BRASS.

1.

FELICITATIS. PVBLICAE. (*or* FELICITAS. REIPVBLICAE.) Felicity, standing.

The obverse has two heads, with the legend DEO. ET. DOMINO. CARO. AVG.

2.

PAX. AETERNA. Peace, standing.

3.

PAX. AVGVSTORVM. Peace, marching.

No. 1 is by far the rarest. Mionnet values it at forty francs.

THIRD BRASS, WITH RARE REVERSES.

1.

DIVO. CARO. PARTHICO. Radiated head of Carus.—*Rev.* CONSE-CRATIO. An altar. In the field, A. In the exergue, SMSXXR. *or* SMSXXI.

2.

DEO. ET. DOMINO. CARO. AVG. The radiated heads of Carus and the Sun, face to face.—*Rev.* FELICITATIS. PVBLICAE. (*or* FELICITAS. REIPVBLICAE.) Felicity standing, holding the caduceus and hasta. In the exergue, XI. *or* XII. (See *Banduri*).

3.

FIDES. MILITVM. A woman standing, holding two ensigns. In the field, P. In the exergue, XXI. With the legend, DEO. ET. DOMINO. CARO. INVIC. AVG. on obverse.

4.

IOVI. VICTORI. Jupiter standing, naked, holding a victory and the hasta; at his feet, an eagle. In the exergue, KAB.

5.

RESTITVT. ORBIS. The emperor standing, holding a globe and the hasta; before him, a woman presenting a garland. In the field, a star and P. *or* II. In the exergue, XXI.

6.

VIRTVS. AVGG. A military figure standing, with spear and shield. (Size of the quinarius).

7.

Same legend. Carus and Carinus, supporting a figure of Victory. In the field, A. *or* B. *or* Γ. *or* Δ. or Z. *or* H. *or* ΕΔ. *or* ϛ. In the exergue, XXI.

No. 2 is very rare. No. 3, though by no means so rare, is much more so than the remaining types.

[CARUS AND CARINUS.]

1.

CARVS. ET. CARINVS. AVGG. The heads of Carus and Carinus.— *Rev.* SAECVLI. FELICITAS. The emperor, standing.

2.

SPES. PVBLICA. Carus and his son, on horseback.

3.

CARVS. ET. CARINVS. AVGG. Heads of Carus and Carinus.—*Rev.* VICTORIA. AVGG. Victory, and two captives.

Mionnet values Nos. 1 and 3 at thirty francs each; the other at eight francs only.

NUMERIANUS.

[Marcus Aurelianus Numerianus, the son of Carus, was born about the year of Rome 1007 (A. D. 254), and created Caesar by his father in 1035 (A. D. 282). He accompanied Carus in his Persian expedition, when he received the title of emperor, without, however, that of Augustus. Upon the death of his father, the army saluted him emperor and Augustus, together with Carinus, his elder brother. Numerianus was assassinated by the Praetorian praefect, Aper, his father-in-law, near Heraclea, in Thrace, in the year of Rome 1037 (A. D. 284).

STYLE:——M. AVR. NVMERIANVS. C. [On reverse, sometimes, PRINCEPS. IVVENT. (*or* IVVENTVT.)] —— NVMERIANVS. NOB. CAES.——M. AVR. NVMERIANVS. NOB. C. [On reverse, sometimes, PRINCEPS. IVVENT. (*or* IVVENTVT.)]——IMP. C. M. AVR. NVMERIANVS. NOB. C.——IMP. NVMERIANVS. AVG. [On reverse, sometimes, UNDIQVE. VICTORES.]——IMP. C. NVMERIANVS. AVG.——IMP. C. M. AVR. NVMERIANVS.

AVG.——IMP. NVMERIANVS. P. F. AVG. [On reverse, sometimes, PRINCEPS. IVVENTVT.]——IMP. C. NVMERIANVS. P. F. AVG.——IMP. NVMERIANVS. INVICT. AVG.—— DIVVS. NVMERIANVS.

Gold - R 6
Quinarii of silver (very doubtful if any exist): that in the *Cab. d'Ennery*, No. 712, is doubted.
Brass medallions - - - - - - - - - - - - - - - R 4
Second brass - - - - - - - - - - - - - - - - - - R 4
Third brass - - - - - - - - - - - - - - - - - - C
Brass, of the quinarius size - - - - - - - - - - - - - R 1

GOLD.
1.
ORIENS. AVGG. The Sun, standing: a star in the field.

2.
PRINCIPI. IVVENT. Numerianus standing, in a military habit, holding the hasta and an olive branch.

3.
SALVS. AVGG. Hygeia seated, feeding a serpent on an altar. (*Plate x, No. 7*).

At the sale of Mr. Miles' collection, in 1820, this type, very fine, brought 7*l.* 2*s.* 6*d.* That in the Henderson collection, sold in 1830, was extremely fine, but brought only 5*l.*

4.
SPES AVGG. Hope.

5.
VENERI. VICTRICI. Venus-Victrix, holding a child.

6.
VICTORIA. AVGG. Victoria, marching.

7.
VIRTVS. AVGG. Hercules, standing.

Nos. 2, 3, 4, 7 are much rarer than the other numbers.

[NUMERIANUS AND CARINUS.]
CARINVS. ET. NVMERIANVS. AVGG. The laureated heads of Numerianus and Carinus, side by side, to the right.—*Rev.* VICTO-RIA. AVGG. Victory, marching.

Valued by Mionnet at 300 francs.

BRASS MEDALLIONS.

1.

ADLOCVTIO. AVGG. The usual type.

2.

MONETA. AVGG. The three Monetæ, standing.

3.

TRVNFV. *(sic)*. QVADOR. *(or* TRIVMPHVS. QVADORVM.) The two emperors, in a quadriga, preceded by Victory; above, two captives, secured to a trophy; below, two other captives, seated on the ground, their hands bound behind their backs : arms scattered in the field.

4.

VIRTVS. AVGVSTORVM. Two horsemen, both full-faced, trampling on six enemies; above, two Victories, presenting garlands.

Valued by Mionnet at 100, 30, 150, and 120 francs.

SECOND BRASS, WITH RARE REVERSES.

1.

MARS. VICTOR. Mars, marching.

2.

PAX. AVGG. Peace, standing. In the field, B.

Valued by Mionnet at fifteen francs each.

THIRD BRASS, WITH RARE REVERSES.

1.

ABVNDANTIA. AVGG. A woman standing, reversing a cornucopia. (Size of the quinarius).

2.

CONSECRATIO. An eagle, with expanded wings. In the exergue, KAA.

3.

FIDES. EXERCIT. AVGG. A woman seated, holding a patera and a standard: before her, two other standards : in the field Γ. In the exergue, SMSXXI.

4.

MARS. VICTOR. Mars, marching. In the field, C.

5.

ORIENS. AVGG. The Sun, marching. In the exergue, KAϛ.

6.

PAX. AVGG.   Peace, walking.   In the exergue, Δ.   (Very small size),

7.

PIETAS. AVGG.   Mercury, standing.   In the exergue, Δ *or* a star. (Very small).

8.

P. M. TR. P. COS. P. P.   The emperor in a quadriga.   *(Tanini).*

9.

VIRTVS. AVGG.   Hercules, standing.   (Very small size).

10.

VNDIQVE. VICTORES.   The emperor, standing: two captives at his feet.   In the exergue, KAϛ.

11.

Same legend.   The emperor, standing.   In the exergue, KAϛ.

12.

VOTA. PVBLICA.   Two emperors, sacrificing on a tripod: two standards.   In the exergue, SMS XXIΓ. *or* SMS XXIϛ.

No. 1 is the rarest type; the next in rarity are Nos. 5, 6, 7, 9, and 11.

[NUMERIANUS AND CARINUS].

CARVS. ET. NVMERIANVS.   The laureated heads of Carinus and Numerianus, side by side.—*Rev.* VICTORIA. AVGG.   Victory, marching.

Valued by Mionnet at twenty francs.

CARINUS.

[Marcus Aurelius Carinus, the eldest son of Carus, was born in the year of Rome 1002 (A. D. 249), and created Caesar with his brother Numerianus in 1035 (A. D. 282).   He governed the provinces of the East (while his father and brother were maintaining the war against the Persians) with the title of Emperor, but without that of Augustus: this latter title he assumed upon the death of Carus, while his brother was also saluted Augustus by the army under his command, 1036 (A. D. 283).   Carinus was assassinated by a tribune, after a battle with Diocletian, who, upon the death of Numerianus, had been elected emperor by the legions of the East, in the year of Rome 1038 (A. D. 285)].

STYLE:——M. AVR. CARINVS. CAES.——CARINVS. (*or* KA-
RINVS.) NOBIL. CAES. [On reverse, sometimes, PRINCEPS.
IVVENT. (*or* IVVENTVT. *or* IVVENTVTIS.)] —— M. AVR. CARINVS.
(*or* KARINVS.) N. (*or* NOB.) C. (*or* CAES.) [On reverse, some-
times, PRINCEPS. IVVENT. (*or* IVVENTVT. *or* IVVENTVTIS.)]——M. AVR.
CARINVS. P. F. NOB. CAES.——IMP. C. M. AVR. CARINVS.
——IMP. C. M. AVR. CARINVS. NOB. C.——IMP. CARI-
NVS. AVG.——IMP. C. M. AVR. CARINVS. AVG.——IMP.
CARINVS. P. F. AVG.——IMP. M. AVR. CARINVS. P. F.
AVG.——IMP. C. CARINVS. P. F. AVG.——IMP. C. M. AVR.
CARINVS. P. F. AVG.

CARINUS, AND HIS BROTHER, ASSOCIATED:——CARINVS. ET. NVME-
RIANVS. AVGG.

Gold medallion - - - - - - - - - - - - - - - - *unique*
„ of the usual size - - - - - - - - - - - - - R 6
Silver (supposed none).
Brass medallions - - - - - - - - - - - - - - - R 4
Second brass - - - - - - - - - - - - - - - - - R 4
Third brass - - - - - - - - - - - - - - - - - C
Brass, of the size of the quinarius - - - - - - - - - - R 3

GOLD MEDALLIONS.

1.

VIRTVS. AVGVSTOR. Carus and Carinus standing, holding between
them a globe; one holds the hasta pura; the other the parazonium :
Hercules crowning one, Victory the other.

Valued by Mionnet at 1200 francs.

[CARUS AND CARINUS].

IMPP. CARVS. ET. CARINVS. AVGG. The bust of Carinus and his
brother, face to face: one with the paludamentum ; the other with
the Aegis. — *Rev.* VICTORIAE. AVGVSTI. Two Victories
standing, supporting a buckler, inscribed VOTIS. X. In the
exergue, SIS. (See *M. Steinbuchel's Notice sur les médallons d'or
du Cabinet de Vienne,** where it is engraved).

Valued by Mionnet at 1500 francs.

---

* This work contains several plates of rare and singular medallions in the
Imperial Cabinet.

GOLD, OF THE USUAL SIZE.

1.

ABVNDANTIA. AVGG.   Abundance, standing.

2.

PAX. AETERNA.   Peace, marching.

3.

FIDES. MILITVM.   A woman, holding two standards.

4.

P. M. TRI. P. COS. P. P.   The emperor, in a quadriga.

5.

PRINCIPI. IVVENTVT.   The emperor, in a military habit, standing in the midst of four ensigns.

PRINCIPIS. IVVENTVTI. *(sic)*.   The emperor standing, in a military habit, holding a spear and a globe.   In the exergue, ꙩ.

7.

VENERI. VICTRICI.   Venus standing, holding a Victory and a globe. *(Plate x, No 8)*.

8.

VICTORIA. AVG.   Victory, standing on a globe.

9.

Same legend.   Victory marching, with garland and palm-branch: a captive at her feet.   In the exergue, A.

Mionnet says the coin of this type described as of pure silver in the Catalogue D'Ennery, was no doubt cast from the mould of the third brass.

10.

VICTORIA. AVGG.   Victory, marching.

11.

Same legend.   The emperor crowned by Victory : two captives.

12.

VICTORIA. AVGVSTORVM.   Victory supported between the two emperors, placing a garland on the head of each.

13.

VIRTVS. AVG.   Hercules, standing.

Nos. 3, 4, and 11 are the rarest: the next in rarity is 5.

[CARUS AND CARINUS].

IMP. C. M. AVR. KARVS. AVG. (*or* P. F. AVG.).   Laureated head of Carus, with the paludamentum. — *Rev.* KARINVS. NOBIL. CAES.   Laureated head of Carinus to the right, with the paludamentum.

Valued by Mionnet at 200 francs.

[CARUS AND NUMERIANUS].

CARINVS. ET. NVMERIANVS. AVGG. The laureated heads of Carinus and his brother, side by side, to the right. — *Rev.* VICTORIA. AVGG. Victory, marching.

Valued by Mionnet at 300 francs.

BRASS MEDALLIONS.

1.

IOVI. VICTORI. Jupiter, standing: an eagle. *(Tanini).*

2.

MONETA. AVGG. The three Monetæ.

3.

TRAIECTVS. AVGG. A Praetorian galley, with rowers: above, the emperor and five Praetorian soldiers.

4.

VIRTVS. AVGVSTOR. Carus and Carinus standing, in the paludamentum; the first crowned by Hercules, the other by Apollo.

5.

Same legend. A similar type. (Very small size).

No. 3 is a very rare type, and valued by Mionnet at 100 francs.

[CARUS AND CARINUS].

IMP. CARO. AVG. ET. CARINO. N. CAES. The laureated heads of Carus and Carinus, face to face.—*Rev.* SAECVLI. FELICITAS. The four Seasons.

Valued by Mionnet at 200 francs.

SECOND BRASS.

PAX. AVGVSTORVM. Peace, standing.

THIRD BRASS, WITH RARE REVERSES.

1.

ADVENTVS. AVG. The emperor on horseback.

2.

CLEMENTIA. TEMP. Two figures standing, holding a Victory. In the field, A. *or* B. *or* Γ. *or* Δ. In the exergue, XXI.

3.

FIDES. MILITVM. A woman standing, holding two ensigns. In the exergue, KAЄ *or* KAςЄ .

4.

PAX. AETERNA. Peace, marching. (Size of the quinarius).

This type is errroneously described in the Catalogue d'Ennery, as of silver.

5.

VIRTVS. AVGG. Hercules, standing. (Size of the quinarius).

6.

VOTA. PVBLICA. Two figures, in military habits, sacrificing on a tripod. In the exergue, SMSXXIA. *or* SMSXXIB.

Those of the size of the quinarius are much the rarest. No. 1 is rarer than the others.

[CARINUS AND NUMERIANUS].

CARINVS. ET. NVMERIANVS. AVGG. The laureated heads of Carinus and Numerianus, side by side.—*Rev.* VICTORIA. AVGG. Victory, marching.

Valued by Mionnet at twenty francs.

[CARINUS AND MAGNIA URBICA].

IMP. CARINUS. AVG. Helmeted bust of Carinus; the right hand holding a horse by the bridle, a buckler on the left arm. — *Rev.* MAGNIA. VRBICA. AVG. Head of Magnia Urbica.

This coin is of the size of the quinarius. Mionnet values it at fifty francs.

MAGNIA URBICA.

[This lady is known only by her coins. She was formerly supposed to be the wife of some other emperor or usurper; but Khell and Eckhel assign her to Carinus].

STYLE:——MAGNIA. VRBICA.——MAGN. (*or* MAGNIA.) VR-
BICA. AVG.

Gold - R 8
Brass medallions - - - - - - - - - - - - - - - R 6
Second brass *(Beauvais and Eckhel)*. - - - - - - - - - R 4
Third brass - - - - - - - - - - - - - - - - - - R 2

GOLD.

1.

CONCORDIA. AVGG.   Concord, seated.

2.

PVDICITIA. AVG.   Pudicitia, seated.

3.

VENVS. GENETRIX.   Venus, standing.

4.

VENERI. VICTRICI.   A similar type.

These are valued at 400 francs each, by Mionnet.

BRASS MEDALLIONS.

1.

PVDICITIA. AVG.   Pudicitia, seated; two children before her: behind, a woman standing, holding a caduceus and cornucopia.

2.

VENVS. VICTRIX.   Venus-Victrix, standing.

Mionnet values No. 1 at 200, and the other at 150 francs.

THIRD BRASS.

1.

SALVS. PVBLICA.   Health seated, feeding a serpent rising from an altar.   In the field, A.   In the exergue, SMS XXI.

2.

VENVS. CELEST.   Venus standing, in the stola, holding a globe and the hasta.   In the exergue, SXXI.

3.

VENVS. GENETRIX.   A similar type.   In the field, D.

4.

VENVS. VICTRIX.   Venus-Victrix, standing.   In the exergue, KAς. or KAUς. or KUAς. or SXXIZ. or SXXIT. or IUA.

The first three numbers are much rarer than the other.

[MAGNIA URBICA AND CARINUS].

MAGNIA. VRBICA. AVG.   Head of Magnia Urbica.—*Rev.* IMP. CARINVS. AVG.   Helmeted bust of Carinus; the right hand holding a horse by the bridle, a buckler on the left arm.   (Size of the quinarius).   *(Tanini).*

Valued by Mionnet at fifty francs.

NIGRINIANUS.

[Nigrinianus is supposed to have been the son of Carinus, but is known only by the coins here described. Some writers have imagined him to have been the son of the tyrant Alexander, who assumed the purple in Africa, in the reign of Maxentius].

STYLE:——DIVVS. NIGRINIANVS.

Gold - R 8
Silver and second brass (very doubtful if any).
Third brass - - - - - - - - - - - - - - - - - - - R 4

GOLD.

DIVO. NIGRINIANO. Bare head of Nigrinianus to the right.—*Rev.* CONSECRATIO. A biga placed on the summit of a funeral pile. (*Mus. Gotha.*)

Valued by Mionnet at 400 francs only.

THIRD BRASS.

1.

CONSECRATIO. An eagle with expanded wings. In the exergue, KAꞶA.* *or* KAA. *or* R. III. III.

2.

Same legend. An altar, with the fire kindled. In the exergue, KAꞶA.

JULIANUS.

[Marcus Aurelianus Julianus was governor of Venetia in Italia, during the reign of Carus and his sons. He assumed the purple, upon the death of Numerianus; and Pannonia acknowledged his claim, in the year of Rome 1037 (A. D. 284). He maintained his usurpation for five or six months, when he was defeated by Carinus, and slain near Verona, in the following year].

STYLE:——IMP. C. IVLIANVS. P. F. AVG.——IMP. C. M. AVR. IVLIANVS. P. F. AVG.

Gold - R 8
Brass medallions - - - - - - - - - - - - - - - - R 8
Third brass - - - - - - - - - - - - - - - - - - - R 8

GOLD.

LIBERTAS. PVBLICA. Liberty, standing: a star in the field.

BRASS MEDALLION.

MONETA. AVGG. N. The three Monetæ, standing.

Valued by Mionnet at 200 francs.

THIRD BRASS.

1.

FELICITAS. TEMPORVM. Felicity standing, with her attributes. In the field, S. B. In the exergue, XXI.

2.

LIBERTAS. PVBLICA. Liberty, standing.

3.

PANNONIAE. AVG. Two women standing : one of them holding an ensign.

4.

VICTORIA. AVG. Victory, marching. In the exergue, S. A. *or* XXI.

5.

Same legend. Victory standing, holding a garland and a palm branch : in the field, S. A.; in the exergue, XXI. (Unpublished; in the cabinet of the *King of France*). (*Plate x, No.* 9).

Mionnet values Nos. 1 and 2 at sixty francs each ; No. 3 at seventy-two ; and No. 4 at fifty-five francs.

DIOCLETIANUS.

[Caius Valerius Diocletianus was born a slave, at Dioclea, or Doclia, in Dalmatia, in the year of Rome 998 (A. D. 245). He was General of the army in Maesia, under Probus ; and having accompanied Carus in his war against the Persians, he, upon the death of that emperor, served under Numerianus. In 1037, the army of the East proclaimed him emperor, the deaths of Numerianus and Carinus having removed the only obstacles to his elevation. In 1039 (A. D. 286) he took as his colleague in the empire, Maximianus Herculius, to whom the government of the West was confided, while Diocletian ruled the

provinces of the east.   In 1045 (A. D. 292), Diocletian adopted
Galerius Maximianus, and created him Caesar, while Maximianus
Herculius conferred the same title on Constantius Chlorus.   In the
year of Rome 1058 (A. D. 305), Diocletian abdicated the empire,
having nominated Galerius Maximianus, Augustus, and Maximianus
Daza, Caesar.   At the same time, Maximianus Herculius retired
from the government, having declared as his successor Constantius
Chlorus, and nominated Severus, Caesar.   Diocletian died at Salona,
in Dalmatia, whither he had retired upon his abdication, in the year
of Rome 1066 (A. D. 313)].

STYLE:——DIOCLETIANVS. AVG. (or AVGVSTVS.) [On reverse,
sometimes, P. P.]——IMP. DIOCLETIANVS. AVG. [On re-
verse, sometimes, P. P.]——IMP. C. DIOCLETIANVS. AVG.
——IMP. C. VAL. DIOCLETIANVS. AVG.——IMP. C. C.
VAL. DIOCLETIANVS. AVG.——DIOCLETIANVS. P. F.
AVG. [On reverse, sometimes, P. P.]——IMP. DIOCLETIANVS.
P. F. AVG.——IMP. C. DIOCLETIANVS. P. F. AVG.——
IMP. C. VAL. DIOCLETIANVS. P. F. AVG.——IMP. C. C.
DIOCLETIANVS. P. F. AVG.——IOVIVS. DIOCLETIANVS.
AVG.——DIOCLETIANVS. SEN. AVG.——D. N. DIOCLE-
TIANUS. P. F. S. AVG.——D. N. DIOCLETIANVS. BEATIS-
SIMVS. SEN.——D. N. DIOCLETIANVS. B. (or BEATISS. or
BEATISSIMVS. or BAEATISSIMVS.) S. (or SEN. or SENI.)
AVG.——D. N. DIOCLETIANVS. FELICISSIMVS. SENI.
——D. N. DIOCLETIANVS. FELICISSIMVS. SEN. AVG.——
D. N. DIOCLETIANVS. AETER. AVG.

The coins on which this emperor is styled SENIOR, BEATISSIMVS, FELI-
CISSIMVS, and AETERNVS, were, in all probability, struck after his abdication.

Gold medallions - - - - - - - - - - - - - - -	R 7
„ of the usual size - - - - - - - - - - - - -	R 4
„ with the Consulates - - - - - - - - - - - -	R 6
Silver medallions - - - - - - - - - - - - - -	R 8
Fine silver, of the usual size - - - - - - - - - -	R 1
Brass medallions - - - - - - - - - - - - - -	R 4
Second brass - - - - - - - - - - - - - - - -	VC
Third brass - - - - - - - - - - - - - - - -	VC
Brass, of the size of the quinarius - - - - - - - -	R 1

GOLD AND SILVER MEDALLIONS.

[DIOCLETIANUS AND MAXIMIANUS HERCULES].

1.

IMPP. DIOCLETIANO. ET. MAXIMIANO. AVGG. The busts of the two emperors, holding the Roman eagle.—*Rev.* IMPP. DIO-CLETIANO. III. ET. MAXIMIANO. COSS. The two emperors, Victory crowning them, in a triumphal car, drawn by four elephants. (*Mus. Florent.*). - - - - - - - - - - - - - - AU
Valued by Mionnet at 600 francs.

2.

DIOCLETIANVS. ET. MAXIMIANVS. AVGG. The laureated heads of the emperors, face to face.—*Rev.* IOVIO. ET. HERCVLIO. The two emperors, sacrificing on a tripod : above, two small figures of Jupiter and Hercules, standing on an estrade, or pedestal. AU
Valued by Mionnet at 480 francs.

3.

IMP. DIOCLETIANVS. AVG. Bust of Diocletian, with coat of mail and laureated head.—*Rev.* MAXIMIANVS. NOB. CAES. Laureated head of Maximianus Hercules, - - - - - - AR

4.

IMP. DIOCLETIANVS. P. F. AVG. The head to the right.—*Rev.* MAXIMIANVS. NOB. CAES. Head of Maximianus Her-cules. - - - - - - - - - - - - - - - - - - AR
The last two are valued by Mionnet at 200 francs each.

GOLD, AND FINE SILVER, OF THE USUAL SIZE.

1.

ADVENTVS. AVGVSTORVM. The two emperors, on horseback. (*Tanini*). - - - - - - - - - - - - - - - AU
Valued by Mionnet at 200 francs.

2.

COMITATVS. AVGG. A similar type. In the exergue, PR. - AU
Valued by Mionnet at 150 francs.

3.

CONCORDIAE. AVGG. NN. The two emperors, standing : Victory.
AU

4.

Same legend. The two emperors seated, crowned by Victory. (*Khell*).
AR

5.

COS. III. (or IIII.)   The emperor on horseback.   - - - - - AU

6.

CONSVL. IIII. P. P. PROCOS.   A figure, seated. - - -   AU & AR

7.

Same legend.   The emperor standing, in the toga, holding a globe.   In the field, ☒.   In the exergue, ⸿MA. - - - - - - - - AR

8.

Same legend.   The emperor-standing, in the toga, holding a globe and a wand. - - - - - - - - - - - - - - - - - AU

9.

CONSVL. VI. P. P. PROCOS.   A similar type.   In the exergue, SMA☒. - - - - - - - - - - - - - - - - - AU

10.

FATIS. VICTRICIBVS.   The three Parcæ, standing: S. C.   - AU

Valued by Mionnet at 150 francs.

11.

FEL. (or F.) ADVENT. AVGG. NN.   A woman standing, in the stola, holding a   and an ensign; a lion and a bull at her feet. In the exergue, D. (or P. or P. K.) - - - - - - AU & AR

This type, in gold, was sold at Dr. Mead's sale, in 1755.   In the catalogue, the woman is described as holding the labarum and an elephant's tooth, with the proboscis of an elephant on her head.

12.

IOVI. CONSER. AVGG.   Jupiter standing, holding the hasta and a thunderbolt; an eagle at his feet: a star in the field.   In the exergue, ALE. - - - - - - - - - - - - - - AU

13.

IOVI. CONSERVAT. AVGG.   Jupiter standing, holding the thunder-bolt and hasta. - - - - - - - - - - - - - - - AU

14.

Same legend.   A similar type.   In the exergue, PR. - - - - AU

15.

Same legend.   Similar type.   In the exergue, PR.   (Size of the quinarius). - - - - - - - - - - - - - - - AU

16.

IOVI. CONSERVAT. AVGG.   A similar type, but without the letters PR. in the exergue.   (Mionnet). - - - - - - - - AU

17.

IOVI. CONSERVATORI. Jupiter, standing. S. C. - - - AU

18.

Same legend. Jupiter, standing; an eagle at his feet. In the exergue, SMA. *or* ZSMA. - - - - - - - - - - - - - - - AU

19.

Same legend. A similar type, with ΣT. in the exergue. - - - AU

20.

Another, with PR. In the exergue. - - - - - - - - - - AU

21.

Same legend. Jupiter, seated; an eagle at his feet. PR. in the exergue. - - - - - - - - - - - - - - - - - AU

22.

IOVI. CONSERVATORI. AVG. Jupiter, standing. - - - - AU

23.

IOVI. CONSERVATORI. AVGG. A similar type. - - - - AU

24.

IOVI. CONSERVATORI. ORBIS. Jupiter standing, holding in his right hand a globe surmounted by a figure of Victory, and in his left the hasta pura. - - - - - - - - - - - - AU

25.

IOVI. FVLGERATORI. Jupiter standing, hurling a thunderbolt at a Titan. PR. in the exergue. *(Plate x, No.* 10 *).* - - - - AU

Brought, fine, 2*l.* 12*s.* 6*d.* at the Trattle sale.

26.

MARS. VICTOR. Mars, marching with a trophy and a spear. - AU

This type, fine, brought but 2*l.* 12*s.* 6*d.* at the Trattle sale.

27.

PIETAS. AVGG. ET. CAES. NN. A woman, standing, holding a child: another child at her feet. In the exergue, TR. - - AU

28.

PRIMIS. X. MVLTIS. XX. Two Victories supporting a buckler, on which is inscribed VOT. X. FEL. In the exergue, XXI. Є. *(Khell).* - - - - - - - - - - - - - - - - - - AU

29.

PRIMI. XX. IOVI. AVGVSTI. Jupiter, standing. In the exergue, TR. - - - - - - - - - - - - - - - - - - - AU

30.

Same legend. Jupiter, seated. In the exergue, TR. - - - - AU

31.

PROVIDENTIA. AVGG. The Praetorian camp. In the exergue,
PR. - AU

32.

Same legend. Four soldiers, sacrificing before the gate of the Praetorian
camp. - - - - - - - - - - - - - - - - - - - AR

33.

Same legend. A similar type, but with R. in the exergue - - - AR

34.

ROMAE. AETERNAE. Rome, seated. - - - - - - - - AU

35.

VICTORIA. AVG. Victory, standing. - - - - - - - - AU

36.

Same legend. Victory, marching. In the exergue, SMA. - - AU

37.

Same legend. The Praetorian camp. - - - - - - - - AR
Valued by Mionnet at eighty francs.

38.

Same legend. Four soldiers, sacrificing before the gate of the Praetorian
camp. In the exergue, SIS✳ - - - - - - - - - AU

39.

VICTORIA VG. (sic). Victory, in a biga. - - - - - - - AU

40.

VICTORIA. SARMAT. A similar type. - - - - - - - AR

41.

Another, similar, but with A. or B. or HA. in the exergue. - - AR

42.

VICTORIAE. SARMATICAE. The gate of the Praetorian camp.
In the exergue, SMNΓ. - - - - - - - - - - - - - AR

43.

Same legend. Four figures, sacrificing before the camp. In the
exergue, HA. - - - - - - - - - - - - - - - - AR

44.

VIRTVS. AVGG. Hercules, overpowering a stag. In the exergue,
TR. - AU

45.

VIRTVS. ILLYRICI. An equestrian figure, on a galley. In the
exergue, TR. - - - - - - - - - - - - - - - - AU
Valued by Mionnet at 100 francs.

46.

VIRTVS. MILITVM. The Praetorian camp. In the exergue,
⁂ ANTH.⁂ - - - - - - - - - - - - - - - - AR

47.

Same legend. Four figures, sacrificing before the Praetorian camp. AR

48.

Another, similar. In the exergue, A. or C. or D. or Γ. or Z. or Q. - AR

49.

VOTA. XX. AVGG. within a garland. - - - - - - - - AU

50.

VOTA. XX. SIC. XXX. within a garland. - - - - - - - - AU

51.

VOTIS. ROMANORVM. Two Victories, supporting a shield, inscribed
SIC. XX. SIC. XXX.. In the exergue, AQ. - - - - - - AU

52.

XCVI. or XCVIAQ. or XCVIT. or XCVIIT. within a garland. - AR

53,

XX. DIOCLETIANI. AVG. SMT. in five lines within a garland. AU

In gold, No. 1 is much the rarest. The next in rarity are Nos. 2 and
10; then No. 45. Nos. 3, 8, 9, 25, 27, 28, 31, 38, 39, 44, 51, and 53,
are the rarest of the remaining numbers. In silver, No. 37 is by far the
rarest. Nos. 7 and 11 are very rare types; and Nos. 46 and 52 are
rarer than the remaining numbers.

BRASS MEDALLIONS.

1.

ADVENTVS. AVG. The emperor on horseback, preceded by Victory,
and followed by two foot-soldiers bearing standards.

2.

CONCORDIA. CAES. AVGG. NN. The two emperors standing, each
in the paludamentum; between them a veiled figure, standing before
an altar; a Victory behind each emperor, placing a crown upon
his head.

3.

GENIO. POPVLI. ROMANI. The Genius standing, the modius on
his head; a garland (or patera?) in his right hand, and in his left
a cornucopia.

A very common type on the second brass of this emperor.

4.

HERCVLIO. MAXIMIANO. AVG. The emperor in the paludamentum, seated; in his right hand a globe, surmounted by a figure of Victory, which places a garland upon his head : Hercules, also seated, holding the lion's skin and club; to the left, a bow.

5.

HERCVLIO. MAXIMIANO. AVG. ROM. Maximianus and Hercules seated, each crowned by a Victory, behind.

6.

IOVI. CONSERVATORI. Jupiter seated, holding the thunderbolt and the hasta.

7.

IOVI. CONSERVATORI. AVG. Statue of Jupiter, seated within a a temple.

8.

Same legend. Statue of Jupiter, seated within a temple: on the front of the temple, IOVI. O. M. V. C.

9.

MONETA. AVG. *or* AVGG. The three Monetæ, standing.

The medallions with this type, vary in size. The above is valued by Mionnet at twelve francs only, but the large size at thirty francs. The large medallion described by Vaillant, with the head bare, Mionnet values at 100 francs.

10.

MONETA. IOVI. ET. HERCVLI. AVGG. Moneta, standing between Jupiter and Hercules.

11.

PROVIDENTIA. DEORVM. QVIES. AVG. (*or* AVGG.). Two women, standing. In the field, to the right, S.: to the left, F. In the exergue, PTR.

12.

VOTA. PVBLICA. Serapis, seated on a galley: Victory, standing before him, holding a sail.

The above are thus valued by Mionnet: No. 1, sixty francs; No. 2, seventy francs; No. 3, twenty-four francs; No. 4, 100 francs; No. 5, 150 francs; No. 6, twenty francs; No. 7, sixty francs; No. 8, 150 francs; and Nos. 10, 11, and 12, 120 francs each.

[DIOCLETIANUS AND MAXIMIANUS.]

1.

IMPP. DIOCLETIANO. ET. MAXIMIANO. AVGG. NN. The

heads of Diocletianus and Maximianus, face to face : the first radiated ; the other, laureated.—*Rev.* IMP. DIOCLETIANO. III. ET. MAXIMIANO. COSS. The two emperors in a triumphal car, drawn by four elephants: Victory behind, placing a garland on their heads: eight soldiers accompanying, bearing palm branches. (*Musei Theupoli*, Vol. ii, page 819).

2.

IMP. DIOCLETIANVS. AVG. Laureated head of Diocletianus.—*Rev.* IMP. MAXIMIANVS. P. F. AVG. Head of Maximianus Hercules.

3.

DIOCLETIANVS. ET. MAXIMIANVS. AVGG. The laureated heads of the emperors, face to face.—*Rev.* MONETA. IOVI. ET. HERCVLI. AVGG. Moneta standing, between Jupiter and Hercules.

These are valued by Mionnet at 200 francs each.

SECOND BRASS, WITH RARE REVERSES.

1.

D. N. DIOCLETIANO. AETER. AVG. Head of Diocletianus.—*Rev.* GENIO. POP. ROM. Genius standing, with patera and cornucopia.

2.

IOVI. CONS. CAES. Jupiter, standing: in the field, S. P. Γ. *or* S. P. Δ. In the exergue, ALE.

3.

MAXIMIANVS. AVG. Head of Maximianus Hercules.

4.

M. SACRA. AVGG. ET. CAESS. NN. Moneta, standing. In the field, a star, *or* S. F. In the exergue, ATR. *or* BTR. *or* ITR.

5.

D. N. DIOCLETIANO. FELICISSIMO. SEN. AVG. Head of Diocletianus.—*Rev.* PROVIDENTIA. DEORVM. QVIES. AVG. Two women, standing. In the field, S. F. In the exergue, ANT. *or* PTR.

6.

QVIES. AVGG. A woman in the stola, standing.

7.

Same legend. A similar type. In the exergue, PLC. *or* PLN.

Nos. 1 and 3 are the rarest; the next in rarity is No. 5.

[DIOCLETIANUS AND MAXIMIANUS].

DIOCLETIANO. ET. MAXIMIANO. AVGG.   The heads of Dio-
cletianus and Maximianus, with radiated crowns, face to face.—*Rev.*
CONSERVATORES. AVGG.   Jupiter and Hercules, standing.
In the exergue, SMS.   (*Tanini*).

Valued by Mionnet at fifty francs.

THIRD BRASS, WITH RARE REVERSES.

1.

AETERNITAS. AVGG.   An elephant, mounted by its driver.   In the
exergue, A.

2.

AVSPIC. FEL.   The goddess standing, holding a tessera and a caduceus: a small figure at her feet.

3.

CLARITAS. AVGG.   The Sun, standing; a captive at his feet.   In the
field, D.   In the exergue, PTR.

4.

CONSERVATOR. AVGG.   Jupiter and the emperor, standing before
a tripod.   In the field, B. Γ.   In the exergue, XXIBI. *or*
ΓXXIBI. *or* XXIΓBI. *or* XXIBO. *or* XXIO.

5.

IOVI. CONSERVAT.   Jupiter, standing: at his feet, an eagle.

This coin is of the size of the quinarius, and has on the obverse the
bust of the emperor, holding the Roman eagle.

6.

IOVI. CONSERVAT. AVGG.   Jupiter, standing.   (Size of the
quinarius).

7.

IOVI. TVTATORI. AVGG.   Jupiter, standing: an eagle at his feet.
In the exergue, D.

8.

MAXIMIANVS. AVG.   Laureated head of Maximianus.   (Size of
the quinarius).

9.

PAX. AVGGG.   Peace, standing, with her attributes.   In the field, S. P.
In the exergue, MLXXI.

The coins of Maximianus and Diocletianus, with these types, deserve especial notice. We learn from history that these emperors recognised the title which Carausius had assumed; but we know at the same time that they were not enabled to depose and punish the usurper. Mionnet, either doubting the authenticity of coins of these princes with AVGGG., or passing them over through inadvertence, does not notice the types here described, although they are of considerable rarity. But we have no proof that they were struck by authority of Diocletianus and Maximianus; while, on the other hand, there appear some grounds for believing that they were minted by the usurper himself. Many coins of Carausius bear AVGGG.: and this is not surprising, for he would naturally publish the recognition of his title by Diocletianus and his colleague: but those of the emperors, though very common with AVGG., are of rare occurrence with AVGGG. Now it is somewhat singular, that the two coins in the British Museum with PAX. AVGGG. are in fabric exceedingly like the rude coins of Carausius; so much so, that they might, if it were not for the legends, by a careless observer be supposed to belong to that personage. Eckhel (see *Doct. Num. Vet.*), after quoting a coin with VIRTVS. AVGGG., observes that it bears testimony to the truth of the account of the recognition of Carausius by Diocletianus and Maximianus: but he does not notice that on the Continent these coins are of great rarity, and even in England are of unfrequent occurrence; a circumstance certainly in favour of the supposition that they were minted by Carausius.

10.

P. M. TR. P. VIII. COS. IIII. P. P.   A lion walking, with a thunderbolt in his mouth.   In the exergue, A. and a star.

11.

PRINCIPI. IVVENTVT.   The emperor in a military habit, standing, holding an ensign and a spear.   In the exergue, XXIΓ. *or* XXIϛ.

12.

PROVIDENT. DEOR.   A figure half naked, seated, touching with a staff a globe on the ground, and holding the hasta.   In the exergue, II.

13.

VTILITAS. PVBLICA.   A woman, standing.   In the exergue, T. (Size of the quinarius).

14.

VICTORIA. AVGG.   Victory, standing.   (Size of the quinarius).

15.

VIRTVS. AVGG. Hercules standing, with the lion's skin, club, and
bow. (Size of the quinarius).

The rarest type is No. 8.; the next in rarity are Nos. 2 and 5; then
Nos. 1, 12, 14, and 15.

[DIOCLETIANUS AND MAXIMIANUS].

DIOCLETIANVS. AVG. Laureated head of Diocletian, with the
paludamentum.—*Rev.* MAXIMIANVS. AVG. Laureated head·
of Maximianus Hercules, with the paludamentum. (Size of the
quinarius).

Valued by Mionnet at six francs.

MAXIMIANUS HERCULES.

[Marcus Aurelius Valerius Maximianus was born near Sirmium, in
Pannonia, in the year of Rome 1003 (A. D. 250). His parents were
peasants, and he served as a common soldier in the Roman army.
He was associated in the empire with Diocletian, in the year of Rome
1039 (A. D. 286), having, as is supposed, been created Caesar in the
preceding year. Maximianus abdicated the empire at Milan at the
same time as his colleague Diocletian, in the year of Rome 1058
(A. D. 305); after nominating as his successor Constantius Chlorus,
and creating Severus, Caesar, Diocletian having raised to the Eastern
Empire Galerius Maximianus, and created Maximinus Daza, Caesar.
At the persuasion of his son Maxentius, Maximianus resumed the
government at Rome in the following year; but having failed in his
attempt to deprive his son of the imperial dignity, the troops mutinied
and drove him from the city (1061). He fled to Gaul, to the court of
Constantine, whom he had created Caesar in the preceding year, and
to whom he had given his daughter Faustina in marriage. Here, in the
absence of Constantine, he again attempted to regain the imperial
dignity (1062), A.D. 309, but was obliged to take refuge in the city of
Marseilles, where he was made prisoner, and deprived of the purple.
Constantine, nevertheless, allowed him apartments in his own palace :
but, having attempted the life of that prince, he was compelled to
choose the manner of his death. Maximianus terminated his eventful
life at the age of sixty by strangling himself, in the year of Rome
1063 (A. D. 310)].

STYLE : —— VAL. MAXIMIANVS. NOB. CAES. —— MAXIMI-
ANVS. AVG. (*or* AVGVSTVS.) [On reverse, often, P. P.]——

IMP. MAXIMIANVS. AVG.——IMP. M. AVR. VAL. MAXI-
MIANVS. AVG.——IMP. C. VAL. MAXIMIANVS. AVG.——
IMP. C. M. A. MAXIMIANVS. AVG.——IMP. C. M. A. (or
AVR.) VAL. MAXIMIANVS. AVG.——IMP. MAXIMIANVS.
P. AVG.——MAXIMIANVS. P. F. AVG.——IMP. MAXI-
MIANVS. P. F. AVG.——IMP. C. MAXIMIANVS. P. F. AVG.
[On reverse, sometimes, CONSERVATOR. AFRICAE. SVAE. (or CONSER-
VATORES. KART. SVAE.*)]——IMP. C. VAL. MAXIMIANVS. P.
F. AVG.——IMP. C. M. A. (or AVREL.) MAXIMIANVS. P. F.
AVG.——IMP. C. M. A. (or AVR. or AVREL.) V. (or VAL.)
MAXIMIANVS. P. F. AVG.——HERCVLEVS. MAXIMI-
ANVS. AVG.——IMP. MAXIMIANVS. SEN. AVG. [On
reverse, sometimes, CONSERV. (or CONSERVATORES.) VRB. (or VRBIS.)
SVAE.]——D. N. MAXIMIANVS. SEN. AVG.——D. N.
MAXIMIANVS. P. S. AVG.——MAXIMIANVS. SEN. P. F.
AVG.——D. N. MAXIMIANVS. P. F. S. AVG.——D.
N. MAXIMIANVS. BEATISS.——D. N. MAXIMIANVS.
BEATISSIMVS. SEN.——D. N. MAXIMIANVS. BAEATISS.
(or BAEATISSIMVS. or BEATISSIMVS.) SEN. AVG.——D.
N. MAXIMIANVS. FELICISSIMVS. SEN. AVG.——DIVVS.
MAXIMIANVS. IMP.——DIVVS. MAXIMIANVS. PATER.
——DIVVS. MAXIMIANVS. OPTIMVS.——DIVVS. MAXI-
MIANVS. P. OPTIMVS.——DIVVS. MAXIMIANVS. FOR.
IMP.——DIVVS. MAXIMIANVS. SEN. FORTIS. (or FOR-
TISSIMVS.)——DIVVS. MAXIMINIANVS. SOCER. (perhaps
MAXENTII.)

Gold medallions - - - - - - - - - - - - - - - - R 8
  ,, of the usual size - - - - - - - - - - - - - R 4
  ,, with the Consulates - - - - - - - - - - - R 7
Silver medallions - - - - - - - - - - - - - - R 6
  ,, of the usual size - - - - - - - - - - - - - R 1
Brass medallions - - - - - - - - - - - - - - R 4
Second brass - - - - - - - - - - - - - - - - VC
  ,, with his head and the head of Hercules on obverse - R 4
Third brass - - - - - - - - - - - - - - - - VC
Brass, of the size of the quinarius - - - - - - - - - S

---

* Perhaps Maximianus, Maxentius, and Constantius.

GOLD AND SILVER MEDALLIONS.

1.

GENIO. AVGVSTI. Genius, standing: a star. - - - - - AR

2.

GENIO. POPVLI. ROMANI. Genius standing, holding a cornucopia and a patera; an owl at his feet. In the exergue, AQR. (*d'Ennery —Mionnet*). - - - - - - - - - - - - - - - AR

3.

AVR. VAL. MAXIMIANVS. P. F. AVG. The bare bearded head of Maximianus.—*Rev.* HERCVLI. CONSERVATORI. AVGG. Bust of Hercules, with lion's skin and club. - - - - - - AU

This medallion is of large size, and has a loop. It is engraved in a work on the gold medallions of the Cabinet of Vienna, by Steinbuchel.

4.

IOVI. CONSERVAT. AVGG. Jupiter, standing. - - - - AU

5.

VOTIS. X. The two emperors, sacrificing: C. - - - - AU & AR

The gold are valued by Mionnet at 600, 300, and 100 francs. The first two numbers, in silver, at forty-eight francs each; and No. 5 at sixty francs.

[MAXIMIANUS AND DIOCLETIANUS].

1.

IMPP. DIOCLETIANO. ET. MAXIMIANO. AVGG. The busts of the emperors, in their royal habits, holding the Roman eagle.— *Rev.* IMPP. DIOCLETIANO. III. ET. MAXIMIANO. COSS. The two emperors, crowned by Victory, on a car drawn by four elephants. (*Mus. Florent.*) - - - - - - - - - AU

2.

MAXIMIANVS. NOB. CAES. The laureated head of Maximianus to the right.—*Rev.* IMP. DIOCLETIANVS. AVG. The bust of Diocletianus, with coat of mail, to the left. (*Mionnet*). - AR

3.

DIOCLETIANVS. ET. MAXIMIANVS. AVGG. The laureated heads of the emperors, face to face.—*Rev.* IOVIO. ET. HERCVLIO. The two emperors, sacrificing: above, two small figures of Jupiter and Hercules, standing on an estrade or pedestal - - - - AU

Mionnet values the gold at 600 and 480 francs. The silver at 200 francs.

PLATE II.

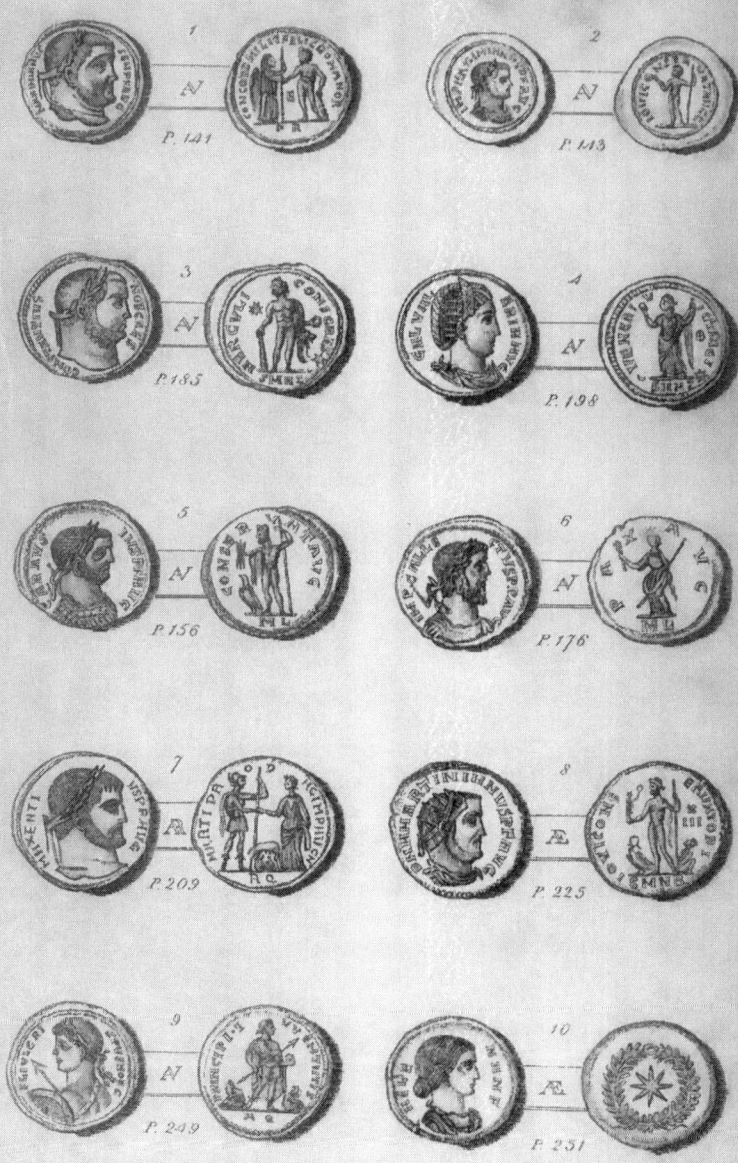

GOLD AND SILVER, OF THE USUAL SIZE.

1.

ADVENTVS. AVGG. The two emperors, on horseback. - - AR

2.

ADVENTVS. AVGVSTORVM. A similar type. - - - - - AR

3.

CONCORDIA. AVGG. The two emperors. - - - - - - - AU

4.

CONCORDIA. AVGG. ET. CAESS. NNNN. Concord seated, with her attributes. *(Mus. Vindob.)* - - - - - - - - - AU

5.

CONCORDIA. MILITVM. A woman, holding two ensigns. In the exergue, SC. *or* SC*. *or* ST. - - - - - - - - - - AU

6.

CONCORD. MILIT. FELIC. ROMANOR. Hercules and a veiled woman, standing. In the exergue, EPR. *(Mionnet).* - - AU
Valued by Mionnet at 100 francs.

7.

CONCORD. MILIT. FELIC. ROMANOR. Hercules standing, holding his club and joining hands with a veiled woman, who holds the hasta pura; in the field between them, E. In the exergue, PR. *(Plate xi, No. 1)*.

8.

CONSVL. AVGG. NN. The emperor, standing. In the field, Z. In the exergue, SMSD. - - - - - - - - - - - - - AU

9.

COS. II. The emperor, on horseback. - - - - - - - - AU

10.

COS. III. A similar type. - - - - - - - - - - - - AU

11.

COS. III. P. P. PROCOS. A similar type. - - - - - - - AU

12.

CONSVL. III. P. P. PROCOS. The emperor seated, holding a globe surmounted by a Victory, and the parazonium. (With a loop). *(Steinbuchel's notice of the gold medallions of the Cabinet of Vienna,* pl. 1, No. 1). - - - - - - - - - - - - - - AU
Valued by Mionnet at 100 francs.

13.

CONS. IIII. P. P. PROCOS. The emperor standing, in the toga, holding a globe and a staff. - - - - - - - - - - - AU

14.

CONSVL. IIII. P. P. PROCOS. The emperor in the toga, standing: a star. In the exergue, SMAZ. *or* SMA✳. - - - - - AU

15.

CONSVL. V. P. P. PROCOS. A similar type. In the exergue, SMAZ✳. - - - - - - - - - - - - - - - - - AU

16.

CONS. VI. *or* VII. *or* VIII. P. P. PROCOS. The emperor, standing.
AU

17.

CONSVL, VI. *or* VIII. P. P. PROCOS. The emperor, standing. A star in the field. In the exergue, SMAZ✳. - - - - - AU

18.

FATIS. VICTRICIBVS. The three Parcæ, standing. In the field, Z. *or* F. In the exergue, SMA. - - - - - - - - AU
Valued by Mionnet at 150 francs.

19.

FEL. ADVENT. AVGG. NN. A woman standing, in the stola, holding an elephant's tooth and a standard: at her feet, a lion and a bull. In the exergue, S. *or* P. - - - - - - - - - - AR

20.

FELIX. INGRESSVS. SEN. AVG. Rome seated, holding a buckler inscribed VOT. XXX: a buckler on the ground. In the exergue, PR. - - - - - - - - - - - - - - - - - - - AU
This and the following No. are valued by Mionnet at 100 francs.

21.

FELIX. KARTHAGO. A woman, standing. In the exergue, PK. - AU

22.

GAVDETE. ROMANI. Two Victories, holding a buckler inscribed SIC. XX. *or* SIC. XXX. In the exergue, AQ. (Size of the quinarius). - - - - - - - - - - - - - - - - AU
Valued by Mionnet at 150 francs.

23.

GAVDIVM. ROMANORVM. A female captive, at the foot of a trophy. In the exergue, PR. - - - - - - - - - AU
Valued by Mionnet at 150 francs.

24.

HERCVLI. COMITI. AVGG. ET. CAESS. NN. Hercules, standing.
In the exergue, PK. - - - - - - - - - - - - - - AU

25.

HERCVLI. CONSER. AVGG. ET. CAESS. NN. Hercules, standing. In the exergue, TR. - - - - - - - - - - - - AU

26.

HERCVLI. CONSERVAT. Hercules standing, leaning on his club. AU

27.

HERCVLI. DEBELLAT. Hercules destroying the Hydra. In the
exergue, P. ROM. *(Khell).* - - - - - - - - - - - AU

28.

HERCVLI. DEBELLATORI. A similar type. *(Vaillant. Khell).*
AU & AR

29.

HERCVLI. IMMORTALI. Hercules bearing away Cerberus in
chains. In the exergue, TR. - - - - - - - - - - - AU

30.

HERCVLI. INVICTO. AVGG. Hercules destroying the Hydra. AU

31.

HERCVLI. PACIFERO. Hercules standing, holding an olive branch
in his right hand, and in his left the club and lion's skin. In the
exergue, PR. *(Mionnet).* - - - - - - - - - - AU

32.

HERCVLI. VICTORI. Hercules destroying the Hydra. On some,
PR. in the exergue. - - - - - - - - - - - - - - AU
This type, fine, brought 3*l.* 1*s.* at the sale of the Trattle collection.

33.

Same legend. Hercules seated, leaning on his club : on one side, a
quiver. In the exergue, PR. - - - - - - - - - - AU

34.

Same legend. Hercules, standing. In the exergue, PR. *or* SMN. AU

35.

IOVI. CONSERVAT. AVGG. Jupiter, seated. - - - - - AU

36.

Same legend. Jupiter, standing. In the exergue, SMT. - - - AU

37.

IOVI. CONSERVAT. AVGG.   Jupiter standing, holding in his right hand a thunderbolt, and in his left the hasta pura. - - - - AU

This quinarius is unpublished, and, in all probability, unique.   It is in the cabinet of *T. Thomas, Esq.* (See *Plate xi, No.* 2).

38.

IOVI. CONSERVATORI.   Jupiter standing, holding a globe surmounted by a Victory, and the hasta.   In the field, Γ.   In the exergue, ALE. - - - - - - - - - - - - - - - AU

39.

Same legend.   Jupiter, seated: an eagle at his feet. - - - - AU

40.

IOVI. CONSERVATORI. AVGG.   Jupiter standing, holding the thunderbolt and hasta.   In the field, Z.   In the exergue, SMA.
AU

41.

IOVI. CONSERVATORI. N. K. *or* N. K. L. Y. K. C.   Jupiter, with the pallium, standing, holding the thunderbolt and the hasta.   In the exergue, SMN. - - - - - - - - - - - - - AU

42.

IOVI. FVLGERATORI.   Jupiter, hurling a thunderbolt at a Titan.   In the exergue, IAN. - - - - - - - - - - - - AU

43.

Another, without the letters in the exergue. *(Tanini).* - - - AU

44.

IOVIS. CONSERVATOR.   Jupiter standing, holding the thunderbolt and the hasta: an eagle at his feet.   In the field, Z.   In the exergue, SM. SD. - - - - - - - - - - - - - - AU

45.

PIETAS. AVGG.   A woman standing, holding a child: two children at her feet.   In the exergue, PTR. - - - - - - - AU

46.

P. M. TR. P. P. P.   The emperor standing, holding two ensigns. *(Cabinet of Vienna).* - - - - - - - - - - - - AU

47.

PROVIDENTIA. AVGG.   The Praetorian camp.   In the exergue, PR. - - - - - - - - - - - - - - - - - - AU

This type, in fine preservation, brought 2*l.* 2*s.* at the Trattle sale.

48.

PROVIDENTIA. AVGG. Four soldiers sacrificing before a camp. In the exergue, Γ. - - - - - - - - - - - - - - - AR

49.

SALVS. AVGG. Hygeia, feeding a serpent. - - - - - - AU

The obverse has the head covered with the lion's skin.

50.

VICTORIA. AVGG. The Praetorian camp. In the exergue, SIS. - AR

51.

VICTORIA. SARMAT. Four soldiers, sacrificing before a camp. In the exergue, D. *or* Є. - - - - - - - - - - - - - AR

Some have no letters in the exergue.

52.

VICTORIA. SARMATICA. Four soldiers, sacrificing before a camp. In the exergue, HB. - - - - - - - - - - - AU & AR

53.

VICTORIA. SARMATICAE. The Praetorian camp. In the exergue, SMNΓ. - - - - - - - - - - - - - - - - - - AR

54.

VIRTVS. AVGG. Hercules, strangling the Nemæan lion. In the exergue, PR. - - - - - - - - - - - - - - - AU

55.

Same legend. Hercules, seizing a stag. In the exergue, PR. - AU

56.

Same legend. Hercules, standing. - - - - - - - - - - AU

57.

Same legend. Hercules and Jupiter, standing. - - - - - - AU

Valued by Mionnet at 100 francs.

58.

VIRTVS. (*or* VIRTVTI. AVGG.) Hercules, killing a monster. AU & AR

59.

VIRTVS. AVGG. ET. CAESS. The emperor on horseback, trampling on an enemy. In the exergue, SIS. - - - - - - - - AU

60.

VIRTVS. ILLYRICI. The emperor, on horseback : below, a vessel. In the exergue, TR. - - - - - - - - - - - - - AU

This type, fine, brought 4*l*. 6*s*. at the sale of the Trattle collection.

61.

VIRTVS. MILITVM. The Praetorian camp. In the exergue, ANTH.
(*or* ✱ANTH✱. *or* AQS. *or* RS. *or* TSA.) - - - - - - - AR

62.

Same legend. A similar type. In the exergue, TR. (Size of the
quinarius). - - - - - - - - - - - - - - - - - - AR

63.

Same legend. Four soldiers, sacrificing before a camp. Sometimes
a club in the exergue, or various letters. - - - - - - - AR

64.

VIRTVTI. AVGG. Hercules, carrying the carcass of the Erymanthean
boar. In the exergue, PT. - - - - - - - - - - - - AU

65.

VIRTVTI. HERCVLIS. Hercules, standing. In the exergue, of
some, SC. - - - - - - - - - - - - - - - - - AU

66.

VIRTVTI. MILITVM. The Praetorian camp. In the exergue,
SMNꞩ. - - - - - - - - - - - - - - - - - - AR

67.

VOT. (*or* VOTA.) XX. AVGG. within a garland. - - - - - AU

68.

VOT. XX. AVGG. NN. within a garland. - - - - - AU & AR

69.

XX. MAXIMIANI. AVG. SMAQ. within a garland. - - - - AU

In gold, Nos. 18 and 22 are the rarest, excepting, of course, the
unique quinarius. The next in rarity is No. 23; then Nos. 6, 7, 12, 21,
27, 31, and 57.

In silver, No. 28 is by far the rarest. The next in rarity is No. 2;
then No. 1. The least rare are Nos. 61 and 63.

BRASS MEDALLIONS.

1.

AETERNAE. MEMORIA. A circular temple with six columns,
surmounted by the figure of an eagle. In the exergue, MOSTR.

2.

FELIX. ADVENT. AVGG. NN. A woman in the stola standing,
holding the hasta pura.

3.

HERCVLI. DEBELLATORI. Hercules, destroying the Hydra. In the exergue, *SIS.

4.

IOVI. CONSERVATORI. AVG. Statue of Jupiter, with an eagle at his feet, standing within a temple.

5.

Same legend. Statue of Jupiter standing, within a temple: on the peristyle, IOVIVS. AVG. The obverse has the emperor's head covered with the lion's skin.

6.

MAXIMIANVS. NOB. CAES. ET. CONSVL. Bust of Galerius Maximianus.

Valued by Mionnet at 150 francs.

7.

MONETA. AVGG. The three Monetæ, standing.

8.

Same legend. A similar type. The obverse has the bust of the emperor holding the Roman eagle.

9.

Same legend. A similar type. The obverse has the bust of Maximianus, armed with a spear and buckler: legend, VIRTVS. MAXIMIANI. AVG.

10.

Same legend. A similar type. The obverse has the bust of the emperor with a spear and buckler, holding a horse by the bridle: legend, VIRTVS. MAXIMIANI. AVG.

11.

MONETA. IOVI. ET. HERCVLI. AVGG. Moneta, standing between Jupiter and Hercules.

12.

Same legend. A similar type. (Of various sizes).

13.

PROVIDENTIA. DEORVM. QVIES. AVGG. Two women in the stola, standing, with different attributes. In the exergue, ST.

14.

SACRA. MONETA. AVGG. ET. CAESS. NOSTR. Moneta standing, with her attributes. In the exergue, AQS.

15.

SALVIS. AVGG. ET. CAESS. FEL. ORBIS. TER.   Moneta, standing between a woman and Mars, holding a Victory. The obverse
has the bust of Maximianus, with a buckler, and holding a horse by
the bridle : legend, VIRTVS. MAXIMIANI. AVG.

Of the above, No. 6 is by far the rarest. Nos. 5 and 15 are the next
in rarity: then Nos. 1, 2, 3, 13, and 14. Nos. 7 and 8 are by no means
so rare as the others.

[MAXIMIANUS, AND DIOCLETIANUS].

1.

IMP. MAXIMIANVS. P. F. AVG.   Head of Maximianus Hercules.
—*Rev.* IMP. DIOCLETIANVS. AVG.   Laureated head of
Diocletianus.

2.

IMPP. DIOCLETIANO. ET. MAXIMIANO. AVGG. NN.   The
heads of the two emperors, face to face; one with radiated crown, the
other laureated, and holding a sceptre.—*Rev.* IMPP. DIOCLE-
TIANO. III. ET. MAXIMIANO. COSS.   The two emperors in a
car, drawn by four elephants : Victory behind, crowning them : eight
foot soldiers attending, bearing palm branches. (*Mus. Theupoli*).

3.

DIOCLETIANVS. ET. MAXIMIANVS. AVGG.   Laureated heads
of the emperors, face to face.—*Rev.* MONETA. IOVI. ET. HER-
CVLI. AVGG.   Moneta, standing between Jupiter and Hercules.
The above are valued by Mionnet at 200 francs each.

[MAXIMIANUS HERCULES, AND GALERIUS MAXIMIANUS].

IMP. MAXIMIANVS. AVG. COS. IIII.   Head of Maximianus
Hercules, covered with the lion's skin.—*Rev.* MAXIMIANVS.
NOB. CAES. ET. CONSVL. Bust of Gal. Maximianus to the right.

Valued by Mionnet at 150 francs.

SECOND BRASS, WITH RARE REVERSES.

1.

AETERNA. MEMORIA.   A circular temple.   In the exergue,
MOSTQ. (*or* MOSTS.)   The obverse has the veiled head of
Maximianus, and the legend, DIVO. MAXIMIANO. PATRI.
MAXENTIVS. AVG.

2.

CONCORDIA. MILITVM. The emperor and Jupiter standing, supporting a Victory. In the field, Δ. (or κ. Δ.) In the exergue, XXI. ·

3.

CONSERV. VRB. SVAE. A statue, within a temple.

4.

FORTVNAE. REDVCI. CAESS. NN. Fortune, standing: a star in the field. In the exergue, AT.

5.

IMP. MAXIMIANVS. P. F. AVG. The heads of the emperor and Hercules, side by side. — *Rev.* GENIO. POPVLI. ROMANI. Genius standing, sacrificing: a star in the field. In the exergue, TR.

6.

HERCVLI. CONSERVATORI. Hercules standing, with bow, club, and lion's skin. In the exergue, PLN.

7.

HERCVLI. VICTORI. Hercules, standing; his right hand on his club; his left, holding the apples of the Hesperides. In the field, B. S. *or* P. S. In the exergue, ALE.

8.

MARS. VICTOR. Mars marching, with a spear and a trophy. In the exergue, PLN.

9.

QVIES. AVG. A woman standing, holding a laurel branch and the hasta pura. In the field, S. A. In the exergue, PTR.

10.

ROMAE. AETER. Rome seated, within a temple. In the exergue, PLN.

11.

S. M. VRB. AVGG. ET. CAESS. NN. Equity, standing. A star in the field. In the exergue, RS.

12.

VIRTVS. AVGG. ET. CAESS. NN. The emperor on horseback, with a spear and a shield: two figures below. In the exergue, AQP.

13.

D. N. MAXIMIANO. FELICISSIMO. SEN. AVG. Bust of Maximianus.—*Rev.* VOTA. PVBLICA. Serapis in a vessel, and Isis-Pharia holding the sail.

14.

MAXIMIANVS. NOB. CAES. Laureated head of Maximianus
Hercules.—*Rev.* MAXIMIANVS. NOB. CAES. The same head,
but rather smaller. (See *Catalogue d'Ennery*).

No. 5 is extremely rare, and valued by Mionnet at eighty francs. Of the
others, Nos. 13 and 14 are the rarest. The next in rarity, are 2, 4, 6.

[MAXIMIANUS, AND DIOCLETIANUS].

DIOCLETIANO. ET. MAXIMIANO. AVGG. Radiated heads of
the emperors, face to face.—*Rev.* CONSERVATORES. AVGG.
Jupiter and Hercules, standing. In the exergue, SMS.

(Quoted from *Tanini*, by *Mionnet*, who values it at fifty francs).

THIRD BRASS, WITH RARE REVERSES.

1.

ADVENTVS. AVGG. The emperors on horseback. In the exergue,
XXI.

2.

IMP. MAXIMIANVS. AVG. The laureated heads of the emperors,
side by side.—*Rev.* AEQVITAS. AVGG. The three Monetæ,
standing.

3.

AETERN. MEMOR. A similar type. (Size of the quinarius).

4.

AETERNIT. AVGG. A similar type. (Size of the quinarius).

5.

AETERNITAS. AVGG. An elephant, mounted by its driver; A.

6.

AVSPIC. FEL. A woman standing, holding a tessera and a caduceus:
before her, a figure, stretching out its hands.

7.

CLARITAS. AVGG. The Sun, standing: at his feet, a captive. In
the exergue, PTR.

8.

DIOCLETIANVS. AVG. Laureated head of Diocletianus. (Size of
the quinarius).

9.

FIDES. MILIT. A woman standing, holding two ensigns. In the exergue, PTR.

10.

IMP. MAXIMIANVS. AVG. Laureated bust of Maximianus, with a coat of mail.—*Rev.* IMP. MAXIMIANVS. AVG. Laureated bust of Maximianus, holding the club and lion's skin of Hercules. (Size of the quinarius).

11.

IOVI. CONSERVAT. AVGG. Jupiter, standing. (Size of the quinarius).

12.

IOVI. CONSERVATORI. AVGG. Jupiter and Victory, standing.

13.

IMP. MAXIMIANVS. AVG. The heads of Maximianus and Hercules, side by side.—*Rev.* MONETA. AVG. (*or* AVGG.) The three Monetæ, standing.

14.

PAX. AVGG. Peace, standing. In the field, S. P. In the exergue, MLXXI.

15.

PAX. AVGGG. A similar type, with the same letters in the field and the exergue.

16.

PIETAS. AVGG. Piety, sacrificing on an altar. In the exergue, R.

17.

PRIMIS. X. MVLTIS. XX. Hercules standing, with his attributes. In the exergue, XXIA.

18.

Same legend. Victory standing, inscribing VO. XX. on a buckler. In the exergue, XXIϹ. (*or* XXIZ).

19.

PRINCIPI. IVVENT. The emperor, holding two ensigns. (Size of the quinarius).

20.

REQVIES. OPTIMOR. MERIT. A figure seated on a curule chair. In the exergue, R. *or* RQ. *or* RS. *or* RT.

The obverse has the laureated and veiled head of Maximianus: DIVO. MAXIMIANO. SEN. FORT. IMP.

21.

Same legend. A figure seated on a curule chair. In the exergue, various letters. (Size of the quinarius).

22.

SAECVLARES. AVGG. A cippus, inscribed COS. X. (Sometimes, in the exergue, IAXX.)

23.

VTILITAS. PVBLICA. A woman standing, in the stola. In the exergue, R. (Size of the quinarius).

24.

VICTORIA. AVGG. Victory, standing; her right foot resting on a helmet, or a globe, holding a buckler resting on her knee, inscribed VOTIS. X. (Size of the quinarius).

25.

VIRTVS. AVGG. Hercules strangling the Nemæan lion. (Size of the quinarius).

26.

Same legend. Hercules overpowering a stag, which he holds by the horns.

27.

Same legend. Hercules, engaged in combat with Antæus. (Size of the quinarius).

28.

Same legend. The emperor, overpowering an enemy. In the field, Є. In the exergue, PTR.

29.

VIRTVS. AVGGG. Mars standing, holding a spear and a shield resting on the ground. In the field, SP. In the exergue, MLXXI.

30.

VIRTVTI. AVGG. Hercules, strangling the Nemæan lion: Victory placing a garland upon his head : a club on the ground.

31.

VOT. AVG. XX. within a garland. (Size of the quinarius).

32.

VOT. XXX. AVGG. NN. within a garland. (Same size).

33.

VOTIS. XXX. within a garland. (Same size).

No. 2 is much the rarest; the next in rarity are Nos. 7, 8, 10, 12, 14, 15, 22, 25, 26 and 29 : Nos. 5, 9, 17, 19, 20, 27, and 28, are the least rare.

[MAXIMIANUS, AND DIOCLETIANUS].

MAXIMIANVS. AVG. Laureated bust of Maximianus, with the paludamentum.—*Rev.* DIOCLETIANVS. AVG. Laureated head of Diocletianus. (Size of the quinarius).

EUTROPIA.

[Eutropia, the wife of Maximianus Hercules, was a Syrian lady. But little is known of her; and the coins given by Goltzius, legend GAL. VAL. EVTROPIA. AVG. are not authenticated. Vidua has attributed to her a coin, which Eckhel informs us is one of Placilla, wife of Theodosius the Great, altered to an Eutropia].

AMANDUS.

[Amandus assumed the purple in Gaul in 1038 (A. D. 285); but was encountered by Maximianus Hercules, and killed in battle, in the year of Rome 1040. Banduri and others have given coins of this usurper, but their authenticity is doubted. (See *Banduri*, vol. ii, p. 87. Also *Tanini*].

AELIANUS.

[Aelianus, another usurper in the reigns of Diocletianus and Maximianus, was born of an obscure family in Gaul. He associated with Amandus in the usurpation, and was slain about the same time as that personage].

There are no authenticated coins of Aelianus. That given by Goltzius, on which he is styled AVLVS. POMPONIVS. AELIANVS. is not accredited.

CARAUSIUS.

[Marcus Aurelius Valerius Carausius was born in Belgic Gaul, of obscure parents.* He had enjoyed the reputation of a skilful pilot and a brave soldier, when he was appointed by Maximianus to the command

---

* Gibbon, in his account of this usurper, observes that Eutropius, Aurelius Victor, and Eumenius leave us in doubt as to his origin. Their words are " Vilissime natus," " Bataviæ alumnis," and " Menapiæ civis." The reader will therefore perhaps allow the term " obscure," if he be not a disciple of Stukeley, whose *Medallic History of Carausius* is one of the most extraordinary works in existence. This writer, by the help of Richard of Cirencester, discovers Carausius to have been a British prince, and a native of St. David's ! The work will ever remain a proof that great learning is at best but an indifferent gift, when unaccompanied by discretion and judgment.

of the fleet stationed at Boulogne, to suppress the piratical ravages of
the Franks.   If we may credit the Roman historians, the admiral did
not faithfully discharge his trust; but suffering the German pirates to
sail from their harbours, he seized upon them as they returned from
their expeditions, and appropriated a considerable share of the spoil to
his own use.   Maximian, informed of his cupidity, gave orders for his
death, when Carausius, having secured to his interest the fleet which
he commanded, sailed over to Britain, in the year of Rome 1040,
(A. D. 287).   Here he was well received, and assumed the purple
and the title of Augustus.   Unable, from the loss of their fleet, to
cope with the usurper, Maximianus and his colleague Diocletianus
consented to acknowledge his claim, in 1042 (A. D. 289).   Carausius
held his title with eclat; his fleet swept the seas; his troops re-
pulsed the Caledonians in the North, and the bravest of the Franks
were proud to enlist under his banner: but in the year 1046 (A. D.
293), this bold and successful usurper, who had defied the power of
Rome, fell by the hand of his own minister, Allectus].

Style: —— CARAVSIVS. —— CARAVSIVS. AVG. —— IMP. CA-
RAVSIVS. AVG.——IMP. C. CARAVSIVS. A.——IMP. C. M.
CARAVSIVS. AVG.——IMP. C. M. AVR. CARAVSIVS. P.
AVG.——IMP. CARAVSIVS. P. AVG.——IMP. C. CARAV-
SIVS. P. AVG.——IMP. C. M. AVR. V. CARAVSIVS. P.
AVG.——CARAVSIVS. P. F. AVG.——IMP. CARAVSIVS.
P. F. AVG.   [On reverse, sometimes, GERMANICVS. MAXV. (or
PACATOR. ORBIS. or PRINCEPS. IVVENTVT.)] —— IMP. C. CARAV-
SIVS. P. F. AVG.   [On reverse, sometimes, INVICTVS.] ——
CARAVSIVS. ET. FRATRES. SVI.

Gold - R 8
Silver medallions, of small size - - - - - - - - - - - R 8
„ of the usual size* - - - - - - - - - - - - - R 6
Third brass - - - - - - - - - - - - - - - - - R 2

SILVER MEDALLION.

PAX. AVG. Peace, standing.

GOLD AND SILVER, OF THE USUAL SIZE.

1.

ADVENTVS. AVG. The emperor on horseback, his right hand elevated, his left holding the hasta: before, a captive seated on the ground. In the exergue, a thunderbolt. (Cabinet of *J. Brumell, Esq.*) - - - - - - - - - - - - - - - - - - - AR

2.

Same legend. A similar type. In the exergue, The obverse has the laureated bust of Carausius, holding a sceptre surmounted by an eagle. - - - - - - - - - - - - - - - - AR

In the *Hunter* collection.

3.

Same legend. A similar type on reverse, with M. L. in the exergue. AR

4.

ADVENTVS. AVGG. (*or* AVG.) The emperor casting a javelin, and riding over two figures seated on the ground. In the exergue, M. (*Stukeley*). - - - - - - - - - - - - - - - - - AR

5.

. . . . AVGG. Jupiter and Hercules standing, both naked; the former holding the hasta and thunderbolt, the other his club and the lion's skin. In the exergue, +++. (In the *British Museum*). AR

6.

CONCORDIA. AVG. Two hands, joined. (*Haym.*) - - - AR

---

* The silver of Carausius is sometimes tolerably good, but there are many coins of very base quality. The coins of this usurper and his successor Allectus, are much more rare in France and Italy than in England. Those of Carausius are generally of barbarous fabric. In the *Catalogue d'Ennery*, page 631, there is a description of a coin of Carausius struck on one of Quintillus.

7.

CONCORDIA. MILITVM.   Two women, standing.   *(Mionnet)*.

AU & AR

8.

Same legend.   Two hands, joined.   In the exergue, RSR. (*or* C.)   AR

9.

CONCORD. MILIT.   A woman, holding two standards.   In the
exergue, RSR. (*or* RS.) - - - - - - - - - - - - - AR

10.

CONSERVATORI. AVGGG.   Hercules standing, with club and lion's
skin (or bow).   In the exergue, ML.   - - - - - - - AU

11.

CONSERVAT. AVG.   Jupiter standing, holding the hasta and thunderbolt: at his feet, an eagle.   In the exergue, M. L.   *(Plate xi,
No. 5)*. - - - - - - - - - - - - - - - - - - - AU

12.

CONS. AVG.   A woman standing, holding an anchor and the hasta.
In the exergue, RSR.   - - - - - - - - - - - - - AR

13.

EXPECTATE. VENI.   The emperor, joining hands with a woman,
who holds a trident.*   In the exergue, RSR.   *(Vignette*, p. 154).

AU & AR

Some are without letters in the exergue.

14.

FELICITAS. (*or* FELICITA.)   A galley, with rowers.   In the
exergue, RSR. (*or* PSA.) - - - - - - - - - - - AR

15.

FELICITAS.   Four children, representing the four Seasons. - - AR

16.

FELICITA. AVG.   A galley, with four rowers.   In the exergue,
RSR.   - - - - - - - - - - - - - - - - - - - AR

17.

FIDEM. MILITVM. NN.   A woman standing, holding a pair of scales
and a cornucopia. - - - - - - - - - - - - - - AR

---

* This coin is erroneously described by Genebrier, who calls the trident a
caduceus.   We are warranted in believing that the female figure represents the
genius of Britain. The coin from which the vignette is engraved, is in the
cabinet of *T. Thomas, Esq.*

18.

FORTVNA. AVG.   Fortune with her attributes, standing.   In the
exergue, RSR. - - - - - - - - - - - - - - - - AR

19.

IXPECTATE. VENI. *(sic)*.   The emperor holding a spear, and delivering a standard to a woman.   *(British Mus.)*. - - - - - AR

20.

LAETITIA. AVG.   A galley, with rowers.   In the exergue, RSR. - AR

21.

LEG. IIII. FL.   A lion walking, holding ears of corn in his mouth.   In
the exergue, MRS.   *(Mionnet)*. - - - - - - - - - AU

22.

LEG. IIII. F. . . .   A centaur walking to the left, bearing a long club (or
pedum), which he holds with both hands, and rests on his shoulders.
In the exergue, C. - - - - - - - - - - - - - AR
Unpublished: in the cabinet of *J. Brumell, Esq.*   *(Vignette,* p. 159).

23.

LEG. V. . . . AVG.   A bull, standing.   *(Stukeley)*. - - - - AR

24.

LEG. VII. . : . . .   A similar type.   *(Ibid.)* - - - - - - - AR

25.

LEG. VIII. . . . IN.   A ram, standing.   In the exergue, ML.   *(Stukeley)*.
AR

26.

LEG. VIII. . . . INV.   A similar type, with or without ML. in the
exergue.   *(Ibid.)* - - - - - - - - - - - - - AR

27.

LIB. III. . . . III. SPPC. *(sic)*.   The emperor, on horseback.   In the
exergue, RSR.   *(Brit. Mus.)*. - - - - - - - - - - AR

28.

MONETA. AVG.   Moneta, standing.   *(Ibid.)* - - - - - - AR

29.

ORIENS. AVG.   The Sun, standing; his right hand raised, his left
holding a globe.   In the exergue, RSR. - - - - - - AR

30.

. . ORTVNA. *(for* FORTVNA.) AVG.   A female bust to the right,
within a garland, holding a garland and a branch. - - - - AR

31.

PAX. AVG.   Peace, standing, with olive branch and cornucopia.   M. L.
in the exergue.   On some, L. in the field. - - - - - - AR

32.

PRINCIPI. IVVENT. The emperor standing, holding a spear. AR

33.

RENOVAT. ROMA. A similar type to No. 30. In the exergue, RSR. - - - - - - - - - - - - - - - - - - - AR

34.

RENOVA... ROMANO. Romulus and Remus, suckled by the wolf. In the exergue, RSR. (In the *Hunter* collection). - - - AR

35.

ROMA. RENOV. A similar type. RSR. - - - - - - - AR

36.

ROMA. RENOV. (*or* RENOVA.) A similar type. In the exergue, RSR. - - - - - - - - - - - - - - - - - AR

37.

ROMANO. RENOVA. A similar type. The obverse has the helmeted bust of Carausius: legend, VIRTVS. CARAVSI. - - AU & AR

38.

ROMAE. AETERNAE. Victory standing, presenting a garland to Rome, seated. In the exergue, CXXI. - - - - - - - AR

39.

ROMAE. AETERNAE. Rome seated, within a temple. In the exergue, RSR. - - - - - - - - - - - - - - - - AR

40.

SALVS. AVG. Salus feeding a serpent, rising from an altar. - AR

41.

Same legend. Salus, feeding a serpent entwined around an altar, and holding the hasta in her right hand. - - - - - - - - AR

42.

VBERTAS. AVG. Neptune standing on the prow of a vessel, joining hands with the emperor, who holds a spear. In the exergue, RSR. (*Stukeley*). - - - - - - - - - - - - - - - - AR

43.

VBERTAS. (*or* VBERTA.) AVG. A figure, milking a cow. In the exergue, of some, RSR. - - - - - - - - - - - - AR

44.

VLTO. PAX. AVG. (*sic*). The emperor in a military habit, joining hands with a woman, who holds a patera; between them an altar. AR

45.

VICTORIA. . . . A. Victory marching, with a garland. - - - AR

46.

VIRTVS. IM. .. AVG. *(sic)*. A military figure standing, holding a globe and a javelin. In the exergue, L. - - - - - - - AR

47.

VOTO. PVBLICO. A garland, within which is inscribed, MVLTIS. XX. IMP. In the exergue, of some, RSR. - - - - - - AR

48.

Same legend. An altar, inscribed MVLTIS. XX. IMP. *(Brit. Mus.)* AR

49.

VOTVM. PVBLIC. A similar type. In the exergue, RSR. (In the *Hunter* collection.) - - - - - - - - - - - - - - AR

50.

VOTVM. PVBLICVM. A similar type, without the letters in the exergue. - - - - - - - - - - - - - - - - - - - AR

In gold, Nos. 10 and 37 are the rarest. In silver, Nos. 1 to 6, 18, 19, 21, 22 to 29, 32, 40 to 45, and 46, are much the rarest, some of them being perhaps unique. Nos. 40 and 41 are the least rare.

THIRD BRASS.

1.

ABVNDANTI. AVG. A woman emptying a cornucopia.

2.

ADIVTRIX. AVG. Half-length bust of Victory, holding a garland and a palm branch.

3.

Same legend. Victory standing, with garland and palm branch.

4.

ADVENTVS. AVG. Felicity standing, with a long caduceus and a cornucopia.

5.

ADVENTVS. CARAVSI. The emperor on horseback; his right hand raised, holding a globe. In the exergue of some, RSP. (*or* ML.)

6.

AEQVITAS. AVG. Equity, with her attributes. (In the *Hunter* collection.

7.

.... AVG. The emperor and a woman, joining hands.

8.

APOLLINI. CO. AVG. A griffin. In the exergue, MSC. (*or* MS.)

9.

APOLLINI. CONS. A griffin. In the exergue, MC.

10.

APOLLINI. CONS. AVG. A griffin.

11.

COHH... Four standards. In the exergue, ML.

12.

COHR. PRAET. Four standards. (In the *Hunter* collection).

13.

COMES. AVG. Victory marching, with garland and palm branch. In the exergue, C. (*or* L. *or* ML.)

14.

Same legend. A similar type, with ML. in the exergue. The obverse has the helmed head of Carausius, with javelin and buckler : legend, CARAVSIVS. AVG.

15.

Same legend. Minerva standing, holding the hasta and an olive branch.

16.

Same legend. Neptune standing : his right foot on a galley in the sea, his left on a dolphin ; a dolphin in his right hand, and a trident reversed in his left. On some, S. P. in the field.

17.

COMES. AVGGG. Minerva, standing. In the field, S. P. In the exergue, MLXXI. *(Tanini).*

18.

Same legend. Victory marching, with garland and palm branch. In the field, S. P. In the exergue of some, C.

19.

CONCORD. AVGG. A woman, holding two standards.

20.

CONCORDIA. AVGG. A woman standing, holding thehasta and a cornucopia.

21.

CONCORDIA. MIL. Two right hands, joined. In the exergue, RS.

22.

CONCORD. MILIT. A similar type. In the exergue, RSR.

23.

CONCORD. MILITVM. A similar type. In the exergue, C.

24.

CONCORDIA. MILITI. (or MILIT.) The emperor, in the toga, joining hands with a woman. In the exergue, C.

25.

CONCORD. MILITVM. A similar type. In the exergue, C.

26.

CONCORDIA. MILITVM. N. N. A similar type; with O. in the field, and XXX. in the exergue.

27.

CONCORDIA. MILITVM. P. C. A similar type. In the exergue, X.

28.

CONSERVAT. AVG. Neptune, seated : in his right hand, an anchor ; in his left, a trident reversed.

29.

Same legend. A naked figure, standing : in his right hand, in his left, the hasta pura. In the field, S. C.

30.

CONSERVATOR. A woman seated, her elbow resting on a cippus.

31.

CONSTANT. AVG. A naked male figure, standing ; in his right hand the hasta. In the field, S. C. In the exergue, S. C.

32.

CONSTANT. (or CONSTAVNT.) (sic) AVG. Hercules, standing. In the field, S. In the exergue, C. (Mionnet).

33.

COS. IIII. A woman standing, holding a globe. (Stukeley).

34.

DIANA. Diana, seated.

35.

DIANAE. CONS. (or DINAE.) (sic). AVG. A stag. In the exergue, XX.

36.

EXPECTA...... Victory placing a garland upon the emperor's head.

37.

EXPECTATE. VENI. Two figures standing, joining hands. In the exergue, RSA.

38.

FELICITAS. AVG. A woman standing, holding an ensign and a cornucopia.

39.

Same legend. A galley on the sea, with rowers. In the exergue of some, CXXI.

40.

FELICIT. PVPLI. *(sic)*. Felicity holding a caduceus, leaning on a column. In the exergue, C.

41.

FELICITAS. Four children, representing the four Seasons.

42.

FIDES. MILITVM. A woman, holding two standards.

43.

FIDES. MILIT. A similar type. In the exergue, C.

44.

FIDEM. MILITVM. A similar type. (Cabinet of *F. Douce, Esq.*)

45.

FORTVNA. AVG. Fortune, standing: in her right hand the hasta, in her left a cornucopia. In the exergue, C.

46.

Same legend. Fortune, standing, with rudder and cornucopia. In the exergue of some, C.

47.

Same legend. Fortune seated, holding a rudder and a cornucopia.

48.

Same legend. Fortune seated upon a wheel, holding the hasta. (Cabinet of *F. Douce, Esq.*)

49.

FORT. REDVX. (*or* RAEDVX.) *(sic)*. Fortune seated on a wheel, with rudder and cornucopia.

50.

Same legend. Fortune standing, with rudder and cornucopia.

51.

GENIO. AVG. A woman standing, holding a globe and a cornucopia.

52.

GERMANICVS. MAXV. A trophy and two captives. In the exergue, L. *(Mionnet)*.

53.

HERCVLI. INVICT. Hercules standing, with his club.

54.

HILARITAS. AVG. A woman standing, holding a branch and a cornucopia. In the exergue, M. L. (In the *Hunter* collection).

55.

Same legend. A woman standing, holding a garland and a cornucopia.

56.

HILARITAS. AVGGG. A woman standing, holding a branch and a cornucopia.

57.

IAPR. . . . VICTOR. *(sic)*. A woman standing, holding an olive branch and the hasta.

58.

INVICTVS. The Sun, marching. *(Mionnet)*.

59.

INVICTVS. AVG. A similar type.

60.

I. O. X. The emperor, in a military habit, on horseback; his right hand holding a spear, his left hand raised aloft.

61.

IOVI. AVG. Jupiter standing, holding the hasta and thunderbolt. In the field, S. F. In the exergue, ML.

62.

IOVI. CONSER. . . A similar type. In the field, SP.

63.

IOVI. CONSER. AVG. A similar type.

64.

IOVI. CONS. Jupiter and Carausius, standing: the first delivering a globe to the emperor.

(See *Stukeley*, who supposes the figure of Jupiter to be *Venus with the apple!*).

65.

IOVI. STATORI. Jupiter standing, with hasta and thunderbolt.

66.

LAETIT. AVG. A woman, standing: in her right hand a garland, in her left, ears of corn. In the field, S. P. In the exergue, C.

67.

LAETITIA. AVG. A similar type. In the field, SC. (Some are without the SC.)

68.

Same legend. A woman standing, holding a garland and the hasta. In the field, F. O. In the exergue, ML.

69.

Same legend. A similar type. In the exergue, MC.

70.

Same legend. A similar type, without letters in the field, or in the exergue.

71.

Same legend. A galley, with rowers. In the exergue, MC.

72.

LAETITIA. AVGGG. A woman standing, holding a garland and ears of corn. In the field, S. P. In the exergue, C.

73.

Same legend. A woman standing, holding an anchor; her hand resting on an anchor.

74.

LAETITIA. FVND. A woman standing, holding the hasta and a garland. In the exergue, XXI.

75.

LEG. II. AVG. Capricorn. In the exergue, ML.

76.

LEG. II. PARTH. A centaur, holding a globe and a rudder. In the exergue, M. *or* ML.

77.

Same legend. A centaur walking to the right, holding with both hands a long club or pedum, which he rests on his shoulders. (Cabinet of *J. Brumell, Esq.*)

78.

Same legend. A centaur, standing. In the exergue, MI.

79.

Same legend. A centaur walking to the right, holding a club and a garland.

80.

LEG. II. PAR. A centaur walking, holding a globe and a club. In the exergue, ML.

81.

LEG. IIII. FLAVIA. P. F. Two lions meeting; above, a human head with the ancient diadem. *(Stukeley).*

82.

LEG. IIII. FL. A lion, walking. In the exergue of some, MC.

83.

LEG. VII. CL. A bull. In exergue of some, ML.

84.

LEG. VII. CLA. A bull: above, D. X. In the exergue of some, M.

85.

LEG. VIII. A ram. In the exergue, ML.

86.

LEG. VIII. AVG. A bull. In the exergue of some, ML.

87.

LEG... IN .. A ram. In the exergue, ML.

88.

LEG. XXI. VLPIA. Neptune standing, holding the hasta and a dolphin. (*Stukeley*).

89.

LEG. XXV. V. A boar, standing.

90.

LEG. ... VLPIA. A male figure, standing; in his right hand, ; in his left, the hasta. (In the *Hunter* collection).

91.

L. .... VLPIA. VI. *(sic)*. Neptune, standing: in his right hand, a dolphin; in his left, a trident. *(Brit. Mus.)*

92.

...... LITIT. AV. *(sic)*. A woman, holding the hasta, standing before an altar. *(Idem).*

93.

MAR. PAC. .... A woman, holding a long caduceus and a cornucopia. *(Stukeley).*

94.

MARTI. PACIF. Mars marching, with a laurel branch and a javelin.

95.

MARTI. PACIFER. Mars marching, with shield and olive branch.

96.

MARTI. PACIFERO. Mars marching, with a laurel branch and ears of corn. In the field, S. C. In the exergue, C.

97.

MARS. VICTOR. Mars marching, with a trophy. In the field of some, S. C.

98.

MARS VICTOR. Mars standing, holding the hasta pura and a buckler. (In the *Hunter* collection).

99.

MARS. VLTOR. Mars marching, holding a javelin and a buckler.

100.

MARS. . . . . . . Mars, standing; his right hand holding a spear, his left holding a horse by the bridle. (Cabinet of *F. Douce, Esq.*).

101.

. . . . . MILITVM. Two women standing, joining hands. *(Brit. Mus.)*

102.

MONETA. AVG. Moneta standing, with her attributes. In the exergue, MC. *or* MSP.

103.

Same legend. Moneta, standing. In the field, S. C.

104.

Same legend. Moneta, standing. In the exergue, RSR.

105.

Same legend. Moneta, standing. In the field, S. C. In the exergue, C.

106.

MONETA. AVGG. Moneta, standing.

107.

Same legend. Moneta, standing. In the field, S. P. In the exergue, C.

108.

MONETA. AVGGG. Moneta, standing. In the field, B. P. In the exergue, C. *(Brit. Mus.)*

109.

ORIENS. AVG. The Sun, standing; his right hand raised, his left holding a globe. In the field, S. P.

110.

Same legend. A similar type, without letters in the field or exergue.

111.

Same legend. The Sun, marching; his right hand raised, his left holding a globe. In the field, a star.

112.

Same legend. The Sun, marching; his right hand elevated, his left holding a whip.

113.

Same legend. A similar type. In the field, S. P. In the exergue, MLX.

114.

ORIENS. AVG. A similar type. In the field, S. P. In the exergue, C.

115.

Same legend. A similar type, without letters in the field. In the exergue, C.

116.

Same legend. The Sun, standing; his right hand raised; his left holding a globe: at his feet, a captive.

117.

Same legend. The Sun, standing between two captives; a globe in his left hand. *(Stukeley).*

118.

PACATOR. ORBIS. Radiated head of the Sun. (In the *Hunter* collection).

119.

PACATO. . . . The same type.

120.

PAX. AETERN. AVG. Peace standing, holding an olive branch and the hasta.

121.

PAX. AVG. Peace standing, holding an olive branch and the hasta. In the exergue, ML.: on others, SP. in the field, and C. in the exergue.

122.

Same legend. A similar type, with FO. ML. *or* L. ML. *or* EO. ML. *or* L. VII. *or* SP. C. *or* various other letters.

123.

Same legend. A similar type, with BE. in the field, and MLXXI. in the exergue. The obverse has the radiated head of Carausius, with coat of mail, javelin, and buckler.

124.

Same legend. A similar type, with ML. in the exergue. The obverse has the helmed bust of Carausius, with coat of mail, holding a javelin resting on his shoulder, and a buckler: legend, CARAV-SIVS. AVG.

125.

Same legend. A similar type, without letters in the field. In the exergue, CXXI. The obverse has the radiated heads of Carausius and the Sun, side by side: legend, IMP. CARAVSIVS. P. F. AVG. (In the *Hunter* collection).

126.

PAX. AVG. A similar type, with . . . in the field, and CXXI. in the exergue. The obverse has the helmed bust of Carausius, with radiated crown, javelin, and a buckler: legend, VIRTVS. CA-RAVSI.

127.

Same legend. Peace, standing, holding a branch and a cornucopia. In the exergue, ML. *or* XXXX.

128.

PAX. AVGG. Peace, standing, holding a flower, or a branch, and the hasta erect.

129.

PAX. AVGGG. A similar type. In the field, S, P. In the exergue, C. On some SP. in the field, and MLXXI. *or* C. in the exergue. The obverse of some, has the bust with paludamentum; on others, a coat of mail.

It is generally believed that the coins of Carausius, with this legend, were struck in commemoration of the treaty between the Usurper and the emperors Diocletianus and Maximianus.

130.

PAX. AVGVSTA. Peace, walking, holding a flower and the hasta. In the exergue, CXXI. The obverse has the heads of Carausius and the Sun, side by side: legend, IMP. CARAVSIVS. P. F. AVG. (In the *Hunter* collection).

131.

Same legend. Bust of Peace. (Cabinet of *F. Douce, Esq.*)

132.

PAX. GALLI. IVG. *(sic)*. Peace, standing, holding the hasta.

133.

PIAETAS. AVG. *(sic)*. A woman, standing: a child at her feet. In the field, S. P. In the exergue, ML.

134.

Same legend. A woman standing, holding a branch (or garland) and a cornucopia.

135.

PIETAS. AVG. A veiled woman, standing before an altar. (In the *Hunter* collection).

136.

Same legend. A woman, standing before an altar, holding a cornucopia.

137.

Same legend, a woman, standing before an altar, holding the hasta.

138.

PIETUS. *(sic)* AVG. A woman, sacrificing on an altar. In the field, S. P. In the exergue,

139.

PRINCIPI. IVVENTVT. A military figure standing, bare-headed, holding a standard and a spear.

140.

PROVID. AVG. A woman standing, holding a globe and the hasta transversely. In the field, S. P. In the exergue, C.

141.

Same legend. A woman standing, holding a globe and the hasta. In the field, S. C.

142.

Same legend. A woman standing, holding the hasta and a cornucopia. In the field, S. C. In the exergue, C.

143.

Same legend. A woman standing, touching a globe on the ground; on her left arm, a cornucopia. In the field, S. P.

144.

PROVID. AVGGG. A woman standing, holding a globe and a cornucopia. In the field, S. P. In the exergue, C.

145.

Same legend. A woman standing, holding a globe and the hasta transversely. In the field, S. P.

146.

Same legend. A woman standing, touching with a wand a globe on the ground; on her left arm, a cornucopia. In the field, S. P. In the exergue of some, C.

147.

PROVIDE. AVG. A woman standing, holding a globe and a cornucopia. In the field, S. P. *or* S. C.

148.

PROVIDEN. AVG. A woman standing, touching a globe with a wand; on her left arm, a cornucopia. In the exergue, C.

149.

PROVIDENT. AVG. A woman standing, holding a globe and the hasta transversely. In the field, B. In the exergue, MLXXI.

150.

PROVIDENTIA. AVG.   A woman standing, holding a garland (or a branch) and a wand.

151.

Same legend.   A woman standing, holding in each hand a military ensign.

152.

Same legend.   A woman standing, holding a wand and a cornucopia.

153.

Same legend.   A woman standing, holding a branch and a cornucopia.

154.

Same legend.   A woman standing, holding a globe and a cornucopia. In the field, S. P.

155.

RENOVAT. ROMA.   Romulus and Remus suckled by the wolf.   In the exergue, C. *or* RSR.

156.

RESTITVT. SAECVL.   The emperor standing, holding a globe and the hasta pura; Victory standing behind.

157.

RESTITVT. SAECVLI.   The emperor, in a military habit, standing, holding a spear: Victory behind, placing a garland on his head.   In the exergue, C.

158.

ROMAE. AETER.   A temple with six columns: within, a figure seated, full-faced.   In the exergue, SPC.

159.

Same legend.   A figure standing: Rome seated on spoils : CXXI.

160.

ROMANORVM. RENOV.   Romulus and Remus, suckled by the wolf.

161.

SAECVLARES. AVG.   A lion, walking.   In the exergue, MC.   (In the *Hunter* collection).

162.

SAECVLARES. AVGG.   A lion, standing.   *(Stukeley)*.

163.

SAECVLI. FELICITAS.   The emperor marching, bearing a javelin and a globe.

164.

Same legend.   The emperor standing, holding a javelin and a globe.

165.

Same legend.   Felicity standing, with a caduceus and cornucopia.

166.

SAECVLI. FELICIT. A naked figure standing, holding a javelin and a globe. In the field, S. C. In the exergue, C.

167.

SALVS. AVG. Salus standing, holding the hasta, and feeding a serpent rising from an altar. In the field, S. C.

168.

Same legend. A similar type, with B. E. in the field, and MLXXI. in the exergue.

169.

Same legend. A similar type, without letters in the field or in exergue.

170.

Same legend. A similar type. In the field, S. F. In the exergue, MLXXI.

171.

Same legend. Salus standing, holding a serpent feeding from a patera, which she holds in her left hand. In the field, S. P. In the exergue, MLXXI. *or* MLXX.

172.

Same legend. Salus, seated before an altar, feeding a serpent.

173.

SALVS. AVGGG. Salus feeding a serpent out of a patera. In the field, S. P. In the exergue, C. *(Cabinet of J. Brumell, Esq.)*

174.

SALVS. PVBLICA. Salus standing, feeding a serpent out of a patera. In the field, BE. In the exergue, MLX.

The obverse has the radiated bust of Carausius, with coat of mail, a spear, and a round shield, ornamented with three equestrian figures: legend, IMP. CARAVSIVS. P. F. AVG. *(Cabinet of F. Douce, Esq.)*

175.

SECVRIT. . . . . . Security, leaning on a column.

176.

SECVRITAS. ORBIS. Security, seated.

177.

SOLI. INVICTO. The Sun, in a quadriga, his right hand elevated. In the exergue, VC.

The obverse has the radiated bust of Carausius, with javelin and buckler: legend, IMP. CARAVSIVS. AVG.

178.

SPES. PVBL. . . . . . *(sic)*. Hope. In the field, S. P.

179.

SPES. PVBL. . . . . . .   Hope.   In the field, S. P.   In the exergue, C.

180.

SPES. PVBLICA.   Hope.   In the field, S. C.

181.

Same legend.   Hope.   In the exergue, M.

182.

TEMPO. FELIC.   Felicity standing, holding a long caduceus and a cornucopia.

183.

TEMPORVM. FEL.   A similar type.   In the field, S. C.

184.

TEMPORVM. FELI.   A similar type.   In the field, S. P.   In the exergue, C.

185.

TEMPORVM. FELICITAS.   A woman standing, holding a garland and a cornucopia.

186.

TVTELA. AVG.   A woman standing, holding a patera over an altar : on her left arm, a double cornucopia.   (In the *Hunter* collection).

187.

Same legend.   A similar type, but the woman holds a single cornucopia.

188.

TVTELA. . . . P. . . . .   A woman standing, holding a flower and a cornucopia.

189.

VBERITAS. AVG.   The emperor, in a military habit, joining hands with Neptune, who stands on the prow of a vessel.   *(Stukeley)*.

190.

Same legend.   The emperor and a woman, joining hands, each holding the hasta pura.   In the exergue, RSR.   The obverse has the laureated bust of Carausius, with the trabea, holding a sceptre surmounted by an eagle : legend, IMP. CARAVSIVS. P. F. A.

191.

VBERTAS. AVG.   Neptune, standing on the prow of a vessel, joining hands with the emperor, in a military habit.

192.

Same legend.   A woman milking a cow.   In the exergue, RSR.

193.

VICTORIA. AVG.   Victory walking, holding a garland and a palm branch.   In the exergue, CXXI.

194.

VICTORIA. AVG. A similar type. In the field, S. P. In the exergue, ML.

195.

Same legend. Victory marching, holding a garland and a palm branch : at her feet, a captive. In the field, C.

196.

Same legend. A similar type. In the field,   In the exergue, MC.

197.

Same legend. A similar type, without letters in the field. In the exergue, MC.

198.

Same legend. A similar type. In the field, E. In the exergue, MLXXI.

199.

VICTORIA. AVGG. Victory marching, holding a garland and palm branch. In the field, +.

200.

Same legend, A woman standing, holding the hasta, and sacrificing on an altar. *(Stukeley)*.

201.

Same legend. Victory marching, holding a garland and a palm branch. In the field, +.

202.

VICTORIA. . . . . . A trophy, between two captives.

203.

VICTORIA. . . . . . Victory standing, holding the hasta and a palm branch. In the exergue, ML.

204.

VITORIA. *(sic)* AVG. A woman standing, holding a flower and the hasta.

205.

VICTORIA. GER. A trophy, between two captives.

206.

VICTORIA. PR. (The legend from right to left). A woman standing, holding the hasta and a palm branch. In the exergue, ML.

207.

VIRTVS. AVG. A military figure standing, with shield and spear. In the field, S. C. In the exergue, C.

Some are without letters in the field and the exergue.

208.

VIRTVS. AVG. Mars naked, marching, with javelin and buckler. In the field, S. C.

209.

VIRTVS. AVG. Mars marching, with spear and trophy. In the field of some, S. C.

210.

Same legend. A military figure marching, with spear and shield.

211.

Same legend. Victory marching, with garland and palm branch. *(Stukeley)*.

212.

Same legend. Victory standing, with garland, or palm branch.

213.

VIRTVS. AV. A woman standing, holding a globe and a cornucopia.

214.

VIRTVS. AVGG. A military figure standing, with spear and shield.

215.

Same legend. A military figure standing, holding an inverted javelin and a buckler. In the exergue, C. The obverse has the radiated bust of Carausius, with the paludamentum: legend, IMP. C. M. AVR. CARAVSIVS. P. AVG.

The coin which bears this uncommon legend on the obverse, is in the cabinet of *F. Douce, Esq.*

216.

VIRTVTE. AVG. Hercules, strangling the Nemæan lion; a club on the ground. In the field, S. P. In the exergue, C.

217.

VIRTVTI. AVG. Hercules standing; a club in his right hand, a bow in his left.

218.

Same legend. A galley, with rowers. *(Mionnet)*.

219.

VIRTVS. INV. AVG. A military figure standing, holding a javelin and a globe. In exergue, L.

220.

VITAVI. A woman standing, holding in each hand a serpent. (Cabinet of *F. Douce, Esq.)*

This most extraordinary type is believed to be the only one of the kind in the Roman series, and the coin itself is probably unique. The singularity of the device encourages an attempt at an explanation of its meaning. The female figure would appear to be the good Genius of Carausius, and she grasps in each hand the enemies of her protegé, the emperors Diocletian and his colleague, represented as serpents. May we not suppose, therefore, that this very curious coin was struck by Carausius immediately upon his arrival in Britain, before the recognition of his title by the emperors? It seems to confirm the account of the historians, who inform us that the rebel admiral, previous to his carrying off the Roman fleet, had received intelligence of some meditated punishment from the emperors.

221.

VOTVM. PVBLIC. An altar, with the fire kindled, inscribed XX. IMP. In the exergue, RSR.

222.

. . . . X. . VG. A woman standing; holding in her right hand a garland; in her left, a head with a mural crown. (*Stukeley*).

Nos. 1 to 6, 11, 17, 34, 38, 41, 46, 51, 53 to 55, 58, 59, 60, 64, 65, 72 to 74, 77, 81, 88 to 93, 98, 117, 118, 119, 125, 130, 131, 139, 155 to 157, 161, 162, 174, 189 to 191, 205, 215, 218, 220, and 222, are the rarest types, some of them being, in all probability, unique; the least rare are those with PAX., SALVS., SPES., PROVIDENTIA., and VICTORIA.·

[CARAUSIUS, DIOCLETIANUS, AND MAXIMIANUS].

CARAVSIVS. ET. FRATRES. SVI. The heads of the emperors, side by side—*Rev.* PAX. AVGGG. Peace standing, to the right, holding an olive branch and the hasta pura. In the field, S. P. In the exergue, G.

ALLECTUS.

[This usurper having assassinated Carausius, in the year of Rome 1046 (A. D. 293), assumed the purple in Britain. Allectus did not possess the ability of his predecessor; during the latter part of whose reign, Boulogne was captured by Constantius Chlorus, who had made great preparations for recovering the island. The armament at length was completed, and the landing having been made on two different parts of the coast, Allectus was encountered by Asclepiodotus, the general of Constantius, and slain in the battle, in the year of Rome 1049 (A. D. 296)].

STYLE : ——IMP. C. ALLECTVS. P. AVG.——ALLECTVS. P. F. AVG.——IMP. ALLECTVS. P. F. AVG.——IMP. C. ALLEC-TVS. P. F. AVG. ——IMP. C. ALLECTVS. P. F. I. (*invictus*). AVG.

Gold - - - - - - - - - - - - - - - - - - - R 8
Silver* - - - - - - - - - - - - - - - - - - R 8
Third brass - - - - - - - - - - - - - - - - - R 2

---

* Fine silver of Allectus is of extreme rarity : his denarii are generally of a very base quality.

GOLD AND SILVER.

1.

COMES. AVG.   Minerva standing, holding in her right hand a branch, in her left a javelin and buckler.   In the exergue, ML.   *(Hunter)*.

AU

2.

ORIENS. AVG.   The Sun, standing between two captives seated on the ground; his right hand elevated, his left holding a globe.   In the exergue, ML. *(Mead's Catalogue, p. 13)*.   - - - - - - AU

3.

PAX. AVG.   Peace, standing; her right hand holding aloft an olive branch, her left holding the hasta transversely.   In the exergue, ML. - - - - - - - - - - - - - - - AU & AR*

The gold coin is in the cabinet of *J. Brumell, Esq.*, and is in all probability unique.   *(Plate xi, No. 6)*.

4.

Same legend.   Same type, with S. P. in the field, and ML. in the exergue. - - - - - - - - - - - - - - - - - AR

5.

PROVIDENTIA. AVG. (*or* DEOR.)   Providence, standing.   In the field, S. P.   In the exergue, M. SL.   *(Mionnet)*. - - - - AR

6.

SALVS. AVG.   Salus standing, holding a serpent, which she feeds out of a patera.   In the exergue, ML.   *(Haym)*. - - - - - AR

7.

SALVS. AVG.   Hygeia, feeding a serpent out of a patera.   In the exergue of some, ML. - - - - - - - - - - - - AU

There is a modern forgery of this type in silver, which has been probably cast in a mould formed from the gold coin.

8.

SPES. AVG.   Hope.   In the exergue, MI. *or* ML.   - - - - AU

9.

VIRTVS. AVG.   The emperor on horseback, armed with a javelin, riding over a prostrate enemy.   In the exergue,
(In the *Hunter* collection). - - - - - - - - - - AU

---

* This coin is in Mr. Brumell's cabinet; it is plated with silver.

10.

VIRTVS. AVG. Mars, standing. In the exergue, MSL. - - AU
This unique coin was purchased at the Trattle sale, by the Duke de
Blacas, for 74*l.*!

In gold, Nos. 1, 2, 3, 9, and 10, are probably unique. In silver, No.
6, if really existing, is by far the rarest.

THIRD BRASS.

1.

ADVENTVS. AVG. Allectus on horseback, his right hand raised, his
left holding a staff. In the exergue, SPC. *(See Vignette).*

2.

AEQVITAS. AVG. Equity standing, with her attributes. In the
field, S. P. In the exergue, C.

3.

Same legend. A similar type: S. A. in the field; ML. in the exergue.

4.

COMES. AVG. Minerva, standing.

5.

DIANAE. REDVCI. Diana, standing.

6.

FELICITAS. SAECVLI. Felicity, standing before an altar, holding
in her hands a patera and a cornucopia. S. P. In the exergue, C.

7.

FIDES. MILITVM. A woman standing, holding an ensign in each
hand. In the field, S. P. In the exergue, C.

8.

FIDES. MILITVM. A similar type: S. P. in the field; CL. in the exergue.

9.

HILARITAS. AVG. A woman standing, holding a branch and a cornucopia. In the field, S. P. In the exergue, ML.

10.

Same legend. A similar type: S. A. in the field; M. in the exergue.

11.

Same legend. A similar type: S. P. in the field; C. in the exergue.

12.

IOVI. CONSERVATORI. Jupiter standing, holding the hasta and a thunderbolt. In the field, S. P.

13.

LAETITI. . AVG. Laetitia standing, holding in her right hand a branch or a garland, and in her left an inverted javelin. In the field, S. P. In the exergue, C.

14.

Same legend. A similar type: S A. in the field; MSL. in the exergue.

15.

LAETITIA. AVG. A similar type: S. P. in the exergue, CL.

16.

Same legend. A similar type. In the field, S. A. In the exergue, ML.

17.

Same legend. A similar type. In the field, S. P. In the exergue, C.

18.

Same legend. A similar type. In the field, S. A. In the exergue, MSL.

19.

Same legend. A similar type, with ML. in the exergue.

20.

Same legend. A similar type. In the field, S. P. In the exergue, CL.

21.

Same legend. A similar type. In the field, S. A. In the exergue, ML.

22.

Same legend. A galley with a mast, and with four rowers. In the exergue, Q. C.

23.

Same legend. A galley, with six rowers. In the exergue, QC.

24.

Same legend. A galley without mast, and four rowers. In the exergue, QL.

25.

LAETITIA. AVGVSTI. A woman standing, holding in her right hand a branch or a garland, and in her left a javelin reversed. In the exergue, C.

26.

MONETA. AVG. Moneta standing, with her attributes. In the field, SP. In the exergue, C.

27.

MONETA. AVG. A similar type; with S. A. in the field, and ML. in the exergue: (or S. A. in the field, and MSL. in the exergue).

28.

ORIENS. AVG. The Sun standing; his right hand raised, his left holding a globe. In the field, S. P. (In the *Hunter* collection).

29.

PAX. AVG. Peace standing, holding a flower in her right hand, and the hasta pura erect in her left. In the field, SP. In the exergue, C.

30.

Same legend. A similar type; with SP. in the field, and ML. in the exergue: (or S. A. in the field, and ML. in the exergue).

31.

Same legend. Peace standing, holding in her right hand a flower, and in her left the hasta transversely. In the field, S. A. In the exergue, ML.

32.

Same legend. A similar type; with S. P. in the field, and C. in the exergue.

33.

Same legend. Similar types, with SA. in the field, and ML. in the exergue: (or S. M. in the field, and ML. in the exergue: or SP. in the field, and ML. in the exergue: or SA. in the field, and MSL. in the exergue).

34.

Same legend. A similar type; with SA. in the field, and ML. in the exergue. The obverse has the bust of Allectus, with radiated crown and coat of mail, holding a javelin and a buckler: legend, IMP. ALLECTVS. P. F. AVG. (In the *Hunter* collection).

35.

Same legend. Same type and letters. The obverse has the bust of Allectus, with radiated head and the trabea, holding a sceptre, surmounted by an eagle: legend, IMP. ALLECTVS. P. F. AVG. (In the *Hunter* collection).

36.

PIETAS. AVG. Piety, holding a cornucopia and a patera, sacrificing on an altar. In the field, S. A. In the exergue, ML.

37.

PROVID. AVG.   A woman, standing; in her right hand a globe, in her left a cornucopia.   In the field, S. P.   In the exergue, C. : (or SP. in the field, and M.L. in the exergue : or S. A. in the field, and M.L. in the exergue).

38.

PROVIDENTIA. AVG.   A woman standing, holding a globe in her right hand, and the hasta-pura in her left.   In the the field, S. P. In the exergue, C.

39.

Same legend.   A similar type; with S.A. in the field, and MSL. in the exergue.

40.

Same legend.   A woman standing, holding in her right hand a globe, and in her left the hasta pura transversely.   SP.; in the exergue, C.

41.

Same legend.   A woman standing, holding in her right hand a globe, and in her left a cornucopia.   In the field, SP.   In the exergue, C.

42.

Same legend.   A similar type; with SA. in the field, and ML. in the exergue.

43.

Same legend.   A similar type; with S. A. in the field, and ML. in the exergue.   The obverse has the bust of Allectus, with radiated head, buckler, and coat of mail, holding a javelin resting on his shoulder.   (British Museum).

44.

Same legend.   A woman standing, touching with a wand, which she holds in her right hand, a globe on the ground, and holding a cornucopia in her left.   In the field, S. P.   In the exergue, C.

45.

Same legend.   A similar type; with S. P. in the field, and CL. in the exergue.

46.

ROMAE. AETERN.   A temple with eight columns: within, a sedent figure.   In the exergue,   (In the Hunter collection).

47.

SAECVLI. FELICITAS.   The emperor standing, holding in his right hand the hasta transversely, and in his left a globe.   In the field, S. P.   In the exergue, ML.

48.

SALVS. AVG.   Salus standing, feeding a serpent out of a patera.   In the field, S. A.   In the exergue, ML.

49.

Same legend. A similar type. In the field, S. P. In the exergue, ML.

50.

SALVS. AVG. Salus standing before an altar, holding in her right hand a patera, and in her left the hasta pura. In the field, S. C. In the exergue, ML.

51.

Same legend. Salus feeding a serpent, rising from an altar; her left hand holding the hasta. In the field, S. A. In the exergue, ML.

52.

SPES. AVG. The usual type of Hope. S. A.; in the exergue, ML.

53.

Same legend. Same type; with S. A. in the field, and ML. in the exergue: (or S.P. in the field, and ML. in the exergue).

54.

SPES. PVBLICA. Same type; with S. P. in the field, and ML. in the exergue.

55.

Same legend. Same type; with S. P. in the field, and C. in the exergue.

56.

TEMPORVM. FELIC. Felicity standing, holding in her right hand a caduceus, and in her left the hasta pura. S. P.; in the exergue, CL.

57.

Same legend. Felicity standing, holding a long caduceus and a cornucopia. In the field, S. P. In the exergue, C.

58.

TEMPORVM. FELICIT. A similar type: S. P. in the field: C. in the exergue.

59.

TEMPORVM. FELICITAS. A similar type: S. A. in the field: MSL. (or CL.) in the exergue.

60.

VICTORIA. AVG. Victory marching, with garland and palm branch: S. P. and ML.

61.

VIRTVS. AVG. Mars standing, with spear and buckler: S. P. and C.

62.

Same legend. Same type: S. A. and ML.

63.

Same legend. A galley with a mast, and four rowers. In the exergue, QC.

64.

VIRTVS. AVG. A galley, with a mast and six rowers. In the exergue,
QC.

65.

Same legend. A similar type, with seven rowers. In the exergue, QC.

66.

Same legend. A similar type, with five rowers; the emperor, standing
on the prow. In the exergue, QC. (In the *Hunter* collection).

67.

Same legend. A galley, with mast and four rowers, on the sea. In the
exergue, QL.

68.

Same legend. A similar type, with five rowers.

69.

Same legend. A galley on the sea, without mast, and with six rowers.
In the exergue, QL.

Nos. 1, 2, 3, 4, 5, 6, 28, 34, 35, 46, and 47, are the rarest, some of
them being, in all probability, unique; the next in rarity are Nos. 52, 53,
54, 55, 60, and 66: the galley is the commonest type, excepting No. 66,
which is singular.

ACHILLEUS.

[An usurper in Egypt, in the reign of Diocletian, defeated and put to
death by that emperor].

The small brass coin, in imitation of Egyptian fabric, is a modern
forgery. No certain coins are known of Achilleus. Those given by
Goltz are considered spurious.

DOMITIUS DOMITIANUS.

[Lucius Domitius Domitianus, an usurper in the reign of Diocletianus,
assumed the purple at Alexandria probably about the time of that
emperor's abdication. The time of his death is not known, and the
period of his revolt is only surmised from the circumstance, that when
Latin coins began to be struck at Alexandria, those of Greek fabric
and legend were discontinued. The last Greek coins struck in that
city are of Diocletian, and bear the date IG (15) A. U. C. 151].

STYLE:——IMP. C. L. DOMITIVS. DOMITIANVS. AVG.

Second brass - - - - - - - - - - - - - - - - - - R. 4
GENIO. POPVLI. ROMANI. Genius standing, naked; the modius
on his head; a patera in his right hand, and a cornucopia in his

left; an eagle at his feet. In the field, A. *or* B. *or* Γ. In the exergue,
ALE.

Valued by Mionnet at fifteen francs. One of these coins, in good
condition, brought but 9s. 6d. at a sale in London in 1831.

CONSTANTIUS I.

[Flavius Valerius Constantius, surnamed Chlorus,* the son of Eutropius,
a nobleman of Dardania, and Claudia, the daughter of Crispus, brother
of Claudius Gothicus, was born in Moesia Superior, about the year of
Rome 1003 (A. D. 250). He was appointed governor of Dalmatia
by Carus in 1035 (A. D. 282); adopted and created Cæsar by Max.
Hercules in 1045, and proclaimed Augustus by that emperor at Milan
1058 (A. D. 305). Constantius died at York in the following year,
having first declared his son Constantine Cæsar].

STYLE:——CONSTANTIVS. C. (*or* CAES. *or* CAESAR.) [On reverse,
sometimes, VNDIQVE. VICTORES.]——CONSTANTIVS. N. (*or* NOB.
or NOBIL.) C. (*or* CAES.) [On reverse, sometimes, PRINCEPS.
IVVENT. (*or* IVVENTVT. *or* IVVENTVTIS. *or* VNDIQVE. VICTORES)].——
FL. VAL. CONSTANTIVS. N. (*or* NOB.) C. (*or* CAE. *or*
CAES.) [On reverse, sometimes, PRINCEPS. IVVENTVT.]——
CONSTANTIVS. AVG. (*or* AVGVSTVS.)——IMP. CONSTAN-
TIVS. AVG.——IMP. CONSTANTIVS. P. AVG.——CON-
STANTIVS. P. F. AVG. [On reverse, sometimes, CONSERV. VRB.
SVAE.]——IMP. CONSTANTIVS. P. (*or* PIVS.) F. (*or* FEL. *or*
FELIX.) AVG.——IMP. C. CONSTANTIVS. P. F. AVG.——
IMP. C. FL. VAL. CONSTANTIVS. P. F. AVG.——DIVVS.
CONSTANTIVS.——DIVVS. CONSTANTIVS. AVG.——
DIVVS. CONSTANTIVS. PIVS.——DIVVS. CONSTANTIVS.
PIVS. PRIN. (*or* PRINC. *or* PRINCEPS.)——DIVVS. CON-
STANTIVS. ADFINIS. (*or* COGN. *or* COGNAT.) perhaps, of
Maxentius.

Gold - - - - - - - - - - - - - - - - -	R 6
Silver medallions - - - - - - - - - - - -	R 4
,, of the usual size - - - - - - - - - -	R 2
Brass medallions - - - - - - - - - - - -	R 6
Second brass - - - - - - - - - - - - - -	VC
Third brass - - - - - - - - - - - - - -	VC
Brass, of the size of the quinarius - - - - - - - -	R 1

* He received this name, it is said, on account of the paleness of his com-
plexion : Tillemont, however, finds it only among the modern Greek writers.

SILVER MEDALLIONS.

1.

GENIO. POPVLI. ROMANI. Genius standing, with his attributes. In the exergue, ATR.

2.

MONETA. AVGG. The three Monetæ, standing. *Obverse.* VIRTVS. CONSTANTI. AVG. T. Bust of Constantius Chlorus, with spear and buckler.

No. 1 is valued by Mionnet at forty francs. The other at twenty francs.

GOLD AND SILVER.

1.

COMITATVS. AVG. Two horsemen. In the exergue, PT. - AU

2.

CONCORDIA. AVGG. ET. CAESS. Two emperors, standing. AU

3.

CONCORDIA. AVGG. NOSTR. Concord, seated. In the exergue, AQ. - AU

4.

CONSECRATIO. A funeral pile, surmounted by the chariot of the Sun. In the exergue, PTR. The obverse has the bare head of the emperor: legend, DIVVS. CONSTANTIVS. - - - - AU

Valued by Mionnet at 200 francs.

5.

CONSVL. AVGG. NN. The emperor standing, in the paludamentum, holding a globe and the parazonium. - - - - - - - - - AU

Valued by Mionnet at 150 francs.

6.

CONSVL. CAES. A similar type - - - - - - - - - - - AU

7.

CONSVL. V. P. P. PROCOS. A similar type. In the exergue, SMAⵎ. - - - - - - - - - - - - - - - - - - AU

8.

FELICITAS. AVGG. NOSTR. (*or* NOSTROR.) A woman, seated. In the exergue, AQ. *or* SMT. - - - - - - - - - - AU

9.

FE. ADVENT. AVGG. NN. (*or* FELIX. ADVENTVS. AVGG. NN.) Africa, standing; a lion at her feet. - - - - - - - - AR

10.

HERCVLI. CONSERVATORI. Hercules, standing. In the exergue, SMAQ. - - - - - - - - - - - - - - - - AU

11.

HERCVLI. CONS. CAES✳. Hercules, standing. In the field, a star. In the exergue, SMAN. (or SMAZ.) (Plate xi, No. 3). AU

12.

IOVI. CONSERVAT. AVGG. Jupiter, standing. In the exergue, PR. - - - - - - - - - - - - - - - - - AU

13.

IOVI. FVLGERATORI. Jupiter thundering, on a Titan. In the exergue, PTR. - - - - - - - - - - - - - - - AU

14.

MARTI. PROPVGNATORI. A helmed head: below, TR. - - AU

15.

Same legend. Mars, fighting. In the exergue, TR. - - - - AU

16.

ORIENS. AVGG. The Sun, standing. In the exergue, SIS. - AU

17.

PIETAS. AVGG. ET. CAESS. NN. A woman standing, holding a child: another child standing at her feet. In the exergue, TR. AU

18.

PRINCIPI. IVVENTVTIS. The emperor standing, in a military habit, holding a globe, &c. In the exergue, PROM. or PROV. or ✳SIS.
AU & AR

19.

PROVIDENTIA. AVGG. The Praetorian camp. In the exergue, PR. or SMNΓ. - - - - - - - - - - - - - - AU

20.

Same legend. Four figures sacrificing before the gate of the Praetorian camp. In the exergue, CM. or HP. or NΓ. - - - - - AR

21.

VICT. CONSTANT. AVG. Victory marching, and two captives. In the exergue, SMT. - - - - - - - - - - - - - AU

22.

VICTORIA. SARMAT. Four soldiers sacrificing on a tripod before the camp. On the obverse, DN. - - - - - - - - AR
Valued by Mionnet at eighty francs.

23.

Same legend. Four figures sacrificing before the camp. - - - AR

24.

VIRTVS. AVG. Hercules, standing. - - - - - - - - AU

25.

VIRTVS. HERCVLI. CAESARIS. The emperor on horseback. In the exergue, TR. - - - - - - - - - - - - - - - AU

26.

VIRTVS. ILLYRICI. The emperor on horseback, on a Praetorian galley. *(Banduri).* - - - - - - - - - - - - - - AU

27.

VIRTVS. MILITVM. The Praetorian camp. In the exergue, ANTH✳. - - - - - - - - - - - - - - - - - - - AR

28.

Same legend. The Praetorian camp. In the field, H. and a star. In the exergue, ANT. - - - - - - - - - - - - - - AR

29.

Same legend. Four soldiers sacrificing before the camp : a club in the exergue. - - - - - - - - - - - - - - - - AR

30.

Same legend. A similar type, without the club in the exergue. - AR

31.

Same legend. A similar type. In the exergue, A. *or* Γ. *or* C. *or* D. *or* Z. *or* SIS. - - - - - - - - - - - - - - - AR

32.

VIRTVTI. AVGG. Hercules destroying the Hydra. In the exergue, TR. - - - - - - - - - - - - - - - - - - - AU

33.

VOT. X. within a garland. (Size of the quinarius). - - - - AU

34.

VOT. X. *(sic)* XX. within a garland. - - - - - - - - - AR

35.

XC. VI. within a garland. - - - - - - - - - - - - - AR

36.

X. CONSTANTI. AVG. SMN. within a laurel garland : above, NK. in monogram. - - - - - - - - - - - - - - - - - AR

In gold, Nos. 4, 14, and 15, are much the rarest; the next in rarity are Nos. 5, 7, 13, 24, 25, and 26 ; then Nos, 1, 2, 6, and 21. In silver, No. 22 is much the rarest; Nos. 18 and 35 are the rarest of the remaining numbers.

BRASS MEDALLIONS.

1.

FELIX. ADVENTVS. AVGG. NN.   A figure, with the pileus, standing; his right hand holding a vexillum, his left a cornucopia : a bull couchant, at his feet.   In the field, to the right, Γ.   In the exergue, PKT.

2.

FIDES. MILITVM.   A woman helmeted, seated, holding a standard in her right hand, and the hasta in her left.   In the exergue, TT.

3.

GENIO. POPVLI. ROMANI.   Genius standing, with the modius on his head, before an altar with the fire kindled : a patera in his right hand, and a cornucopia on his left arm.   In the field to the left, A.   In the exergue, PLC.

4.

MEMORIA. DIVI. CONSTANTI.   A circular temple, surmounted by the figure of an eagle with expanded wings.   The obverse has the veiled head of Constantius : legend, DIVO. CONSTANTIO. AVG.

5.

MONETA. AVG. (or AVGG.)   The three Monetæ, standing.

6.

SACRA. MONETA. AVGG. ET. CAESS. NOSTR.   Moneta standing, holding a pair of scales and a cornucopia.   In the exergue, ST.

7.

SALVIS. AVGG. ET. CAESS. AVCTA. KART.   A woman standing, holding a branch in her right hand, and ears of corn in her left.   In the exergue, I.

8.

VICTORIA. BEATISSIMORVM. CAESS.   Victory seated on spoils, inscribing on a buckler, VOT. X.   (*Mus. Theupoli*, vol. ii).

The last four are much the rarest.

[CONSTANTIUS CHLORUS, AND GALERIUS MAXIMIANUS].

CONSTANTIVS. NOBIL. C.   Laureated head of Constantius.—*Rev.* MAXIMIANVS. NOB. C.   Laureated bust of Maximianus, with a spear on his shoulder.

Valued by Mionnet at 200 francs.

SECOND BRASS, WITH RARE REVERSES.

1.

ADLOCVTIO. AVG. N. The usual type. In the exergue, STR. (*Tanini*).

2.

AETERNA. MEMORIA. A circular temple, surmounted by the figure of an eagle. In the exergue, MOSTP. *or* MOSTQ. *or* MOSTS. The obverse has the veiled head of Constantius : legend, IMP. MAXENTIVS. DIVO. CONSTANTIO. ADFINI. (*or* COGN.)

3.

AETERNAE. MEMORIAE. A similar type. In the exergue, AET. The obverse has the veiled head of Constantius : legend, IMP. MAXENTIVS. DIVO. CONSTANTIO. COGN.

4.

CONSECRATIO. An eagle, with expanded wings. In the exergue, PLC.

5.

FIDES. MILITVM. AVGG. ET. CAESS. NN. A woman, standing between two ensigns. In the exergue, AQP. *or* AQS.

6.

FORTVNAE. REDVCI. AVGG. NN. Fortune, seated (or standing). In the field, B. and a star. In the exergue, TR.

7.

GENIO. POPVLI. ROMANI. Genius standing, with his attributes. The obverse has the head of Constantius : legend, VIRTVS. CON-STANTI. NOB. C.

The coin with this reverse, but with the legend CONSTANTIVS. NOBIL. C. on the obverse, is very common.

8.

HERCVLI. VICTORI. Hercules, standing; his right hand on his club, and his left holding the apples of the Hesperides and the lion's skin. In the field, VI. In the exergue, SISA.

9.

IOVI. CONSERVAT. Jupiter standing, holding a Victory on a globe, and the hasta pura. In the field, VI. In the exergue, SISB.

10.

IOVI. CONSERVATORI. A similar type : at the foot of Jupiter, an eagle. In the field, Z. In the exergue, SMK.

11.

MEMORIA. DIVI. CONSTANTI. A circular temple, surmounted
by the figure of an eagle with expanded wings. In the exergue,
PT. *or* ST. *or* TT. The obverse has the veiled head of Constantius:
legend, DIVO. CONSTANTIO. AVG.

12.

Same legend. An eagle with expanded wings, standing on an altar.
In the exergue, AQΓ. *or* AQS.

13.

MEMORIA. FELIX. An eagle with expanded wings, within a temple,
on the frieze of which is another eagle with expanded wings. In the
exergue, PLC. The obverse has the veiled head of Constantius:
legend, DIVO. CONSTANTIO. PIO.

14.

Same legend. Two eagles, standing on each side an altar with the fire
kindled. In the exergue, PLN. *or* PLC. *or* PTR.

15.

VIRTVS. AVGG. ET. CAESS. NN. The emperor on horseback,
riding over two prostrate figures. In the exergue, AQS.

16.

VIRTVS. PERPETVA. AVG. Hercules strangling the Nemæan
lion. In the exergue, PT.

No. 1 is much the rarest; the next in rarity is No. 3; then Nos. 4,
13, and 16. Nos. 5, 6, 11. 12, and 14, are the least rare.

[CONSTANTIUS CHLORUS, AND GALERIUS MAXIMIANUS].

1.

CONSTANTIVS. ET. MAXIMIANVS. NB. *(sic)* C. The laureated
busts of Constantius and Galerius Maximinianus, side by side.—*Rev.*
GENIO. POPVLI. ROMANO. Genius with his attributes, standing. In the field, B. and a star. In the exergue, TR. (Some
are without these marks).

2.

CONSTANTIVS. ET. MAXIMINIANVS. AVGG. The heads of the
emperors.—*Rev.* GENIO. POPVLI. ROMANI. A helmed head.

Valued by Mionnet at ten francs each.

THIRD BRASS, WITH RARE REVERSES.

1.

AETERNA. MEMORIA. A circular temple. The obverse has the head of Maxentius: legend, IMP. MAXENTIVS. DIVO. CON-STANTIO. ADFINI.

2.

DIOCLETIANVS. AVG. Head of Diocletianus.

3.

MEMORIA. FELIX. An altar, with the fire kindled, between two eagles with expanded wings. In the exergue, PTR. The obverse has the veiled and laureated head of Constantius: legend, DIVO. CONSTANTIO. PIO.

4.

Same legend. A similar type. (Small size).

5.

PIETAS. AVGG. The emperor raising up a woman with a turreted crown, who kneels at his feet. In the field, C. In the exergue, PTR.

6.

CONSTANTIVS. N. C. Laureated head of Constantius to the right.— *Rev.* PIETAS. AVGG. Romulus and Remus, suckled by the wolf. (Quoted by *Mionnet*, from the cabinet of the *Bibliotheque of Autun*).

7.

PRAESIDIA. REIPVBLIC. Two soldiers, joining hands, each holding a spear, supporting together a figure of Victory: between them, a captive on his knees. *(Mus. Vindob.).*

8.

PRINCIPI. IVVENTVT. The emperor standing, in a military habit, holding a globe. (Size of the quinarius).

9.

REQVIES. OPTIMORVM. MERITORVM. A figure seated on the curule chair. In the exergue, AQ. The obverse has the veiled and laureated head of the emperor: legend, DIVO. CONSTANTIO. PIO. PRINCIPI. (Size of the quinarius).

10.

VNDIQVE. VICTORES. The emperor standing, in a military habit, holding a globe, surmounted by a Victory, and the hasta. In the exergue, B.

Nos. 2 and 6 are the rarest. The next in rarity are Nos. 1 and 8.

HELENA.

[Flavia Julia Helena, the first wife of Constantius Chlorus, was born at Drepanum in Bithynia, of an obscure family, in the year of Rome 1001 (A. D. 248). She married Constantius many years before his elevation to the rank of Caesar, and when that event took place, she was repudiated, to make way for Theodora, the daughter in law of Maximianus Hercules. Helena was afterwards invested with the title of Augusta, by her son Constantine. She died, as is supposed, at Rome, in the year of that city 1081 (A. D. 328)].*

STYLE :——FL. (or FLAVIA.) HELENA. AVGVSTA.——FL. IVL. (or IVLIA.) HELENA. AVG. or AVGVSTA.

Brass medallions - - - - - - - - - - - - - - - R 1
Third brass - - - - - - - - - - - - - - - - - - C

BRASS MEDALLIONS.

1.

FELICITAS. AVGVSTA. A woman standing, wearing the stola; holding in her right hand a branch, and in her left the hasta pura transversely. (Tanini).

2.

PIETAS. AVGVSTAE. A woman standing, holding a child, and presenting a globe to another child standing by her side. (Tanini).

Valued by Mionnet at 100 francs each.

THIRD BRASS.

PROVIDENTIA. AVGG. The Praetorian camp.

THEODORA.

[Flavia Maxima Theodora, daughter of Eutropia, and daughter-in-law of Maximianus Hercules, the second wife of Constantius Chlorus, was married to that prince when he was invested with the title of Caesar, in the year of Rome 1045 (A. D. 292)].

STYLE :——FL. MAX. THEODORA. AVG.

Silver denarii (doubtful if any).
  ,, quinarii - - - - - - - - - - - - - - - - - R 6
Third brass - - - - - - - - - - - - - - - - - - S

---

* Another Helena was wife of the emperor Julianus, and a third, as appears by the Theodosian code, was the consort of Crispus. (See the observations of *Eckhel Doct. Num. Vet.* Vol. viii. p. 143).

SILVER.

1.

PIETAS. ROMANA.   A woman holding a stag : (dubious).

2.

K. in the field.   A *quinarius* : (dubious).

GALERIUS MAXIMIANUS.

[Galerius Valerius Maximianus, the son-in-law of Diocletianus, was
born near Sardica, in Dacia, and was originally a herdsman.   In the
year of Rome 1045 (A. D. 292), he was adopted, and declared
Caesar by Diocletianus, and governed Thrace and Illyria till 1058,
when he was proclaimed Augustus at Nicomedia by the same emperor.
Maximianus died in the year of Rome 1064 (A. D. 311)].

STYLE:——MAXIMIANVS. CAES. (or CAESAR.)——GAL. MAXI-
MIANVS. CAES.——G. (or GAL.) VAL. MAXIMIANVS.
CAES.——MAXIMIANVS. N. (or NOB. or NOBIL.) C. (or
CAES. or CAESAR.)   [On reverse, sometimes, PRINCEPS. IVVENT.
(or IVVENTVT. or IVVENTVTIS.]——G. (or GAL.) VAL. MAXIMI-
ANVS. N. (or NOB.) C. (or CAES.)   [On reverse, sometimes, as
in the preceding.]——MAXIMIANVS. AVGVSTVS.——IMP.
MAXIMIANVS. AVG.——MAXIMIANVS. IVN. AVG.——
IMP. MAXIMIAN. (or MAXIMIANVS.) IVN. AVG.   [On
reverse, as in the preceding.]——IMP. C. GAL. VAL. MAXI-
MIANVS. IVN. AVG.——MAXIMIANVS. P. F. AVG.——
GAL. MAXIMIANVS. P. F. AVG.——GAL. VAL. MAXI-
MIANVS. P. F. AVG.——IMP. MAXIMIANVS. P. F. AVG.
——IMP. GAL. VAL. MAXIMIANVS. P. F. AVG.——IMP.
C. MAXIMIANVS. P. F. AVG.——IMP. C. GAL. MAXIMI-
ANVS. P. F. AVG.——IMP. C. GAL. VAL. MAXIMIANVS.
P. F. AVG.——DIVVS. MAXIMIANVS.——DIVVS. GAL.
VAL. MAXIMIANVS. —— DIVVS. GAL. MAXIMIANVS.
AVG.—— DIVVS. MAXIMIANVS. SOCER. (by implication,
Maxentii).

Gold - - - - - - - - - - - - - - - - - - -	R 6
Silver medallions - - - - - - - - - - - - - -	R 6
,, of the usual size - - - - - - - - - - - - - -	R 2
,, quinarii - - - - - - - - - - - - - - - -	R 3
Brass medallions - - - - - - - - - - - - - - -	R 6

Second brass - - - - - - - - - - - - - - - - - - VC
Third brass - - - - - - - - - - - - - - - - - - C
Brass, of the size of the quinarius - - - - - - - - - - R 2

SILVER MEDALLION.

GENIO. AVGVSTI. Genius standing, holding a patera and a cornucopia. In the field, a star, and Γ. In the exergue, SIS.
Valued by Mionnet at sixty francs.

GOLD AND SILVER.

1.

CLARITAS. AVG. The Sun standing, holding a globe: at his feet,
a captive. In the exergue of some, PTR. - - - - - - AR

2.

CONSVL. CAESS. Galerius Maximianus standing, in the toga. In
the exergue, T. S. - - - - - - - - - - - - - - AU

3.

FEL. ADVENT. AVGG. NN. Africa standing, holding an elephant's
tooth and an ensign : a lion and a bull at her feet. In the exergue,
S. or T. - - - - - - - - - - - - - - - - - - AR

4.

FELICITAS. SAECVLI. AVGG. NN. Two Victories holding a
buckler, inscribed VIC. AVG. In the exergue, SM. AQ. AU

5.

IOVI. CONS. CAES. Jupiter standing, and an eagle at his feet. In
the exergue, SMAT. - - - - - - - - - - - - - - AU

6.

IOVI. CONSERVAT. AVGG. ET. CAESS. NN. Jupiter, seated. In
the exergue, TR. - - - - - - - - - - - - - - - AU

7.

IOVI. CONSERVAT. NC. (or NK. in monogram). Jupiter, standing.
In the exergue, SMN. - - - - - - - - - - - - - AU

8.

IOVI. CONSERVATORI, Jupiter, standing. In the exergue, SMN.
AU

9.

IOVI. CONSERVATORI. AVGG. Jupiter, seated. In the exergue,
PR. - - - - - - - - - - - - - - - - - - - AU

10.

MARTI. PROPVGNATORI. Helmed head of Mars. In the exergue, TR. - - - - - - - - - - - - - - - - AU

This type, very fine, brought eight guineas at the sale of the Trattle
collection. It is valued by Mionnet at 200 francs.

11.

ORIENS. AVG. The Sun. - - - - - - - - - - - - - AU

12.

ORIENS. AVGVSTOR. The Sun, standing. In the exergue, PR. *or*
SIS. - - - - - - - - - - - - - - - - - - - AU

13.

PRINCIPI. IVVENTVT. A figure standing, holding an ensign. AU

14.

Same legend. A figure standing, holding a globe. - - - - - AU

15.

VICTORIA. AVGG. The Praetorian camp. In the exergue SIS. AR

16.

VICTORIA. SARMAT. Four military figures, sacrificing before the
Praetorian camp. - - - - - - - - - - - - - - - AR

17.

VIRTVS. AVGG. ET. CAESS. The emperor marching, with a trophy:
Two captives. In the exergue, SIS. - - - - - - - - AU

18.

VIRTVS. IOVI. CAESARIS. Maximianus on horseback: TR. AU

This, and No. 17, are valued by Mionnet at 100 francs each.

19.

VIRTVS. MILITVM. Four soldiers, sacrificing before the Praetorian
camp. - - - - - - - - - - - - - - - AU & AR

20.

Same legend. A similar type, with different letters in the exergue. AR

21.

Same legend. The Praetorian camp. - - - - - - - AU & AR

22.

Same legend. A similar type: sometimes *ANTH*. *or* TSΓ. in the
exergue. - - - - - - - - - - - - - - - - AR

23.

Same legend. A similar type. In the exergue, TR. (Size of the
quinarius). - - - - - - - - - - - - - - AR

24.

VOT. X. CAESS. within a garland. - - - - - - - - - - AU

Valued by Mionnet at 100 francs.

25.

XC. VI. A. Q. within a garland. - - - - - - - - - - - AR

26.

XC. VI. T. within a garland. - - - - - - - - - - - - AR

In gold, No. 10 is by far the rarest; Nos. 17, 18, and 24, are much rarer than the remainder; No. 2 is the least rare. In silver, the rarest types are, Nos. 21, 22. 25, and 26; the next in rarity are Nos. 1 and 23; then Nos. 3, 15, 16, and 19.

BRASS MEDALLIONS.

1.

GENIO. POPVLI. ROMANI. Genius standing, holding a patera and a cornucopia. In the field, S. C.

2.

Same legend. A similar type; with B. in the field, and SIS. in the exergue.

3.

IOVI. CONSERVATORI. Jupiter, seated: at his feet an eagle. (*Tanini*).

4.

MONETA. AVGG. The three Monetæ, standing. (The size varies)·

5.

Same legend. A similar type. The obverse has the bust of Maximianus, with the attributes of Hercules.

6.

SALVIS. AVGG. ET. CAESS. FEL. KARTH. An armed figure, with the paludamentum, holding a branch in his right hand, and ears of corn in his left.

Valued by Mionnet at from forty to sixty francs each.

[GALERIUS MAXIMIANUS, AND MAXIMIANUS HERCULES].

MAXIMIANVS. NOB. CAES. ET. CONSVL. Bust of Galerius Maximianus to the right.—*Rev.* IMP. MAXIMIANVS. AVG. COS. IIII. The bust of Maximianus Hercules, with the lion's skin.

Valued by Mionnet at 150 francs.

o 2

[GALERIUS MAXIMIANUS, AND CONSTANTIUS CHLORUS].

MAXIMIANVS. NOB. C.   Laureated bust of Galerius Maximianus, with a spear resting on the shoulder. — *Rev.* CONSTANTIVS. NOBIL. C.   Laureated head of Constantius Chlorus.

Valued by Mionnet at 200 francs.

SECOND BRASS, WITH RARE REVERSES.

1.

AETERNA. MEMORIA.   A temple with six columns, surmounted by an eagle. In the exergue, MOSTP. *or* MOSTQ. The obverse has the veiled head of Galerius Maximianus : legend, DIVO. MAXIMIANO. SOCERO. MAXENTIVS. AVG. (*or* IMP. MAXENTIVS. DIVO. MAXIMIANO. SOCERO.)

2.

AETERNAE. MEMORIAE.   A similar type. In the exergue, RLQ. The obverse has the veiled head of Galerius Maximianus : legend, IMP. MAXENTIVS. DIVO. MAXIMIANO. SOCERO.

3.

AETERNAE. MEMORIAE. GAL. MAXIMIANI.   An altar. The obverse has the head of Maximianus : legend, DIVO. MAXIMI- ANO. MAXIMIANVS. AVG. FIL.

4.

CONCORDIA. FELIG. DD. NN.   The two emperors, standing. The obverse has the head of Maximianus : legend, MAXIMIANVS. IVN. AVG.

5.

CONCORD. IMPERII.   A woman standing, in the stola, with the modius on her head, and holding the hasta pura. In the field, SPΓ. *or* SPΔ. In the exergue, ALE.

6.

FORTI. FORTVNAE.   Fortune standing, holding a globe and a rudder. In the field, a crescent and a star. In the exergue, SIS. The obverse has the veiled head of Galerius Maximianus : legend, DIVO. GAL. VAL. MAXIMIANO.

7.

HERCVLI. VICTORI.   Hercules standing, leaning on his club. In the field, A. and a crescent. In the exergue, ANT.

8.

IOVI. CONS. CAES. Jupiter, standing. In the field, S. A. P. In the exergue, ALE.

9.

MONETA. S. AVGG. ET. CAESS. NN. Moneta, standing. In the field, S. F. In the exergue, ITR.

The rarest types are Nos. 4 and 6; the least rare, Nos. 7. 8, and 9.

THIRD BRASS, WITH RARE REVERSES.

1.

FORTI. FORTVNAE. Fortune, standing: the Sun and the Moon. In the field, L. In the exergue, SIS.

2.

IOVI. ET. HERCVLI. CONS. CAES. Jupiter and Hercules, standing; the first holding a globe and the hasta, the other a Victory and his club. In the field, Γ. In the exergue, XXI.

3.

PAX. AVGG. Peace, standing. In the exergue, A. *or* C.

4.

PRIMO. AVSP. The infant Hercules strangling the two serpents. (Size of the quinarius).

The last is much the rarest type.

VALERIA.

[Galeria Valeria, the daughter of Diocletianus and second wife of Galerius Maximianus, was married to that prince at the time he was created Caesar; namely, in the year of Rome 1045 (A. D. 292). Valeria was, with her mother, beheaded by order of Licinius, in the year of Rome 1068 (A. D. 315)].

STYLE:——GAL. (*or* GALERIA.) VALERIA. AVG.

Gold - - - - - - - - - - - - - - - - - - -	R 6
Silver - - - - - - - - - - - - - - - - - -	R 6
Second brass - - - - - - - - - - - - - - -	R 1
Third brass - - - - - - - - - - - - - - -	R 2

GOLD AND SILVER.

1.

VENERI. VICTRICI. Venus standing, holding a globe. In the field, a star, and ⊠. or ⊠. In the exergue, ALE. or SM. S. or SM. SD. - AU

2.

Same legend. A similar type; with a symbol in the field, and a crescent and a star. In the exergue, SMNΣ. (*Plate xi, No. 4*). - - AU

3.

Same legend. A woman, standing. - - - - - - - - - - - AR

SECOND BRASS.

VENERI. VICTRICI. A woman standing, holding a globe. In the field, a star and Δ. In the exergue, SMSD. or various other letters and emblems.

THIRD BRASS.

1.

VENERI. VICTRICI. A woman standing, as on the second brass.

2.

Another, with a monogram, composed of the letters QMH.

No. 2 is much rarer than the other number.

SEVERUS II.

Flavius Valerius Severus was born of an obscure family in Illyria; declared Caesar by Maximianus Hercules, in the year of Rome 1058 (A. D. 305), and proclaimed Augustus by Galerius Maximianus upon the death of Constantius Chlorus, in 1059 (A. D. 306). Severus having failed in his expedition against Maxentius, who had assumed the purple at Rome, retired to Ravenna, where he was besieged by Maximianus, and finally reduced to surrender. This unfortunate prince was compelled to choose the manner of his death; and, having caused his veins to be opened, expired in the year of Rome 1060 (A. D. 307)].

STYLE:——SEVERVS. NOB. (*or* NOBILIS. *or* NOBILLISSIMVS.) C. (*or* CAE. *or* CAES. *or* CAESAR.) [On reverse, sometimes, PRINCEPS. IVVENT. (*or* IVVENTVT. *or* IVVENTVTIS.]——FL. (*or* FLA.) VAL. SEVERVS. NOB. (*or* NOBIL.) C. (*or* CAES. *or* CAESAR.)

---- SEVERVS, AVG. (*or* AVGVST.) —— IMP. SEVERVS.
AVG.——SEVERVS. P. F. AVG.——IMP. SEVERVS. P. F.
AVG——IMP. FL. VAL. SEVERVS. P. F. AVG.——IMP. C.
SEVERVS. P. F. AVG.——IMP. C. FL. VAL. SEVERVS. P.
F. AVG.

Gold - R 6
Silver medallions, of small size - - - - - - - - - - - R 6
Brass medallions - - - - - - - - - - - - - - - - R 4
Second brass - - - - - - - - - - - - - - - - - - S
Third brass - - - - - - - - - - - - - - - - - R 3
Brass, of the size of the quinarius - - - - - - - - - - R 4

SILVER MEDALLION.

GENIO. POPVLI. ROMANI. Genius standing, holding a patera and
cornucopia. In the field, S. F. In the exergue, PTR.

GOLD.

1.

CONCORD. AVGG. ET. CAES. A woman, seated. In the field, A.
In the exergue, ALE.

2.

CONCORDIA. AVGG. ET. CAESS. NN. A similar type. In the
exergue, TR.

3.

CONCORDIA. CAES. NOSTR. A similar type. In the exergue, TR.

4.

FELICITAS. CAESS. NOSTR. Felicity seated, holding a caduceus
and a cornucopia. In the exergue, AQ.

5.

FELICITAS. SAECVLI. AVGG. NN. Two Victories standing,
holding a garland, within which is inscribed VIC. AVGG. In the
exergue, SMAQ.

6.

HERCVLI. CONSER. AVGG. ET. CAES. NN. Hercules, standing.
In the exergue, TR.

7.

HERCVLI. VICTORI. Hercules standing, holding an apple in his
right hand, and the lion's skin in his left. In the field, Z. In the
exergue, SMSD.

8.

IOVIS. CONSECRATOR. Jupiter, standing; at his feet, an eagle. In the field, ⇆. In the exergue, SMSD.

Nos. 5, 6, and 7 are much less rare than the other numbers, which are valued at 200 francs each by Mionnet.

BRASS MEDALLIONS.

1.

VIRTVS. AVG. The emperor on horseback, galloping to the right, and bearing a spear and a buckler.

2.

VIRTVS. AVGG. ET. CAESS. NN. The emperor on horseback, bearing down two captives. In the exergue, AQT. or AQP.

3.

VIRTVS. AVGG. ET. CESS. (sic) NN. A naked figure, helmeted, holding a spear and a trophy. In the exergue, PT.

The first two numbers are the rarest.

SECOND BRASS, WITH RARE REVERSES.

1.

FIDES. MILITVM. AVGG. ET. CAESS. NN. A woman standing, holding two ensigns. In the exergue, AQS.

2.

FIDES. MILITVM. AVϵϵ (sic) ET. CAESS. NN. A similar type. In the exergue, AQS.—The obverse has the helmed head of Severus, with coat of mail, buckler, and lance · legend, IMP. C. SEVERVS. P. F. AVG.

3.

HERCVLI. VICTORI. Hercules standing, in the lion's skin; his right hand on his club, an apple in his left. In the field, S. P. B. In the exergue, ALE.

4.

SAC. MON. VRB. AVGG. ET. CAESS. NN. Moneta standing, with her attributes. In the exergue, RT.

5.

SALVIS. AVGG. ET. CAESS. FEL. KART. A woman standing, holding fruit in each hand. In the field, H. In the exergue, B. or Γ.

6.

VIRTVS. AVGG. ET. CAESS. NN.   Mars marching, with spear and
trophy.   In the exergue, AQΓ. *or* PT. *or* ST. *or* TT.

7.

Same legend.   The emperor on horseback, bearing down two enemies.
In the exergue, various letters.

Nos. 1, 2, 3, are the rarest; and Nos. 6, 7, are the least rare.

THIRD BRASS.

1.

CONCORDIA. MILITVM.   The emperor and Jupiter standing, holding together a Victory, on a globe.   In the field, A. *or* B.   In the
exergue, ALE. *or* ALH.

2.

GENIO. POPVLI. ROMANI.   Genius standing, holding a patera and
cornucopia.   In the exergue, SIS.

3.

PRINCIPI. IVVENTVT.   The emperor standing, in a military habit,
holding a globe and a spear.   (Size of the quinarius).

4.

VTILITAS. PVBLICA.   A woman in the stola, standing.   (Size of the
quinarius).

5.

VOT. X. CAESS. in three lines, within a laurel garland.   (Size of the
quinarius).

The last three are much rar *r* than the others.

MAXIMINUS DAZA.

[Galerius Valerius Maximinus, surnamed Daza, the son of Galerius
Maximianus' sister, was born of an obscure family, in Illyria, and
declared Caesar by Diocletian, previous to the abdication of that
emperor; Galerius Maximianus having been raised to the rank of
Augustus, in the year of Rome 1058 (A. D. 305).   Upon the death of
Severus, Galerius Maximianus created Licinius, Caesar; and Maximi-
nus and Constantine received the titles of *Sons of the Augusti*, 1060
(A. D. 307).   In the following year, Maximinus assumed the purple in

the east, and was subsequently routed in a battle with Licinius, in Thrace, when he fled to Tarsus in Cilicia, where he died of poison, or probably of grief, in the year of Rome 1066 (A. D. 313).

STYLE:——MAXIMINVS. CAESAR.——MAXIMINVS. NOB. (*or* NOBIL. *or* NOBILIS. *or* NOBILISSIMVS.) C. (*or* CAES. *or* CAESAR.) [On reverse, sometimes, PRINCEPS. IVVENT. (*or* IVVEN-TVT. *or* IVVENTVTIS.)]——GAL. VAL. MAXIMINVS. N. (*or* NOB. *or* NOBIL.) C. (*or* CAES.)——IOVIVS. MAXIMINVS. NOB. CAES. (*or* CAESAR.)——MAXIMINVS. FIL. AVGG. ——MAXIMINVS. AVG. (*or* AVGVSTVS.)——GAL. VAL. MAXIMINVS. AVG.——IMP. MAXIMINVS. AVG.——IMP. MAXIMINVS. P. (*or* PIVS.) AVG. [On reverse, sometimes, OPTIMVS. PRINCEPS.]——MAXIMINVS. P. F. AVG. [On reverse, sometimes, P. P.]——GAL. VAL. MAXIMINVS. P. F. AVG. ——IMP. MAXIMINUS. P. F. AVG. [On reverse, sometimes, OPTIMVS, PRINCEPS.]——IMP. C. MAXIMINVS. P. F. AVG.—— IMP. GAL. VAL. MAXIMINVS. P. F. AVG.——IMP. C. GAL. (*or* GALER.) VAL. (*or* VALER.) MAXIMINVS. P. F. AVG. [On reverse, sometimes, OPTIMVS. PRINCEPS.]——IMP. C. GAL. VAL. MAXIMINVS. INV. AVG.——IMP. GAL. VAL. MAX-IMINVS. P. F. INV. AVG.——IMP. C. GAL. VAL. MAX-IMINVS. P. F. INV. AVG.

Gold -	R 6
Silver medallions - - - - - - - - - - - - - - - -	R 6
Silver, of the usual size - - - - - - - - - - - - - -	R 8
„ quinarii - - - - - - - - - - - - - - - - - -	R 8
Brass medallions - - - - - - - - - - - - - - - -	R 4
Second brass - - - - - - - - - - - - - - - - - -	VC
„ with the title of FILIVS. AVGG. - - - - - - - -	R 2
Third brass - - - - - - - - - - - - - - - - - -	C

SILVER MEDALLIONS.

1.
GENIO. POPVLI. ROMANI. Genius, standing.

2.
IOVI. CONSERVATORI. Jupiter, standing. In the field, a garland, and B. In the exergue, SIS.

3.

VIRTVS. AVGG. ET. CAESS. NN. Mars marching, with a spear and a.trophy.

No. 2 is the rarest.

GOLD AND SILVER, OF THE USUAL SIZE.

1.

CONSVL. P. P. PROCONSVL. The emperor, standing. In the exergue, SMAZ. a crescent, and a star. - - - - - - - - AU

2.

FELICITAS. SAECVLI. CAESS. NN. Two Victories, holding a garland, within which is inscribed, VIC. CAESS. In the exergue, SMAQ. - - - - - - - - - - - - - - - - - - - AU

3.

GAVDIVM. ROMANORVM. A woman seated, suckling a child at the foot of a trophy. In the exergue, PR. - - - - - AU

4.

HERCVLI. COMITI. CAESS. NOSTR. Hercules, standing. In the exergue, AQ. - - - - - - - - - - - - - - AU

5.

HERCVLI. COMIT. CAESS. NOSTR. Hercules, standing. In the exergue, AQ. - - - - - - - - - - - - - - - - AU

6.

HERCVLI. VICTORI. Hercules, standing. - - - - - - AR

Valued by Mionnet at 100 francs.

7.

IOVI. CONSERVATORI. AVGG. Jupiter, seated. In the exergue, PR. - - - - - - - - - - - - - - - - - - - AU

8.

IOVI. CONSERVATORI. AVGG. ET. CAESS. NN. Jupiter, seated. In the exergue, TR. - - - - - - - - - - - - - AU

9.

IOVI. CONSERVATORI. Jupiter standing, holding the hasta and a thunderbolt : at his feet an eagle. In the exergue, SMA. (*Mead's Catalogue*). - - - - - - - - - - - - - - - - - AU

10.

PRINCIPI. IVVENT. (*or* IVVENTVT.) A figure standing, holding an ensign and a spear. In the exergue, PA. *or* PR. - - - AU

11.

PRINCIPI. IVVENTVTIS. A military figure and two standards. AU

12.

Same legend. The emperor in a military habit, holding a spear and a globe. In the exergue, PT. *or* PTR. - - - - - - - AU

13.

SOLI. INVICTO. The Sun standing, holding a Victory. In the exergue, SMAZ., a crescent, and a star. - - - - - - - AU

14.

Same legend. The Sun, holding the head of Serapis. In the field, Δ. In the exergue, ALE. - - - - - - - - - - - - - AU

15.

Same legend. A similar type, but without letters in the field. In the exergue, SMAH., a crescent, and a star. - - - - - - AU

16.

SOLI. INVICTO. AVG. The Sun, in a quadriga. - - - - - AU

17.

SOLI. INVICTO. COMITI. A similar type. - - - - - - AU

18.

SOLI. INVICTO., and NK. in monogram. The Sun, standing. In the exergue, SMN. - - - - - - - - - - - - - - - AU

19.

SOLI. INVICT. CONSERVAT. AVGG. ET. CAESS. NN. A similar type. In the exergue, TR. - - - - - - - - - - - AU

20.

VBIQVE. VICTORES. The emperor standing, in a military habit, holding a spear and a globe: two captives at his feet. In the exergue, PTR. - - - - - - - - - - - - - - - AU

21.

VICTORIA. CONSTANTINI. AVG. Victory, marching: a captive at her feet. In the exergue, PR.* - - - - - - - - AU

22.

VIRTVS. AVGG. ET. CAESS. The emperor, marching, and two captives. In the exergue, SIS. - - - - - - - - - AU

---

* A coin of a similar type, but with " Victory standing," is described in Mead's catalogue ; but *quæry* if there be any difference ?

23.

VIRTVS. MILITVM. The Praetorian camp. In the exergue, TR. (A *quinarius*). - - - - - - - - - - - - - - - - AR

Valued by Mionnet at ninety francs.

24.

X. MAXIMINI. AVG. SMA. within a laurel garland. - - - AU

This type, fine, brought 3*l*. 13*s*. 6*d*. at the Trattle sale. It is valued by Mionnet at 120 francs.

In gold, the rarest types are Nos. 20 and 24. The next in rarity are Nos. 1, 2, 3, 10, 18, 19, and 21.

BRASS MEDALLIONS.

1.

MONETA. AVGG. ET. CAESS. NN. The three Monetæ, standing. In the exergue, AC.

2.

SALVIS. AVGG. ET. CAESS. FEL. KART. A woman in the stola standing, holding ears of corn in her left hand. In the field, I. In the exergue, M.

3.

VIRTVS. AVGG. ET. CAESS. NN. Mars marching, with a trophy and a spear.

No. 3 is the rarest.

SECOND BRASS, WITH RARE REVERSES.

1.

BONO. GENIO. PII. IMPERATORIS. Genius standing, holding a patera and a cornucopia. In the field, various letters. In the exergue, ALE.

2.

CONCORD. (*or* CONCORDIA.) IMPERII. A woman standing, holding the hasta pura. In the field, S. B. P. (*or* VI.) In the exergue, ALE. (*or* SISA. *or* SISB. *or* SISΓ.)

3.

GENIO. AVGVSTI. Genius, standing: the modius on his head, and the head of Serapis in his right hand; on his left arm a cornucopia. In the field, X. B. (*or* X.Γ.) In the exergue, ALE.

4.

GENIO. CAESARIS. Genius standing, holding a patera and a cornucopia. In the field, a star, and Δ. In the exergue, SMTS. The obverse has the legend: MAXIMINVS. FIL. AVGG.

5.

HECVLI. VICTORI. Hercules standing, leaning on his club. In the field, S. In the exergue, ANT.

6.

IOVIO. PROPAGAT. ORBIS. TERRARVM. The emperor in the toga, standing before an altar with the fire kindled: in his right hand a globe, surmounted by a Victory, who places a garland on his head. In the field, A. and a star. In the exergue, ANT. The obverse has the bust of Maximinus in the imperial habit: legend, MAXIMINVS. NOB. CAES.

7.

SECVRIT. PERPET. DD. NN. Security leaning on a column, holding the hasta. In the exergue, PLC.

8.

SOLI. INVICTO. The Sun standing in a female dress; his right hand raised, his left holding the head of Serapis. In the field, S. In the exergue, ANT.

9.

VIRTVS. AVGG. ET. CAESS. NN. The emperor on horseback, bearing down two enemies. In the exergue, AQΓ.

10.

VIRTVS. MILITVM. The gate of the Praetorian camp. In the exergue, MKΓ.

11.

VIRTVS. EXERCITVS. and a monogram. Mars marching, with spear buckler, and trophy. In the exergue, SMNΔ.

The rarest types are Nos. 4 and 5. The next in rarity is No. 6. The least rare, Nos. 1, 2, and 3.

THIRD BRASS, WITH RARE REVERSES.

1.

MAXIMINVS. AVG. Laureated head of Maximinus Daza.—*Rev.* The same head, *incuse.* (Size of the quinarius).

Quoted by Mionnet from the cabinet of the Library of *Autun.*

2.

GENIO. EXERCITVS. A naked figure, standing before an altar, holding a patera and a cornucopia. In the field, a crescent and A. In the exergue, ANT.

3.

MARTI. CONSERVATORI. A military figure standing; his right hand resting on a javelin, reversed; his left on a buckler. In the exergue, ST.

4.

VIRTVS. EXERCITVS. A military figure marching, with a trophy, spear, and buckler. In the field, a star and A. In the exergue, ANT.

5.

VIRTVTI. EXERCITVS. A similar figure dragging a captive by the hair. In the field, a star and Z. In the exergue, ANT.

No. 1 is the rarest; Nos. 2 and 3 are rarer than the others.

MAXENTIUS.

[Marcus Aurelius Valerius Maxentius, the son of Maximianus Hercules and his wife Eutropia, was born about the year of Rome 1035 (A. D. 282). According to historians, he assumed the purple, together with his father, in the year 1059 (A. D. 306); but if the coins which give to Maxentius the title of Cæsar only, are received as evidence, it would appear that he was not raised to the empire until some time after. Maxentius maintained his usurpation against Severus and Galerius Maximianus, and secured Africa, in the year 1061 (A. D. 308). Having become embroiled with Constantine, the result was, an appeal to arms; and, in a battle near Rome, the army of Maxentius was routed, and he himself drowned while crossing the Tiber in his flight. 1065 (A. D. 312)].

STYLE:——MAXENTIVS. NOB. C.——M. VAL. MAXENTIVS. NOB. CAESAR. —— M. AVR. MAXENTIVS. NOB. C. (*or* CAES.)——IMP. MAXENTIVS.——IMP. MAXENTIVS. AVG. [On reverse, sometimes, CONSERV. VRB. SVAE.]——MAXENTIVS. P. F. AVG. [On reverse, sometimes, CONSERVATOR. AFRICAE. SVAE. *or* CONSERVATORES. KART. SVAE. (probably Max. Hercules Maxentius and Constantine), *or* CONSER. (*or* CONSERV. *or* CONSERVAT. *or* CONSERVATOR. *or* CONSERVATORES.) VRB. (*or* VRBIS.) SVAE. *or* P. P. *or* PRINCEPS. IMPERII. ROMANI. *or* PRINCEPS. IVVENTVTIS. *or* VICTOR.

OMNIVM. GENTIVM.]——IMP. MAXENTIVS. P. F. AVG. [On re-
verse, as in the preceding.]——IMP. C. MAXENTIVS. P. F. AVG.
[On reverse, as in the last two.]——IMP. C. M. A. VAL. MAX-
ENTIVS. P. F. AVG. [On reverse, sometimes, CONSERVATORES.
VRB. SVAE. (or PRINCEPS. IVVENTVTIS. or VICTOR. OMNIVM. GENTIVM.]
——MAXENTIVS. P. F. INV. AVG.——IMP. MAXENTIVS.
P. F. INV. AVG.——IMP. C. MAXENTIVS. P. F. INV. AVG.
——MAXENTIVS. PRINC. (or PRINCEPS.) INVICT. (or
INVICTVS.) [On reverse, sometimes, CONSERVATOR. AFRICAE.
SVAE. (or CONSERV. VRB. SVAE.)] —— MAXENTIVS. PRINC.
IVVENT. [On reverse, sometimes, CONSERVATOR. AFRICAE. SVAE.]

Gold - - - - - - - - - - - - - - - - - - R 6
   „ with PRINC. INVICT. on obverse - - - - - - - - R 8
   „ with PRINC. IVVENT. (doubtful).
Silver - - - - - - - - - - - - - - - - - - R 8
Brass medallions - - - - - - - - - - - - - - R 6
Second brass - - - - - - - - - - - - - - - - VC
Third brass - - - - - - - - - - - - - - - - C

GOLD AND SILVER.

1.

CONSERV. VRB. SVAE. Statue of Rome, seated within a temple.
In the field, H. In the exergue, AET. *(Tanini Sup. to Band.)* AU

2.

CONSERVAT. VRB. SVAE. Rome seated, holding a globe surmounted
by a Victory. In the exergue, PR. - - - - - - - - AU

3.

CONSERVATOR. VRBIS. SVAE. Rome seated on a buckler, holding
a globe surmounted by a Victory, and the hasta. In the exergue,
PR. The obverse has the laureated head of Maxentius: legend,
MAXENTIVS. PRINC. INVICT. - - - - - - - AU

4.

Same legend. A similar type, but with E. in the field, and PR. in the
exergue. - - - - - - - - - - - - - - - AU

5.

Same legend. Rome, seated within a temple. In the exergue, RS. or
RT. - - - - - - - - - - - - - - - - - AR

6.

CONSERVATORI. VRB. SVAE. A similar type. In the field, E.
In the exergue. PR. - - - - - - - - - - - - - AU

7.

FELIX. KARTHAGO. A woman in the stola, standing, holding fruit in each hand. In the exergue, PK. - - - - - - - - AU

8.

FELIX. PROCESS. CONSVLAT. AVGG. N. The emperor in the toga, standing, holding a globe. In the exergue, PR. AU & AR

9.

HERCVLI. COMITI. AVG. N. Hercules, standing. In the exergue, PR. - - - - - - - - - - - - - - - - - - - AU

10.

HERCVLI. COMIT. or COMITI. AVGG. NN. (or AVG. ET. CAES. N. or AVGG. ET. CAESS. NN.). Hercules, standing. In the exergue, PR. - - - - - - - - - - - - - - - - AU

11.

MARTI. CONSERV. AVGG. ET. CAESS. NN. Mars, marching. In the field, E. In the exergue, PR. The obverse has the laureated head of Maxentius: legend, MAXENTIVS. PRINC. INVICT.
AU

12.

MARTI. PROPAG. IMP. AUG. N. Mars and a woman standing, joining hands: at their feet, Romulus and Remus suckled by the wolf. In the exergue, AQ. or RQ. (Plate xi, No. 7). - - AR

13.

PAX. AETERNA. AVG. N. Maxentius and three figures, standing. In the exergue, POST. - - - - - - - - - - AU & AR

14.

PRINCIPI. IMPERII. ROMANI. Mars marching, with trophy and spear. In the exergue, PΘ. (Musei Theupoli). - - - - AU

15.

PRINCIPI. IVVENTVTIS. Maxentius, in a military habit, standing. In the exergue, PTR. - - - - - - - - - - - - AU

16.

TEMPORVM..FELICITAS. AVG. N. Romulus and Remus suckled by the wolf. In the exergue, POST. or PR. The obverse has the bare head of Maxentius, full-faced: legend, MAXENTIVS. P. F. AVG. - - - - - - - - - - - - - - AU & AR

The gold is valued by Mionnet at 300 francs; the silver at 200 francs. At the sale of Lord Morton's collection this type, in silver, brought 18*l.*

17.

TEMPORVM. FELICITAS. AVG. N. A similar type. In the exergue, MOSTA. *or* MOSTB. The obverse has the laureated head of Maxentius to the right. - - - - - - - - AR

18.

VICTORIA. AETERNA. AVG. N. The emperor seated, and Victory standing. In the exergue, PR. - - - - - - - - - AU

19.

Same legend. A similar type, but with POST. in the exergue. The obverse has the head of Maxentius with a helmet, on which is represented the chariot of the Sun. - - - - - - - - AU

20.

Same legend. A similar type. Victory, marching. In the exergue MOSTN. - - - - - - - - - - - - - - - - AU

21.

VIRTVS. MILITVM. The Praetorian camp. In the exergue, RS. The obverse has the laureated head of Maxentius: legend, MAX-ENTIVS. PRINC. INVICT. - - - - - - - - - - AR

In gold, No. 16 is much the rarest; the next in rarity is No. 19; then No. 13: Nos. 2, 18, and 20, are the least rare. In silver, No. 16 is the rarest; the next in rarity is No. 21.

BRASS MEDALLIONS.

1.

AETERNITAS. AVG. N. Castor and Pollux, with their horses and attributes. In the exergue, MOSTS.

Valued by Mionnet at 100 francs.

2.

FIDES. MILITVM. A woman, holding two standards. In the exergue, AQS.

3.

MONETA. AVG. N. (*or* AVGG.). The three Monetæ, standing, with their attributes.

The first is much the rarest.

[MAXENTIUS AND ROMULUS].

IMP. C. MAXENTIVS. P. F. AVG. The helmeted and laureated bust of Maxentius, with coat of mail, buckler, and spear. — *Rev.* M. AVR. ROMVLVS. NOBILIS. CAES. Bust of Romulus, with bare head, and with the chlamys.

Valued by Mionnet at 200 francs.

SECOND BRASS, WITH RARE REVERSES.

1.

AETERNITAS. AVG. N. Romulus and Remus suckled by the wolf. In the exergue, MOSTS.

2.

CONSERV. VRB. SVAE. A statue of the emperor within a temple : a captive at the feet of the statue: before, Rome, seated. In the exergue, AQF. *or* AQP. *or* AQS. *or* BS.

3.

Same legend. A Statue of Rome, crowned by Victory, seated within a temple. In the exergue, PT. *or* ST.

4.

Same legend. Statue of Rome within a temple, crowned by Victory, as in the preceding: a captive on the ground. In the exergue, PT. *or* ST. *or* TT.

5.

CONSERVATOR. AFRICAE. SVAE. A woman standing, in the stola, her head covered by an elephant's skin ; holding a labarum in her right hand, and the tooth of an elephant in her left. At her feet, a bull and a lion. In the field, S. E. F. In the exergue, Γ.

6.

CONSERVATORES. KART. SVAE. A statue of a woman standing within a temple. In the exergue, PKΓ.

7.

FEL. PROCES. CONS. IN. AVG. N. *(sic).* The emperor, in a quadriga of elephants. In the exergue, RBP. *or* RBQ.

8.

FEL. PROCESS. CONSVL. AVG. N. The emperor, in a car drawn by six horses. In the exergue, ABT.

9.

MARTI. COMITI. AVG. N.   The emperor on horseback, preceded by Mars, who bears a trophy.   In the exergue, R.

10.

MARTI. CONSERVAT. AVG. N.   Mars marching, with a buckler and spear.   In the exergue, RES.

11.

MARTI. VICTORI. AVG. N.   Mars, with spear and buckler, dragging a prisoner by the hair of his head.   In the exergue, RES.

12.

PRINCIPI. IVVENTVTIS.   The emperor, in a military habit, holding two standards.   In the exergue, PLC.

13.

SAECVLI. FELICITAS. AVG. N.   Romulus and Remus suckled by the wolf.   In the exergue, MOSTT.

14.

SALVIS. AVGG. ET. CAESS. FEL. KART.   A woman standing, in the stola, holding fruit in each hand.   In the field, H.   In the exergue, Δ.

15.

VICTOR. OMNIVM. GENTIVM. AVG. N.   The emperor standing, in a military habit, receiving a globe surmounted by Victory, from the hands of Mars: a prostrate figure on the ground.   In the exergue, MOSTQ.

16.

VICTORIA. AETERNA. AVG. N.   Victory standing, full-faced, holding a garland and a palm branch: six prisoners kneeling on the ground, their hands bound.   In the exergue, MOST₹.

No. 8 is much the rarest: the next in rarity is No. 16; then No. 7: the least rare are Nos. 2 to 6, and Nos. 10, 11, 12, and 14.

THIRD BRASS, WITH RARE REVERSES.

1.

ADLOCVTIO.   The emperor, addressing his troops.   In the exergue, POSTO.

2.

CONSERV. VRB. SVAE.   A statue, seated within a temple.   (Size of the quinarius).

3.

CONSERV. VRB. SVAE. Rome, seated within a temple, presenting a globe to Maxentius. In the exergue, AQ. S.

4.

HERCVL. COMITI. AVG. N. Hercules, standing.

5.

MARTI. CONSERVATORI. AVG. N. Mars marching, with spear and buckler.

6.

SAECVLI. FELICITAS. AVG. N. Romulus and Remus suckled by the wolf.

No. 1 is a very rare type; Nos. 3 and 6 are the rarest of the others.

ROMULUS.

[Marcus Aurelius Romulus, the son of Maxentius, was born, as is supposed, about the year of Rome 1059 (A. D. 306), declared Caesar by his father in the following year, and Augustus a short time afterwards. Romulus died in the year of Rome 1062 (A. D. 309)].

STYLE:——M. AVR. ROMVLVS. NOBILIS. CAES.——DIVVS. ROMVLVS. NV. (or NVBIS.) C. (or COS. or CONS.)——DIVVS. ROMVLVS. NVB. AVG.——DIVVS. ROMVLVS. NV. F. (or FILIVS.)——DIVVS. ROMVLVS. NV. CONS. FILIVS.

The words NVBIS. CONS., NVB. AVG., &c., have puzzled all the numismatists. Jobert thinks that the legend should stand NOSTRAE. VRBIS. CONS. and that the R is by accident omitted; but this could not happen in all the coins of Romulus. Cardinal Noris speaks of a coin with NOB. CONS. (*Nobilissimo Consulis*), but this is not authenticated. Mionnet says, "On ignore, absolument le sens des mots ' NVBIS. CONS.' &c."—See the remarks of the *Baron Bimard* on this legend, in the *Science de Medailles, tom ii, p.* 197.

Gold medallion - - - - - - - - - - - - - - - - -	*unique*
,, of the usual size - - - - - - - - - - - - - -	R 8
Brass medallions - - - - - - - - - - - - - - -	R 8
Second brass - - - - - - - - - - - - - - - - -	R 4
Third brass - - - - - - - - - - - - - - - - -	R 4

GOLD MEDALLION.

AETERNAE. MEMORIAE. A circular temple with a dome, surmounted by the figure of an eagle, with expanded wings. In the
exergue, POST. The obverse has the bust of Romulus to the left,
with bare head, and in the toga: legend, DIVO. ROMVLO.
NVBIS. CONS.

Valued by Mionnet at 1200 francs.

This fine medallion is as large in circumference as the second brass of
the Caesars.

SILVER ?

AETERNAE. MEMORIAE. A circular temple: AQ. in the exergue.
The obverse has the bare head of Romulus: legend, DIVO.
ROMVLO. NVBIS. CONS. (A *quinarius*).

This coin is described in the *Catalogue d'Ennery* as of silver; but
Mionnet says, " Je crois ce quinaire moulé sur le petit bronze."

BRASS MEDALLION.

M. AVR. ROMVLVS. NOBILIS. CAES. Bust of Romulus, with the
chlamys; the head bare.—*Rev.* IMP. C. MAXENTIVS. P. F.
AVG. Helmeted bust of Maxentius, with spear and buckler.

Valued by Mionnet at 200 francs.

SECOND BRASS.

1.

AETERNAE. MEMORIA. A circular temple with a dome, surmounted by the figure of an eagle with expanded wings. In the
exergue, MOSTP. *or* MOSTS. *or* REP. The obverse has the bare
head of Romulus, with the legend, IMP. MAXENTIVS. DIVO.
ROMVLO. NV. FILIO.

2.

AETERNAE. MEMORIAE. A similar type, with various letters in
the exergue. The obverse has the bare head of Romulus: legend,
DIVO. ROMVLO. NVB. AVG. (*or* NVBIS. CONS.)

The first is by far the rarest.

THIRD BRASS.

AETERNAE. MEMORIAE. A similar type to the second brass, with various letters in the exergue. The obverse has the bare head of Romulus: legend, DIVO. ROMVLO. NVBIS. CONS.

ALEXANDER.

[Alexander, an usurper in Africa, in the reign of Maxentius, was born of an obscure family in Pannonia, or, according to Zosimus,* in Phrygia. He was lieutenant of the praefect of Africa, under Maxentius, and having become embroiled with that tyrant, he, to avoid the consequences, caused himself to be proclaimed emperor at Carthage, in the year of Rome 1061 (A. D. 308). The army of Alexander was encountered by that of Rufius Volusianus, whom Maxentius had sent against him, and he himself taken prisoner and strangled, 1064 (A. D. 311)].

STYLE:——IMP. ALEXANDER. P. F. AVG.

Silver - R 8
Second brass - - - - - - - - - - - - - - - - - - R 8
Third brass - - - - - - - - - - - - - - - - - - R 6

SILVER.

1.

INVICTA. ROMA. FELIX. KARTHAGO. Africa, standing. In the exergue, PK. (Banduri).

2.

ROMAE. AETERNAE. A military figure standing, holding a Victory and the hasta. (Pembroke).

SECOND BRASS.

1.

GLORIA. EXERCITVS. KART. (or KARTH.) An equestrian figure. In the exergue, PK. or PRT.

2.

INVICTA. ROMA. FELIX. KARTHAGO. A woman standing in the stola, holding fruit in each hand. In the exergue, PK.

---

* This author says that Alexander was a timid, cowardly man, and far advanced in years at the time that he assumed the purple.

3.

ROMAE. AETERNAE.   A military figure standing, holding a globe and the hasta.

4.

VICTORIA. ALEXANDRI. AVG. N.   Victory, standing.   In the exergue, PK.

Valued at seventy-two francs each by Mionnet.

THIRD BRASS.

1.

ROMAE. AETERNAE.   A military figure standing, holding a globe, surmounted by a Victory, and the hasta.   In the exergue, PK.

2.

Same legend.   Statue of Rome, seated within a temple.   In the exergue, PK.

3.

S. P. Q. R. OPTIMO. PRINCIPI.   Three standards.   In the exergue, K.

Valued at sixty francs each by Mionnet.   A coin of this usurper, in third brass, brought 5*l.* 12*s.* 6*d.* at the sale of the Tyssen Cabinet in 1802.

LICINIUS.

[Publius Flavius Claudius Galerius Valerius Licinianus Licinius, the brother-in-law of Constantine the Great, and son-in-law of Constantius Chlorus, was born of an obscure family in Dacia, in the year of Rome 1046 (A. D. 263).   Upon the death of Severus he was declared Caesar and Augustus, and associated in the empire with Galerius Maximianus, 1060 (A. D. 307).   In the year of Rome 1066, he espoused the sister of Constantine (Constantia); but his persecutions of the Christians led to a rupture between them, and an appeal to arms was the consequence.   Licinius was worsted in several engagements; when he offered terms to the victor, and it was finally arranged that Constantine should remain emperor of the West, while Licinius governed the East.   But in the year 1076 (A. D. 323), the flame was rekindled; Licinius was again unfortunate; and, after losing two battles, he fled to Thessalonica, where, by order of Constantine, he was strangled, in the year of Rome 1077 (A. D. 324)].

The coins given by Banduri, on which this prince is styled Caesar only, whereby it would appear that Galerius had first given him that title alone, are thought by Eckhel to be either false, or to belong to Licinius, junior.

STYLE:——LICINIVS. AVG. (*or* AVGVSTVS.)——P. LICINIVS. AVG.——IMP. LICINIVS. AVG.——IMP. LIC. (*or* LICIN. *or* LICINIANVS.) LICINIVS. AVG. —— IMP. C. LICINIVS. AVG.——IMP. C. VAL. LICIN. LICINIVS. AVG.——LICINIVS. P. AVG.——IMP. LICINIVS. P. (*or* PIVS.) AVG.—— IMP. C. LICINIVS. P. AVG.——IMP. LIC. LICINIVS. P. F. ——LICINIVS. P. F. AVG. [On reverse, sometimes, P. P. (*or* PRINCEPS. PROVIDENTISSIMVS. *or* VBIQVE. VICTORES.)] —— VAL. LICINIVS. P. F. AVG.——VAL. C. LICINIVS. P. F. AVG. ——VAL. LICINNIANVS. *(sic)* LICINNIVS. *(sic)* P. F. AVG. ——P. LIC. LICINIVS. P. F. AVG.——IMP. LICINIVS. P. (*or* PIVS.) F. AVG. [On reverse, sometimes, FVNDAT. (*or* FVNDATOR.) PACIS. (*or* LIBERATOR. ORBIS. *or* OPTIMVS, PRINCEPS.)] ——IMP. LIC. (*or* LICIN. *or* LICINIANVS.) LICINIVS. P. F. AVG.——IMP. VAL. LICINIVS. P. F. AVG.——IMP. VAL. LICIN. LICINIVS P. F. AVG.——IMP. FL. CL. LICINIVS. P. F. AVG. [On reverse, PIVS. IMPERATOR.]——IMP. C. LICI-NIVS. (*or* LICINNIVS.) P. F. AVG. [On reverse, sometimes, OPTIMVS. PRINCEPS.]——IMP. C. LIC. LICINIVS. (*or* LICIN-NIVS.) P. F. AVG.——IMP. C. VAL. LICINIVS. P. F. AVG. ——IMP. C.VAL. (*or* VALER.) LIC. (*or* LICIN. *or* LICINIAN.) LICINIVS. (*or* LICINNIVS.) P. F. AVG.—— IMP. C. F. VAL. LICIN. LICINIVS. P. F. AVG. [On reverse, sometimes, OPTIMVS. PRINCEPS.] —— IMP. C. GAL. VAL. LICINIANVS. P. F. AVG.——IMP. C. P. LIC. LICINIVS. P. F. AVG.

LICINIVS AND HIS SON:——DD. NN. IOVII. LICINII. AVG. ET. CAES. —— DD. NN. IOVII. LICINII. INVICT. AVG. ET. CAES.

Gold medallions (of small size) - - - - - - - - - - -	R 8
,, of the usual size - - - - - - - - - - - - - -	R 6
Silver medallion (quoted by *Beauvais*) - - - - - - - - -	R 6
Base silver, of the usual size - - - - - - - - - - - -	R 2
Fine silver, of the usual size - - - - - - - - - - - -	R 7
Brass medallions - - - - - - - - - - - - - - -	R 6
Second brass - - - - - - - - - - - - - - - - -	C
Third brass - - - - - - - - - - - - - - - - -	VC

GOLD MEDALLION.

VIRTVS. AVGG. NN. Rome, seated on a coat of mail; before, a military figure standing; behind, a Victory, placing a garland on her head. In the exergue, S. . . T.

Valued by Mionnet at 300 francs.

GOLD, AND BASE SILVER.

1.

CONSVL. P. P. PROCONSVL. The emperor, standing.   -   -   AU

2.

IOVI. CONS. LICINI. AVG. Statue of Jupiter, with an eagle at his feet, standing on a pedestal. In the field, a garland: on the pedestal, SIC. X. SIC. XX. In the exergue, SMNЄ. - - - - - - AU

3.

Same legend. Statue of Jupiter, with an eagle at his feet, seated on a pedestal, inscribed SIC. X. SIC. XX. In the exergue, SMNГ.

4.

Same legend. A similar type, but with SMND. in the exergue. The obverse has the full face of Licinius: legend, LICINIVS. AVG. OBDV. FILII. SVI. *(Mus. Vindob.)*   - - - - - - AU

5.

IOVI. CONSERVATORI. Jupiter standing; an eagle at his feet. In the field, X. In the exergue, SIS.   - - - - - - - - AU

6.

IOVI. CONSERVATORI. AVG. Jupiter seated. In the exergue, PTR. - - - - - - - - - - - - - - AU & B.

7.

IOVI. CONSERVATORI. AVGG. Jupiter, standing. In the field, ⇌. In the exergue, SM. TS.   -   - - - - - - - - AU

8.

Same legend. Jupiter standing; an eagle at his feet. In the exergue, SMN. *or* SM. TS. - - - - - - - - - - - AU & B.

9.

MARTI. CONSERVATORI. Mars standing, with spear and buckler. In the exergue, PR. - - - - - - - - - - - - - AU

10.

PERPETVA. VIRTVS. AVG. The emperor on horseback, with the paludamentum, etc., attended by a soldier. In the exergue, SIS.
AU

11.

PRINCIPIS. PROVIDENTISSIMI. An owl, standing on a column inscribed SAPIENTIA; on each side, arms. In the exergue, QAB. - - - - - - - - - - - - - - - - - - - AU

12.

PROFECTIO. AVGG. The emperor on horseback. In the exergue, SIS. - AU

13.

PROVIDENTIAE. AVGG. The Praetorian camp. - - - - B

14.

SECVRITAS. AVGG. The emperor, in a quadriga. In the exergue, SIS. - AU

15.

SIC. X. SIC. XX. inscribed on a buckler: an eagle. In the exergue, SMNB. *(Fine silver).* - - - - - - - - - - AU & AR

The gold is valued at 120 francs; the fine silver at eighty francs, by Mionnet.

16.

VBIQVE. VICTORES. The emperor, in a military habit, standing; a javelin in his right hand, and a globe in his left: on each side, two captives seated on the ground. In the exergue, PTR. AU & B

This type in gold, fine, brought 3*l.* 12*s.* at the Trattle sale. It is valued at 100 francs by Mionnet.

17.

VICTORIAE. LAETAE. PRINC. PERP. Two Victories standing, sustaining a buckler resting on a cippus; on the buckler, VOT. X. In the exergue, PR. - - - - - - - - - - - AU & B

18.

VOT. XX. D. N. LICINI. AVGVSTI. within a laurel garland. - B

19.

VOTA. XX. MVLT. XXX. within a laurel garland. In the exergue, TSA. - - - - - - - - - - - - - - - - - - - B

In gold, Nos. 11 and 14 are by far the rarest. The next in rarity is No. 4; then No. 15. The least rare are Nos. 1, 5, 6, 7, 8, and 17. In base silver, Nos. 13, 18, and 19, are the rarest: the next in rarity are Nos. 16 and 17.

BRASS MEDALLIONS.

1.

IOVI. CONSERVATORI. Jupiter, standing; an eagle at his feet.

2.

Another, similar, but with a captive at the feet of Jupiter; and XIII. in the field.

Valued at seventy-two francs each by Mionnet.

SECOND BRASS, WITH RARE REVERSES.

GENIO. CAESARIS. Genius standing, with the modius on his head, holding a patera, cornucopia, and the chlamys. In the exergue, AHTΔ.

[LICINIUS, AND HIS SON LICINIUS].

1.

DD. NN. IOVII. LICINII. INVICT. AVG. ET. CAES. The busts of the elder and younger Licinius, supporting a Victory.—*Rev.* I. O. M. ET. VICT. CONSER. DD. NN. AVG. ET. CAES. Jupiter standing, crowned by Victory. In the exergue, SMKΓ.

2.

I. O. M. ET. FORT. CONSER. DD. NN. AVG. ET. CAES. Jupiter and Fortune, standing. In the exergue, SMKA. *or* SMNA. Obverse, the same as the preceding.

3.

Same legend. The busts of the elder and the younger Licinius, supporting a figure of Fortune and a trophy.—*Rev.* I. O. M. ET. VIRTVTI. DD. NN. AVG. ET. CAES. Jupiter, standing before a trophy, at the foot of which are two captives. In the exergue, SMNTA. *or* SMATE.

Valued by Mionnet at twelve francs each.

THIRD BRASS, WITH RARE REVERSES.

1.

FVNDAT. PACIS. An armed figure dragging a captive by the hair. In the exergue, RQ. *or* RS.

2.

GLORIA. PERPET. Two Victories marching, each holding the hasta transversely, and a garland: between them, the labarum. In the exergue, RT. (Size of the quinarius).

3.

ROMAE. AETERNAE. Rome, seated on a buckler, holding another buckler, which she rests on her knees, inscribed X.V. In the field, P. R. In the exergue, RP. or RS.

4.

SAPIENTIA. PRINCIPIS. An owl, standing on an altar: on one side the labarum; on the other a helmet. In the exergue, RP. or RS. (Size of the quinarius).

5.

VICTORIA. AVGG. NN. Victory, marching. In the exergue, TSA.

6.

VIRT. EXERC. The plan of a camp, on which stands the figure of the Sun. In the exergue, TSA.

Nos. 2, 4. and 6, are the rarest; No. 3 is the least rare.

[LICINIUS, AND HIS SON].

1.

DD. NN. IOVII. LICINII. INVICT. AVG. ET. CAES. The busts of the elder and the younger Licinius, supporting a globe surmounted by a Victory, who places a garland on their heads.—*Rev.* I. O. M. ET. VICT. CONSER. DD. NN. AVG. ET. CAES. Jupiter and Victory, standing. In the exergue, various letters.

2.

Same legend. The busts of the Licinii, supporting a trophy.—*Rev.* I. O. M. ET. VIRTVTI. DD. NN. AVG. ET. CAES. Jupiter standing near a trophy, at the foot of which are two captives.

CONSTANTIA.

[Flavia Constantia, the daughter of Constantius Chlorus, sister of Constantine the Great, and wife of Licinius, was born in Britain, and married to the emperor, in the year of Rome 1066 (A. D. 313). She died about the year 1083 (A. D. 330)].

The coins of this princess, given by Goltzius, are not authenticated.

LICINIUS THE YOUNGER.

[Flavius Valerianus Licinianus Licinius, the son of the elder Licinia by Constantia, was born in the year of Rome 1068 (A. D. 315). He was declared Caesar * in 1070 (A. D. 317). Upon the death of his father, in 1076, he was stripped of his title; and, in 1079 (A. D. 326), executed, by order of Constantine].

STYLE:——LICINIAN. LICINIVS. IVN.——FL. VAL. LICINIVS. CAES.——LICIN. (or LICINIVS.) IVN. CAES.——LICINIVS. NOB. CAES.——FL. LICIN. LICINIVS. NOB. CAES.—— LICIN. (or LICINIVS.) IVN. N. (or NOB.) C. (or CAES. or CAESAR.) [On reverse, sometimes, PRINCEPS. IVVENTVTIS.] ——VAL. LICINIVS. NOB. CAES.——LICIN. LICINIVS· IVN. NOB. CAES.——D. N. VAL. LICINIVS. NOB. C. (or CAES.)——D. N. VAL. LICIN. LICINIVS. NOB. C.——DN. FL. LICIN. LICINIVS. NOB. C.

Gold - - - - - - - - - - - - - - - - - - -	R 6
„ quinarii - - - - - - - - - - - - - - - -	R 6
Silver - - - - - - - - - - - - - - - - - -	R 3
Brass medallions - - - - - - - - - - - - - - -	R 8
Third brass - - - - - - - - - - - - - - - -	VC

GOLD AND SILVER.

1.

FILICIA. TEMPORA. Four children, representing the four Seasons. In the exergue, T. S. - - - - - - - - - - - - - AU

2.

IOVI. CONSERVATORI. Jupiter, standing. An eagle at his feet. In the field, N. In the exergue, SMNЄ - - - - - - - AU

3.

IOVI. CONSERVATORI. CAES. Statue of Jupiter seated on a pedestal, and holding the hasta and a globe surmounted by a Victory; an eagle at his feet. On the pedestal, SIC. V. SIC. X. In the exergue, SMNЄ. The obverse has the bust of the younger Licinius, with bare head, full-faced, and with the chlamys. - AU

---

* Eckhel, Doct. Num. Vet. tom. 8, page 69, restores to Licinius the father, a coin bearing the title of Augustus, which, by Banduri, is erroneously assigned to the younger Licinius.

4.

SECVRITAS. REIPVBLICAE. Security, leaning on a column. In the exergue, TR. (A *quinarius*). - - - - - - - - - AU

5.

VIRTVS. EXERCIT. A trophy, or the labarum, between two captives. In the exergue, X. - - - - - - - - - - - - - - AR

6.

Same legend. The labarum, inscribed VOT. X.: two captives at the foot. In the field, a monogram, and SF. In the exergue, A. SIS. The obverse has the bust of Licinius the younger, with coat of mail, holding a globe surmounted by a Victory. - - - - - - - AR

[LICINIUS THE YOUNGER, CRISPUS, AND CONSTANTINUS THE YOUNGER].

LICINIVS. NOB. CAES. The laureated bust of Licinius the younger, with coat of mail, holding a globe surmounted by a figure of Victory. —*Rev.* CRISPVS. ET. CONSTANTINVS. CC. The bare heads of Crispus and the younger Constantinus, face to face. In the exergue, SIRM.

Valued by Mionnet at 240 francs.

BRASS MEDALLION.

EXERC. AVGVSTORVM. The emperor, sacrificing on a tripod: behind, an armed figure, placing a garland on his head; before, two figures; one of them in the toga, the other holding the lictor's rods. The obverse has the bust of Licinius in the toga, and holding the Roman eagle: legend, D. N. LICINIVS. NOB. C.

Valued by Mionnet at 200 francs.

THIRD BRASS, WITH RARE REVERSES.

1.

CONCORDIA. AVGG. NN. A woman, holding a cornucopia and caduceus. In the exergue, AQS.

2.

PAX. PERPETVA. A woman standing, leaning on a column, holding a branch and the hasta transversely.

3.

SAECVLI. FELICITAS. A garland placed on a cippus, within which is inscribed, AVG. In the field, P. R. In the exergue, AQ.

4.

VIRTVS. MILITVM. DD. NN. Mars marching, with a trophy and a spear. In the exergue. TSG.

Valued at three francs each by Mionnet.

[LICINIUS, AND HIS FATHER].

DD. NN. IOVII. LICINII. AVG. ET. CAES. Busts of the Licinii, supporting a globe surmounted by a Victory, who places a garland on their heads.—*Rev.* I. O. M. ET. VICT. CONSER. DD. NN. AVG. N. AVG. ET. CAES. Jupiter and Victory, standing. In the exergue, various letters.

VALENS.

[Aurelius Valerius Valens, an officer in the army of Licinius, was declared Caesar by that emperor, when about to engage in the war with Constantinus, in the year of Rome 1067 (A.D. 314); though if the coin described below, is authentic, it would appear that he also received the title of Augustus. Upon the reestablishment of peace between the two princes, the first article of the treaty, was the abdication of this new associate; Constantine sternly refusing to acknowledge him. Valens was deprived of his title, and shortly afterwards fell by the hand of Licinius himself].

STYLE :——IMP. C. AVR. VAL. VALENS. P. F. AVG.

A coin of Valens in third brass, occurs in the catalogue of d'Ennery, (p. 635, No. 4660); but its authenticity is doubted. It is thus described :—

IMP. C. AVR. VAL. VALENS. Laureated head of Valens.—*Rev.* IOVI. CONSERVATORI. AVGG. Jupiter standing, holding the hasta and a Victory: an eagle at his feet, holding a garland in its beak. In the field to the right, K., to the left, a garland, and X. A. In the exergue, ALE.

The same type is given by Goltzius.

MARTINIANUS.

[Marcus Martinianus was *magister officiorum* at the court of Licinius, who conferred upon him the titles of Caesar and Augustus, previous to the battle of Chrysopolis, the war having been rekindled between that prince and Constantine, in the year of Rome 1076 (A. D. 323). The disastrous issue of that engagement destroyed for ever the hopes of Licinius, and Martinianus was sacrificed to the vengeance of the conqueror].

Style ——D. N. MARTINIANVS. P. F. AVG.——D. N. M. MARTINIANUS. P. F. AVG.

Third brass - R 6

The silver, with an altar ; legend, consecratio; is a modern fabrication.

IOVI. CONSERVATORI. Jupiter standing, holding a Victory on a globe, and the hasta : at his feet, on one side, an eagle ; on the other, a figure kneeling in an attitude of supplication. In the field, XIIB. (*or* XIII′. *or* XIII.) In the exergue, SMNA. (*or* SMNB. *or* SMNΓ. *or* SMNΔ. *or* SMNT.) The obverse has the radiated head of Martinianus: legend, D. N. (*or* D. N. M.) MARTINIANVS. P. F. AVG. (*or* D. N. *or* D. N. M.) MARTINIANO. P. F. AVG. (*Plate xi, No. 8*).

Valued by Mionnet at sixty francs; but with the legend in the dative case, at seventy-two francs.

CONSTANTINUS MAGNUS.

[Flavius Galerius Valerius Constantinus, the son of Constantius Chlorus and Helena, son in law of Maximianus Hercules, and brother in law of Licinius, was probably born at Dardania in Dacia, in the year of Rome 1027 (A. D. 214); although Britain and Drepanum have each been mentioned as the place of his birth. Upon the death of his father at York, he was proclaimed Caesar and Augustus by the legions of Britain, in 1059 (A. D. 306). Galerius Maximianus, however, refused him the latter title, and conferred it upon Severus. In the following year Maximianus Hercules created him Augustus, and gave him his daughter Fausta in marriage ; but Constantinus prudently contented himself with the title of Son of the Augusti, which was also conferred upon Maximinus Daza. The latter having assumed the purple in 1061 (A. D. 308), Constantinus was created Augustus by

Galerius. In 1064 (A. D. 311) he embraced the Christian religion, and having survived his rivals, remained sole master of the empire in 1076 (A. D. 323). Constantinus quitted Rome for Byzantium, having taken umbrage at the lampoons of the citizens, in 1083 (A. D. 330), and named the city Constantinople. He ended his eventful life at Nicomedia in Bithynia, when about to march against the Persians, in the year of Rome 1090 (A. D. 337)].

STYLE : —— CONSTANTINVS. CAESAR. —— CONSTANTINVS. NOB. C. (or CAES.) [On reverse, sometimes, CONSERVATOR. (or CONSERVATORES.) KART. SVAE. (or CONSERV. or CONSERVATORES.) VRB. SVAE. or PRINCEPS. IVVENT. (or IVVENTVTIS.)]——FL. VAL. CONSTANTINVS. N. (or NOB. or NOBIL.) C. (or CAES.) [On reverse, sometimes, CONSERVATOR. AFRICAE. SVAE. or PRINCEPS. IVVENTVTIS.]——FL. VAL. CONSTANTINVS. FIL. AVG.—— CONSTANTINVS. FIL. AVGG.——AVGVSTVS. [On reverse, CAESAR.]——CONSTANTINVS. AVG. (or AVGVSTVS.) [On reverse, sometimes, PRINCEPS. IVVENTVTIS. or RECVPERATOR. VRBIS. SVAE.]——FL. VAL. CONSTANTINVS. AVG.——IMP. CON-STANTINVS. AVG. [On reverse, sometimes, FVNDATOR. PACIS. (or PRINCEPS. IVVENTVTIS. or VBIQVE. VICTORES.)]——D. N. CON-STANT. (or CONSTANTINVS.) AVG. (or AVGVST.)——CON-STANTINVS. P. AVG. [On reverse, sometimes, PRINCEPS. IVVENTVTIS.] —— IMP. CONSTANTINVS. P. AVG. [On reverse as in the preceding].——CONSTANTINVS. P. F. AVG. [On reverse, sometimes, CONSERV. (or CONSERVATORES.) VRB. (or VRBIS.) SVAE. (or OPTIMVS. PRINCEPS. or P. P. or PRINCEPS. IVVEN-TVTIS. or PRINCEPS. PROVIDENTISSIMVS. or RESTITVTOR. LIBERTATIS. or VBIQVE. VICTOR. (or VICTORES.) or VICTOR. OMNIVM. GENTIVM.] ——FL. VAL. (or VALER. or VALERIVS.) CONSTANTINVS. P. F. AVG.——IMP. CONSTANTINVS. P. F. AVG. [On reverse, sometimes, CONSERV. (or CONSERVATOR.) VRB. (or VRBIS.) SVAE. or FVNDAT. PACIS. or LIBERATOR. ORBIS. or LIBERATOR. VRBIS. SVAE. or OPTIMVS. PRINCEPS. or PRINCEPS. IVVENTVTIS. or VBIQVE. VICTORES.]——IMP. GAL. VAL. CONSTANTINVS. P. F. AVG. ——IMP. C. CONSTANTINVS. P. F. AVG. [On rev. sometimes, CONSERVATORES. KART. SVAE. (or CONSERV. VRB. SVAE. or OPTIMVS. PRINCEPS. or PRINCEPS. IVVENTVTIS.)]——IMP. C. FL. VAL. CON-STANTINVS. P. F. AVG. —— D. N. CONSTANTINVS. P. F. AVG.—— CONSTANTINVS. PP. (perpetuus) AVG. ——

IMP. CONSTANTINVS. PP. AVG.——CONSTA. (or CON-
STANTINVS.) MAX. (or MAXIMVS.) AVG. [On reverse,
sometimes, EXVPERATOR. OMNIVM. GENTIVM.] —— IMP. CON-
STANTINVS. MAX. AVG. [On reverse, sometimes, DEBELLATOR.
GENTIVM. BARBARARVM. or P. P.]——D. N. CONSTANTINVS.
MAX. AVG. [On reverse, sometimes, EQVIS. (sic) ROMANVS.]
—— CONSTANTINVS. MAX. P. F. AVG. —— IMP. CON-
STANTINVS. MAX. P. F. AVG.——IMP. CAES. FL. CON-
STANTINVS. MAX. P. F. AVG.——CONSTANTINVS. P. F.
IN. AVG.——IMP. CONSTANTINVS. P. F. INV. AVG.——
VIC. (or VICT. or VICTOR.) CONSTANTINVS. AVG. [On
reverse, sometimes, DEBELLATOR. GENT. (or GENTT. or GENTIVM.) BAR-
BAR. or BARBARR. or BARBARARVM. or VICTOR. GENTIVM. BARBARAR.)]
——DIVVS. CONSTANTINVS. —— DIVVS. CONSTANTI-
NVS. AVG.——DIVVS. CONSTANTINVS. P.—— DV. (or
DIV.) CONSTANTINVS. P. T. AVGG.

The last legend has been thus explained by Eckhel: DIVUS. venerabilis.
CONSTANTINVS. P. Trium. AVGGustorum. It is founded on an inscription given by Maffei. Mionnet thinks it probable that the letters DV.
are by mistake placed thus by the engraver, and that they probably signify
DIVVS.

Gold medallions, of large size	- - - - - - - - - -	R 5
,, ,, of small size	- - - - - - - - - - -	R 4
,, ,, of the usual size	- - - - - - - - - -	R 1
,, quinarii	- - - - - - - - - - - - - - -	R 2
Silver medallions, of large size	- - - - - - - - - -	R 6
,, small size	- - - - - - - - - - - - - -	R 4
,, of the usual size	- - - - - - - - - - - - -	R 3
,, quinarii	- - - - - - - - - - - - - - -	R 1
Brass medallions	- - - - - - - - - - - - - -	R 2
,, contorniati	- - - - - - - - - - - - - -	R 1
Second brass	- - - - - - - - - - - - - - - -	C
,, with the title of Son of the Augusti on reverse	- -	R 4
Third brass	- - - - - - - - - - - - - - - -	VC

GOLD AND SILVER MEDALLIONS.

1.

ADVENTVS. AVG. N. The emperor on horseback, preceded by
Victory. In the exergue, SMNΓ. - - - - - - - - AU

2.

ADVENTVS. AVGVSTI. N. The emperor, in a civil habit, on horseback. In the exergue, CONS. - - - - - - - - - AU

3.

CAESAR. within a garland. The obverse has the head of Constantine, with diadem: legend, AVGVSTVS. - - - - - - - - - AR

Valued by Mionnet at sixty francs. (It is of large size).

4.

CONSTANTINI. AVG. Two Victories standing, supporting a garland, within which is inscribed VOT. XXX. In the exergue, T. - AU

5.

Same legend. A similar type. (A large medallion with a loop.)—See *Steinbuchel's Notice of the Gold Medallions in the Cabinet of Vienna.*
AU

6.

CONSTANTINVS. AVG. (*or* CONSTANTINVS.) CAES. NN. Four standards. In the exergue, CONS. (*or* CONST.) - - - - AR

7.

EQVES. (*or* EQVIS.) *(sic)*. ROMANVS. The emperor, on horseback. In the exergue, SMN. - - - - - - - - - - - - - AU

8.

FELICITAS. PERPETVA. AVGG. ET. CAESS. NN. Two women, standing. In the exergue, SMN. - - - - - - - - - AU

9.

FELICITAS. PERPETVA. AVGEAT. REM. DD. NN. Two women, standing. - - - - - - - - - - - - - - - - AU

10.

FELICITAS. ROMANORVM. Three military figures, standing beneath an arch supported by two columns. In the exergue, SIRM. *or* SMH. - - - - - - - - - - - - - - AR

11.

GAVDIVM. AVGVSTI. NOSTRI. Two winged Genii, holding a garland of flowers. In the exergue, CONS. - - - - - - AU

12.

GLORIA. CONSTANTINI. AVG. The emperor bearing a trophy, and dragging a captive by the hair: another captive at his feet. In the exergue, SIS. The obverse has the head of Constantine, without legend. (*Plate F. No. 2*). - - - - - - - - AU

13.

GLORIA. CONSTANTINI. AVG. The emperor, standing between two captives, holding a trophy and a spear. In the exergue, SMN. *or* SMTS. - - - - - - - - - - - - - - - - - AU

14.

GLORIA. ROMANORVM. Rome seated, holding a globe surmounted by a Victory. In the exergue, CONS. - - - - - - - AU

15.

MARTI. PATRI. COSERVATORI. Mars, standing. - - - AR

16.

PIETAS. AVGVSTI. NOSTRI. The emperor, standing between Victory, who places a garland upon his head, and a soldier: a prostrate woman at his feet. In the exergue, SMN. (Large size). - AU

17.

PRINCIPI. IVVENTVTIS. Constantine, in a military habit, holding two standards. In the field, S. A. In the exergue, PTR. - AR

18.

SALVS. ET. SPES. REIPVBLICAE. The emperor, seated between two military figures, standing. In the exergue, CONS. (Very large size). - - - - - - - - - - - - - - - - - AU

Valued by Mionnet at 600 francs.

19.

SECVRITAS. AVGG. Security, standing. - - - - - - - AR

20.

SENATVS. The emperor, in the imperial habit, richly ornamented, holding in his right hand a globe, and in his left, a sceptre. In the exergue, SMTS. *(Vignette*, Vol. ii.) - - - - - - - AU

This very fine medallion is in the cabinet of *T. Thomas, Esq.* It is most probably unique.

21.

VICTORIBVS. AVGG. NN. VOTIS. X. ET. XX. Victory, in a quadriga, full-faced. In the exergue, PTR. - - - - - AU

Valued by Mionnet at 150 francs.

22.

VOTA. ORBIS. ET. VRBIS. SEN. ET. PR. A cippus, inscribed XX. XXX. AVG. and placed on a square pedestal. In the exergue, AQS. *(Mus. Vindob.)* - - - - - - - - - AR

In gold, Nos. 5, 9, 11, 14, 16, and 21, are the rarest, except No. 18, which is of a much larger size, and No. 20, probably unique; the next in rarity are Nos. 1, 8, 12, and 13. In silver, No. 3 is the rarest; the next in rarity is No. 17.

GOLD AND SILVER, OF THE USUAL SIZE.

1.

ADVENTVS. (or AVENTVS.) (sic) AVGVSTI. N.   The emperor
on horseback.   In the exergue, SMAN. or SMN. - - - - AU

2.

BEATA. TRANQVILLITAS. with VOTIS. XX. inscribed on an altar.
AR

3.

CONCORDIA. AVGG. N.   Concord, seated.   In the exergue, SMT.
AU & AR

4.

CONSERVATOR. KART. SVAE.   A statue within a temple.   In
the exergue, XCVI. - - - - - - - - - - - - - - AR

5.

CONSTANTINIANA. DAFNE.   Victory, seated: a captive and a
trophy.   In the field, B.   In the exergue, CONS*.   - AU & AR

6.

CONSTANTINVS. AVG.   Victory marching, with garland and palm
branch.   In the exergue, CONS. - - - - - - - - - - AU

7.

CONSTANTINVS. AVG.   Victory, marching.   In the exergue, R. or
SM. or SMTN. - - - - - - - - - - - - - AU & AR

The obverse of this and the four following types has the head of Constantine, without legend.

8.

Same legend.   Victory seated.   In the exergue, SIRM. or SMT.   AU

9.

Same legend.   Two laurel garlands.   In the exergue, N. - - - AU

10.

Same legend.   Victory marching, holding a trophy and a palm branch.
In the exergue, SMN. or SMTS. - - - - - - - AU & AR

11.

CONSTANTINVS. AVGVSTVS. Victory marching, holding a garland
and a palm branch.   In the exergue, C•A. or C•Γ.   - - - AR

12.

CONSTANTINVS. CAESAR.   The modius holding three ears of
corn.   The obverse has two laurel garlands: legend, CONSTAN-
TINVS. AVGVSTVS. - - - - - - - - - - - - - AR

13.

CONSVL. DD. NN. The emperor standing in the toga, holding a globe and the parazonium. In the field, ⇋. In the exergue, SM. TS. The obverse has the laureated head of Constantinus: legend, CONSTANTINVS. FIL. AVGG. - - - - - - - - - - - AU

14.

CONSVL. PP. PROCONSVL. The emperor in a military habit, standing, holding a globe and a sceptre. In the field, Q. II. In the exergue, VSMA⇋. - - - - - - - - - - - - - AU

15.

CRISPVS. CAESAR. Victory, marching. In the exergue, SIRM. The obverse has the diademed head of Constantinus, without legend.
AU

16.

DEBELLATORI. GENTIVM. BARBARARVM. Two military figures, standing, the hand of one resting on the head of a youth who stands by his side. In the exergue, GOTHIA. and TR. - AU

17.

DELMATIVS. NOB. CAESAR. Victory, marching. In the exergue, AQP. *or* TES. The obverse has the laureated or diademed head of Constantinus, without legend. - - - - - - - - - AR

Valued by Mionnet at sixty francs.

18.

FELICIA. TEMPORA. Four children, representing the four Seasons. In the exergue, ✳T✳ • - - - - - - - - - - - - - AU

19.

FELICITAS. PERPETVA. SAECVLI. Two figures, supporting a globe surmounted by a Victory; a captive kneeling at their feet. In the exergue, PARL. - - - - - - - - - - - - AU

20.

FELICITAS. REIPVBLICAE. The emperor, seated on an estrade or tribune, and six figures. In the exergue, PTR. - - - - AU

21.

Same legend. A similar type. (A *quinarius*). - - - - - - AU

22.

FELIX. PROCESSVS. COS. IIII. AVG. N. The emperor standing. In the exergue, SMT. - - - - - - - - - - - - - AU

23.

FELIX. PROCESSVS. COS. VI. AVG. N. The emperor standing in the toga, holding a globe and a staff. In the exergue, AQ. AU

24.

FIDES. EXERCITVS. A woman, seated between two standards. In
the exergue, SMT. - - - - - - - - - - - - - - AU

25.

GAVDIVM. POPVLI. ROMANI. A laurel garland; within which
is inscribed, SIC. XX. SIC. XXX. In the exergue, SIS*. AU

26.

GAVDIVM. REIPVBLICAE. A trophy and two captives. In the
exergue, PTR. - - - - - - - - - - - - - - - - - AU

27.

Same legend. Constantinus and his two sons, standing. In the exergue,
PTR. - AU

28.

GAVDIVM. ROMANORVM. A woman, seated at the foot of a
trophy. In the exergue, ALAM. *or* ALAMANNIA. *or* FRANC.
or FRANCIA. - - - - - - - - - - - - - - - AU

29.

GLORIA. EXERCITVS. GALL. The emperor, on horseback. In
the exergue, PTR. - - - - - - - - - - - - AU & AR

30.

GLORIA. ROMANORVM. The emperor, seated: Victory, standing.
In the exergue, SMT. - - - - - - - - - - - - - AU

31.

GLORIA. SAECVLI. VIRTVS. CAES. Two figures, standing.
AU & AR

32.

IOVI. CONSERVATORI. Jupiter, standing: at his feet, an eagle.
In the field, Є. In the exergue, SIS. - - - - - - - AR

33.

IOVI. CONSERVATORI. AVGG. A similar type. A star in the
field, and SMN. in the exergue. - - - - - - - - - AU

34.

LIBERATOR. ORBIS. The emperor on horseback, piercing a lion
with a javelin. In the exergue, AQP*. - - - - - - - AR
Valued by Mionnet at fifty francs.

35.

MARTI. PATRI., and NK. in monogram. Mars, standing. In the
exergue, SMN. - - - - - - - - - - - - - - - - AU

36.

PIETAS. AVGVSTI. NOSTRI. The emperor standing, Victory placing a garland on his head; a woman kneeling at his feet, and a military figure, standing. In the exergue, SMN. - - - - AU

37.

P. M. TRIB. P. COS. IIII. P. P. PROCOS. The emperor, seated. In the exergue, PTR. - - - - - - - - - - - - AU

38.

Same legend. The emperor, standing. In the exergue, PTR. - AU

39.

P. M. TRIB. P. COS. VI. P. P. PROCOS. The emperor, seated. AU

40.

PONT. MAX. TRIB. P. P. P. PROCOS. A similar type. In the exergue, TR. (A *quinarius*). - - - - - - - - - - - AU

41.

PRINCIPI. IVVENTVT. A military figure, holding a standard. In the exergue, PR. - - - - - - - - - - - - - - AU

42.

PRINCIPI. IVVENTVTIS. The emperor in a military habit, standing, holding a globe and a spear. In the exergue, PTR. *or* SMT. AU

43.

Same legend. A similar type. In the exergue, PTR. (A *quinarius*). AU

44.

Same legend. The emperor standing, or seated, between two standards. AU & AR

45.

Same legend. The emperor, standing between two ensigns. In the exergue, TR. - - - - - - - - - - - - - - - - AU

46.

PRINCIPIS. PROVIDENTISSIMI. An owl, standing on a cippus, inscribed SAPIENTIA. A helmet, spear, and buckler in the field. In the exergue, PARL. - - - - - - - - - - AU & AR

47.

RESTITVTORI. LIBERTATIS. Rome, seated; and the emperor, standing - - - - - - - - - - - - - - - - - - AU

48.

SALVS. ET. SPES. REIPVBLICAE. The emperor standing, holding a globe surmounted by a Victory: a woman and Victory, standing; the latter placing a garland on the head of the emperor. - - AU

49.

SALVS. REIP. DANVBIVS. A bridge, with three arches. - - AU

50.

SARMATIA. DEVICTA. Victory, and a captive. - - - - - AR

51.

SECVRITAS. REIPVBLICAE. Security, leaning on a column. In
the exergue, TR. *or* PTR. - - - - - - - - - - - - AU

52.

Same legend. A similar type. In the exergue, TR. (A *quinarius*). AU

53.

SIC. X. SIC. XX. within a quadruple garland: above, an eagle.
In the exergue, SMHB. - - - - - - - - - - - - - AU

54.

S. P. Q. R. OPTIMO. PRINCIPI. Three standards. In the exergue,
PTR. *or* SMT. - - - - - - - - - - - - - - - - AU

55.

SOLI. COMITI. AVG. N. The Sun and the emperor, standing :
a captive kneeling at the feet of the latter. In the exergue, SMT.
AU

56.

SOLI. INVICTO. COMITI. The Sun, placing a garland on the head
of the emperor. In the exergue, AQ. - - - - - AU & AR

57.

Same legend. The Sun, standing; a captive at his feet. In the exergue,
SIS. The obverse has the radiated head of Constantine: legend,
IMP. CONSTANTINVS. MAX. AVG. - - - - - - - AU

58.

VBIQVE. VICTOR. The emperor, standing between two captives.
In the exergue, PTR. - - - - - - - - - - - - AU

59.

Same legend. The emperor, marching. - - - - - - - - AU

60.

VBIQVE. VICTOR. *or* VBIQVE. VICTORES. The emperor, standing between two captives. In the exergue, PTR. *or* TR. - AU

61.

Same legend. A similar type. In the exergue, PTR. (A *quinarius*).
AU

62.

VICTOR. OMNIVM. GENTIVM. The emperor standing, in a military habit, holding the labarum and a buckler: two figures, kneeling. In the exergue, PTR. *or* SMTSA. *or* SMTSR. *or* TR.
AU

63.

VICTORE. AVG. N. VOTIS. Victory seated, holding a buckler, inscribed X. MVL. XX.: a trophy, and two captives. In the exergue, PT. - - - - - - - - - - - - - - - - AU

64.

VICTORIA. AVGVSTI. Victory, marching. In the exergue, SIS. (A *quinarius*). - - - - - - - - - - - - - - - AU

65.

VICTORIA. AVGVSTORVM. Victory, placing a garland on the head of the emperor. In the exergue, SM. TS. - - - - - AU

66.

VICTORIA. AVGG. NN. Victory standing, or marching. In the exergue, TRS. - - - - - - - - - - - - - - AR

67.

VICTORIA. CONSTANTINI. AVG. A Genius, presenting to Victory a buckler, inscribed VOT. XX. In the exergue, CONS. - - AU

68.

Same legend. Victory marching, with a trophy. In the field, VOT. XXX. In the exergue, SMAN. - - - - - - - - - AU

69.

Same legend. A similar type, with the monogram of Christ, and LXXII. in the field. In the exergue, SMAN. - - - - AU

70.

Same legend. Victory, bearing a trophy. In the exergue, MTS. *or* TSƏ. - - - - - - - - - - - - - - - - - - AU

71.

Same legend. Victory marching, holding a garland and a palm branch. In the exergue, POSΓ. - - - - - - - - - - - - AU

72.

Same legend. Victory, marching; a captive on the ground. In the exergue, PR. - - - - - - - - - - - - - - - AU

73.

Same legend. Victory, marching; two captives on the ground. In the exergue, SIS. *or* SM. TS. - - - - - - - - - - AU

74.

Same legend. Victory seated on arms, and a Genius supporting a shield, inscribed VOT. XXX. In the exergue, SMNC. *or* SMNM. The obverse has the diademed head of Constantine, without legend. AU

75.

VICTORIA. CONSTANTINI. AVG. A similar type. In the exergue, SMNC. - - - - - - - - - - - - - - - - AU

76.

Same legend. A similar type. In the exergue, CONS. *or* MTS. (A *quinarius*). - - - - - - - - - - - - - - - - AU

77.

Same legend. A similar type, but with VOT. XXXX. and P. CONS. in the exergue. *(A quinarius).—Mionnet*, from *Cat. d'Ennery.* AU

78.

Same legend. Victory, seated on arms, holding a buckler, incribed VOT. XXX. In the exergue, SIS. - - - - - - - - - *AU

79.

VICTORIA. CONSTANTIS. AVG. Victory seated on a coat of mail, holding a shield, inscribed VOT. V. MVLT. X.: before, a Genius. In the exergue, SIS ✱. - - - - - - - - - - AU

80.

VICTORIA. DD. NN. AVGG. Victory, standing. - - - - AR

81.

VICTORIAE. LAETAE. PRIN. PERP. Two Victories standing, supporting a shield resting on a cippus, and inscribed VOT. X. In the exergue, PR. - - - - - - - - - - - - - - AU

82.

VICTORIAE. PERPETVAE. Victory seated, holding   AU

83.

VICTORIB. AVGG. ET. CAESS. NN. Victory seated, holding a buckler, inscribed VOT. XX.: before, a trophy and two captives. In the exergue, SIRM. - - - - - - - - - - - - - AU

84.

VICTORIBVS. AVGG. NN. VOTIS. Victory standing, full-faced, holding a buckler, inscribed XX. In the exergue, PTR. - AU

85.

VICTORIOSO. SEMPER. The emperor standing, in the toga, between a woman with a turreted crown, and Victory, who places a garland on his head. In the exergue, SMT. The obverse has the full-faced bust of Constantine, with bare head and military habit; his right hand raised, and a globe in his left: legend, CONSTANTINVS. AVG. - - - - - - - - - - - - - - - AU

Valued by Mionnet at 200 francs.

86.

VIRTVS. AVGVSTI. A lion and a club. In the exergue, PARL. AU

87.

VIRTVS. CONSTANTINI. AVG. The emperor, in a military habit, standing; his right hand holding a trophy, and his left resting on his shield: two captives at his feet. In the exergue, SMTS. The obverse has the diademed head of Constantine, without legend. AU

88.

VIRTVS. EXERCITVS. GALL. Mars, marching; two captives on the ground. In the exergue, PTR. *or* SIS. *or* SM. TS. - - AU

89.

VIRTVS. MILITVM. The Praetorian camp. In the exergue, RQ. AR

90.

Same legend. A similar type. In the exergue, TR. *or* PTR. (A *quinarius*). - - - - - - - - - - - - - - - - - AR

91.

VOTA. PVBLICA. The emperor and two women, standing: PTR. AU

92.

VOTIS. V. MVLTIS. X. Victory seated, inscribing on a buckler, VICTORIA. AVG. In the exergue, PTR. - - - AU & AR

93.

Same legend. Victory standing, holding a buckler resting on a column, and inscribed VICTORIA. AVG. In the exergue, PTR. - AU

94.

VOT. XV. MVLT. XX. within a garland. In the exergue, ANT. *(Mionnet, from Cat. d'Ennery).* - - - - - - - - - AR

95.

VOT. XX. MVLT. XXX. within a garland. In the exergue, ANT. *(Mionnet, from Cat. d'Ennery).* - - - - - - - - - AR

In gold, No. 85 is by far the rarest. The next in rarity is No. 1; then Nos. 13, 18, 36, and 49; of the remaining Nos., 14, 15, 16, 19, 20, 21, 22, 35, 47, 55, 57, and 91, are the rarest. In silver, No. 17 is the rarest; the next in rarity is No. 34; then Nos. 4, 66, and 80.

[CONSTANTINUS MAGNUS, CRISPUS, AND CONSTANTINUS THE YOUNGER.]

CONSTANTINVS. MAX. AVG. The bare head of Constantinus.— *Rev.* CRISPVS. ET. CONSTANTINVS. CC. (*or* CRISPVS. ET. CONSTANTINVS. IVN. NOB. CAES.) The bare heads of Crispus and Constantinus, junior, face to face. In the exergue, SIRM.

The gold is valued by Mionnet at 120 francs; the silver at twenty-four francs.

BRASS MEDALLIONS.

1.

DEBELLATORI. GENT. BARBARR.   The emperor on horseback, piercing an enemy with a spear, and trampling down another figure.

2.

Same legend.   The emperor on horseback, bearing down an enemy.

3.

EXVPERATOR. OMNIVM. GENTIVM.   The emperor seated on a coat of mail, between two captives seated on the ground.

4.

GLORIA. SAECVLI. VIRTVS. CAESS.   The emperor, seated on a coat of mail : before him, a man standing, holding a trophy and a globe surmounted by a phœnix, which he presents to Constantine ; a panther at his feet.   In the exergue, PR.

5.

GLORIA. SAECVLI. VIRTVS. CAESARIS. (or VIRTVS. CAESA-RIS. GLORIA. SAECVLI.)   A similar type.

6.

IN HOC. SIN. (sic) VIC.   The monogram of Christ, surmounted by a star.   In the field, S.C.   (Mus. Pisanum).

7.

MONETA. AVGG. (or AVGVSTORVM.)   The three Monetæ, standing.

8.

P. *(sic)*. VICTORIAE. AVGVSTI. A woman with turreted crown, seated; holding a palm branch and a cornucopia: behind, Victory placing a garland on her head.

Given by Mionnet, who describes it as " retouché."

9.

SALVS. REIP. A bridge with three arches: at one end, a captive kneeling; above, the emperor marching, preceded by Victory; below, a river-god, seated. In the exergue, DANVBIVS.

10,

SALVS. ET. SPES. REIPVBLICAE. The emperor seated, full faced, between his two sons, standing. In the exergue, PR.

11.

SECVRITAS. AVGVSTI. N. Security, leaning on a column; a captive on either side, seated on the ground.

12.

SECVRITAS PERPETVA. A similar type.

13.

SECVRITATI. PERPETVAE. A similar type.

14.

VICTOR. GENTIVM. BARBARR. The emperor on horseback, piercing an enemy with his spear, and trampling on another figure.

15.

VICTOR. GENTIVM. BARBARR. A similar type.

16.

VICTORIA. AVGVSTI. Victory seated on spoils, holding a buckler, inscribed VOT. XX. MVL. XXX.

17.

Same legend. A woman with turreted crown, seated; her foot placed on the prow of a vessel; Victory behind, placing a garland on her head.

18.

VICTORIA. GOTHICA. Rome, seated on arms; Victory, presenting to her a garland; a captive, on the ground.

19.

VICTORIAE. AVGVSTI. A woman with turreted crown, seated; behind, Victory, placing a garland on her head.

20.

VIRTVS. AVG. N. The emperor on horseback, bearing down two enemies; one of whom he has pierced with his spear.

. No. 9 is the rarest. The next in rarity are Nos..6 and 10: then Nos. 3 and 5. Nos. 1, 11, and 18, are much rarer than the remainder.

[CONSTANTINOPOLIS].

1.

FEL. TEMP. REPARATIO. A woman standing, in the stola, holding a branch in her right hand, and the labarum in her left: at her feet, the prow of a vessel. The obverse of this and the following coins has the helmeted bust of the city of Constantinople, personified; the hasta pura on her shoulder: legend, CONSTANTINOPOLIS.

2.

RESTITVTOR. REIP. The emperor, standing, raising up a woman with turreted crown, prostrate at his feet: on his left, a captive.

Valued by Mionnet at thirty francs.

3.

VICTORIA. AVG. A galley, with rowers: above, the emperor seated, surrounded by military standards; Victory standing on the prow.

4.

Same legend. Victory, with a turreted crown, seated; her left foot on the prow of a vessel, holding a laurel branch and a cornucopia.

5.

VICTORIA. AVGG. NN. Victory, winged, and with turreted crown, seated, holding a branch and a cornucopia.

6.

VICTORIA. AVGVSTI. Victory, seated, with a turreted crown, holding a branch and a cornucopia.

7.

VICTORIA. (or VICTORIAE.) AVGVSTI. A woman, with turreted crown, seated, holding a branch and a cornucopia: Victory, behind, placing a garland on her head.

No. 2 is the rarest. The next in rarity are Nos. 1 and 7.

[URBS ROMA].

1.

ANNONA. AVGVSTI. CERES. Ceres seated, holding a sceptre, (?) and extending her hand to Abundance, who stands before her. The obverse has the helmed head of Rome: legend, VRBS. ROMA. (These are *contorniati*).

Valued by Mionnet at thirty francs.

2.

SECVRITAS. ROMAE. Constantinus seated, full-faced, between two women and two children, standing.

Valued by Mionnet at thirty francs.

3.

VIRTVS. AVG. The emperor, standing between two captives.

4.

Without legend. Romulus and Remus, suckled by the wolf. In the field, two stars.

5.

Without legend. A similar type. (*Contorniati*).

The first two are the rarest, and No. 3 is the next in rarity; then No. 4.

SECOND BRASS, WITH RARE REVERSES.

1.

ADVENTVS. AVG. N. The emperor on horseback; a captive before, seated on the ground. A star in the field. In the exergue, PLN.

2.

CONCORDIA. FELIX. DD. NN. Two military figures, joining hands, each holding a spear. In the exergue, PLC.

3.

CONSERVATOR. AFRICAE. SVAE. A woman in the stola, standing, her head covered by the elephant's skin; holding a vexillum in her right hand, and the tooth of the elephant in her left: a lion and a bull at her feet. In the field, S. E. F. In the exergue, A. *or* Δ.

4.

CONSERVATORES. KART. SVAE. A statue, within a temple. In the exergue, PKΔ.

5.

CONSTANTINO. P. AVG. B. R. P. NAT. The emperor in a military habit standing, holding a globe and a spear. In the field of some, CI. H. S. In the exergue, PLC.

6.

GENIO. AVGVSTI. Genius standing, holding a patera and a cornucopia. In the field, a crescent, and A. *or* Δ. In the exergue, SIS.

7.

GENIO. CAESARIS. A similar type. In the field, K. A. P. In the exergue, ALE.

8.

GENIO. FIL. AVGG. A similar type. In the field, OE. In the
exergue, ... *(Mionnet, from Mus. Vindob.).*

9.

GENIO. IMPERATORIS. A similar type. In the field, a crescent,
and K. A. P. In the exergue, ALE.

10.

MARTI. PATR. SEMP. VICTORI. Mars, marching.

11.

PERPETVA. VIRTVS. A military figure, marching. In the
exergue, ST.

12.

PRINCIPI. IVVENTVTIS. B. R. P. NAT. The emperor, standing.

13.

SECVRIT. PERPET. DD. NN. Security, leaning on a column. In
the exergue, PLC.

14.

TEMPORVM. FELICITAS. Felicity, standing. In the exergue, PLC.

15.

VIRTVS. CONSTANTINI. CAES. The emperor on horseback,
trampling on two enemies. In the exergue, AQΓ.

16.

VIRTVS. PERPETVA. AVG. Hercules strangling the Nemæan lion;
his club on the ground. In the exergue, ST. *or* PT.

No. 8 is much the rarest. The next in rarity are Nos. 2, 10, 11, 12,
and 16. Then Nos. 1, 3, 5, and 15.

THIRD BRASS, WITH RARE REVERSES.

1.

BEATI. TRANQVILLITAS. An altar, inscribed VOTIS. XX. In
the exergue, P. LON.

This type is common, with other letters in the exergue.

2.

CONSTANTINIANA. DAFNE. A woman trampling on a captive,
and holding in each hand a palm-branch: on one side, a trophy.
In the field, A. *or* B. *or* Δ. *or* Є. *or* Z. *or* H. In the exergue,
CONS✳.

3.

CONSTANTINVS. AVG. SMANTS. Above, a laurel garland. The obverse has the laureated head of Constantine, without garland.

4.

FVNDAT. PACIS. An armed figure, bearing a trophy on his shoulder, and dragging a captive by the hair. In the exergue, RP. *or* RS. *or* RT.

5.

Same legend. A similar type; with RT. in the exergue. (Size of the quinarius).

6.

GENIO. CAESARIS. Genius, standing, holding a patera and a cornucopia. In the field, a star, and Δ. In the exergue, SMTS.

7.

GENIO. FEL. AVGG. A similar type; with O. G. in the field. In the exergue, ANT.

8.

GLORIA. PERPET. Two Victories, marching; between them, a standard. In the exergue, AV. *or* RP. *or* RS.

9.

GLORIA. ROMANORVM. Rome, seated, holding a Victory and a sceptre. In the field, A. *or* Δ. In the exergue, CONS.

10.

HERCVLI. VICTORI. Hercules, standing: the apples of the Hesperides in his right hand, and the lion's skin on his arm; his left hand resting on his club. In the exergue, MOSTS.

11.

LIBERTAS. PVBLICA. Victory, standing on a galley. In the field, B. In the exergue, CONS.

12.

MARTI. CONSERV. (*or* CONSERVATORI.) Mars, standing. In the exergue, PTR. *or* TT.

13.

PACI. PERPET. A woman, standing, holding an olive branch and a standard. In the field, XII. In the exergue, RP. *or* RQ.

14.

PACIS. FVND. Mars, with a trophy on his shoulder, dragging a captive by the hair. In the exergue, RP. (Size of the quinarius).

15.

PAX. PERPETVA. AVGG. NN. Peace, standing, holding an olive branch and a standard. In the exergue, R∗P.

16.

P. M. TR. P. COS. II. P. P. A woman, seated on a double cornucopia, holding a wand in her right hand. In the field, a star. In the exergue, PLN.

17.

PRINCIPI. IVVENTVTIS. The emperor, standing between two ensigns, holding a spear. In the exergue, TR.

18.

Same legend. The emperor standing, holding two ensigns. A star, *or* SR. in the field. In the exergue, PLN. *or* PTR.

19.

PROVIDENTIA. AVG. A globe, placed on an altar inscribed VOTIS. XXX. In the exergue, P. LON.

This type is common, with other letters in the exergue.

20.

PLVRA. NATAL. FEL. within a garland.

21.

RECVPERATOR. VRBIS. SVAE. The emperor, seated: a soldier presenting to him a figure of Victory. In the exergue, SARI. (*Mionnet—Cat. d'Ennery*).

22.

ROMAE. AETERNAE. Rome, seated on a buckler, inscribing $\frac{X}{V}$ on a shield, which she rests on her knees. In the exergue, PCRCS. (*sic*). *or* RP. *or* RS. In the field of some, P. R.

23.

ROMAE. RESTITVAE. Rome, seated, holding a globe. (*Mionnet*, from *Mus. Vindob.*).

24.

SAEC. VOTA. MVLT. DD. NN. within a garland. (Size of the quinarius).

25.

SAPIENTIA. PRINCIPIS. An owl, standing on a cippus: a helmet, buckler, and spear. In the exergue, RP. *or* RS. *or* RTP. *or* RTS. (Size of the quinarius).

26.

SAPIENTIAE. PRINCIPIS. A similar type. (Size of the quinarius).

27.

SARMATIA. DEVICTA. Victory, marching : a captive on the ground. In the exergue, P. LON.

This type is common, with other letters in the exergue.

28.

SECVRITAS. AVGG. Security, leaning on a column. In the field, a star. In the exergue, PLN.

29.

SOLI. INVICTO. COMITI. Radiated head of the Sun.

30.

Same legend. The Sun, standing; his right hand raised, his left holding a globe : a captive on the ground. In the exergue, ⌒S.

There are varieties of this type.

31.

SPES. PVBLICA. The labarum, surmounted by the monogram of Christ, placed upon a serpent. In the exergue, CONS. *(Mionnet).*

32.

SPES. REIPVBL. The emperor on horseback, trampling down a captive. In the exergue, PLN.

33.

TRIB. P. CONS. IIII. P. P. . . . The emperor seated, holding a globe and a sceptre. In the exergue, TARL. *(Mionnet—Mus. Vindob.)*

34.

VIRT. EXERCIT. A figure, holding a globe in the left hand, viewing the plan of a camp.

35.

VIRT. EXERCIT. GALL. A military figure, standing. In the field, XVI. In the exergue, RS.

36.

VIRTVS. AVGVSTI. A military figure, standing. In the exergue, PTR.

37.

VOTA. PVBLICA. Isis-Pharia, standing on a galley and holding the sail. (Size of the quinarius).

38.

VOT. X. MVLT. XX. within a garland. (Size of the quinarius).

39.

VOTIS. X. within a garland. (Size of the quinarius).

40.

V. N. MR. Constantinus standing, in the toga. In the exergue, various
    letters. The obverse has the veiled head of Constantinus: legend,
    D. N. CONSTANTINVS. P. F. AVGG. (*sic*). (Size of the
    quinarius).

No. 31 is much the rarest type: the next in rarity is No. 20; then
Nos. 16, 35, and 37. Nos. 6, 7, 10, 14, 25, 26, and 34, are the rarest
of the remaining numbers.

[CONSTANTINUS, AND LICINIUS THE ELDER].

IMP. CONSTANTINVS. P. F. AVG. The bare head of Constantinus.—
    Rev. IMP. LICINIVS. AVG. Bare head of Licinius. (*Cat.
    d'Ennery*).

[POPULUS ROMANUS.]
1.

POP. ROMANVS. A youthful laureated bust, with a cornucopia on
    the shoulder.—*Rev.* CONS. A. (*or* CONS. B. *or* CONS. Γ. *or* CONS.
    Ε. *or* various other letters). A star: the whole within a garland.

2.

POP. ROMANVS. A similar head.—*Rev.* CONS. C. (*or* CONS. Ε. *or*
    various other letters). A bridge, with a tower at each end, resting
    on boats.

No. 2 is the scarcest. They are both of the size of the quinarius.

FAUSTA.

[Flavia Maxima Fausta, the daughter of Maximianus Hercules and
    Eutropia, sister of Maxentius, and wife of Constantine the Great, was
    born at Rome, in the year ——, and married to the emperor in 1060
    (A. D. 307). Fausta was suffocated in a warm bath, by order of her
    husband (he having previously put to death his son Crispus, whom
    the empress had falsely accused of a design upon her chastity), in the
    year of Rome 1079 (A. D. 326)].

STYLE :——FL. (*or* FLAV.) MAX. FAVSTA.——FL. (*or* FLAV. *or*
    FLAVIA.) MAX. (*or* MAXIMA.) FAVSTA. AVG. (*or* AV-
    GVSTA.).

Gold medallion (if authentic) - - - - - - - - - - - - *unique*
    „ of the usual size - - - - - - - - - - - - - - - R 8

Fine silver - - - - - - - - - - - - - - - - - - R 4
Brass medallions - - - - - - - - - - - - - - - R 6
Third brass - - - - - - - - - - - - - - - - - - C

GOLD MEDALLION.

PIETAS. AVGVSTA. The empress, seated between two women, holding a child in her arms; the one on the right holds a long caduceus: below, two Genii, holding a garland. In the exergue, PTR. (*Morell. Specim.* p. 53).

GOLD AND SILVER, OF THE USUAL SIZE.

1.

SALVS. REIPVBLICAE. A veiled woman standing, suckling two children. In the exergue, B. SIS. *or* PⱯT. - - - AU & AR

2.

SPES. REIPVBLICAE. A similar type. In the exergue, SIRM. AU & AR

Mionnet values the gold at 500 francs; and the silver at fifty francs.

BRASS MEDALLION.

FLAV. MAX. FAVSTA. AVG. The head of Fausta.—*Rev.* PIETAS. AVGVSTE. *(sic).* A woman standing, holding a child on her left arm : another child standing by her side.

Valued by Mionnet at seventy-two francs.

CRISPUS.

[Flavius Julius Crispus, the son of Constantinus Magnus, by Minervina a concubine, was born in the East about the year of Rome 1053 (A. D. 300). The title of Caesar was conferred upon him and Licinius by Constantinus, at the same time that the younger Constantinus and the younger Licinius were raised to that dignity, 1070 (A.D. 317). Crispus was put to death by order of Constantinus, on a false accusation of having attempted the chastity of his mother-in-law Fausta, in the year of Rome 1079 (A.D. 326)].

STYLE:——CRISPVS. CAESAR.——IVL. CRISPVS. CAESAR.—— CRISPVS. N. (*or* NOB. *or* NOBIL. *or* NOBILISS. *or* NOBILIS-SIMVS. C. *or* CAE. *or* CAES. *or* CAESAR.) [On reverse, sometimes, PRINCEPS. IVVENT. (*or* IVVENTVTIS.)]——IVL. CRISPVS. NOB. (*or* NOBILISS.) C. (*or* CAE. *or* CAES.) [On reverse, sometimes, as on the preceding.]——FL. IVL. CRISPVS. NOB. C. (*or* CAES.) [On reverse, sometimes, PRINCEPS. IVVENTVTIS. (*or* VBIQVE. VICTORES. *or* VICTOR. OMNIVM. GEN.)]——D. N. CRISPVS. NOB. (*or* NOBILISS.) CAES. [On reverse, sometimes, PRIN-CEPS. IVVENTVTIS.]——D. N. FL. CRISPVS. NOB. CAES.—— D. N. FL. IVL. CRISPVS. NOB. CAES.

CRISPUS AND CONSTANTINUS THE YOUNGER : —— CRISPVS. ET. CON-STANTINVS. CC.——CRISPVS. ET. CONSTANTINVS. NOB. (*or* NOBB.) CAES. (*or* CAESS.)

Gold -	R 6
„ quinarii - - - - - - - - - - - - - - - -	R 8
Fine silver (very doubtful if any).	
Brass medallions - - - - - - - - - - - - - - -	R 4
Third brass - - - - - - - - - - - - - - - - -	VC
„ with Consulate - - - - - - - - - - - - -	R 1

GOLD.

1.

CONCORDIA. AVGG. NN. Concord seated, holding a caduceus and a cornucopia. In the exergue, SMNK. *or* SMNM. *or* SMNP. *or* SMKϵ.

2.

CRISPVS. NOB. CAES. in the middle of the field : above, a laurel garland ; below, SM.

3.

GAVDIVM. ROMANORVM. A captive, seated before a trophy. In the exergue, ALAMANNIA.

4.

Same legend. A similar type. In the exergue, FRANCIA. (A *quinarius*).

"Ce quinaire," says Mionnet, "paroit moulé sur le petit bronze."

5.

GLORIA. ROMANORVM. Rome, seated. In the exergue, CONS.

6.

PRINCIPI. IVVENTVTIS. Crispus standing, with the paludamentum, holding a spear and a buckler. In the exergue, SMT.

7.

PRINCIPI. IVVENTVTIS.   Crispus standing, in a military habit, holding a spear and a standard.   In the field, two other standards. In the exergue, SIRM.

8.

Same legend.   The prince, 'in a military habit, standing to the right, between two captives seated on the ground: in his right hand, a javelin, held transversely; in his left, a globe.   In the exergue, AQ.   The obverse has the laureated bust of Crispus to the left, with the shoulders bare, holding a javelin and a buckler : legend, FL. IVL. CRISPVS. NOB. C.   *(Plate xi, No. 9).*—Cabinet of *T. Thomas, Esq.*

9.

VBIQVE. VICTORES.   The prince, standing between two captives, holding a spear and a globe.   In the exergue, TR.   *(Banduri).*

10.

VICTOR. OMNIVM. GEN. *(retrograde).*   Mars marching, with spear and trophy : two captives on the ground.   In the exergue, PTR. *(Khell).*

No. 8 is the rarest; the next in rarity is No. 9; then Nos. 3, 6, 7.

BRASS MEDALLIONS.

1.

FELICIT. SAECVL. . . . . . . A figure standing, holding a sceptre and a branch.   In the exergue, PR.   *(Mionnet).*

2.

IVVENTVS.   The prince standing; his right hand on a trophy, his left holding a spear.   *(Banduri).*

3.

MONETA. CAESARVM.   The three Monetæ, standing.

4.

MONETA. VRBIS. VESTRAE.   A similar type.

5.

PRINCIPI. IVVENTVTIS.   The prince standing, in the paludamentum, holding an ensign in his right hand : two captives seated on the ground.

6.

SALVS. ET. SPES. XRPVBLICAE. *(sic).*   The effigy of Christ, fullfaced, seated; the right hand raised, the left holding a cross : on each side, a soldier, standing.   In the exergue, S. P.   *(Mionnet, from the Mus. Sanclementiani,* p. 182).

7.

VICTORIAE. BEATISSIMORVM. CAESS.   Victory seated, holding
a buckler, inscribed VOT. X.

No. 6 is much the rarest; the next in rarity are Nos. 1, 2, 5, and 7.

THIRD BRASS, WITH RARE REVERSES.

I.

ALAMANNIA. DEVICTA.   Victory, holding a trophy and a palm
branch.

2.

BEATA. TRANQVILLITAS.   A globe charged with three stars,
and placed on a cippus, inscribed VOTIS. XX.   In the field, C. R.
In the exergue, PLC.   The obverse has the bust of Crispus, holding
a Victory on a globe: legend, CRISPVS. N. C. COS. II.

3.

IOVI. CONSERVATORI. CAESS.   Jupiter, standing.   In the field,
a garland and A. *or* Γ. *or* Є.   In the exergue, SMK.

4.

SAECVLI. FELICITAS.   A cippus: above, a buckler, inscribed AVG.
In the field, R. *or* PR.   In the exergue, PT. *or* RP. *or* RQ.

5.

VOTA. PVBLICA.   Isis standing, holding the sistrum in her right
hand, and a fan in her left.

6.

Same legend.   Anubis standing, holding an ear of corn in his right
hand, and in his left the chlamys and a caduceus.

7.

Same legend.   Isis standing on a galley.   (Size of the quinarius).

8.

VOT. XV. FEL. XX. R. C. within a laurel garland.

No. 2 is the rarest: the next in rarity are Nos. 1, 5, 6, 7, 8.   Of the
other third brass of Crispus, those with P. LON. in the exergue, are the
least common.   They are interesting from the supposition that they, like
the other coins of this family, with the same letters, were struck in
London.

HELENA.

[This princess is not alluded to in history, but from the mention of her
name together with that of Crispus, in the Theodosian code, she is
supposed to have been the wife of that prince, although it does not

clearly state that she was. The supposition is strengthened by the style of the coin described below, which bears a strong resemblance to that of Fausta, the supposed wife of Constantius the Second].

Third brass - - - - - - - - - - - - - - - - - - R 6

HELENA. N. F. Head of Helena.—*Rev.* Without legend. A large star within a garland. *(Plate xi, No. 10).*

DELMATIUS.

[Flavius Julius Delmatius (or Dalmatius), the nephew of Constantinus and grandson of Constantius Chlorus, was born at Toulouse, or according to others, at Narbonne. He was created Caesar by Constantine in the year of Rome 1088 (A. D. 335), and obtained the government of Thrace, Macedonia, and Achaia : upon the death of that emperor in 1090, he was assassinated by the soldiers, who would acknowledge no rulers but the sons of Constantinus].

STYLE:——DELMATIVS. CAESAR.——DELMATIVS. NOB. CAE. (*or* CAESAR.) —— FL. DELMATIVS. (*or* DALMATIVS.) NOB. C. (*or* CAES.) [On reverse, sometimes, PRINCEPS. IVVEN-TVTIS.]——FL. IVL. DALMATIVS. NOB. C.

Gold - R 8
Fine silver - - - - - - - - - - - - - - - - - R 6
Third brass - - - - - - - - - - - - - - - - - R 1

GOLD AND SILVER.

1.

DELMATIVS. CAESAR. Victory marching, with garland and palm branch. In the exergue, CONS. The obverse has the diademed head of Delmatius : legend, FL. DELMATIVS. NOB. CAES. AU

2.

DELMATIVS. NOB. CAE. *or* CAESAR. A similar type. In the exergue, AQP. *or* TES. The obverse has the laureated head of Constantine the Great, without legend. - - - - - AU & AR

3.

PRINCIPI. IVVENTVTIS. Delmatius standing, holding a military ensign and a spear : behind, two ensigns. In the exergue, TSE.
AU

In gold, No. 2 is much the rarest.

THIRD BRASS.

1.

GLORIA. EXERCITVS.   Two military figures standing, with spears and bucklers: between them a standard, bearing sometimes the monogram of Christ.   In the exergue, various letters.

2.

Same legend.   A similar type, but with two standards in the middle.   In the exergue, CONST.

No. 2 is much the rarest.

HANNIBALLIANUS.

[Flavius Claudius Hanniballianus, the brother of Delmatius, was born at Toulouse, in the year of Rome ——.   This prince received from his uncle Constantine, the title of King, and the government of Pontus Cappadocia and Armenia were assigned to him, in the year of Rome 1088 (A. D. 335).   Hanniballianus perished, with his brother Delmatius, in 1090 (A. D. 337)].

Gold (no authentic coins).
Third brass - - - - - - - - - - - - - - - - - - - R 6

THIRD BRASS.

1.

SECVRITAS. PVBLICA.   A river-god, seated, his right hand holding a wand: an urn, from which water escapes, by his side. In the exergue, CONS. *or* CONSP. *or* CONSS. *or* SIS.

2.

SECVRITAS. REIPVBLICAE.   A similar type.

No. 2 is much the rarest.

COSTANTINUS II.

[Flavius Claudius Julius Constantinus, the son of Constantine the Great and his wife Fausta, was born at Arles, in the year of Rome 1069 (A. D. 316), and declared Cæsar in the following year by his father and Licinius, at which time Crispus and the younger Licinius were raised to the same dignity.   When Constantine the Great made the division of the empire, in 1088 (A. D. 335), this prince received for his share the provinces of Gaul, Spain, and Britain; and, upon the death of his father, in 1090 (A. D. 337), the senate and the army proclaimed him emperor. The second Constantine, however, enjoyed his power but a short period. A rupture between him and his brother Constans, led to a war; and Constantine was defeated and killed near Aquileia, in the year of Rome 1093 (A. D. 340)].

STYLE:——CONSTANTINVS. CAES. (or CAESAR.)——CONSTAN-
TINVS. IVNIOR. C. (or CAES.)——CONSTANTINVS. NOB.
C. (or CAES.)——FL. CL. CONSTANTINVS. N. C.——FL.
IVL. CONSTANTINVS. NOB. C. —— CONSTANTINVS.
IVN. (or IVNIOR.) N. (or NO. or NOB.) C. (or CAES. or
CAESAR.) [On reverse, sometimes, PRINCEPS. IVVENTVTIS. or
VBIQVE. VICTORES.]——FL. CONSTANTINVS. IVN. N. C.——
FL. IVL. CONSTANTINVS. IVN. NOB. C. —— FL. CL.
CONSTANTINVS. IVN. (or IVNIOR.) N. (or NOBILISS.)
C. (or CAES.) [On reverse, as in the preceding.]——D. N. CON-
STANTINVS. IVN. (or IVNIOR.) N. (or NOB.) C. (or CAES.)
[On reverse, sometimes, PRINCEPS. IVVENTVTIS.]——D. N. FL. CL.
CONSTANTINVS. NOB. C.——FL. CL. CONSTANTINVS.
AVG. [On reverse, VICTOR. OMNIVM. GENTIVM.] —— FL. CL.
CONSTANTINVS. P. (or PIVS.) F. (or FELIX.) AVG.

The coins bearing the last title are not easily to be distinguished from those of the elder Constantine; all those, however, which have the name of *Claudius*, are assigned to the son, because it is never found on the coins of Constantine the Great.

Gold medallions, large size - - - - - - - - - - - -	R 5
,, small size - - - - - - - - - - - -	R 4
,, of the usual size - - - - - - - - - - - - - -	R 4
,, quinarii - - - - - - - - - - - - - - - -	R 6
Silver medallions - - - - - - - - - - - - - -	R 6
,, of the usual size - - - - - - - - - - - - - -	R 2
Brass medallions - - - - - - - - - - - - - - -	R 4
Third brass - - - - - - - - - - - - - - - - - -	VC

GOLD AND SILVER MEDALLIONS.

1.

FELICITAS. PERPETVA. AVG. ET. CAESS. NN. The emperor seated, between two soldiers standing. In the exergue, CONS. or SMN. (Large size).   - - - - - - - - - - - AU
Valued by Mionnet at 500 francs.

2.

PRINCIPI. IVVENTVTIS. The emperor standing, holding the labarum and a spear: on one side, two standards. In the exergue, CONS. - - - - - - - - - - - - - - - - - - - AU

Valued by Mionnet at 300 francs.

3.

FL. CL. CONSTANTINVS. IVN. NOB. CAES. Laureated bust of Constantinus the younger, to the right.—*Rev.* PRINCIPIA. IV- VENTVTIS. The prince standing, in a military habit, bare headed: in his right hand a globe, in his left a javelin reversed; his right foot on a captive in a suppliant attitude. In the exergue, SARMATIA. and TR. *(Plate F, No. 3)*.

This fine medallion is in the cabinet of *T. Thomas, Esq.*

4.

SALVS. ET. SPES. REIPVBLICAE. The emperor, seated between two soldiers standing. (Large size). - - - - - - - - - AU

Valued by Mionnet at 500 francs.

5.

VIRTVS. CONSTANTINI. CAES. Constantine, standing between two captives, holding a trophy and a spear. In the exergue, SMNT. *or* SMNP. - - - - - - - - - - - - - - - - - - AU

Valued by Mionnet at 100 francs.

6.

D. N. CONSTANTINVS. IVN. NOB. CAES. Laureated head of Constantinus the younger, to the right.—*Rev.* VOTIS. X. CAESS. NN. MNT. in four lines, in the centre of a quadruple garland, ornamented with a medallion bearing the figure of an eagle. *(Plate F No. iv)*.

In the cabinet of *T. Thomas, Esq.*

7.

XX. within a laurel garland. In the exergue, AQ. *or* CONST. - AR

Valued by Mionnet at sixty francs.

GOLD AND SILVER, OF THE USUAL SIZE.

1.

CLARITAS. REIPVBLICAE. The Sun standing, wearing the pallium; his right hand raised, and a globe in his left. In the exergue, SMTS. - - - - - - - - - - - - - - - - - - - AU

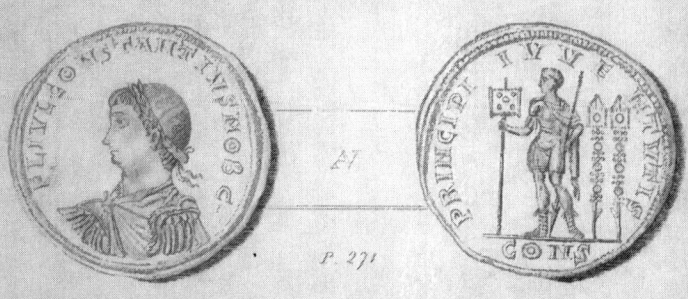

P. 271

P. 271

CONSTANTIUS THE SECOND.

Engraved by Henry A. 1839

London Published by Effingham Wilson 1st Jany 1834

2.

CONSTANTINVS. AVG. Victory seated, holding a Victory on her right hand, and a cornucopia on her left arm. In the exergue, SIRM. The obverse has the diademed head of Constantine the younger, without legend. - - - - - - - - - - AU

3.

CONSTANTINVS. CAES. (or CAESAR.) Three palm branches: a star above. In the exergue, R. - - - - - - - - - - AR

4.

CONSTANTINVS. CAESAR. (or IVN. NOB. CAES.) Victory marching, with garland and palm branch. In the exergue, SMT. or CONS. On some, the obverse has no legend. - - - - AU

5.

FELIX. PROCESSVS. COS. II. AVG. The emperor in the toga, standing, holding a globe and a sceptre. In the exergue, SIRM. AU

6.

GAVDIVM. ROMANORVM. A woman, seated by a trophy. In the exergue, SARMATIA. - - - - - - - - - - - AU & AR

7.

PRINCIPI. IVVENTVTIS. The emperor in a military habit, holding a globe, and a spear transversely. In the exergue, N. (A *quinarius*). AU

8.

Same legend. A similar type. In the exergue, PTR. - - - - AU

9.

Same legend. The emperor standing, in a military habit, holding the labarum and a spear. In the field, two standards. In the exergue, SIRM. or TR. - - - - - - - - - - - - - - - - AU

10.

Same legend. A similar type. In the field, a standard. In the exergue, SMNK. - - - - - - - - - - - - - - AU

11.

SECVRITAS. REIPVBLICAE. Security, leaning on a column. In the exergue, PTR. - - - - - - - - - - - - - - - AU

12.

SIS., only, in the field of the coin. - - - - - - - - - - AU

13.

VBIQVE. VICTORES. The emperor standing, in a military habit, holding a globe and a spear: two captives at his feet. In the exergue, TR. (A *quinarius*). - - - - - - - - - - AU

14.

VICTORIA. CAESAR. NN.   Victory, marching, with garland and palm branch. In the exergue, SMAN. - - - - - - - AU

15.

VICTORIA. CONSTANTINI. CAES.   Victory, seated on a coat of mail, holding a buckler inscribed VOT. X. In the exergue, SIRM.
                                         AU

16.

Same legend.   Victory seated, inscribing on a buckler held by a Genius, VOT. XX. In the exergue, CONS. (A *quinarius*). - - - - AU

17.

Same legend.   Victory seated on a coat of mail, holding a buckler, inscribed VOT. X. In the exergue, SIRM. *(Mus. Vindob.)*.   AU

In gold, Nos. 14 and 15 are the rarest types: the next in rarity is No. 4; then Nos. 5 and 10. Nos. 1, 6, 8, 9, 11, and 17, are rarer than the remaining numbers. The two types in silver are equally rare, and are valued by Mionnet at thirty francs each.

BRASS MEDALLIONS.

1.

MONETAE. VRBIS. VESTRAE.   The three Monetæ, standing.

2.

PRINCIPI. IVVENTVTIS.   The emperor in the paludamentum, standing, holding a spear: two captives at his feet.

3.

SACRA. MONETA. VRBIS.   The three Monetæ, standing.

4.

VICTORIA. AVG.   A galley, with five rowers; above, the emperor, seated between two standards: Victory, standing on the prow.

5.

VICTORIA. BEATISSIMORVM. CAESS.   Victory, seated on a coat of mail, holding a buckler inscribed VOT. X.

6.

VICTORIA. CONSTANTINI. AVG.   A similar type.

7.

VIRTVS. AVGG.   A figure, dragging a captive, and bearing a trophy.

8.

VIRTVS. CAESS.   The emperor on horseback, riding over two enemies.

9.

Same legend.   The emperor, standing by a trophy: two captives at his feet.

10.

VIRTVS. CAESS. The emperor standing, in a military habit; his right
hand holding a spear, his left on a trophy: a captive at his feet.

11.

VOT. CAESS. Two Victories standing, supporting a buckler inscribed
VOT. XV.

Nos. 2 and 4 are the rarest types. Nos. 5, 6, and 10 are the
least rare.

THIRD BRASS, WITH RARE REVERSES.

1.

CAESARVM. NOSTRORVM. In the field of the coin, VOTIS. V.
In the exergue, PL. *or* QA.

2.

CONSTANTINVS. CAESAR. SMANTG. A star. The obverse has
the head of the younger Constantine, without legend.

3.

CONSTANTINVS. IVN. NOB. C. SMRT. A garland. The obverse
has the head of the emperor, without legend.

4.

FELICITAS. ROMANORVM. Three military figures standing within
a temple. In the exergue, THES.

"Je crois," says Mionnet, "que cette medaille a été moulée sur l'or
ou sur l'argent."

5.

IOVI. CONSERVATORI. CAESS. Jupiter standing, holding a
Victory and the hasta: a captive at his feet. In the field, B.
In the exergue, AHANT.

6.

Same legend. Jupiter standing, holding a globe and the hasta. In the
field, a crescent, and A. In the exergue, SMAL.

7.

VICTORIA. CAESS. Victory, marching. (Size of the quinarius).

8.

VIRT. EXERC. The Sun, overlooking the plan of a camp. In the
exergue, TSB.

9.

VOTA. PVBLICA. The emperor in a military habit, holding a globe
and a spear. (Size of the quinarius).

10.

VOTA. PVBLICA. Isis, standing.

11.

Same legend. Anubis, standing. (Size of the quinarius).

12.

VOTA. VICENNALIOR. *(sic)*. The emperor in the toga, seated; holding in his right hand a human head, and in his left a wand. (Size of the quinarius).

13.

VOT. X. ET. XV. F. RT. within a laurel garland.

Nos. 2, 9, and 12, are much the rarest; and Nos. 1, 3, and 4, are the least rare.

CONSTANS.

[Flavius Julius Constans, the son of Constantine the Great and Fausta, was born about the year of Rome 1073 (A. D. 320). In 1086 (A. D. 333) he was invested with the title of Caesar, and two years afterwards obtained the government of Illyria, Italy, and Africa. Upon the death of his father, he participated in the division of the empire with his brothers, 1090 (A.D. 337). The death of the second Constantine, near Aquileia, in 1093 (A. D. 340), left him master of the East. Constans was assassinated at Helena, at the foot of the Pyrenees, by the partisans of Magnentius, who had usurped the purple at Autun, in Gaul, in the year of Rome 1103 (A. D. 350)].

STYLE: ——FL. IVL. CONSTANS.——CONSTANS. CAESAR.—— FL. CONSTANS. CAES.——CONSTANS. N. (*or* NOB.) C. (*or* CAES. *or* CAESAR.)——FL. (*or* FLAVIVS.) CONSTANS. NOB. CAES. (*or* CAESAR.) [On reverse, sometimes, PRINCEPS. IVVENTVTIS.]——FL. I. (*or* IVL.) CONSTANS. NOB. C. (*or* CAE. *or* CAES.). [On reverse, sometimes, PRINCEPS. IVVENTVTIS.] ——D. N. CONSTANS. NOB. CAES.——CONSTANS. IVN. NOB. C.——FL. CONSTANS. BEA. C. (*or* CAES.) [On reverse, sometimes, PRINCEPS. IVVENTVTIS.] —— CONSTANS. AVG. (*or·* AVGVSTVS.)——FL. IVL. CONSTANS. AVG. [On reverse, sometimes, PRINCEPS. IVVENTVTIS.]——IMP. CONSTANS. AVG. ——D. N. CONSTANS. AVG. (*or* AVGVSTVS.)——D. N. FL. CONSTANS. AVG. [On reverse, sometimes, DEBELLATOR. GENTT. BARBARR. (*or* BARBARAR.) *or* VICTOR. OMNIVM. GENTIVM.]——D. N.

CONSTANS. P. AVG.——CONSTANS. P. F. AVG. [On
reverse, sometimes, VICTOR. GENTIVM. BARBARR. (*or* VICTOR. OMNIVM.
GENTIVM.)]——FL. CONSTANS. P. F. AVG.—— FL. IVL.
CONSTANS. P. (*or* PIVS.) F. (*or* FEL. *or* FELIX.) AVG.
[On reverse, sometimes, TRIVMFATOR. GENTIVM. BARBARARVM.]——
D. N. CONSTANS. P. F. AVG.——D. N. FL. CONSTANS. P.
F. AVG.——FL. IVL. CONSTANS. PERP. AVG.

Gold medallions, of large size - - - - - - - - - - - -	R 6
,, small size - - - - - - - - - - -	R 4
,, of the usual size - - - - - - - - - - - - - - -	C
,, quinarii - - - - - - - - - - - - - - - - - -	R 2
Silver medallions, of large size - - - - - - - - - - -	R 2
,, ,, small size - - - - - - - - - - - -	R 2
,, of the usual size - - - - - - - - - - - - - -	R 1
Brass medallions - - - - - - - - - - - - - - - -	R 1
Second and third brass - - - - - - - - - - - - - -	VC

GOLD AND SILVER MEDALLIONS.

1.

CONSTANS. P. F. AVG. Three standards. In the exergue, TES. AR

2.

FELICIA. DECENNALIA. Two Genii holding a garland; within
which is inscribed, VOTIS. X. MVLTIS. XX. In the exergue,
TES. - - - - - - - - - - - - - - - - - AU

Valued by Mionnet at 400 francs.

3.

FELICITAS. PERPETVA. Three figures seated, full faced: below,
VOT. V. In the exergue, SIS. and ☽. (Large size). - - AR

Valued by Mionnet at 150 francs.

4.

GAVDIVM. POPVLI. ROMANI. A garland, within which is
inscribed, SIC. V. SIC. X. In the exergue, SIS. *or* TES. (Large
size). - - - - - - - - - - - - - - - - - AR

5.

Same legend. A similar type. In the exergue, SIS. - - - - AR

6.

Same legend. A similar type, with TSE. in the exergue. - - - AU

7.

GAVDIVM. POPVLI. ROMANI. A garland, within which is inscribed SIC. X. SIC. XX. Two palm branches. In the exergue, SIS.
AR

8.

Same legend. Two captives, at the foot of the labarum, on which is inscribed, VOT. X. MVLT. XV. In the exergue, TR. - - AR

9.

Same legend. A similar type, with VOT. X. MVLT. XX. *(Mionnet)*.
AR

10.

GLORIA. REIPVBLICAE. Two figures, with the nimbus, seated on a tribune, and two others standing: the monogram of Christ in the field. In the exergue, *SIS* - - - - - - - - AU

11.

TRIVMFATOR. GENTIVM. BARBARARVM. The emperor standing, holding the labarum charged with the monogram of Christ, and a spear. In the exergue, SIS. (Large size). - - - - - AR

12.

Same legend. A similar type, but without the monogram of Christ. In the exergue, TES. - - - - - - - - - - - - - AR

13.

Same legend. A similar type, but of a much smaller size. - - AR

14.

Same legend. The emperor standing in a military habit, holding the labarum charged with the monogram of Christ; his right foot on the prow of a vessel: Victory behind, placing a garland on his head. In the exergue, TR. (Large size). - - - - - - - - AU

15.

VICTORIA. AVGVSTORVM. Victory marching, with garland and palm branch; another palm branch at her feet. In the exergue, SIS. - - - - - - - - - - - - - - - - - - - AR

16.

VICTORIAE. DD. NN. AVGG. Two Victories, supporting a garland; within which is inscribed, VOT. X. MVLT. XX. In the exergue, TR. - - - - - - - - - - - - - - - - - - AU

17.

Same legend. Victory, seated on a heap of arms, inscribing on a buckler, VOT. X. MVLT. XX. In the exergue, *AQ. *or* LXAQ.
AR

18.

VIRTVS. CONSTANTIS. AVG. The emperor in a military habit, standing, holding the labarum charged with the monogram of Christ, and a spear: a captive at his feet. In the exergue, SMAQ✳. - - - - - - - - - - - - - - - AU

19.

VIRTVS. DD. NN. AVGG. The emperor standing, holding the labarum, with monogram. In the exergue, TR. - - - - AR

20.

VIRTVS. EXERCITVM. *(sic)*. Four standards; the two middle ones charged with the letters alpha and omega : above, the monogram of Christ. In the exergue, P. *(Mionnet—Khell)*. - - - - AR

21.

Same legend. An armed figure standing, holding a trophy and a buckler: two captives on the ground. In the exergue, TES. AU

In gold, No. 14 is much the rarest; the next in rarity is No. 2; No. 10 is much rarer than the remainder. In silver, No. 3 is by far the rarest; the next in rarity are Nos. 4 and 20; then, Nos. 11 and 12 ; the least rare are, Nos. 1, 5, 8, 9, 13, 15, 17, and 19.

GOLD AND SILVER, OF THE USUAL SIZE.

1.

CONSTANS. AVG. within a laurel garland. In the exergue, ALЄ . AR

2.

Same legend. Three palm branches and a star. In the exergue, SIS. ☺. - - - - - - - - - - - - - - - - AR

3.

CONSTANS. CAESAR. Victory marching, with garland and palm branch. In the exergue, SMAN. The obverse has the diademed head of Constans, without legend. - - - - - - - - - AR

4.

CONSTANS. NOB. CAESAR. A similar type. In the exergue, CONS. *(Mionnet, Cat. d'Enn.)* - - - - - - - - - AU

5.

FELICITAS. PERPETVA. Victory marching, with a trophy and a garland. In the exergue, ✳AQ. - - - - - - - - - AR

6.

Same legend. The emperor seated on the tribune, with the nimbus around his head; his right hand raised: on front of the tribune is inscribed, VOT. V.: a youthful figure togated, seated on each side. In the exergue, SIS. *(Khell)*. - - - - - - - - - AU

7.

FEL. TEMP. REPARATIO. Victory standing, inscribing on a buckler, supported by a kneeling figure, VOT. XX. In the exergue, P. *or* R. - - - - - - - - - - - - - - - - - - AR

8.

GAVDIVM. POPVLI. ROMANI. A laurel garland, within which is inscribed, SIC. V. SIC. X. In the exergue, TSЄ. - - - - AR

9.

Same legend. A similar type, but with PARL. in the exergue. (A *quinarius*). - AU

10.

Same legend. A laurel garland, within which is inscribed, VOT. V. MVLT. X. In the exergue, TSЄ. - - - - - - - - - - AU

11.

Same legend. A laurel garland, within which is inscribed, SIC. X. SIC. XX. In the exergue, SIS. ◡. - - - - - - - - - - AR

12.

MT. ES. in the centre of the field, without type. The obverse has the radiated head of Constans. - - - - - - - - - - - - - - AU

13.

OB. VICTORIAM. TRIVMFALEM. Two Victories, supporting a buckler, inscribed VOT. X. MVLT. XV. In the exergue, SIS* *or* SMAQ. *or* TR. - - - - - - - - - - - - - - - - - AU

14.

PRINCIPI. IVVENTVTIS. The emperor standing, in a military habit, holding the labarum and a spear. In the field, two standards. In the exergue, SIS. *or* TR. - - - - - - - - - - - - - AU

15.

SECVRITAS. REIPVBLICAE. Security, leaning on a column. In the exergue, TR. - - - - - - - - - - - - - - - - - - AU

16.

SIS. in the centre of the field, without type. The obverse has the radiated head of Constans. - - - - - - - - - - - - - - AU

17.

SPES. REIPVBLICAE. The emperor in a military habit standing, holding the labarum charged with the monogram of Christ in his right hand, and a spear in his left: Victory standing behind, holding a palm branch, and placing a garland on his head. In the exergue, *SIS.* - AU

18.

TR. in the middle of the field, without type. The obverse has the radiated head of Constans. - - - - - - - - - - - - - - AU

19.

VICTORIA. AVGVSTORVM. Victory seated on arms, holding with a child, a buckler inscribed VOT. V. MVLT. X. In the exergue, S. M. AN. S. *(Khell)*. - - - - - - - - - - - - - - - AU

20.

Same legend. Victory marching, holding in her right hand a garland, within which is inscribed, XXV.; and a palm branch and a trophy in her left: a captive on the ground. In the exergue, S. M. N. C. *(Khell)*. - AU

21.

Same legend. Victory marching, with a garland and trophy. In the exergue, SIS. ⌣. - - - - - - - - - - - - - - - - - AR

22.

VICTORIA. CONSTANTIS. AVG. Victory standing, inscribing on a buckler, VOT. V. MVLT. X.: a captive seated on the ground. In the exergue, MHR. - - - - - - - - - - - - - - - - AU

23.

Same legend. Victory seated on arms, inscribing on a buckler, supported by a Genius, VOT. X. In the exergue, CONS. - - AU

24.

Same legend. A similar type, with VOT. XV. on the buckler. In the exergue, SMAQ. (A *quinarius*). - - - - - - - - - - - AU

25.

VICTORIA. DD. NN. AVGG. Victory, with garland and palm branch, dragging a captive. In the exergue, R. - - - - - AR

26.

Same legend. Victory marching, with trophy and palm branch. In the exergue, TES. - - - - - - - - - - - - - - - - - - - AU

27.

Same legend.. Victory marching, with garland and trophy. In the exergue, TES. (*or* TR.) - - - - - - - - - - - - - - - AR

28.

Same legend. Victory marching, with garland and palm branch. In the exergue, TR. (A *quinarius*). - - - - - - - - - - - AU

29.

VICTORIA. DDD. NNN. AVG.   Victory marching, with a buckler, inscribed VOT. V. MVLT. X.: a captive.   In the exergue, M. NR.   *(Khell).* - - - - - - - - - - - - - - - AU

30.

VICTORIAE. D. N. AVG.   Two Victories, supporting a buckler, inscribed VOT. X. MVLT. XV.   In the exergue, TR. - - AR

31.

VICTORIAE. DD. NN. AVGG.   Victory, seated on arms, inscribing on a buckler, supported by a winged Genius, VOT. X. MVLT. XX.   In the exergue, TES. - - - - - - - - - - - AU

32.

Same legend.   Victory seated on arms, holding a buckler, supported by a winged Genius, inscribed VOT. X. MVLT. XX.   In the exergue, TES.   (A *quinarius*).—*Khell.* - - - - - - - - AU

33.

VICTOR. OMNIVM. GENTIVM.   The emperor standing, in a military habit, his right hand holding the labarum, his left resting on a shield: three figures on the ground.   In the exergue, TR. AU

34.

VIRTVS. EXERCITVM. *(sic).*   The emperor standing, in a military habit, holding a trophy in his right hand, his left resting on a buckler: two captives at his feet.   In the exergue, TES. - - AU

35.

VIRTVS. EXERCITVS. GALL.   Mars marching, with spear and buckler: two captives on the ground.   In the exergue, TR. - AU

In gold, No. 6 is by far the rarest: the next in rarity are Nos. 15, 19, 20, 29, and 33; then Nos. 8, 10, 14, 17, 22, 23, 31, 34, and 35.   In silver, No. 1 is the rarest: the next in rarity are Nos. 2, 3, 7, 21, 25, and 30.

BRASS MEDALLIONS.

1.

BONONIA. OCEANEN.   A galley, with rowers : the emperor, armed with spear and buckler, standing on the deck; behind him, two standards; Victory on the prow, with garland and palm branch: a figure swimming: a light-house, or tower, on a rock on the shore.

Valued by Mionnet at 200 francs.

Bononia is the modern Boulogne, from which Constans, in the winter of 342-3, set sail for Britain, to repress the incursions of the Picts, who were wasting the province.

2.

DEBELLATORI. GENTT. BARBARR. The emperor on horseback, bare-headed, riding over two enemies, one of whom he pierces with his spear. (The size varies).

3.

GAVDIVM. POPVLI. ROMANI. A laurel garland, within which is inscribed SIC. V. SIC. X.

4.

GAVDIVM. ROMANORVM. Victory, seated on a coat of mail, inscribing on a buckler VOT. XX.

5.

GLORIA. ROMANORVM. The emperor togated, standing, holding the hasta and a globe.

6.

Same legend. The emperor togated, standing, holding a branch and the parazonium.

7.

Same legend. The emperor helmeted, standing, holding ears of corn and the labarum, his right foot on a captive.

The medallion engraved in Banduri, has a helmeted Victory holding ears of corn and the labarum.

8.

Same legend. Rome, and a woman with turreted crown, standing; between them a cippus, on which is placed a buckler, inscribed VOT. XXX. MVLT. XXXX. In the exergue, R. The obverse has the armed bust of Constans, with a spear: legend, D. N. CONSTANTI. AVGVSTI. *(sic)*.

9.

ROMA. AETERNA. Rome, seated.

10.

ROMA. BEATA. Rome, seated on a buckler.

11.

VRBS. ROMA. Rome seated, holding a spear and a globe surmounted by a Victory.

12.

VRBS. ROMA. BEATA. A similar type.

13.

VICTORI. GENTIVM. BARBARR. The emperor riding over two enemies, one of whom he pierces with his spear.

14.

VICTORIA. AVGG. The emperor on horseback, preceded by Victory.

15.

VICTORIA. AVGG. NN. Victory seated on arms, holding a buckler, inscribed VOT. X.

16.

Same legend. Victory seated, holding a buckler on her knees. In the exergue, CONS.

17.

VICTORIA. AVGVSTI. Victory, marching; two captives, seated on the ground.

18.

Same legend. A woman with turreted crown, seated, holding a cornucopia and a garland.

19.

VICTORIA. AVGVSTORVM. Victory, marching; a palm branch on the ground. In the exergue, SIS. Q.

20.

Same legend. The emperor on horseback, preceded by Victory.

21.

VIRTVS. AVG. The emperor, standing; a captive at his feet.

22.

VIRTVS. AVG. N. The emperor on horseback, piercing an enemy with his spear.

23.

VIRTVS. AVGG. The emperor, seated near a trophy, and Victory standing.

24.

VIRTVS. AVGG. NN. The emperor standing, holding a spear and a globe.

25.

VIRTVS. CAESARVM. The emperor standing, his hand resting on a trophy, at the foot of which is a captive.

No. 1 is by far the rarest; of the others, Nos. 3, 6, and 20, are the rarest; and Nos. 10, 11, 12, 13, 15, 16, 19, 21, 24, and 25, are the least rare.

SECOND BRASS.

TRIVMFVS. *(sic)* CAESARVM. Victory in a quadriga, full faced. In the exergue, TR. *(Tanini)*.

THIRD BRASS.

VOTA. PVBLICA. Isis-Pharia, standing on a galley. (Size of the quinarius).

SATURNINUS III.

[History does not mention this usurper, whose revolt, if the coin-given by Banduri is genuine, must have been in the time of Constans or Constantius; for it is at this period that the legend, FELIX. TEMPORVM. REPARATIO. first appears on the Roman coins. Mionnet observes that this Saturninus should not be confounded with the usurpers of the same name in the reigns of Gallienus and Probus].

A coin is thus described by Banduri, but its authenticity is doubted.

THIRD BRASS.

FEL. TEMP. REPARATIO. A soldier striking with a spear a horse-man, who appears falling beneath the blow. In the exergue, B. SIS.

CONSTANTIUS II.

[Flavius Julius Constantius, the second son of Constantinus and Fausta, was born at Sirmium in Pannonia, in the year of Rome 1070 (A. D. 317), and declared Caesar by his father in 1076 (A. D. 323). He obtained the government of the East in 1088 (A. D. 335). Upon the death of Constantine the Great, in 1090 (A. D. 337), he shared in the division of the empire, of which, by the murder of Constans, in 1103 (A. D. 350), he became sole master. Constantius died at Mopsucrene, near Tarsus in Cilicia, when about to oppose his cousin Julianus, in the year of Rome 1114 (A. D. 361)].

STYLE:——CONSTANTIVS. CAESAR.——CONSTANTIVS. NOB. C. (*or* CAES.) [On reverse, sometimes, PRINCEPS. IVVENTVTIS.] ——FL. CONSTANTIVS. NOB. C.——FL. IVL. CONSTAN-TIVS. NOB. C. (*or* CAES.) [On reverse, sometimes, CONSTANTIVS. CAESAR. *or* PRINCEPS. IVVENTVTIS.)]——D. N. CONSTANTIVS.

NOB. C. (*or* CAES.)——D. N. FL. CONSTANTIVS. NOB. C.
——CONSTANTIVS. AVG. (*or* AVGVSTVS.) [On reverse,
sometimes, CONSTANTIVS. AVG.]——FL. IVL. CONSTANTIVS.
AVG. [On reverse, sometimes, CONSTANTINVS. AVG. (*or* VICTOR.
OMNIVM. GENTIVM.)]——IMP. CONSTANTIVS. AVG.——D. N.
CONSTANTIVS. AVG.——D. N. FL. CONSTANTIVS. AVG.
[On reverse, sometimes, DEBELLATOR. GENT. (*or* GENTT. *or* GENTIVM.)
BARBARAR. (*or* BARBARARVM.) *or* VICTOR. OMNIVM. GENTIVM.]——
CONSTANTIVS. P. F. AVG. [On reverse, sometimes, CON-
STANTIVS. AVG. *or* DEBELLATOR. GENTT. BARBAR. *or* TRIVMFATOR.
GENTIVM. BARBARARVM.] —— FL. IVL. CONSTANTIVS. P. (*or*
PIVS.) F. (*or* FELIX.) AVG. [On reverse, sometimes, CON-
STANTIVS. AVG. (*or* CONSTANTIVS. P. F. AVG. *or* TRIVMFATOR. GENTIVM.
BARBARARVM.)]——IMP. CONSTANTIVS. P. F. AVG.——IMP.
C. CONSTANTIVS. P. F. AVG.——D. N. CONSTANTIVS. P.
(*or* PIVS.) F. (*or* FEL.) AVG. [On reverse, sometimes, CON-
STANTIVS. AVG. (*or* DEBELLATOR. GENTT. *or* GENTI. *or* GENTIVM.)
BARBARR. (*or* BARBARAR.) *or* VICTOR. OMNIVM. GENTIVM.]——D. N.
FL. CONSTANTIVS. P. F. AVG. [On reverse, sometimes,
DEBELLATOR. GENTT. BARBARR.]——D. N. IVL. CONSTANTIVS.
P. F. AVG.——D. N. CONSTANTIVS. VICTOR. AVG.——D.
N. CONSTANTIVS. VICT. P. F. AVG. —— FL. IVL. CON-
STANTIVS. PER. (*or* PERP.) AVG. (*or* AVGV.) [On reverse,
sometimes, CONSTANTIVS. AVG.]——D. N. CONSTANTIVS. PERP.
AVG.——D. N. FL. CONSTANTIVS. PERP. AVG.——FL.
IVL. CONSTANTIVS. P. F. PERP. AVG. [On reverse, some-
times, VICTOR. OMNIVM. GENTIVM.] —— D. N. CONSTANTIVS.
MAX. AVG. (*or* AVGVSTVS.) [On reverse, sometimes, CON-
STANTIVS. VICTOR. SEMPER. AVG.]

Gold medallions, large size - - - - - - - - - - - - -	R 6
„ small size - - - - - - - - - - - - - - - -	R 3
„ of the usual size - - - - - - - - - - - - -	C
„ quinarii - - - - - - - - - - - - - - - -	C
Silver medallions, large size - - - - - - - - - - - -	R 6
„ small size - - - - - - - - - - - - - - - -	R 2
„ of the usual size - - - - - - - - - - - - -	R 2
„ quinarii - - - - - - - - - - - - - - - -	R 1
Brass medallions - - - - - - - - - - - - - - -	R 2
Second and third brass - - - - - - - - - - - - -	VC

GOLD AND SILVER MEDALLIONS.

1.

CONSTANTIVS. AVG. Four standards. In the exergue, S. CONS.
(or SMTR.) - - - - - - - - - - - - - - - - AR

2.

COSTANTIVS. CAESAR. Four standards. In the exergue, CONSI.
(or SMTR.) - - - - - - - - - - - - - - - - AR

3.

CONSTANTIVS. P. F. AVG. Three standards. In the exergue,
TES. - - - - - - - - - - - - - - - - - - - AR

4.

D. N. CONSTANTIVS. VICTOR. SEMPER. AVG. The emperor,
standing in a car, full-faced, drawn by six horses; his right hand
raised, and a globe in his left: on each side, a Victory placing a
garland on his head. In the exergue, AN., with various symbols.
(Large size). - - - - - - - - - - - - - - - AU

Valued by Mionnet at 600 francs.

5.

FELICITAS. PERPETVA. A garland, within which is inscribed
VOT. XX. MVLT. XXX. In the exergue, AQ.   - - - AR

6.

FELICITAS. ROMANORVM. The emperor Constantius and Julianus,
in military habits, standing beneath a kind of portico. In the
exergue, AQ. (Mionnet, Cat. d'Ennery). - - - - - - AR

7.

Same legend. A similar type. In the exergue, SIRM. (Mus. Vind.)
AR

8.

FELIX. ADVENTVS. AVG. N. The emperor on horseback, his
right hand raised. In the exergue, S. M. AN. (Khell).   - AU

9.

GAVDIVM. POPVLI. ROMANI. A garland, within which is
inscribed, SIC. X. SIC. XX. In the exergue, SIS. ☒. (Large
size). - - - - - - - - - - - - - - - - - - AR

10.

Same legend. A similar type; but of a much smaller size. - - AR

11.

GAVDIVM. POPVLI. ROMANI. A garland, within which is inscribed,
SIC. XX. SIC. XXX. In the exergue, TES. (Large size). AR

12.

Same legend. A similar type. In the exergue, two palm branches.
In the field, SIS. ☽. Sometimes two palm branches in the field.
(Small size). - - - - - - - - - - - - - - - - - AR

13.

GAVDIVM. ROMANORVM. Two captives, at the foot of the
labarum, on which is inscribed, VOT. XX. MVLT. XXX. In
the exergue, TR. - - - - - - - - - - - - - - - - AR

14.

Same legend. Three figures, standing: the middle one is crowned by a
celestial hand; that to the right is embraced by a military figure;
that to the left, is crowned by Victory. In the exergue, M. CONS.
The obverse has the laureated bust of Constantius, with spear and
buckler: on the latter, the prince is represented on horseback,
bearing down his enemies, preceded by Victory and followed by his
legions. The legend is, FL. IVL. CONSTANTIVS. NOB. CAES.
(Large size).—*Mus. Vindob.* - - - - - - - - - - AU
Valued by Mionnet at 600 francs.

15.

Same legend. Three figures, standing; the middle one crowned by a
celestial hand: Victory places a garland on the head of the figure
to the right, and that to the left is crowned by Virtue. In the
exergue, M. CON. - - - - - - - - - - - - - - AU

This extremely rare medallion is of a very large size, and has a wide
border.—See *Steinbuchel's Notice* of the gold medallions in the *Cabinet
of Vienna*, where it is engraved.

Valued by Mionnet at 2000 francs.

16.

GLORIA. ROMANORVM. Rome seated, holding a globe surmounted by a Victory, and a spear: a buckler on the ground. In
the exergue, TR. *or* TS. - - - - - - - - - - - - AU

17.

Same legend. A similar type; with the prow of a vessel at the feet of
Rome. In the exergue, RM. - - - - - - - - - - AU

18.

GLORIA. ROMANORVM. Rome seated, holding a globe surmounted by a Victory, which places a garland on her head : her right foot on the prow of a vessel, and a spear on her shoulder. In the exergue, ... ANT. (*Steinbuchel.*) - - - - - - - - - - - - AU

This medallion is mounted in a border, and has a loop. It is valued by Mionnet at 600 francs.

19.

Same legend. Rome, and a woman with turreted crown, seated on the same seat, each holding a globe surmounted by a Victory and the hasta pura; the latter resting her foot on the prow of a vessel. In the exergue, SMANT. - - - - - - - - - - - - AU

20.

Same legend. A woman seated on a throne, her hair bound with a fillet; holding in her right hand a globe surmounted by a Victory, about to place a garland on her head; in her left hand, the hasta:* her right foot resting on the prow of a vessel. In the exergue, SMN. The obverse has the full-faced bust of Constantius, with coat of mail, and a helmet richly ornamented, surmounted by peacocks' feathers: a Victory, holding a garland on his right hand, a spear in his left: legend, D. N. CONSTANTIVS. MAX. AVG. (*Plate G, No. 2*). Cabinet of *T. Thomas, Esq.*

21.

OB. VICTORIAM. TRIVMPHALEM. Two Victories standing, holding a buckler, inscribed VOT. X. MVL. XX. (*Mus. Vindob.*)
AU

22.

PRINCIPI. IVVENTVTIS. The prince, in a military habit, standing to the left; in his right hand the labarum, in his left a javelin reversed: behind, two standards. In the exergue, CONS. (*Plate G, No. 1*). Unique: in the cabinet of *T. Thomas, Esq.*

23.

SALVS. ET. SPES. REIPVBLICAE. Three military figures, standing. In the exergue, TES. (Large size). - - - - - - - - AU

Valued by Mionnet at 400 francs.

---

* This hasta, if it be really that symbol, resembles the thyrsus of Bacchus. The female figure may probably be a portrait of the empress Fausta. She wears embroidered shoes; an article of princely luxury first used by Diocletianus, as we learn from Eutropius.

24.

SALVS. ET. SPES. REIPVBLICAE. The emperor seated, between
two military figures standing. In the exergue, CONS. (This
medallion is larger than the preceding). - - - - - - - AU
Valued by Mionnet at 600 francs.

25.

SECVRITAS. PERPETVAE. (sic). The emperor standing, in a
military habit; his right hand resting on a trophy, a spear in his
left. In the exergue, BMN. - - - - - - - - - - AU

26.

TRIVMFATOR. GENTIVM. BARBARARVM. The emperor
standing, holding the labarum (sometimes charged with the monogram of Christ) and a spear, or a buckler. In the exergue, ✻AQ.
or TES. (Large size). - - - - - - - - - - - - - AR
There is a modern forgery of this medallion.

27.

Same legend. A similar type. In the exergue, TES. - - - - AR

28.

VICTORIA. AVGVSTORVM. Victory marching, with garland and
palm branch: a palm branch at her feet. In the exergue, SIS.
and sometimes a garland. - - - - - - - - - - - AR

29.

VICTORIAE. DD. NN. AVGG. Two Victories standing, holding a
shield, on which is inscribed, VOT. XX. MVLT. XXX. In the
exergue, SIS. between two palm branches. (Khell). - - - AU

30.

VIRTVS. CONSTANTI. (sic) CAES. Constantius standing between
two captives, holding a trophy and a spear. In the exergue,
SMN. or SMNM. or SMNP. - - - - - - - - - - AU

31.

VIRTVS. CONSTANTI. (sic) AVG. The emperor, in a military
habit, standing to the left: in his right hand the labarum charged
with the monogram of Christ; in his left, a javelin reversed; at his
feet, a captive. In the exergue, ✻SMAQ. (Plate F, No. 5).
AR
This medallion is in the collection of T. Thomas, Esq.

32.

VIRTVS. DD. NN. AVGG. The emperor standing, holding the
labarum charged with the monogram of Christ. In the exergue,
TR. - - - - - - - - - - - - - - - - - - AR

31.

VIRTVS. EXERCITVS. The emperor standing ; holding a javelin reversed in his right hand, his left resting on his shield. In the exergue, C. Z. (*or* TES.) - - - - - - - - - - - AR

GOLD AND SLVER, USUAL SIZE, WITH RARE REVERSES.

1.

CONSTANTIVS. AVG. Three palm-branches: above, a star. In the exergue, SIS. - - - - - - - - - - - - - - AR

2.

CONSTANTIVS. CAESAR. Victory marching, holding a garland and palm-branch. In the exergue, CONS. *or* TR. The obverse has the diademed head of the emperor, without legend. - - AU

3.

Same legend. A similar type ; but with M. sometimes in the field. In the exergue, ... NSI. *or* TSϾ. - - - - - - - - - AR

4.

FELICITAS. PERPETVA. Victory seated on a coat of mail, holding a buckler, supported by a winged Genius, inscribed VOT. X. MVLT. XX. In the exergue, SMAQ. - - - - - - - AU

5.

Same legend. Victory, marching with a garland and trophy. In the exergue, ✳AQ. - - - - - - - - - - - - - - AR

6.

Same legend. Victory, marching with a palm branch and a garland. In the exergue, ✳AQ. - - - - - - - - - - - - AR

7.

FELICITAS. ROMANORVM. A laurel garland, within which is inscribed, VOT. XV. MVLTIS. XX. In the exergue, SMANΔ. *or* SMANI. *or* SMANJ. - - - - - - - - - - - AU

8.

Same legend. Four military figures, standing under a portico, or arch. In the exergue, SMK. *(Banduri)*. - - - - - - - AR

9.

FELICITAS. REIPVBLICAE. A laurel garland, within which is inscribed, VOT. XV. MVLT. XX. In the exergue, C.Γ. - AR

10.

Same legend. A laurel garland, within which is inscribed, VOT. XX. MVLT. XXX. In the exergue, C.B. *or* C.Γ. - - - - - AR

11.

FEL. TEMP. REPARATIO. Victory, standing, her left foot on a helmet, holding a buckler, inscribed VOT. XX.: a kneeling woman supporting the buckler. In the exergue, R. - - - - - - - AR

12.

GAVÐIVM. POPVLI. ROMANI. A laurel garland, within which is inscribed SIC. X. SIC. XX. In the exergue, SIS. between two stars. - AU

13.

GLORIA. EXERCITVS. A woman leaning on a column, holding a laurel branch and the hasta. In the exergue, C. Γ. - - - AR

14.

GLORIA. REIPVBLICAE. The emperor, on horseback: before, a prostrate woman, holding a torch. In the exergue, SMANZ. AU

15.

Same legend. Two women, seated; one helmeted, the other with turreted crown, supporting a shield, inscribed VOT. XXX. MVLT. XXXX. In the exergue, CON. - - - - - - - - - AR

16.

Same legend. A similar type, but with VOT. XXXV. MVLT. XXXX. In the exergue, SIRM✳. - - - - - - - - - - - - AU

17.

Same legend. A similar type, but with VOT. XXXX. on the buckler. In the exergue, TES. between two stars. - - - - - - - - AU

18.

PAX. AVGVSTORVM. The emperor, in a military habit, standing, holding the labarum charged with the monogram of Christ. In the exergue, TR. - - - - - - - - - - - - - - - AR

19.

PRINCIPI. IVVENTVTIS. The emperor standing, in a military habit, holding the labarum and a spear. In the field, two standards. In the exergue, SIS. *or* BR. *or* TSЄ. - - - - - - - - - AU

20.

Same legend. The emperor, in a military habit, standing, holding a spear and a globe. In the exergue, TR. - - - - - - AU

21.

Same legend. A similar type, with SIS. in the exergue. (A *quinarius*). AU

22.

SECVRITAS. REIPVBLICAE. Security standing, leaning on a column. In the exergue, TR. - - - - - - - - - - AU

23.

SPES. REI. PVBLICE. *(sic)*. The emperor in a military habit, holding a javelin reversed, and a globe. In the exergue, TES. *(Khell)*. - - - - - - - - - - - - - - - - - AR

24.

VICTORIA. AVG. NOSTRI. The emperor in a military habit, holding a globe, and a spear transversely; Victory flitting before him with a garland and palm branch. In the exergue, TR. - AU

25.

VICTORIA. AVGVSTI. Victory marching, with a garland and palm branch. In the exergue, R. - - - - - - - - - - AU

26.

VICTORIA. AVGVSTI. N. A similar type. In the exergue, R. between two stars. - - - - - - - - - - - - - AR

27.

VICTORIA. AVGVSTORVM. Victory marching, with palm branch and trophy. In the exergue, SIS. *or* SIC. and ⌣. - - - AR

28.

Same legend. Victory marching, with garland and branch. In the exergue, SIS. (A *quinarius*). - - - - - - - - - - AU

29.

Same legend. Victory, seated on a coat of mail, holding a buckler supported by a Genius, on which is inscribed, VOT. X. In the exergue, LVG. (A *quinarius*). - - - - - - - - - AU

30.

Same legend. A similar type, with VOT. XV. MVLT. XX. on the buckler. In the exergue, SMANE. - - - - - - - - - AU

31.

Same legend. A similar type, with VOT. XXX. on the buckler. In the exergue, SMANI. - - - - - - - - - - - - AU

32.

Same legend. A similar type, with VOT. XXXX. on the buckler. In the exergue, KONSA. *or* SMAN. *or* SMN. *(Quinarii)*. - - AU

33.

VICTORIA. CONSTANTI. (*sic*) AVG. Victory, seated on a coat of mail, holding a buckler supported by a Genius, on which is inscribed VOT. X. MVLT. XX. In the exergue, SMAN. - - - - AU

34.

Same legend. A similar type, but with VOT. XV. on the buckler. In the exergue, CONS. - - - - - - - - - - - - - AU

35.

Same legend. A similar type, but with VOT. XX. MVLT. XXX. on the buckler. In the exergue, CONS. - - - - - - - AU

36.

Same legend. A similar type, with VOT. XXXX. on the buckler. In the exergue, SRM. (A *quinarius*). - - - - - - - - AU

37.

VICTORIA. DD. NN. AVG. Victory, seated on a coat of mail, inscribing on a buckler supported by a winged Genius, VOT. X. MVLT. XX. In the exergue, SIS. and a star. - - - - AU

38.

Same legend. Victory, seated on a coat of mail, inscribing on a buckler SIC. X. SIC. XX. In the exergue, SIS. and a star. - - - AU

39.

Same legend. Victory marching, holding a garland and a palm branch. In the exergue, LVG. (A *quinarius*). - - - - - - - AR

40.

VICTORIA. DD. NN. AVGG. Victory standing, holding a trophy and a palm branch. In the exergue, TR. - - - - - - AU

41.

Same legend. Victory marching, with garland and palm branch. In the exergue, TR. - - - - - - - - - - - - - AR

42.

Same legend. Victory marching, with garland and trophy. In the exergue, TES. - - - - - - - - - - - - - - AR

43.

VICTORIAE. DD. NN. AVGG. Victory, seated on a coat of mail, inscribing on a buckler supported by a winged Genius, VOT. XX. MVLT. XXX. In the exergue, SMAQ.: the whole within a laurel garland. - - - - - - - - - - - - - - - - AU

44.

VICTORIAE. DD. NN. AVGG. Two Victories, supporting a buckler, inscribed VOT. XX. MVLT. XXX. In the exergue, TR. *or* TES. - - - - - - - - - - - - - - - - - - - AU

45.

Same legend. A similar type, but with VOT. MVLT. XXX. In the exergue, TR. and a palm branch. - - - - - - - - - AU

46.

VICTOR. OMNIVM. GENTIVM. The emperor in a military habit, standing, holding the labarum and a buckler: on one side, two suppliant figures, kneeling; on the other, a captive. (*Mus. Vindob.*).
AU

47.

VIRTVS. EXERCITVS. A military figure, standing; his right hand resting on a javelin reversed, his left on a shield. In the exergue, P. CON. *or* S. CON. *or* TES. - - - - - - - - - - - AR

48.

VIRTVS. EXERCITVS. GALL. Mars, naked, marching with a spear and trophy: two captives on the ground. In the exergue, TR.
AU

49.

VOT. XXXX. within a laurel garland. In the exergue, C.Θ. - AR

50.

Without legend. The monogram of Christ, between the letters A. Q. The obverse has the radiated bust of Constantius, with coat of mail, and the paludamentum: legend, CONSTANTIVS. P. F. AVG. - AU

In gold, No. 50 is the rarest; the next in rarity are, Nos. 14 and 24; then Nos. 2, 4, 12, 20, 22, 35, 46, and 48; the least rare are, Nos. 16, 28, 29, 32, 37, 38, 44, and 45. In silver, Nos. 1, 3, 11, 13, 15, and 18, are much the rarest; the next in rarity are Nos. 8 and 49.

BRASS MEDALLIONS.

1.

DEBELLATORI. GENTT. BARBARR. The emperor on horseback, riding over two enemies, one of whom he pierces with his spear.

2.

Same legend. The emperor on horseback, riding over two enemies.

3.

FEL. TEMP. REPARATIO. The emperor, standing on a galley, holding a globe surmounted by a phoenix, and the labarum charged with the monogram of Christ: on his left, Victory, seated. In the exergue, SHKB.

Mionnet, who describes this medallion, states it to be retouched.

4.

GAVDIVM. ROMANORVM. Victory, seated on a coat of mail, inscribing on a buckler, VOT. XX.

5.

GLORIA. ROMANORVM. Rome, seated, inscribing on a buckler, resting on a column. In the exergue, R.

6.

Same legend. Victory, standing, inscribing on a buckler, VOT. V. MVLT. X.

7.

Same legend. Victory, marching, with garland and palm branch.

8.

LARGITIO. Constantius, seated, joining hands with a woman on his right; to the left, Rome.

9.

MONETA. AVG. The three Monetæ, standing.

10.

Same legend. A similar type; with R. in the exergue.

11.

ROMA. BEATA. Rome, seated on spoils, holding a Victory and a spear.

12.

SABINAE. The rape of the Sabines; three obelisks in the midst, as on the medallions of the earlier emperors.

13.

VRBS. ROMA. Rome, seated on arms, holding a spear, and a globe surmounted by a figure of Victory.

14.

Same legend. Rome, seated, but without the Victory.

15.

VRBS. ROMA. BEATA. A similar type.

16.

VICTORIA. AVG. Victory, with turreted crown, seated, holding a cornucopia, and ears of corn: the prow of a vessel at her feet.

17.

VICTORIA. AVG. Victory, seated on arms, inscribing on a buckler, VOT. XX.

18.

VICTORIA. AVG. N. Victory, marching, holding a garland: a captive on each side, seated on the ground.

19.

VICTORIA. AVGG. NN. Victory, seated, holding a buckler, on which is inscribed, VOT. X.

20.

VICTORIA. AVGVSTI. Victory, standing, her left foot on a globe, inscribing on a buckler resting on a column, VOT. XXX. MVLT. XXXX. (Tanini).

21.

Same legend. A woman, with turreted crown, holding a branch and a cornucopia: Victory, behind, placing a garland on her head.

22.

Same legend. Victory, marching.

23.

VICTORIA. AVGVSTORVM. The emperor, in a military habit, attended by Victory.

24.

Same legend. Victory, marching: two captives on the ground.

25.

VICTORIA. BEATISSIMORVM. CAESS. Victory, seated on arms, holding a buckler, inscribed VOT. X.

26.

VIRTVS. AVG. The emperor standing, in a military habit, holding a spear and a globe: a captive seated on the ground.

27.

VIRTVS. AVG. N. Victory, standing, holding a garland with both hands: two captives on the ground.

28.

Same legend. The emperor standing, in a military habit, holding a spear and a globe: two captives at his feet.

29.

VIRTVS. AVG. NOSTRI. The emperor standing, holding a javelin reversed, and an olive branch.

30.

VIRTVS. AVGG. The emperor standing, holding a spear and a globe: a captive at his feet.

31.

Same legend. The emperor on horseback, casting his javelin at an enemy.

32.

VIRTVS. AVGVSTI. The emperor standing, holding a spear and the parazonium; his left foot on a captive: behind, Victory placing a garland on his head.

33.

VIRTVS. AVGVSTI. N. The emperor standing, holding an olive branch and a spear: a captive at his feet.

34.

Same legend. A military figure marching, with a javelin and a globe: two captives, seated on the ground.

35.

Same legend. An armed figure, holding a spear and a globe.

36.

VIRTVS. CAESS. A woman standing, holding the hasta; her right hand resting on a trophy, at the foot of which is a captive.

37.

Same legend. The emperor, standing by a ·trophy: a captive on the ground.

38.

VIRTVS. CAESARVM. The emperor standing, holding a spear; his right hand resting on a trophy, at the foot of which is a captive.

39.

Same legend. A naked figure marching, bearing a spear, and dragging a captive by the hair.

Nos. 8 and 12 are by far the rarest. The next in rarity is No. 20; then Nos. 1, 3, 11, 18, 25, 29, 31, and 32. The least rare are Nos. 9, 10, and 14.

SECOND BRASS, WITH RARE REVERSES.

1.

CONCORDIA. MILITVM. The emperor standing, in a military habit, holding in each hand a labarum charged with the monogram of Christ: above his head, a star. In the field, A. In the exergue, Γ. SIS. *or* R. SIS*.

2.

FEL. TEMP. REPARATIO. The emperor with his foot on a captive, and a globe surmounted by a Victory. In the field, Γ. and a star. In the exergue, *TSA.

3.

FELICITAS. REIPVBLICAE. The emperor in a military habit, standing, holding in his right hand a globe, surmounted by a Victory, and in his left the vexillum. In the field, F. In the exergue, SAR.

4.

HOC. SIGNO. VICTOR. ERIS. The emperor in a military habit, standing, holding in his right hand the standard of the cross : Victory placing a garland on his head. In the field, A. or III. In the exergue, A. SIS. or B. SIS. or Γ. SIS. or SIRM.

5.

MONETA. AVG. The three Monetæ, standing. In the exergue, R.

6.

SALVS. AVGVSTI. The monogram of Christ, between the letters alpha and omega. In the exergue, TRS.

7.

SALVS. AVG. NOSTRI. A similar type. (*Mus. Vindob.*).

The rarest type is No. 5. The next in rarity is No. 2 ; then Nos. 1, 3, and 7.

THIRD BRASS.

1.

VICTORIA. AVGG. Victory marching, with garland and palm branch. In the field, the monogram of Christ. In the exergue, B. SIS.*

2.

VOTA. PVBLICA. Anubis standing, holding the sistrum in his right hand, and a caduceus in his left. (*Banduri*).

No. 2 is the rarest.

FAUSTA.

[This lady is supposed to have been the wife of Constantius II., although historians speak of the empress, without making mention of her name. The coin here described, cannot belong to the wife of Constantine the Great, and is therefore assigned to the wife of Constantius II. Fausta was the daughter of Julius Constantius, brother of the first Constantine].

STYLE :——FAVSTA. N. F.

Third brass - R 6

FAVSTA. N. F.   Head of Fausta.—*Rev.* No legend. A star. In the
exergue, TSA. *(Mus. Vindob).*

A coin is given by Banduri, with a large star within a laurel garland.

NEPOTIANUS.

[Flavius Popilius Nepotianus Constantinus, son of Eutropia, the sister of
Constantine the Great, assumed the purple at Rome, upon the death
of his cousin Constantius, in the year of that city 1103 (A. D. 350).
This prince rendered himself odious by his cruelty; and twenty-eight
days after his usurpation, was killed in a battle with Marcellinus,
an adherent of Magnentius].

STYLE:——FL. NEPOTIANVS. AVG.——FL. NEP. CONSTAN-
TINVS. AVG.——FL. POP. NEPOTIANVS. P. F. AVG.

Second brass - - - - - - - - - - - - - - - - - - R 6

SECOND BRASS.

1.

GLORIA. ROMANORVM.   Nepotianus on horseback, launching a
javelin at a kneeling figure : a broken buckler and spear on the
ground. A star in the field. In the exergue, R. *or* RQ. *or* RS.

2.

VRBS. ROMA.   Rome seated, holding a globe surmounted by a
Victory, and the hasta. In the exergue, RQ. *or* RS.

VETRANIO.

[Vetranio was born in Mæsia Superior, and held the post of general of
infantry under Constantinus the Second. Upon the death of Constans,
in the year of Rome 1103 (A.D. 350), he assumed the purple at
Sirmium in Pannonia. He was, however, compelled by Constantius
to renounce his claim at the end of ten months, and retired to Prusa
in Bithynia, where he died, in 1109 (A. D. 356)].

STYLE:——D. N. VETRANIO. P. F. AVG.   [On reverse of some
coins, SALVATOR. REIPVBLICAE.]

1

P. 283

2

P. 307

3

P. 321

4

P. 334

5

P. 338

6

P. 348

7

P. 350

8

P. 351

9

P. 353

10

P. 377

Engraved by Henry A. Ogg.

London, Published by Effingham Wilson, 1st. Jan.y 1834.

Gold - R 8
Silver medallions *(quoted by Beauvais)* - - - - - - - - R 8
Silver of the usual size - - - - - - - - - - - - - - R 8
Second brass - - - - - - - - - - - - - - - - - - R 4
Third brass - - - - - - - - - - - - - - - - - - R 6

GOLD AND SILVER.

1.

SALVATOR. REIPVBLICAE.   The emperor with the paludamentum,
holding the standard of the cross and a spear : Victory standing,
placing a garland on his head. In the exergue, A. SIS. *or* SIS.
only.* - - - - - - - - - - - - - - - - - - - AU

2.

VICTORIA. AVGVSTORVM. Victory marching, holding a trophy
and a garland. In the exergue, SIS. (In the cabinet of *M.
Gosselin*, of Paris). *(Plate xii, No.* 1*)*. - - - - - - - - AR
Mionnet values the gold at 600, and the silver at 200 francs.

SECOND BRASS.

1.

CONCORDIA. MILITVM. The emperor in a military habit standing,
holding in each hand a standard charged with the monogram of
Christ : above, a star. In the field, A. *or* A. B. In the exergue,
A. SIS. *or* B. SIS.* *or* TSA.

2.

HOC. SIGNO. VICTOR. ERIS. The emperor standing, in a military
habit, holding the standard of the cross in his right hand, and a
spear transversely in his left : behind, Victory placing a garland on
his head. In the field, A. In the exergue, *A. SIS.* *or* Γ.
SIS.* *or* Є. SIS.

3.

VIRTVS. EXERCITVM. *(sic)*. Vetranio standing, with the paludamentum ; his right hand holding the standard of the cross, his
left resting on a shield. In the exergue, TSΔ. *(Mus.Vindob)*.

The above are valued by Mionnet at thirty francs each.

---

* A gold Vetranio was at one time in the French cabinet.   It was obtained in
the year 1755, by Barthelemy, from the Abbé Boule at Marseilles, after a week's
negotiation.   The Abbé refused all offers of price, but at length presented it to
Barthelemy as a bribe, to procure his election as a corresponding member of the
French Academy.

THIRD BRASS.

1.

CONCORDIA. MILITVM. A figure standing, holding the labarum and a spear.

2.

GLORIA. ROMANORVM. A military figure standing, holding the standard of the cross, and a spear tranversely. In the exergue, B. SIS. *or* Γ. SIS. *or* Є. SIS.

3.

HOC. SIGNO. VICTOR. ERIS. The emperor standing, holding the labarum, and crowned by Victory.

4.

SALVS. AVGVSTORVM. The emperor in a military habit, marching, and bearing a globe, and a spear transversely. In the exergue, Δ. SIS.

5.

VIRTVS. AVGVSTORVM. The emperor standing, holding a spear and a globe, and trampling on a captive. In the exergue, A. SIS. *or* Γ. SIS. *or* H. SIS.

6.

VIRTVS. EXERCITVS. The emperor standing, holding the standard of the cross, his left hand resting on a shield. In the exergue, TRS. *or* TRSB.

7.

VIRTVS. EXERCITVM. *(sic).* A similar type. In the exergue, TESA. *or* TRSΓ.

Valued by Mionnet at fifteen francs each.

NONIUS?

[A usurper, of whom history makes no mention, but whose revolt probably took place in the reign of Constantius II. Beauvais is of opinion that the coins described below, were struck for Regalianus, a usurper in the reign of Gallienus, and states that this personage bore the name of Nonnius, which name, however, is found only on the coins given by Goltzius, and not on any authentic pieces struck by Regalianus: besides, one of the barbarous coins here described, has the standard of the cross, which proves it to be of a later period than the reign of Gallienus. Eckhel thinks that these coins belong in reality to some prince whose name is known, but that they are the work of ignorant moneyers, who were incapable of producing a legible coin].

The following are described in the catalogue *d'Ennery,* p. 641.

THIRD BRASS.

1.

D. N. NONIIVS. AVG. *(sic)*. Male head, with chaplet of pearls, and the paludamentum.—*Rev.* FELICITAS. REIPVBLICE. *(sic)*. A military figure standing, holding a globe surmounted by a Victory, and the labarum. In the exergue, R. P. L. C.

2.

D. N. VONIIVS. *(sic)*. M. N. V. Bare head, with the paludamentum. In the field, A.—*Rev.* VICTOR. . . . . NONA? *(sic)*. Two Victories standing, holding a buckler attached to a tree: on the buckler, OVI. AV. Q. In the exergue, H. M. R.

MAGNENTIUS.

[Flavius Magnus Magnentius, a usurper in the reign of Constantius II. was born of obscure parents, either in Britain or Germany, about the year of Rome 1056 (A. D. 303). It is said that he was made a prisoner of war; and that to avoid perpetual servitude, he enlisted under the Roman standard, and was much distinguished for his bravery. He became after a time, commander of the Jovian and Herculean legions, established on the banks of the Rhine. In 1103 (A. D. 350), he assumed the purple, at Augustodunum (the modern *Autun*), and the murder of Constans followed immediately after. Constantius offered him the provinces of Gaul, Spain, and Britain; but Magnentius rejected his terms: a war was the consequence, and after two engagements, in which the army of the usurper was worsted, Magnentius fled to Lyons, and stabbed himself, in the year of Rome 1106 (A. D. 353)].

STYLE:——MAGNENTIVS. AVG.——MAG. (*or* MAGN.) MAG-NENTIVS. AVG. —— IMP. MAGNENTIVS. AVG. [On reverse, sometimes, LIB. ROMANORVM.]——IM. (*or* IMP.) C. (*or* CAE. *or* CAES.) MAGNENTIVS. AVG. [On reverse, sometimes, LIBERATOR. REIPVBLICAE. *or* LIB. ROMANOR. (*or* ROMANORVM.)]——D. N. MAGNENTIVS. AVG. [On reverse, LIB. ROMANOR. (*or* LIB. ROM. ORB.)]——FL. MAGNENTIVS. P. F. AVG.——IM. CAE. MAGNENTIVS. P. F. AVG.——D. N. MAGNENTIVS. P. F. AVG. [On reverse, sometimes, LIB. ROMANOR. (*or* ROMANORVM)].——FL. MAGNENTIVS. TR.* P. F. AVG. [On reverse, sometimes, RESTITVTOR. LIBERTATIS.)]

---

* The signification of the letters TR. has not been explained.

Gold medallions, of large size - - - - - - - - - - - - R 7

„   of the usual size - - - - - - - - - - - - - R 2

„   quinarii - - - - - - - - - - - - - - - - R 6

Silver medallions, large size - - - - - - - - - - - R 8

„   „   small size - - - - - - - - - - - R 8

„   of the usual size - - - - - - - - - - - - - R 4

Brass medallions - - - - - - - - - - - - - - - R 2

Contorniati - - - - - - - - - - - - - - - - R 1

Second and third brass - - - - - - - - - - - - - VC

GOLD AND SILVER MEDALLIONS.

1.

LIBERATOR. REIPVBLICAE. The emperor on horseback; before, a prostrate woman. In the exergue, SMAQ.—*Obv.* IM. CAE. MAGNENTIVS. AVG. Bust of Magnentius. - - - - AU

Valued by Mionnet at 400 francs.

2.

SECVRITAS. REIPVBLICAE. Security, leaning on a column. In the exergue, TR. (*Catalogue d'Ennery*, p. 309, No. 1080.) - AR

3.

VICTORIAE. DD. NN. AVGG. Victory, seated on a coat of mail, holding a buckler, on which is inscribed VOT. V. MVLT. X. In the exergue, *AQ*. - - - - - - - - - - - - AR

Mionnet values No. 2, at 200, and No. 3 at 100 francs.

GOLD AND SILVER, OF THE USUAL SIZE.

1.

FELICITAS. PERPETVA. Victory marching, with garland and palm branch. In the exergue, SMAQ. (A *quinarius*). - - AU

2.

Same legend. Victory marching, holding a garland and a trophy. In the exergue, AQ. *or* LVG. - - - - - - - - - - - AR

3.

GLORIA. ET. REPARATIO. TEMPORVM. The emperor standing, in a military habit, holding a Victory and the labarum. In the exergue, PAR. - - - - - - - - - - - - - - AU

4.

LIBERATOR. REIPVBLICAE. The emperor on horseback : before, a prostrate woman. In the exergue, SMAQ. - - - - - AU

5.

RESTITVTOR. LIBERTATIS. The emperor, with the paludamentum, standing, holding a Victory and the monogram of Christ. In the exergue, SMAQ. *(Mus. Vindob)*. - - - - - - - AU

6.

VICT. AVG. LIB. ROM. ORB. Victory, and a woman supporting a trophy; the latter holding a spear transversely. In the exergue, NAR. *or* N. LVG. - - - - - - - - - - - AU & AR

7.

VICTORIA. AVG. LIB. ROMANOR. Victory and a woman standing, supporting a trophy. In the exergue, NAR. *or* RT. *or* SMAQ. *or* TR. - - - - - - - - - - - - - - - - - - AU

Brought, in fine condition, 1*l*. 13*s*. and 1*l*. 11*s*. at the Trattle sale.

8.

VICTORIA. DD. NN. AVGG. Victory marching, with garland and palm branch. In the exergue, TR. (A *quinarius*). - - - AU

9.

VICTORIAE. DD. NN. AVG. ET. CAES. Two Victories standing, supporting a buckler, on which is inscribed VOT. V. MVLT. X. In the exergue, PTR. *(Mionnet)*. - - - - - - - - - AR

10.

VIRTVS. EXERCITI. A military figure, standing : his right hand on a javelin, reversed; his left resting on a buckler. In the exergue, TR. - - - - - - - - - - - - - - - - - - - AR

In gold, Nos. 4 and 5 are the rarest: the next in rarity is No. 3 ; then Nos. 1 and 8. In silver, Nos. 2 and 9 are much the rarest.

BRASS MEDALLIONS.

1.

GLORIA. ROMANORVM. Victory, helmeted, standing, holding the labarum and a laurel branch; her right foot on a captive.

2.

SALVS. DD. NN. AVG. ET. CAESS. The monogram of Christ between the letters alpha and omega. In the exergue, TRP.

3.

VICTORIA. AVGG. A woman, standing, with the paludamentum, holding in her right hand a figure of Victory, and a spear in her left: Victory, behind, placing a garland on her head, and holding a palm branch in her left hand.

4.

Same legend. Victory, standing, holding a garland and a palm branch: her right foot on a kneeling captive.

5.

Same legend. Magnentius, standing, holding a globe surmounted by a Victory, and a spear: Victory, behind, placing a garland on his head.

6.

VICTORIA. AVGVSTORVM. Victory, marching to the right, holding a laurel garland and a palm branch.

7.

VIRTVS. AVGVSTORVM. Magnentius, standing, holding a spear and a laurel branch.

Nos. 1 and 5 are the rarest.

SECOND BRASS, WITH RARE REVERSE.

RENOBATIO. *(sic)*. VRBIS. ROME. *(sic)*. Rome, seated: RE. in the exergue. *(Tanini, Supp. ad Band.)*.

Valued by Mionnet at ten francs.

THIRD BRASS.

1.

BEATITVDO. PVBLICO. Magnentius, in the toga, seated; his right hand raised, the hasta in his left. In the exergue, ANS. *(Mus. Vindob.)*.

2.

FEL. TEMP. REPARATIO. Magnentius, standing on the deck of a galley, holding a Victory and a spear; a winged Genius kneeling at his feet. In the field, A. In the exergue, TRE.

3.

SALVS. D. AVG. ET. CAES. The monogram of Christ, between the letters alpha and omega. In the exergue, LP.

4.

VICTORIA. AVG. LIB. ROMANOR. Magnentius, in a military habit, holding the standard of the cross, and a laurel branch: a captive kneeling at his feet. In the field, N. In the exergue, PR.

Valued by Mionnet at two francs each.

DECENTIUS.

[Magnus Decentius, the brother of Magnentius, was created Caesar by that usurper at Milan, in the year of Rome 1104 (A.D. 351). Decentius strangled himself, upon hearing the news of the defeat and death of his brother, in 1106 (A.D. 353)].

STYLE:——D. N. DECENTIVS. CAESAR.——MAG. (or MAGN.) DECENTIVS. N. (or NOB.) CS. (or CAE. or CAES.) —— D. N. DECENTIVS. NOB. C. (or CAE. or CAES.) [On reverse, sometimes, PRINCEPS. IVVENTVTIS.]—— DECENTIVS. FOR. (or FORT.) CAES. —— D. N. DECENTIVS. FORT. CAES. [On reverse, sometimes, LIB. ROMANOR. or PRINCEPS. IVVENTVTIS.]

A coin of Decentius, with the title of *Augustus*, has been produced, but it is not authenticated.

Gold medallions, of small size - - - - - - - - - - - R 8
„ of the usual size - - - - - - - - - - - - - - R 4
Quinarii - - - - - - - - - - - - - - - - - - R 6
Silver medallions, small size - - - - - - - - - - - R 8
„ of the usual size - - - - - - - - - - - - - - R 6
Brass medallions - - - - - - - - - - - - - - - R 4
Second and third brass - - - - - - - - - - - - - VC

GOLD AND SILVER MEDALLIONS.

1.

GLORIA. ROMANORVM. Rome-Nicephore, seated. In the exergue, TR. - - - - - - - - - - - - - - AU

Valued by Mionnet at 200 francs.

2.

PRINCIPI. IVVENTVTIS. Decentius, standing, holding a spear and a globe. In the exergue, TR. - - - - - - - - - - AR

3,

PRINCITI. *(sic)*. IVVENTVTIS. A similar type. In the exergue,
TR. The obverse has the bare head of Decentius: legend, D. N.
DECENTIVS. NOB. CAES. - - - - - - - - - - - AR

The last two are valued at 150 francs each by Mionnet.

GOLD AND SILVER, WITH RARE REVERSES.

1.

VICTORIA. AVG. LIB. ROMANOR. Victory and a woman, standing, supporting a trophy: the latter holding a spear transversely.
In the exergue, TR. - - - - - - - - - - - - - - AU

Brought, in fine condition, 3*l.* 3*s.* at the Trattle sale.

2.

VICTORIA. CAES. LIB. ROMANOR. *or* VICT. CAES. LIB. ROM.
ORB. A similar type. In the exergue, TR. - - - - - AU

3.

VICTORIA. DD. NN. AVGG. Victory, marching, with garland and
palm branch. In the exergue, TR. (A *quinarius*). - - - AU

Brought 3*l.* 4*s.* at the Trattle sale.

4.

VIRTVS. EXERCITI. A military figure, standing: his right hand
resting on a javelin reversed; his left, on a shield. In the exergue,
TR. - AR

In gold, Nos. 1 and 2 are valued at seventy-two francs, by Mionnet;
the quinarius at sixty francs; the silver, at seventy-two francs.

BRASS MEDALLIONS.

1.

VICTORIA. AVGG. Decentius standing, in a military habit, holding
in his right hand a Victory, and in his left a spear: Victory, holding
a palm branch, placing a garland on his head.

2.

Same legend. Victory, with garland and palm branch, trampling on a
captive, bound and kneeling.

3.

VICTORIA. AVGVSTORVM.   Decentius, marching with a spear and laurel branch : Victory preceding him.

There are varieties of this type.

4.

VIRTVS. AVGG.   Decentius on horseback, striking an enemy with his spear.

The size of these medallions varies.   The largest are, of course, the most valued.

5.

Same legend.   Decentius on horseback, bearing down two captives.

No. 2 is the least rare.

THIRD BRASS, WITH RARE REVERSE.

SALVS. DD. NN. AVG. ET. CAES.   The monogram of Christ, between the letters alpha and omega.   In the field, S. and a star, *or* PS.   In the exergue, F. . . . LC.

Valued by Mionnet at eight francs.

DESIDERIUS.

[Desiderius was created Caesar at the same time as Decentius, by his brother Magnentius; by whom he was stabbed, in the year of Rome 1106 (A.D. 353)].

Goltzius gives coins of Desiderius, but they are not authenticated.

CONSTANTIUS GALLUS.

[Flavius Claudius Julius Constantius Gallus, the son of Julius Constantius (brother of Constantine the Great) and Galla, was born in the year of Rome 1078 (A.D. 325). The emperor Constantius created him Caesar in 1104 (A. D. 351), and gave him his sister Constantina in marriage : But Gallus shewed himself unfit for so high a dignity; his insolence and cruelty provoked the indignation of his cousin the emperor, by whose order he was beheaded in prison, at Pola in Istria, in the year of Rome 1107 (A.D. 354)].

STYLE:——CONSTANTIVS. CAES.——FL. IVL. CONSTANTIVS.
CAES.——CONSTANTIVS. NOB. CAES.——FL. IVL. CON-
STANTIVS. NOB. CAES.——D. N. CONSTANTIVS. NOB. C.
(*or* CAES.)——D. N. FL. CL. CONSTANTIVS. NOB. CAES.
——D. N. CONSTANTIVS. IVN. NOB. C.

Gold medallions, of small size   - - - - - - - - - - - - R 8
„   of the usual size - - - - - - - - - - - - - - - R 6
Quinarii - - - - - - - - - - - - - - - - - - R 6
Silver medallions, of small size   - - - - - - - - - - - R 6
„   of the usual size - - - - - - - - - - - - - - R 4
Brass medallions   - - - - - - - - - - - - - - - R 4
Second and third brass - - - - - - - - - - - - - - C

GOLD AND SILVER MEDALLIONS.

1.

FELICITAS. ROMANORVM.   Two military figures, standing within a
temple.   In the exergue, SMN.   - - - - - - - - - AR

2.

GLORIA. EXERCITVS.   Four standards. In the exergue, SMN. - AR

3.

GLORIA. ROMANORVM.   Rome-Nicephore, seated, her right foot
on the prow of a vessel.   In the exergue, SMANT.   (*Thesaur.
Brandenb, tom. ii*, p. 817). - - - - - - - - - - - AU

4.

Same legend.   Rome, and a woman with turreted crown, seated, each
holding a Victory on a globe, and the hasta pura: the foot of the
latter on the prow of a vessel.   In the exergue, TES. - - - AU

5.

VIRTVS. EXERCITVS.   Three standards.   In the exergue, SMKΔ.
(*Mus. Vindob*).   - - - - - - - - - - - - - - AR

6.

XX. within a garland.   The obverse has the bare head of Gallus:
legend, CAESAR.   (*Mus. Vindob*). - - - - - - - - AR

Valued by Mionnet at 100 francs.

The gold are equally rare, and valued by Mionnet at 200 francs each.
In silver, No. 6 is much rarer than the others.

GOLD AND SILVER, OF THE USUAL SIZE.

1.

FELICITAS. ROMANORVM. Two figures, each holding a spear, standing beneath a portico. In the exergue, SMN. *(Banduri).*
AU & AR

2.

GLORIA. REIPVBLICAE. Rome, and a woman, with turreted crown, seated, supporting a shield inscribed, VOTIS. V. In the exergue, SMNB. *or* SMNR. *or* SMNS. - - - - - - - - AU

3.

Same legend. A similar type, with VOT. V. MVLT. X. In the exergue, SM. LVG. - - - - - - - - - - - - - - - AU

The above types brought, in fine condition, 1*l.* 10*s.* to 2*l.* 2*s.* at the Trattle sale.

4.

VICTORIA. AVGVSTORVM. Victory seated on a coat of mail, holding a buckler inscribed, VOT. V.: a genius at her feet. In the exergue, CONOB. (A *quinarius).*—*Mus. Theupoli, vol. i, p.* 347. AU

5.

VOTIS. V. MVLT. X. within a garland. In the exergue, AQ. *or* SIRM. *(Mionnet,* from the cabinet of *M. Gossellin).* - - AR

6.

Without legend. A star, within a laurel garland. In the exergue, ANT. *or* LVG. *or* PAR. - - - - - - - - - - - - AR

In gold, No. 1 is much the rarest. In silver, No. 1 is also the rarest.

BRASS MEDALLIONS.

1.

GLORIA. ROMANORVM. Victory marching, with garland and palm branch.

2.

Same legend. Victory standing, inscribing on a buckler resting on her knees, VOT. V. MVLT. X.

3.

Same legend. Victory marching, with garland and palm branch: a captive on the ground.

4.

VRBS. ROMA. Rome-Nicephore, seated on a buckler.

5.

VICTORIA. AVGG. The emperor standing, in a military habit, holding a globe surmounted by a Victory, and a spear: Victory behind, placing a garland on his head.

6.

VICTORIA. ROMANORVM. Victory marching, with garland and palm branch : a captive kneeling on the ground.

7.

VIRTVS. AVG. Gallus standing, holding a globe surmounted by a Victory, and a spear: on each side, a captive on the ground.

8.

VIRTVS. AVGVSTORVM. A military figure, holding a Victory and a spear: a captive on each side.

Nos. 2, 7, and 8, are the rarest.

CONSTANTINA.

[Constantina, the daughter of Constantinus the Great, by his wife Fausta, was first married to her cousin Hanniballianus, in the year of Rome 1088 (A. D. 335), and subsequently, in 1104 (A. D. 351), to Constantius Gallus. This princess died a short time before the execution of her second husband, 1107 (A. D. 354)].

The coins of Constantina, given by Goltzius, are not authenticated.

SYLVANUS.

[Sylvanus, an usurper, in the reign of Constantius II., was the son of a Gaulish captain, and under that emperor, employed to check the barbarians who threatened Gaul. Sylvanus fell a victim to the foulest treachery. He was accused of a conspiracy against the emperor, which, however, to the satisfaction of Constantius, was proved to be entirely false; but in the mean time Sylvanus endeavoured, by assuming the defensive, to avoid the impending danger, and invested himself with the purple at Cologne, in the year of Rome 1108 (A. D. 355). He was assassinated by those who had assisted him in his usurpation, at the end of a month; and the troops he had commanded, returned to their allegiance].

Goltzius gives coins of Sylvanus, but they are not authenticated.

JULIANUS II.

[Flavius Claudius Julianus, commonly called Julian the Apostate, son of Julius Constantius and Basilina, nephew of Constantine the Great, and brother of Constantius Gallus, was born at Constantinople, in the year of Rome 1084 (A. D. 331). In 1108 (A. D. 355), he was created Caesar, by Constantius II., who gave him in marriage, his sister Helena. Julian was compelled by the legions of Gaul, to assume the purple at Lutetia (Paris), in the year of Rome 1113 (A. D. 360), and the death of Constantius in the following year left him sole master of the empire. He died of a wound received in a battle with the Persians, near the Tigris, three years after his election].

STYLE:——D. N. IVLIANVS. CAES.——IVLIANVS. NOB. CAES. ——CL. IVLIANVS. N. (*or* NOB.) C. (*or* CAES.)——FL. CL. IVLIANVS. N. (*or* NOB.) C. (*or* CAES.)——D. N. IVLIANVS. N. (*or* NOB.) C. (*or* CAES. *or* CAESAR.)——D. N. CL. IVLIANVS. N. (*or* NOB.) C. (*or* CS. *or* CAES.)——D. N. FL. IVLIANVS. N. C.——D. N. FL. CL. IVLIANVS. N. (*or* NOB.) C. (*or* CAES.)——IMP. IVLIANVS. N. (*or* NOB.) C. (*or* CAES.) ——IVLIANVS. AVG.——D. N. CL. IVLIANVS. AVG.—— D. N. FL. CL. IVLIANVS. AVG.——FL. CL. IVLIANVS. P. AVG.——FL. CL. IVLIANVS. P. F. AVG.——IMP. C. IVLIANVS. P. F. AVG.——D. N. IVLIANVS. P. F. AVG.—— D. N. CL. IVLIANVS. P. F. AVG.——D. N. FL. IVLIANVS. P. F. AVG.——D. N. FL. CL. IVLIANVS. P. F. AVG.—— FL. CL. IVLIANVS. P. P. (*or* PER. *or* PERP.) AVG.——D. N. CL. IVLIANVS. PP. (*or* PERP.) AVG. —— D. N. FL. CL. IVLIANVS. PP. AVG.——D. N. CL. IVLIANVS. SEMP. AVG.

Gold medallion, of small size - - - - - - - - - - - - -	R 8
„ of the usual size - - - - - - - - - - - - -	R 2
„ quinarii - - - - - - - - - - - - - - - - -	R 4
Silver medallions, of small size - - - - - - - - - -	R 6
„ of the usual size - - - - - - - - - - - - - -	C
„ quinarii - - - - - - - - - - - - - - - -	R 4
Brass medallions - - - - - - - - - - - - - - -	R 4
Contorniati - - - - - - - - - - - - - - - -	R 8
Second and third brass - - - - - - - - - - - -	C

GOLD AND SILVER MEDALLIONS.

1.

D. N. IVLIANVS. CAES. Three standards. In the exergue, T. CON. - AR

2.

GLORIA. ROMANORVM. Rome, and a woman with turreted crown, seated, each holding a Victory on a globe. In the exergue, KONSTAN. - - - - - - - - - - - - - - - - AU

Valued by Mionnet at 200 francs.

3.

VICTORIA. ROMANORVM. Julian crowned by Victory, standing within a temple. In the exergue, *SIRM. - - - - - - - AR

4.

VOTA. PVBLICA. Anubis standing, holding the sistrum and a caduceus. (In the cabinet of the *Prince of Waldeck*). - - AR

In silver, No. 4 is by far the rarest.

GOLD AND SILVER, OF THE USUAL SIZE.

1.

GLORIA. REIPVBLICAE. Rome helmeted, and a woman with turreted crown, seated, supporting a buckler inscribed, VOTIS. V. A palm branch in the field. In the exergue, KONSTAN. - AU

2.

Same legend. A similar type, but with *V.* MVLT. X. on the buckler. The same letters in the exergue. - - - - - - AU

3.

Same legend. A similar type; a large star on the buckler. In the exergue, CONS. *or* SMAN. II. - - - - - - - - - AU

4.

SPES. REI. PVBLICE. *(sic)*. The emperor standing, in a military habit, holding a globe, and a javelin reversed. In the exergue, CM. . . . (A *quinarius*, given by *Khell*). - - - - - - - AR

5.

VICTORIA. AVGVSTI. N. Victory marching, with a garland and palm branch. In the exergue, R. - - - - - - - - AR

6.

VICTORIA. AVGVSTORVM.   Victory, seated on a coat of mail, inscribing on a buckler, supported by a Genius, VOT. V.   In the exergue, KONSTAN.   (A *quinarius*). - - - - - - - AU

7.

VICTORIA. DD. NN.   Victory, marching.   In the exergue, CON. A. (A *quinarius*). - - - - - - - - - - - - - - - - AU

8.

VICTORIA. DD. NN. AVG.   Victory marching, with garland and palm branch.   In the exergue, LVG.   - - - - - - - AR

9.

VICTORIA. ROMANORVM.   Victory, seated on a coat of mail, inscribing on a buckler, supported by a Genius, VOT. XX.   In the exergue, ANT.   (A *quinarius*). - - - - - - - - - AU

10.

VIRTVS. EXERC. GALL.   The emperor standing, in a military habit; his right hand resting on the head of a kneeling captive, his left holding a trophy: a garland in the field, or an eagle holding a garland on its beak.   In the exergue, KONSTAN.   AU

11.

VIRTVS. EXERCITVS. ROMANORVM.   A similar type, with various letters in the exergue. - - - - - - - - - - AU

This type brought 3*l*. at the Trattle sale.

12.

T. AOVIS. VITIS. X. *(sic)*. within a garland.   In the exergue, IIVAC. (A barbarous coin). - - - - - - - - - - - - - AR

13.

Without legend.   A star within a laurel garland.   - - - - - AR

Mionnet values the *aurei* at forty francs each, excepting No. 11, which is valued at thirty francs only; and the quinarii at twenty-four francs each.   In silver, Nos. 4 and 5 are much the rarest.

BRASS MEDALLIONS.

1.

BONIFATIVS.   A woman standing, holding a Victory: an altar on her right, a child on her left.

The medallions of this type are of large size, and are *Contorniati*.

2.

MONETA. AVG. The three Monetæ, standing. In the exergue, R.

3.

SECVRITAS. REIP. The bull Apis, standing; two stars above his head, and an eagle on a garland at his feet. In the exergue, P. CONST.

4.

SECVRITAS. REIPVB. A similar type, without the eagle, and with AQVIL. P. in the exergue.

5.

VIRTVS. AVG. N. A military figure, with the paludamentum, standing, holding the labarum and a laurel branch, and trampling on a captive.

6.

VIRTVS. CAESARIS. Julian in a military habit, holding a globe, and a javelin reversed : two captives at his feet. In the exergue, R.

7.

VIRTVS. ROMANORVM. The emperor standing, in a military habit, holding a Victory on a globe, and a spear. In the exergue, ANTS.

8.

Without legend. A car on the sea, drawn by two sphinxes, preceded by a dog : Isis above, holding the sistrum. *(Tanini's Sup. ad Band.)*

No. 8 is by far the rarest. Nos. 1 and 7 are the rarest of the other numbers.

SECOND BRASS, WITH RARE REVERSES.

1.

VOTA. PVBLICA. Isis, full-faced, seated, suckling Orus.

2.

Same legend. Isis, holding the sistrum and hasta, seated on a dog running.

3.

Without legend. A similar type to the medallion No. 8. *(Banduri).*

No. 3 is by far the rarest.

THIRD BRASS, WITH RARE REVERSES.

1.

ISIS. FARIA. Bust of Julian without beard, wearing a diadem ornamented with pearls. *(Banduri).*

2.

SPES. REIPVBLICAE. A military figure standing, holding a globe and spear. In the exergue, CONS. A. *or* N.

3.

II. (*or* III. *or* IV. *or* VIII. *or* XIII.) in indented characters.

4.

VOTA. PVBLICA. Isis and Osiris, their forms terminating in serpents, supporting a vase holding an asp. *(Banduri*, from *Ducange).*

Nos. 1 and 4 are much the rarest.

THIRD BRASS.

With various representations of Egyptian deities, supposed to have been struck during the reign of Julianus the Second.

[SERAPIS].

1.

DEO. SERAPIDI. The radiated head of Serapis.—*Rev.* VOTA. PVBLICA. A figure in the stola, walking, holding transversely the hasta, surmounted by the figure of a hippopotamus. (*Tanini*).

2.

DEO. SERAPIDI. (*or* SARAPIDI. *sic*). The radiated head of Serapis.—*Rev.* Same legend. Isis standing, holding the sistrum in her right hand, and the fan in her left.

3.

Same legend, with the head of Serapis radiated, or not radiated. (Size of the quinarius).

4.

DEO. SARARIDI. *(sic).* Radiated head of Serapis.—*Rev.* Same legend. A similar type.

5.

DEO. SERAPIDI. *(sic).* Head of Serapis.—*Rev.* A woman standing, holding a globe. (Size of the quinarius).

6.

Same legend. Same head.—*Rev.* Same legend. A woman standing in a suppliant posture.

7.

Same legend. Same head.—*Rev.* Same legend. Isis standing, suckling Orus.

8.

DEO. SARAPIDI. *(sic).* The head of Serapis radiated, or not radiated. —*Rev.* Anubis standing, holding the sistrum and a caduceus.

9.

Same legend. Head of Serapis.—*Rev.* A similar type. (Size of the quinarius).

10.

Same legend. Head of Serapis.—*Rev.* VOTA. PVBLICA. Isis-Pharia, standing on a galley.

11.

Same legend. A similar type.—*Rev.* A similar type. (Size of the quinarius).

12.

DEO. SERAPIDI. Full-faced head of Serapis.—*Rev.* Isis-Pharia on a galley. *(Ibid.)*

13.

DEO. SARAPIDI. *(sic).* Head of Serapis. *Rev.* Same legend. Isis seated, suckling Orus.

14.

DEO. SERAPIDI. *(or* SARAPIDI.) Radiated head of Serapis.— *Rev.* Same legend. Harpocrates standing, with his attributes.

15.

Same legend. The head of Serapis radiated, or not radiated.—*Rev.* Same legend. A similar type. (Size of the quinarius).

16.

Same legend. The head of Serapis, radiated, or not radiated.—*Rev.* A sphinx.

17.

DEO. SERAPIDI. Head of Serapis.—*Rev.* A similar type. (Size of the quinarius).

18.

Same legend. Head of Serapis, radiated or not radiated.—*Rev.* Two human figures, their bodies terminating in serpents, holding the præfericulum. (?)

19.

DEO. SERAPIDI. *(or* SARAPIDI.) Head of Serapis, radiated or not radiated.—*Rev.* Isis in a biga, holding the sistrum.

20.

DEO. SERAPIDI. Head of Serapis.—*Rev.* Isis, holding the sistrum and the hasta, seated on a dog running.

21.

DEO. SERAPIDI. (*or* SARAPIDI.) Radiated head of Serapis.—*Rev.*
Same legend. The Nile personified, seated on the ground; a
cornucopia on his arm.

22.

DEO. SERAPIDI. Head of Serapis, radiated or not radiated.—*Rev.*
Same legend. The Nile, seated on the ground, holding a bulrush,
or a boat, in his right hand, and sometimes an oar in his left. (Size
of the quinarius).

23.

DEO. SANCTO. SAR. . . . . . (*or* SARAPIDI.). The head of Serapis.
—*Rev.* DEO. SANCTO. NILO. The Nile, seated, holding a
bulrush in his right hand, and a cornucopia or a sceptre in his left.
(Size of the quinarius).

24.

VOTA. PVBLICA. Head of Serapis.—*Rev.* Same legend. The Nile,
seated, holding a vessel in his right hand, and a bulrush in his left.
(Size of the quinarius).

25.

Same legend. A similar type.—*Rev.* Same legend. Isis, seated,
suckling Orus. (Size of the quinarius).

26.

Same legend. Head of Serapis.—*Rev.* Same legend. Anubis, marching,
holding a caduceus and the sistrum.

The above are valued by Mionnet at from two to six francs each.
Nos. 1, 8, 18, 19, 20, 23, 24, and 26, are the rarest.

[ISIS FARIA].

1.

DEA. ISIS. FARIA. Bust of Isis-Faria with the lotus-flower, to the
left, holding the sistrum.—*Rev.* VOTA. PVBLICA. Isis-Faria
on a galley. (Size of the quinarius.—*Mionnet*, from *Tanini*).

2.

ISIS. FARIA. Bust of Isis with the lotus-flower, sometimes holding
the sistrum.—*Rev.* VOTA. PVBLICA. A similar type.

3.

Same legends and types, with the bust of Isis, sometimes veiled and
holding the sistrum. (Size of the quinarius).

4.

ISIS. FARIA.   Full-faced head of Isis, crowned with the lotus-flower.
Rev. Same legend.   Isis-Pharia, standing on a galley and holding
the sail.

5.

Same legend.   Head of Isis, crowned with the lotus-flower.—*Rev.*
Same legend.   A woman standing, holding in each hand an altar.

6.

Same legend.   The head of Isis, crowned with the lotus-flower.—*Rev.*

7.

Same legend.   The head of Isis, crowned with the lotus-flower.—*Rev.*
Same legend.   Harpocrates standing, holding a cornucopia.

8.

Same legends and same type.   (Size of the quinarius).

9.

ISIS. FAIRA. *(sic)*.   Head of Isis, with the lotus-flower.—*Rev.* Same
legend.   A similar type.

10.

ISIS. FARIA.   Bust of Isis, with the sistrum and lotus-flower.—*Rev.*
Same legend.   A similar type.   (Size of the quinarius).

11.

Same legend.   Bust of Isis, full-faced, crowned with the lotus-flower, and
holding the sistrum.—*Rev.* Anubis, standing.   (Size of the quinarius).

12.

Same legend.   Head of Isis, with the lotus-flower.—*Rev.* Same legend.
Anubis standing, holding a branch and a caduceus.

13.

Same legend.   A similar type.   (Size of the quinarius).

14.

Same legend.   A similar type, but with Anubis holding a sistrum and a
caduceus.

15.

Same legend.   Head of Isis.—*Rev.* VOTA. PVBLICA.   The Nile,
seated on the ground, holding a cornucopia.

16.

Same legend.   Same head.—*Rev.* Same legend.   The Nile, seated on
the ground, holding a galley in his right hand, and a bull-rush in
his left.

17.

Same legend. Bust of Isis, crowned by the lotus-flower; sometimes holding the sistrum.—*Rev.* Same legend. Isis standing, holding the sistrum and the fan.

18.

Same legend. Bust of Isis, crowned by the lotus-flower.—*Rev.* Same legend. A similar type. (Size of the quinarius).

19.

Same legend. Bust of Isis, crowned by the lotus-flower, with the sistrum.—*Rev.* Same legend. Serapis, standing.

20.

Same legend. Bust of Isis, holding the sistrum.—*Rev.* Same legend. Isis seated, full faced, suckling Orus.

21.

Same legend. A similar type.—*Rev.* Same legend. Isis seated on a dog running, holding in her right hand the sistrum, and in her left the hasta.

22.

Same legend. A similar type; sometimes without the sistrum.—*Rev.* Isis in a biga, holding the sistrum.

23.

Same legend. Bust of Isis, holding the sistrum.—*Rev.* Same legend. Isis, in a car drawn by two hippopotami, holding a cornucopia.

24.

Same legend. Same bust; sometimes without the sistrum.—*Rev.* Isis walking, her right hand raised, her left enveloped in her stola.

25.

Same legend and type, without the sistrum on the head. (Size of the quinarius).

26.

Same legend. The same bust, with the sistrum.—*Rev.* Same legend. A winged sphinx. (Size of the quinarius).

27.

VOTA. PVBLICA. Bust of Isis, crowned by the lotus-flower, and holding the sistrum.—*Rev.* VOTA. PVBLICA. A figure holding a cornucopia, seated in a car drawn by two hippopotami.

28.

Same legend. Same bust.—*Rev.* Same legend. Isis-Pharia, standing on a galley. (*Mionnet—Tanini*).

29.

VOTA. PVBLICA. Same bust, without the sistrum.—*Rev.* Same legend. Harpocrates standing, holding a cornucopia. (Size of the quinarius).

30.

Same legend. Same bust.—*Rev.* Same legend. Anubis, standing. (*Mionnet*, cabinet of *M. Gossellin*).

Nos. 6 and 23 are the rarest. The next in rarity are Nos. 1 and 24, to 30: then Nos. 2, 4, 5, and 10. The rarest are valued by Mionnet at twelve francs each.

[SERAPIS AND ISIS-FARIA].

1.

DEO. SERAPIDI. *or* SARAPIDI. The heads of Serapis and Isis, side by side.—*Rev.* VOTA. PVBLICA. Isis seated on a wolf, or a dog, running, holding the sistrum and the hasta transversely. (Large size).

2.

Same legend. Same heads.— *Rev.* Same legend. Isis-Faria, standing on a galley.

3.

Same legend. Same heads.—*Rev.* Isis marching, holding the sistrum and the fan.

4.

DEO. SARAPIDI. (*sic*). The same heads.—*Rev.* Same legend. Isis standing in the stola, holding the hasta, and resting her hand on the head of a prostrate figure.

5.

DEO. SERAPIDI. *or* SARAPIDI. The same heads.—*Rev.* Same legend. The Nile seated on the ground, holding in his right hand a vessel, and in his left a bulrush.

6.

Same legend. Same heads.—*Rev.* SANCTO. NILO. A similar type.

7.

DEVS. SARA. . . . The heads of Serapis and Isis, face to face.—*Rev.* VOTA. PVBLICA. Isis, suckling Orus.

8.

VOTA. PVBLICA. The heads of Serapis and Isis.—*Rev.* Same legend. Anubis standing, holding the sistrum.

9.

VOTA. PVBLICA. The heads of Serapis and Isis, face to face.—*Rev.* Same legend. Isis seated, suckling Orus.

Nos. 1, 7, 8, and 9, are the rarest. The next in rarity is No. 6. The rarest are valued by Mionnet at twelve francs each.

THIRD BRASS.

[Struck at Antioch in Syria, during the reign of Julian].

1.

GENIO. ANTIOCHENI. *(sic).* A veiled woman, with turreted crown, seated on a rock : a river-god at her feet.—*Rev.* APOLLINI. *(sic).* SANCTO. Apollo wearing the stola, holding in his right hand a patera, and in his left a lyre. In the field, A. *or* B. *or* I. In the exergue, SMA.

2.

GENIO. CIVITATIS. A female head, with turreted crown and a veil. *Rev.* APOLLONI. *(sic).* SANCTO Apollo, as in the preceding. In the field, B. In the exergue, SMA. *(Tanini).*

Valued by Mionnet at twenty-four francs each.

HELENA.

[Flavia Helena, the daughter of Constantinus the Great and Fausta, was married to Julianus when that prince was declared Caesar, in the year of Rome 1108 (A. D. 355). She died a short time after her husband had been proclaimed Augustus; namely, in the year of Rome 1113 (A. D. 360)].

STYLE:——FL. HELENA. AVGVSTA.

Gold - - - - - - - - - - - - - - - - - - R 8
Third brass - - - - - - - - - - - - - - - - Ct

GOLD.

SECVRITAS. REIPVBLICAE. A woman in the stola, standing. In the exergue, SMT.

This type brought 23*l.* at the sale of the Trattle collection. It is valued by Mionnet at 1000 francs. "On connoit," says this writer, "une medaille de coin moderne, avec l'exergue, SMR."

---

† The coins of this lady have been assigned erroneously to Helena, wife of Constantius Chlorus. *(See Eckhel, tom. viii.)*

JOVIANUS.

[Flavius Jovianus, the son of Varronianus, was born at Singidonum in
Pannonia, in the year of Rome 1084 (A. D. 331). He was head
officer in the palace of Julian; and upon the death of that prince, was
elected emperor; "not so much on account of his own merit," says
Eutropius, "as on that of his father, who was a great favourite of the
soldiers," 1116 (A.D. 363). Jovianus died at Dardastana in Bithynia,
having concluded a dishonourable peace with Sapor, king of Persia, in
the year of Rome 1117 (A. D. 364), after a short reign of seven
months and twenty days].

STYLE:——D. N. IOVIANVS. AVG.——D. N. IOVIANVS. P. F.
AVG.——D. N. FL. C. IOVIANVS. P. F. AVG. (only on a
Contorniate medal, published by *Ducange*].——D. N. IOVIANVS.
PERP. AVG.——D. N. IOVIANVS. PP. P.——D. N. IOVI-
ANVS. P. F. P. (*or* P. F. PP. *or* P. F. PERP.) AVG.

Gold medallions, of large size - - - - - - - - - - - - -	R 8
,, of the usual size - - - - - - - - - - - - - -	R 6
,, quinarii - - - - - - - - - - - - - - - - -	R 6
Silver medallions, of small size - - - - - - - - - - - -	R 6
,, of the usual size - - - - - - - - - - - - - -	R 2
,, quinarii - - - - - - - - - - - - - - - -	R 2
Brass medallions - - - - - - - - - - - - - - -	R 3
,, *Contorniati* - - - - - - - - - - - - - -	R 3
Second brass - - - - - - - - - - - - - - - - - -	S
Third brass - - - - - - - - - - - - - - - - - -	R 1

GOLD AND SILVER MEDALLIONS.
1.

GAVDIVM. ROMANORVM.   The emperor in military habit, seated
on a buckler, presenting his hand to a prostrate woman; his right
hand holding a spear: Victory standing by, with garland and palm
branch.   In the exergue, CONS. A. *or* CONS. P.   (Very large
size). - AU

Valued by Mionnet at 1000 francs.

2.

GLORIA. ROMANORVM.   The emperor, standing under a portico,
holding a globe and a spear.   - - - - - - - - - - AR

Valued by Mionnet at 100 francs.

GOLD AND SILVER, OF THE USUAL SIZE.

1.

CONCORDIA. MILITVM. A male and female figure, supporting a shield, on which is a Victory. (A *quinarius*). - - - - AR

2.

N. OVIANVS. *(sic)*. P. F. AVG. around a sort of garland. The fabric is barbarous. - - - - - - - - - - - - - - - AR

3.

SECVRITAS. REIPVBLICAE. Rome, and a woman with turreted crown; the latter holding the hasta, and her foot resting on the prow of a vessel, supporting together a buckler inscribed, VOT. V. MVLT. X. In the exergue, ANє. *or* ANTO. *or* CONS. P. *or* RSMQ. *or* *SIRM. *or* SIRM., and a palm branch. - - - - - - AU

4.

Same legend. The emperor, standing in a military habit, holding the standard of the cross and a globe : a captive seated at his feet. In the exergue, *SIRM. - - - - - - - - - - - - - - AU

5.

SECVRITAS. REIPVBLICE. *(sic)*. A similar type. In the exergue, SIRM., and a palm branch. *(Plate xii, No. 2)*. - - AU

6.

VICTORIA. AVGVSTORVM. Victory, marching with a garland and a globe, surmounted by a cross. In the field, R. V. In the exergue, CON. (A *quinarius*). - - - - - - - - - AU

7.

VOT. V. MVLT. X. within a garland. In the exergue, ANT. - AR

8.

Same legend. A similar type. In the exergue, S. CONST. *or* T. CONST. (*Quinarii*). - - - - - - - - - - - - - AR

9.

VOT. X. MVLT. XX. within a garland. In the exergue, T. CONST. (*Mionnet*, from the cabinet of *M. Gosselin*). - - - - - - AR

In gold, Nos. 4 and 5 are by far the rarest: the next in rarity is No. 3. In silver, No. 9 is the rarest; the next in rarity is No. 1.

BRASS MEDALLIONS.

1.

ADVENTVS. AVGVSTI. The emperor on horseback as Pacificator, preceded by a soldier bearing the standard of the cross, and followed by Victory, who places a garland on his head. In the exergue, ROMA.

Valued by Mionnet at forty francs.

2.

MONETA. AVG.   The three Monetæ, standing.   (*Mionnet, Mus. Florent*).

3.

VICTORI. AVGVS.   The labarum, terminating in a cross, with the monogram of Christ : two captives seated at the foot.

4.

VICTORIA. ROMANORVM.   The emperor with the paludamentum, holding the standard of the cross, and a globe surmounted by a Victory.   (*Tanini*).

5.

VRBS. ROMA.   Rome-Victrix, seated.   (*Baldini, add. Vaillant*).

6.

Without legend.   The emperor on horseback, piercing a lion with his javelin.   (The medallions of this type are *Contorniati*).

No. 1 is the rarest.

SECOND BRASS.

1.

VICTORIA. ROMANORVM.   The emperor standing, in a military habit, holding the standard of the cross, and a globe surmounted by a Victory.   In the exergue, ANT. B. *or* ANT. Γ. *or* TES. B. *or* TES. Δ.

2.

VOTA. PVBLICA.   Isis seated, suckling Orus.

3.

Same legend.   Two women ; their bodies terminating in serpents, supporting a vase, from which a serpent, or an asp, is escaping.

The last two types, and the following in third brass, are rather singular for the coins of a Christian emperor, as they resemble the money of Julian. (See pp. 304, 5). The existence of such types on the reverse of money bearing the head of Jovian, who professed the Christian religion, can only be accounted for by supposing that they were struck in some distant province, and that the reverses which may have been designed for the coins of Julian, were adopted for those of the new emperor, whose religion might not have been known to the mint masters.

No. 3 is much the rarest; and No. 2 is much rarer than No. 1.

THIRD BRASS.

1.

VOTA. PVBLICA. Anubis standing, holding the sistrum in his right hand, and in his left a caduceus.

2.

Same legend. Isis in a biga of mules, holding the sistrum.

3.

Same legend. A similar type : Anubis, preceding the biga.

4.

Same legend. Isis Faria, standing on the prow of a vessel.

5.

Same legend. Harpocrates, standing.

Nos. 2 and 3 are the rarest.

VALENTINIANUS. I.

[Flavius Valentinianus, the son of Gratianus, was born at Cibalæ in Pannonia, in the year of Rome 1074 (A. D. 321). He was an officer under Jovianus; and upon the death of that emperor at Nicæa, was invested with the purple, 1117 (364). Valentinianus died at Brigitio in Pannonia, in the year of Rome 1128 (A. D. 375)].

STYLE : ——D. N. VALENTINIANVS. AVG.——VALENTINI-ANVS. P. AVG.——D. N. VALENTINIANVS. P. AVG.——VALENTINIANVS. P. F. AVG. —— D. N. VALENTINI-ANVS. P. F. AVG.——D. N. FL. VALENTINIANVS. P. F. AVG. [On reverse, sometimes, RESTITVTOR. REIP. (or REIPVB-LICAE.) or TRIVMFATOR. GENT. BARB. (or BARBAR.)].

Gold medallions, of small size - - - - - - - - - - - -	R 6
„ of the usual size - - - - - - - - - - - - - -	C
„ quinarii - - - - - - - - - - - - - - - - -	R 2
Silver medallions, of small size - - - - - - - - - - -	R 2
„ of the usual size - - - - - - - - - - - - - -	VC
„ quinarii - - - - - - - - - - - - - - - - -	R 1
Brass medallions - - - - - - - - - - - - - - -	R 6
„ Contorniati - - - - - - - - - - - - - - -	R 3
Second brass - - - - - - - - - - - - - - - - -	S
Third brass - - - - - - - - - - - - - - - - -	VC

GOLD AND SILVER MEDALLIONS.

1.

FELIX. ADVENTVS. AVG. N. The emperor on horseback, as
Pacificator. In the field, L. D. In the exergue, COM. - - AU

2.

FELIX. ADVENTVS. AVG. M. *(sic).* A similar type. In the
exergue, SMAQ. *(Mionnet).* - - - - - - - - - - - AU

3.

FELIX. ADVENTVS. AVGGG. A similar type. In the exergue,
SMTR. - - - - - - - - - - - - - - - - - - AU

4.

GLORIA. ROMANORVM. Rome, and a figure with turreted crown,
seated; the latter with her foot on the prow of a vessel, holding a
globe surmounted by a Victory, and the hasta. In the exergue,
CONOB. *or* TR. OB. - - - - - - - - - - - - - AU

5.

Same legend. The emperor standing, with the nimbus around his head,
holding a spear in his right hand; his left on his buckler. In the
exergue, CON. - - - - - - - - - - - - - - AR

6.

Same legend. The emperor standing, holding the labarum and a
buckler. In the exergue, LVGPS. - - - - - - - - AR

7.

Same legend. The emperor in a quadriga, full-faced. In the field, TR.
In the exergue, COM. - - - - - - - - - - - - AU

8.

RESTITVTOR. REIPVBLICAE. The emperor standing, holding the
labarum and a Victory. In the exergue, ANTꟅ. - - - - AR

9.

SALVS. REIPVBLICAE. Four standards. In the exergue, LVG. *or*
T. CON. - - - - - - - - - - - - - - - - AR

10.

SECVRITAS. REIP. Valentinian and Valens, standing, holding the
labarum, and supporting a Victory, who places a garland on their
heads. In the exergue, CONS. PR. - - - - - - - AR

11.

VICTORIA. AVGVSTORVM. Victory, leading a captive, and bearing
a trophy. In the exergue, ROMA. - - - - - - - AR

12.

VICTORIA. AVGVSTORVM. Victory, standing, inscribing on a buckler, VOT. V. MVLT. X. In the exergue, RT. - - AR

13.

Same legend. A similar type; with VOT. X. MVLT. XV. In the exergue, SMKAP. - - - - - - - - - - - - - AR

14.

VICTORIA. D. N. AVGVSTI. Victory seated, inscribing on a buckler, supported by a winged Genius, VOT. V. MVLT. X. In the exergue, TES. OB. - - - - - - - - - - - - - - AU

This medallion has a loop. It is engraved in *Steinbuchel's* description of the gold medallions of the Cabinet of Vienna.

15.

VIRTVS. EXERCITVS. The emperor standing, holding the standard of the cross, and a buckler. In the exergue, SISCP. - - - AR

16.

Same legend. A similar type; but without the monogram of Christ on the labarum. In the exergue, TRPS. - - - - - - - AR

17.

VOTIS. V. MVLTIS. X. within a laurel garland. In the exergue, SMTR. - - - - - - - - - - - - - - - - - - AR

18.

VOTIS. V. MVLT. XV. within a laurel garland. In the exergue, SMLAP. - - - - - - - - - - - - - - - - - AR

19.

VOT. XV. MVLTIS. XX. within a laurel garland. In the exergue, SISCP. *or* SISCPS. - - - - - - - - - - - - - AR

In gold, the first four are the rarest. In silver, Nos. 10 and 11 are the rarest; the next in rarity are Nos. 9, 12, and 13; Nos. 5, 8, 18, and 19, are the least rare.

GOLD AND SILVER, USUAL SIZE, WITH RARE REVERSES.

1.

PAX. PERPETVA. Victory, seated on a coat of mail, holding a buckler supported by a winged Genius, inscribed, VOT. V. MVLT. X. In the exergue, TES. (A *quinarius*).—*Khell.* - - - AU

2.

PAX. PERPETVA. Victory standing, full-faced, waving in each hand a laurel garland. In the exergue, TESOB. (A *quinarius*).—*Mus. Vindob.* - - - - - - - - - - - - - - - - - - - AU

3.

SALVS. REIP. The emperor, standing, in a military habit; his right foot on a kneeling captive; his right hand holding the standard of the cross; in his left, a globe surmounted by a Victory : a star in the field. In the exergue, SMSISC. and a palm branch.   - AU

4.

TRIVMFATOR. GENT. BARB. The emperor, in a military habit, standing, holding the labarum and a globe: a captive at his feet. In the exergue, TH. OB. *or* TR. OB. - - - - - - - - AU

5.

VICTORIA. AVGG. Victory, marching, with garland and palm branch. In the exergue, RP. (A *quinarius*). - - - - - AR

6.

VICTORIA. AVGVSTORVM. Victory, seated on a coat of mail, inscribing on a buckler, VOT. V. MVL. X. In the field, B. In the exergue, CONS✱. - - - - - - - - - - - - - AU

7.

Same legend. Same type; but with VOT. X. MVLT. XX.: the monogram of Christ in the field; and ANOB. Θ. in the exergue.
AU

8.

Same legend. Victory marching, bearing a garland and a palm branch. In the field, L. P. In the exergue, CON. (A *quinarius*). - AU

9.

VIRTVS. ROMANORVM. Two military figures, standing, supporting a globe surmounted by a Victory, who places a garland on their heads. In the exergue, CONS. P. - - - - - - - - AU

10.

VOTA. PVBLICA. Two figures seated, each with the nimbus, holding a book and a sceptre: a captive at their feet. In the exergue, ✱CONS. and a garland. - - - - - - - - - - - - AU

11.

VOTIS. V. MVLTIS. X. within a laurel garland. In the exergue, SIRM. - - - - - - - - - - - - - - - - - - AR

12.

VOT. X. MVLT. XX. within a garland. In the exergue, CONS. AR

13.

Same legend, within a garland. In the exergue, MDPΔ. *or* MDPS.
(A *quinarius*). - - - - - - - - - - - - - - AR

14.

VOTIS. XV. MVLT. XX. within a garland. In the exergue, SISCPE.
(*Mionnet*). - - - - - - - - - - - - - - - AR

15.

Without legend. A cross, within a laurel garland. In the exergue,
CONOB. (A *quinarius*). - - - - - - - - - - AU

In gold, No. 4 is by far the rarest. In silver, No. 14 is the rarest.

BRASS MEDALLIONS.

1.

MONETA. AVG. *or* AVGG. The three Monetæ, standing, with their
attributes.

2.

RESTITVTOR. REIPVBLICAE. The emperor standing, with the
paludamentum; the labarum in his right hand, and a globe
surmounted by a Victory, in his left. In the exergue, PR. *or* RT.
or SNNB.

3.

VICTORIA. AVGGG. An armed figure standing, holding a staff
surmounted by a cross in his right hand, and a Victory in his left;
his right foot on a helmet; on his left a buckler.

4.

VRBS. ROMA. Roma-Victrix, seated.

The first is valued by Mionnet at twelve francs: the last three at
twenty francs each.

THIRD BRASS.

1.

VOT. PVB. The Praetorian camp: beneath the portico, O. (Size of
the quinarius).

2.

VOTA. PVBLICA. Isis, seated on a dog, holding the sistrum and the
hasta.

3.

VOTA. PVBLICA.　Isis scated, suckling Orus.

4.

Same legend.　Harpocrates, standing.

No. 3 is the rarest; and No. 1 is the least rare.

SEVERA.

[Valeria Severa was married to the emperor Valentinianus before his elevation, and repudiated by him about the year of Rome 1121 (A. D. 368).　Severa died, as is supposed, in the reign of her son Gratianus].

Goltzius gives coins of this lady, but they are not authenticated.

JUSTINA.

[Flavia Justina, the second wife of Valentinianus the First, was born in Sicily.　She was the widow of Magnentius, and married the Emperor Valentinianus, in the year of Rome 1121 (A.D. 368).　Justina died at Thessalonica in Macedonia, in the year of Rome 1140 (A.D. 387)].

The coins of Justina, described by Goltzius, are not authenticated.

VALENS.

[Flavius Valens, the brother of Valentinianus the First, was born near Cibalæ in Pannonia, in the year of Rome 1081 (A. D. 328).　He was associated with his brother in the empire in the year 1117 (A. D. 364), and appointed to the government of the East with the title of Augustus, while Valentinianus ruled the provinces of the West. Valens, according to Claudianus, was burnt to death in a house in which he had shut himself up, after his defeat by the Goths near Adrianople, in the year of Rome 1131 (A. D. 378).　Other accounts vary; but he was never seen after the battle].

STYLE:——D. N. VALENS. AVG.——D. N. VALENS. P. A.—— D. N. VALENS. P. F. AVG.　[On reverse, sometimes, RESTITVT. ORBIS. (or RESTITVTOR. REIP. or REIPVBLICAE. or TRIVMFATOR. GENT. BARB.]——IMP. CE. (sic) VALENS. P. F. AG. (sic). —— D. N.

VALENS. PERP. AVG. [On reverse, sometimes, RESTITVTOR.
REIPVBLICAE.]——D. N. VALENS. PER. F. AVG.   [On reverse,
as in the preceding.]——D. N. VALENS. MAX. AVGVST. (*or*
AVGVSTVS.) [On reverse, sometimes, D. N. VALENS. VICTOR.
SEMPER. AVG.]

Gold medallions, of large size	R 6
,, ,, small size	R 6
,, of the usual size	C
Quinarii	R 3
Silver medallions, of large size	R 6
,, ,, small size	R 4
,, of the usual size	VC
Brass medallions	R 2
Second brass	C
Third brass	VC

GOLD AND SILVER MEDALLIONS.

1.

D. N. VALENS. VICTOR. SEMPER. AVG.   Valens, with the
nimbus encircling his head, in a car drawn by six horses; on each
side, a Victory placing a garland on his head. In the exergue, RM.
with the modius and other attributes. (Very large size).—*Mus.
Vindob.* - - - - - - - - - - - - - - - - - AU

Valued by Mionnet at 1500 francs.

2.

Same legend. A similar type; with RM. in the exergue. - - - AU

This medallion is rather smaller than the preceding, and has a loop.
It is engraved in Steinbüchel's notice of the gold medallions in the
cabinet of Vienna. Mionnet values it at 1500 francs.

3.

FELIX. ADVENTVS. AVGGG.   The emperor, on horseback. In
the exergue, SMTR. - - - - - - - - - - - - - AU

4.

GLORIA. ROMANORVM.   The emperor on horseback, with the
nimbus: before, a woman; another woman seated on the ground;
a cornucopia, &c.: A. and N. (Very large size). - - - - AU

Quoted by Mionnet from the Mus. Vindob., and valued by him at 2000
francs.

5.

GLORIA. ROMANORVM. The emperor on horseback, with the
nimbus: before, a prostrate woman, with turreted crown: a figure
on the ground. In the exergue, AN. - - - - - - - AU

This medallion is of a very large size, and has a loop. (See
Steinbuchel). It is valued by Mionnet at 4000 francs.

6.

Same legend. A similar type, but of a smaller size. *(Steinbuchel)*. AU

Valued by Mionnet at 2000 francs.

7.

Same legend. Two emperors seated on the same throne, each with the
nimbus, their right hands raised, and a globe in their left. In the
exergue, R. N.: between which are symbols. - - - - - AU

8.

Same legend. A woman seated to the left, holding a globe surmounted
by a Victory, and the hasta transversely; her feet resting on the
prow of a vessel. In the exergue, ROMA. - - - - - - AU

This medallion is described by Steinbuchel. It is mounted in an ornamented circle with a loop. Mionnet values it at 600 francs.

9.

Another, of a similar type, with a border and loop, but of a rather smaller
size. *(Steinbuchel)*. - - - - - - — - - - - - - - - AU

10.

Same legend. A female seated, her right foot resting on the prow of a
vessel, holding the hasta, and a globe surmounted by a Victory. In
the exergue, ROMA. - - - - - - - - - - - - - AU

11.

Same legend. Rome seated, holding a spear, and a Victory on a globe.
In the exergue, TROBS. *or* TROSS. - - - - - - - - AU

12.

Same legend. Two military figures standing, holding the standard of the
cross and a globe. In the exergue, SIS. and a star. - - - AR

13.

LIBERATOR. REIPVBLICAE. The emperor on horseback, with
the nimbus: before, a woman, holding a cornucopia. In the
exergue, S. M. A. Q. *(Steinbuchel)*. - - - - - - - - AU

14.

PIETAS. DDD. NNN. AVGVSTORVM. Three figures standing, with the paludamentum, each holding a spear and a buckler; the middle figure with the nimbus. In the exergue, TESOB. *(Mionnet,* from *Mus. Vindob.).* - - - - - - - - - AU

15.

Same legend. A similar type. In the exergue, TESOB. *(Steinbuchel).*

AU

This medallion has a border and loop, and is of a large diameter. Mionnet values it at 800 francs.

16.

RESTITVTOR. REIP. The emperor standing, holding a globe surmounted by a Victory, and the standard of the cross. In the exergue, TCONST. - - - - - - - - - - - - - AR

17.

RESTITVTOR. REIPVBLICAE. The emperor standing, holding the labarum and a Victory. In the field, to the right, a cross. In the exergue, ANTI. - - - - - - - - - - - - - - - AR

18.

SALVS. REIPVBLICAE. Four standards. In the exergue, S. CON.*

AR

19.

TRIVMFATOR. GENT. BARB. The emperor standing, holding the labarum and a globe; a captive on his right. In the exergue, TRPS. - - - - - - - - - - - - - - - - - AR

Valued by Mionnet at 100 francs.

20.

VICTORIA. AVGVSTORVM. Victory, bearing a trophy and dragging a captive. In the exergue, RP. - - - - - - - - - AR

21.

Same legend. Victory standing, inscribing on a buckler VOT. V. MVLT. X. In the exergue, RB. - - - - - - - - - AR

22.

VIRTVS. EXERCITVS. The emperor standing, holding the labarum and a buckler. In the exergue, TRPS. - - - - - - - AR

23.

Same legend. A military figure standing, holding a spear and a buckler. In the exergue, P. CON. - - - - - - - - AR

24.

VOT. V. MVLT. X. within a garland. In the exergue, SM. AQ. - AR

25.

VOT. X. MVLT. XV. within a garland. - - - - - - - - - AR

26.

VOTIS. V. MVLTIS. X. within a garland. In the exergue, TRPS. - AR

27.

VOTIS. X. MVLTIS. XV. within a garland. In the exergue, S. M.

L. P. and a palm branch. - - - - - - - - - - - - AR

28.

VOTIS. XV. MVLTIS. XX. within a garland. In the exergue,

SISCPZ. - - - - - - - - - - - - - - - - - AR

In gold, most of the medallions above described, are of extreme rarity, and some of them, in all probability, are unique. The least rare are Nos. 3, 11, and 13. In silver, No. 19 is by far the rarest.

GOLD AND SILVER, USUAL SIZE, RARE REVERSES.

1.

GLORIA. ROMANORVM. Two helmeted women, seated; one of whom rests her foot on the prow of a vessel, and holds the hasta pura, supporting a buckler inscribed, VOT. X. MVLT. XX.: above the buckler, the monogram of Christ. In the exergue, ANOBΔ. - AU

2.

RESTITVT. ORBIS. The emperor standing, with the paludamentum, holding the standard of the cross, and a Victory. In the exergue, PLVS. (*Tanini's Supplement*). - - - - - - - - - AR

3.

RESTITVTOR. REIP. The emperor standing, in a military habit, holding the standard of the cross and a globe, surmounted by a Victory. In the field, OF. I. *or* II., and a star. In the exergue, CONST. *or* P. LVG. - - - - - - - - - - - - - AR

4.

RESTITVTOR. REIPVBLICAE. A similar type. In the field, a cross. In the exergue, *ANTA.* - - - - - - - - - AR

5.

SALVS. REIP. The emperor standing, in a military habit, holding the standard of the cross, and a Victory on a globe; his right foot on a kneeling captive. In the field, one or two stars. In the exergue, SMTES. - - - - - - - - - - - - - - - - AU

6.

SECVRITAS. REIPVBLICAE. Victory marching, with garland and palm branch. In the exergue, R. TERTIA. (A *quinarius*). AU

7.

SPES. R. P. Two emperors seated, each with the nimbus, and holding the hasta and a globe; a figure standing between them: above, a buckler, on which is inscribed VOT. V. MVL. X. In the exergue, ANTΓ..... - - - - - - - - - - - - - - - AU

8.

VICTORES. AVGVSTI. Two emperors seated, supporting a globe: above, Victory placing a garland on their heads. In the exergue, TR. OB• - - - - - - - - - - - - - - - - AU

9.

VICTORIA. AVGVSTI. N. Victory marching, holding a garland and a palm branch. In the exergue, TR. (A *quinarius*). - - AU

10.

VICTORIA. AVGVSTORVM. Victory, seated on a coat of mail, inscribing on a buckler supported by a Genius, VOT. V. MVLT. X. In the exergue, TROB. (A *quinarius*). - - - - - AU

11.

Same legend. A similar type; but without the Genius. In the field, OB. In the exergue, CON. - - - - - - - - - - - AU

12.

Same legend. Victory seated on arms, inscribing on a buckler VOT. X. MVL. XX. In the field, the monogram of Christ. In the exergue, AN. OBH. *or* P. AN. OB. - - - - - - - - AU

13.

Same legend. Victory seated on a coat of mail, inscribing on a buckler supported by a Genius, VOT. X. In the exergue, R. and a palm branch; *or* SMRP. (A *quinarius*). - - - - - - - - AU

14.

Same legend. Victory marching, with garland and palm branch. In the exergue, TROB. (A *quinarius*). - - - - - - - - AU

15.

VIRTVS. ROMANORVM. Two emperors standing, supporting a globe, each in a military habit, and holding a spear : Victory placing a garland on their heads. In the exergue, CONS. and two palm branches ; *or* TR. OBS. - - - - - - - - - - AU

16.

VOT. V. within a laurel garland. In the exergue, COB. - - - AR

17.

VOT. V. MVLT. X. within a garland. In the exergue, RB. - - AR

18.

VOT. X. MVLT. XX. within a garland. In the exergue, ANT. *or*
  ANT. A. *or* LVG. *or* SISCP. - - - - - - - - - - - AR

19.

VOT. XX. MVLT. XXX. within a garland. In the exergue, CON.
  CM. - AR

In gold, Nos. 7 and 8 are the rarest. The next in rarity are Nos. 6
and 12. In silver, Nos. 2, 4, and 19, are the rarest; the next in rarity
are Nos. 3 and 17.

BRASS MEDALLIONS.

1.

MONETA. AVGG. *or* AVGGG. The three Monetæ, standing. In
 the exergue, RQ.

2.

RESTITVTOR. REIPVBLICAE. The emperor standing, with the
 paludamentum, holding the labarum, and a Victory on a globe. In
 the exergue, RP. *or* SMQP.

Valued by Mionnet at ten and twenty francs.

THIRD BRASS, WITH RARE REVERSES.

1.

VOT. XX. MVLT. XXX. within a laurel garland. Various letters in
 the exergue. (Size of the quinarius).

2.

VOTA. PVBLICA. Isis seated, suckling Orus. (Same size).

3.

Same legend. The Nile, seated on the ground.

4.

Same legend. Harpocrates, standing.

5.

Same legend. Anubis standing, holding the sistrum and a caduceus.

Those bearing the figures of Egyptian deities, are much rarer than the
others.

DOMINICA.

[Albia Dominica, the wife of Valens, was married to the emperor before
 his elevation, and died, as is supposed, in the reign of Theodosius].

Goltzius gives coins of this lady, but they are not authenticated.

PROCOPIUS.

[Procopius was born of an illustrious family, in the year of Rome 1087 (A. D. 334), and was himself a man of learning, and a friend of the emperor Julianus, under whom he served as an officer. During the absence of Valens, in Syria, Procopius assumed the purple at Constantinople, 1118 (A. D. 365), but at the end of eight months was reduced by Valens, and given up by his own men to the conqueror, who caused him to be beheaded.*

Style :———D. N. PROCOPIVS. P. F. AVG.

Gold - R 8
Silver - R 6
Brass medallion - - - - - - - - - - - - - - - - R 8
Second brass - - - - - - - - - - - - - - - - - - R 8
Third brass - - - - - - - - - - - - - - - - - - R 6

GOLD AND SILVER, OF THE USUAL SIZE.

1.

SECVRITAS. REIPVBLICAE. *or* REIPVB. The emperor standing, in the paludamentum; his right hand holding a spear, his left resting on a shield. - - - - - - - - - - - - - - - AU

2.

VICTORIA. AVG. Victory, seated on a coat of mail, inscribing on a buckler, supported by a winged genius, VOT. V. In the exergue, CONS. (A *quinarius*). - - - - - - - - - - - - AU

3.

VOT. V. within a laurel garland. - - - - - - - - - - AR

4.

VOT. V. within a laurel garland. In the exergue, C. Δ. *or* . . . . Є. *or* C. Γ. *or* CS. *or* CT. *or* SMN. *or* KVB. *(Plate xii, No. 3).* AR

Mionnet values the gold at 250 francs, and the silver at fifty francs each.

---

* The account which Zosimus gives of Procopius (Book iv.) is curious and interesting; and, if it may be credited, would incline us to pity this unfortunate usurper, who, it would appear, assumed the purple as the only probable means of preserving his life. He had been forced by his enemies from the retirement he had sought, to struggle for the empire.

BRASS MEDALLION.

REPARATIO. FEL. TEMP. Procopius, standing in the toga, holding a spear in his right hand, his left resting on a shield. In the exergue, SMHT.

Valued by Mionnet at sixty francs.

SECOND BRASS.

FEL. TEMP. REPARATIO. *or* REPARATIO. FEL. TEMP. The emperor in the paludamentum, holding the standard of the cross; his left hand on a buckler, and his right foot on the prow of a vessel. *(Mus. Vindob.)*.

Valued by Mionnet at fifty francs.

THIRD BRASS.

1.

FEL. TEMP. REPARATIO. *or* REPARATIO. FEL. TEMP. The emperor standing, wearing the paludamentum, holding in his right hand the labarum; his left resting on a buckler: a captive seated on the ground. The monogram of Christ, in the field. In the exergue, CONS. B.

2.

FEL. TEMP. REPARATIO. The emperor standing, in a military habit, holding a spear and a buckler. In the exergue, CONS. T.

3.

Same legend. The emperor standing, with the labarum and a buckler.

4.

GLORIA. EXERCIT. Two military figures standing, and an ensign.

5.

GLORIA. ROMANORVM. The emperor, on horseback. (Size of the quinarius).

6.

REPARATIO. PVBLICA. A military figure standing, holding the labarum and a buckler. In the field, the monogram of Christ. In the exergue, SMHA.

7.

Without legend. A cross, within a laurel garland. (Size of the quinarius). *(Tanini's Supplement to Banduri)*.

Nos. 1, 6, and 7, are the rarest.

GRATIANUS.

[Gratianus, the son of Valentinianus I. and Severa, was born at Sirmium in Pannonia, in the year of Rome 1112 (A. D. 359), and at the age of eight years was created Caesar by his father, at Ambianum (Amiens). Upon the death of that emperor, Gratianus succeeded him in the government of the West, 1128 (A. D. 375). Gratianus was killed by the troops of Magnus Maximus, against whom he had marched, in the year of Rome 1136 (A. D. 383)].

STYLE:——D. N. GRATIANVS. AVG.——D. N. GRATIANVS. P. F. AVG. [On reverse, sometimes, PRINCEPS. IVVENTVTIS. (or RESTITVTOR. REIPVBLICAE.)]——D. N. GRATIANVS. PP. AVG. ——D. N. GRATIANVS. PPP. AVG.——D. N. GRATIANVS. AVGG.* AVG.

Gold medallions, of large size - - - - - - - - - - - - -	R 8
„ „ small size - - - - - - - - - - - -	R 6
„ of the usual size - - - - - - - - - - - - - - -	C
„ quinarii - - - - - - - - - - - - - - - - -	R 1
Silver medallions, of small size - - - - - - - - - - -	R 6
„ of the usual size - - - - - - - - - - - - - -	C
„ quinarii - - - - - - - - - - - - - - - - -	R 4
Brass medallions - - - - - - - - - - - - - - - -	R 4
Second brass - - - - - - - - - - - - - - - - -	C
Third brass - - - - - - - - - - - - - - - - -	C

GOLD AND SILVER MEDALLIONS.

1.

GLORIA. ROMANORVM. Rome seated, full faced, holding a spear and a globe. In the exergue, TROBC. or TROBS. - - - AU

2.

Same legend. A similar type. In the exergue, TROBS. - - - AU

This medallion is given by Steinbuchel, in his account of the gold medallions of the Vienna cabinet. It is mounted in a wide circle, and has a loop. Mionnet values it at 800 francs.

---

* Various interpretations have been given of this legend. Hardouin was of opinion that, if not contracted, it would read GRATIANVS. AVGVSTI. GENER. AVGVSTVS.; and Spanheim supposes it to have the same meaning. (See the "Remarques" of the Baron Bimard de la Bastie, in Jobert's *Science des Medailles*, tom. ii, pp. 324-6. Also, the observations of Eckhel, *Doct. Num. Vet.* tom. viii, p. 158.

3.

GLORIA. ROMANORVM. The emperor in a military habit, standing, holding a spear transversely, and a globe. In the exergue, ANT. - AR

4.

Same legend. Rome, and a woman with turreted crown, seated, holding a Victory on a globe; the latter rests her foot on the prow of a vessel. In the exergue, TROBS. or TROBT. - - - - - AU

5.

VICTORIA. AVGG. Gratianus and the younger Valentinianus, seated, supporting a globe, and crowned by Victory. In the exergue, TROBT. - - - - - - - - - - - - - - AR

6.

VIRTVS. EXERCITVS. The emperor standing, holding the labarum and a buckler. In the exergue, SMTR, or TRPS. *(Vignette).* AR

7.

VOTIS. V. MVLTIS. X. within a laurel garland. In the exergue, S. M. L. A. P. - - - - - - - - - - - - - - - AR

8.

VOTIS. X. MVLTIS. XX. within a garland. In the exergue, TRPS. AR

9.

VOTIS. XV. MVLTIS. XX. within a garland. In the exergue, SISCPZ. - - - - - - - - - - - - - - - - AR

In gold, No. 2 is much the rarest; the next in rarity is No. 1. In silver, No. 5 is the rarest, and No. 8 is the least rare.

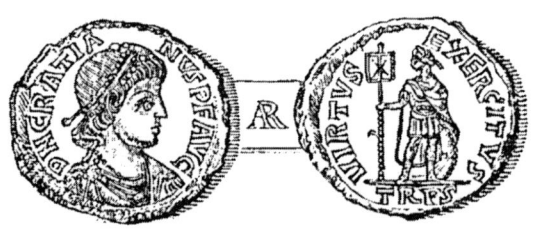

GOLD AND SILVER, USUAL SIZE, WITH RARE REVERSES.

1.

CONCORDIA. AVGG. Є. Rome, holding a spear and a globe, seated
on a throne placed on the prow of a vessel. In the exergue,
CONOB. - - - - - - - - - - - - - - - - - - AU

2.

GLORIA. NOVIS. (sic). or NOVI. SAECVLI. The emperor in a
military habit, holding in his right hand a figure of Victory standing
on a globe, and in his left the labarum charged with the monogram
of Christ, and surmounted by another Victory, who supports with
the first a laurel garland above the head of the emperor. In the
exergue, LVG. - - - - - - - - - - - - - - - AU

3.

GLORIA. NOVI. SAECLI. (sic). A military figure standing,
holding the standard of the cross, and resting his hand upon a
shield. In the exergue, T. CON. (Mionnet.—Cabinet of M.
Gosselin). - - - - - - - - - - - - - - - - - AR

4.

GLORIA. ROMANORVM. Rome seated, holding a globe and a
spear. In the exergue, LVGPS. - - - - - - - - - AR

5.

PRINCIPIVM. IVVENTVTIS. The emperor standing, in a military
habit, wearing the diadem, and holding a globe and a lance transversely. In the exergue, *CONS. and a garland ; or SMTR. AU

6.

RESTITVTOR. REIPVBLICAE. The emperor standing, in a
military habit, holding the standard of the cross, and a globe surmounted by a Victory, who places a garland on his head: on the
ground, an eagle. In the exergue, SMRB. - - - - - - AU

7.

VICTORIA. AVGG. Victory marching, holding a garland and palm
branch. In the exergue, AQPS. - - - - - - - - - AR

8.

VICTORIA. AVGVSTORVM. Victory seated on a coat of mail,
inscribing on a buckler VOT. V. MVLT. X.: the monogram of
Christ, in the field. In the exergue, ANOBЄ. or KANOBЄ. AU

9.

Same legend. Victory seated, holding a buckler supported by a Genius,
on which is inscribed VOT. X. In the exergue, ... NT.
(A quinarius).—Mionnet.- - - - - - - - - - - - AU

10.

VICTORIA. AVGVSTORVM. A similar type. In the exergue, TRORT. (A *quinarius*). - - - - - - - - - - - AU

11.

VIRTVS. ROMANORVM. Rome seated, holding a globe and a spear. In the exergue, TRPS. (A *quinarius*). - - - - AU

12.

Same legend. A similar type. In the exergue, AQPS. *or* TRP. *or* TRPS. - - - - - - - - - - - - - - - - - - AR

13.

VOTA. PVBLICA. Two figures seated, each with the nimbus, holding a book. In the exergue, TR. OB. *or* TROBT. - - AU

14.

VOTA. PVBLICA. Hercules standing, with club and lion's skin (A *quinarius*).—*Banduri*. - - - - - - - - - - - AR

15.

VOT. V. MVLT. X. within a garland. In the exergue, SAN. *or* SN. AR

16.

VOT. X. MVLT. XX. in four lines within a laurel garland. In the exergue, SISCP. - - - - - - - - - - - - - - AR

17.

VOT. XV. MVLT. XX. within a garland. In the exergue, SISCP. *or* SISCPS. - - - - - - - - - - - - - - - - - AR

18.

VOTIS. X. MVLTIS. XX. within a garland. In the exergue, AQPS. AR

19.

VOTIS. XV. MVLT. XX. within a garland. In the exergue, LVGN. *or* SISCPZ. (*Mionnet*, from the cabinet of *M. Gosselin*). - AR

In gold, Nos. 2, 5, 6, and 13, are the rarest. In silver, No. 14 is the rarest; the next in rarity are Nos. 3 and 19; then Nos. 7 and 18.

BRASS MEDALLIONS.

1.

VRBS. ROMA. Roma-Victrix, seated.

2.

Same legend. Rome seated, holding a globe and a spear : on one side, a buckler. In the exergue, RT.

Valued by Mionnet at twenty francs each.

THIRD BRASS, WITH RARE REVERSES.

1.

FELICITAS. TEMPORVM.   Victory, marching.   In the exergue, SMAQS.

2.

GLORIA. NOVI. SAECVLI.   A military figure standing, holding the standard of the cross, and resting his hand on a buckler.   In the exergue, CON. *or* T. CON.

3.

VOTA. PVBLICA.   Isis, holding the hasta and a vase.

4.

VOTA. PVBLICA.   Isis, in a car drawn by two mules.

5.

Same legend.   Anubis standing, holding a branch and a caduceus.

Nos. 2 and 4 are the rarest.

CONSTANTIA.

[There are no authentic coins of this lady.   She was married to the emperor Gratianus, in 1127 (A. D. 374), and died some months before him].

VALENTINIANUS II.

[Flavius Valentinianus, the son of Valentinianus the First and Justina, was born at Acincum in Pannonia, in the year of Rome 1124 (A.D. 371).   Upon the death of his father, he was saluted Augustus by the legions of Pannonia, and ruled jointly with his brother and his uncle 1128 (A. D. 375): Valentinianus having the government of Illyria, Africa, and Italy; Gratianus that of the Western Provinces; and Valens still ruling the East.   Upon the death of Gratianus, Valentinianus succeeded to the government of the East, in 1136 (A. D. 383).   This emperor was assassinated at Vienna, in the year of Rome 1145 (A. D. 392)].

STYLE: —— D. N. VALENTINIANVS. IVN. P. AVG. —— D. N. VALENTINIANVS. IVN. P. F. AG. (*or* AVG.)   [On reverse, sometimes, RESTITVTOR. REIPVBLICAE.] —— D. N. VALENTINIANVS. P. F. AVG.

The coins of this emperor without the word IVNior. cannot be distinguished from those of his father.   In consequence of this, all those which bear simply, D. N. VALENTINIANVS. P. F. AVG., are assigned to the elder

Valentinianus. The common coins bearing a helmeted bust,—*Rev.* a figure standing on a galley; legend, GLORIA. ROMANORVM.,—are supposed to belong to Valentinianus the Second. It should also be observed that the coins of Valentinianus the Third are only known to belong to him when they bear the name, PLAC*idius.*

Gold medallions, of large size - - - - - - - - - - -	R 8
„ „ small size - - - - - - - - - - -	R 8
„ of the usual size - - - - - - - - - - - - - - - -	C
„ quinarii - - - - - - - - - - - - - - - - -	R 1
Silver medallions, of small size - - - - - - - - - -	R 8
„ of the usual size - - - - - - - - - - - - -	VC
Brass medallion (*Beauvais, Hist. des Emp. tom ii.* p. 316) - - -	R 6
Second brass - - - - - - - - - - - - - - - - - -	S
Third brass - - - - - - - - - - - - - - - - - -	VC

GOLD AND SILVER MEDALLIONS.

1.

FELIX. ADVENTVS. AVG. *or* AVG. N. *or* AVGVST. N. The emperor, on horseback. In the exergue, TROBT. - - - AU

Valued by Mionnet at 200 francs.

2.

RESTITVTOR. REIPVBLICAE. The emperor standing, holding the standard of the cross, and raising up a woman with turreted crown who kneels at his feet. In the exergue, TROBS. (Large size). AU

Valued by Mionnet at 600 francs.

3.

Same legend. A similar type. In the exergue, TROBT. (Same size). (*Mionnet*). - - - - - - - - - - - - - - - - - - AU

4.

VIRTVS. EXERCITVS. The emperor standing, with the labarum and a buckler. In the exergue, AQ. PS. - - - - - - AR
Valued by Mionnet at 100 francs.

GOLD AND SLVER, USUAL SIZE, WITH RARE REVERSES.

1.

CONCORDIA. AVGGG. A helmeted woman, seated, her right foot resting on the prow of a vessel, holding a spear, and a shield inscribed VOT. XV. MVLT. XX. In the exergue, COMOB. AU

2.

GLORIA. ROMANORVM. Two women, seated. *(Mus. Vindob.)*. AU

3.

PERPETVETAS. *(sic)*. A phœnix, with radiated head, standing on a globe. *(Banduri)*. - - - - - - - - - - - - - - - AR

4.

VICTORIA. AVGGG. Victory, marching. In the exergue, AQPS. *or* LVGP3. *or* TRPS. - - - - - - - - - - - - - - AR

5.

VICTORIA. AVGVSTORVM. Victory, seated on a coat of mail, inscribing on a buckler, VOT. V. In the field, the monogram of Christ. In the exergue, ANOBI. *or* ANOBS. - - - - - AU

6.

Same legend. Victory marching, with garland and palm branch. In the exergue, CON. (A *quinarius*). - - - - - - - - - AU

7.

VIRTVS. ROMANORVM. Rome, seated, holding a spear and a globe. In the exergue, AG. PS. - - - - - - - - - - AR

8.

VOT. V. MVLT. X. within a garland. In the exergue, TE. *or* TH. and the monogram of Christ. *(Mus. Vindob.)*. - - - - - AU & AR

9.

VRBS. ROMA. Rome, seated, holding a Victory and a spear. In the field, sometimes, a star. In the exergue, AQ. PS. - AU & AR

In gold, No. 9 is the rarest type, and No. 6 is the least rare. In silver, Nos. 3 and 7 are the rarest, and Nos. 4 and 9 are the least rare.

SECOND BRASS.

REPARATIO. REIPVB. The emperor standing, in a military habit, holding in his right hand a globe surmounted by a Victory, and raising up a female with turreted crown, who kneels at his feet. In the exergue, TCON.

Valued by Mionnet at twenty-four francs.

THIRD BRASS, WITH RARE REVERSES.

1.

CONCORDIA. AVGG. Rome seated, holding a globe. In the exergue, LVGZ. *or* ꜱ.

2.

GLORIA. ROMANORVM. The emperor in a military habit, holding the labarum in his right hand, his left resting on a kneeling captive. In the exergue, SMARP.

3.

VRBS. ROMA. Roma-Victrix, seated. In the field, Θ.Φ. In the exergue, ANTB. *or* ANTΔ.

Valued at four francs each by Mionnet.

THEODOSIUS MAGNUS.

[Theodosius, surnamed the Great, was born of an illustrious family, at Italica in Spain, in the year of Rome 1099 (A.D. 346). He was associated in the empire with Gratianus, and succeeded Valens in the government of the East in 1132 (A.D. 379). Theodosius died at Mediolanum *(Milan)*, in the year of Rome 1148 (A.D. 395)].

STYLE:——D. N. THEODOSIVS. P. F. AV. (*or* AVG.) [On reverse, sometimes, TRVMFATOR. GENT. BARB.]

The coins which bear the name of Theodosius have always the same legend on the obverse; and it is difficult to distinguish to which of the two princes of this name they should be attributed. Some of them, however, without doubt, belong to the younger Theodosius; and these are the coins which bear on the reverse IMP. XXXXII. COS. XVII. P. P.; the first number evidently signifying the year of the reign of this prince, from the period that he was raised to the rank of Augustus; namely, in the year of Rome 1155 (A.D. 402). The forty-second year of his reign commenced in 1196 (A.D. 443), and the younger Theodosius had been exactly seventeen times consul. This cannot be applied to Theodosius the Great, who reigned only sixteen years. It should be observed, that legends like those in question are not found on the coins of the period in which the younger Theodosius reigned. Banduri and Mediobarba give other coins, which, however, have not been authenticated, bearing the legends, TR. P. XXXVII. COS. XVII. P. P., and TR. P. XXXXII. COS. XVIII. P. P. No coins with these legends are at present known : if really genuine, these also belong to the younger Theodosius; the numbers agreeing with the times that he had held the consulship and the tribunitian power. Again, the coins which bear the inscriptions, VOT. XX. MVLT. XXX., and VOT. XXX. MVLT. XXXX., are given to the same emperor; the elder Theodosius having reigned but sixteen years. A great many of the coins alluded to, bear on the obverse, the full-faced and helmeted bust of the emperor, with spear and buckler; and it is believed that all those which have a similar bust, whatever may be the legend on the reverse, belong to the younger Theodosius. In conclusion, the coins which bear on the reverse the letters xr. within a laurel garland, are also assigned to the second Theodosius; this description of type occurring for the first time on the coins of Placidia, wife of Constantius Patricius, and being, as is supposed, adopted after the reign of the first Theodosius, to whom the coins not bearing the legends above quoted, are given, although some of them may possibly belong to the other emperor of the same name.

Gold, of the usual size - - - - - - - - - - - - - - C
    „   quinarii - - - - - - - - - - - - - - - - - R 1
Silver medallions - - - - - - - - - - - - - - - R 4
    „   of the usual size - - - - - - - - - - - - - - C
Brass medallions - - - - - - - - - - - - - - - R 3
Contorniati - - - - - - - - - - - - - - - - - R 2
Second brass - - - - - - - - - - - - - - - - - C
Third brass - - - - - - - - - - - - - - - - - C

SILVER MEDALLIONS.

1.

CONCORDIA. AVGGG. Theodosius seated, holding a spear and a globe. In the exergue, COMOB.

2.

GLORIA. ROMANORVM. The emperor standing, with the nimbus, and holding a globe; his right hand extended. In the exergue, COM. *or* MRPS.

3.

TRIVMFATOR. . . . . ARB. . . . The emperor standing, wearing the paludamentum, holding the labarum and a globe: a captive at his feet. In the exergue, TR.

4.

VICTORIA. AVGG. Two emperors seated, supporting a globe: behind, Victory, placing a garland on their heads. In the exergue, L D. CON.

No. 3 is the rarest.

GOLD AND SILVER, USUAL SIZE, WITH RARE REVERSES.

1.

CONCORDIA. AVGGG.   A woman with turreted crown, seated, her
   right foot on the prow of a vessel, holding a spear and a cornucopia.
   In the exergue, AQPS. or TRPS. - - - - - - - - AR

2.

CONCORDIA. AVGGG. B. or Γ. or Θ.   A helmed woman, seated,
   her right foot on the prow of a vessel, holding a spear and a buckler
   inscribed, VOT. X. MVLT. XV.   In the exergue, CONOB. - AU

3.

GLORIA. ORVIS. (sic). TERRARVM.   The emperor standing,
   wearing the paludamentum, holding the labarum and a globe
   surmounted by a cross. (Banduri). - - - - - - - - AR

4.

GLORIA. ROMANORVM.   The emperor, on horseback.   In the
   exergue, ANT. A. or T. - - - - - - - - - - - - - AR

5.

VICTORIA. AVGG.   Victory, seated on a coat of mail, inscribing on
   a buckler, XX. XXX.   A star in the field, and the monogram of
   Christ.   In the exergue, CONOB. (A quinarius).   - - - AU

6.

VICTORIA. AVGGG.   The emperor standing, in a military habit,
   holding in his right hand a staff surmounted by a cross, and in his
   left two javelins; his right foot on a lion.   In the field, R. V.   In
   the exergue, COB.   - - - - - - - - - - - - - - AU

7.

Same legend.   Victory marching, with garland and palm branch.   In
   the exergue, AQPS. (Mionnet, Cat. d'Ennery). - - - - AR

8.

VICTORIA. AVGVSTORVM.   Victory marching, holding in her
   right hand a garland, and in her left a globe, surmounted by a cross.
   In the exergue, CONOB. (A quinarius).   - - - - - AU

9.

Same legend.   Victory marching, with garland and palm branch.   In
   the field, TR.   In the exergue, CON. (A quinarius).   - - AU

10.

VIRT. EXERC. ROM.   The emperor standing, wearing the paludamentum; his right hand holding a captive by the hair, his left
   holding a trophy, which he rests on his shoulder.   In the exergue,
   CONOB. (Tanini's Supp.)   - - - - - - - - - - AU

11.

VIRTVS. ROMANORVM. Roma-Victrix, seated. In the exergue, MDPS. *or* TRPS. - - - - - - - - - - - - - AR

12.

VOT. V. MVLT. X. within a garland. In the exergue, SISCPZ. *(Mionnet, cabinet of M. Gosselin).* - - - - - - - - AR

13.

VOT. X. MVLT. XX. within a garland. In the exergue, CONS. *or* MDPS. *or* TES. *or* TR. - - - - - - - - - - - - - AR

14.

VOT. XV. MVLT. XX. within a garland. - - - - - - - - AR

15.

VRBS. ROMA. Roma-Victrix, seated. In the exergue, R✳P. *or* R✳T. *or* LVGPS. - - - - - - - - - - - - - - - AR

16.

Without legend. A trophy. (A *quinarius*).—*Mus. Vindob.* - - AU

In gold, Nos. 10 and 16 are much the rarest. In silver, Nos. 3 and 7 are the rarest. The next in rarity is No. 4.

BRASS MEDALLIONS.

1.

VIRTVS. AVGVSTORVM. The emperor standing, wearing the paludamentum, holding the hasta or the labarum in his right hand; his left resting on a shield.

2.

EVTIMI. VINICAS. *(sic)*. A military figure in a quadriga, full-faced. In the exergue, MVSALLIGER. *(sic)*. and two palm branches. *(Tanini)*.

3.

Without legend. The emperor on horseback, piercing an enemy with his javelin.

The last two are *Contorniati*.

THIRD BRASS, WITH RARE REVERSES.

1.

GLORIA. ROMANORVM. Three military figures, standing. In the exergue, ANTA. (Size of the quinarius).

2.

GLORIA. AVGGG. Two Victories standing, full faced. (Same size).

FLACCILLA.

[Aelia Flaccilla, the daughter of Antonius, Praefect of Gaul, and wife of the emperor Theodosius, was born in Spain. She was married to Theodosius before his elevation to the empire, and died in Thrace, in the year of Rome 1141 (A.D. 388)].

STYLE:——AEL. FLACCILLA. AVG.

Gold, of the usual size - - - - - - - - - - - - - - - R 6
„ quinarii - - - - - - - - - - - - - - - - - R 6
Silver, of the usual size - - - - - - - - - - - - - R 6
Second brass - - - - - - - - - - - - - - - - - - - R 1
Third brass - - - - - - - - - - - - - - - - - - - R 1

GOLD AND SILVER.

1.

SALVS. REIPVBLICAE. ⚹. Victory seated on a buckler, inscribing the monogram of Christ on another buckler. In the exergue, CONOB. or QSISC. - - - - - - - - - - - - AU & AR

2.

Without legend. The monogram of Christ within a laurel garland. In the exergue, CONOB. P. or CONS. (A *quinarius*).—*Plate xii, No.* 4. - - - - - - - - - - - - - - - - - - - AU

Mionnet values the gold at eighty and at seventy-two francs. The silver at fifty francs.

SECOND BRASS.

1.

SALVS. REIPVBLICAE. A woman standing with the stola, her hands joined. In the exergue, ALEB. or ANT. or ✳ or ANTϹ.

2.

Same legend. A similar type, with the monogram of Christ in the field. In the exergue, CONS. Ϲ. or SMKΓ.

3.

Same legend. Victory seated on a cippus, inscribing on a buckler the monogram of Christ. In the exergue, ANTB. or ANTR. or ASISCO. or CONΓ. or CONϹ.

4.

Same legend. A similar type. In the field, T. In the exergue, ANTS. or CONϹ. or SMNΓ.

These types are of equal rarity.

THIRD BRASS.

1.

SALVS. REIPVBLICAE.   A woman wearing the stola, standing, her hands clasped together.   In the field, sometimes a cross or a star. In the exergue, SMHA.

2.

Same legend.   Victory seated, inscribing on a buckler the monogram of Christ.   In the exergue, SMHA. *or* TESΔ.

MAGNUS MAXIMUS.

[Magnus Maximus was a Spaniard by birth, and commander of the legions in Britain under the emperor Gratianus.   He raised the standard of revolt, and set out for Gaul with an immense army, in the year of Rome 1136 (A. D. 383).   He subsequently procured the murder of Gratianus, and obtained by treaty as his portion of the empire the provinces on this side the Alps; but his insatiate ambition prompted him to invade Italy, from which the younger Valentinianus fled precipitately, 1140 (A. D. 387).   Maximus was encountered and defeated by Theodosius in the following year, and fled to Aquileia, where he was seized and beheaded by order of that emperor].

STYLE:——D. N. MAG. MAXIMVS. P. AVG.——D. N. MAG. MAXIMVS. P. F. AVG.   [On reverse, sometimes, RESTITVTOR. REIPVBLICAE.]——D. N. MAG. MAXIMVS. PP. AVG.

Gold - - - - - - - - - - - - - - - - - - -	R 1
„ quinarii - - - - - - - - - - - - - - -	R 2
Silver medallions - - - - - - - - - - - - - -	R 8
„ of the usual size - - - - - - - - - - - -	C
„ quinarii - - - - - - - - - - - - - - -	S
Second brass - - - - - - - - - - - - - - - -	R 1
Third brass - - - - - - - - - - - - - - -	S

SILVER MEDALLIONS.

1.

RESTITVTOR. REIPVBLICAE.   Maximus standing, wearing the paludamentum, holding the labarum and a Victory.   In the exergue, SM.

2.

VIRTVS. EXERCITVS.   The emperor standing, holding the labarum in his right hand, and a buckler on his left.   In the exergue . .

Valued by Mionnet at 150 francs each.

GOLD AND SILVER, OF THE USUAL SIZE.

1.

RESTITVTOR. REIPVBLICAE.   The emperor standing, holding the
standard of the cross, and a globe surmounted by a Victory.   In
the exergue, SMTR. - - - - - - - - - - - - - AU

2.

Same legend.   A similar type, with a star in the field.   - - - AU

3.

SPES. ROMANORVM.   The gate of the Praetorian camp: above, a
star. - - - - - - - - - - - - - - - - - - - AR

4.

VICTORIA. AVGG.   Two figures in imperial habits, seated on the
same throne, full-faced, supporting together a globe : a winged
Victory behind.   In the exergue, AVCOB. *or* ORT. *or* TROB. AU

5.

VICTORIA. AVGVSTORVM.   Victory marching, with garland and
palm branch.   In the exergue, SMTR. *(A quinarius).* - - AU

6.

Same legend.   A similar type.   In the exergue, ACPS. *or* AQPS.
(Quinarii). - - - - - - - - - - - - - - - - AR

7.

VIRTVS. ROMANORVM.   A helmed woman seated, holding a globe
and a spear.   In the exergue, AQPS. *or* MDPS. *or* TRPS.
(Quinarii). - - - - - - - - - - - - - -

In gold, Nos. 1 and 2 are much the rarest.   In silver, No. 3 is much
the rarest.

VICTOR.

[Flavius Victor, the son of Magnus Maximus, was declared Caesar by
his father, in the year of Rome 1136 (A. D. 383).   He perished shortly
after his father, by the hands of the soldiers of Theodosius, 1141
(A. D. 388)].

STYLE:——D. N. FL. VICTOR. P. F. AVG.

Gold - - - - - - - - - - - - - - - - - - -	R 6
„ quinarii - - - - - - - - - - - - - - - -	R 6
Silver - - - - - - - - - - - - - - - - - -	R 1
„ quinarii - - - - - - - - - - - - - - - -	R 2
Third brass - - - - - - - - - - - - - - - -	R 2

GOLD AND SILVER, OF THE USUAL SIZE.

1.

BONO. REIPVBLICE. *(sic)*. NATI. Two figures wearing the paludamentum, seated on the same throne, full-faced, supporting together a
globe: a winged Victory behind. In the exergue, TROB. - AU & AR

2.

SPES, ROMANORVM. The Praetorian camp. In the exergue,
ANLOP. - - ` ~ - - - - - - - ` - - - - - - AR

3.

VICTORIA. AVGVSTORVM. Victory marching, with garland and
palm branch. In the exergue, AQPS. (A *quinarius*). - - AR

4.

Same legend. Victory seated on a coat of mail, holding a buckler
inscribed, VOT. V. MVLT. X.: a winged genius, standing. In the
exergue, M. D. OB. (A *quinarius*).—*Mus. Vindob.* - - - AU

5.

VIRTVS. ROMANORVM. A helmeted woman, seated, holding in her
right hand a globe, and in her left a spear reversed. In the
exergue, AQPS. *or* MDPS. *or* TRPS. - - - - - - - AR

6.

Same legend. A similar type. In the exergue, AQPS. (A *quinarius*).
AR

Unpublished: in the cabinet of *Alexander Mills, Esq.*

In gold, No. 1 is much the rarest. In silver, No. 2 is by far the rarest;
and No. 6 is the next in rarity.

THIRD BRASS.

SPES. ROMANORVM. The Praetorian camp. In the exergue, LVG.
or P. CON. *or* SM. *or* SMQP. *or* SMRP.

EUGENIUS.

[Eugenius was originally a teacher of grammar and rhetoric, and subsequently master of the palace. He was proclaimed Augustus, at
Vienne, by Arbogastes, the murderer of Valentinianus the younger, in
the year of Rome 1145 (A. D. 392). Eugenius had his title
acknowledged by the western provinces, but was vanquished and put
to death at Aquileia, by order of Theodosius, two years afterwards].

STYLE :——D. N. EVGENIVS. P. F. AVG.

Gold medallions, of small size - - - - - - - - - - - - R 8

　„　of the usual size - - - - - - - - - - - - - - R 4

　„　quinarii - - - - - - - - - - - - - - - - - 'R 4

Silver medallions, of small size - - - - - - - - - - - R 8

　„　of the usual size - - - - - - - - - - - - - - R 2

　„　quinarii - - - - - - - - - - - - - - - - - R 3

Third brass - - - - - - - - - - - - - - - - - - R 7

GOLD AND SILVER MEDALLIONS.

1.

GLORIA. ROMANORVM.　Rome and Constantinople personified, seated.　In the field, T. R.　In the exergue, COM. - - - AU

2.

Same legend.　Eugenius, standing, holding the labarum.　In the exergue, MDPS. - - - - - - - - - - - - - - - AR

Mionnet values the gold at 200, and the silver at fifty francs.

GOLD AND SILVER, OF THE USUAL SIZE.

1.

VICTORIA. AVGG.　Two figures in regal habits, each with the nimbus, seated on the same throne, full faced, supporting together a globe: Victory behind.　In the field, L. D. or M. D.　In the exergue, COM. (*Plate xii, No. 5*). - - - - - - - - AU

2.

VICTORIA. AVGVSTORVM.　Victory marching, with garland and palm branch.　In the field, TR.　In the exergue, COM. or CON. (*Quinarii*). - - - - - - - - - - - - - AU & AR

3.

VIRTVS. ROMANORVM.　Roma-Victrix, seated on a coat of mail. In the exergue, TRPS. - - - - - - - - - - - - AR

4.

Same legend.　A similar type.　In the exergue, MDPS. or TRPS. (*Quinarii*). - - - - - - - - - - - - - - - AR

5.

VRBS. ROMA.　Rome, seated on a coat of mail, holding a globe surmounted by a Victory, and a spear.　In the exergue, LVGPS. - AR

6.

Same legend.　A similar type.　(A *quinarius*). - - - - - - AR

In gold, No. 1 is the rarest.　In silver, Nos. 3 and 5 are the rarest.

THIRD BRASS.

VIRTVS. ROMANORVM. Victory marching, with garland and palm branch.

This coin is valued by Mionnet at forty francs.

ARCADIUS.

[Arcadius, the son of Theodosius Magnus and Flaccilla, was born in Spain, about the year of Rome 1130 (A. D. 377). He was declared Caesar by his father, in 1136 (A. D. 383), and succeeded to the government of the East (his brother Honorius ruling the West), in the year 1148 (A. D. 395). Arcadius died at Constantinople, in the year of Rome 1161 (A. D. 408)].

STYLE:——D. N. ARCADIVS. P. F. AVG. (*or* AVGVSTVS). [On reverse of some coins, TRIVMFATOR. GENT. BARB.].

Gold medallions, of large size - - - - - - - - - - - -	R 6
„ of the usual size - - - - - - - - - - - - - - -	C
„ quinarii - - - - - - - - - - - - - - - - -	R 1
Silver medallions - - - - - - - - - - - - - - -	R 2
„ of the usual size - - - - - - - - - - - - -	R 1
„ quinarii - - - - - - - - - - - - - - - -	R 2
Brass medallions - - - - - - - - - - - - - - -	R 4
Second brass - - - - - - - - - - - - - - - - - -	S
Third brass - - - - - - - - - - - - - - - - -	C

GOLD AND SILVER MEDALLIONS.

1.

GLORIA. ROMANORVM. The emperor, in a chariot drawn by six horses, full faced. In the field, the monogram of Christ. In the exergue, CO. . . OB. (Large size). - - - - - - - - AU

Valued by Mionnet at 400 francs.

2.

Same legend. A woman seated, her right foot resting on the prow of a vessel, holding a globe and a spear. In the field, the monogram of Christ. In the exergue, CONO. . . - - - - - - - - AU

Valued by Mionnet at 300 francs.

3.

GLORIA. ROMANORVM. The emperor standing, the nimbus encircling his head; his right hand raised, and a globe in his left. In the exergue, AQP. - - - - - - - - - - - - - AR

4.

TRIVMFATOR. *(sic)*. GENT. BARB. The emperor standing, wearing the paludamentum, and holding the labarum and a globe : a captive at his feet, in a suppliant posture. *(Mus. Vindob).* - - - AR

5.

VICTORIA. AVGGG. The emperor standing, holding the labarum and a Victory, and trampling on a captive. In the field, M. P. In the exergue, COMOR. *(Mionnet, Cat. d'Ennery).* - - - AR

6.

VIRTVS. EXERCITVS. An armed figure, standing; his right hand on a javelin reversed, his left resting on a buckler. In the exergue, RVPS. *(Tanini's Supplement).* - - - - - - - - - - AR

In gold, No. 1 is the rarest. In silver, Nos. 3 and 6 are much the rarest.

GOLD AND SILVER, OF THE USUAL SIZE.

1.

CONCORDIA. AVGGG., and a numeral letter : Rome seated, holding a buckler, inscribed VOT. X. MVLT. XV. In the exergue, CONOB. - - - - - - - - - - - - - - AU

2.

NOVA. SPES. REIPVBLICAE. Victory seated on arms, inscribing on a buckler, XX. XXX. In the exergue, CONOB. - - AU

3.

NOVA. SPES. REIPVBLICAE. B. A similar type: a star in the field. In the exergue, CONOB. - - - - - - - - - - - - AU

4.

VICTORIA. AVGG. Two figures in imperial habits, each with the nimbus, supporting together a globe: behind, Victory. In the exergue, COM. - - - - - - - - - - - - - - - - AU

5.

VICTORIA. AVGGG. Victory marching, with garland and palm branch. In the exergue, RM. (A *quinarius*). - - - - AR

6.

VICTORIA. AVGVSTORVM. Victory marching, holding aloft in her right hand a garland, and on her left a globe surmounted by a cross. In the exergue, COM. *or* CONOB. *(Quinarii).* - - AU

7.

VICTORIA. AVGVSTORVM. A similar' type: with M. D. in the
field; *or* M. *or* R. In the exergue, COM. (*Quinarii*). - - AU

8.

VIRTVS. ROMANORVM. Roma-Victrix, seated. In the exergue,
MDPS. *or* . . . . QPS. *or* TRPS. - - - - - - - - - - AR

9.

VOT. V. MVLT. X. within a garland. In the exergue, MD. P. S.
(*Khell*). - - - - - - - - - - -.- - - - - - - AR

10.

VOT. X. MVLT. XX. within a garland. In the exergue, CONS. *or*
MDPS. - - - - - - - - - - - - - - - - - - - AR

11.

VRBS. ROMA. Roma-Victrix, seated. In the exergue, LVG. PS.
AR

In gold, Nos. 2, 3, and 4, are the rarest. In silver, No. 9 is the
rarest; the next in rarity is No. 11.

BRASS MEDALLION.

VOTA. ROMANORVM. The emperor standing, holding the labarum
and a buckler: a captive on the ground. In the exergue, A.
(*Tanini*).

Valued by Mionnet at twenty-four francs.

THIRD BRASS, WITH RARE REVERSES.

1.

GLORIA. REIPVBLICAE. The Praetorian camp. In the exergue,
TES. (Size of the quinarius).

2.

GLORIA. ROMANORVM. Three military figures, standing. In the
exergue, ANT. B. (Same size).

3.

VIRTVS. AVGG. The emperor standing on a galley, holding the
labarum and a globe: Victory seated on a rudder. . In the exergue,
MRS. . (*Tanini's Supp.*). .

EUDOCIA.

[Aelia Eudoxia, or Eudocia, daughter of Bauto, a General of the Franks in the pay of the Romans, was married to Arcadius in the year of Rome 1148 (A. D. 395), and died in 1157 (A D. 404)].

There are no certain coins of this lady. (See those described under Eudocia, or Eudoxia, wife of Theodosius the Second).

HONORIUS.

[Honorius, son of Theodosius and Flaccilla, was born at Constantinople, in the year of Rome 1137 (A. D. 384), and created Augustus by his father in 1146 (A. D. 393). He succeeded to the empire of the West in 1148 (A. D. 395), and died at Ravenna in 1176 (A. D. 423)].

STYLE: —— HONORIVS. AVGVSTVS. —— D. N. HONORIVS. AVG.——D. N. HONORIVS. P. AVG.——D. N. HONORIVS. P. F. AVG. [On reverse, sometimes, TRIVMFATOR. GENT. (or GENTT.) BARB. (or BARBAR.)].

Gold medallions, of large size - - - - - - - - - - - -	R 8
„ „ small size - - - - - - - - - - - -	R 8
„ of the usual size - - - - - - - - - - - - - - -	C
„ quinarii - - - - - - - - - - - - - - - - -	R 1
Silver medallions, of large size - - - - - - - - - - -	R 6
„ „ small size - - - - - - - - - - -	R 4
„ of the usual size - - - - - - - - - - - - -	C
„ quinarii - - - - - - - - - - - - - - - -	R 1
Brass medallions - - - - - - - - - - - - - - -	R 4
„ Contorniati - - - - - - - - - - - - - - -	R 4
Second brass - - - - - - - - - - - - - - - -	S
Third brass - - - - - - - - - - - - - - - -	C

GOLD AND SILVER MEDALLIONS.

1.

GLORIA. ROMANORVM. Rome seated, full-faced, holding a globe and a spear. In the field, R. V. In the exergue, COMOB. (Large size). - - - - - - - - - - - - - - - - - - AU

2.

GLORIA. ROMANORVM. A similar type. In the field, M. B.
In the exergue, COMOB. - - - - - - - - - - - AU

This medallion, which is of large diameter, is mounted in an ornamented circle of gold with festoons, and has a loop, Mionnet values at
600 francs.

3.

Same legend. The emperor, in a car drawn by six horses. *(Banduri).*
AU

4.

TRIVMFATOR. GENT. BARB. The emperor standing, holding in
his right hand the standard of the cross, and in his left a globe : a
captive at his feet. In the exergue, MDPS. *or* RMPS. (Large
size). - - - - - - - - - - - - - - - - - AR

5.

VOT. V. MVLT. X. within a garland. In the exergue, MBPS. *or*
MDPS. - - - - - - - - - - - - - - - - AR

In gold, No. 2 is much the rarest; the next in rarity is No. 1. In
silver, No. 4 is much the rarest.

GOLD AND SILVER, USUAL SIZE, WITH RARE REVERSES.

1.

ANNO. IIII. A woman, standing, holding ears of corn. In the field,
A. In the exergue, a star, between two palm branches. (A *quinarius*).—*Mionnet*, from *Cat. d'Ennery.* - - - - - - - AR

2.

GLORIA. ROMANORVM. Rome, seated, holding a spear and a
globe. In the exergue, RVPS. (A *quinarius*). - - - - AR

3.

IVSSV. RICHIARI. REGES. *(sic).* round a garland, within which is
a cross, between the letters B. R. In the exergue, a garland.
(*Mionnet*, from the cabinet of *M. Gosselin*). - - - - - - AR

" Cette medaille unique," observes Mionnet, "paroit être le seul
monument que l'on ait des Suèves."

4.

VICTORIA, AVGG. Rome, seated, holding a Victory and a spear.
(*Mionnet*, from *Cat. d'Ennery*). - - - - - - - - AR

5.

VICTORIA. AVGGG. Victory, marching, with garland and palm branch. In the exergue, MD. *or* RM. *or* RV. *(Quinarii)*. AR

6.

Same legend. The emperor trampling on a captive, holding in his right hand the labarum, inscribed VOT. X., and a buckler on his left arm, inscribed MVLT. XX. In the field, N. D. In the exergue, CONOB. *(Khell)*. - - - - - - - - - - - - - - AU

7.

Same legend. The emperor standing, in a military habit, crowned by a hand which issues from the clouds; his right foot on a panther; in his right hand a staff surmounted by the monogram of Christ; in his left, two javelins. In the field, R. V. In the exergue, COB. AU

8.

Same legend. Victory, seated on a cuirass, inscribing on a buckler, XX. XXX. In the field, a star, and the monogram of Christ. In the exergue, CONOB. (A *quinarius*). - - - - - - - AU

9.

VICTORIA. AVGVSTORVM. Victory, seated on a coat of mail, inscribing on a buckler, which a winged Genius supports, VOT. X. MVLT. XX. In the field, R. V. In the exergue, COMOB. (A *quinarius*). - - - - - - - - - - - - - - - - AU

10.

Same legend. A similar type; but with VOT. XX. MVLT. XXX. In the exergue, COMOB. (A *quinarius*). - - - - - - AU

11.

Same legend. Victory, marching, with a garland, and a globe surmounted by a cross. In the exergue, CONOB. (A *quinarius*). AU

12.

Same legend. A similar type. In the field, R. M. *or* R. V. In the exergue, COM. *or* COMOB. *(Quinarii)*. - - - - - - AU

13.

VIRTVS. ROMANORVM. Roma-Victrix, seated. In the exergue, MDPS. *or* RMPS. *or* RVPS. *(Quinarii)*. - - - - - - AR

14.

VOT. X. (*or* XV.) MVLT. XX. within a laurel garland. In the exergue, CONS. - AR

15.

VRBS. ROMA. Roma-Victrix, seated. In the exergue, RVPS. AR

16.

Without legend. Two helmeted women, seated on a coat of mail, supporting a buckler, on which is inscribed, VOT. XXX. MVLT. XXXX. In the field, R. V. In the exergue, COMOB. - AU

In gold, Nos. 6 and 16 are the rarest; the next in rarity is No. 7. In silver, Nos. 1, 4, and 14, are the rarest, excepting, of course, No. 3.

BRASS MEDALLIONS.

1.

EVTIMI. VINCAS. A full-faced male figure, in a quadriga, holding a garland and a palm branch.

2.

SPECIOSVS. DIGNVS. EVGENIVS. ACHILL. DESIDEREVS. A similar type.

This, and the preceding medallion, are *Contorniati.*

3.

Without legend. Honorius, in a quadriga, holding a garland and a palm branch.

4.

Without legend. The emperor on horseback, wearing the paludamentum; his right hand raised: beneath the horse, a lion.

5.

Without legend. No type on the reverse.

Nos. 1, 2, and 4, are the rarest.

THIRD BRASS, WITH RARE REVERSES.

1.

ASINA. An ass, suckling its colt.

See the observations of *Tanini* on this curious type.

2.

GLORIA. ROMANORVM. The emperor, on horseback. In the exergue, ALE. (Size of the quinarius).

3.

Same legend. Three military figures, standing. In the exergue, SMKA.

4.

DDD. NNN. GGG. The heads of Arcadius, Honorius, and the younger
Theodosius, full-faced and without beard, each with the diadem.
—*Rev.* GLORIA. ROMANORVM. A woman standing, in the
stola: a pair of scales in her right hand, and a cornucopia on her
left arm. In the exergue, effaced letters.

No. 4 is much the rarest.

[EXAGIUM SOLIDI].

1.

D. N. HONORIVS. P. F. AVG. Bearded head of Honorius.—*Rev.*
EXAGIVM. SOLIDI. Moneta standing, with her attributes.

2.

DDD. NNN. AAAVVVGGG. The heads of Arcadius, Honorius, and
Theodosius the younger, without beard, and with the diadem:
above, a cross.—*Rev.* EXAG. SOL. SVB. V. INL. IOANNI.
(*sic*) COM. S. L. Moneta standing: a star in the field. In the
exergue, CONS. (*Tanini*).

3.

Same legend. The same heads.—*Rev.* EXAGIVM. SOLID. A
similar type.

4.

DDD. NNN. GGG. The same heads.—*Rev.* EXAGIVM. SOLIDI.
A similar type. (*Tanini*).

CONSTANTIUS III.

[Constantius, surnamed Patricius, was born at Naissus in Illyria, in the
year of Rome, ——. In 1164 (A. D. 411), he was raised to the
rank of General; and in 1174 (A. D. 421), created Augustus, and
associated with Honorius in the government of the West. Constantius died seven months after his elevation].

STYLE:——D. N. CONSTANTIVS. P. F. AVG.

Gold -	R 6
„ quinarii - - - - - - - - - - - - - - - -	R 7
Silver quinarii - - - - - - - - - - - - - - - -	R 8

GOLD AND SILVER.

1.

VICTORIA. AVGGG. The emperor standing, wearing the paludamentum, holding the labarum, and a globe surmounted by a Victory; his left foot on a captive. In the field, R. V. In the exergue, COMOB. - - - - - - - - - - - - - - - - - AV

2.

VICTORIA. AVGVSTORVM. Victory marching, with a garland and a globe, surmounted by a cross. In the field, R. V. In the exergue, CON. (A *quinarius*).—*Mus. Vindob.* - - - - AU

3.

VICTORIA. ROMANORVM. Victory marching, with garland and palm branch. In the exergue, SMN. (A *quinarius*). - - AR

4.

VOTIS. V. MVLTIS. X. within a laurel garland. In the exergue, LVG. (A *quinarius*).—*Mionnet, Cab. of M. Gosselin.* - - AR

The above are thus valued by Mionnet:—No. 1, 400 francs: No. 2, 300 francs: the silver at 100 francs each.

PLACIDIA.

Galla Placidia, daughter of Theodosius the Great, by Galla his second wife, and wife of Constantius the Third, was widow of Adolphus, king of the Visigoths, and married Constantius in the year of Rome 1170 (A.D. 417). She died at Rome, in the year of that city 1203 A. D. 450)].

STYLE :——GALLA. PLACIDIA. P. F. AV. (*or* AVG.)——D. N. GALLA. PLACIDIA. P. F. AVG.

Gold medallion, - - - - - - - - - - - - - - - R 8
  „ of the usual size - - - - - - - - - - - - - R 6
  „ quinarii - - - - - - - - - - - - - - - R 6
Silver - - - - - - - - - - - - - - - - - R 6
  „ quinarii - - - - - - - - - - - - - - - R 4
Brass medallions (Beauvais) - - - - - - - - - - R 6
Second brass - - - - - - - - - - - - - - - R 8
Third brass - - - - - - - - - - - - - - - R 8

GOLD MEDALLION.

SALVS. REIPVBLICAE. A woman, full-faced, seated on a throne, holding a globe. *(Tanini)*.

This medallion is of small size, but it is mounted in an ornamented circle.

GOLD AND SILVER, OF THE USUAL SIZE.

1.

SALVS. REIPVBLICAE. Victory seated on a coat of mail, inscribing on a buckler the monogram of Christ. In the field, R. V. In the exergue, COMOB. *(Plate xii, No. 6)*. - - - - - - - - AU

2.

Same legend. Victory seated on spoils, holding a laurel garland, within which is the monogram of Christ. In the exergue, DMPS. *(Mionnet, Cab. M. Gosselin)*. - - - - - - - - - - - AU & AR

3.

Same legend. Victory marching, with a staff surmounted by a cross. In the field, R. V. In the exergue, COMOB. - - - - - AU

4.

Same legend. The empress, seated on a throne, holding with both hands a globe. - - - - - - - - - - - - - - - - - AU

5.

Same legend. The monogram of Christ, within a laurel garland. In the exergue, COMOB. *(Quinarii)*. - - - - - - - - AU

6.

VICTORIA. AVGGG. A figure standing, wearing the paludamentum. *(Banduri)*. - - - - - - - - - - - - - - - - AU

7.

VOT. XX. MVLT. XXX. Victory standing, holding a staff surmounted by a cross. In the field, a star, and A. Q. *or* R. M. *or* R. V. In the exergue, COMOB. - - - - - - - - - - - - AU

8.

Without legend. The monogram of Christ, or a cross, within a laurel garland. In the exergue, COMOB. *(Quinarii)*. - - AU & AR

9.

Without legend. The monogram of Christ, within a garland. In the exergue, V. *or* RV. *(Quinarii)*. - - - - - - - - AR

10.

Without legend.   A cross, within a garland.   In the exergue, COMOB.

(A *quinarius*). - - - - - - - - - - - - - - - - AU

11.

Without legend.   A cross within a laurel garland.   (A *quinarius*).   AR

In gold, No. 6 is the rarest ; the next in rarity are Nos. 2, 3, 4, and 7, In silver, Nos. 2 and 9 are the rarest.

SECOND BRASS.

A coin is described in the Pembroke collection ; but quæry its authenticity.   Tanini quotes it from that collection.

THIRD BRASS.

SALVS. REIPVBLICAE.   A cross.   In the field, Q.

CONSTANTINUS III.

[Flavius Claudius Constantinus, a private soldier, was proclaimed Augustus by the legions of Britain, and acknowledged by those of Gaul, in the year of Rome 1160 (A. D. 407).   This usurper was encountered by Constantius, the general of Honorius, defeated and taken prisoner.   His death followed soon after, 1164 (A. D. 411)].

Style:——D. N. CONSTANTINVS. P. F. AVG.——FL. CL. CONSTANTINVS. AVG.*

Gold . - - - - - - - - - - - - - - - - - - - R 2

Silver - - - - - - - - - - - - - - - - - - - R 2

Third brass *(Beauvais)*. - - - - - - - - - - - - R 6

---

* The last legend is found on the gold coin described below from Banduri. The coins of this usurper have frequently been confounded with those of the emperors of the same name; but it is now agreed, that those which bear AVGGG. or AVGGGG. belong to this usurper, as legends of this description were not used so early as the reigns of the two preceding emperors of the same name. Those, therefore, which are assigned by Bergerus to Constantinus the younger, and others given by Banduri to Constantinus Magnus, are restored to Constantinus III. Those also, which are similar to the denarius with VICTORIA. AVGGGG., although differing from it in the legend of the obverse, but with the same type on the obverse, and having on the reverse the same type of the female sedent figure, are appropriated to this usurper, as they resemble in fabric the coins of Constans II., his successor. Eckhel is of this opinion. (See *Doct. Num. Vet.*, tom. *viii*, p. 177).

GOLD AND SILVER.

1.

VICTORIA. AVG. Constantinus standing, wearing the paludamentum, and holding in his right hand the labarum ; in his left hand, a globe surmounted by a Victory: his foot on a captive.   In the exergue, TROAS. *or* TROBS. - - - - - - - - - - AU & AR

2.

VICTORIA. AAVGGG.   A similar type.   In the field, A. R. *or* L. D. In the exergue, COMOB. *or* CONOB. *or* KONOB.   - - - AU

3.

Same legend.   A similar type.   In the exergue, TROBS. - - - AU

4.

VICTORIA. AAAVGGGG.   A similar type.   In the field, L. D. In the exergue, COMOB. *(Plate xii, No. 7).* - - - - AU

5.

VICTORIA. AAAVGGG. *or* AAAVGGGG.   A helmed woman seated, holding a Victory and the hasta.   In the exergue, KONT. *or* LDPV. *or* SMAR. *or* SMLD. *or* TRMS.   - - - - - AR

Mionnet values the gold at thirty francs, and the silver at six francs each.

CONSTANS II.

[Constans, the son of the usurper Constantinus, was created Augustus by his father, in the year of Rome 1161 (A. D. 408). He was murdered, at Vienna (Vienne) in Gaul, shortly after the death of his father].

Style :——D. N. CONSTANS. P. F. AVG.

Silver quinarii - - - - - - - - - - - - - - - - R 6

VICTORIA. AAAVGGG.   A helmeted female seated, holding a Victory on a globe, and the hasta pura.   In the exergue, CON. *or* KON.

The coins of this Constans, are often confounded with those of Constans the son of Constantine the Great.   Mionnet observes, that they are rarer in France than in Italy, a circumstance for which it is difficult to account.

MAXIMUS.

[Maximus was proclaimed emperor in Spain by Count Gerontius, one of the generals of the usurper Constantinus, in 1162 (A. D. 409) ; but the Count having been reduced, and forced to lay violent hands upon himself, the life of Maximus was spared for a time.   " The caprice," says Gibbon, " of the barbarians who ravaged Spain once more seated this imperial phantom on the throne; but they soon resigned him to the justice of Honorius; and the tyrant Maximus, after he had been shewn to the people of Ravenna and Rome, was publicly executed, 1164 (A. D. 411)."]

STYLE:——D. N. MAXIMVS. P. F. AVG.

Silver - R 6

1.

VICTORIA. AAVGGG. A helmeted woman, seated, holding a globe surmounted by a Victory, and the hasta.

2.

VICTORIA. ROMANOR. A similar type.

Given in error by *Banduri* to Petronius Maximus.

JOVINUS.

[Jovinus was a Gaulish captain, who assumed the purple at Mayence, in the year of Rome 1164 (A.D. 411). He was defeated by Adolphus, the Gothic king, by whose orders he was beheaded, in 1166 (A.D. 413)].

STYLE:——D. N. IOVINVS. P. F. AVG. [On reverse of some coins, RESTITVTOR. REIP. *or* RESTITVTOR. ROM].

Gold - R 6
„ quinarii - - - - - - - - - - - - - - - - - R 6
Silver - R 2
„ quinarii - - - - - - - - - - - - - - - - - R 2
Third brass (if genuine) - - - - - - - - - - - - - - R 8

GOLD AND SILVER.

1.

RESTITVTOR. REIP. Jovinus standing, holding the labarum, and a globe surmounted by a Victory; his foot on a captive. In the field, L. D. *or* T. R. *or* A. R. In the exergue, COMOB. *or* CONOB. *(Plate xii, No. 8).* - - - - - - - - - - AU

2.

Same legend. A helmed woman, seated, holding a globe surmounted by a Victory, and the hasta-pura. In the exergue, COMOB. *or* KONT. *or* CON. *or* TR. *(Quinarii)* - - - - - AU & AR

3.

RESTITVTOR. ROM. A similar type. In the exergue, KONT. (A *quinarius*).—*Mionnet, Cat. d'Ennery.* - - - - - - - AR

4.

VICTORIA. AVG. *or* AVGG. *or* AVGGG.   A helmed woman seated,
  holding a Victory on her right hand, the hasta in her left.   In the
  exergue, SMLP. *or* SMLDV. *or* SMLD. *or* MLDA. *or* RMS.
  or TRMS. - - - - - - - - - - - - - - - AU & AR

5.

VOT. V. MVLT. X. within a garland.   - - - - - - AU & AR

  In gold, No. 2 is the least rare.   In silver, No. 3 is the rarest; and
No. 2 is the least rare.

THIRD BRASS.

VICTORIA. AVGG.   A woman seated, holding a globe and a spear.
  In the exergue, TRMS.   *(Cat. d'Ennery)*.

Valued by Mionnet at forty francs.

SEBASTIANUS.

[Sebastianus, the brother of Jovinus, was associated with him, after his
  usurpation, in the year of Rome 1165 (A. D. 412), but was seized at
  Narbonne, and beheaded by order of Adolphus, king of the Goths,
  in the following year].

STYLE:——D. N. SEBASTIANVS. P. F. AVG.

Silver denarii - - - - - - - - - - - - - - - - - R 7

VICTORIA. AVGG.   A helmed woman seated, holding in her right
  hand a globe surmounted by a Victory; in her left the hasta.   In
  the exergue, CON. *or* KONT.

Valued by Mionnet at sixty francs.

PRISCUS ATTALUS.

[Priscus Attalus, born of a family of Ionia, was praefect of Rome in the
  reign of Honorius, and upon the taking of that city by Alaric, was
  raised to the empire in 1162 (A. D. 409).   He was, however, in the
  following year deprived of the purple, but reassumed it in Gaul, upon
  the death of the Gothic king, in the same year, 1163 (A. D. 410).
  Attalus was captured by Constantius, in 1169 (A. D. 416), and sent
  to Honorius, who after causing two fingers of his right hand to be
  amputated, banished him to the island of Lipari, where he terminated
  his life].

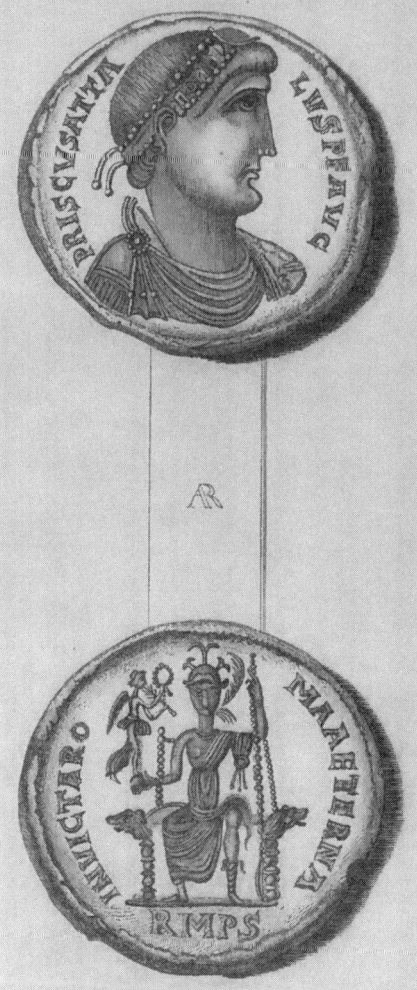

P 353

cz . dial . gr
Weight 2 . 10 . 4

PRISCUS ATTALUS.

_____ London, Published by Effingham Wilson. 1st Jany 1831.

Style :——PRISC. (*or* PRISCVS.) ATTALVS. P. F. AVG.——IMP.
PRISCVS. ATTALVS. P. F. AVG.

Gold - R 6
Silver medallion, of very large size - - - - - - - - - - R 8
  ,,   of the usual size - - - - - - - - - - - - - - - R 6
  ,,   quinarii - - - - - - - - - - - - - - - - - R 6
Third brass - - - - - - - - - - - - - - - - - - - R 6

SILVER MEDALLION.

INVICTA. ROMA. AETERNA. Rome seated, full-faced, holding in
her right hand a globe surmounted by a Victory, and in her left the
hasta. In the exergue, RMPS. *(Plate H)*.

This medallion, which is of very large size, and much thicker than
the medallions of this period, is probably unique. It is in the collection
of the British Museum.

GOLD AND SILVER, OF THE USUAL SIZE.
1.

INVICTA. ROMA. AETERNA. A similar type to that of the
medallion. In the field, R. M. In the exergue, COMOB. *(Plate
xii, No. 9).* - - - - - - - - - - - - - - - - AU
2.

Same legend. Rome, seated on a coat of mail, holding a Victory on a
globe, and the hasta. In the exergue, PST. - - - - - - AR
3.

RESTITVTIO. REIP. Attalus, in a military habit, holding the
labarum, and raising up a woman prostrate at his feet. In the field,
N. B. In the exergue, COMOB. - - - - - - - - - AU
4.

VICTORIA. AVGVSTI. Attalus, in a military habit, holding the
labarum, and a globe surmounted by a Victory : his foot on a
captive. In the field, R. M. In the exergue, COMOB. - - AU
5.

VICTORIA. ROMANORVM. Victory marching, with garland and
palm branch. In the field, a star. In the exergue, PST. (A
quinarius). - - - - - - - - - - - - - - - - AR
6.

VOT. V. MVLT. X. within a garland. In the exergue, PST. *(Cat.
d'Ennery).* - - - - - - - - - - - - - - - AR

The gold are valued at seventy-two francs each by Mionnet. In
silver, Nos. 2 and 6 are the rarest.

THIRD BRASS.

1.

BONO. REIPVBLICAE. NATI. Two figures in imperial habits, seated, supporting a globe: Victory behind them. In the exergue, TR. (*Catalogue d'Ennery*).

2.

GLORIA. ROMANORVM. Attalus, dragging a captive by the hair.

3.

VICTORIA. ROMANORVM. Victory, marching. (Size of the quinarius).

THEODOSIUS II.

[Theodosius, the son of Arcadius and Eudoxia, was born at Constantinople, in the year of Rome 1154 (A.D. 401), and created Augustus by his father in the following year. In 1161 (A.D. 408), he succeeded to the empire of the East; and in 1191 (A.D. 438) published the celebrated code known by his name. Theodosius the Second died at Constantinople, in the year of Rome 1203 (A.D. 450)].

STYLE :——D. N. THEODOSIVS. P. F. AVG.

Gold - - - - - - - - - - - - - - - - -	C
„ quinarii - - - - - - - - - - - - - - -	R 2
Silver medallions - - - - - - - - - - - - -	R 4
„ of the usual size - - - - - - - - - - - -	R 8
Brass *Contorniati* - - - - - - - - - - - - -	R 8
Third brass - - - - - - - - - - - - - - - -	R 6

SILVER MEDALLION.

D. N. P. F. AVG. Bust of Theodosius, full-faced, holding a spear and a buckler.—*Rev.* CONCORDIA. AVGG. The emperor seated, holding a globe and a spear. In the field, a star. In the exergue, COMOB.

In the *Catalogue d'Ennery* this medallion is erroneously ascribed to Theodosius Magnus.

GOLD AND SILVER, OF THE USUAL SIZE.

1.

GLORIA. ORBIS. TERRAE. *or* GLOR. ORVIS. *(sic)* TERRAR. *or* GLORIA. ORVIS. *(sic)* TERRAR. The emperor in a military habit, standing, full-faced, holding the labarum, and a globe surmounted by a cross. In the field, a star. In the exergue, CON. *or* TESOR. - - - - - - - - - - - - - - - - AU

2.

IMP. XXXXII. COS. XVII. P. P. Rome seated, her left foot on the prow of a vessel, holding a globe surmounted by a cross, and the hasta. In the field, a star. In the exergue, COMOB. - - AU

3.

SALVS. REIPVBLICAE. Two figures, wearing the paludamentum, one seated on a curule chair, the other standing; each holding a scroll in his right hand, and in his left a cross: above, a star. In the exergue, CONOB. - - - - - - - - - - - - AU

4.

Same legend. Two similar figures, but each with the nimbus : a star above: at the end of the legend, a numeral letter. In the exergue, CONOB. - - - - - - - - - - - - - AU

5.

SECVRITAS. REIPVBLICAE. Theodosius seated in the consular habit, with the nimbus, holding a scroll and a sceptre terminating in a cross. In the exergue, CONOB. - - - - - - - - AU

6.

VIRT. ЄXЄRC. *(sic)* ROM. Δ. The emperor in a military habit, dragging a captive by the hair, and bearing a trophy on his shoulder. A star in the field. In the exergue, CONOB. - - - - - AU

7.

VIRT. EXERC. ROM. A similar type. In the exergue, CONOB.
AU

Quoted by Mionnet as a " médaille incertaine."

8.

VRTIS. *(sic)* ROMANORVM. Roma-Victrix, seated. In the field, a star. In the exergue, TRPS. The obverse has the head of Theodosius, with a diadem surmounted by a raised crown : legend, D. N. THEODOSIVS. P. F. AVG. - - - - - - - - AR

Quoted by Mionnet, from the cabinet of *M. Gosselin.*

9.

VOT. XX. MVLT. XXX. Γ. *or* Z.   Victory, marching; in her right
hand, a long cross.   In the field, a star.   In the exergue, CONOB.
AU

10.

VOT. XXX. MVLT. XXXX.   Victory, seated.   In the field, a star.
In the exergue, CONOB. - - - - - - - - - - - - AU

11.

Without legend.   A cross within a garland.   In the exergue, CONOB.
(A *quinarius*). - - - - - - - - - - - - - - - - AU

12.

Without legend.   A cross within a garland: above and below, CONOB.
(A *quinarius*).—*Mus. Vindob.* - - - - - - - - - - AU

In gold, Nos. 1, 5, 6, 7, and 10 are the rarest.   The silver is valued by
Mionnet at 100 francs.

BRASS MEDALLION.

MAR. . . . . . INC. . . . .   A woman in the stola, standing, holding a
garland, and attended by four girls and two soldiers.

The medallions of this type are *Contorniati*.

THIRD BRASS.

1.

CONCORDIA. AVGG.   Roma-Victrix, full-faced, seated.   In the
exergue, ANT.   The obverse has the bust of the emperor, full-
faced and helmeted, with a spear and buckler.

2.

Same legend.   Rome, seated; her right foot on the prow of a vessel.
In the exergue, SMAQ.

3.

GLORIA. ROMANORVM.   A military figure standing, holding the
labarum and a globe.   In the exergue, ALE.

No. 3 is much rarer than the other numbers.

EUDOXIA.

[Aelia Eudoxia, or Eudocia, daughter of Leontius, an Athenian Sophist, was
born about the year of Rome 1146 (A. D. 393), and married to the
emperor Theodosius the younger, in 1174 (A. D. 421).   Eudoxia died
in retirement at Jerusalem, having been disgraced by her husband, in
the year 1213 (A. D. 460)].

STYLE:——AEL. (*or* AELIA.) EVDOXIA. (*or* EVDOCIA.) AVG.
——AEL. EVDOXIA. FE.

Two ladies, of the name of Eudocia, or Eudoxia, each of whom bear the family name of Aelia, are mentioned by historians. The present was the wife of Theodosius the younger; the other was the consort of Arcadius. Banduri endeavours to distinguish their coins by supposing that those which bear the name of Eudocia belong to one empress, and those with Eudoxia to the other; but this has been refuted by Eckhel. There are coins which must belong to this lady; but it is not certain that there are any of the wife of Arcadius, although Nos. 1, 4, 5, 6, may probably belong to that empress.

Gold - R 6
„ quinarii - - - - - - - - - - - - - - - R 6
Silver - - - - - - - - - - - - - - - - - - R 6
„ quinarii - - - - - - - - - - - - - - - R 6
Third brass - - - - - - - - - - - - - - - - R 4

GOLD AND SILVER.

1.

GLORIA. ROMANORVM. A woman seated, her hands crossed on her breast. In the field, a cross. In the exergue, ANTZ. The obverse has the head of Eudoxia: legend, AEL. EVDOXIA. AVG. (*Catalogue d'Ennery*). - - - - - - - - - - - - AR

2.

IMP. XXXXII. COS. XVII. P. P. Rome, seated; her right foot on the prow of a vessel, holding the hasta, and a globe surmounted by a cross: a buckler on the ground. In the field, a star. In the exergue, CONOB. The obverse has the legend, AEL. EVDOCIA. AVG. - - - - - - - - - - - - - - - - - - AU

3.

Same legend. Victory seated, holding a globe surmounted by a cross, and a sceptre. In the exergue, CONOB. The obverse has the legend, AEL. EVDOXIA. AVG. (*Banduri*). - - - - - AU

4.

SALVS. REIPVBLICAE. Victory seated on spoils, inscribing on a buckler the monogram of Christ. In the exergue, CONOB. The obverse has the same legend as on the preceding. - - AU & AR

5.

SALVS. REIPVBLICAE. Δ. Victory seated, inscribing on a buckler,
which she rests on a column, the monogram of Christ. The obverse
has the legend as on the preceding. - - - - - - - - AU

6.

Same legend and type, with the exception of the numeral letter. - AU

7.

VOT. XX. MVLT. XXX. B. Victory standing, holding a long cross.
In the field, a star. In the exergue, CONOB. The obverse has
the legend, AEL. EVDOCIA. AVG. - - - - - - - - AU

8.

VOT. XXX. MVLT. XXXX. B. Victory standing, holding a cross.
In the field, a star. In the exergue, CONOB. The obverse has
the same legend as on the preceding. - - - - - - - - AU

9.

VOT. XXX. MVLT. XXXX. Θ. Rome seated, her left foot on the
prow of a vessel, holding a globe surmounted by a cross and the
hasta; a buckler on the ground. In the field, a star. In the exergue, CONOB. The obverse has the legend, AEL. EVDOXIA.
AVG. - - - - - - - - - - - - - - - - - AU

10.

Without legend. A cross within a garland. In the exergue, COB. or
CONOB. The obverse has the legend, AEL. EVDOXIA. AVG.
or AEL. EVDOCIA. AVG. (Quinarii). - - - - - - AU

11.

Without legend. The monogram of Christ within a laurel garland. The
obverse has the legend AEL. EVDOXIA. AVG. FE. (A
quinarius). - - - - - - - - - - - - - - - - AR

In silver, Nos. 1 and 4 are the rarest.

THIRD BRASS.

1.

GLORIA. ROMANORVM. A woman seated, full-faced, her hands
clasped together. In the field, a cross. In the exergue, ALEA. or
ANTΔ. The obverse has the legend, AEL. EVDOXIA. AVG.

2.

SALVS. REIPVBLICAE. Victory seated, inscribing on a buckler the
monogram of Christ. In the exergue, ANTΓ. or CONSΔ. or
SMKA. The obverse has the legend as on the preceding.

These coins may also belong to the wife of Arcadius.

JOHANNES.

[Johannes, an usurper in the reign of Theodosius the Second, was born about the year of Rome 1133 (A. D. 380). He was secretary to the emperor Honorius, and upon the death of that prince, invested himself with the purple, 1176 (A. D. 423). He was besieged in Ravenna by the army of Theodosius, and being reduced, paid the forfeit of his usurpation with his life, 1178 (A. D. 425)].

STYLE :——D. N. IOHANNES. P. F. AVG.

Gold medallions, of small size - - - - - - - - - - - -	R 8
„ of the usual size - - - - - - - - - - - - - - -	R 4
„ quinarii - - - - - - - - - - - - - - - - -	R 6
Silver medallions, of small size - - - - - - - - - - - -	R 8
„ of the usual size - - - - - - - - - - - - - -	R 6
„ quinarii - - - - - - - - - - - - - - - -	R 6
Third brass - - - - - - - - - - - - - - - - - -	R 8

GOLD AND SILVER MEDALLIONS.

VICTORIA. AVGGG. Johannes standing, holding the labarum and a Victory, and trampling on a captive. In the field, R. V. In the exergue, COMOB. - - - - - - - - - - - AU & AR

Mionnet values the gold at 200, and the silver at sixty francs.

GOLD AND SILVER, OF THE USUAL SIZE.

1.

VRBS. ROMA. Roma-Victrix, seated. In the exergue, RVPS. (*Mionnet*, Cabinet of *M. Gosselin*). - - - - - - - - - AR

2.

Same legend. A similar type; with TR. PS. in the exergue. (*Mead's Catalogue*). - - - - - - - - - - - - - - - AR

3.

VICTORIA. AVGG. Victory marching, with garland and palm branch. In the exergue, R. V. (A *quinarius*). - - - - - - - AR

4.

VICTORIA. AVGGG. Johannes standing, wearing the paludamentum; his left foot on a captive, his right hand holding the labarum, his left a globe surmounted by a Victory. In the field, R. V. In the exergue, COMOB. - - - - - - - - - - - - - AU

5.

VICTORIA. AVGGG.   A similar type.   In the exergue, CONOS.
(*Mead's Catal.*) - - - - - - - - - - - - - - - AR

6.

VICTORIA. AVGVSTORVM.   Victory marching, with a garland,
and a globe surmounted by a cross.   In the field, R. V.   In the
exergue, COMOB.   (A *quinarius*). - - - - - - - - - AU

7.

Same legend.   Victory seated on a coat of mail: before, a, buckler
attached to a tree, and supported by a small figure; on the buckler
the monogram of Christ.   (*Banduri*). - - - - - - - - - AU

8.

Without legend.   A cross within a garland.   (*Banduri*). - - - AU

In silver, Nos. 1, 2, and 5, are the rarest.

THIRD BRASS.

SALVS. REIPVBLICAE.   Victory marching, bearing a trophy, and
dragging a captive.   In the field, the monogram of Christ.
(*Mionnet.*—Cabinet of *M. Gosselin*).

VALENTINIANUS III.

[Placidius Valentinianus, the son of Constantius Patricius and Galla
Placidia, was born at Ravenna in Cisalpine Gaul, in the year of Rome
1172 (A. D. 419).   Upon the death of his father in 1174 (A. D. 421),
he was taken by his mother to the court of Theodosius the younger.
In 1177 (A. D. 424), he received the title of Caesar at Thessalonica;
and was sent under the guardianship of his mother into Italy by the
emperor Theodosius, when he took in the following year the style of
Augustus, his troops having defeated and destroyed the usurper
Johannes.   Valentinianus the Third was murdered at Rome by the
partizans of the senator Petronius Maximus, whose wife he had basely
seduced, in the year of that city 1208 (A. D. 455)].

STYLE:——D. N. PLA. VALENTINIANVS.   AVG. —— D. N.
VALENTINIANVS. P. F. AVG.——D. N. PLA. VALENTINI-
ANVS. P. AVG.——D. N. PL. (*or* PLA. *or* PLAC. *or* PLA-
CIDIVS.) VALENTI. (*or* VALENTINIAN. *or* VALENTINI-
ANVS.) P. F. AVG.

The coins of Valentinianus the Third, when the legends on the obverse are unaccompanied by the prenomen, PLACIDIVS., cannot be properly distinguished from those of the two other emperors of the same name. (See *Eckhel*, vol. viii, pp. 187, 188).

Gold medallions, of small size - - - - - - - - - - - -	R 6
„ of the usual size - - - - - - - - - - - - - - -	C
„ of the middle size - - - - - - - - - - - - - -	R 3
„ quinarii - - - - - - - - - - - - - - - -	R 2
Silver medallions, of small size - - - - - - - - - - - -	R 6
„ of the usual size - - - - - - - - - - - - - -	R 4
„ quinarii - - - - - - - - - - - - - - - -	R 3
Brass medallions (*Contorniati*) - - - - - - - - - - -	R 2
Third brass - - - - - - - - - - - - - - - - - -	R 3

GOLD AND SILVER MEDALLIONS.
1.
VICTORIA. AVGGG. The emperor standing, full-faced, holding a cross and a Victory. In the field, R. V. In the exergue, COMOB.

AR
2.
VOT. XXX. MVLT. XXXX. The emperor standing, wearing the consular habit, and a diadem surmounted by a cross; presenting his right hand to a prostrate woman, his left holding a sceptre surmounted by a cross. In the field, R. M. In the exergue, COMOB.

AU

Mionnet values the gold at 120 francs, and the silver at fifty francs.

GOLD AND SILVER, OF THE USUAL SIZE.
1.
GLORIA. ROMANORVM. A helmed figure, seated; holding in her right hand a garland, and in her left a cross. In the field, R. V. In the exergue, COMOB. (*Banduri*). - - - - - - . AU
2.
Same legend. Victory marching, holding a long cross. In the exergue, A. . . S. (*Banduri*). - - - - - - - - - - - - - AR
3.
IMP. XXXXII. COS. XVII. P. P. A helmeted woman, seated: in her right hand a globe surmounted by a cross, a spear in her left; her left foot on the prow of a vessel; a buckler by her side. In the field, a star. In the exergue, CONOB. - - - - - - - AU

4.

SALVS. REIPVBLICAE.   The monogram of Christ within a laurel
garland.   In the exergue, COMOB.   (Middle size.) - - - AU

5.

VICTORIA. AVGG.   Victory marching, with garland and palm
branch.   In the exergue, R. M. *or* R. V.   *(Quinarii)*. - - AR

6.

VICTORIA. AVGGG.   Victory seated, holding a long cross.   In the
exergue, COMOB.   (A *quinarius*). - - - - - - - - - AU

7.

Same legend.   A figure standing, holding a cross, and a globe surmounted
by a Victory;   his right foot on a serpent. *(Mead's Catalogue*, p. 15).
AU

8.

Same legend.   A figure standing, holding a cross, and a globe surmounted
by Victory;   his right foot on a serpent with a human head.   In the
field, R. V.   In the exergue, CONOB.   *(Mead's Catalogue*, p. 104).
AR

9.

VICTORIA. AVGVSTORVM.   Victory marching, holding a garland
and a globe surmounted by a cross.   In the field, R. M.   In the
exergue, COMOB,   (A *quinarius*). - - - - - - - - AU

10.

VOT. X. MVLT. XX.   The emperor seated, holding a book in his
right hand and a cross in his left.   In the field, R. V.   In the
exergue, COMOB.   *(Mus. Vindob.).* - - - - - - - - AU

11.

VOT. XXX. MVLT. XXXX.   Rome seated, holding a globe surmounted by a cross, and a spear;   her left foot on the prow of a
vessel.   In the exergue, COMOB.   *(Mionnet,* from *Viezay).* - AU

12.

VRBS. ROMA.   Roma-Victrix seated.   In the exergue, RMPS.
(Mionnet, from the cabinet of *M. Gosselin).* - - - - - - AR

13.

Without legend.   A cross within a laurel garland.   In the exergue,
COMOB. *or* CONOB.   (A *quinarius*). - - - - - - - AU

In gold, Nos. 7 and 10 are the rarest: the next in rarity is No. 1;
then No. 9.   In silver, Nos. 2, 8, and 12 are the rarest.

BRASS MEDALLIONS.

1.

BONIFATIVS. A man in a quadriga, holding a garland and a palm branch: below, four monograms.

2.

MARGARITA. VINCAS. A woman standing, in the stola, holding a garland: before her, a small figure of Victory, holding a garland and a palm branch. In the exergue, two palm branches.

3.

PETRONIVS. MAXIMVS. *(sic)* V. C. CONS. Petronius Maximus in the consular habit, seated; holding a volume and a sceptre surmounted by an eagle. In the exergue, two bags full of coin.

4.

VICTORIA. AVGGG. A military figure, standing: in his right hand, the labarum; in his left, a figure of Victory; his right foot on a helmet; on his left, a buckler.

5.

Without legend or type on the reverse.

The above are all *Contorniati.* The first three are by far the rarest, and are valued by Mionnet at thirty francs each.

THIRD BRASS.

1.

DD. NN. AVG. OBN. *(sic)*. Moneta, standing.

2.

SALVS. REIPVBLICAE. Victory marching, dragging a captive. In the exergue, R. M.

3.

VICTORIA. AVGG. Victory marching. In the exergue, RM.

4.

Same legend. Two Victories, standing. In the exergue, RM.

5.

VOT. PVB. The Praetorian camp. In the exergue, RM. *or* RS.

Nos. 1, 2, and 5 are the rarest.

LICINIA EUDOXIA.

[Licinia Eudoxia, the daughter of Theodosius the Second and Aelia
Eudoxia, and wife of the emperor Valentinianus the Third, was
born at Constantinople, in the year of Rome 1176 (A. D. 423).
Her marriage with the emperor took place in 1190 (A. D. 437).
Petronius Maximus having caused Valentinianus to be assassinated,
compelled Eudoxia to accept him as her husband; but the empress,
having solicited the aid of Genseric, the Vandal king, was, after the
sack of Rome, carried away captive to Carthage by the Barbarian.
Eudoxia returned to Constantinople in the year of Rome 1215,
(A. D. 462), where she passed the remainder of her life].

STYLE:——LICINIA. EVDOXIA. P. F. AVG.

Gold, of the usual size - - - - - - - - - - - - - - - R 6

1.

SALVS. REIPVBLICAE.   A woman seated, holding a globe surmounted by a cross, and a staff likewise surmounted by that
emblem.   In the exergue, COMOB.

2.

VOT. XXX. MVLT. XXXX.   Valentinianus and Eudoxia, standing.
In the exergue, COMOB.

Valued by Mionnet at 100 francs each.

HONORIA.

[Justa Grata Honoria, the sister of Valentinianus the Third, was born at
Ravenna, about the year of Rome 1170 (A. D. 417).   She received
from her brother the title of Augusta, about the year 1186 (A.D. 433),
and is supposed to have died somewhere in Italy, after the year 1207
(A. D. 454)].

STYLE:——D. N. IVST. (or IVSTA.) GRAT. (or GRATA.) HO-
NORIA. P. F. AVG.

Gold - R 8
   „   quinarii   - - - - - - - - - - - - - - - - - R 8
Silver quinarii - - - - - - - - - - - - - - - - - R 8

GOLD AND SILVER.
1.

BONO. REIPVBLICAE.   Victory standing, holding a staff surmounted
by a cross.   In the field, R. V.   In the exergue, COMOB. - AU

2.

SALVS. REIPVBLICAE. The monogram of Christ within a laurel garland. In the exergue, COMOB. (A *quinarius*). - - - AU

3.

VOT. XX. MVLT. XXX. Victory standing, holding a cross. (*Banduri*).

AU

4.

Without legend. A cross within a laurel garland. In the exergue, COMOB. (A *quinarlus*). - - - - - - - - - - - - AR

ATTILA.

[Attila succeeded to the government of the Huns, in the year of Rome 1187 (A. D. 434). In 1195 (A. D. 442), he ravaged the provinces of the East, and exacted tribute from the emperor Theodosius the Second. In 1204 (A. D. 451), he subdued the northern tribes, and ravaged Gaul; and, in the following year, rendered Valentinianus the Third tributary. Attila ended his eventful life in the year of Rome 1206, (A. D. 453)].

The coins described below have been given by numismatists to this celebrated warrior, but they have always been doubted by some, who have assigned them to the Gaulish chiefs of a much earlier period. Eckhel is of this opinion; and, indeed, their legend and types do not warrant their appropriation to Attila; nevertheless, they are here given for the satisfaction of the curious.

1.

ATEVLA. *or* ATIVLA. *(sic)*. A youthful winged bust.—*Rev.* VLATOS. A horse.

2.

ATIL. *(sic)*. A diademed head.—*Rev.* Without legend. A winged horse, or pegasus, running.

PETRONIUS MAXIMUS.

[Petronius Maximus was born of an ancient family, in the year of Rome 1148 (A. D. 395). He assumed the purple after the assassination of Valentinianus, and compelled Eudoxia to give him her hand, in 1208,

(A. D. 455), but was murdered three months afterwards by the people of Rome, on the approach of Genseric, whom the widow of Valentinianus had invited from Africa to avenge the death of her husband].

Gold - R 6
Silver - R 6
„ quinarii - - - - - - - - - - - - - - - - - - R 6
Third brass (quoted by *Beauvais*) - - - - - - - - - - R 8

GOLD AND SILVER.

1.

VICTORIA. AVGGG.   Petronius Maximus, in a military habit, holding a staff surmounted by a cross, and a globe surmounted by a Victory; his right foot on the head of a dragon.   In the field, R. M. *or* R. V.   In the exergue, COMOB.   - - - - AU & AR

2.

Same legend.   Victory seated, holding a Victory and a javelin reversed. (A *quinarius*).—*Mionnet, Cat. d'Ennery.* - - - - - - - - AR

3.

VICTORIA. ROMANOR.   A woman wearing the stola, seated on spoils, holding a globe surmounted by a Victory, and a javelin reversed.   In the exergue, SM.   *(Banduri).* - - - - - AR

In silver, Nos. 1 and 3 are the rarest.

MARCIANUS.

[Marcianus, the husband of Pulcheria, sister of Theodosius the Second, was born in Illyria, and raised from the rank of a soldier to that of a senator, and subsequently to the empire of the East, by his marriage, in 1203 (A. D. 450).   Marcianus died at Constantinople, in 1210 (A. D. 457)].

STYLE :——D. N. MARCIANVS. AVG.——D. N. MARCIANVS. P. F. AV. (*or* AVG.)

Gold medallions, of small size - - - - - - - - - - - R 8
„ of the usual size - - - - - - - - - - - - - - - R 4
„ quinarii - - - - - - - - - - - - - - - - - - R 4
Silver quinarii - - - - - - - - - - - - - - - - - R 6
Third brass - - - - - - - - - - - - - - - - - - - R 6

GOLD MEDALLION.

ADVENTVS. S. D. N. AVG. The emperor on horseback, as Pacificator, wearing the diadem. In the field, a star. In the exergue,
CONOB.

GOLD AND SILVER.

1.

FELICITER. NVBTIIS. *(sic)*. Marcian and Pulcheria, each with the
nimbus, joining hands : Christ between them, standing, with the
nimbus surmounted by a cross. In the exergue, CONOB. - AU

2.

GLORIA. ORVIS. *(sic)*. TERRAR. The emperor in a military habit,
standing, holding the labarum, and a globe surmounted by a cross.
In the exergue, TESOB. - - - - - - - - - - - - - AU

3.

VICTORIA. AVGGG. The emperor standing, in a military habit; his
right foot on the head of a dragon, his left hand holding a globe
surmounted by a Victory. In the field, R. V. In the exergue,
COMOB. - - - - - - - - - - - - - - - - - - AU

4.

Same legend. Victory, standing, holding a staff surmounted by a cross.
A star in the field. In the exergue, CONOB. - - - - - AU

5.

VICTORIA. AVGGG. A. *or* B. *or* ϛ. *or* Z. *or* H. *or* Θ. *or* I. A similar
type. In the exergue, CONOB. - - - - - - - - - AU

6.

VICTORIA. AVGVSTORVM. Victory, marching; in her right hand
a garland, in her left a globe surmounted by a cross. In the
exergue, CONOB. (A *quinarius*). - - - - - - - - AU

7.

Without legend. A cross, within a garland. In the exergue, CONOB.
(A *quinarius*). - - - - - - - - - - - - - - - - AU

8.

Without legend. A cross within a garland. (A *quinarius*). - - AR

In gold, No. 1 is by far the rarest type. No. 2 is the next in rarity ;
then No. 3.

THIRD BRASS.

Without legend. A laurel garland surrounding a cross, a monogram, and the letter S. In the exergue, CON. *or* ЄYT. (Size of the quinarius).

PULCHERIA.

[Aelia Pulcheria, the sister of Theodosius the Second, and wife of Marcianus, was born at Constantinople, in the year of Rome 1152, (A. D. 399). She was associated in the empire with her brother, who gave her the title of Augusta, 1167 (A. D. 414), and after his death, married Marcianus, whom she raised to the throne, 1203 (A. D. 450). Pulcheria died in the year of Rome 1206 (A. D. 453)].

STYLE:——AEL. PVLCHERIA. AVG.

Gold -	R 6
„ quinarii - - - - - - - - - - - - - - - - -	R 6
Silver quinarii - - - - - - - - - - - - - - - - -	R 6
Third brass - - - - - - - - - - - - - - - - -	R 6

GOLD AND SILVER.

1.

IMP. XXXXII. COS. XVII. P. P. A helmed woman seated: a globe surmounted by a cross in her right hand, a spear in her left; her left foot on the prow of a vessel; on one side a buckler. In the exergue, CONOB. *(Mionnet,* from the Cabinet of the *Prince of Waldeck).* - - - - - - - - - - - - - - - - - AU

2.

Same legend. A similar type, with a star in the field, and without letters in the exergue. *(Mead's Catalogue).* - - - - - AU

3.

SALVS. REIPVBLICAE. Victory seated on arms, inscribing on a buckler the monogram of Christ. In the field, a star. In the exergue, CONOB. - - - - - - - - - - - - - - - AU

4.

VICTORIA. AVGGG. Victory standing, holding a long cross. In the field, a star. In the exergue, CONOB. *(Mus. Vindob.)* AU

5.

VOT. XX. MVLT. XXX. Victory standing, holding a long cross in her right hand, and the stola in her left. In the exergue, COMOB. *(Tanini).* - - - - - - - - - - - - - - - - - AU

6.

Without legend. A cross within a garland. In the exergue, CONOB*.

(*Quinarii*). - - - - - - - - - - - - - - AU & AR

In gold, Nos. 1 and 2 are much the rarest.

THIRD BRASS.

1.

SALVS. REIPVBLICAE. Victory seated on spoils, inscribing on a buckler the monogram of Christ. In the exergue, ANT.

2.

Same legend. Victory standing, her right hand supporting a buckler resting on a column ; on the buckler, the monogram of Christ. In the exergue, RM.

The above are given by Tanini. They are valued at twenty francs each by Mionnet.

AVITUS.

[Marcus Maecilius Avitus was born of a noble family in Aquitaine. He held the office of Praetorian praefect in Gaul, under Valentinianus the Third, and that of general of the horse under Petronius Maximus, upon whose death he assumed the purple at Arles, in the year of Rome 1208 (A. D. 455). His title was acknowledged at Rome, and by the emperor Marcianus ; but after a reign of fourteen months, Avitus was deposed by Ricimer, one of his generals. His life was spared, and the usurper Avitus became bishop of Placentia].

STYLE :——M. MAECIL. AVITHVS. (*sic*) P. F. AVG. (see *Banduri*) D. N. AVITVS. (*or* AVITHVS.) P. F. AVG.——D. N. AVITVS. PERP. (*or* PERPE.) AVG.——D. N. AVITVS. PERP. F. AVG.

Gold - - - - - - - - - - - - - - - - - - - R 6

„ quinarii - - - - - - - - - - - - - - - - R 6

Silver - - - - - - - - - - - - - - - - - - R 6

Third brass - - - - - - - - - - - - - - - R 6

GOLD AND SILVER.

1.

VICTORIA. AVGGG. The emperor in a military habit, his left foot on a captive ; a cross in his right hand, and a globe surmounted by a Victory in his left. In the field, A. R. *or* M. D. In the exergue, COMOB. - - - - - - - - - - - - - - - AU

2.

VRBIS. *(sic)* ROMA. Roma-Victrix, seated. *(Mionnet,* from the
Cabinet of *M. Gosselin).* - - - - - - - - - - - - AR

3.

Without legend. A cross within a garland. In the exergue, CONOB.
(A *quinarius).* - - - - - - - - - - - - - - - - AU

THIRD BRASS.

Without legend. ·A cross within a garland. In the exergue, COMOB.
(Size of the quinarius).

LEO I.

[Leo was born in Thrace, but historians do not mention the rank of his
family. He was a tribune in the army of Marcianus; and after the
death of that prince, was raised to the empire of the East, in the year
of Rome 1210 (A. D. 457). Leo died in 1227 (A. D. 474)].

STYLE: D. N. (*or* NO.) LEO.——D. N. LEO. P. F. AVG.——D. N.
LEO. PERP. (*or* PERPET. *or* PERPETV. *or* PERPETVVS.)
AVG.——D. N. LEO. PERP. (*or* PERPET. *or* PERPETV. *or*
PERPETVVS.) F. AVG.

Gold - C

„ quinarii - - - - - - - - - - - - - - - - - C

Third brass   - - - - - - - - - - - - - - - - R 4

GOLD, WITH RARE REVERSES.

1.

IMP. XXXXII. COS. XVII. P. P. A helmed woman, seated.

2.

VICTORIA. AVGG. Victory seated on arms, inscribing on a buckler
XV. XXX. In the field, a star, and the monogram of Christ. In
the exergue, CONOB. (A *quinarius).*

3.

VICTORIA. AVGVSTORVM. Victory marching, holding a garland,
and a globe surmounted by a cross. In the field, a star. In the
exergue, CONOB. (A *quinarius).*

4.

VIRTVS. AGVSTI. *(sic).* The emperor standing, wearing the paludamentum, holding a cross in his right hand, and in his left the
labarum. In the field, M. D. In the exergue, COMOB. *(Mus.
Vindob.)*

THIRD BRASS.

1.

Without legend.　A lion couchant.　In the exergue, CON.　(Size of the quinarius).

2.

Without legend.　Leo standing, holding a globe and a sceptre.　(Size of the quinarius).

3.

Without legend.　Leo holding a cross, and dragging after him a captive: H. I. (Same size).

Vaiued by Mionnet at eight francs each.

VERINA.

[Aelia Verina, the wife of Leo the First, was married to the emperor before his elevation, in the year of Rome 1227 (A. D. 474). She ended her turbulent life in exile, in 1237 (A. D. 484)].

STYLE:——AEL. (*or* AELIA.) VERINA. AVG.

Gold, denarii and quinarii　- - - - - - - - - - - - R 6

GOLD.

1.

VICTORIA. AVGGG. A.　Victory standing, holding a long cross.　In the field, a star.　In the exergue, CONOB.　The obverse has the diademed head of Verina: legend AEL. ЧERINA. *(sic).* AVG.

2.

Without legend.　A cross within a laurel garland.　In the exergue, CONOB. (A *quinarius*).

MAJORIANUS.

[Julius Majorianus was commander of the legions of the West, and assumed the purple at Ravenna in Cisalpine Gaul, after the deposition of Avitus, in the year of Rome 1210 (A. D. 457). His title was recognised by the emperor Leo and by the senate, but he was assassinated four years after, by Ricimer, the general of his troops].

2 B 2

Style:——D. N. MAIORIANVS. AVG.——D. N. MAIORIANVS.
P. F. AVG.——D. N. IVL. (*or* IVLIVS.) MAIORIANVS. P.
F. AVG.——D. N. IVLIVS. MAIORIANVS. FELIX. AVG. P.
(*Tanini*).*

Gold -	R 2
„ quinarii - - - - - - - - - - - - - - - - -	R 4
Silver -	R 4
„ quinarii - - - - - - - - - - - - - - - - -	R 4
Brass medallion - - - - - - - - - - - - - - - -	R 8
Third brass - - - - - - - - - - - - - - - - - -	R 4

GOLD AND SILVER.

1.

VICTORIA. AVGGG. The emperor standing, in a military habit;
his left foot on the head of a dragon, holding in his right hand a long
cross, and a globe surmounted by a Victory. In the field, A. R.
or Δ. R. *or* R. D. *or* R. V. In the exergue, COMOB. - AU & AR

2.

VIRT. EXERC. ROM. The emperor, wearing the paludamentum,
bearing a trophy, and dragging after him a captive. In the
exergue, CONOB. (*Tanini*).- - - - - - - - - - AU

3.

VIT. (*sic*). AVGG. Victory standing, holding a long cross. In the
exergue, two stars. (A *quinarius*). - - - - - - - - AR

4.

VOTIS. MVLTIS. Two emperors seated, full-faced, each holding a
volume and a cross. In the field, R. V. In the exergue, COMOB.
AU

5.

Same legend. A military figure standing, armed with a spear and
a buckler. In the field, (A *quinarius*). - - - AR

6.

Without legend. A cross, within a garland. In the exergue, CONOB.
(A *quinarius*). - - - - - - - - - - - - - - - AU

In gold, Nos. 2 and 4 are the rarest. In silver, No. 1 is the rarest.

---

* Tanini quotes a medallion with this legend on the obverse, and the full-
faced bust of Majorianus, but without legend or type on the reverse. (See
page 371).

THIRD BRASS.

VICTORIA. AVGG. Victory, standing. In the exergue, NM. *or* RV. (Size of the quinarius).

SEVERUS III.

[Libius Severus was a native of Lucania. He owed his elevation to Ricimer, who caused him to be proclaimed emperor of the West at Ravenna, in the year of Rome 1214 (A. D. 461), immediately after the death of Majorianus. Severus was probably poisoned by Ricimer, in 1218 (A. D. 465)].

STYLE :——D. N. LIB. SEVERVS. AVG.——D. N. LIBIVS. SEVE-RVS. P. AVG.——D. N. SEVERVS. P. F. AVG.——D. N. LIB. (*or* LIBIVS.) SEVERVS. P. F. AV. (*or* AVG.) —— IMP. SEVERVS. P. F. AVG.——D. N. SEVERVS. PP. AVG.——D. N. LIBIVS. SEVERVS. PP. (*or* PERPET.) AVG.

Gold - - - - - - - - - - - - - - - - - - - R 2
  „ quinarii - - - - - - - - - - - - - - - - R 2
Silver medallions, of small size - - - - - - - - - - - R 6
  „ of the usual size - - - - - - - - - - - - - - - R 4
  „ quinarii - - - - - - - - - - - - - - - - - R 4
Third brass - - - - - - - - - - - - - - - - - - R 8

SILVER MEDALLION.

VICTORIA. AVGG. The emperor standing, full-faced, holding a large cross and a Victory. In the field, R. M. *or* R. V. In the exergue, COMOB.

Valued by Mionnet at thirty francs.

GOLD AND SILVER.

1.

SALVS. REIPVBLICAE. The monogram of Christ, within a garland. In the exergue, CONOB. (*Banduri*). - - - - - - - - AU

2.

VICTORIA. AVGGG. The emperor in a military habit; his right foot on the head of a dragon, holding a long cross, and a globe surmounted by a Victory. In the field, various letters. In the exergue, COMOB. *or* CONOB. - - - - - - - - - - AU

3.

VICTORIA. AVGGG.   Victory standing, holding a long cross.   In the
exergue, CONOB.   (A *quinarius*). - - - - - - - - - - AU

4.

VRBS. (*or* VRBIS.) *(sic)*. ROMA.   Roma-Victrix, seated.   In the
exergue, RMPS. - - - - - - - - - - - - - - AR

5.

Without legend.   The monogram of Christ, within a laurel garland.   In
the exergue, RM.   (A *quinarius*). - - - - - - - - - AR

6.

Without legend.   A cross, within a laurel garland.   In the exergue,
COMOB.   (A *quinarius*). - - - - - - - - - - - - AU

In gold, No. 1 is much the rarest.

THIRD BRASS.

Without legend.   A cross (or the monogram of Christ), within a laurel
garland.   In the exergue, R. M.   (Size of the quinarius).

Valued by Mionnet at forty francs.

ANTHEMIUS.

[Procopius Anthemius, the son-in-law of Marcianus, was born at Constantinople, of the same family as the usurper Procopius, who assumed
the purple in the reign of Valens.   He was general of the army under
Marcianus and Leo, and being sent by the latter into Italy with the
title of Caesar, the senate and the people of Rome proclaimed him
Augustus, 1220 (A. D. 467), the city having been under the controul
of Ricimer, since the death of Severus.   Anthemius was assassinated
by command of Ricimer, in the year of Rome 1225 (A. D. 472)].

STYLE:——D. N. ANTHEMIVS. PI. AVG.——D. N. ANTHEMIVS.
(*or* ANTHMIVS.) *(sic)*. P. F. AVG.——D. N. PROC. ANTHE-
MIVS. P. F. AVG.——D. N. ANTHEMIVS. PP. (*or* PERPE. *or*
PERPET.) AVG.——D. N. ANTEHEMIVS. *(sic)*. PERPET.
AVG.——D. N. ANTHEMIVS. PER. F. AVG.

Gold - - - - - - - - - - - - - - - - - - - R 2
„ quinarii - - - - - - - - - - - - - - - - R 2
Silver, quinarii - - - - - - - - - - - - - - - R 8
Brass, *Contorniati* - - - - - - - - - - - - - - R 8

GOLD AND SILVER.

1.

SALVS. REIPVBLICAE. Two military figures standing, supporting between them a globe surmounted by a cross; each holding a spear. In the field, the monogram of Christ, or a star. In the exergue, CORMOB. - - - - - - - - - - - - - - - - - AU

2.

Same legend. A similar type. In the field, sometimes, M. B. *or* N. D. *or* R. M. *or* R. V. In the exergue, COMOB. - - - - - - AU

3.

Same legend. Two figures standing, wearing the paludamentum, and joining hands; one of them holding a globe, surmounted by a Victory; between them a garland, surmounted by a cross; within the garland is inscribed, PAX. In the field, R. M. In the exergue, COMOB. - - - - - - - - - - - - - - - AU

4.

Same legend. Two figures standing, each with the nimbus and the paludamentum, supporting together a long cross. In the field, R.V. In the exergue, COMOB. - - - - - - - - - - - - - AU

5.

Same legend. The monogram of Christ, within a laurel garland. In the exergue, COMOB. (A *quinarius*). - - - - - - - - AU

6.

Without legend. A similar type. In the exergue, RM. (A *quinarius*). AR

7.

Without legend. A similar type, without letters in the exergue. (*Cat. d'Ennery*). - - - - - - - - - - - - - - - AR

8.

Without legend. A cross, within a laurel garland. In the exergue, COMOB. *or* CONOB. (*Quinarii*). - - - - - - - - AU

In gold, No. 3 is the rarest. The next in rarity are Nos. 1 and 4. Of the quinarii, No. 8 is the least rare. The silver quinarii are valued by Mionnet at 120 francs each.

BRASS MEDALLION.

...... OS. HERACLEOS. Hercules naked, standing; his right hand on his club, his left holding a child, seated on the lion's skin. In the exergue, ANDREA. (*Vaillant*).

Valued by Mionnet at 100 francs. The medallions of this type are *Contorniati*.

EUPHEMIA.

[Aelia Marciana Euphemia, was married to the emperor Anthemius at the time that he was appointed by Marcianus, general of the legions of the East. The time of her death is not known].

STYLE:——D. N. AEL. MARC. EVFEMIA. AVG.——D. N. AEL. MARC. EVFEMIA. PP. AVG.

Gold, of the usual size - - - - - - - - - - - - - - - R 8

VICTORIA. AVGGG.* Victory, holding a long cross. In the exergue, CORMOB. (*Banduri*, vol. ii, p. 628).

OLYBRIUS.

[Anicius Olybrius, the son-in-law of Valentinianus the Third, whose youngest daughter he married, was descended from the ancient family which fled from Rome after the sack of that city by Genseric. He was sent into Italy by the emperor Leo, to suppress the tyrant Ricimer, who, upon his advance, caused Anthemius to be assassinated, and proclaimed Olybrius emperor of the West, in the year of Rome 1225 (A. D. 472). Olybrius died in the same year, after a short reign of three months].

STYLE:——D. N. ANICIVS. OLYBRIVS. AVG.——D. N. ANIC. (*or* ANICIVS.) OLYBRIVS. P. F. AVG.

Gold - R 6
„ quinarii - - - - - - - - - - - - - - - - - R 8
Silver - - - - - - - - - - - - - - - - - - - R 8
Lead - R 8

GOLD AND SILVER.

1.
SALVS. MVNDI. A large cross. In the exergue, COMOB. - AU

2.
VIRTVS. ROMANORVM. Rome seated, holding a globe surmounted by a Victory. In the exergue, MD. (*Tanini*). - - - - AR

3.
Without legend. A cross within a garland. In the exergue, COMOB. (A *quinarius*). - - - - - - - - - - - - - - - AU

LEAD.

DD. NN. AVGG. Full-faced heads of Olybrius and Placidia: above, a cross.—*Rev.* SALVS. MVNDI. A large cross. (*Tanini*).

Valued by Mionnet at thirty francs.

PLACIDIA.

[Placidia, the daughter of Valentinianus the Third and Eudoxia, was married to the emperor Olybrius in the year of Rome 1215 (A.D. 462)].

Style:——AEL. PLACIDIA. AVG.

Gold, of the usual size - - - - - - - - - - - - - - - R 8
Lead (see the coins of her husband). - - - - - - - - - R 8

VOT. XX. MVLT. XXXI. Victory, standing to the left, holding a long cross: above, a star. In the exergue, CONOB. (*Plate xii, No. 10*). - - - - - - - - - - - - - - - - - - AU

This aureus is in the collection of the British Museum. The continental numismatists doubt its authenticity; but it is certainly a genuine coin. It is, however, not so certain that it belongs to the wife of Olybrius, since the coins of Galla Placidia, wife of Constantius the Third, have legends and types very similar. The wife of Constantius III. may have borne the name of Aelia as well as that of Galla, in which case the coin in question would certainly appear to belong to her, instead of to the consort of Olybrius.

GLYCERIUS.

[Glycerius held high situations in the palace of the emperors of the West, and upon the death of Olybrius, assumed the purple at Ravenna, in Cisalpine Gaul, in the year of Rome 1226 (A. D. 473). He was dethroned by Julius Nepos in the following year, and became Bishop of Salona. Glycerius died in the year of Rome 1233 (A. D. 480)].

Gold - R 6
  „ quinarii - - - - - - - - - - - - - - - - - R 6
Silver quinarii - - - - - - - - - - - - - - - - - R 8

1.

VICTORIA. AVG. (*or* AVGG. *or* AVGGG.) Glycerius standing, in a military habit; his right foot on a pedestal, holding in his right hand a long cross; in his left, a globe surmounted by a Victory. In the field, R. V. In the exergue, COMOB. - - - - - AU

2.

Without legend. A cross within a laurel garland. In the exergue COMOB. (A *quinarius*). - - - - - - - - - - - - - AU

3.

Without legend. A similar type. (A *quinarius*).—*Mionnet*, from the cabinet of *M. Gosselin.* - - - - - - - - - - - - - AR

LEO II.

[Leo, the son of Zeno Isaurus and Ariadna, was born about the year of Rome 1212 (A. D. 459), and succeeded Leo I. in the empire of the East in 1227 (A. D. 474). He died, after a reign of six months].

STYLE, ASSOCIATED WITH HIS FATHER:———D. N. LEO. ET. ZENO. PP. AVG.

If any coins exist on which the style of this emperor is found alone, they are confounded with those of Leo the First.

Gold - R 6

„ quinarii - - - - - - - - - - - - - - - - R 6

GOLD.

[LEO, AND ZENO].

1.

D. N. LEO. ET. ZENO. P. P. AVG. Helmed bust of Leo II. with coat of mail, spear, and ornamented buckler. — *Rev.* SALVS. REIPVBLICAE. Zeno and Leo seated on the same throne, full-faced, each with the nimbus. In the field, a star and a cross. In the exergue, CONOB. (*Mionnet;* cabinet of *M. Gosselin*).

2.

Same legends. A similar type; but the figures without the nimbus; and the numeral Θ. (*Banduri*).

3.

D. N. LEO. ET. ZENO. PP. AVG. The diademed head of Leo. II.
to the right, with the paludamentum.—*Rev.* VICTORIA. AVGVS-
TORVM. Victory marching, holding a garland and a globe. In
the field, a star. In the exergue, CONOB. (A *quinarius*).

Mionnet values the above at from sixty to seventy-two francs.

ZENO.

[Zeno, son-in-law of Leo I. and father of Leo II., was born in the year of
Rome 1179 (A. D. 426). In 1227 (A. D. 474), he was associated in
the Eastern empire with his son Leo, whose death, six months after,
left him sole possessor of the throne. Zeno was compelled to abdicate
by his uncle Basiliscus, in 1229 (A. D. 476); but he regained the
sovereignty in the following year. This prince died in the year of
Rome 1244 (A. D. 491).

STYLE:——D. N. ZENO. AVG.——IMP. ZENO. SEMPER. AVG.
——D. N. ZENO. SEMPER. AVG.——D. N. ZENO. PERP.
NC.*——D. N. ZENO. PERP. (*or* PERPE.) AVG.——IMP.
ZENO. FEL. PERP.——ZENO. PERP. F. AVG.——D. N.
ZENO. PER. (*or* PERP. *or* PERPET.) F. AVG.——ZENO.
PERP. P. F. AVG.

ZENO AND HIS SON ASSOCIATED:——D. N. ZENO. ET. LEO. NOV. (*for*
NOB.) CAE. (*or* CAES.)

This last legend has been commented upon by M. Labus and the Baron
Marchant; but, as their interpretations are not conclusive, they shall not
be here discussed. The reader is, however, referred to the letter of the
Baron Marchant, addressed to the " Société des Recherches, utiles de la
Ville de Treves."—*Metz. Nov.* 2, 1821."

Gold, denarii and quinarii - - - - - - - - - - - - -	C
Silver, quinarii - - - - - - - - - - - - - - - - - -	R 4
First brass - - - - - - - - - - - - - - - - - - -	R 4
Second brass - - - - - - - - - - - - - - - - - -	R 2
Third brass - - - - - - - - - - - - - - - - - - -	R 4

---

* Mionnet supposes these letters to signify NOBILISSIMVS. CAESAR., which is
confirmed by the legend, in which Zeno and Leo are styled together, NOBILIS-
SIMI. CAESARES. Why these princes are merely styled Caesars, while they held
the rank of Augustus, is difficult to explain.

1.

SALVS. REIPVBLICE. *(sic)*. The monogram of Christ, within a laurel garland. In the exergue, COMOB. (A *quinarius*).—*Tanini.*
                                                                    AU

2.

VICTORIA. AVGGG. Victory, standing, holding a long cross. In the field, a star. In the exergue, CONOB. (A *quinarius*).   AU

3.

Same legend. Victory, seated on arms, inscribing on a buckler, XXXX. In the field, the monogram of Christ, and a star. In the exergue, CONOB. (A *quinarius*). - - - - - - - - AU

4.

Same legend. The monogram of Christ, within a garland. In the exergue, COMOB. (A *quinarius*). - - - - - - - - - AU

5.

Without legend. Victory marching, with garland and palm branch. (A *quinarius*). - - - - - - - - - - - - - - - AR

6.

Without legend. An eagle with wings expanded : a cross. (A *quinarius*).
                                                                    AR.

7.

Without legend. A military figure standing, his right foot on the prow of a vessel, holding a spear and a cornucopia. In the field, R. V. *or* M. D. (A *quinarius*). - - - - - - - - - - - - AR

In gold, Nos. 1 and 3 are the rarest.

FIRST BRASS.

1.

ZENO. ET. LEO. NOV. CAES. The bearded and diademed head of Zeno. In the exergue, IIII.—*Rev.* INVICTA. ROMA. Victory marching, bearing a garland and a trophy. In the field, S. C. In the exergue, XL.

2.

IMP. ZENO. FEL. PERP. (*or* IMP. ZENO. SEMPER. AVG.) A similar type.

No. 1 is much the rarest.

BASILISCUS.

[Basiliscus, the brother of Verina, wife of Leo I., was general of the army of the Western empire under that emperor. He drove from the throne in 1229 (A. D. 476), his nephew Zeno, by whom he was subsequently vanquished and imprisoned in Cappadocia, with his family, who, with Basiliscus, were suffered to die of hunger, in the year of Rome 1230 (A. D. 477)].

STYLE.——D. N. ·BASILISCVS. P. AVG.——D. N. BASILISCVS. P. F. AVG.——D. N. BASILISCVS. PP. (or PERP.) AVG.

BASILISCUS AND HIS SON MARCUS ASSOCIATED :——D. N. BASILISCVS. ET. MARC. P. AVG.——D. N. BASILISC. (or BASILISCVS.) ET. MARC. P. F. AVG.

Gold - - - - - - - - - - - - - - - - - - - R 4
„ quinarii - - - - - - - - - - - - - - - - R 3
Silver, quinarii - - - - - - - - - - - - - - - R 6
Third brass - - - - - - - - - - - - - - - - *unique*

GOLD AND SILVER.

1.

VICTORIA. AVGGG. (or AVGGG. B. or Γ. or Δ. or Є. or Z. or H.) Victory standing, holding a long cross. In the field, a star. In the exergue, CONOB. or TMSOB. - - - - - - - - AU

2.

VICTORIA. AVGGG. A similar type. In the exergue, CONOB. (A *quinarius*). - - - - - - - - - - - - - - AU

3.

VICTORIA. AVGG. Victory seated on arms, inscribing on a buckler XXXX. In the field, a star, and the monogram of Christ. In the exergue, CONOB. (A *quinarius*). - - - - - - - AU

4.

Without legend. A military figure standing, with his right foot on the prow of a vessel, holding a spear and a cornucopia. In the field, R. V. (A *quinarius*). - - - - - - - - - - - - AR

5.

Without legend. A cross within a laurel garland. In the exergue, COMOB. or CONOB. (*Quinarii*). - - - - - - - - AU

In gold, No. 3 is the rarest; the next in rarity is No. 1.

[BASILISCUS, AND HIS SON MARCUS].

D. N. BASILISCVS. (*or* BASILISCI. ET. MARC. P. AVG. The
helmeted and armed bust of Basiliscus.—*Rev.* SALVS. REIPVB-
LICAE. Γ. Basiliscus and Marcus seated on the same throne,
each holding a volume and a globe. In the exergue, CONOB.
(*Mus. Vindob.*) - - - - - - - - - - - - - - - - AU

Valued by Mionnet at sixty francs.

THIRD BRASS.

GLORIA. ROMANORVM. Basiliscus marching, holding the
labarum, and dragging after him a captive. In the exergue, . SM.

Mionnet gives this coin as from the Cabinet of M. Gosselin of Paris,
and values it at fifty francs.

AELIA ZENONIS.

[Aelia Zenonis, the wife of Basiliscus, was married to that prince long
before his usurpation. She died of hunger, with her husband and
children, as before related, in the year of Rome 1230 (A.D. 477)].

Style:——AEL. ZENONIS. AVG.

Gold - R 6

VICTORIA. AVGGG. Victory standing, holding a long cross. In
the field, a star. In the exergue, CONOB.

Valued by Mionnet at eighty francs.

MARCUS.

[Marcus, son of Basiliscus and Aelia Zenonis, was declared Augustus
by his father, in the year of Rome 1229 (A.D. 476). - He shared the
horrible fate of his family in 1230 (A. D. 477)].

See the coins of Basiliscus.

LEONTIUS.

[Leontius was governor of Syria in the reign of Zeno, and usurped the
purple at Tarsus in Cilicia, in the year of Rome 1235 (A. D. 482).
He was defeated by the troops of Zeno, and suffered death at Constantinople, in the year 1241 (A. D. 488)].

STYLE :——D. N. LEONTIVS. P. F. AVG.——D. N. LEONTIVS. PERP. (*or* PERPET.) AVG.——D. N. LEOTIO. (*sic*) PERPS. (*sic*) AVG.

Ducange has confounded the coins of this usurper with those of Leontius, who deposed Justinianus the Second.

Gold - R 4

1.

VICTORIA. AVGG. *or* VICTORA. (*sic*). AЧGG. (*sic*). Victory standing, holding a long cross. In the exergue, ANT. *or* ANTIC.

2.

VICTORIA. AVGЧ. Victory standing, full-faced, holding a cross surmounted by the monogram of Christ, and a globe surmounted by a cross. In the exergue, CONOB. (*Mus. Vindob.*).

Valued by Mionnet at seventy-two francs each.

JULIUS NEPOS.

[Julius Nepos was born in Dalmatia. His father Nepotianus was general in that country; his mother was a sister of Marcellinus. Nepos was created emperor of the West, by Leo the First, and he ascended the throne in the year of Rome 1227 (A. D. 474), having first deposed Glycerius. This prince was himself deposed by Orestes, and subsequently murdered, at Salona in Dalmatia, in the year of Rome 1233, (A. D. 480)].

STYLE :——D. N. IVLIVS. NEPOS. AVG.——D. N. IVL. (*or* IVLI. *or* IVLIVS.) NEPOS. P. F. AVG.——D. N. IVL. NEPOS. PERP. P. F. AVG.

Gold - R 4
„ quinarii - - - - - - - - - - - - - - - - - R 2
Silver - - - - - - - - - - - - - - - - - - R 6
„ quinarii - - - - - - - - - - - - - - - - - R 6
Third brass - - - - - - - - - - - - - - - - - R 8

GOLD AND SILVER.

1.

SALVS. REIP. The monogram of Christ, within a laurel garland. In the exergue, CONOB. (A *quinarius*)—*Tanini.* - - - - AU

2.

VICTORIA. AVGGG.   Victory standing, holding a long cross.   In
the field, A. R. or M. D. or R. V.   In the exergue, COMOB. or
CONOB.   - - - - - - - - - - - - - - - - AU

3.

VOT. V. MVLT. X.   In the exergue, P. CON.   *(Tanini).* - - AR

4.

VOTIS. V. MVLTIS X. within a garland: below, P. CON.   *(Mead's
Catalogue,* p. 104*).*   - - - - - - - - - - - - - - AR

5.

VRBIS. *(sic).* ROMA.   Rome, seated.   In the exergue, RV. PS. - AR

6.

Without legend.   A cross, or the letters XP., within a garland.   In the
exergue, KOMO. or COMOB. or CONOB.   *(Quinarii).* - - AU

7.

Without legend.   A military figure, standing, his right foot on the prow
of a vessel, holding a spear and a cornucopia.   In the field, R. V.
In the exergue, COMOB.   (A *quinarius*).—*Mus. Vindob.*   - AR

THIRD BRASS.

1.

SALVS. REIPVBLICAE.   Victory marching, bearing a trophy, and
dragging after her a captive.

2.

VICTORIA. AVGGG.   Victory, marching,   In the exergue, MR. . .

The above are quoted by Tanini.   Mionnet values them at forty
francs each.

ROMULUS AUGUSTUS.

[Romulus Augustus, the son of Orestes, was proclaimed emperor by his
father, in the year of Rome 1228 (A. D. 475).   This puppet was
deposed by Odoacer, king of the Heruli, in the following year, and
banished to Campania.   With Romulus Augustus, the Roman empire
ended in the West].

STYLE : —— D. N. ROMVLVS. AVGVSTVS. P. AVG. —— D. N.
ROMVLVS. AVGVSTVS. P. F. AVG.

The coins given by Goltzius, on which this emperor is styled AVGVS-
TVLVS. and MOMYLVS., are either false (which is most probable) or have
been erroneously described.   Eckhel is of this opinion.

Gold - - - - - - - - - - - - - - - - - - - R 6

  ,, quinarii - - - - - - - - - - - - - - - - R 6

Third brass - - - - - - - - - - - - - - - - R 8

GOLD AND SILVER.

1.

VICTORIA. AVGGG. Victory standing, holding a long cross. In the field, RM. or a star. In the exergue, COMOB.

2.

Without legend. A cross within a laurel garland. In the exergue, COMOB. (A *quinarius*).

3.

Without legend. A soldier standing, holding in his right hand a spear, and a cornucopia in his left. In the field, R. V. (*Banduri*).

No. 3 is the rarest.

THIRD BRASS.

1.

SALVS. REIPVBLICAE. Victory marching, holding a trophy resting on her shoulder, and dragging after her a captive : the monogram of Christ. In the exergue, RP.

2.

VICTORIA. AVG. . . . . . Victory marching. In the exergue, RP. (Size of the quinarius).

The above are quoted by Tanini, and are valued by Mionnet at forty francs.

ANASTASIUS.

[Anastasius was born of an obscure family, at Dyrrhachium in Illyria, in the year of Rome 1183 (A.D. 430). He was an officer of the imperial palace under Zeno, upon whose death he ascended the throne of Constantinople, and married Zeno's widow, Ariadne, 1244 (A. D. 491). Anastasius was killed by thunder, in the year of Rome 1271 (A.D. 518)].

STYLE :——D. N. ANASTASIVS.—— D. N. ANASTASIVS. AVG. —— D. N. ANASTASIVS. P.——D. N. ANASTASIVS. P. A. (*or* AVG.) —— D. N. ANASTASIVS. P. F. AV. (*or* AG. *or*

AVG.)——IMP. ANASTASIVS. PP. AVG.——IMP. ANAS-
TASIVS. PP. A. (*or* AV. *or* AVG.)——D. N. ANASTASIVS.
PERP. AVG.——D. N. ANASTASIVS. PERP. P. F. AVG.——
D. N. ANASTASIVS. P. PI. AVG.——D. N. ANASTASIVS.
PR. (*sic*)——D. N. ANASTASIVS. PR. N. C. (*sic*)——D. N.
ANASTASIVS. PR. (*sic*) AVG.——D. N. ANASTASIVS. PR.
(*sic*) F. AV. (*or* AVG.)

Gold, quinarii and denarii - - - - - - - - - - - - - - C
Silver, quinarii - - - - - - - - - - - - - - - - - R 1
  ,,   with the name of THEODORICUS - - - - - - - - - R 1
  ,,   with the name of BADUILA - - - - - - - - - - - R 2
  ,,   with the name of THEIA. - - - - - - - - - - - R 3
Brass medallions - - - - - - - - - - - - - - - - C
First, second, and third brass - - - - - - - - - - - C

GOLD AND SILVER.

1.

VICTORIA. AVGGG. Γ. *or* H. *or* I. Victory holding a staff, surmounted by the monogram of Christ. In the field, a star. In the
exergue, CONOB. - - - - - - - - - - - - - AU

2.

Same legend and same numerals. Victory seated on arms, inscribing
on a buckler XXXX. In the field, a star, and the monogram of
Christ. In the exergue, CONOB. - - - - - - - - AU

3.

VICTORIA. AVGVSTORVM. Victory seated on a coat of mail,
holding a buckler supported by a winged Genius, on which is inscribed VOT. P. C. In the exergue, COMOB. (A *quinarius*).
Quoted by *Tanini.* - - - - - - - - - - - - - AU

4.

INVITA. (*sic*) ROMA. Victory marching, bearing a cross on her
shoulders, and a garland. In the field, S. C. (A *quinarius*)—*Mus.
Vindob.* - - - - - - - - - - - - - - - - - AR

5.

Without legend. The monogram of Christ within a garland. (A
quinarius). - - - - - - - - - - - - - - - AR

In gold, No. 3 is the rarest. In silver, No. 4 is the rarest.

[ANASTASIUS, AND THEODORICUS, KING OF THE OSTRO-GOTHS].

SILVER.

1.

D. N. ANASTASIVS. PP. AVG. Diademed head of Anastasius.—
Rev. INVITA. (*sic*) ROMA. C. M. In the middle of the field,
THEODORS. (*for.* THEODORICVS.) in monogram: a cross
and a star. (A *quinarius*).

2.

Another, with INVICTA. ROMA. and the same monogram. (A
ꞌ quinarius).

3.

THDORS. in monogram, within a garland. (A *quinarius*).

No. 1 is much the rarest.

[ANASTASIUS AND BADUILA].

SILVER.

D. N. ANASTASIVS. AVG. *or* P. F. AVG. Diademed head of
Anastasius—*Rev.* D. N. BADVILA. REX. (*or* RIX.) in four
lines, within a laurel garland. (*Quinarii*).

[ANASTASIUS, AND THEIA (or THELA)].

SILVER.

D. N. ANASTASIVS. P. AG. *(sic)* or D. N. ANASTASIVS. AV.
Diademed head of Anastasius.—*Rev.* DOMNVS. *(sic)* THEIA. P.
(sic) REX. *or* D. N. THELA. REX. in three or four lines, within
a laurel garland. (*Quinarii*).

JUSTINUS.

[Justinus was born a peasant, at Bederiana, in Thacia, in the year of
Rome 1203 (A. D. 450). He was Praetorian praefect in the reign
of Anastasius; upon whose death he was raised to the empire, in
1271 (A.D. 518). This emperor died in the year of Rome 1280,
(A. D. 527)].

STYLE:——D. N. IVSTINVS. AV. (*or* AVG.)——D. N. IVSTINVS. P.
(*or* PI.)——D. N. IVSTINVS. P. AVG.——D. N. IVSTINVS.
P. F. AVG.——D. N. IVSTINVS. PP. A. (*or* AV. *or* AVG. *or*
AG.)——D. N. IVSTINVS. PP. AVGS. *(sic).*——D. N. IVSTI-

NVS. PP. PIV.——D. N. IVSTINVS. V. PP. AVG. *(sic)* ——
D. N. IVSTINVS. PP. VI. *(sic)*——D. N. IVSTINVS. PP.
VII. *(sic)*.

JUSTINUS AND JUSTINIANUS, ASSOCIATED: —— D. N. IVSTIN. ET.
IVSTINI. (*or* IVSTINIAN.) PP. AV. (*or* AVG.)——D. N.
IVSTINVS. IVSTINI. AVG.

Gold, with the head of Justinus only - - - - - - - - - C
,, with the effigies of Justinus and Justinian - - - - - - R 6
,, quinarii - - - - - - - - - - - - - - - - - R 1
Silver medallion - - - - - - - - - - - - - - - R 6
,, of the usual size - - - - - - - - - - - - - - R 1
,, quinarii, with the monogram of Theodoric - - - - - - R 1
,, quinarii, with the name of Athalaric - - - - - - - R 2
Brass medallions - - - - - - - - - - - - - - - - C
First, second, and third brass - - - - - - - - - - - - C

SILVER MEDALLION.

GLORIA. ROMANORVM. The emperor standing, holding a globe;
his right hand raised. In the field, a star. In the exergue, COB.
(*Cat. d'Ennery*).

Valued by Mionnet at thirty francs.

GOLD AND SILVER, OF THE USUAL SIZE.

1.

VICTORIA. AVGGG. Victory seated on arms, inscribing on a buckler
XXXX. In the field, a star, and the monogram of Christ. In the
exergue, CONOB. - - - - - - - - - - - - - AU

2.

VICTORIA. AVGVSTORV. (*sic*). A globe, surmounted by a cross.
In the field, A. R. In the exergue, CONOB. (A *quinarius*). AU

3.

C. N. within a laurel garland. (A *quinarius*). - - - - - - AR

4.

P. K. within a laurel garland. (A *quinarius*).—*Tanini.* - - - AR

5.

Without legend. The monogram of Christ between two stars, within a
garland. (A *quinarius*). - - - - - - - - - - - - AR

6.

Without legend. A star, within a laurel garland. (A *quinarius*). AR

7.

Without legend. The monogram of Christ, within a laurel garland. (A *quinarius*).—Cabinet of *M. Gosselin.* - - - - - - - AR

In silver, No. 4 is the rarest.

[JUSTINVS I., AND THEODORICUS, KING OF THE OSTRO-GOTHS].

SILVER.

1.

D. N. IVSTINVS. P. AVG. (*or* IVSTINVS. AVG.) The diademed head of Justinus the First. — *Rev.* D. N. Theodoricus, in monogram; a cross, and a star: the whole within a laurel garland. (*Quinarii*).

2.

THEODORICVS. in monogram; a cross: the whole within a laurel garland. (A *quinarius*).

The first is much the rarest.

[JUSTINUS I., AND ATHALARICUS, KING OF THE OSTRO-GOTHS].

D. N. IVSTINVS. AVG.—Diademed head of Justinus the First.—*Rev.* D. N. ATHALARICVS. REX. (*or* RIX.) in four lines, within a laurel garland. (*Quinarii*).

FIRST BRASS.

ANNO. PRIMO. In the midst of the field, XP. (*Banduri*).

SECOND BRASS.

FLVRENS. (*sic*) SEMPER. A woman standing, holding a spear in her right hand, her left resting on a buckler. (*Banduri*).

THIRD BRASS.

1.

CONCORP. (*sic*) Є-I. bound together, and supporting a cross between two stars. (*Mus. Vindob.*).

2.

VOT. XIII. within a garland. (*Mus. Vindob.*).

EUPHEMIA.

[Euphemia, the wife of Justinus the First, was born in one of the
barbarous countries tributary to the Romans. She was a slave, and
purchased by Justinus, who caused her to change her real name for
that of Euphemia, and married her before his elevation to the throne.
This empress died before her husband].

There are no coins of Euphemia. Ducange and Banduri have erroneously attributed to her the coins of Euphemia, wife of Athemius.

VITALIANUS.

[Vitalianus, the nephew of Aspar, was master of the militia, under
Anastasius, and in the year of Rome 1267 (A. D. 514), was elected
emperor by the people of Constantinople. Anastasius, however, prevailed
upon Vitalianus to retire. Justinus recalled him to court upon the
death of Anastasius, and honoured him with the consulate, in the year
of Rome 1273 (A. D. 520); but he was assassinated in the seventh
month of his office, at the instigation of Justinianus, nephew of Justinus].

STYLE:——D. N. VITALIANVS PP. AV. (or AVG.).

Gold, quinarii - - - - - - - - - - - - - - - R 8

1.

VICTORIA. AVGVSTOR. (sic). Victory, standing; her right hand
holding a garland, her left, a globe surmounted by a cross. In the
exergue, CONONV. (sic). (Catalogue d'Ennery).

2.

VICTORIA. AVSTO. (sic). Victory marching. (Tanini).

Valued by Mionnet at 300 francs each.

JUSTINIANUS.

[Justinianus, the nephew of Justinus, was born at Thauresium in
Dardania, in the year of Rome 1236 (A.D. 483). In 1280 (A.D. 527),
he received from his uncle the title of Augustus, and succeeded to the
throne four months afterwards. Justinia died of apoplexy, in the
year of Rome 1318 (A. D. 565)].

Style:——D. N. IVSTINI. (or IVSTINIA. or IVSTINIAN. or IVSTINIANVS.)——D. N. IVSTINIANVS. C.——D. N. IVS-TINI. (or IVSTINIAN. or IVSTINIANVS.) A. (or AV. or AVG.)——D. N. IVSTINIAN. (or IVSTINIANVS.) P.——D. N. IVSTINIANVS. PI. C.——D. N. IVSTINIAN. (or IVSTINIA-NVS.) P. A. (or AV. or AG. or AVG.)——D. N. IVSTINIANVS. AVG. P.——D. N. IVSTINIAN. (or IVSTINIANVS.) P. F. A. (or AVG.)——D. N. IVSTINIANVS. PP.——D. N. IVSTI-NIAN. (or IVSTINIANVS.) PP. A. (or AV. or AG. or AVG.) ——D. N. IVSTINIANVS. PP. P.——D. N. IVSTINIANVS. V. PP. C. (sic).

Gold medallion, of very large size - - - - - - - - - -	unique
„ denarii and quinarii - - - - - - - - - - - - - -	C
Silver, denarii and quinarii - - - - - - - - - - - -	R 1
„ quinarii, with the name of ATHALARIC, THEODOBAT, or WITIGES.	R 2
„ „ with the name of BADUILA - - - - - - - -	R 6
Brass medallion - - - - - - - - - - - - - - - -	C
First, second, and third brass - - - - - - - - - - -	C
Third brass, Greek, erroneously attributed to CAESAREA, in Palestine	R 6

UNIQUE GOLD MEDALLION.

D. N. IVSTINIANVS. PP. AVG. The bust of Justinianus, full-faced, with helmet and nimbus, holding a spear and a buckler.—*Rev.* SALVS. ET. GLORIA. ROMANORVM. The emperor armed, on horseback, with the nimbus around his head, preceded by Victory, bearing a trophy. In the field, a star. In the exergue, CONOB. (*Mionnet*).

GOLD AND SILVER, USUAL SIZE, WITH RARE REVERSES.

1.

GLORIA. ROMANORVM. The emperor standing, wearing the palu-damentum, holding a spear, and a globe surmounted by a cross. In the field, a star. (*Banduri*). - - - - - - - - - AR

2.

VICTORIA. AVGGG. Victory, seated on arms, inscribing on a buckler, XXXX. In the field, the monogram of Christ, and a star. In the exergue, CONOB. - - - - - - - - - AU

3.

VICTORIA. PRINCIPVM. Victory, marching. In the field, S. C. (*Banduri*). - - - - - - - - - - - - - - - AR

4.

VOT. MVLTHTI. (*sic*) within a garland. In the exergue, CONOS. (A' *quinarius*).—*Mionnet*, from cabinet of *M. Gosselin.* - - AR

$$\begin{pmatrix} O & V \\ + \\ T & N \end{pmatrix}$$

5.

In the exergue, CONSI. (A *quinarius*). - - - - - AR

6.

C. N.: above, or below, a cross or a star; the whole within a garland. (A *quinarius*). - - - - - - - - - - - - - - - - AR

7.

P. K. within a garland: a star. (A *quinarius*). - - - - - - - AR

8.

Without legend. A globe, surmounted by a cross, within a laurel garland. (A *quinarius*). - - - - - - - - - - - - - AR

9.

Without legend. The monogram of Christ, within a laurel garland. (A *quinarius*). - - - - - - - - - - - - - - - - AR

10.

Without legend. The monogram of Christ, between two stars: the whole within a garland. (A *quinarius*). - - - - - - - - AR

11.

Without legend. The monogram of Christ, between the letters alpha and omega. (A *quinarius*). - - - - - - - - - - - - AR

12.

Without legend. A monogram, a cross, and S: the whole within a garland. (A *quinarius*). - - - - - - - - - - - - - AR

13.

Without legend. A monogram: S. and O.: all within a garland. (A *quinarius*). - - - - - - - - - - - - - - - - AR

14.

Without legend. A monogram: S. and C: all within a garland. (A *quinarius*). - - - - - - - - - - - - - - - - AR

15.

Without legend. D. N.: and a monogram; a cross, and a star: the whole within a garland. (A *quinarius*). - - - - - - - AR

In silver, Nos. 1, 3, and 4 are the rarest: the next in rarity are Nos. 5 and 11.

[JUSTINIANUS I. AND ATHALARICUS].

D. N. IVSTINI. AV. *or* AVG. (*or* IVSTINIANVS. AVG.) Diademed head of the emperor.—*Rev.* D. N. ATHALARICVS. REX. (*or* RIX.), in four lines, within a laurel garland. (*Quinarii*). - AR

Valued by Mionnet at six francs.

[JUSTINIANUS AND THEODOHATUS].

D. N. IVSTINIAN. AVG. Diademed head of Justinianus.—*Rev.* D. N. THEODOHATVS. REX. (*or* RIX.), in four lines, within a laurel garland. - - - - - - - - - - - - - - - - - AR

Valued by Mionnet at six francs.

[JUSTINIANUS AND WITIGES].

D. N. IVSTINIAN. AVG. (*or* IVSTINIANVS. AVG.) Diademed head of Justinianus.—*Rev.* D. N. VVITIGES. *or* VVITIGIS. (*sic*) REX., in four lines, within a laurel garland. (A *quinarius*). - AR

Valued by Mionnet at nine francs.

[JUSTINIANUS AND BADUILA].

D. N. IVSTINIAN. AVG. Diademed head of Justinianus.—*Rev.* D. N. BADVILA. REX. (*or* RIX.), within a garland. (*Eckhel, Doctrina Num. Vet.*).

Valued by Mionnet at fifty francs.

SECOND BRASS.

ΘΥ. ΠΟΛΙC. A cross, and K. In the field, Δ. (*Tanini*).

THIRD BRASS.

Without legend. A lion walking.

GOTHIC KINGS.

THEODORICUS.

[The character of Theodoricus has been minutely drawn by Gibbon. He assisted in deposing Basiliscus, and gained the esteem and confidence of the emperor Zeno, in the year of Rome 1230 (A. D. 477). Having obtained from that prince permission to invade Italy and expel Odoacer, he accordingly entered that country, in 1242 (A. D. 489). Odoacer was worsted in several engagements, and having at length been subdued, a treaty of friendship was made between the conqueror and the conquered, but Odoacer was basely assassinated at a banquet. Theodoricus ended his eventful life at Ravenna, in the year of Rome 1279 (A. D. 526)].

STYLE:——D. N. THEODORICV. REX.

ON COINS OF ANASTASIUS AND JUSTINUS:——THEODORICVS. (in monogram).——D. N. THEODORICVS. (the last word in monogram)].

Silver quinarii, with the head of ANASTASIUS - - - - - - - R 1
      ,,   with the head of JUSTINUS - - - - - - - - R 1
Third brass - - - - - - - - - - - - - - - - R 4

SILVER.
1.
INVITA. (*sic*). ROMA. C. M. In the middle of the field, THEODORICVS., in monogram: above, a cross: below, a star.—*Rev.* D. N. ANASTASIVS. PP. AVG. Diademed head of Anastasius, with the paludamentum. (A *quinarius*).

2.
INVICTA. ROMA. A similar type. (A *quinarius*).

3.
THEODORICVS., in monogram, within a laurel garland.—*Rev.* D. N. ANASTASIVS. PP. AVG. Head of Anastasius. (A *quinarius*).

[THEODORICUS, AND JUSTINUS I].

1.

D. N. THEODORICVS. (the last word in monogram), within a garland.
—*Rev.* D. N. IVSTINVS. P. AVG. (*or* IVSTINVS. AVG.)
Diademed head of Justinus. (*Quinarii*).

2.

THEODORICVS., in monogram. A cross : the whole within a laurel
garland.—*Rev.* Same legend. Head of Justinus. (Λ *quinarius*).

THIRD BRASS.

D. N. THEODORICVS. REX. within a garland.—*Rev.* INVICTA.
ROMA. Helmed head of Rome. (*Pembroke Catal.*)

Valued by Mionnet at twenty francs.

BADUILA.

[History makes no mention of this king. Some coins of Justinianus
bear the name of Baduila, but it is another prince. Whether the
Baduila in question was associated with Theodoricus, or was king of
some other barbarous nation in the time of Anastasius, is not known.]

STYLE :——BADVILA. REX. (*or* RIX.)

Silver, with the head of Anastasius - - - - - - - - - - - R 2

D. N. BADVILA. REX. (*or* RIX.), in four lines, within a laurel garland.
—*Rev.* D. N. ANASTASIVS. AVG. (*or* P. F. AVG.) Diademed
head of Anastasius. (*Quinarii*).

Mionnet says there is a modern forgery.

THEIA.

[Theia, or Thela, is another king whom history does not mention, but
whose name occurs on coins of Anastasius. It is obvious that these
coins were not struck by the Gothic king Theias, who succeeded
Baduila or Totila, in the year of Rome 1305. The Baron Marchant
is of a different opinion].

STYLE, ON COINS OF ANASTASIUS: —— D. N. THELA. REX. ——
DOMNVS. *(sic)* THEIA. REX.——DOMNVS. THEIA. P.
REX.

Silver quinarii - - - - - - - - - - - - - - - - - R 3

[THEIA (or THELA), AND ANASTASIUS.]

1.

DOMNVS. *(sic)* THEIA. P. *(sic)* REX. in four lines, within a laurel
garland.—*Rev.* D. N. ANASTASIVS. P. AG. *(sic)*.   Diademed
head of Anastasius, with the paludamentum.   (A *quinarius*).

2.

D. N. THELA. REX. in three lines, within a laurel garland.—*Rev.*
D. N. ANASTASIVS. AV.   The head of Anastasius, as before.
(A *quinarius*).

No. 1 is the rarest.

ATHALARICUS.

[Athalaricus, the grandson of Theodoricus, ascended the throne of the
Goths in Italy, upon the death of his grandfather, in the year of Rome
1279 (A. D. 526).   Athalaricus died in 1287 (A. D. 534)].

STYLE:——D. N. ATHALARICVS. (*or* ATALARICVS.)——D. N.
ATHALARICVS. REX.

ON COINS OF JUSTINUS AND JUSTINIANUS:——D. N. ATHALARICVS.
REX. (*or* RIX.)

Silver quinarii, with the head of Justinus, - - - - - - - - R 1
     „   with the head of Justinianus - - - - - - - - R 2
Third brass (with the effigy of Athalaricus, standing) - - - - R 3
     „   with the head of Rome on one side, and his name
          on the other - - - - - - - - - - - - - R 1

SILVER.

[ATHALARICUS, AND JUSTINUS I.]

D. N. ATHALARICVS. REX. (*or* RIX.) in four lines, within a laurel
garland.—*Rev.* D. N. IVSTINVS. AVG.   Diademed head of
Justinus, with the paludamentum.   (*Quinarii*).

[ATHALARICUS, AND JUSTINIANUS.]

D. N. ATHALARICVS. REX. (*or* RIX.) in four lines, within a laurel garland.—*Rev.* D. N. IVSTINI. AV. (*or* AVG. *or* IVSTINIANVS. AVG.) Diademed head of Justinianus, with the paludamentum. (*Quinarii*).

THIRD BRASS.

1.

D. N. ATHALARICVS. REX. within a laurel garland.—*Rev.* INVICTA. ROMA. Helmed bust of Rome.

2.

D. N. ATHALARICVS. REX. In the centre of the field, V.—*Rev.* INVICTA. ROMA. Helmed bust of Rome. (*Tanini*).

3.

D. N. ATHALARICVS. . . . . . Athalaricus standing, wearing the paludamentum, holding a spear; his left hand resting on a buckler. In the field, S. C. and X. *Rev.* INVICTA. ROMA. Helmed bust of Rome.

THEODOHATUS.

[Theodohatus, the grandson of Theodoricus, was raised to the throne by his cousin Amalasuntha, who gave him her hand, in the year of Rome 1287 (A.D. 534). Theodohatus, however, shewed himself unworthy of these favours, and caused his wife to be murdered. This deed brought upon him the resentment of the soldiers, who elected Witiges in his stead. The death of Theodohatus followed immediately after, in the year of Rome 1289 (A. D. 536)].

STYLE:——D. N. THEODOHATVS. (*or* THEODOHATHVS. *or* THEODAHATHS. *or* THEODATVS.) REX.

ON COINS OF JUSTINIANUS:——D. N. THEODAHATVS. (*or* THEO-DAHATHVS.) REX. (*or* RIX.)

Silver quinarii, with the head of Justinianus - - - - - - - - R 2
Brass medallions   - - - - - - - - - - - - - - - - R 6
Second brass - - - - - - - - - - - - - - - - - - R 2
Third brass - - - - - - - - - - - - - - - - - - R 1

SILVER.

[THEODAHATUS, AND JUSTINIANUS.]

D. N. THEODAHATVS. REX. (*or* RIX.) in four lines, within a laurel garland.—*Rev.* D. N. IVSTINIAN. AVG. Diademed head of Justinianus, with the paludamentum. (*Quinarii*).

BRASS MEDALLION.

D. N. THEODAHATVS. REX. The crowned bust of Theodohatus.— *Rev.* VICTORIA. PRINCIPIS. Victory, on the prow of a vessel.

Valued by Mionnet at fifty francs.

·SECOND BRASS.

D. N. THEODAHATVS. REX. The crowned bust of Theodohatus.— *Rev.* VICTORIA. PRINCIPVM. Victory, on the prow of a vessel. In the field, S. C.

THIRD BRASS.

INVICTA. ROMA. Helmed bust of Rome.—*Rev.* D. N. THEODA- HATVS. (*or* THEODAHATHS.) (*sic*) REX. within a garland.

WITIGES.

[Witiges was General of the army of Theodohatus, and having destroyed that prince, he was proclaimed king by the Goths, in the year of Rome 1289 (A. D. 536); but in the year 1293 (A. D. 540), Witiges was defeated and made prisoner by Belisarius, the General of Justinianus, and sent to the Roman emperor at Constantinople, who gave him the command of some troops stationed on the Persian frontiers].

STYLE:——D. N. VVITIGES. (*or* VVITICES.) REX. (*or* RIX.)

ON COINS OF JUSTINIANUS :——D. N. VVITIGES. (*or* VVITIGIS. *or* VVITICES. *or* VVITTICES.) REX.

Silver quinarii, with the head of Justinianus - - - - - - - R 3

Third brass - - - - - - - - - - - - - - - - - R 4

[WITIGES, AND JUSTINIANUS].

D. N. VVITIGES. REX. in four lines, within a laurel garland.—*Rev.* D. N. IVSTINIAN. AVG. (*or* IVSTINIANVS. AVG.). The diademed bust of Justinianus to the right. (*Quinarii*).

THIRD BRASS.

D. N. VVITIGES. REX. (*or* RIX.) within a garland.—*Rev.* INVICTA.
ROMA. Helmed bust of Rome.

HILDIBADUS.

[Hildibadus or Hildibaldus, was proclaimed king of the Goths after the
capture of Witiges, in the year of Rome 1293 (A. D. 540). He fell
by the hands of his own soldiers, in the following year].

No coins are known of Hildibadus.

ARARICUS.

[Araricus, or Eraricus, was elected king of the Goths upon the murder of
Hildibadus, and was assassinated six months afterwards by Baduila, or
Totila].

No coins are known of this prince.

BADUELA.

[Baduela, or Baduila, or, as he is called by the Greek writers, Totila,
ascended the throne of the Goths after his murder of Araricus, in the
year of Rome 1294 (A. D. 541). He fell in a battle with Narses, the
General of Justinianus, in 1305 (A. D. 552)].

STYLE :——D. N. BADVELA. (*or* BADVIL. *or* BADVILA. *or*
BADVILLA.) REX. (*or* RIX. *or* RX.)

ON COINS OF JUSTINIANVS :——D. N. BADVILA. REX. (*or* RIX.)

Silver - - - - - - - - - - - - - - - - - - -	R 8
„ quinarii, with the head of Justinianus - - - - - - -	R 8
Third brass - - - - - - - - - - - - - - - - -	R 3

SILVER.

1.

INVICTISSIMV. AV. *(sic)*. Bust of Baduila, with coat of mail, to
the left, with a diadem surmounted by a cross.—*Rev.* D. N.
BADVILA. RIX. *(sic)*, within a garland. (A *quinarius*.).—*Tanini.*

2.

D. N. BADVILA. (or BADVELA. REX.)   Bust of Baduela.—*Rev.*
D. N. BADVILA. REX. within a garland.   (*Eckhel*).

3.

FELIX. TICINVS.   Turreted female head.—*Rev.* BADVILA. REX.
within a garland.   (*Hunter*).

[BADVILA, AND JUSTINIANUS.]

D. N. BADVILA. REX. (or RIX.) within a garland.—*Rev.* D. N.
IVSTINIAN. AVG. Diademed head of Justinianus. (A *quinarius*).
—*Eckhel.*

THIRD BRASS.

1.

D. N. BADVELA. REX.   Full-faced bust of Baduela.—*Rev.* D. N.
BADVELA. REX. within a garland.   (*Cat. d'Ennery*).

2.

D. N. BADVILLA. REX. within a laurel garland.—*Rev.* FELIX.
TICINVS.   Turreted female head.   (*Banduri*).

3.

D. N. BADVILA. REX.   Full-faced bust of Baduela.—*Rev.* FLORIAS.
(or FLVRIAS.) SEMPER.   A soldier standing, holding a spear,
his left hand resting on a buckler.   In the field, X.

4.

D. N. BADVELA. REX.   Bust of Baduela.—*Rev* VIRTVS. EX-
ERCIT.   A similar type to the preceding.   (*Banduri*).

5.

D. N. BADVIL. RX. (*sic*).   Bust as before.—*Rev.* Without legend.
A lion, walking.   (*Tanini*).

Nos. 2 and 5 are much the rarest.

THEIAS.

[Theias was raised to the throne by the Goths, after the death of Baduela,
in the year of Rome 1305 (A. D. 552), and was defeated and slain by
Narses, in the following year.   With Theias, ended the dominion of
the Goths in Italy].

There are no certain coins of this prince.   The Baron Marchant is of
opinion that Theia and Theias are the same persons, and that it is the
same with Baduela and Baduila.

VANDAL KINGS.

The history of this barbarous people, and their encroachments upon the more civilized nations of Europe, has been given by Gibbon. The names of several of their kings are recorded in history; but the first of whom we have coins, is

GUNTHAMUNDUS.

[Gunthamundus, or Gondamond, succeeded Hunneric in the government of the Vandals in Africa, in the year of Rome 1237 (A. D. 484), and died in the year 1249 (A. D. 496)].

STYLE:——D. N. R. (or RX. or REX.) GVNTHA. (or GVNTHA-MVND. or GVNTAMVNDVS.)

Silver, denarii and quinarii - - - - - - - - - - - - R 6

1.

D. N. R. (or RX.) (sic). GVNTHA. or GVNTHAMVND. The head of Gunthamundus, with a diadem and paludamentum.—Rev. D. N. or $\overline{D.\,N.}$ XXV. within a myrtle garland. (Quinarii).—Mionnet.

2.

D. N. REX. GVNTHAMVND. (or GVNTHAMVNDV.) The same head.—Rev. $\overline{D.\,N.}$ within an olive garland. (Mionnet).

TRISAMUNDUS.

[Trisamundus, or Trasamond, or Trasimond, the brother of Gunthamundus, ascended the Vandal throne upon the death of the latter, in the year of Rome 1249 (A. D. 496). This prince died in 1276 (A. D. 523)].

STYLE:——D. N. RG. THISAMVNDS. (or TRHSAMVNDS. or TRSAMVNS).

Silver quinarii - - - - - - - - - - - - - - - - R 4

D. N. RG. THISAMVNDS. (*sic*) *or* D. N. RG. (*sic*) TRHSAMVNDS. (*sic*) *or* TRSAMVNS. (*sic*).   Diademed head, with the paludamen-tum.—*Rev.* D. N. within a myrtle crown.

The above are quoted by Mionnet, from the cabinet of M. Gosselin of Paris.

HILDERICUS.

[Hildericus succeeded his cousin Trisamundus, in the year of Rome 1276 (A. D. 523). He was deposed and imprisoned by Gelimarus in 1283 (A. D. 530)].

STYLE:——D. N. HILDERICVS. (*or* HILDERIK. *or* HILDERIX. *or* HILDIRIX.) REX.·

Silver quinarii - - - - - - - - - - - - - - - - - R 6

1.

D. N. DILDIRIX. (*sic*) *or* HILDERIX. REX. The head of Hildericus with a diadem and the paludamentum.—*Rev.* FELIX. KARTG. *(sic).* A female wearing the stola, full-faced, holding ears of corn in each hand. *(Quinarii).*

2.

D. N. HILD. . . RI. REX. The same head.—*Rev.* XXV. within a garland. (A *quinarius*).—*Mionnet.*

No. 2 is the rarest.

GELIMARUS.

[Gelimarus, or Geilamir, deposed his cousin Hildericus, and ascended the throne, in the year of Rome 1283 (A. D. 530), but four years afterwards was defeated and taken prisoner by Belisarius. This event ended the dynasty of the Vandals in Africa: Gelimarus was sent by the victorious general to Constantinople, and Justinianus assigned him some lands in Galatia].

STYLE:——D. N. R. (*or* RX. *or* REX.) GELAMA. (*or* GEILAMIR.)

Silver quinarii - - - - - - - - - - - - - - - - R 5

1.

D. N. R. (*or* REX.) GELAMIR. The bust of Gelimarus, with diadem and paludamentum.—*Rev.* D. N. within a myrtle garland.

2.

D. N. RX. ҀELIMA. *(sic)*. The bust as before.—*Rev.* $\overline{\text{D . N.}}$ within
a laurel garland. *(Mus. Hedervar, p. 331).*

No. 2 is much the rarest.

THEODEBERTUS.

[The coins of Theodebertus belong to the suite of Merovingian monarchs,
but as they bear the title of *Augustus,*[*] having probably been struck
when this king invaded Italy, they are ranged with those of the
emperors. Theodebertus was born in the year A. D. 534, and died of
a hurt received in combat with a wild bull while hunting, when about
to invade Thrace, A. D. 548. Some of the French historians say he
died of a fever].

STYLE (on coins probably struck in Italy):——D. N. THEODEBERTVS.
——D. N. THEODEBERTVS. C.——D. N. THEODEBERTVS.
VICTOR.—— TEODIBERTI. A. —— D. N. THEODEBERTI.
P. P. AVG.——THEODOBERCIA.——THVDEBERTIACO.

Gold - - - - - - - - - - - - - - - - - - R 4
„ quinarii - - - - - - - - - - - - - - - - R 3
Silver quinarii - - - - - - - - - - - - - - - *dubious*

1.

VICTORIA. AVGGG. *(or* AVGGG. I). Victory standing, full-faced,
holding a long cross, and a globe surmounted by a cross. In the
field, $\overline{\text{ҁAV.}}$ *or* B. O. *or* L. V.: and a star. In the exergue,
CONOB. *or* ICON. . . B. . . *or* RI.

2.

VICTORIA. AGGG. *(sic)* NN. Victory marching, holding a garland. In the field, a star, and P. E. In the exergue, CONOB.
(A *quinarius*, of barbarous fabric).

There are several varieties of this type, says Mionnet, and the legend
is always blundered.

---

[*] The title Augustus was assumed by Theodebertus in consequence of Justinianus' assumption of that of Franciscus, implying that he was the conqueror
of France.

3.

THEODOBERCIA.   Head of Theodebert.— *Rev.* + IOHANNES. ഗ
A cross.   (A *quinarius*, of barbarous fabric).

4.

THVDEBERTIAEO.   Head of Theodebert. — *Rev.* LHADVLFO.
Three crosses surmounted by a P. and two stars.   (A *quinarius*, of
barbarous fabric).   *Cat. d'Ennery*, p. 279.

JUSTINUS II.

[Justinus the Second, son of Dulcissimus and Vigilantia, sister of Justinianus the emperor, was born in Illyria.   He held the office of master
of the palace under his uncle Justinianus, upon whose death he was
elected emperor of the East, in the year of Rome 1318 (A. D. 565).
Justinus died in 1331 (A. D. 578)].

STYLE:——D. N. IVSTINVS.——D. N. IVSTINVS. PI.——IVSTI-
NVS. PIVS. C. *(Khell).* —— D. N. IVSTINVS. PP. ——-- D. N.
IVSTINVS. P. A. (*or* AVG.)——D. N. IVSTINVS. P. F. AVG.
——D. N. IVSTINVS. PP. A. (*or* AV. *or* AVG. *or* AG.)——D.
N. IVSTINVS. PPS. (*sic*) AV.—— D. N. IVSTINVS. PP.
AVGS. (*sic*)——D N. IVSTINVS. IVN. AVG.——D. N. IVS-
TINVS. IVN. PP. AVG.

JUSTINUS AND SOPHIA:——D. N. IVSTIN. ET. SOFIA.—— D. N.
IVSTINVS. ET. SOFIA. A. (*or* AVG.)

Gold -	C
„ with the title of IVNIOR. - - - - - - - - - - -	R 6
„ quinarii - - - - - - - - - - - - - - - - -	R 4
„ „ with the legend GABALORVM. - - - - - -	R 6
Silver quinarii - - - - - - - - - - - - - - - -	R 6
Brass medallion, with the names of IVSTINVS. and SOPHIA - - -	R 8
First and second brass - - - - - - - - - - - - - - -	C
Second brass, with the names of IVSTINVS. and SOPHIA. - - - -	R 4
Third brass - - - - - - - - - - - - - - - - - -	C

GOLD AND SILVER.

1.

FELIX. CARTHA.   A woman wearing the stola, standing; holding in
each hand poppies and ears of corn. - - - - - - - - - AR

This denarius, in the cabinet of M. Gosselin, of Paris, was formerly
attributed to the first Justinian.

2.

FELIX. RESPVBL. within a myrtle garland. (*Mionnet*). - - AR

3.

GABALORVM.' In the centre of the field, a cross placed on steps. (*Banduri*). - - - - - - - - - - - - - - - - - AU

4.

Without legend. The monogram of Christ within a garland. (*Banduri*).
AR

The above are quinarii. The silver is valued by Mionnet at from twenty-four to thirty francs: the gold at 150 francs.

THIRD BRASS.

CONCORDI. In the centre of the field, I. In the exergue, CON. (*Banduri*).

The coins of Justinus the Second are difficult to distinguish from those of the elder Justinus; but those which are supposed to belong to the latter are more common than the others.

SOPHIA.

[Sophia, wife of Justinus the Second, was born in the year of Rome —— and died in the reign of Mauricius].

Brass medallion - - - - - - - - - - - - - - - - R 8
Second brass - - - - - - - - - - - - - - - - - - R 8

BRASS MEDALLION.

[JUSTINUS AND SOPHIA].

1.

D. N. IVSTINO. ET. SOFIE. (*sic*) AVG. Justinus and Sophia seated:

between them, a cross.—*Rev.*

$$\begin{matrix} & + & \\ \text{A} & \text{X} & \text{K} \\ \text{N} & & \\ \text{N} & \text{M} & \text{A} \\ \text{O} & & \\ & \text{B} & \end{matrix}$$
In the exergue, effaced letters.

Valued by Mionnet at 120 francs.

SECOND BRASS.

1.

D. N. IVSTIN. ET. SOPHIA. The emperor and empress seated: between them, a cross. — *Rev.* Without legend. Two Victories standing, supporting a buckler, upon which is a star, and X. In the exergue, HM. *(Tanini)*.

2.

D. N. IVSTIN. ET. S. . . . . . Full-faced busts of Justinus and

Sophia.—*Rev.*
A + V
N **K** . . . : *(Mionnet)*.
N
N
O   S
K A . . .

TIBERIUS II.

[Tiberius Constantinus, the son-in law of Justinus, was born in Thrace, of an unknown family. Justinus made him captain of his guards, and finally created him Caesar, and took him as his colleague in the empire, in the year of Rome 1327 (A.D. 574). In 1331 (A.D. 578) he was raised to the dignity of Augustus; and the death of Justinus in the same year, left him master of the empire of the East. Tiberius died in the year of Rome 1335 (A. D. 582)].

STYLE :——D. N. TIBERIVS. P. A.——D. N. TIBERIVS. P. F. AVG.——D. N. TIBERIVS. PP.——D. N. TIBERI. (*or* TI-BERIVS.) PP. AV. (*or* AVG.) —— D. N. CONSTANTIN. —— D. N. CONSTANTINVS. P.——D. N. CONSTANTINVS. P. F. AVG. —— D. N. (*or* m.) CONSTANTINVS. PP. A. (*or* AV. *or* AVG.)——D. N. TIB. CONSTANT. (*or* CONSTANTINVS.) P. F. AVG. —— D. N. TI. (*or* TIB.) CONSTANTI. PP.——D. N. (*or* m.) TIB. CO. (*or* CONST. *or* CONSTAN. *or* CONSTANT. *or* CONSTANTINVS.) PP. A. (*or* AV. *or* AVG. *or* AG.) —— TIBERIVS. CONSTANTINVS. PERPETVVS. AVG. (*or* AV-GVSTVS.)

Gold - - - - - - - - - - - - - - - - - - -	R 2
„ quinarii - - - - - - - - - - - - - - -	R 3
Silver - - - - - - - - - - - - - - - - -	R 6
„ quinarii - - - - - - - - - - - - - - -	R 2
Brass medallions - - - - - - - - - - - - -	C
First, second, and third brass - - - - - - - - - -	C

GOLD AND SILVER.

1.

LVX. MVNDI. A cross; the whole within a myrtle garland. (A *quinarius*). - - - - - - - - - - - - - - - - AR

2.

VICTORIA. AVGG. B. (*or* Γ. *or* S. *or* Z. *or* H. *or* T. (*sic*). A cross placed on steps. In the exergue, CONOB. *or* C+N+B. (*sic*). AU

3.

VICTOR. TIBERI. AVS. (*sic*). A cross in the centre of the field. In the exergue, CONOB. (A *quinarius*). - - - - - - - - AU

4.

VICTOR. MAVRI. AVS. (*sic*). A cross. In the exergue, CONOB. (A *quinarius*).—*Mus. Vindob.* - - - - - - - - - - - AU

5.

Without legend. A cross, placed on steps, within a myrtle garland. (A *quinarius*). - - - - - - - - - - - - - - - AU & AR

6.

Without legend. Two crosses, one larger than the other. In the exergue, RTSS. (*Tanini*). - - - - - - - - - - - - AR

MAURICIUS.

[Mauricius Tiberius, son-in-law of Tiberius Constantinus, was born at Arabissus, in Cappadocia, of a family originally of Rome, in the year of that city 1292 (A. D. 539). Mauricius at first followed the profession of a notary, but, quitting it for a military life, he became general of the army sent against the Persians by Tiberius, by whom he was declared Caesar and Augustus, in 1335 (A. D. 582), and whose daughter, Constantina, he married. This emperor was, with his wife and family, most barbarously murdered by the usurper Phocas, who had been invested with the purple by the soldiers, in the year of Rome 1355 (A. D. 602)].

STYLE:——D. N. MAV. (*or* MAVRICI.)——D. N. MAVRI. AVG. ——D. N. MAVRIC. (*or* MAVRICIVS.) P. F. AVG.——D. N. MAVR. (*or* MAVRICI. *or* MAVRICIVS. *or* MAVRIT. *or* MAVRITIVS.) P. P. A. (*or* AV. *or* AVG.)——D. N. MAVRICI. PERP. AVG.——D. N. MAVR. (*or* MAVRIC.) N. P. (*sic*) A. (*or* AV. *or* AVT. *sic*)——D. N. MAVRIT. D. PP. (*sic*)——D. N. MAVRICI. T.——D. N. MAVRI. TIB. AVG.——D. N. MAVRI.

TIBER. P.——D. N. MAVR. (or MAVRI. or MAVRIC.) TIB.
P. AVG. —— D. N. MAVRIC. TIBER. P. F. AVG. —— D. N.
MAVR. (or MAVRI.) TIBE. (or TIBER.) PP.——D. MAV-
RICIVS. TIBERI. PP. AVG.—— D. N. MAVR. (or MAVRI.
or MAVRIC. or MAVRICI.) T. (or TIB. or TIBE. or TIBER.)
PP. A. (or AV. or AVG. or AG.)——D. N. TIB. MAVRICI. P.
——D. N. TIBER. MAVRI. PP.——D. N. TIB. (or TIBER.)
MAVR. (or MAVRI. or MAVRIC. or MAVRICI.) PP. A. (or
AV.)——D. N. MAVRIC. PP. AVG. AVG. (sic).

The last legend appears on a brass coin of this emperor, bearing, on
the obverse, two figures standing, which Mionnet supposes to be those of
Mauricius and his consort; and another figure, on the reverse, to be
Theodosius, their son, who was created Augustus by his father. This
writer is of opinion that the double AVG. refers to the emperor and empress, and not to the figure on the reverse.

Gold - C
,, quinarii - - - - - - - - - - - - - - - - - R 3
Silver - R 4
,, quinarii - - - - - - - - - - - - - - - - - R 5
Brass medallions - - - - - - - - - - - - - - - - C
First, second, and third brass - - - - - - - - - - - - - C

GOLD AND SILVER.
1.
SALVS. MVNDI. ✳   A cross within a diadem of pearls. (A quinarius)
(Mionnet). - - - - - - - - - - - - - - - - - AR
2.
VICTOR. TIBERI. AVG.   A cross.   In the exergue, CONOB.
(Mus. Theupoli). - - - - - - - - - - - - - - - - AU
3.
VICTOR. (or VICTORI.) MAVRI. AVG.   A cross.   In the exergue,
CONOB.   (A quinarius). - - - - - - - - - - - AU
4.
VICTORIA. AVGGV.   A globe surmounted by a cross, within a
garland.   In the field, MA. or MAS. XXI.   In the exergue.
CONOB. - - - - - - - - - - - - - - - - - AU
5.
VICTORIA. AVGTOR. (sic).   A globe surmounted by a cross.   In
the field, MA. VII.   In the exergue, CONOB. (A quinarius).   AU

6.

VICTORIA. AVGVSTORVM. Victory marching, with a garland, and globe surmounted by a cross. In the exergue, CONOB. *(*A *quinarius)*. - - - - - - - - - - - - - - - - - - AU

7.

VIIVORI. AVTOAV. A globe surmounted by a cross, within a garland. In the field, M. A. VII. In the exergue, CONOB. *or* ONOB. (*Quinarii*). - - - - - - - - - - - - - - AU

There are various of this barbarous type.

8.

VIENNA. DE. OFFICINA. LAVRENTI. +. A globe surmounted by the monogram of Christ, between the letters alpha and omega. (A *quinarius*). - - - - - - - - - - - - - - - - AU

Valued by Mionnet at fifty francs.

9.

VIRTVS. ROMANORVM. Rome seated, holding a globe and a spear. In the exergue, MDPS. *(Tanini)*. - - - - - - - - - AR

10.

Without legend. A cross placed on steps, within a garland. (A *quinarius*).—*Cat. d'Ennery.* - - - - - - - - AU & AR

In gold, No. 8 is much the rarest. The next in rarity is No. 4.

FIRST BRASS, WITH RARE TYPES.

[MAURICIUS, CONSTANTINA, AND THEODOSIUS]. (?)

1.

D. N. MAVRIC. PP. AVG. AVG. (*sic*). The emperor standing, with the nimbus, holding in his right hand a globe surmounted by a cross; by his side, to the left, a woman with the nimbus, holding a cross.—*Rev*. Without legend. A youth standing in the toga, the nimbus encircling his head, holding in his right hand a staff surmounted by the monogram of Christ: on one side, H. *(Eckhel, Doctr.)*.

2.

Ꙩ. N. MAV. . . . . A similar type. In the field, a cross.——*Rev.* Without legend. A similar type. In the field, H.

Valued by Mionnet at twelve francs each.

SECOND BRASS, WITH RARE REVERSE.

A   +   Q
N   V
N   M   I   In the exergue, RAVEN.   *(Musei. Hedervarii)*.
O   Є. N
        T

Valued by Mionnet at twenty-four francs.

CONSTANTINA.

[Constantina, daughter of Tiberius Constantinus, and wife of Mauricius, was married to the emperor in the year of Rome 1335 (A. D. 582). She perished, shortly after her husband and her children, in 1355 (A. D. 602)].

See the coins of Mauricius in first brass.

THEODOSIUS.

[Theodosius, the son of Mauricius and Constantina, was associated with his father in the empire, in 1343 (A. D. 590).   He shared the fate of his parents at Chalcedon].

See the coins of Mauricius.

PHOCAS.

[Phocas was born at Chalcedon in Bithynia, of an obscure family.   He was centurion in the army of the Eastern empire, when the soldiers revolted in his favour, and placed him on the throne, in the year of Rome 1355 (A. D. 602).   The usurper caused the deposed emperor Mauricius and the whole of his family to be murdered.   Phocas was besieged in Constantinople by Heraclius, son of Heraclius the governor of Africa, and being obliged to surrender, his head was struck from his body, in the year of Rome 1363 (A. D. 610)].

STYLE :——FOCA.——D. N. FOCA. (*or* FOCAS.)——D. N. FOCAS. AVG.——D. N. FOCA. (*or* FOCAS.) P. AVG.——D. N. FOCA. (*or* FOCAS. P. F. AVG.——D. N. FOCAS. PP. A. (*or* AV. *or* AVG.)——D. N. FOCA. IMP. PP. A.——D. N. FOCA. (*or*FOCAS.

PER. *or* PERP.) AV. (*or* AVG.)——D. NN. (*sic*) FOCAS.
PERP. AVG. —— FLAVIII. (*sic*) FOCAS. PERP. AVG.
(*Banduri*). ——D. N. (*or* m.) FOCA. NEP. (*or* NEPE.) AV.
(*or* AVG.)

The legend with the name of FLAVIVS, was first published by Ducange,
and afterwards by Banduri, who, however, never saw the coin. Mediobarba has also given coins of Phocas with the name of Flavius, but they
are considered dubious. The last legend with NEP. *or* NEPE. is found on
those coins only which present us with the effigies of Phocas and his wife,
but her name was Leontia, and this contracted word requires explanation.
Banduri is of opinion that the letters ΦK. on the silver quinarii of Phocas
furnish the abbreviation of his name, and that it is the same with the
coins of Heraclius, which bear HK.; but as the letters CN. occur on the
money of Justinianus the First, this opinion is not conclusive.

Gold - C
  „ quinarii - - - - - - - - - - - - - - - - R 2
Silver, quinarii - - - - - - - - - - - - - - - R 4
First, second, and third brass - - - - - - - - - - - - C

GOLD AND SILVER.

1.

VICTORIA. AVGVSTORVM. Victory marching, holding a garland
and a globe surmounted by a cross. In the field, a star. In the
exergue, CONOB. (A *quinarius*). - - - - - - - - AU

2.

VICTORI. FOCAS. AV. (*or* AVG.) A cross. (*Quinarii*). - - AU

3.

ΦK. within a garland. (A *quinarius*). - - - - - - - - - AR

4.

The monogram of Christ between the letters alpha and omega. (A
quinarius).—*Mionnet*, cabinet of *M. Gosselin.* - - - - - AR

In gold, No. 2 is the rarest. In silver, No. 4.

FIRST AND SECOND BRASS, WITH RARE REVERSES.

(The two sizes are not always distinguishable).

[PHOCAS, AND LEONTIA].

1.

D. N. FOCA. NEPЄ. AV.   Phocas and Leontia standing, each in the imperial habit, and wearing a diadem surmounted by a cross. Phocas holds a globe, surmounted by a cross: Leontia holds a long cross.   Above, a cross.

Rev. $\overset{\text{A}}{\underset{\text{O}}{\overset{\text{N}}{\underset{\text{N}}{}}}}$ $+$ m   I. *or* II. *or* III. *or* $\frac{\text{II}}{\text{II}}$ *or* V. *or* VI. *or* VII. *or* IIG.

for VIII.   In the exergue, ƷHЄUP.

2.

D. N. *or* ᴆ. m. (*sic*) FOCA. . . . .   A similar type to the preceding, with the head of Leontia, surrounded by the nimbus.

Rev. $\overset{\text{A}}{\underset{\text{O}}{\overset{\text{N}}{\underset{\text{N}}{}}}}$ $+$ m   I.

CONЄ

3.

ᴆ. m. FOCA. NЄPЄ.   A similar type.

Rev. $\overset{+}{\text{XX}}$

CONB.

No. 2 is the rarest.

THIRD BRASS.

[PHOCAS, AND LEONTIA].

1.

D. N. FOCA. IMP. P. P. A.   Phocas and Leontia, standing; the first with the diadem, the other with the nimbus: above, a cross.

Rev. $\overset{\text{A}}{\underset{\text{O}}{\overset{\text{N}}{\underset{\text{N}}{}}}}$ $+$ X   I.

R

2.

D. N. FOCA. NЄPЄ. AV.   A similar type to the preceding.

Rev. $\overset{\text{A}}{\underset{\text{O}}{\overset{\text{N}}{\underset{\text{N}}{}}}}$ $+$ XX   II.

R.

LEONTIA.

[Leontia, the wife of Phocas, was married to that emperor before his usurpation. The time and manner of her death are not known].

See the coins of Phocas.

HERACLIUS I.

[Heraclius, son of Heraclius, praefect of Africa, was born about the year of Rome 1328 (A.D. 575). He dethroned, and caused Phocas to be beheaded in 1363 (A.D. 610), after which he was proclaimed emperor of the East. Heraclius died in the year of Rome 1394 (A.D. 641)].

STYLE:——D. N. HERACL.——D. N. HERACLIVS. (or ERA-CLIVS.) AV. (or AVG.)——D. N. HERACLIVS. P.——D. N. HERACLIVS. P. AV. (or AVG.)——D. N. HERACLI. (or HERA-CLIVS.) P. F. AVG.——D. N. HERACLIVS. PP.——HERACLI. PP. AVG.——D. N. HERACLIVS. (or ERACLIVS.) PP. A. (or AV. or AVG.)——D. N. HERAC. (or HERACL. or HERACLI. or ERACLI.) PERP. A. (or AVG.)——D. NN. (sic). HERACLI. (or HERACLIVS.) PERP. AVG——D. N. HERACLI. PERP. P. AVG.

HERACLIUS THE FATHER, AND HERACLIUS THE SON, ARE STYLED:—— DD. NN. (or D. N.) HERACLII.——DD. NN. (or D. N.) HERA. (or HERACLIV. or HERACLIVS. or ERACLI. or ERACLIVS.) ET. HERA. (or ERA.) CO. (or CON. or CONST.) ——D. N. ERACLIVS. ET. ERA. CON. A.——D. N. ERACLI. ET. CONST. P. A.——DD. NN. HERACLIVS. HERA. CONS. P. F. A.——DD. NN. (or D. N.) HERACLIVS. ET. HERA. (or ERA.) CONS. (or CONST.) P. F. A. (or AVG.)——DD. NN. (or (D. N.) HERA. (or HERACLI. or HERACLIVS.) ET. HERA. (or ERA.) CONS. (or CONST.) PP. —— D. N. ERACLIVS. ERA. CONS. PP. A.——DD. NN. (or D. N.) HERACLIVS. (or ERACLI. or ERACLIV.) ET. HER. (or HERA. or ERA. or ERAC.) CO. (or CON. or CONS. or CONST.) PP. A. (or AV. or AVG.) —— DD. NN. HERACLIVS. ET. HERA. CONST. PERP. AVG.

Gold medallion, of large size (modern fabric).

  ,,   of the usual size, with his head only - - - - - - - - C

  ,,   with the head of his son   - - - - - - - - - - - R 1

  ,,   quinarii, with head of Heraclius only   - - - - - - - C

Silver medallions, of small size - - - - - - - - - - - R 4

  ,,   quinarii   - - - - - - - - - - - - - - - - - R 4

Brass medallions   - - - - - - - - - - - - - - - R 3

First, second, and third brass - - - - - - - - - - - - C

Third brass, with the heads of Heraclius and his son   - - - - R 4

SILVER MEDALLIONS.

DD. NN. HERACLIVS. ET. HERA. CONST. P. P. A. (*or* AVG. *or* ꞇ. N.) hERACILꞍS. (*sic*) EꙆ. hERA. CO. (*or* CONSꙆ. P. P. A. *or* AꞍG. Heraclius, and his son Heraclius Constantinus seated, full-faced, each holding a globe surmounted by a cross. In the field, a small cross.—*Rev.* DEVS. ADIVTA. ROMANIS. (*or* ꞇEꞍS. AꙅIꞍꙆA. ROMANIS. A globe surmounted by a cross, placed on the summit of a flight of steps: sometimes, in the field, the letter K.

Valued by Mionnet at twenty-four francs.

QUINARII OF GOLD AND SILVER.

1.

VICTORI. HERACLI. AVG. A cross. In the exergue, CONOB. (*Mus. Vindob.*)   - - - - - - - - - - - - - - - AU

2.

VIRTVS. Victory, marching. (*Tanini*).   - - - - - - - AR

3.

Without legend. A cross within a garland. - - - - - - - AR

THIRD BRASS.

1.

HK. bound together in the centre of the field: above, XX. In the exergue, RAV. (*Banduri*).

2.

I. M. ET. XX. (*Eckhel*).

3.

INDICTIONE. Ƶ III. A globe surmounted by a cross: below, XX. (*Banduri*).

[HERACLIUS, AND HERACLIUS HIS SON].

DD. NN. ЄRACLIORVM. Full-faced busts of the two Heraclii.

+

Rev. XX.

ROM.

FLAVIA EUDOCIA.

[Flavia Eudocia, wife of Heraclius the First, was married to him in the year of Rome 1363 (A. D. 610). She died in 1365 (A. D. 612), shortly after the birth of Heraclius Constantinus].

There are no coins of this lady.

MARTINA.

[Martina, the niece of Heraclius the First, was married to her uncle, in the year of Rome 1366 (A. D. 613). Upon the death of her husband, she took off her son-in-law Heraclius Constantinus by poison in 1394 (A. D. 641), and assumed the reigns of government, associating her son Heracleonus in the empire, in which her other son Tiberius, and Constans son of Heraclius Constantinus, had a share. The career of this bold woman was, at length, checked by the senate, who caused her tongue to be torn out, and banished her to Cappadocia in the same year].

There are no coins of this empress; but the Baron Marchant, who has devoted much time and talent to the study of the coins of this period, supposes that she is represented on some coins, with her husband and her son Heraclius Constantinus.

HERACLIUS II.

[Heraclius the Second, son of the elder Heraclius and Flavia Eudocia, was born at Constantinople, in the year of Rome 1365 (A. D. 612), and created Augustus in the following year. He was consul in 1370 (A. D. 617), and succeeded his father in 1394 (A. D. 641). Heraclius the Second was poisoned by his mother-in-law Martina, four months after his succession].

STYLE:——ERACLIVS. CONSVL.——D. N. ERA. (*or* ERACLIVS. *or* ERAKLIVS.) CONST. (*or* KONST.)——D. N. ERACLI. P. ——D. N. CONSTANTINVS. P. A.——D. N. ERACLIVS. (*or* ERAKLIVS.) KONT. *(sic)*. P. AV.—— . . . . ER. CONSTANTINVS. PP. AVG.——D. N. HERACLIVS. PP. AV.

Gold, quinarii, with his head and those of Heracleonus and Constans	R 8
Silver medallions - - - - - - - - - - - - - - - -	R 6
,, quinarii - - - - - - - - - - - - - - - - -	R 4
Silver quinarii, with the heads of Constans and Gregoria - - -	R 4
Third brass - - - - - - - - - - - - - - - - -	R 3
,, with the head of the elder Heraclius - - - - -	R 4
,, with heads of his father and his brother - - - - -	R 6

SILVER MEDALLION.

. . . GR. CONSZANZINYS. PP. AVG. Bust of the second Heraclius, full-faced, with a diadem surmounted by a cross, wearing the chlamys, and holding in the right hand a cross.—*Rev.* dGYS. AdIYZA. ROMANIS. A globe surmounted by a cross, placed on a flight of steps. *(Tanini)*.

Valued by Mionnet at 100 francs.

GOLD AND SILVER, OF THE USUAL SIZE.

1.

GRACAIO. CONSVA. Full-faced bust of Heraclius surmounted by a cross, with the paludamentum and a sceptre, also surmounted by a cross.—*Rev.* V. TORA. C. in three lines, within a myrtle garland. (A *quinarius*).—*Mionnet,* from the cabinet of *M. Gosselin.* - AR

2.

D. N. ЄRACAI. P.   Full-faced bust, with a diadem surmounted by a
cross.   In the field to the right, another cross.—*Rev.* VIRTVS.
Victory marching to the left, holding a garland and a palm branch.
(A *quinarius*).—*Mionnet,* from the cabinet of *M. Gosselin.*   -   AR

3.

D. N. CONSTANTINVS. P. A.   Youthful head, with diadem.—*Rev.*
Without legend.   A cross placed on steps; between the letters,
CON.   (A *quinarius*).—*Tanini.* - - - - - - - - - AR

Valued by Mionnet at fifty francs each.

[HERACLIUS II., GREGORIA, AND THEIR SON CONSTANS].

1.

D. N. ЄRACÁIO. PP. AV.   Full-faced bust of Heraclius, with a diadem
surmounted by a cross.—*Rev.* Without legend.   Two full-faced
busts of Gregoria and her infant son Constans, each with the diadem
surmounted by a cross : above, another cross.   (A *quinarius*). AR

2.

D. N. ЄRACLIO. KONT. *(sic).* P. AV.   Full-faced heads of Heraclius
II., Constans, or Heracleonas.—*Rev.* VICZORIA. AVG.   A cross
placed on a flight of three steps.   In the exergue, CONOB.   (A
quinarius). - - - - - - - - - - - - - - - - - - AU

THIRD BRASS.

1.

ЄRACAIO. CONSVAI. *(sic).*   Youthful bust, surmounted by a cross;
a sceptre in the right hand.

$$\text{+}$$
$$Rev. \text{ N } \mathbf{X} \text{ M}$$
$$*$$

2.

M. *or* XX. in the centre of the field, with various letters in the field or
the exergue.

No. 1 is the rarest.

GREGORIA.

[Gregoria, daughter of Nicetas a Patrician, and wife of the second
Heraclius, was married to the emperor in the year of Rome 1381,
(A. D. 628)].

See the coins of Heraclius the Second.

HERACLEONAS.

[Heracleonas, son of Heraclius the First and Martina, was born at
Colchis, in the year of Rome 1379 (A. D. 626), and declared Caesar
by his father, in 1384 (A. D. 631). He received the title of Augustus
shortly afterwards, and succeeded his father with his brother Heraclius
Constantinus, in 1394 (A. D. 641). Heraclius having been poisoned
by his mother-in law shortly afterwards, this prince remained sole
emperor, but in the same year Heracleonas was dethroned by the
senate, his nose was cut off, and he was condemned to exile in Cappa-
docia].

See the coins of Heraclius the Second.

TIBERIUS.

[Tiberius, the brother of Heracleonas, was created Caesar by Heraclius
the First, in the year of Rome 1393 (A. D. 640), and in the following
year succeeded to the empire, which he shared with his brother
Heracleonas. The death of Tiberius probably happened soon after,
but is not mentioned by the Byzantine historians].

There are no coins of Tiberius.

CONSTANS II.

[Constans, the son of Heraclius the Second and Gregoria, was born at
————, in the year of Rome 1383, (A. D. 630) ; and in 1394
(A. D. 641), received, with his uncles Tiberius and Heracleonas, the
title of Augustus. The deposition of Heracleonas shortly after, and
the death of Tiberius, left him sole possessor of the throne. Constans
was assassinated in a bath at Syracuse, in the year of Rome 1421
(A. D. 668)].

STYLE:——D. N. CONSTAN. (or CONSTANT. or CONSTANTI.
or CONSTANTIN.)——CONSTANTINVS. P. F. AVG.——D. N.
CONSTANTINVS. PP. AV. (or AVG.)

CONSTANS, AND HIS SON CONSTANTINUS POGONATUS ASSOCIATED, ARE
STYLED : —— D. N. CONSTANS. CONSTANTIN. —— D.
CONSTANTINVS. CO. —— D. N. CONSTANTINVS. ET.
CONSTANS.——DD. NN. CONSTANS. ET. CONST. AVG.
—— D. N. CONSTANTINVS. (or CONSTANTINOS.) C.
CONSTA. (or CONSTAN. or CONSTANTINO.)

PLATE 13.

London Published by Effingham Wilson 1st Jany 1834.

Gold, with his head only - - - - - - - - - - - - - R 1

" with his head, and that of his son Pogonatus - - - - - R 2

" with the effigies of his children, Pogonatus, Heraclius and
Tiberius - - - - - - - - - - - - - - - - R 3

" with the effigies of Heraclius and Tiberius - - - - - R 1

Silver medallions, with his head, and that of Const. Pogonatus - R 4

Brass medallions - - - - - - - - - - - - - - - - R 4

Second brass - - - - - - - - - - - - - - - - - R 4

Third brass - - - - - - - - - - - - - - - - - R 2

SILVER MEDALLION.

[CONSTANS II., AND HIS SON POGONATUS].

ꙮ. N. CONSꙀANꙀINꙬS. C. CONSꙀ. . . . Full-faced busts of the
emperor and his son; the first with a long beard, the other
with a short beard. In the field, a small cross.—*Rev.* ꙂЄꙬS.
AꙂIꙬꙀA. ROmANIS. A cross, placed on steps. In the
field, B.

Valued by Mionnet at thirty francs.

GOLD, OF THE USUAL SIZE.

1.

ꙮ. N. CONSꙀANꙀINꙬS. PP. AV. Full-faced bust of Constans or
Constantinus, with a diadem surmounted by a cross, and a long
beard; the right hand holding a globe surmounted by a cross.—
Rev. VICTORIA. AVGꙬ. A. A cross placed on a flight of steps.
In the exergue, CONOB. *or* CONOB+.

2.

A similar legend and type, with the numerals Г. *or* Δ. *or* Є. *or* H. *or* I.

[CONSTANS, AND CONSTANTINUS POGONATUS].

1.

ꙮ. N. CONSꙀANꙀINꙬS. C. CONSꙀAN. Full-faced heads of Constans
the Second and Constantinus Pogonatus, the first with a long
beard, each wearing a diadem surmounted by a cross: another
cross in the field.—*Rev.* VICTORIA. AVGꙬ. Г. *or* A. A cross
placed on a flight of steps. In the field, sometimes, the monogram
of Christ, or the letter C. In the exergue, CONOB. *or* CONOB+.
(*Plate xiii, No.* 1).

2.

Others, with the numerals Δ. *or* ϛ. *or* H. *or* Θ. *or* I. *or* ΘI.

[CONSTANS II., POGONATUS, HERACLIUS, AND TIBERIUS].

1.

Ⴢ. N. CONSƵAN. *or* CONSƵANƵ. *or* CONSƵANƵINI. CO. Full-faced heads of Constans the Second and Pogonatus, the first with a long beard, and a helmet surmounted by a cross; the other with a short beard, and a diadem surmounted by a cross.—*Rev.* VICTORIA. AVG५. A. *or* Γ. *or* Z. *or* H. *or* I. Heraclius and Tiberius standing, each with a diadem surmounted by a cross, and each holding a globe surmounted by a cross: between them, a cross placed on a flight of steps. In the exergue, CONOB.   - - AU

2.

A blundered legend. Two full-faced busts; one with a long beard, the other smaller than the first, and without beard. — *Rev.* Without legend. Two full-faced busts, without beard: between them, a cross. (*Eckhel*). - - - - - - - - - - - - - - AU

GOLD AND SILVER.

[CONSTANS II., HERACLIUS, AND TIBERIUS].

1.

Without legend. Constans the Second, standing between his sons Heraclius and Tiberius, each in the imperial habit, wearing a diadem surmounted by a cross, and holding a globe surmounted by a cross.—*Rev.* VICTORIA. AVG५. A. *or* B. *or* Γ. *or* Є. *or* ς. *or* Z. *or* H. *or* Θ. *or* I. A cross placed on steps. In the field the monogram of Christ, and the numerals Λ. *or* B. *or* I. *or* Θ. In the exergue, CONOB. - - - - - - - - - - - - - - AU

2.

VICTORIA. AVG५. Θ. Full-faced bust of Constans the Second, with a long beard, the right hand holding a globe surmounted by a cross. —*Rev.* Without legend. Constans the Second, standing between his sons Heraclius and Tiberius. In the exergue, CONOB.

AU & AR

This type in silver is dubious.

BRASS MEDALLION.

[CONSTANS, AND CONSTANTINUS POGONATUS].

Without legend. The emperor and his son Pogonatus, standing; the first in a military habit, and with a long beard, wearing a diadem surmounted by a cross, holding in his right hand a long cross; the other with a short beard, and wearing the imperial habit, holding a globe surmounted by a cross.   In the field, a cross.—

$$Rev. \quad \begin{matrix} & \overset{+}{C} & \\ A & & \\ N & M & X \\ N & & X \\ O & A & \\ & CON. & \end{matrix}$$

Valued by Mionnet at twenty-four francs.

SECOND BRASS.

[CONSTANS AND HIS WIFE].

1.

Without legend.   Constans the Second standing, with a long beard, and a diadem surmounted by a cross; holding in his right hand a long cross; on his left, the empress standing, with a head dress surmounted by a cross, holding in her right hand a globe surmounted by the same emblem.   In the field, a cross, and the letter K.—

$$Rev. \quad \begin{matrix} A & \overset{+}{M} & X \\ N & & X \\ N & \Gamma & \\ O & CON. & \end{matrix} \quad (Marchant).$$

2.

$$\text{Another, with} \quad \begin{matrix} A & & \\ N & & X \\ N & \Lambda & X \\ O & A & \\ & CON. & \end{matrix} \quad (Ibid).$$

CONSTANTINUS IV.

[Constantinus, surnamed Pogonatus,* the son of Constans the Second, was born in the year of Rome, ——.   In 1407 (A. D. 654),

---

* According to Zonarus, the surname of Pogonatus (bearded) was given to this prince from the following circumstances : — When Constantinus IV. quitted Constantinople for Sicily, with his father, he had but a youthful beard, and that on his return after the death of his father it was long and ample.   By other writers, however, it does not appear that Constantinus accompanied his father to Sicily.   Besides, the effigy on the coins of Constans the Second, has a very large beard, while that of his son Constantinus is short and youthful; so that the surname, as Mionnet observes, may with more propriety have been given to the father of this prince.

he was associated with his father in the empire; and in 1421 (A. D. 668), he succeeded that prince. Constantinus IV. died in the year of Rome 1438 (A. D. 685)].

STYLE: —— CONSTANTINVS. —— D. N. CONSTANTINVS. —— CONSTANTINVS. AVG.——D. N. CONSTANTIN. (or CONSTANTINV. or CONSTANTINVS.) P.——CONSTANTINVS. P. AVG.——D. N. CONSTANTINVS. P. AV.——CONSTANTINVS. PP.——D. N. CONSTANTIN. (or CONSTANTINVS.) PP.——CONSTANTINVS. PP. A.——D. N. CONSTANTINVS. PP. A. (or AV. or AVG.)

The legends on the coins of this emperor are frequently blundered and barbarous; reading often, CONSTANTNVS. CONSTANVS. CONTNVS. COSTNVS. &c.

Gold, quinarii and denarii - - - - - - - - - - - - - - - C
Silver medallions, of small size - - - - - - - - - - - - - R 6
  ,, quinarii - - - - - - - - - - - - - - - - - R 3
Brass medallions - - - - - - - - - - - - - - - - - R 6
First brass - - - - - - - - - - - - - - - - - - - R 4
Second and third brass - - - - - - - - - - - - - - - R 4

SILVER MEDALLIONS.

1.

D. N. CON7ANЧS. (sic) PP.　Bust of the emperor, full-faced, with a spear and a buckler.—Rev. DЄЧS. АdIЧ2A. ROmANIS. A globe surmounted by a cross placed on three steps, between Constantinus Pogonatus and Justinianus the Second, both standing. (Cat. d'Ennery).

2.

ᴐ. N. CONS2ANЧ. (sic) or ᴐ. N. CONS2NЧS. (sic) P. (or a still more barbarous legend). Full-faced bust of Pogonatus, holding a spear and a buckler.—Rev. A blundered legend. A similar type.

3.

ᴐ. N. CONS2AN2INЧS. PP. AL. (sic). Full-faced bust of Constantinus Pogonatus holding a globe surmounted by a cross.—Rev. ᴐЄЧS. Aᴐ IЧ2A. ROmANIS. A globe, surmounted by a cross placed on a flight of steps.

Nos. 1 and 3 are by far the rarest.

GOLD AND SILVER.

1.

ᴐ. CONSƵANᴎS. *(sic)* PP. A. *or* ᴐ. N. CONSƵNᴎS. *(sic)* P. *or* ᴐ. N. CONSƵANƵINI. Full-faced bust, helmeted, with spear, coat of mail, and buckler.—*Rev.* VICTORA. *(sic)* AVGᴎ. B. *or* Є. *or* ᴢ. *or* I. A cross placed on steps, between Constantinus Pogonatus and his son Justinianus the Second, both standing. In the exergue, CONOB. - - - - - - - - - - - - - - - - Aᴜ

2.

D. N. CONSTANTINI. The same bust as in the preceding.—*Rev.* VICTORIA. ᴧᴎGᴎ. A similar type to the preceding. In the field, a crescent, a cross, and the letter Є. In the exergue, CONOB. *(Mus. Vindob).* - - - - - - - - - - - - AU

3.

P. CONSƵANᴎS. *(sic).* PP. A. The same bust as on the preceding. *Rev.* VICTORA. *(sic).* AVGᴎ. B. *or* Z. A cross, placed on steps, In the exergue, CONOB. A. - - - - - - - - - - AU

4.

Without legend. The head of Constantinus Pogonatus, full-faced, with a long beard.—*Rev.* Rᴍ. in the field, surmounted by a cross: below, a star. (A *quinarius).—Catalogue d'Ennery.* - - - - - AR

In gold, No. 3 is the rarest.

BRASS MEDALLION.

M : above, a cross, between two emperors, standing : between the strokes of the letter, A. *or* B. *or* Є.

Valued by Mionnet at twelve francs.

HERACLIUS AND TIBERIUS.

[Heraclius and Tiberius were created Caesars by their father, in the year of Rome 1412 (A. D. 659) ; and after his death, were associated in the empire with their brother Pogonatus, by whose order they were mutilated, and as is supposed, secretly put to death].

See the coins of Constans the Second.

JUSTINIANUS II.

[Justinianus, son of Constantinus Pogonatus and Anastasia, was born in
the year of Rome 1423 (A. D. 670). He received the title of Augustus
in 1435 (A. D. 682), and the death of his father three years after, left
him sole possessor of the empire. His monstrous cruelty roused the
fury of the people, who, headed by Leontius the Patrician, seized him
in his palace, and after burning alive his ministers, cut off the nose of
the tyrant, and exiled him to Chersonesus, in 1448 (A. D. 695). He
obtained from this circumstance, the name of *Rhinotmetus.* By the
aid of the Bulgarians, he was replaced on the throne, in 1458 (A. D.
705), but was again deposed, and put to death by Bardanes, in the
year of Rome 1464 (A. D. 711).

Style :——D. N. IVSTINIANVS.——D. N. IVSTINIANVS. PE.
——IVSTINIANVS. PE. V.——D. N. IVSTINIAN. (*or* IVS-
TINIANVS.) PP. A. (*or* AV.)——D. N. IVSTINIANVS. PPE.
AV. (*or* V.) —— IVSTINIANVS. SERV. CHRISTI. —— D.
(*or* D. N.) IVSTINIANVS. SERV. (*or* SERVVS.) CHRISTI.——
D. N. IVSTINIANVS. MVLTVS. A. (*or* AN. *or* AV. *or* AVG.)

Justinianus and Tiberius are styled :——D. N. IVSTINIANVS.
ET. TIBERIVS. P.——D. N. IVSTINIANVS. ET. TIBERIVS.
PP.——D. N. IVSTINIANVS. ET. TIBERIVS. PP. A. (*or* AV.)

Gold, denarii and quinarii - - - - - - - - - - - - - R 1
Silver medallions, of small size - - - - - - - - - - - - R 8
Third brass - R 6

SILVER MEDALLION.

D. IVSTINIANVS. SERV. ChRI. . . . . B. The emperor in the imperial
habit, standing, holding in his right hand a long cross, resting on a
flight of steps. In the exergue, CONOB.—*Rev.* . . . . . SVOS. REX.
REGNANTIVM. The bust of Christ, holding the book of the
Evangelists.

Valued by Mionnet at 200 francs.

GOLD, OF THE USUAL SIZE.
1.

D. N. IVSTINIANVS. MVLTVS. A. *or* AN. *or* AV. *or* AVG. Full-
faced bust of the emperor with a diadem, ornamented by a cross,
holding a cross resting on a flight of steps, and a buckler surmounted

by a double cross, inscribed, PAX.—*Rev.* ᴐ. N. IhS. ChS. REX. REGNANTIчM. Full-faced bust of Christ, backed by a cross, holding the book of the Evangelists.

2.

D. *or* ᴐ. N. IчSZINIANчS. SERч. ChRISZI. B. *or* Δ. *or* Є., &c. The emperor standing in the imperial habit, holding a cross resting on steps, and a scroll. In the exergue, CONOB.—*Rev.* IhS. CRISZ. D. S. *or* D. F. REX. RFGNANZIчM. The bust of Christ, backed by a cross; the right hand raised, the left holding the book of the Evangelists.

3.

ᴐ. N. IчSINIANVS. PP. A. *or* IчSZINIANS. *(sic)* PчЄ. AV. (*or* IчSZINIANчS. PP. Є. AV. (*or* PP. ЄV.) Full-faced bust of Justinianus the Second, holding a globe surmounted by a cross. —*Rev.*VICTORIA. AVGч. A. *or* Є. *or* ⸗. or other numerals. A cross placed on a flight of steps. In the exergue, CONOB. In the field of some, R.

4.

ᴐ. N. IчSZINIANчS. PЄ. *or* IчSZINIANS. *(sic)* PЄV. Diademed head of Justinianus to the right.—*Rev.* VICTORIA. AчGч. *or* AчGч. ⸗. A cross. In the field, of some, K. In the exergue, CONOB. *(Quinarii)*.

No. 1 is the rarest.

[JUSTINIANUS, AND TIBERIUS].

ᴐ. N. IчSTINIANчS. ЄT. TIbЄRIчS. PP. *or* PP. A. Full-faced busts of Justinianus and his son Tiberius, holding together a cross; the one bearded, the other without beard.—*Rev.* ᴐ. N. IhS. ChS. *or* CRISTчS. REX. REGNANTIчM. The bust of Christ, backed by a cross; the right hand raised, the left holding the book of the Evangelists. - - - - - - - - - - - - - AU

Valued by Mionnet at thirty francs.

THIRD BRASS.

K. between two crosses. In the exergue, PAX. *(Tanini)*.

[JUSTINIANUS, AND TIBERIUS.]

1.

d. N. IUSTINIANUS. ET. TIBERIVS. P.   Busts of Justinianus the
Second, and his son Tiberius; between them, a double cross, placed
on a pedestal, inscribed PAX.

Rev.   A N N / +M / X X   In the exergue, O.   *(Tanini).*

2.

Another, similar, but with the letter K. in the centre.

TIBERIUS IV.

[Tiberius, son of Justinianus and Theodora, was born in the year of
Rome 1454 (A. D. 701).   He was created Caesar, and immediately
after, Augustus, by his father, in 1459 (A. D. 706).   Tiberius perished
with his father, in 1464 (A. D. 711)].

Gold, with his head and the head of his father - - - - - - - R 4
Third brass (same heads) - - - - - - - - - - - - - R 6

See the coins of Justinianus the Second.

LEONTIUS II.

[Leontius was born of a patrician family, originally of Isauria.   He was
general of the armies of the East, and subsequently governor of Greece
under Justinianus the Second, whom he drove from the throne, in the
year of Rome 1448 (A. D. 695).   He was in his turn dethroned by
Tiberius Absimarus, and forced to enter a monastery, after being
deprived of his nose and his ears, 1451 (A. D. 698).   Leontius was
put to death by Justinianus the Second, when that prince regained
the throne, in 1458 (A. D. 705)].

STYLE :——D. LEONTI. A.——D. N. LEONCIVS. *(sic)* P. F. AVG.

Gold, quinarii - - - - - - - - - - - - - - - - R 8
Third brass - - - - - - - - - - - - - - - - *unique*

GOLD.

D. LEONTI. A.   Full-faced bust of Leontius, holding a globe surmounted by a cross.—*Rev.* VICTORIA. AVGVℼ   A long cross.
In the exergue, CONOB. *(Tanini).*

Valued by Mionnet at 300 francs.

The other gold coins attributed to Leontius the Second, belong to
Leòntius the First. ' (See *Eckhel,* tom. viii, p. 201).

THIRD BRASS.

D. N. LEONCIVS. *(sic)* P. F. AVG.   Helmed bust of Leontius,
holding a spear in the right hand.—*Rev.* CONCORDIA. . . . . .
Roma-Victrix, seated.   In the exergue, CONO. . . .   *(Mionnet,*
from the cabinet of *M. Gosselin).*

Mionnet observes that this coin belongs rather to the first Leontius, of
which there can be little doubt.

TIBERIUS V.

[Tiberius, whose real name was Absimarus, was hailed as emperor of
the East by the soldiers of Leontius in the Isle of Crete, when he
caused Leontius to descend from the throne, in the year of Rome 1451
(A. D. 698).   Tiberius was put to death by order of Justinianus,
who regained the throne by the aid of the Bulgarians, in the year of
Rome 1458 (A. D. 705).

STYLE :——D. TIBERIVS.P. A.——D. N. TIBERIVS. P. F. AVG.——
D. (*or* D. N.) TIBERIVS. PP.——D. TIBERIVS. PP. AV.——
D. N. TIBERIVS. AVG. PP. —— N. TIBERIVS. PER. —— D.
TIBE. (*or* TIBERIVS.) PE. (*or* PER.) A. (*or* AV.)——N. TI-
BERIVS. PRTV. (for *perpetuus*)—See *Tanini.*

Gold, denarii and quinarii - - - - - - - - - - - - R 4
Silver - - - - - - - - - - - - - - - - - R 8
Third brass - - - - - - - - - - - - - - - - R 8

1.

N. ƵIBE. PE. A. *or* N. ƵIbERIUS. PER. *or* PE. AV. *or* PE. A. *or* P.
A. *or* PRTV. *(sic) or* PP.   Full-faced bust of Tiberius V., with a
diadem surmounted by a cross, holding a buckler and a spear, the

former bearing the figure of a horseman.—*Rev.* VICTRA. *(sic)*
or VICTORIA. AVGЧ. or AVGЧ. B. or Δ. or ς. or X.   A cross
placed on steps: on some, an M. in the field, and. In the exergue,
CONOB. - - - - - - - - - - - - - - - AU & AR

2.

D. ZIBЄRIЧS. PЄ. AV.   A similar bust to the preceding.—*Rev.*
VICTRA. *(sic)* VVЧ *(sic)* or VICTORIA. AVGЧ.   A cross. In
the field, S. M. In the exergue, CONOB. (A *quinarius*). - AU

THIRD BRASS.

D. N. TIBERIVS. AVG. P. P.   Full-faced bust of Tiberius, holding a
spear.—*Rev.* RAVE. in the middle of the field. *(Mionnet).*

FILEPICUS.

[Filepicus, whose real name was Bardanes, was born of a patrician
family in Armenia.   He was proclaimed emperor by the soldiers of
the East, in the year of Rome 1464 (A. D. 711), when he ascended
the throne, and put to death Justinianus. Filepicus was deprived of
his sight, and banished, in 1466 (A. D. 713), and died miserably a
short time afterwards].

STYLE:——D. N. FILEPICVS. *(or* FILEPPICVS.) MVLTVS. *(or*
MVLTOS.) AN.

Gold - R 4
 „ quinarii - - - - - - - - - - - - - - - - - R 5
Silver (see *Tanini*) - - - - - - - - - - - - - - R 8

GOLD AND SILVER.

1.

α. N. FILЄPICЧS. *or* FILЄPPICЧS. *(sic)* MЧLTЧS. AN.   Full-
faced bust of Filepicus, with a diadem surmounted by a cross,
holding in his right hand a globe surmounted by a cross, and in his
left a sceptre surmounted by an eagle and a star.—*Rev.* VICTORIA.
AVGЧ. B. *or* Δ. *or* ς. *or* Z. *or* Θ. *or* I.   A cross placed on steps.
In the exergue, CONOB. - - - - - - - - - AU & AR

2.

D. N. FILЄPICЧS. MЧLTOS. AN.   A similar bust to the preceding.
—*Rev.* VICTORIA. IVSTA.   A cross placed on steps. In the
exergue, CONOB. *(Banduri).* - - - - - - - - - AU

ANASTASIUS II.

[Anastasius, whose real name was Artemius, held the situation of Secretary to the emperor Filepicus, after whose deposition he was raised to the throne, in the year of Rome 1466 (A. D. 713). He retired to a monastery, upon hearing that the troops in the island of Rhodes had proclaimed Theodosius emperor, 1469 (A. D. 716). But was encouraged to attempt to regain the crown from Leo Isaurus, who had succeeded Theodosius, when he was seized and murdered by order of Leo, in 1472 (A. D. 719)].

STYLE:——D. N. APTEMIVS. ANASTASIVS. MV. (or MVL.)—— D. N. ANASTASIS. (sic) MVL. AN.

Gold - R 4
„ quinarii - - - - - - - - - - - - - - - - - R 5

GOLD.

1.
ꝺ. N. ΑΡΤЄΜΙꝐS. ANASTASIꝐS. MꝐL. Full-faced bust of Anastasius with a diadem, surmounted by a cross, holding a globe and a book.—*Rev.* VICTORIA. AVGꝐ. B. *or* Δ. *or* Ϛ. *or* Z. *or* Θ. A cross, placed on steps. In the exergue, CONOB.

2.
VICTORIA. AVGꝐ. ϩ. A cross. In the exergue, CONOB. (A *quinarius*).

3.
ꝺ. N. ANASTASIS. (*sic*). MꝐL. AN. Full-faced bust as before.— *Rev.* VICTORI. AVG. A cross, placed on steps. In the field, a star and a cross. In the exergue, CONOB. (Barbarous fabric).

THEODOSIUS III.

[Theodosius Adramytenus, was born at Adramytium, in Mysia, of an obscure family. He was a receiver of the revenue in the reign of Anastasius, and was compelled to assume the purple by the discontented soldiery at Rhodes, in the year of Rome 1468 (A. D. 715). Anastasius abdicated the throne, of which Theodosius took possession, but was in his turn deposed by Leo the Third; and the emperor Theodosius exchanged the regal power, for the life of an ecclesiastic 1470 (A. D. 717)].

STYLE:——D. N. THEODOSIVS. AVG.——D. N. THEODOSIVS.
P. F. AVG.——D. N. THEODOSIVS. PP. A. (*or* AV.)——D. N.
THEODOSIVS. MVL. A.

Gold quinarii - - - - - - - - - - - - - - - - - R 6
Silver quinarii - - - - - - - - - - - - - - - - R 8

GOLD AND SILVER.

1.

ᴆ. N. ƵhЄODOSIⱵS. AⱵG. *or* ThЄOᴆOSIS. *(sic).* AⱵG. *or* ƵhЄO-
ᴆOSIⱵS. MVL. A.   Full-faced bust of Theodosius the Third, with
a diadem surmounted by a cross, holding a globe surmounted by a
double cross, and a volume.—*Rev.* VICTORIA. AVG. *or* AVG.Ⱶ.
A. *or* Δ. *or* I.   A cross, placed on steps.   In the field, of some, L.
and a star.   In the exergue, CONOB. - - - - - - - - AU

2.

D. N. TЄODOSIVS. *(sic)* PP. $\overline{\text{AV}}$.   Full-faced bust of Theodosius,
with a rich diadem and the paludamentum.—*Rev.* Without legend.
Full-faced busts of the wife and son of Theodosius; between them,
a large cross: on each side, a small cross.   In the exergue, ACTI.
(A *quinarius*). - - - - - - - - - - - - - - - AR

This quinarius is described by Mionnet, from the cabinet of M.
Gosselin.   The figures on the reverse are supposed to be those of the
empress and her son, but history does not furnish us with their names.

LEO III.

[Leo, surnamed the Isaurian, from the country of his birth, was
descended from an obscure family, but in the reign of Anastasius II.
and Theodosius III., he held the rank of General of the Eastern
army, which invested him with the purple, when the latter emperor
abdicated the throne, in the year of Rome 1470 (A. D. 717).   Leo
died in 1494 (A. D. 741)].

STYLE:——D. (*or* D. N.) LEO. (*or* LEON.) P. (*or* PE.) A. (*or* AV.)
——D. NO. LEON. MVL.——D. N. LEON. A. MV.——D. (*or*
D. N. *or* D. NO.) LE. (*or* LEO. *or* LEON.) P. A. MV. (*or* MVL.)

LEO AND CONSTANTINUS COPRONYMUS ASSOCIATED: —— LEON. S. CONST.——LEON. S. CONST. A.——D. N. LEO. ET. CONSTANTINVS. P. F. AVG.——LEON. PAP. S. CONSTAN.—— LEON. PA_r (or PAP.) CONSTANTI. (or CONSTANTINOS.) PATHR.

The last two legends are found on some of the coins of Leo. IV., of whom Constantinus Copronymus was the father, and Leo. III. grandfather. Hence the name of ΠΑΠΠΥΣ (signifying in Greek, grandfather) given to Leo.

Gold -	C
„ quinarii - - - - - - - - - - - - - - - - -	R 1
Silver medallion - - - - - - - - - - - - - - - - -	R 4
„ quinarii - - - - - - - - - - - - - - - - -	R 4
Second and third brass - - - - - - - - - - - - - -	R 2

SILVER MEDALLION.

D. NO. LEO. P. A. MUI.   Full-faced bust of Leo. III. holding a globe surmounted by a cross.—*Rev.* D. NO. CONSTANTIN. *(sic).* Full-faced bust of Constantinus Copronymus, holding a globe surmounted by a cross. In the field, various symbols.

Valued by Mionnet at thirty francs. Four medallions of this type are described in the *Catalogue d'Ennery*, p. 314.

GOLD AND SILVER, OF THE USUAL SIZE, RARE TYPES.

D. LEON. PE. AV. *or* D. NO. LEON. P. A. MUL.   Full-faced bust of Leo, with a diadem surmounted by a cross, holding aloft in the right hand a scroll, and in the left, a globe surmounted by a cross. —*Rev.* VICTORIA. AVG q. B. *or* S. (or other numerals). A cross placed on steps. In the exergue, CONOB. - - - - AU

[LEO III. AND CONSTANTINUS COPRONYMUS.]

1.

C. *or* Ꝺ. NO. *or* D. LEON. P. A. MUL. ꞇ. *or* H. *or* MUL. *or* MULꞀ. *or* MULT. Full-faced bust of Leo. III. with a diadem surmounted by a cross, holding a globe surmounted by a cross, and the book of the Evangelists—*Rev.* C. N. CONSꞀANꞀNIUS. *(sic)* or CONSꞀANꞀINUS. *or* CONSꞀANꞀINU. N̅E̅. *or* ᘔ. N. CONSꞀANꞀINU. Θ. The bust of Constantinus Copronymus, with similar attributes. - - - - - - - - - - - - - - - AU

2.

Œ. ND. *(sic)* LEON. PA. MᵾL. Full-faced bust of Leo the Third, holding a globe surmounted by a cross, and a scroll.—*Rev.* CONSƵANƵIN. Full-faced bust of Constantinus V. with similar attributes. (A *quinarius*). - - - - - - - - - - - - AU

3.

꘡. NO. LEON. P. A. MᵾL. Full-faced bust of Leo the Third, holding in his right hand a globe surmounted by a cross, and in his left a scroll.—*Rev.* ꘡. N. CONSƵANƵINᵾS. M. Full-faced bust of Constantine the Fifth, with similar attributes. In the field of some, B. - - - - - - - - - - - - - - - - - - AU

4.

. . . . . . N. LEON. P. A. MᵾL. A similar type to the preceding. In the field, C.—*Rev.* . . . . . . ƵANƵINᵾ. A similar bust. In the field, I. (A *quinarius*). - - - - - - - - - - - - - - AU

5.

Œ. NO. LE. PA. MᵾL. Full-faced bust of Leo the Third, with a diadem surmounted by a cross, and holding a globe surmounted by the same emblem.—D. NO. CONTANTI. *(sic).* Full-faced bust of Constantinus the Fifth, with similar attributes. In the field, two stars. (A *quinarius*)—*Khell.* - - - - - - - - - - - AR

6.

Same legend. A similar bust.—*Rev.* D. N. CONTANTIN. *(sic).* A similar bust to that on the reverse of the preceding. In the field, I. E, and a star. (A *quinarius*). - - - - - - - - - - AR

[LEO III., CONSTANTINUS V., AND LEO IV.]

C. *or* Œ. LEON. P. A. MᵾL. *or* Mᵾ. Θ. *or* MᵾL. Θ. Full-faced bust of Leo III., with a diadem surmounted by a cross, holding in his right hand a cross.—*Rev.* COhSƵAhƵIhOS. S. LEOh. O. hEOS. Full-faced busts of Constantinus V. and Leo IV. A small cross in the field. - - - - - - - - - - - - - - - - - AU

Valued by Mionnet at twenty-four francs.

[LEO III., AND CONSTANTINUS V.]

SECOND BRASS.

1.

D .N. LEO. . . . . . . Full-faced bust of Leo III., with a diadem surmounted by a cross ; his right hand holding a globe also surmounted
by a cross.—*Rev.* D. N. CONSTANTINꞋS. Full-faced bust of
Constantinus V. on a pedestal : on the left, a cross : below, M. : on
one side, ANNO. : on the other, XX. (*Mus. Vindob.*)

2.

LEOh. S. COhSꝀ. Busts of Leo III. and Constantinus V., with similar
attributes.—

Rev. $\begin{matrix} X & + & N \\ X & \mathbf{M} & N \\ X & & N \\ & A & \end{matrix}$ the whole within a garland. (*Tanini.*)

THIRD BRASS.

D. NO. LE. . . . . . Full-faced bust of Leo III., wearing a robe, and
a diadem surmounted by a cross, and holding a globe surmounted
by a cross.—*Rev.* VICTORI. . . . . . A cross placed on steps. In
the field, A., and a star. (*Tanini.*)

[LEO III., AND CONSTANTINUS V.]

d. N. LEON. PA. MV. Full-faced bust of Leo III., with a diadem
surmounted by a cross, holding in his right hand a globe surmounted by a cross, and in his left a volume.—*Rev.* d. N. CON-
STANTINVS. N. Bust of Constantinus V., with the same
attributes, placed on a pedestal. In the field, +. In the exergue,
K. : on one side, ANNO. ; on the other, XX. (*Tanini.*)

CONSTANTINUS V.

[Constantinus the Fifth, son of Leo. III. and Maria, surnamed Copronymus from his having polluted the baptismal font, was born at Constantinople, in the year of Rome 1472 (A. D. 719). He was created
emperor by his father in the following year, and succeeded that prince
in 1494 (A. D. 741). Constantinus Copronymus died in 1528 (A. D.
775)].

Style: ——CONSTANTIN. —— D. (or D. N. or D. NO.) CON-
STANTI. (or CONSTANTIN. or CONSTANTINV. or CON-
STANTINVS.)——D. N. CONSTANTIN. P.——D. N. CON-
STANTINVS. PP.——D. N. CONSTANTINVS. PP. AVG.——
D. N. CONSTANTINVS. M.——D. N. CONSTANTINV. (or
CONSTANTINVS.) M. A.——D. N. CONSTANTINV. (or CON-
STANTINVS.) N. (or NE.)

Constantinus associated with Leo his son:——CONST. LEO.
PP.——CONSTANTINOS. S. LEON. O. NEOS.

Gold (pale) denarii and quinarii - - - - - - - - - - - - R 2
Gold (pale), or silver medallions - - - - - - - - - - - R 6
Silver, quinarii - - - - - - - - - - - - - - - - - R 4
Brass - R 6

GOLD AND SILVER.

1.

d. N. CONSTANTINO. PP. Full-faced beardless bust of Constantinus
V., with a diadem surmounted by a cross, holding in his right hand
a globe surmounted by a cross.—*Rev.* VICTORI. AVGVΔ.
A cross. In the exergue, CONOB. *(Banduri.)* - - - - AU

2.

d. NO. CONSTANTINɥ. Full-faced bust of Constantinus, with a
diadem surmounted by a cross, holding a globe surmounted by a
cross, and a scroll.—*Rev.* VICTORI. AVGTO. *(sic)*. A cross
placed on steps between a star and R. In the exergue, CONOB.
(Barbarous fabric). - - - - - - - - - - - - - AU

3.

D. NO. CONTANTI. *(sic)* or CONTANTIN. *(sic)*. A similar bust,
with similar attributes. — *Rev.* VICTORI. AVGTO. *(sic)* or VIC-
TORIVS. ⊳. *(sic)*. A cross between a star and the letter R. In
the exergue, CONOB. *(Quinarii)*. - - - - - - AU & AR

These quinarii are of very barbarous fabric.

[CONSTANTINUS V., AND LEO IV.]

1.

CONST. LEO. PP. Full-faced busts of Constantinus and Leo, each wearing the diadem surmounted by a cross; the first holding a globe surmounted by a cross : above, a celestial hand.—*Rev.* VIC-TORI. AVGTO. *(sic).* A cross placed on steps, between a star and the letter R. In the exergue, CONOB. (Barbarous fabric).

AU

2.

Same legends, and similar type. (A *quinarius*). - - - - - - AU

IRENE.

[Irene, daughter of a Khan of the Chozars, and wife of Constantinus Copronymus, was married to the emperor in the year of Rome 1486 (A. D. 733). She died shortly after the birth of Leo IV. in 1503 (A. D. 750)].

No coins are known of this princess.

MARIA.

[Maria, the second wife of Copronymus, was married to the emperor in the year of Rome 1503 (A. D. 750), and died shortly afterwards].

No coins.

EUDOCIA.

[Eudocia was the third wife of Copronymus. The time of the marriage of this lady to the emperor is not known. She gave birth to several children, two of whom, Christophorus and Nicephorus, were created Caesars, in the year of Rome 1522 (A. D. 769). The time of her death is not known].

There are no certain coins of this lady. See, however, the third letter of the Baron Marchant.

ARTAVASDUS.

[Artavasdus was son-in-law of Leo III., under whom he held the posts of master of the palace and governor of Armenia. He revolted against Constantinus Copronymus, who fled from the throne, of which Artavasdus took possession, in the year of Rome 1495 (A. D. 742). The deposed emperor, however, succeeded in subduing the usurper in the following year; and Artavasdus, after having his eyes put out, was sent into exile].

STYLE: —— D. NO. ARTAVA. (or ARTAVASDVS.)——D. ARTA-
VASDOS. MVLT.

Gold (pale), with his head, and that of Constantinus Copronymus on
the reverse - - - - - - - - - - - - - - - - - - R 8
„ with his head, and that of Nicephorus on the reverse - - - R 8
Silver - R 8

GOLD AND SILVER.

[ARTAVASDUS, AND CONSTANTINUS COPRONYMUS].

D. NO. APTAЧASDO. Full-faced bust of Artavasdus, holding a scroll, and a globe surmounted by a cross.—*Rev.* D. NO. CONTATINЧ. *(sic).* Full-faced bust of Constantine V., holding a scroll, and a globe surmounted by a cross. In the field, two stars. - - - AU

This coin is of a pale-coloured gold, and of barbarous fabric.

Valued by Mionnet at 400 francs.

[ARTAVASDUS, AND HIS SON NICEPHORUS].

1.

G. *(sic)* APZAЧASDOS. MЧLZ. Full-faced bust of Artavasdus, with a diadem surmounted by a cross, holding a cross in his right hand.—*Rev.* L. NIChFORЧS. *(sic)* MЧLZЧ. A. Bust of Nicephorus, with similar attributes. (Pure gold). - - - - - AU

Valued by Mionnet at 600 francs.

2.

D. NO. ARTAЧASↃO. Full-faced bust of Artavasdus, holding a globe surmounted by a cross.—*Rev.* D. NO. NICIFORO. *(sic).* Full-faced bust of Nicephorus, with the same attributes: two stars in the field. (Pale gold, and of barbarous fabric). - - - - - AU

3.

D. NO. ARTAYASDO. Same type.—*Rev.* Same legend. Same type, with two stars in the field. *(Tanini).* - - - - - - - - AR

4.

Same legend. Same type.—*Rev.* Same legend and type, with I. B. in the field. *(Tanini).* - - - - - - - - - - - - - AR

NICEPHORUS.

[Nicephorus, son of Artavasdus and Anna, the sister of Constantinus the Fifth, was created Augustus, and associated with his father, who usurped the throne in 1495 (A. D. 742). He shared the same fate as his parent, in the following year].

See the coins described under Artavasdus.

CHRISTOPHORUS AND NICEPHORUS.

[Christophorus and Nicephorus, the sons of Constantinus the Fifth and Eudocia, were declared Caesars by their father, in the year of Rome 1522 (A. D. 769). They were mutilated and banished to Athens by Constantinus the Sixth, in 1545 (A. D. 792), and in 1550 (A. D. 797) were put to death by order of Irene, the mother of that prince].

No coins are known of these princes, but the Baron Marchant assigns to them some coins without legends. See his *Mélanges de Numismatique et d'Histoire*, lettre iii.

LEO IV.

[Leo, son of Constantinus Copronymus and Irene, bore the surname of Chazarus, because his mother was the daughter of a Khan of the Chozars. He was born at Constantinople, in the year of Rome 1503 (A. D. 750), and declared emperor in the following year. Leo succeeded his father in 1528 (A.D. 775), and died in 1533 (A.D. 780)].

STYLE :——ΛEO.

LEO AND HIS SON ASSOCIATED : —— LEON. VSSESSON. CONSTANTI. (*or* CONSTANTINOS.) O. NEOS.

The meaning of the word VSSESSON. has never been explained.

Gold - R 6
Third brass (uncertain) - - - - - - - - - - - - - - R 4

GOLD.

[LEO IV. AND CONSTANTINUS VI., LEO III. AND CONSTANTINUS V.].

1.

LΕOh. VSSΕSSOh. COhSΖAhΖIhOS. O. hΕOS. Leo IV. and Constantinus VI. seated, each wearing the diadem surmounted by a cross, and holding a volume: above, a cross.—*Rev.* LΕOh. PAP. COhSΖANΖIhOS. PAΖHR. Busts of Leo III. and Constantinus V., each wearing a diadem surmounted by a cross: a cross between them.

2.

LΕOh. VSSΕSSOh. COhSΖANΖ. *or* COhSΖAhΖIhOS. O. hΕOS. Full-faced busts of Leo IV. and Constantinus VI.: above, a cross.— *Rev.* LΕON. PA. *or* PAP. COhSΖANΖ. *or* COhSΖANΖIhOS. PAΖHR. *or* PAΖH̄R̄. Θ. Full-faced busts of Leo III. and Constantinus V.: above, a cross.

No. 1 is much the rarest.

THIRD BRASS.

1.

ΛΕO. Leo IV. standing, wearing a diadem surmounted by a cross, and holding a long cross, and a globe surmounted by the same emblem. —*Rev.* An Arabic legend. M: above, the monogram of Christ.

2.

ΔAMACKOC. Leo standing, wearing a diadem surmounted by a cross, holding a long cross, and a globe surmounted by that emblem.—*Rev.* Same type and same legend.

3.

ΔAMAͰ KOͰ. The emperor standing, as on the preceding.—

Rev. Λ N O **M** ΔAMΛ. with P, Ω and asterisks

The foregoing types in small brass, are given by Sestini. The Arabic legend gives the name of Leo, and explains that the coins were struck at Damas (Damascus), in Syria, which was taken by this emperor, in his war with the Saracens. The Baron Marchant thinks these coins belong to Leontius the Second, but Sestini assigns them to Leo IV.

IRENE.

[Irene, wife of Leo IV., surnamed Attica, from the country of her birth, was married to the emperor in the year of Rome 1522 (A. D. 769). Upon the death of Leo IV., in 1533 (A. D. 780), she caused herself to be proclaimed Augusta, and ruled the empire in the name of her son Constantinus, who, in 1543 (A. D. 790), removed her from the government. She was recalled, however, in the following year; and, in 1550 (A. D. 797), Constantinus, by her command, was deprived of his eyes, and Irene governed alone, until the year 1555 (A. D. 802), when she was deposed by Nicephorus Logotheta, and banished to the island of Lesbos, where she maintained herself by spinning. This barbarous woman ended her life, in the year of Rome 1556 (A. D. 803)].

STYLE:——EIRINH. BASILISSH.——IRINH. AΓOVSTI. *(sic)*.

Gold -	R 6
Silver (her name occurs on the coins of her son) - - - - - -	R 6
Third brass (see the reverses of her son's coins) - - - - - -	R 8

GOLD.

ЄIRIhH. bASILISSH. Bust of Irene, full-faced, with a diadem surmounted by a cross, holding a long cross, and a globe surmounted by that emblem.—*Rev.* ЄIRIhH. bASILISSH. X. *or* Θ. A similar bust, with the same attributes.

Valued by Mionnet at sixty francs.

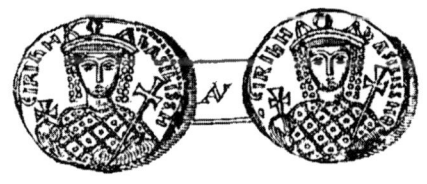

CONSTANTINUS VI.

[Constantinus, son of Leo IV. and Irene, was born in the year of Rome
1524 (A. D. 771), and at the age of five years, was declared Caesar by
his father, whom he succeeded in 1533 (A. D. 780), but the empire
was governed by his mother. This unfortunate prince died shortly
after the cruel injury inflicted upon him by the agents of his mother
Irene, in the year of Rome 1550 (A. D. 797)].

STYLE:——CONSTAN——CONSTANTINOS. BAS.

CONSTANTINUS AND IRENE TOGETHER:——CONSTANTINOS. S. IRINI.
EC. ΘEV. BASILIS.

Gold - R 6
Silver - R 8
Third brass (uncertain) - - - - - - - - - - - - - - R 4
Third brass, with the bust of Irene on reverse - - - - - - - R 8

GOLD AND SILVER.

[CONSTANTINUS VI. AND HIS MOTHER IRENE].

1.

+. COhSZAhZIhOS. CAb. Δ. (sic). Full-faced busts of Constantinus
VI. and Irene his mother: the first with a diadem, surmounted by a
cross; the other with a radiated crown, likewise surmounted by a
cross, holding a long cross in her left hand.—*Rev.* A blundered
legend. Three figures seated, full-faced, each with a diadem surmounted by a cross. - - - - - - - - - - - - - - AU

The Baron Marchant, in his "*Melanges de Numismatique, &c.*," has
given a coin somewhat similar, in small brass; but expresses his doubts
as to its appropriation to Constantinus VI., and supposes it to belong to
Constantinus V. The Baron thinks the two figures represent the emperor
and his third wife Eudocia, and that the three effigies on the other side,
are those of Leo IV., Christophorus, and Nicephorus.

2.

COhSZANZIhOS. bAS. Full-faced bust of Constantinus VI., with a
diadem surmounted by a cross, holding in his right hand a globe,
surmounted by the same emblem.—*Rev.* IRIhH. AΓOVSZI. (sic).
Bust of Irene, with a radiated crown surmounted by a cross, holding
a long cross, and a globe surmounted by a cross.

3.

COhSZAhZIhOS. S. IRIhI. ЄC. ОЧЄ. bASILIS +. in the field of the coin.—*Rev.* IhSЧS. XPISTЧS. hICA. A cross, placed on steps. (*Tanini*). ᐧ - - - - - - - - - - - - - - - - - AR

In gold, No. 1 is by far the rarest.

THIRD BRASS.

+. CШNSZAN. . . . . Bust of Constantinus VI., full-faced, his left hand raised, his right holding a sceptre.—*Rev.* O. A. ΔIMITPI. Full-faced bust of Saint Demetrius, the head surrounded by the nimbus, &c. (*Pellerin*).

[CONSTANTINUS VI. AND IRENE].

Without legend. Full-faced bust of the emperor, on a sceptre, placed horizontally, holding a globe surmounted by a cross: below,

X $\underset{\text{A}}{\text{M}}$ N. In the field, a cross.—*Rev.* Without legend. Full-faced bust of Irene, with the same attributes as on the gold coins.

Valued by Mionnet at forty francs.

NICEPHORUS I.

[Nicephorus, a patrician, born in Seleucia, was treasurer and interpreter (hence his name of Logotheta) in the reigns of Constantinus VI. and Irene, against whom he promoted a successful rebellion, and assumed the purple, in the year of Rome 1555 (A. D. 802). Nicephorus fell in a battle with the Bulgarians, in 1564 (A. D. 811)].

STYLE:——NIK.——NICEFOROS. (*or* NICIFOROS. *or* NICIFO-RVS.) BASI. (*or* BASIL. *or* BASILE.)

Gold - - - - - - - - - - - - - - - - - - R 4
Second and third brass - - - - - - - - - - - - - R 8

GOLD.

[NICEPHORUS AND STAURACIUS].

NICEFOROS. *or* hICIFOROS. bASIL. *or* bASILE. Full-faced bust
of Nicephorus, with a diadem surmounted by a cross, holding a
volume and a cross.—*Rev.* SZAЦRACIS. ՀESPO. Є. (*sic*). *or*
ՀESPO. X. *or* ՀESPO. Ꮎ. Full-faced bust of Stauracius, with
a diadem surmounted by a cross: in his right hand a globe, surmounted by the same emblem.

SECOND BRASS.

[NICEPHORUS AND STAURACIUS.]

1.

NIK. Bust of Nicephorus, full-faced, with a diadem; in his right
hand a globe, surmounted by a cross.—*Rev.* STAЦ. Diademed
bust of Stauracius, full-faced, with the paludamentum. (*Mionnet*).

2.

Another, with CTA. instead of STAЦ. on the reverse. (*Sestini*).

Valued by Mionnet at fifty francs each.

THIRD BRASS.

hICIFORI. bASI. Full-faced bust of Nicephorus, with a diadem surmounted by a cross, and holding in his right hand a long cross. —

Rev.
$$\begin{matrix} X & + & N \\ X & M & N \\ X & A & N \end{matrix}$$
(*Marchant, Lettre ii. fig.* 5).

STAURACIUS.

[Stauracius, son of Nicephorus the First, was created Augustus by his
father, in the year of Rome 1556 (A. D. 803). He accompanied
Nicephorus in his war with the Bulgarians, and after the death of the
emperor, returned to Constantinople, when he was compelled by
Michael the First, to abdicate the throne, in the year 1564 (A. D. 811).
Stauracius entered a monastery, and died in the following year].

STYLE:——STA. (*or* STAV.)——STAVRACIS. DESPO.

Gold   - R 4
Second brass   - - - - - - - - - - - - - - - - R 8

(See the reverses of the coins of his father).

MICHAEL I.

[Michael, Rhangabe, or Curopalata, son of Theophylactus, and son-in-law of Nicephorus the First, was raised to the empire, after the death of that prince, in the room of Stauracius, who abdicated in his favour, in the year of Rome 1564 (A. D. 811). This emperor, upon hearing of the revolt of the troops in favour of Leo V., abdicated the throne, and voluntarily embraced a monastic life, in 1566 (A. D. 813). He died in 1598 (A. D. 845)].

STYLE :——MIXAHL.——MIXAHΛ. (or MIXAHL.) BACIΛ. (or. BASIΛE. or BACIΛOS.)

MICHAEL AND HIS SON THEOPHYLACTUS ASSOCIATED :——MIXAHL. S. ΘEOFYLACTE. EC. Θ. BASILIS. ROMAION.

Gold - R 3
Silver - - - - - - - - - - - - - - - - - - - R 5
Second and third brass, - - - - - - - - - - - - - R 4

GOLD AND SILVER.

1.

MIXAHΛ. BACIΛE. Bust of Michael I., holding the labarum, and a globe, surmounted by a cross.—*Rev.* IC. XC. Bust of Christ. (*Banduri*, p. 712). - - - - - - - - - - - - - - AU

2.

MIXAHL. Bust of Michael, as on the preceding.—*Rev.* MIXAHL. Bust of Christ. (*Banduri*, p. 712). - - - - - - - - - AU

3.

+MIXAHΛ. BACIΛOC. *(sic)*. Bust of Michael, full-faced, holding the labarum and a globe, surmounted by a cross.—*Rev.* I̅C̅. X̅C̅. the bust of Christ, backed by a cross. (*Plate xiii, No.* 2). - - AU

[MICHAEL, AND HIS SON THEOPHYLACTUS].

+. MIXAHL. S. ΘEOFYLACTE. EC. Θ. bASILIS. ROMAIOh. in the middle of the field.—*Rev.* IhSЧS. XRISZЧS. hICA. A cross placed on steps.—*(Sestini and Marchant)*. - - - -- - - AR

THIRD BRASS.

1.

MIXAHL. BASILE.   Full-faced bust of Michael I., with a diadem, surmounted by a cross, holding a globe, surmounted by the same emblem : another cross in the field.

X + N
Rev. X M N   *(Marchant's Mélanges de Numismatique. &c.)*
X A. N

2.

MIXAHL. BASIL. ⊲   Full-faced bust of Michael, with a diadem, surmounted by a cross : a cross in his right hand.—*Rev.* ΘΕΟΦY. Full-faced bust of Theophylactus, with a diadem surmounted by a cross. *(Marchant)*.

Other second and third brass of this emperor have the same type as his gold coins. Those which bear his name, unaccompanied by that of his son Theophylactus, may belong to some of the other emperors of the name of Michael.

THEOPHYLACTUS.

[Theophylactus, son of Michael I. and Procopia, was associated with his father, in the year of Rome 1564 (A. D. 811). He was mutilated by order of Leo V., in 1566 (A. D. 813), and ended his days in a monastery].

See the coins of his father, Michael I.

LEO V.

[Leo, surnamed the Armenian, from the country of his birth, was general of the army of Michael I., and proclaimed emperor by the soldiery, in the year of Rome 1566 (A. D. 813). Michael abdicated, upon the news of the revolt, and Leo V. ascended the throne. He was assassinated in 1578 (A. D. 820)].

STYLE :———ΛΕΟ. ΔΕCΠ.

Third brass - - - - - - - - - - - - - - - - - R 6

ΛΕΟ. ΔΕCΠ.   Leo standing, full-faced.—*Rev.* KΩNS. ΔΕC.   Constantinus, son of Leo V., standing, full-faced. *(Sestini)*.

CONSTANTINUS VII.

[Constantinus, son of Leo V. and Theodosia, was associated with his father, in the year of Rome 1566 (A. D. 813). He was mutilated and exiled to the island of Prote, after the death of his father, by order of Michael Balbus, in 1573 (A. D. 820)].

See the coins of Leo V.

MICHAEL II.

[Michael, surnamed Balbus, or the Stammerer, was born of an obscure family, at Amorium, in Phrygia. He held the post of captain of the guard under Leo, whose murderers proclaimed Michael emperor, in the year of Rome 1573 (A. D. 820). This emperor died in 1582, A. D. 829)].

STYLE: —— MIXAHL. BA. (or BASILEV. or BASILEVS.)——
MIXAHL. BASILEVS. RM.——MIXAHL. EC. ΘEV. PISTOS.
BASILEVS. POMAIωN. —— MIXAHL. PISTOS. MEGAS.
BASILEVS. ROMAION.

MICHAEL, AND THEOPHILUS HIS SON, ASSOCIATED:——MIXAHL. S.
ΘEOF. (or ΘEOFILOS.) —— MIXAHL. S. ΘEOFILE. EC.
ΘEV. BASILIS. ROMAION.

Gold, denarii and quinarii - - - - - - - - - - - - -	R 4
Silver -	R 8
First, second, and third brass - - - - - - - - - - - - - -	R 1

GOLD AND SILVER.

1.

ΙΠIHAIL. bASILEЧS. RM. (sic). Full-faced bust of Michael II. with a diadem surmounted by a cross, holding the labarum, and a globe surmounted by a cross : to the right, a hand issuing from above. —Rev. IHS. XIS. REX. REGNANTIVM. Full-faced bust of Christ. (Tanini). - - - - - - - - - - - - - - - AU

2.

MIXAHL. EC. ΘEY. PISTOS. BASILEVS. POMAIωN. in the middle of the field.—Rev. IHSVS. XRISTVS. NICA. A cross placed on steps. (Tanini.) - - - - - - - - - - - - AR

3.

mIXAHL. PISƵOS. mЄ ꟼAS. bASILЄꟼS. ROmAIOh. in the middle of the field.—*Rev.* IhSꟻS. XRISƵVS. NICA. A cross placed on steps. *(Sestini).* - - - - - - - - - - - AR

The gold is valued by Mionnet at thirty francs; the silver at 100 francs each.

[MICHAEL, AND HIS SON THEOPHILUS].

1.

* mIXAHL. bASILЄꟼS. Full-faced bust of Michael II., with a diadem surmounted by a cross, holding a cross and a book.—*Rev.* ΘЄOFIL. *or* ΘЄOFILO. ᴆЄSP. X. B. *or* Є. *or* IXЄ. Full-faced bust of Theophilus, holding a long cross, and a globe surmounted by the same emblem. *(Plate xiii, No. 3).* - - - AU

2.

+mIXAHL. S. ΘЄOFILЄ. ЄC. ΘЄꟼ. bASILIS. ROmAIOh. in the field of the coin.—*Rev.* IhSꟻS. XPISƵVS. hICA. A cross placed on steps. - - - - - - - - - - - - - - - - AR

3.

mIXAHL. bA. Full-faced bust of Michael II., holding a globe surmounted by a cross.—*Rev.* ΘЄOFILI. .... Full-faced bust of Theophilus, holding a cross. In the field, a small cross. (A *quinarius*). - - - - - - - - - - - - - - - - AU

FIRST, SECOND AND THIRD BRASS.

mIXAHL. S. ΘЄOFILOS. Full-faced busts of Michael and Theophilus his son.—

$$\text{Rev.} \quad \begin{matrix} X \\ X \\ X \end{matrix} \ \overset{+}{\mathbf{M}}_{\Theta} \ \begin{matrix} N \\ N \\ N \end{matrix} \quad \textit{(Mus. Vindob.).}$$

THEOPHILUS.

[Theophilus, son of Michael the Second and Thecla, was probably born at Armorium in Phrygia. He received from his father the title of Augustus, in the year of Rome 1574 (A. D. 821), and succeeded him in 1582 (A. D. 829). Theophilus died in 1595 (A. D. 842)].

Style :——ΘEOFILOS.——ΘEOFIL. (or ΘEOFILOS.) B. (or BA.
or BASI. or BASIL. or BASILE.)——ΘEOFIL. (or ΘEOFILO.)
DESP. —— ΘEOFILOS. DVLOS. XRISTVS. PISTOC. EN.
AVTO. BASILEV. ROMAION.

Theophilus and his son Constantinus associated: —— ΘEOFILOS.
S. CONSTANT.

Gold - R 2
„ quinarii - - - - - - - - - - - - - - - - - - R 3
Silver - R 5
Second and third brass - - - - - - - - - - - - - - - C

GOLD AND SILVER.

1.

ΘEOFILOS. Full-faced bust of Theophilus, with a diadem surmounted
by a cross, holding a globe surmounted by the same emblem.—*Rev.*
ΘEOFILOS. A similar bust. (A *quinarius*). - - - - AU

2.

*ΘEOFILOS. bA. A similar bust as on the preceding.—*Rev.* ΘEO-
FILOS. BA. (A *quinarius*.) - - - - - - - - - - AU

3.

ΘEOFILOS. bASILE. Bust of Theophilus, holding a globe surmounted by a cross.—*Rev.* CVRIE. BOHΘH. ZO. SO.)OVLO.
(*sic)* E. A cross. (*Eckhel).* - - - - - - - - - - AU

4.

+ΘEOFILOS. dЧLOS. XRISZЧS. PISTOC. EN. AVZO. BASILEЧ.
ROMAIOh. in the centre.—*Rev.* IhSЧS. XRISZЧS. NICA. A
cross placed on steps.—*(Sestini).* - - - - - - - - - AR

SECOND BRASS.

[THEOPHILUS, AND HIS SON CONSTANTINUS].

ΘEOFILOS. S. COhSTAhT. Two busts: between them, a small cross.—

Rev.
X + N
X M N   (*Musei Hedervarii*, p. 397).
X ☉ N

If, says Mionnet, this coin be authentic, it does not present us with a
bust of the Constantinus, supposed to be the son of Michael the Third,

since this prince was not born during the lifetime of Theophilus, and it is not probable that Michael III. would strike coins for his son, without placing his own effigy and name on them. It can only be accounted for, by supposing that Theophilus had also a son, whom history does not mention.

THEODORA.

[Theodora, wife of Theophilus, was the daughter of a Tribune, and born at Ebissa, in Paphlagonia.   She was married to the emperor, in the year of Rome 1583 (A. D. 830).   Upon the death of Theophilus, in 1595 (A. D. 842), she governed the empire during the minority of Michael, who, in the year 1610 (A. D. 857), shut her up in a monastery, where she ended her life].

STYLE:——ΘΕODORA. DESPVNA. (or DESPOVNA).

Gold - R 8

[THEODORA, her son MICHAEL III., AND her DAUGHTER THECLA].

+ ΘΕOꝊORA. ꝊESPVhA. or ꝊESPOVhA.   Full-faced bust of Theodora, with a diadem surmounted by a cross, holding in her right hand a globe, surmounted by a double cross, and in her left, a long cross, transversely.—*Rev.* MIXAHL. S. ΘΕCLA. Youthful full length figure of Michael III., with a diadem surmounted by a cross, holding a globe surmounted by the same emblem. Thecla also, standing, with a radiated crown surmounted by a cross, holding a long double cross.

Valued by Mionnet at 300 francs.—See also the coins of her son Michael the Third.

MICHAEL III.

[Michael, the son of Theophilus and Theodora, was born in the year of Rome 1589 (A. D. 836), and created Augustus by his father immediately after. He succeeded Theophilus in 1595 (A. D. 842), and compelled his mother to embrace a religious life in 1610 (A. D. 857). Michael was assassinated in 1620 (A. D. 867), by Basilius, whom he had admitted as an associate in the empire in the preceding year].

STYLE:——MIXAHL.——MIXHAEL. IMPERAT.

MICHAEL AND THEODORA:——MIXAHL. S. ΘEODORA.

MICHAEL, AND HIS SON CONSTANTINUS:——MIXAHL. S. CONSTANT. (or CONSTANTIN.)

MICHAEL AND THECLA:——MIXAHL. S. ΘECLA.

MICHAEL, THEODORA, AND THECLA:——MIXAHL. ΘEODORA. S. ΘECLA. EC. Θ. BASILIS. ROMAION.

Gold . -	R 8
„ quinarii - - - - - - - - - - - - - - - -	R 6
„ quinarii, of base quality - - - - - - - - - - -	R 5
Silver - - - - - - - - - - - - - - - - - - -	R 6
First brass - - - - - - - - - - - - - - - - -	R 8

GOLD AND SILVER.

MIXAHΛ. Full-faced bust of Michael, with a diadem surmounted by a cross, holding a globe, likewise surmounted by a cross.—*Rev.* Same legend. A similar type. (Λ *quinarius*)—*Tanini*, page 421.

AU

[THEOPHILUS, MICHAEL III., AND CONSTANTINUS].

1.

*ΘEOFILOS. bASILE. Θ. or X. or A. Full-faced bust of Theophilus, with a diadem surmounted by a cross, holding a double cross in his right hand, and a book in his left.—*Rev.* +MIXAHL. S. COh-SZAhZIb. Busts of Michael III. and Constantinus: the first bearded, the other without beard; each with a diadem surmounted by a cross: a small cross in the field. - - - - - - - AU

2.

ΘEOFILOS. bASILEO. Full-faced bust of Theophilus, holding a globe surmounted by a cross.—*Rev.* MIXAHL. S. CONSZANZIN. Full-faced bust of Michael III., or Constantinus, holding a double cross. - - - - - - - - - - - - - - - - AU

This coin is of pale gold, and of barbarous fabric.

[MICHAEL III., AND THEODORA].

1.

MIXAHL. S. ΘEODORA. Busts of Michael and his mother: between them, a cross.—*Rev.* IhSυS. XRISTOS.   The bust of Christ backed by a cross, holding the book of the Evangelists. (*Mus. Vindob*). - AU

2.

Same legend.   Same busts.—*Rev.* IIIS. XIS. REX. REGNANTIVM. Bust of Christ. (*Tanini*). - - - - - - - - - - - - - AU

[MICHAEL III., THEODORA, AND THECLA].

+mIXAHL. ΘEOdORA. S.ΘEϹLA. EϹ. Θ. bASILIS. ROmAIOh. in the middle of the field.—*Rev.* IhSVS. XRISTOS. NICA.   A cross placed on steps. (*Sestini*, tom. viii, p. 147). - - - AR

Valued by Mionnet at fifty francs.

[MICHAEL, AND BASILIUS].

MIXAHA.   Full-faced bust of Michael, with a diadem surmounted by a cross, holding a globe likewise surmounted by a cross. — *Rev.* bASIΓEIOS. (*sic*). Full-faced bust of Basilius, with the same attributes. (A *quinarius*, of base gold). - - - - - - - - AU

FIRST BRASS.

+MIXhAEL. IMPERAT.   Full-faced bust of Michael III., holding a globe surmounted by a cross.—*Rev.* +bASILIυS. REX.   Full-faced bust of Basilius. (*Tanini*, page 421).

Valued by Mionnet at 100 francs.

CONSTANTINUS.

This prince is not mentioned by historians. The coins described at page 449, have been ascribed to Constantinus, the supposed brother of Michael III.; but the Baron Marchant is of opinion that this Constantinus was a son of that emperor. *Mionnet* (tom. ii, p. 480), has a long note on the subject of this new attribution, the substance of which is as follows:—Those coins upon which there are two busts, or one only with the legend MIXAHL. S. CONSTANTIN. have raised doubts in the minds of some numismatists, whether these two effigies are those of the two sons of Theophilus, who is represented and named on the other side of these same coins. In the first place, because Michael is portrayed with a beard, whereas he was only five or six years old at the time of his father's death; and in the next, because history does not mention that Theophilus had a son named Constantinus. Some have supposed that the bust on these coins must be that of Michael II., who had received, as his associate in the empire, Constantinus, son of Leo. V., and on the other side that of his own son Theophilus; but it is not probable that Michael II. should receive as his partner in the empire the son of Leo the Armenian, whom he had mutilated and exiled, upon ascending the throne. This opinion being unsupported, and, indeed, discredited, by the recital of historians, the former one has been held by many antiquaries; namely, that Constantinus and Michael were the sons of Theophilus. It appears, however, that there is good reason for supposing that Michael the Third had a son named Constantinus. The Baron Marchant was the first to solve this difficulty.* He discovered in Ducange, who quotes from Leo the grammarian, that it is probable Michael had a son by his wife Eudoxia; and that this prince died very young, at the commencement of the reign of Basilius. It therefore becomes almost a certainty that the two busts are those of Michael III. and his infant son Constantinus, whom he might have taken as his colleague; and that the bearded single portrait is that of his father Theophilus, placed as a memento on the reverse.

(See the coins of Michael the Third).

THECLA.

[Thecla, daughter of Theophilus and Theodora, and sister of Michael the Third, was driven from the imperial palace by Michael, and shut up in a convent with her mother, in the year of Rome 1610 (A. D. 857)].

See the coins of Theodora and Michael III.

---

* See his *Melanges de Numismatique et d'Histoire*, Letter xiv., addressed to the Baron Rühle de Lilienstern.

BASILIUS I.

[Basilius was born of an obscure Thracian family, at Hadrionopolis, in the year of Rome —— Michael the Third adopted and admitted him to a share in the empire, in 1619 (A.D. 866), but he caused Michael to be murdered in the following year. Basilius died in 1639 (A.D. 886)].

STYLE :——BASILIOS. (or BASILEIOS.)——BASILIVS. REX.—— BASILIOS. BASILEVS.——BASILIOS. EN. ΘEO. BASILEVS. ROMEON.

BASILIUS, AND HIS SON CONSTANTINUS, ASSOCIATED :——BASILIOS. ET. CONSTANTIN.——BASILIOS. S. CONST. AVGG.——BA- SILIOS. ET. CONSTANT. (or CONSTANTI.) AVGG. B.—— BASIL. CONST. (or CONSTANTI.) BA. (or BASIL.) —— BASIL. C. CONSTANTI. (or CONSTANTIN.) BA.——BASIL. S. CONST. BA. (or BASIL.)——BASILIOS. CE. CONSTANTIN. BASILIS. ROMEO. —— BASILIOS. CONSTANTINOS. EN. ΘO. BASILEIS. ROMAION.——BASIL. (or BASILO. or BA- SILIVS.) S. CONSTANTINOS. EN. ΘO. (or ΘEO.) BASILEIS. ROMAION.——BASILIOS. CE. CONSTANTIN. PISTV. BA- SILIS. ROMEO. (or ROMEOI. or ROMEON.)——BASILIOS. E. Θ. CONSTANTINI. PISTV. BASILIS. ROMEO.*

BASILIUS, CONSTANTINUS VIII., AND LEO VI., ASSOCIATED :——LEON. BASIL. CONST. AVGG.——LE. BASI. C. CONST. AVGG.—— LEON. BASIL. S. CONST. AV. (or AVGG.)——BASIL. CON- STANT. S. LEON. EN. ΘO. (or Θ̄Ō.) BASILS. (or BASILIS.) ROMEON.

Gold medallions, of small size - - - - - - - - - - - - -	R 4
,, of the usual size - - - - - - - - - - - - - -	R 4
,, middle size - - - - - - - - - - - - - - -	R 5
Quinarii, of base gold - - - - - - - - - - - - - -	R 3
Silver medallions, of small size - - - - - - - - - - -	R 6
,, of the usual size - - - - - - - - - - - - - -	R 6
Second brass - - - - - - - - - - - - - - - - -	C

---

* It has been justly observed that some of the coins with these legends, may possibly belong to Basilius the Second, as that emperor is associated with his brother Constantinus XI.

GOLD AND SILVER.

1.

+ ᏏASILIOS. ᏏASILЄVS.   Basilius seated, full-faced, with a diadem surmounted by a cross, holding   in his right hand.—*Rev.* + ᏏASILIOS. Єh. ӨЄO. ᏏASILЄVS. ROMЄON. in the centre of the field.   (A small medallion). - - - - - - - - - AR

2.

BASILIOS. BASILЄЧS.   Full-faced bust of Basilius, holding in his right hand a long cross, and in his left a globe, surmounted by a cross.—*Rev.* IHS. XPS. REX. REGNANTIVM. The bust of Christ.   (*Banduri*). - - - - - - - - - - - - - AU

[BASILIUS, AND HIS SON CONSTANTINUS VIII.]

1.

+ ᏏASIL. . . C. COᏏSᏃAᏏᏃI. ᏏA.   Basilius and Constantinus, standing, holding, together, a long cross.—*Rev.* +. IᏏS. XIS. RЄX. RЄGNANᏃIᏏm. *(sic).*   The bust of Christ, backed by a cross, holding the book of the Evangelists.   (A small medallion). -   AU

2.

+ ᏏASIL. C. COᏏᏃANᏃI. ᏏA. *or* BASIL. COᏏSᏃANᏃI. ᏏA. *or* BASILIOS. ЄT. COᏏSᏃANᏃ. AЧGG. Ꮟ. The same busts as on the preceding.—*Rev.* +. IᏏS. XPS. RЄX. RЄGNANTIЧM.   Christ seated (or the bust of Christ.) - - - - - - - - - - AU

3.

+ ᏏASILIOS. CЄ. COᏏSᏃAᏏᏃIᏏ. PISᏃV. ᏏASILIS. ROMЄO. in six lines, in the centre of the field.—*Rev.* IᏏSЧS. XRISᏃЧS. ᏏIKA. A cross, placed on steps.   (A small medallion).—*Mionnet.*
AR

4.

+ ᏏASILIOS. Є. Ө. COᏏSᏃAᏏᏃINI. PISᏃV. ᏏASILIS. ROMЄO. in the centre of the field.—*Rev.* IᏏSVS. XPISᏃᏏS. ᏏICA. A cross, placed on steps.   *(Sestini).* - - - - - - - - - AR

5.

* ᏏASILЄIO.   Full-faced head of Basilius, holding a globe surmounted by a cross.—*Rev.* CONSTANT.   Full-faced bust of Constantinus, holding a globe surmounted by a cross.   (A *quinarius*, of base gold).
AU

[BASILIUS I. AND HIS SONS LEO VI. AND ALEXANDER?]

bASILIO). AVZOS. *(sic)*. Full-faced bust of Basilius, with a diadem surmounted by a cross, holding a cross in his right hand.—*Rev.* +LEO. . S. . . . AЧꞬꞬ. *. The busts of Leo VI. and Alexander? full-faced, each with a diadem surmounted by a cross, (middle size). - - - - - - - - - - - - - - - - AU

It is most likely, observes Mionnet, that this coin bears the effigies of Leo VI. and Alexander, instead of those of Constantinus VIII. and Leo. Constantinus being the eldest son of Basilius, would have been mentioned first in the legend, if in company with his brother; but on this coin, Leo is mentioned first. Mionnet thinks this coin was struck after the death of Constantinus, who died young, and before his father.

The coins in brass, on which Constantinus and his brother Leo are associated with their father, are common.

CONSTANTINUS VIII.

[Son of Basilius and Eudocia Ingerina, was born about the year of Rome 1616 (A. D. 863); created Augustus, and associated with his father, in 1621 (A. D. 868), and died in 1632 (A. D. 879)].

See the coins of Basilius, his father.

LEO VI.

[Leo, the second son of Basilius and Eudocia, was born at Constantinople, in the year of Rome 1618 (A.D. 865); created Augustus, and associated with his father, in 1623 (A. D. 870); and succeeded Basilius, in 1639 (A. D. 886). Leo died in 1664 (A. D. 911)].

STYLE:——LEON. BASILEVS. ROM.——LEON. EN. ΘEO. BASILEVS. ROMEON.——LEON. EN. XѠ. BASILEVS. ROM. (*or* ROMѠN.) (*sic*).——LEON. EN. XѠ. EVSEBHS. BASILEVS. RѠMAIѠN.

LEO, AND HIS SON CONSTANTINUS X., ASSOCIATED:——LEON. ET. CONSTANT. AVGG. ROM.-—-LEON. S. CONSTANTINE. EC. ΘEV. BASILIS.——LEON. S. CONSTANTINE. EC. ΘEV. BASILIS. ROMAION.——LEON. CE. CONSTANTIN. EN. XѠ. EVSEBIS. BASILI. ROM.

LEO, AND HIS BROTHER ALEXANDER:——LEON. S. ALEXANDROS.——LEON. S. ALEXANDROS. BASIL. ROMEON.

Gold - - - - - - - - - - - - - - - - - - - R 6
Silver medallions - - - - - - - - - - - - - - - R 4
First, second, and third brass - - - - - - - - - - - - R 2

GOLD AND SILVER.

1.

+LEON. EN. Xω. bASILEUS. ROM. Full-faced bust of Leo. VI.
with a diadem surmounted by a cross, holding the labarum and a
volume.—*Rev.* + IhS. XPS. REX. REGNANƵIVM. Full-faced
bust of Christ, holding the book of the Evangelists. (*Tanini*). AU

2.

+LEωh. Eh. Xω. EUSEbHS. bASILE VS. RωmAIωh. in the centre
of the coin.—*Rev.* IhSUS. XPISƵUS. hICA. A cross, placed on
steps: below, a globe. (A small medallion). - - - - - AR

3.

LEON. EN. Xω. bASILEUS. ROMωN. (*sic*, with a cedille under the
ω). Full-faced bearded bust of Leo. VI. with a diadem surmounted
by a cross, holding a globe surmounted by a double cross.—*Rev.*
+mARIA. +. Full-faced bust of the Virgin Mary, her arms
raised aloft. In the field, $\overline{MHR}$. $\overline{\Theta U}$. - - - - - - - AU

Valued by Mionnet at 150 francs.

[LEO VI. AND HIS SON CONSTANTINUS X.]

1.

+LEOh. S. COhSƵAhƵIhE. EC. ΘEU. bASILIS. in five lines, in the
middle of the field.—*Rev.* IhSUS. XRISTUS. hICA. A cross,
placed on steps. (*Sestini*). - - - - - - - - - - - AR

2.

+LEOh. S. COhSƵAhƵIhE. EC. ΘEU. bASILIS. ROMAIOh. in
the field of the coin.—*Rev.* IhSUS. XRISTUS. hICA. A cross
placed on steps. (*Sestini*). - - - - - - - - - - AR

3.

+LEOh. CE. COhSTAhTIh. Eh. Xω. EVSEbIS. bASILI. ROM. in
five lines, enclosed within an ornamented circle.—*Rev.* IhSUS.
XRISƵUS. bICA. A cross placed on steps: below, a globe. AR

Valued by Mionnet at twenty-four francs each. They are all small
medallions.

FIRST, SECOND, AND THIRD BRASS.

+LEOh. bASILEHS. ROm.   The emperor, standing (or his bust only) with a diadem surmounted by a cross, holding a standard, or a scroll.—*Rev.* +LEOh. Eh. ΘEO. BASILEVS. ROmEOh. in the centre of the coin.

[LEO, AND HIS BROTHER ALEXANDER.]
FIRST AND SECOND BRASS.

+. LEOh. S. ALEΞAhGROS. *(sic)* or ALEXAhdROS.   Leo and Alexander seated, full-faced, each wearing a diadem surmounted by a cross, holding between them the labarum.—*Rev.* +LEOh. S. ALEΞAhGROS. *(sic)* bASIL. ROmEOh. in the centre of the coin.

ZOE.

[Zoe, wife of Leo VI. commonly called Zoe Carbonopsina, was married to the emperor in the year of Rome 1654 (A. D. 901), and after his death, in 1664 (A. D. 911), was exiled by Alexander; but, upon the death of the latter in the following year, she returned to the court, and took charge of the education of her son Constantinus X., by whom she was compelled to enter a monastery, in 1672 (A. D. 919)].

First, second, and third brass (see the coins of her son, Constantinus X.)
R 4

ALEXANDER.

[Alexander, third son of Basilius I. and Eudocia, was born about the year of Rome 1623 (A. D. 870).   He was created Augustus by his father, and associated with that prince; after whose death, in 1639, he reigned with his brother Leo.   Upon the death of Leo, in 1664 (A. D. 911), he superintended the education of his youthful nephew, Constantine X.   Alexander died in the year of Rome 1665 (A. D. 912)].

Gold, of the middle size - - - - - - - - - - - - - R 5
First and second brass - - - - - - - - - - - - - - B 4

See the coins of Leo VI. and those of Basilius I.

ROMANUS.

[Romanus, surnamed Lecapenus, was born in Armenia. He was general of the army of Constantinus X., by whom he was created Augustus, and associated in the empire, when Constantinus married his daughter Helena, in the year of Rome 1672 (A. D. 919). Romanus, in the following year, raised his son Christophorus to the dignity of emperor, when they seized the first and second place in the empire, compelling Constantinus to hold the third. This ambitious man was driven from the throne by his son Stephanus, whom he had taken as his associate after the death of Christophorus, in 1697 (A. D. 944). Romanus died in a monastery, in the year of Rome 1699 (A. D. 946)].

Style:——ROMANOS. DESPOTHS.

Romanus and Christophorus associated:——ROMAN. ET. XPIS-TOFO. AVGG.

Romanus, Christophorus, and Constantinus X.: —— ROMANO. XPISTOFOR. CE. CONSTAN. EN. XѠ. EVSEB. BASIL. R.

Romanus, Constantinus X., Stephanus, and Constantinus IX.:—— ROMANO. CONSTANT. STEFANOS. CE. CONSTA. EN. XѠ. B. R.

Gold medallions, of small size - - - - - - - - - - - R 6
,, of the usual size - - - - - - - - - - - - - - R 4
Silver medallions - - - - - - - - - - - - - - - R 6

[ROMANUS, AND HIS SON CHRISTOPHORUS].

GOLD AND SILVER.

ROMAҺ. ЄT. XPISZOFO. AЧGG. Һ. *or* l. Full-faced busts of Romanus and Christophorus, each with a diadem surmounted by a cross, holding between them a double cross.—*Rev.* + IҺS. XPS. REX. REGNANTIЧM. ❋. The effigy of Christ seated, full-faced, the nimbus surrounding the head; the right hand raised, and the left holding the book of the Evangelists. (*Plate xiii, No. 4*). AU

[ROMANUS, CHRISTOPHORUS, AND CONSTANTINUS X.].

1.

+ ROMAhO. XPISTOFOR. CЄ. COhSTAh. Єh. XѠ. ЄVSЄb. bASIL. R. in five lines in the middle of the field.—*Rev.* IhSꙍS. XRISℤVS. hICA.   A cross, placed on steps : below, a globe.   (A small medallion). - - - - - - - - - - - - - - - AR

2.

+KЄ. BOHѲЄI. ROMAhO. DESPOℤH.   Romanus standing, full-faced, wearing a diadem surmounted by a cross, and holding in his right hand a globe surmounted by a cross; on his left, Christ standing, placing his right hand on the head of Romanus.—*Rev.* XPISℤOF. Єℤ. COhSℤAhℤIh.   Full-faced busts of Christophorus and Constantinus, each with a diadem surmounted by a cross, holding between them a long cross. *(Musei Hedervarii).* AU

Valued by Mionnet at 100 francs.

[ROMANUS I. CONSTANTINUS X. STEPHANUS, AND CONSTANTINUS IX.]

+ ROMAhO. COhSℤAhℤ SℤЄKAhOS. *(sic)* *(or* SℤЄFANOS. CЄ. COhSℤA. *or* COhℤAhℤ. ЄN. XѠ. b. R.) in the centre of the field.—*Rev.* IhSꙍS. XPISℤꙍS. hICA.   A cross charged with a buckler, on which is the effigy of Romanus; on one side, RѠꟽA. (A small medallion).—*Eckhel. Doct. Num. Vet.* - - - - AR

CRISTOPHORUS.

[Christophorus, the son of Romanus the First and Theodora, was created Augustus by his father, and associated with him, in the year of Rome 1673 (A. D. 920).   This prince died in 1684 (A. D. 931)].

(See the coins of Romanus the First).

STEPHANUS.

Stephanus, second son of Romanus the First and Theodora, was declared Augustus, and associated with his father, in the year of Rome 1684 (A. D. 931).   He was banished to the island of Lesbos, by Constantinus X., soon after he had driven his father from the throne, in 1698 (A. D. 945).   He died in exile, in the year 1717 (A. D. 964)].

See the coins of his father, Romanus I.

CONSTANTINUS IX.

[Constantinus, third son of Romanus and Theodora, was created Augustus, and associated with his father, in the year of Rome 1684 (A. D. 931). Constantinus was banished to the island of Samothrace, at the same time as his brother, 1698 (A. D. 945), and murdered by his guard shortly afterwards].

See the coins of Romanus I., his father.

CONSTANTINUS X.

[Constantinus, son of Leo VI. and Zoe, was born at Constantinople, in the year of Rome 1658 (A. D. 905). He received the surname of Porphyrogenitus, in consequence of his having been born in a wing of the palace called Porphyra. This prince succeeded his father in 1664 (A. D. 911). He reigned, associated with Romanus Lecapenus and his sons, twenty-five years; and ruled alone, from the year 1698 (A.D. 945), to the time of his death, in 1712 (A. D. 959)].

STYLE: —— CONSTANTIN. A. —— CONST. (*or* CONSTANT.) BASIL. RѠM. —— CONST. (*or* CONSTANTIN.) EN. ѲEO. BASIL. (*or* BASILEVS.) ROM. (*or* ROMEON.)

CONSTANTINUS, AND HIS MOTHER ZOE :——CONSTANT. ET. ZOH. B. ——CONSTANT. (*or* CONSTANTI.) CE. ZOH. B.——CONSTANTIN. (*or* CONSTANTINO.) CE. ZOH. BASILIS. ROMEON.

CONSTANTINUS X. AND HIS SON ROMANUS II.:——CONSTANT. ET. ROMAN. AVG.——CONSTANT. CE. ROMAN. AVGG.—— CONSTANT. CE. ROMAN. BA. —— CONSTANT. ET. ROMAN. AVGG. B. (*or* BA.) —— CONSTANT. ET. ROMAN. B. ROM.——CONST. CE. ROMAN. B. ROM.——CONSTANT. CE. ROMAN. AVGG. B. R.——CONST. ET. ROMAN. EN. XRIST. B. ROMEO.——CONST. CE. ROMAN. EN. XRIST. B. ROMEO. —— CONSTANTINOS. CE. ROMAN. EN. XѠ. BLIR.*——CONST. HORFVROS. CE. ROMANO. EN. XѠ.

---

* Mionnet supposes these letters to signify Bas*I*LI. R.

EVSEB. RѠMEON.——CONST. ΠORFVROS. CE. ROMANO.
EN. XѠ. ENSEB. B. RѠMEON.—— CONST. ΠORFVROS.
E. Θ. ROMANO. EN. XѠ. EVSEB. B. RѠMEON.

Gold - R 4
　„　quinarii - - - - - - - - - - - - - - - - - - R 5
Silver medallions - - - - - - - - - - - - - - - - R 8
First and second brass, with his head only - - - - - - - R 1
　　　　　„　　　with the heads of Zoe, or of Romanus II. - R 4
Third brass, with his head, and that of Zoe, his mother - - - R 4

GOLD AND SILVER.

CONSZANZIN. A.　Full-faced bust of Constantinus X., wearing a
diadem surmounted by a cross, holding in his right hand a double
cross, and in his left a globe surmounted by a cross.—*Rev.* IhS.
XPS. RЄX. RЄGNAT. *(sic)*.　Full-faced bust of Christ on a
cross; the right hand raised, the left holding the book of the
Evangelists. (A *quinarius*).—*Tanini.* - - - - - - - - AU

[CONSTANTINUS X. AND HIS SON ROMANUS II.]
1.
COḂSZAhZ. CЄ. ROMAh. AVGG. ḃA. *or* IB.　Full-faced busts of
Constantinus and Romanus, holding between them a double cross,
each wearing the diadem surmounted by a cross.—*Rev.* ✠ IhS.
XPS. RЄX. RЄGNANZIꝎM.　Full-faced bust of Christ, with the
nimbus, backed by a cross. - - - - - - - - - - - - AU
2.
COḂSZAhZIhOC. CЄ. ROMAh. ЄN. XѠ. ḃLIR. *(sic)*.　Constan-
tinus and his son standing, holding between them a cross; each
holding a globe surmounted by the same emblem.—*Rev.* IhS.
XPS. RЄX. RЄGhANZIꝎM.　Christ seated, full-faced. *(Tanini)*.
　　　　　　　　　　　　　　　　　　　　　AU
3.
CONSZ. ΠORFYROS. CЄ. ROMANO. ЄN. XѠ. ЄYSḃ. RѠMЄON.
in the field of the coin.—*Rev.* IhSꝐS. XRISZꝐS. ḃICA.　A
cross placed on steps. (A small medallion).—*Tanini.* - - - AR

FIRST BRASS.

+. COhSZ. *or* COhSZANZ. BASIL. RωM.   Full-faced bust of Constantinus X., with a diadem surmounted by a cross, holding a globe surmounted by the same emblem.—*Rev.* + COhSZ. Єh. ƟЄO. bASILЄVS. ROMЄOh. in the field of the coin.

[CONSTANTINUS X. AND HIS MOTHER ZOE.]

+ CONSZANZ. CЄ. ZOH. b.   The busts of Constantinus and his mother, holding between them, a cross.—*Rev.* + COhSZANZINO. CЄ. ZOH. bASILIS. ROMЄOh. in five lines in the middle of the coin.

SECOND BRASS.

+ COhSZ. *or* COhSZAhZ. bASIL. Rωm.   Bust of Constantinus X. with a diadem, as before; his right hand on his breast (or holding a standard), his left holding a globe surmounted by a cross.—*Rev.* + COhSZ. ЄN. ƟЄO. bASILЄЧS. ROMЄOh. in the middle of the coin.

[CONSTANTINUS AND ZOE].

These coins have the same types and legends as the large brass.

[CONSTANTINUS, AND HIS SON ROMANUS].

COhZ. *(sic)* ЄZ. ROMAh. b. ROM.   Constantine and Romanus, each wearing a diadem surmounted by a cross, holding between them a globe surmounted by the same emblem. — *Rev.* COhSZ. ЄZ. ROMAh. ЄN. XPISZ. b. ROMЄO. in the middle of the coin. *(Banduri).*

THIRD BRASS.

The third brass are of Constantine and Zoe, and have the same types as the large brass.

ROMANUS.

[Romanus II. was born at Constantinople, in the year of Rome 1691 (A. D. 938).   He succeeded his father, with whom he had been associated, in 1712 (A. D. 959), and died in 1716 (A. D. 963)].

STYLE :——RωM. (or RωMAN.) BASILEVS. RωM.——RωM. (or
RωMAN.) EN. ΘEω. BASILEVS. RωMAIωN.

First and second brass, with the same types - - - - - - - R 4

The Baron Marchant thinks these coins belong to the first emperor of
this name. He assigns to this Romanus, some coins which have hitherto
been considered uncertain. (See his *Melanges de Numismatique, &c.,
Lettre viii.*)

+. RωmAh. bASIL. or bASILEVS. RωM.   Bust of Romanus II.
  wearing a diadem surmounted by a cross, holding in his right hand
  a sceptre, and in his left a globe surmounted by a cross.—*Rev.*
  +. RωmAh. EN. ΘEω. bASILEVS. RωMAIωh. in the centre
  of the coin.

THEOPHANO.

[Theophano, the second wife of Romanus II., was born of an obscure
  family, in the year of Rome—— She was married to the emperor, in
  1712 (A. D. 959); upon whose death, in 1716 (A. D. 963), she was
  nominated Regent during the minority of her sons, Basilius and Constantinus, when she gave her hand to Nicephorus Phocas, who had
  been proclaimed emperor by the army of the East. Theophano con-
  trived the death of Nicephorus, in 1722 (A. D. 969), when the
  murderer, Johannes Zimisces, possessed himself of the throne, and
  banished her to the island of Prote. She was, however, recalled
  by her sons, who had regained the throne, after the death of Zimisces,
  in 1728 (A. D. 975). The time of her death is not known].

STYLE :——ΘEOΦAN. AVGV.

Second brass - - - - - - - - - - - - - - - - - - - R 4

ΘEOΦAN. AYSOY. *(sic)*.   Full-faced bust of Theophano, holding a
  sceptre, and a globe surmounted by a cross.—*Rev.* ΘEOTOC.
  COMOSA. Bust of the Virgin Mary. *(Banduri—Eckhell)*.

Valued by Mionnet at twenty-four francs.

NICEPHORUS II.

[Nicephorus was born of an illustrious family of Constantinople, about the
  year of Rome 1665 (A. D. 912). He was proclaimed emperor by the

army in Asia, of which he was general, after the death of Romanus, in
the year 1716 (A. D. 963), and was murdered, at the command of
his wife Theophano, by Johannes Zimisces, who usurped the throne in
1722 (A. D. 969)].

STYLE:——NICHF. DES.——NICHF. (*or* NICEF. *or* NICIFR.)
BASIL. (*or* BASILEV.) RꞶ. (*or* RꞶM.)——NICH. (*or* NICHF.
or NICEF. *or* NICIF.) EN. ΘEꞶ. BASILEVS. RꞶMAIꞶN.——
NICHF. EN. XꞶ. AVTOCRAT. EVSE. (*or* EVSEB.) BASI-
LEVS. RꞶMAIꞶ.

NICEPHORUS, AND HIS SON-IN-LAW BASILIUS II. ASSOCIATED:—NICHFOP.
CE. BASIL. AVGG.——NIKHFOP. (*or* NIKHΦOR.) KAI.
BASIL. (*or* BACIΛ.) AVG. (*or* AVΓ.) B. P.

Gold - R 6
Silver medallions - - - - - - - - - - - - - - - R 8
First and second brass - - - - - - - - - - - - - - - R 4

GOLD AND SILVER.

1.

+ΘEOTOC. bHΘ. *(sic)* hICHF. ꞆЄS. Full-faced bust of the Virgin
Mary, with the nimbus; on one side, $\overline{\text{M}}$. Θ.; the bust of Nicephorus, holding between them a double cross.—*Rev.* +IhS. XPS.
REX. REGNANTIꝰm. Full-faced bust of Christ, with the
nimbus, placed on a cross, and holding the book of the Evangelists.

AU

2.

+hICHF. Єh. XꞶ. AVꙄOCRAT. ЄVSE. *or* ЄVSEB. bASILEVS.
RꞶMAIꞶ. in the field of the coin.—*Rev.* + IhSꝰS. XRISꙅꝰS.
hICA. A cross; a buckler bearing the head of Nicephorus attached:
on one side, bꙄCF. (A small medallion). - - - - - - AR

[NICEPHORUS, AND BASILIUS.]

1.

NIKΦHOP. KAI. BACIΛ. AVΓ. B. P. Full-faced busts of Nicephorus
and Basilius, holding between them a cross.—*Rev.* IhS. XPS. REX.
REGNANTIꝰM. Bust of Christ, full-faced and with the nimbus,
holding the book of the Evangelists. *(Khell)*. - - - - - AU

Valued by Mionnet at 120 francs.

2.

NICHFOP. CE. bASIL. AVGG. SA. The busts of Nicephorus and Basilius.—*Rev.* IhS. XPS. REX. REGNANTIЧM. Bust of Christ, with the same attributes as on No. 1. (*Tanini*). - - AU

Valued by Mionnet at thirty francs.

FIRST AND SECOND BRASS.

+. NICIFR. (*sic*) BASILEV. RW. (*or* NICHF. BASILЄV. RWM). Bust of Nicephorus, with a diadem surmounted by a cross, holding the labarum and a globe surmounted by a cross.—*Rev.* +. hICHF. Єh. ӨЄW. BASILЄVS. RWmAIWh. in the middle of the field.

JOHANNES I.

[Johannes, surnamed Zimisces, was descended from a noble Armenian family, and was himself a man of great military reputation. He ascended the throne of Constantinople, after having murdered Nicephorus Focas, in the year of Rome 1722 (A. D. 969). Zimisces is supposed to have died of poison, in the year 1728 (A. D. 975). This usurper has been eulogised by Gibbon; but the murder of Nicephorus, and his treatment of the woman to whom he was indebted for his elevation, represent Zimisces in a very odious light].

STYLE:——IWANN. ЄN. XW. AVTOCRAT. EVSE. (*or* EVSEB.) BASILEVS. RWMAIWN. (*or* RWMAIWN.)

Silver medallion - - - - - - - - - - - - - - - R 7
First, second, and third brass (dubious) - - - - - - - - - C

SILVER MEDALLION.

+ IhSЧS. XRISЗЧS. hICA. +. Bust of Johannes Zimisces, on a shield; with the legend, IWAh. surrounded by four crosses; the whole within a triple circle.—*Rev.* + IWAbh. Єh. XW. AVЗO-CRAЗ. ЄVSЄ. *or* ЄVSЄb. bASILЄVS. RWmAIW. . . in five lines, in the middle of the coin; the whole within a triple circle.

Valued by Mionnet at 120 francs.

We are informed by the historians, that the coins which bear on the obverse the effigy of Christ in the place of that of the emperor; and on the reverse, the legend, *Jesus Christ, King of kings,* were first struck during the reign of this emperor. This is confirmed by the appearance of the coins themselves, but it is doubtful whether some of those described below do not belong to other emperors. Many of the brass coins with the types in question are very common, and are therefore not noticed here.

BRASS COINS ATTRIBUTED TO JOHANNES ZIMISCES.

1.

+ ЄMMANOVHL. I͞C. X͞C. Full-faced bust of Christ on a cross, with the nimbus around his head, holding the book of the Evangelists. — *Rev.* + IhSVS. XRISTVS. bASILЄVS. bASILЄ. in the field of the coin. (Large brass).

2.

+ ЄMMANSHA. The bust of Christ. — *Rev.* No legend. The Virgin seated, with the infant Jesus; three Magi approaching with their offerings: above, a star; below, two doves.

The size and the metal of this coin, which is described by Banduri from Ducange, are not known.

3.

+ ЄMMANSHA. Christ, standing. — *Rev.* A cross, between the compartments of which are the words I͞C. X͞C. NICA. (Middle brass).

4.

I͞C. X͞C. Bust of Christ.—*Rev.* M͞P. ΘY. Bust of the Virgin, with the nimbus round the head, and the hands raised. (Middle brass). —*Mus. Vindob.*

5.

No legend. Bust of Christ, with the nimbus, placed on a cross.—*Rev.* ANACTACIC. A circular temple; on each side, a sleeping soldier.

The last is much the rarest: Tanini describes it under Constantinus Magnus. See his note on this curious type.

BASILIUS II.

[Basilius, son of Romanus the Second and Theophano, was born about the year of Rome 1709 (A. D. 956); and when four years of age, was created Augustus by his father, a title which he held during the reigns of Nicephorus and Johannes Zimisces, succeeding the latter in 1728 (A. D. 975). This prince died in 1778 (A. D. 1025)].

STYLE:——BASILIOS. BASILEVS.

BASILIUS II. AND HIS BROTHER CONSTANTINUS XI. ASSOCIATED:—— BASILEI. C. CѠNST. —— BASILIOS. ET. CONSTANT. AVGGV. ——BASILIOS. CE. CONSTANTIN. PISTV. BA- SILIS. ROMEO. (*or* ROMEOI. *or* ROMEON.)—— BASIL. C. CѠNSTAN. ΠORFYROG. (*or* ΠORFYROS.) ΠISTV. BAS. RѠMAIѠ.

Mionnet justly observes, that the supposed coins of Basilius II., with his name only, may with equal propriety be assigned to Basilius I. The coins upon which the names of Basilius II. and Constantine XI. occur, are also uncertain; as Basilius I., and his son Constantine, were also associated. Those, however, upon which the princes have each the sur- name of Porphyrogenitus, belong exclusively to Basilius II. and Con- stantine XI.

Gold medallions, of small size, with his head, and that of his brother
  Constantine - - - - - - - - - - R 6
  „   „   of small size, with the brothers associated, but without
    their heads - - - - - - - - - R 4
  „   of the usual size, with his head, and that of his brother - - R 4
Silver medallions, of large size, with the same heads - - - - R 7
  „   „   of small size, with the same heads - - - - R 6
Second brass (uncertain) - - - - - - - - - - - - - - C

GOLD AND SILVER.

1.

+ bASILIOS. CE. COhSℤANℤIh: PISℤ⁹. BASILIS. ROMEO. The busts of Basilius II. and Constantinus XI., each with a diadem surmounted by a cross, holding between them a long cross.—*Rev.* IHSVS. KPISℤVS. NIKA. A cross, placed on steps. (*Tanini*).

AU

This is a small medallion.

2.

+ ᑐASILIOS. CϹ. COᴜSƵAhƵIh. PISƵV. ᑐASILIS. ROMϹO. *or* ROMϹOI. *or* ROMϹOᴜ. in five lines.—*Rev.* IhSᑫS. XRISƵᑫS. hICA. A cross, placed on steps: below, a globe. (A small medallion). (*Tanini*). - - - - - - - - - - - - - - - - - AU

3.

Ϲh. ƵOYƵⲰ. hICAƵ. ᑐASILϹI. C. CⲰhSƵ. Full-faced busts of Basilius II. and Constantinus XI.; between them, an ornamented cross placed on steps.—*Rev.* + ᑐASIL. C. CⲰᴜSTAᴜ. ᴨORFYROS. ᴨISTV. ᑐAS. RⲰMAIⲰ. in five lines. (A medallion, of large size). - - - - - - - - - - - - - - - - - AR

4.

Same legend. A similar type. (A medallion; but smaller than the former). - - - - - - - - - - - - - - - - - AR

5.

ᑐASILIOS. ϹƵ. COhSƵAhƵ. AᴜᏀᏀᑫ. The busts of Basil and Constantinus, each with a diadem surmounted by a cross, and holding between them a cross.—*Rev.* IhS. XPS. RϹX. REGhAhƵIVm. Christ, seated. - - - - - - - - - - - - - - AU

CONSTANTINUS XI.

[Constantinus, son of Romanus II. and Theophano, was born in the year of Rome 1714 (A. D. 961). He reigned with his brother Basilius until the year 1778 (A. D. 1025), when the death of Basilius left him sole master of the empire. Constantinus XI. died in 1781 (A. D. 1028)].

STYLE:——CⲰNSTANTIN. BASIL. EVSEB. RⲰM.

Gold medallion (*concave*), with his head only (uncertain) - - - R 4

„ medallion, of small size, with his head and that of Basilius his brother - - - - - - - - - - - - - - R 6

„ medallion, of small size, with the brothers associated, but without their heads - - - - - - - - - - - - - R 4

„ of the usual size, with his head and that of Basilius - - - R 4

Silver medallion, of large size, with the same heads - - - - - R 7

„ „ of small size, with the same heads - - - - R 6

Second brass, with the same heads - - - - - - - - - - C

GOLD MEDALLION.

+ CωhSƷAhƷIh. bASIL. ЄVSEb. RωM. Bust of Constantinus XI., full-faced, and with an ample beard, holding a baton and a volume.—*Rev.* + IHS. XIS. *(sic)* RЄX. RЄGhAhƷIЧM. The bust of Christ with the nimbus, within which is a cross, holding the book of the Evangelists. (Concave).

This medallion is described by Tanini (page 428), who assigns it to Constantine XI. from the circumstance of its being concave, a description of coin not in use until this period. This author observes that the first mention of *nummi scyphati*, or cup-shaped coins, occurs in an instrument of the year A. D. 1024, quoted by Ughelli, at which time Constantine and his brother Basilius were associated.

ROMANUS III.

[Romanus, surnamed Argyrus, was born about the year of Rome 1726 (A. D. 973), and was raised to the throne by his marriage with Zoe, daughter of Constantine XI., whom he espoused a few days before the death of that emperor, in the year 1781 (A. D. 1028). Romanus was poisoned and suffocated in a bath by command of his wife, who raised to the empire Michael Paphlago, in 1787 (A. D. 1034)].

No certain coins are known of this prince. The Baron Marchant has, nevertheless, attributed a coin to Romanus III.—*Mélanges, Lettre ii.*

MICHAEL IV.

[Michael, surnamed Paphlago from the country of his birth, was born of obscure parents. He was raised to the empire by Zoe, whom he married, in 1787 (A. D. 1034). Michael died in a monastery, in the year 1794 (A. D. 1041)].

The Baron Marchant attributes to Michael IV. some coins which have been assigned to the first emperor of this name. No others are known.

MICHAEL V.

[Michael, surnamed Calaphates, son of Maria, sister of Michael Paphlago, was adopted by the infamous Zoe, after the abdication of his uncle, in the year of Rôme 1794 (A. D. 1041); but was shortly banished, and eventually shut up in a monastery, by the empress, after being deprived of sight. He died soon afterwards].

No certain coins. The Baron Marchant thinks otherwise, and assigns to this Michael, coins which have hitherto been supposed to belong to Michael the First. *(Mélanges, Lett. ix.)*

CONSTANTINUS XII.

[Constantinus, surnamed Monamachus (the single combatant), was born of a noble family of Constantinople, and raised to the throne by Zoe, who married him, in 1795 (A. D. 1042). This emperor died in 1807 (A. D. 1054)].

STYLE:——CѠNSTANT. (or CѠNSTANTIN.) BASILE. (or BA-SILEVS.) RѠ. (or RѠM.)——EVSEBHS. MONOMAXOS.

It should be borne in mind that only those coins which bear the surname of Monomachus, belong, without doubt, to this emperor. Those which are without this distinction, may possibly belong to another emperor of the same name.

Gold, of the usual size - - - - - - - - - - - - - R 5
Silver medallions - - - - - - - - - - - - - - - R 8

GOLD AND SILVER.

1.

CѠhAhZ. *(sic)* AOSILЄ. m. *(sic)* or CѠhSZAhZ. AOSILЄ. *(sic)*Rm. or RC. Full-faced bust of Constantinus, with a diadem surmounted by a cross, holding the labarum, and a globe surmounted by a cross. —*Rev.* + IdS. *(sic)* XIS. *(sic)* RЄX. REGNANTIhm. *(sic)*. Full-faced bust of Christ with the nimbus, backed by a cross, holding the book of the Evangelists. *(Plate xiii, No. 5).*   - AU

2.

ЄVSЄBH. mohomAXOh.   The emperor standing, wearing the paludamentum, and a diadem surmounted by a cross, holding a long cross and a sheathed sword.—*Rev.* + ΔЄCΠOIhA. CѠZOIC. The Virgin Mary, standing, her head surrounded by the nimbus, and her hands raised. In the field, $\overline{\text{MH}}$. $\overline{\text{OY}}$.   - - - - AR

The foregoing is a small medallion, described by *Tanini*, (p. 428).—

The two legends make but one, beginning with that on the reverse, ΔΕϹΠΟΙΝΑ. ΜΗΤΗΡ. ΘΕΟΥ. ϹΩΖΟΙϹ. ΕΥϹΕΒΗ. ΜΟΝΟ-ΜΑΧΟΝ.—" O Domina Dei Mater serves pium Monomachum."

3.

· . . . ΜΟhΟΜΑΧ. . . . . The emperor standing, full-faced, holding a long cross, and a globe surmounted by a cross—*Rev.* + $\overline{\text{IHS}}$. $\overline{\text{XC}}$. The figure of Christ seated, full-faced, with the nimbus round the head, holding the book of the Evangelists. (This coin is concave).—See *Tanini*, page 429. - - - - - - - - - - AR.

ZOE.

[Zoe, daughter of Constantinus XI. and Helena, was born in the year of Rome 1731 (A. D. 798). Having caused the death of her first husband, the emperor Romanus III., in 1787 (A. D. 1034), she married Michael Paphlago, who embraced a monastic life, in 1794 (A. D. 1041). Zoe then adopted her nephew, Michael Calaphates, who shortly afterwards sent her into banishment. Michael was, however, driven from the throne in the following year by his aunt, by whose orders he was deprived of his eyes; when Zoe caused herself to be proclaimed empress, with her sister Theodora, having first married Constantinus Monomachus, whom she raised to the purple, 1795 (A. D. 1042). This ambitious woman died in the year of Rome 1803 (A. D. 1050)].

Banduri quotes coins of Zoe from Ducange and Strada, but none are known at this time.

THEODORA.

[Theodora, sister of Zoe, was born in the year of Rome 1734 (A. D. 981). She was driven from the throne, and shut up in a monastery, by her brother-in-law Romanus Argyrus, but was released by Zoe, as above related, in 1795 (A. D. 1042). She succeeded Constantinus Mona-machus, in 1807 (A. D. 1054), having borne the title of Augusta during the reign of that prince. Theodora died in the year of Rome 1809 (A. D. 1056)].

STYLE :——ΘΕΟΔ. (*or* ΘΕΟΔΩ. *or* ΘΕΟΔΩΡ. *or* ΘΕΟΔΩΡΑ.) AVG. (*or* ΛVΓΟ. *or* ΟVΓΟV. *or* ΑVΓΟVϹ. *or* ΑVΓΟVϹΤ. *or* ΑVΓΟVϹΤΑ.)

Gold medallions, of small size - - - - - - - - - - - - R 7
  „ of the usual size - - - - - - - - - - - - - - - R 6

GOLD.

1.

+. ΘΕΟΔѠΡΑ.˛ ΑΥΓΟΥϹΤΑ. The Virgin Mary and Theodora, standing, holding between them the labarum. In the field, M. $\overline{\text{O}}$. —*Rev.* IdS. *(sic).* XIS. *(sic).* RΕX. RΕGNANZIhm. *(sic).* The effigy of Christ standing, full-faced, backed by a cross, holding the book of the Evangelists. (A small medallion).

2.

+ΘΕΟΔ. ΑΥΓΟ. (*or* ΘΕΟΔѠΡ. ΑΥΓΟΥϹΤ. *or* ΘΕΟΔѠΡΑ. ΑΥΓΟΥ. *or* ΑΥΓΟΥϹ. Full-faced bust of Theodora, with a diadem surmounted by a cross, holding a sceptre and a globe surmounted by a cross.—*Rev.* $\overline{\text{IC}}$. $\overline{\text{XC}}$. Full-faced bust of Christ, backed by a cross, holding the book of the Evangelists.

3.

Another, of similar type, with the legend ΘΕΟΔѠ. ΑΥG. (*Mus. Vindob.*).

Mionnet values the first at 150 francs, and the others at 100 francs each.

MICHAEL VI.

[Michael, surnamed Stratioticus, was of noble birth, and designed by Theodora as her successor. He was acknowledged emperor after the death of that empress, in the year of Rome 1809 (A.D. 1056). His troops, however, rebelled against him, and having chosen Isaacius Comnenus for emperor, Michael was compelled to abdicate, and retired to a monastery, in which he died, in the year 1812 (A.D. 1059)].

There are no certain coins of this prince; but the Baron Marchant (*Mélanges, Lettre ix.*), is of opinion that those which bear the effigies of an emperor and an empress, with the legend MIXAHA. S. MAPIA. belong to him. This very zealous numismatist observes, that the male figure on these coins has a beard, and the countenance of a man of advanced age, which attributes cannot belong to Michael VII. He is also of opinion, that the silence of historians respecting the wife of Michael the Sixth ought not to be considered sufficient to discredit this new attribution. This writer gives to Michael VII. those coins only which are described by Banduri from *Ducange*, tom. ii, p. 751. On these the prince is without beard, and has a youthful countenance.

ISAACIUS I.

[Isaacius, surnamed Comnenus, was praefect of the East under Theodora,
when he was proclaimed emperor by the soldiers, who compelled
Michael Stratioticus to abdicate, in the year of Rome 1810 (A.D. 1057).
This prince, enfeebled by age, voluntarily abdicated the throne and
retired to a monastery, in 1812 (A. D. 1059), having nominated
Constantinus Ducas as his successor. Isaacius died in the year of
Rome 1814 (A. D. 1061)].

STYLE:——ICAAKIOC. BACIΛEVS. PѠM.——ICAAKIOC. ΔEC.
(or ΔECΠ. or ΔECΠOTHC).

Gold (concave medallion) - - - - - - - - - - - - - R 6
Second and third brass - - - - - - - - - - - - - - R 6

GOLD.

+ICΛΛKIOC. BACIΛE ЧC. PѠm. The emperor standing, full-faced,
wearing the paludamentum, holding in his right hand a naked sword,
and in his left its sheath.—*Rev.* + IЛS. (*sic*) XPS. RЕX. RЕЧ-
NANTIЬM *(sic)*. The effigy of Christ seated, with the nimbus
encircling the head; the right hand raised, and the left holding the
book of the Evangelists. (*Plate xiii, No.* 6).

Valued by Mionnet at fifty francs.

THIRD BRASS.

ICΛΛKIOC. ΔECΠOZHC. The emperor standing, holding in his
right hand a cross, and in his left a scroll.—*Rev.* $\overline{\text{MHP}}$. $\overline{\text{ΘY}}$. The
Virgin standing, with the nimbus encircling her head, and her hands
raised.

Valued by Mionnet at twelve francs.

CONSTANTINUS XIII.

[Constantinus was of the illustrious house of Ducas, from whom he
took his surname. He was born in the year of Rome 1760 (A.D.
1007), and nominated by Isaacius Comnenus as his successor previous
to his resigning the purple, in the year 1812 (A.D. 1059). Constantinus died in the year of Rome 1820 (A. D. 1067)].

STYLE:——CѠNSTANT. (or CѠNSTANTIN. or CѠNSTANTINOS.)
BASILEVS. RѠ. (or ROM.)——CONSTANTIN. (or CONSTAN-

TINOS.) ΔΟΥΚΑS. (or O. ΔΟΥΚΑS.)——KωN. ΔC. (pro
ΔϵϹποⁱης). O. ΔΟΥΚΑS.——KωN. BAS. (or BAC. or BACIΛ.)
ΔΟΥΚΑ (or O. ΔჰK. or O. ΔΟΥϹΛ. or O. ΔΟΥΚΑϹ.)——KωN.
BACIΛϵΥϹ. PωMAIωN. O. ΔჰK.

Gold medallions (concave) - - - - - - - - - - - - - R 4
„ of the usual size - - - - - - - - - - - - - - - R 4
Silver medallions (concave) - - - - - - - - - - - - R 8
Medallions in lead - - - - - - - - - - - - - - - - R 8

GOLD AND SILVER.

1.

CONSTANTIN. O. ΔΟΥΚΑS. Full-faced bust of the emperor, with a
diadem surmounted by a cross, holding a cross, and a globe surmounted by the same emblem.—*Rev.* IHS. XPS. REX. REG-
NANTIVM. The bust of Christ. *(Eckhel).* - - - - - AU

2.

+ COჰϹჇΑჰϹIჩOS. O. ΔΟΥΚΑS. The emperor standing, holding in
his left hand a globe surmounted by a cross; the Virgin Mary
standing by his side, her right hand raised: the letters M̄. O̅. in
the field.—*Rev.* IჩS. XPS. RϵX. RϵGჩΛჩϹIႱM. Christ seated,
holding the book of the Evangelists. (A concave medallion).—
Tanini. - - - - - - - - - - - - - - - - - AU

3.

+ KωN. BAC,ΛI. *(sic.)* O. ΔΟΥΚΑϹ. The emperor, standing in the
imperial habit, highly ornamented, wearing a diadem surmounted
by a cross, holding the labarum, and a globe surmounted by a
cross.—*Rev.* + IᴅⅠS. *(sic).* XPS. RϵX. RϵGNANϹIჩႶ. *(sic).*
The effigy of Christ, seated, full-faced, backed by a cross, holding
the book of the Evangelists. (A concave medallion). - - - AU

4.

KωNII. *(sic.)* ΔC. *(sic)* O. ΔΟΥΚΑϹ. (or + KωNϹAN. *(sic)* O.
ΔΟΥΚΑϹ. The emperor standing, holding the labarum, and a
globe surmounted by a cross.—*Rev.* IჩS. XPS. RϵX. RϵGჩΛჩ-
ϹIႱM. Christ, seated. *(Plate xiii, No. 7).* - - - - - ΛU

5.

Similar legends; but with the effigy of Christ, standing. *(Tanini,* page
430). - - - - - - - - - - - - - - - - - - - ΛR

6.

KωN. BAC, Λ, *(sic.)* O. ΔჂK. Full-faced bust of Constantinus, holding in his right hand a globe surmounted by a cross.—*Rev.* M̅H̅P̅. Θ̅Y̅. Full-faced bust of the Virgin Mary, with the nimbus surrounding her head, and her arms extended. - - - - - AU

7.

+ CωhSZhZh. *(sic),* BASILEYS. Rωω. Full-faced bust of the emperor, holding a long cross, and a globe surmounted by a cross.— *Rev.* + IhS. XPS. REX. REGNANTIhm. *(sic).* Full-faced bust of Christ, backed by a cross, holding the book of the Evangelists. (A concave medallion). - - - - - - - - - - AU

8.

CωNSZANZIh. bASILEYS. ROM. Full-faced bust of the emperor, holding the labarum in his right hand.—*Rev.* + IhS. XPS. REX. REGNANZIhm. *(sic).* Full-faced bust of Christ, holding the book of the Evangelists. - - - - - - - - - - - - - AU

9.

CωhSZAhZIhOS. BASILEYS. Rm. *(sic).* Bust, full-faced, of the emperor, between two stars, holding a globe and a sword.—*Rev.* + IhS. XPS. REX. REGNANTIhM *(sic.)* Bust of Christ, as in the preceding. - - - - - - - - - - - - - - - - - AU

MEDALLION, IN LEAD.

+ KωN. BACIΛEVC. PωMAIωN. O. ΔჂK. The emperor standing, in the imperial habit, highly ornamented, wearing a diadem surmounted by a cross, holding the labarum and a scroll.—*Rev.* ЄM-MANჂEΛ. Full-faced bust of Christ, with the nimbus, placed on a cross, holding the book of the Evangelists.—*(Mionnet*, from the Baron Marchant's *Mel. de Num. et d'Hist.* lettre iv).

Another medallion in lead, is given by the Baron Marchant to this emperor. It bears on the obverse, a monogram, supposed to be that of Constantine, and the words: Tω. Cω. ΔჂΛω.—On the reverse, the following inscription, in four lines: + ΓЄOPΓIω. ΔICPATOPI.

EUDOCIA.

[Eudocia Dalassena, daughter of Constantinus Dalassenus, was wife of Constantinus Ducas, upon whose death, in the year of Rome 1820, (A. D. 1067), she assumed the reins of government, and ruled the empire in the names of her sons, Michael, Constantinus, and Andronicus. In 1821 (A. D. 1068), she married Romanus Diogenes, upon whom she conferred the title of emperor, leaving that of Augustus to her children, who, however, were associated with their father-in-law. Eudocia, after the death of Romanus, was driven from the throne, and shut up in a monastery, in the year of Rome 1824 (A. D. 1071). She died about the year 1849 (A. D. 1096).

STYLE:——EVΔ. (*or* EVK.)——EVΔOKI.——BACIΛ.

Gold medallion (concave)   - - - - - - - - - - - -   R 6
Second brass - - - - - - - - - - - - - - - - - -   R 8

GOLD MEDALLION.

MIX. ЄVΔK. CЄ. KѠbS. Eudocia standing on a cushion, holding a sceptre, between her two sons, each holding a globe surmounted by a cross.—*Rev.* IbS. XIS. *(sic).* RЄX. RЄ ԳNANZIhm. *(sic).* Christ seated on a throne, full-faced, holding the book of the Evangelists.

Valued by Mionnet at 120 francs.

SECOND BRASS.

[EUDOCIA, AND HER SON CONSTANTINUS].

ЄVΔK. AV. KѠNTAb. *(sic).* Eudocia and her son, standing, holding between them the labarum, resting on a flight of steps.—*Rev.* + ЄMMANȢHΛ. Christ, standing, full-faced, holding with both hands the book of the Evangelists. In the field, $\overline{IC}$. $\overline{XC}$. *(Marchant).*

The Baron Marchant is of opinion that this coin may bear the effigy of Constantinus, son of Michael VII. and Maria, and grandson of Eudocia; and thinks that it is the same with the gold medallion. Mionnet, however, controverts this opinion; and observes, that when the son of Michael was born, Eudocia did not hold the imperial dignity, having been deprived of her rank and shut up in a monastery three years previously.

ROMANUS IV.

[Romanus Diogenes, son of Constantinus Diogenes, held a military command under Constantinus Ducas, and was raised to the throne by Eudocia, widow of that emperor, who gave him her hand, in the year

of Rome 1821 (A. D. 1068). This unfortunate prince was captured
by the Turks in 1824 (A. D. 1071); but being set at liberty in the
same year, he returned to resume the government of the empire, when
he was inhumanly deprived of sight, and immured in a monastery,
where he died, shortly after, from the effects of his wounds].

STYLE:——RⲰMAN. (or PⲰMAN. or RⲰMANOC. or PⲰMANOC.
or POMANOC.)——PⲰ. (or PⲰMAN. or ROMANOC.) DES. (or
DESP. or ΔESP. or ΔECΠ.)——PⲰMANOC. ΔECΠOTHC. O.
ΔIOΓENHC.

Gold medallions (concave)	- - - - - - - - - - - - - - -	R 4
Brass medallions	- - - - - - - - - - - - - - - - -	R 8
Brass, of uncertain size (concave)	- - - - - - - - - - - -	R 4
Lead medallions	- - - - - - - - - - - - - - - -	R 8

GOLD.

1.

ⲐCE. *(sic)* bOHⲐI. RⲰMAhⲰ. The emperor standing, holding in his
left hand a globe surmounted by a cross; the effigy of the Virgin,
also standing, with the nimbus round the head, her hand resting on
the head of the emperor; over the head of the Virgin, $\overline{\text{M. O.}}$ —*Rev.*
+IhS. XIS. *(sic)* or XPS. RⲈX. RⲈGNANZIhm. *(sic)*. The effigy
of Christ seated, full-faced, with the nimbus encircling the head.
(*Plate xiii, No.* 8*)*.

2.

+ ⲐⲈOTOC. bOHⲐ. IⲰ. (*for* PⲰ.) ꞈⲈSP. The bust of the emperor,
holding a double cross, and crowned by the Virgin Mary: above
the head of the emperor, a celestial hand; above that of the Virgin,
the letters $\overline{\text{MⲐ}}$.— *Rev.* IhS. XIS. *(sic)* or XPS. RⲈX. RⲈG-
NANTIhM. *(sic)*. The full-faced bust of Christ, with the nimbus
encircling the head, backed by a cross, and holding the book of the
Evangelists.

Valued by Mionnet at twenty-four francs.

[ROMANUS, AND EUDOCIA].

ΡѠΜΑΝѠ. ΑVVΟΜϹ. *(sic) or* +ΡѠΜΑΝS. *(sic)* ϾVΔΤΑ. *(sic) or* ΡѠΜS. *(sic)* ϾVΔ. ΚΟΙΜΙ. *(sic)*. The emperor and empress standing (half-lengths), holding between them a globe surmounted by a long cross.—*Rev.* + ΘΚϾ. ΒΟΗΘ. The bust of the Virgin Mary, with a hood, holding before her with both hands a circular tablet, bearing an infant head. In the field, $\overline{\text{MP}}$. $\overline{\text{ΘY}}$.

[ROMANUS IV., EUDOCIA, MICHAEL, CONSTANTINUS, AND ANDRONICUS].

ΡѠΜΑh. ϾVΔΚΡΙΝ. *(sic)*. The effigy of Christ, standing on a cushion; one hand placed on the head of Romanus, standing on his right, the other on the head of Eudocia, on his left; each holding a globe surmounted by a cross. In the field, $\overline{\text{IC}}$. $\overline{\text{XC}}$.—*Rev.* ΚѠh. MX. ΑΝΔ. *or* ΔhΔ. Michael, standing between Constantinus and Andronicus, each holding a globe surmounted by a cross. The figure of Michael is larger than the two others, and holds the labarum. (A concave medallion).

Valued by Mionnet at 200 francs.

BRASS MEDALLION.

[ROMANUS IV. AND EUDOCIA].

+ ΡѠΜΑΝ. ΔϾϹΠ. The full-faced diademed bust of the emperor, with the imperial mantle, holding a volume in his right hand, and in his left a globe surmounted by a cross.—*Rev.* ϾYΔΟΚΙ. ΒΑϹΙΛ. Full-faced bust of the empress, holding a sceptre and a globe surmounted by a cross.

Valued by Mionnet at 100 francs.

BRASS, OF UNCERTAIN SIZE.

1.

ΘϾΟΤΟΚΟϹ. RѠΜΑhѠ. The emperor and the Virgin Mary, standing.—*Rev.* $\overline{\text{IC}}$. $\overline{\text{XC}}$. The effigy of Christ, seated: (concave). *(Banduri)*.

2.

OHKO. RѠmAhѠ. ΔCCΠOTH. TѠ. ΔIOΓЄNЄI. in the middle of
the coin.—*Rev.* M̅Ρ̅. Θ̅. The effigies of Christ and the Virgin
Mary, seated. *(Banduri).*

MEDALLION, IN LEAD.

[ROMANUS. IV., EUDOCIA, MICHAEL, CONSTANTINUS,
AND ANDRONICUS.].

PѠMANѠ. ЄVΔKPIAA. *(sic).* Romanus and Eudocia standing,
each holding a globe surmounted by a cross : between them, Christ
standing on a cushion ; his hands placed on their heads. In the
field, I̅C̅. X̅C̅.—*Rev.* KѠN. MX. ANΔ. Constantinus, Michael,
and Andronicus, standing on cushions : the first, who stands in the
middle, holds in his right hand the nartex, and a scroll in his left :
each of the two other figures, which are smaller, holds a cross in
his right hand, and a scroll in his left. *(Marchant, Lettre iv).*

The Baron Marchant attributes to this prince several coins in small
brass, which by Ducange are placed among the incerti of John Zimisces.

MICHAEL VII.

[Michael, surnamed Ducas, son of Constantinus XIII. and Eudocia,
was created Augustus by his father, whom he succeeded, and was
associated with his brothers Constantinus and Andronicus, subject to
the authority of Eudocia, in the year of Rome 1820 (A.D. 1067). In
the following year, the empress married Romanus Diogenes, whom
she raised to the empire, when Michael was associated with his father-
in-law. The captivity of Romanus left Michael master of the empire,
and that unfortunate prince, upon his return, was mutilated, and shut
up in a monastery, 1824 (A.D. 1071). Michael was deposed by
Nicephorus Botoniates; and, embracing a religious life, was shortly
after consecrated Archbishop of Ephesus. This prince died in the
reign of Alexius Comnenus].

STYLE : —— MIXAHΛ. BACIΛ. (*or* BACIΛEVS.) MIXAHΛ.
BACIΛ. AVG.——MIXAHΛ. ΔVKOC. *(sic)* BAC.

MICHAEL, AND HIS WIFE MARIA :——MIXAHΛ. S. MAPIA.——MIX-
AHΛ. KAI. MAPIA.——MIXAHΛ. KAI. MAPIA. ΠICTOI.
BACIΛEIC. PѠMAIѠN.

Gold medallions (concave) - - - - - - - - - - - - R 5
,,   of the usual size, with the head of Maria - - - - - - R 6
Silver medallions, of small size, with the head of Maria   - - - R 8
,,   ,, ¯   ,,   (concave) - - - - - - - R 6

GOLD AND SILVER.

1.

+ MIXAHΛ. BACIΛϵV. (or BACIΛOΔ.) (sic) or BΛCIΛ. ⋈ or BAϵIΛ. (sic). Full-faced bust of Michael VII., with a diadem surmounted by a cross, holding the labarum, and a globe surmounted by a cross.—Rev. IX̄. X̄C̄. Full-faced bust of Christ, with the nimbus, backed by a cross, and holding the book of the Evangelists. (A concave medallion). - - - - - - - AU

2.

ʍIXAHΛ. ΔϵCΠOʒ. The Virgin Mary and Michael, standing, holding between them the labarum.—Rev. + IHS. XIS. (sic) RϵX. RϵGhAhʒIqʍ. Christ, seated. (A concave medallion) Tanini. - - - - - - - - - - - - - - - - - - AU

3.

+ MIXAHΛ. ΔVKOC. (sic) BAC. Michael, standing, crowned by the Virgin Mary. In the field, M̄. Ꝺ̄.—Rev. IHS. XIS. (sic) RϵX. RϵGhAhʒIqʍ. Full-faced bust of Christ, holding the book of the Evangelists. (A concave medallion). - - - - AU

4.

MIXAHΛ. bACIΛO. (sic) AVG. The emperor standing, full-faced, holding a long cross in his right hand: his left resting on a sword. —Rev. ꝊKϵ. BOHꝊϵ. TꙶꙶꙶW. CꙶꙶꙶW. ΔOVΛꙶꙶꙶW. The Virgin, standing. M̄P̄. Ꝺ̄Ȳ. (A small concave medallion).—Musei Hedervárii. AR

5.

+ ʍIXAΛ. (sic). BACIΛO. (sic). AqG. The emperor wearing the paludamentum and a diadem, surmounted by a cross, standing, full-faced, holding a long cross in his right hand; his left resting on (ut videtur) a sword.—Rev. + ꝊKIXΛꝊI. ʒOY. WΔObΛ. (sic). The Virgin, standing, her hands raised. In the field, M̄P̄. Ꝺ̄Ȳ. A concave medallion.—(Tanini, p. 431). - - - - - - AR

[MICHAEL, AND MARIA.]

1.

+ MIXAHA. S. MAPIA. Half-length figures of Michael and the empress, standing, full-faced, holding between them a long cross. —*Rev.* + ΘΚЄ. BOHO. The bust of the Virgin, holding on her breast a circular tablet, on which is the head of the infant Jesus. In the field, $\overline{\text{MHP}}$. $\overline{\text{OY}}$. - - - - - - - - - - - - - - AU

2.

MIX. . . . MAPIA. ЄN. YOCTⱲ. *(sic)* NIKATЄ. An ornamented cross, placed on a flight of three steps, between the busts of Michael and Maria. — *Rev.* +. MIXAHA. KAI. MAPIA. ΠICTOI. BACIΛЄIC. PⱲMAIⱲN. in five lines. (A small medallion).— *Mionnet.* - - - - - - - - - - - - - - - - AR

MARIA.

[Maria, an Iberian princess, and wife of the emperor Michael VII., was shut up with her fifth husband in a monastery, in the year of Rome 1831 (A. D. 1078). She, however, came forth from her captivity shortly after, and remounting the throne, married Nicephorus Botoniates, although Michael was still living. Her second husband was deposed by Alexius Comnenus, in 1834 (A. D. 1081), when Maria re-entered her monastery, where she ended her life].

Gold (see the coins of her husband, Michael) - - - - - - - R 6
Silver medallions *(idem)* - - - - - - - - - - - - - - R 8

CONSTANTINUS.

(SON OF CONSTANTINUS XIII).

[This prince was declared Augustus, with his brother Michael, and succeeded with him to the empire after the death of Constantinus XIII., under the control of their mother Eudocia, in the year of Rome 1820 (A. D. 1067. He abdicated the throne in 1831 (A. D. 1078), and was soon after made præfect of the East, by Nicephorus Botoniates. This prince was slain in a battle with Robert Guichard, Duke of Pouille, in the reign of Alexis Comnenes, in 1835 (A. D. 1082)].

(See the coins of Romanus Diogenes, and those of Eudocia.)

ANDRONICUS.

[Andronicus, third son of Constantinus XIII. and Eudocia, died, as is supposed, at an early age, having borne with his brothers the rank of Augustus].

See the coins of Romanus IV.

CONSTANTINUS

(SON OF MICHAEL VII. AND MARIA).

[This prince was born at Constantinople, in the year of Rome 1827 (A. D. 1074), and shortly after was created Augustus by his father. In 1831 (A. D. 1078), he was deprived of his title by Nicephorus Botaniates, and shut up in a monastery; but, upon the deposition of the usurper by Alexius Comnenus, Constantinus was recalled to the court, and received anew the title of Augustus. Constantinus died in the reign of Alexius I.]

No coins are known of this prince; but the Baron Marchant is of opinion that his effigy occurs on the coins of Eudocia Dalassena.

NICEPHORUS III.

[Nicephorus, surnamed Botaniates, is supposed to have been the son of the praefect of Thessalonica. In the reign of Michael Ducas, he commanded the army of Asia, by which he was proclaimed emperor, when, assisted by the Turks, he possessed himself of the throne, and deposed Michael, in the year of Rome 1831 (A. D. 1078). Nicephorus was, in his turn, dethroned by Alexius Comnenus, in the year 1834 (A. D. 1081), when he retired to a monastery].

STYLE:——NIKHΦOS. ΔΕCΠΟΤ.——NIKHΦ (or NIKHF.) ΔE. (or ΔEC.) O. BOTANI. (or BOTANIAT. or BOTANIATHC.)

Gold medallions (concave) - - - - - - - - - - - - - R 6

1.

+ NIKHΦOS. (sic) ΔECΠΟΤ. (or NIKHΦ. ΔEC. TΩ. BOTANI.) The emperor standing, holding the labarum in his right hand, and in his left, a globe surmounted by a cross.—Rev. I͞C. X͞C. Christ seated, full-faced; his right hand raised, and the book of the Evangelists in his left. - - - - - - - - - - - - AU

2.

NIKIIΘ. *(sic) or* NIKIIF. *(sic)* ΔЄ *or* ΔЄC. ΤѠ. BOTANIAT. *or*
BOTANIATHI. A similar type to the preceding.—*Rev.* $\overline{IC}$. $\overline{XC}$.
A similar type to the preceding. - - - - - - - - - AU

Valued by Mionnet at thirty francs each. The legend on the obverse
is curious, the surname of Botaniates being in the dative case.

ALEXIUS I.

[Alexius, son of Johannes Comnenus, the brother of Isaacius I. and Anna
Dalassena, was born at Constantinople, in the year of Rome 1801
(A. D. 1048). He was created Caesar by Nicephorus Botaniates, but
being shortly after proclaimed emperor by the legions in Thracia, he
deposed Nicephorus, and ascended the throne, in 1834 (A. D. 1081).
Alexius died in 1871 (A. D. 1118)].

Style :———ΑΛΕΞI. (*or* ΑΛΕΞIC. *or* ΑΛΕΞIOC.) ΔЄCΠ. (*or* ΔЄC-
ΠΟΤ. *or* ΔЄCΠΟΤΗC.)———ΑΛΕΞIOC. ΔЄC. (*or* ΔЄCΠΟΤ.
or ΔЄCΠΟΤΗC.) O. ΚΟΜΝΗΝΟC.

Gold medallions - - - - - - - - - - - - - - - - - R 4
Silver - R 6
Third brass - - - - - - - - - - - - - - - - - R 4

GOLD AND SILVER.

1.

ΑΛΕΖIѠ. *or* ΑΛЄΞIѠ. *or* ΔΛЄΞIѠ. ΔЄCΠΟΤ. *or* ΔЄCΠΟΤΗ. ΤѠ.
$\overline{\text{KOMNHN}}$Ѡ. The emperor, standing, wearing an embroidered
mantle, holding the labarum, and a globe surmounted by a cross.
Rev. +KЄ. BOHΘЄI. The effigy of Christ seated, full-faced;
the right hand raised, the left holding the book of the Evangelists.
In the field, $\overline{IC}$. $\overline{XC}$. (A concave medallion). *(Plate xiii, No.*10*)*.

AU

2.

ΔΛЄΞI. . . . . . The bust of Alexius, holding a sceptre, and a globe
surmounted by a cross.—*Rev.* MP. ΘY. The bust of the Virgin
Mary, her hands raised, and the portrait of the infant Jesus at her
breast. - - - - - - - - - - - - - - - - - AR

THIRD BRASS.

ΛΛЄXIOC. ΔЄCΠOTHC. The emperor standing, holding the labarum, and a globe surmounted by a cross.—*Rev.* O. ГЄШPГIOC. *or* AГIOC. ΓЄOP. *(sic).* The bust of Saint George, with the nimbus.

JOHANNES II.

[Johannes Comnenus Porphyrogenitus, son of Alexius I. and Irena Ducaena, was born at Constantinople, in the year of Rome 1841 (A. D. 1088); and at the age of four years, created Augustus by his father, whom he succeeded, in 1871 (A. D. 1118). This prince died in 1896 (A. D. 1143)].

STYLE:——IШ. ΔЄCΠOT. (*or* ΔЄCΠOTHC.)——IШ. ΔЄC. (*or* ΔЄCΠ. *or* ΔЄCΠOT. *or* ΔЄCΠOTHC.) ΠOPΦ. (*or* ΠOPΦYP. *or* ΠOPΦYPOГЄNHT.) ——IШ. ΔЄCΠOT. (*or* ΔЄCΠOTHC. O. ΠOPΦY. (*or* ΠOPΦYPOГ. *or* ΠOPΦYPOTЄN. *or* ΠOPΦYPO-ГЄNN. *or* ΠOPΦYPOГЄNHT.) —— IШ. O. KOMNOC. (*or* KOMNЧNOC.)

Gold medallions (concave) - - - - - - - - - - - - - R 4
Silver medallions - - - - - - - - - - - - - - - - R 4
„   „   (concave) - - - - - - - - - - - - R 4
Second and third brass - - - - - - - - - - - - - - R 2

GOLD AND SILVER.

1.

. . Ш. ΔЄCΠ. . . . C. $\overline{TШ}$. ΠO. . . ΦI. . . ГЄ. . . C. *or* $\overline{IШ}$. ΔЄCΠOT. *or* $\overline{IШ}$. ΔЄCΠOT. $\overline{TШ}$. ΠOPΦYPOГЄNHT. The emperor and the Virgin Mary, standing; the latter placing her hand on the head of Johannes, who holds the labarum, and a globe surmounted by a cross. In the field, $\overline{MP}$. $\overline{OY}$.—*Rev.* $\overline{IC}$. $\overline{XC}$. The effigy of Christ, seated, full-faced; the right hand raised, and the left holding the book of the Evangelists. (A concave medallion). *(Plate xiii, No. 9).* - - - - - - - - - - - - - - - AU

2.

+ $\overline{IШ}$. ΔЄCΠOTH. The full-faced busts of the emperor and the Virgin Mary, holding between them a double cross: a celestial hand above the head of the emperor. In the field, $\overline{OY}$. $\overline{MP}$.—*Rev.* $\overline{IC}$. $\overline{XC}$. The effigy of Christ, seated, as before. (A concave medallion). - - - - - - - - - - - - - - - - AU

3.

IѠ. ΔЄCΠOTH. The emperor and Saint George, holding between them a long cross: the first wearing a diadem surmounted by a cross; the other with the nimbus encircling his head, wearing the paludamentum, and holding a sword in his left hand.—*Rev.* I̅C̅. X̅C̅. Type as before. (Concave medallions).   - AU & AR

4.

J̅Ѡ̅. ΔЄCΠOTH. The emperor wearing the diadem, standing; his right hand on his breast, his left supporting a globe surmounted by a cross: on his left, the Virgin Mary. In the field, ΘY. MR.— *Rev.* KЄ. BOHOЄI. Christ seated, full-faced. In the field, I̅C̅. X̅C̅. (A concave medallion).—See *Tanini.* - - - - AU

5.

IѠ. O. KMNOC. *(sic).* The emperor standing, holding the labarum, and a globe surmounted by a cross.—*Rev.* O. A̅. EVΓENIOC. Saint Eugenius standing, grasping in his right hand a staff surmounted by a cross; and holding his garments with his left. In the field, four globules. (A small medallion).—In the Imperial cabinet of *St. Petersburgh.* - - - - - - - - - - - AR

6.

IѠ. O. KOMNNOC. *(sic).* The emperor standing, as on the preceding. *Rev.* O̅. A̅. EVΓENIOC. A similar type, with a transverse line below, intersecting the staff of the cross held by Saint Eugenius. (Imperial cabinet of *St. Petersburgh*). - - - -   - - - AR

7.

IѠ. O. KOMN. ... The emperor standing, as before.—*Rev.* O. ATIO. EVΓENIO. A similar type, with a star in the field. (A small medallion).—In the Imperial cabinet of *St. Petersburgh.* AR

8.

IѠ. O. KOMNNOC. *(sic).* The emperor standing, as before.—*Rev.* Same legend. Saint Eugenius standing, grasping in his left hand a staff surmounted by a cross, and holding his garments with his right: a cross in the field, between the figure and the staff. (A small medallion).—In the Imperial cabinet of *St. Petersburgh.* - - AR

SECOND BRASS.

1.

IⲰ. ΔЄCΠOTHC. The emperor standing, full-faced, holding a cross in his right hand, and a volume in his left.—*Rev.* $\overline{\text{MP}}$. $\overline{\text{ΘY}}$. The Virgin Mary, seated. (Concave).—*Tanini.*

2.

Same legend. The emperor standing, crowned by the Virgin Mary.— *Rev.* $\overline{\text{IC}}$. $\overline{\text{XC}}$. Christ seated, between two stars. (Concave).— *Tanini.*

3.

IⲰ. ΔЄC. ΠOPΦYP. The emperor standing, holding in his right hand a cross, and in his left a globe, surmounted by the same emblem: on his left, the Virgin, seated on a raised throne, her hands elevated.

—*Rev.* $\overline{\text{MP}}$. The Virgin seated, her right hand raised: before $\overline{\Theta}$. her, three men standing, wearing hoods. (*Banduri*, p. 756).

THIRD BRASS.

IⲰ. ΔЄCΠOT. TⲰ. ΠOPΦYPOΓЄNI. The emperor standing, in the imperial habit, holding in his right hand a sceptre, and in his left a globe surmounted by a cross.—*Rev.* $\overline{\text{MP}}$. $\overline{\text{ΘY}}$. Full-faced bust of the Virgin Mary, with the nimbus; her hands raised.

MANUEL I.

[Manuel, son of Johannes II. and Irene, daughter of Ladislaus, king of Hungary, was born at Constantinople, in the year of Rome 1873 (A. D. 1120). He succeeded his father, to the prejudice of his elder brother Isaac, in the year 1896 (A. D. 1143). This prince died in 1933 (A. D. 1180)].

STYLE:——MANVHΛ. (*or* MANꞨHΛ.)——MAN. (*or* MANVHΛ. *or* MANOVHΛ. *or* MANꞨHΛ.) ΔЄ. (*or* ΔЄC. *or* ΔЄCΠ. *or* ΔЄCΠOT. *or* ΔЄCΠOTHC.) —— MANVHΛ. KMNO.) (*pro* Κομνηνος?) —— MANꞨHΛ. ΔЄCΠOTHC. KOMNHN. (*or* KOMNHNOC.) ΔOYKAC.——MANVHΛ. (*or* MANOVHΛ. *or* MANꞨHΛ.) ΔЄCΠOT. (*or* ΔЄCΠOTHC.) O. ΠOPΦYPOΓ. (*or* ΠOPΦYPOΓЄNNHT. *or* ΠOPΦYPOΓЄNNHTOC.)

Gold medallions (concave)	- - - - - - - - - - - - -	R 4
Silver medallions „	- - - - - - - - - - - -	R 6
„ „ „	- - - - - - - - - - - - -	R 6
Base silver (concave)	- - - - - - - - - - - - -	R 6
Brass medallions	- - - - - - - - - - - - - - -	R 1
Second and third brass	- - - - - - - - - - - - - -	C
„ „ with the effigy of Saint George	- - - -	R 2

GOLD AND SILVER.

1.

MANȢHΛ. *or* MANVHΛ. ΔЄCΠOTH. TⲰ. (*or* T̄Ⲱ. in monogram)
ΠOPΦYPOΓЄNNHTⲰ. *or* ΠOPΦYPOΓNNHT. *(sic)* *or* ΠOP-
ΦYPΓЄN̄N̄HTO. *(sic)*. *or* ΠOPΦYPOΓЄNNIT̄Ⲱ. *(sic)*. *or*
ΠOPΦYPOΓЄNNHT̄Ⲱ. *(sic)*. The emperor standing, holding the
labarum, and a globe surmounted by a cross: above, a celestial
hand, resting on the head of the emperor.—*Rev.* + KЄ. BOHΘЄI.
(*or* ROHΘЄI.) *(sic)*. Full-faced bust of Christ, with the nimbus
encircling the head, backed by a cross, holding a scroll in the right
hand. In the field, I̅C̅. X̅C̅. (Concave medallions). AU & AR

2.

MANȢHΛ. ΔЄCΗ.. The emperor standing, and the Virgin, also standing, placing a crown upon his head.—*Rev.* I̅C̅. X̅C̅. Christ, seated,
(Base concave silver).—*Mus. Vindob.* - - - - - - - - AR

3.

MANVHΛ. O. ΘЄOΔⲰPO. The emperor and Saint Theodorus,
standing, the latter in a short habit, holding between them a double
cross, resting on a globe; each holding a sword.—*Rev.* I̅C̅. X̅C̅.
The bust of Christ, between two stars. (*Tanini*, page 434) - AR

4.

MANVHΛ. O. ΘЄOΔⲰPO. A similar type to the preceding.—*Rev.*
I̅C̅. X̅C̅. Christ, seated between two stars. (A concave medallion in pale gold). - - - - - - - - - - - - - - AU

5.

MANV. . . . KON. . . . The emperor standing, holding the labarum
and a sword.—*Rev.* O. AΓIO. ЄYΓЄNIO. The full-length effigy
of Saint Eugenius, his right hand on a cross, his left on his breast.
(*Tanini*). - - - - - - - - - - - - - - - - AR

6.

MNHΛ. *(sic)*. O. KMNO. *(sic)*. The emperor standing, in the imperial habit, holding the labarum and a sword. In the field, a
transverse line, intersecting the staff of the labarum.—*Rev.* Θ.
ΑΓΙΟ. ΕVΓ̈ΕΝΙΟ. The effigy of Saint Eugenius, standing, holding
the labarum, the nimbus encircling the head. In the field, three ⦁
(Imperial cabinet of *St. Petersburgh*). - - - - - - - - - AR

7.

MN. . . . O. K. . . . The emperor standing, as in the preceding. In
the field, between the labarum and the figure, B.—*Rev.* O. ΑΓΙ.
ΕVΓΕΝΙ. A similar type to the preceding. In the field, B.
(Imperial cabinet of *St. Petersburgh*). - - - - - - - - AR

8.

MNΛ. O. KM. . . . The emperor standing, as in the preceding. In
the field, I.—*Rev.* ΑΓΙΟC. ΕVΓΕΝΙΟ. In the field, three ⦁
(Imperial cabinet of *St. Petersburgh*). - - - - - - - - AR

9.

MN. . . . Λ. O. KOM. The emperor standing, as in the preceding. In
the field, K.—*Rev.* O. ΑΓΙΟ. ΕVΓΕΝΙΟ. A similar type. In
the field, two ⦁ (Imperial cabinet of *St. Petersburgh*). - - AR

10.

MNHΛ. O. K. . . . . . The emperor standing, as before. In the field,
K.—*Rev.* O. ΑΓΙΟ. ΕVΓΕΝΗΟ. *(sic)*. A similar type to the
preceding : K. (A small medallion).—Imperial cabinet of *St.
Petersburgh*). - - - - - - - - - - - - - - - AR

11.

MNHΛ. O. K. . . M. The emperor standing, as before. In the field,
KΛ.—*Rev.* O. ΑΓΟ. ΕVΓΕΝΙ. A similar type to the preceding.
(Same cabinet).—A small medallion. - - - - - - - - AR

12.

MNHΛ. O. KMN. The emperor standing, as before : X.—*Rev.* O.
ΑΓΙΟ. ΕVΓΕΝΙΟ. A similar type to the preceding. (A small
medallion).—Same cabinet. - - - - - - - - - - - AR

13.

O. ΑΓΙΟ. ΕVΓΕΝΙΟ. A similar type to the preceding.—*Rev.* O.
ΑΓΙΟ. ΕVΓΕΝΙΟ. A similar type to the preceding. - - AR

BRASS MEDALLION.

1.

MANЅHL. ΔЄCΠOTHC. KOMNHNO. ΛOYKΛC.　The emperor standing, holding a palm branch in his right hand, and a sceptre in his left.—*Rev.* $\overline{\text{IC}}$. $\overline{\text{XC}}$. O. ЄMANЅHΛ.　The bust of Christ. (*Tanini*).

2.

MANЅHΛ. ΔЄCΠOTHC. KOMNHN. ΛOYKΛC.　The emperor standing, holding in his right hand a sceptre, his left hand on his breast: a celestial hand, placing a crown upon his head.—*Rev.* $\overline{\text{IC}}$. $\overline{\text{XC}}$. O. ЄMMANVHΛ.　The bust of Christ.　(*Tanini*).

ALEXIUS II.

[Alexius, son of Manuel the First and Maria, was born in the year of Rome 1920 (A. D. 1167); or, according to some authors, two years later. When two years of age, he was created Augustus by his father, whom he succeeded, in 1933 (A. D. 1180), but under the regency of his mother. This prince was strangled at the command of his cousin Andronicus Comnenus, who usurped the regency; and his mother Maria having shortly afterwards shared the same fate, Andronicus possessed himself of the throne, in 1936 (A. D. 1183)].

STYLE :——ΛΛЄXIVS.——ALE. (*or* ΛΛEZ.) O. KOMN.

The silver coins described below were not known to Eckhel. They have been published by the Conservator of the Imperial Cabinet of Russia,* and from the circumstance of their bearing the figure of St. Eugenius, which appears for the first time on the money of Johannes the Second, are assigned to the Second Alexius. Hitherto the coins of the three emperors of this name were confounded, and there are now several which cannot be distinguished. The gold concave medallion must belong to this emperor, because it bears the name and effigy of Andronicus, who had usurped the regency of the empire.

---

* " Medailles Grecques, etc.," par M. Koehler, Saint Petersburgh : N. Gretsch. (*s. d.*) 1 vol. 8vo., plates.

GOLD AND SILVER.

1.

ALEZ. O. KOMN. The emperor on horseback, to the left (the head full-faced), holding a sceptre in his right hand. In the field to the right, a star.—*Rev.* O. A. EVΓ. N. . . . Saint Eugenius on horseback, to the right (the head full-faced), holding a cross. In the field to the right, a star. *(Koehler)*. - - - - - - - AR

2.

ALEZ. MN. A similar effigy of the emperor: below, a letter, obliterated.—*Rev.* O. A. EVΓ. NO. A similar type to the preceding; a cross in the letter O: below, an initial letter. (Small medallion). —*Koehler.* - - - - - - - - - - - - - - - - - AR

3.

ALE. K. MN. The emperor on horseback, as before; but to the right. *Rev.* O. A. ЄVΓ. A similar type to the preceding. (A small medallion).—*Koehler.* - - - - - - - - - - - - AR

4.

ALЄ. KMN. The emperor, on horseback, as before.—*Rev.* O. A. ЄV. ΓЄ. A similar type to the preceding: flowers between the legs of the horse. (A small medallion).—*Koehler.* - - - - - - AR

5.

ALЄ. KM. The emperor on horseback, as before.—*Rev.* O. A. Є VΓ. O. A similar type: between the legs of the horse, a star. (A small medallion).—*Koehler.* - - - - - - - - - - - - - AR

6.

ALЄ. MN. The emperor on horseback, as before: between the legs of the horse, a star.—*Rev.* O. A. ЄVΓ. NO. A similar type: between the legs of the horse, a letter or numeral. (A small medallion).— *Koehler.* - - - - - - - - - - - - - - - - - - - AR

[ALEXIUS II. AND ANDRONICUS I.]

ΛΛЄXIVS. ANΔP. . . . . The effigies of Alexius and Andronicus, standing; between them Christ, also standing, backed by a cross, extending his arms over each figure. In the field, $\overline{\text{IC. }}$ $\overline{\text{XC.}}$ *Rev.* Without legend. Full-faced bust of the Virgin Mary, the nimbus encircling the head, and the hands raised aloft, in the midst of the fortifications of Constantinople. (A concave medallion.)— *Khell, Supp. to Vaillant.* - - - - - - - - - - - - AU

Valued by Mionnet at 150 francs.

ANDRONICUS I.

[Andronicus, son of Isaacius Comnenus, the brother of Johannes II., was general of the army in the reigns of Manuel and Alexius II. He possessed himself of the throne, after the murder of Alexius, in the year of Rome 1936 (A. D. 1183), having first obtained the regency, by the murder of the empress Maria. This cruel usurper was deposed by Isaac Angelus, whom he had doomed to death; and being delivered into the hands of the populace, was executed with great barbarity, in 1938 (A. D. 1185)].

Style:——ANΔPON. (or ANΔPONIKOC.)——ANΔPONIKOC. ΔECПOTHC.

Gold medallion (concave) - - - - - - - - - - - - - - - R 6
Second brass - - - - - - - - - - - - - - - - - - - R 2
Third brass - - - - - - - - · - - - - - - - - - - R 2

GOLD CONCAVE MEDALLION.

ANΔPONIKOC. ΔECПOTHC.   The emperor standing, holding a sceptre in his right hand, and a globe surmounted by a cross, in his left; Christ standing, placing a garland on his head.—*Rev.* $\overline{\text{MP}}$. $\overline{\Theta Y}$. The Virgin seated, her arms enveloped in her robe. *(Tanini)*.

The second and third brass have the same type.

ISAACIUS II.

[Isaacius, son of Andronicus Angelus, was raised from the scaffold to the empire by the populace, in the year of Rome 1938 (A. D. 1185). In the year 1948 (A. D. 1195), he was deposed by his brother, Alexius Angelus, who shut him up in prison, after depriving him of his eyes. He was, however, replaced on the throne by the Crusaders, who took Constantinople, in 1956 (A. D. 1203), and associated with his son Alexius IV. This unfortunate prince died in the following year, after the murder of his son by Alexius Murzuphlus, who usurped the throne].

Style:——— ICAAKIOC. ——— ICAAKIOC. ΔЄCΠ (*or* ΔЄCΠΟΤ. *or*
ΔЄCΠΟΤΗC.)———ISAAKIOC. BACIL.*

Gold medallions (concave) - - - - - - - - - - - - R 6
Silver medallions   ,,   - - - - - - - - - - - - R 6
Second and third brass (same type as the gold, with or without the
      angel) - - - - - - - - - - - - - - - - - R 2

GOLD AND SILVER.

1.

ICAAKIOC. ΔЄCΠ. The emperor and an angel, standing, holding
between them a sheathed sword : the emperor holds a cross, and is
crowned by a celestial hand; the angel has a nimbus encircling
the head. In the field, X. Ω. X. MI.—*Rev.* $\overline{\text{MHP.}}$ $\overline{\text{ΘY.}}$ The
Virgin seated, full-faced, with the nimbus; the infant Jesus on her
knees. - - - - - - - - - - - - - - - - - - AU

2.

Same legends. Similar types, but with MAI. XM. *or* XOXM. *or* XXM.
AU & AR

SECOND BRASS.

ICAAKI. . . . . . Isaacius II. standing, holding a cross.—*Rev.* $\overline{\text{MP.}}$ $\overline{\text{ΘY.}}$
The Virgin seated, full-faced. (Concave).

ALEXIUS III.

[Alexius was brother of Isaacius II., whom he dethroned, mutilated,
and imprisoned, in the year of Rome 1948 (A. D. 1195); but being
deposed by the French and Venetian crusaders, in 1956 (A. D. 1203),
he fled from Constantinople, when he was captured, deprived of sight,
and shut up in a monastery, where he ended his life].

No coins.

———————

* A leaden seal of this emperor, in the collection of the British Museum,
is engraved at page 504 of this volume. It bears on the obverse the full-
length figure of the emperor, holding a cross and a scroll, and crowned
by a celestial hand: legend, + ICAAKIOC. BACIΛΕVC. POMЄIωN.
O. AΓΓЄΛOC. : on the reverse, the sedent figure of Christ, with $\overline{\text{IC.}}$ $\overline{\text{XC.}}$

ALEXIUS. IV.

[Alexius, son of Isaacius II., was crowned emperor and associated with his father, who had been replaced on the throne, by the Crusaders, in the year of Rome 1956 (A. D. 1203). This prince was strangled, by order of the usurper Alexius Murzuphlus, in the year of Rome 1957, (A. D. 1204)].

No certain coins.

ALEXIUS V.

[Alexius Murzuphlus, was master of the wardrobe, in the reign of Isaacius Angelus and Alexius, his son. He usurped the throne, in 1957 (A. D. 1204), and caused the latter to be strangled; but in the same year was obliged to fly for safety from the scene of his cruelties. He was captured by the Crusaders, who had possessed themselves of Rome for the second time, and condemned to be cast from the Theodosian column. A new empire was now established for some years at Constantinople].

No certain coins are known of this usurper.

FRENCH EMPERORS AT CONSTANTINOPLE.

BALDUINUS I.

[Baldwin, son of Baldwin VIII., Count of Flanders, and Margaret of Alsace, was elected emperor by the Crusaders of Venice and France, who had possessed themselves not only of Constantinople, but also of the whole empire of the Greeks in Europe, in the year of Rome 1957 (A. D. 1204). This prince was defeated by the Bulgarians, who kept him for some months in close captivity, and finally put him to death, in the year of Rome 1959 (A. D. 1206)].

STYLE:——BΔOIN. *(sic).* Δ.

Third brass - R 8

The coin described below, is published by the Baron Marchant, in his " *Melanges de Numismatique, &c.*" *Lettre vii.*

BΔOIN. *(sic).* Δ. Baldwin, standing, wearing a crown and a short habit, holding a small cross in his right hand, and a sword in his left.—*Rev.* Without legend. An ornamented cross.

HENRICUS.

[Henry, brother of Baldwin, was elected regent of the empire, after the defeat of the latter, in the year of Rome 1958 (A. D. 1205). Upon the death of Baldwin, he was created emperor. This prince died in 1969 (A. D. 1216)].

STYLE:——HNPI. O. ΦΛΑΝ.

Third brass - - - - - - - - - - - - - - - - - - - R 8

HNPI. O. Φ$\overline{\Lambda\Lambda}$Ν. (?) Henry, on horseback, to the right, wearing the diadem, and holding a sceptre in his right hand.—*Rev.* O. Λ. ΝΙ. . . St. Nicholas (?) on horseback, to the right; the nimbus encircling his head, and holding a cross in his right hand. *(Marchant).*

PETRUS.

[Peter de Courtenai, Count of Auxerre, and husband of Iolande, sister of
the preceding emperors, was elected emperor of Constantinople upon the
death of Henry, in the year of Rome 1969 (A. D. 1216). He caused
himself to be crowned at Rome by Pope Honorius III.; but, upon his
return, was taken prisoner by Theodorus Angelus, Prince of Epirus,
and died in captivity, not without suspicion of having been assassinated by command of that prince, in the year of Rome 1971 (A. D.
1218). During his captivity, Iolande held the reins of government].

No coins are known of this emperor.

ROBERTUS.

[Robert, son of Peter de Courtenai and Iolande, was crowned emperor
of Constantinople, after the throne had been for some time vacant, and
the government administered by the regent, Conon de Bethune, in the
year of Rome 1974 (A. D. 1221). Robert died in 1981 (A. D.
1228)].

No coins are known of Robertus.

BALDUINUS II.

[Baldwin, brother of Robert de Courtenai, was elected emperor, after
the death of the preceding, in the year of Rome 1981 (A. D. 1228).
Baldwin was dethroned by Michael Paleologos, who retook Constantinople from the French, in 2014 (A. D. 1261), and retired into Italy,
in which country he died, in the year of Rome 2025 (A. D. 1272)].

No coins are known of this emperor.

THEODORUS I.

[Theodorus, husband of Anna Comnena, the daughter of Alexius III., was born in the year of Rome 1929 (A. D. 1176). He retired into Asia upon the taking of Constantinople by the Crusaders, and having possessed himself of Bithynia and some other provinces, he caused himself to be proclaimed Emperor of the East at Nicæa, where he established his court, in the year 1958 (A. D. 1205). This prince died in 1975 (A. D. 1222)].

"Three princes of the name of Theodorus," says Mionnet, "reigned at Thessalonica and at Nicæa, during the occupation of Constantinople by the Crusaders; and it is difficult to say to which of these princes belong the coins which bear their name." This author prefers placing them to the reign of the second Theodorus.

THEODORUS II.

[Theodorus, the son of Johannes Angelus, held possession of a part of Epirus and other provinces, after the death of his brother Michael, who had formed a state, after the taking of Constantinople by the Crusaders. He took the title of emperor, and caused himself to be crowned, at Thessalonica in Macedonia, in the year of Rome 1976 (A. D. 1223). In 1983 (A. D. 1230) he was defeated and made prisoner, by Azan, king of the Bulgarians. This barbarian caused the captive emperor to be deprived of sight; but Theodorus shortly after regaining his liberty, returned to Thessalonica, when he found that his brother Manuel had usurped the sovereignty. Manuel was driven from the throne, when Theodorus renounced in favour of his son Johannes, who was soon deposed by Johannes Vatatzes].

STYLE :——ΘΕΟΔѠΡΟC. ΔΕCΠΟΤΗC.——ΘΕΟΔѠΡΟC. ΔȣΚΑC. ——ΘΕΟΔѠΡΟC. ΔΕCΠΟΤΗC. Ο. ΔΟΥΚΑC.——ΘΕΟΔѠ- ΡΟC. ΔΕCΠΟΤΗC. ΚΟΜΝΗΝΟC. Ο. ΔȣΚΑC. [But, quære, the appropriation of these titles?]

Silver medallions - - - - - - - - - - - - - - - R 8
First, second, and third brass (concave) - - - - - - - - - R 4

SILVER.

+OEOΔⲰPOC. ΔꙞKAC. O. AΓIOC. ΔHMHTPIOC. Theodorus and St. Demetrius standing, holding between them a long cross; the first wearing the imperial habit, the other with the paludamentum and the nimbus.—*Rev.* ĪC. X̄C. Christ seated. In the field, IC. on one side; and AK. . . . on the other. *(Sestini).*

FIRST BRASS.

OEOΔⲰPOC. ΔECΠOTHC. KOMNHNOC. O. ΔꙞKAC. The emperor, standing, holding a sceptre and a globe surmounted by a cross; a celestial hand above the head of the emperor.—*Rev.* ĪC. X̄C. EMMANꙞHA. The bust of Christ. (Concave).—*Tanini.*

SECOND BRASS.

1.

OEOΔⲰPOC. ΔECΠOTHC. O. AΓIOC. MI. A cross placed on steps, between the busts of the emperor and St. Michael.—*Rev.* +. OEOΔⲰPOC. ΔECΠOTHC. O. ΔOYKAC. in the field of the coin. *(Tanini).*

2.

OEOΔⲰPOC. ΔECΠOTHC. The emperor, standing.—*Rev.* ĪC. X̄P. (*sic*). Bust of Christ. (Concave coin).—*Tanini.*

THIRD BRASS.

. . . OΔⲰP. . . . . . A cross placed on steps, between the busts of the emperor and the Virgin Mary. — *Rev.* + OEOΔⲰPOC. ΔEC-ΠOTHC. O. ΔOYKAC. in five lines. *(Eckhel—Mus. Vindob.)*

JOHANNES III.

[Johannes, son-in-law of Theodorus I., was born at Didimotichos in Thrace, in the year of Rome 1946 (A. D. 1193). He succeeded to the empire formed by his father, and was crowned at Nicæa, the capital, in 1975 (A. D. 1222). This prince died at Nymphæa in Bithynia, in the year 2008 (A. D. 1255)].

STYLE:——IѠ. ΔЄ..... O. Δ8KAC.

Third brass - - - - - - - - - - - - - - - - - - - R 8

IѠ. ΔЄ. . . . O. Δ8KAC. The emperor standing, full-faced, with the imperial mantle and diadem, holding the labarum (or a long cross) in his right hand, and a scroll in his left.—*Rev.* O̅. A̅. Γ̅Ѡ̅P̅. (in two monograms, for O. Aγιos ΓεΩPγιos.) The full-faced bust of Saint George, with coat of mail, and the nimbus encircling the head, holding in the right hand a spear.

Banduri and Ducange give a coin with a similar type to the above; but instead of IѠ, a contraction, thus, Ѡ̅. These writers are of opinion that a K preceded this contracted word, and therefore assign the coin to Constantinus XIII. (Ducas). The Baron Marchant, however, thinks otherwise, and remarks that there is no room for another letter, and supposing the horizontal line to be intended for an iota, attributes this piece to Johannes Vatatzes. A coin quoted by Mionnet, in the cabinet of the French king, warrants this new attribution.

THEODORUS III.

[Theodorus, son of Johannes Vatatzes and Helena, daughter of Theodorus I., was born in the year of Rome 1976 (A. D. 1223). He succeeded his father at Nicæa, in 2008 (A. D. 1255), and died in the year 2012 (A. D. 1259)].

No coins.

JOHANNES IV.

[Johannes, son of Theodorus III. and Helena, daughter of Asan, king of the Bulgarians, was born about the year of Rome 2004 (A. D. 1251). He succeeded his father, in 2012 (A. D. 1259), and was dethroned by Michael Paleologos, who deprived him of sight, and banished him to Bithynia, in 2014 (A. D. 1261). This unfortunate prince died in the place of his exile, in the reign of Andronicus the Second].

No coins.

MICHAEL VIII.

[Michael, son of Andronicus Paleologos, usurped the regency of the empire established at Nicæa, after having murdered Muzalo, the guardian of the young prince Johannes IV., with whom he associated himself, but whom he shortly after banished to Bithynia, about the year of Rome 2012 (A. D. 1259). He retook from the French the city of Constantinople, in which he re-established the seat of the Greek empire, in 2014 (A. D. 1261). This usurper died in 2035 (A. D. 1282)].

Style: —— MIXAHΛ. ΔΕCΠΟΤΗC. ΠΑΛ. . . —— MIXAHΛ. ΔΕCΠΟΤ. Ο. ΠΑΛΕΟ.

Gold medallions (concave) - - - - - - - - - - - - - - R 8
Third brass - R 8

GOLD.

MIXAHΛ. ΔΕCΠΟΤ. Ο. ΠΑΛΕΟ.   The Virgin, presenting the emperor, who kneels to Christ, seated.   In the field, $\overline{\text{IC}}$. $\overline{\text{XC}}$. and M.—*Rev.* $\overline{\text{MP}}$. $\overline{\text{ΘY}}$.   Bust of the Virgin, with her arms extended, in the midst of the walls of Constantinople. *(Pellerin).*

THIRD BRASS.

[MICHAEL, AND ANDRONICUS].

MIXAHΛ. ΔΕCΠΟΤΗC. ΠΑΛ....   The emperor standing, full-faced, holding a volume in his left hand.—*Rev.* ΑΝΔΡΟΝΙΚΟC. ΔΕCΠ... ΠΑΛ.   A similar type. *(Tanini).*

The legends on this coin are retrograde.

ANDRONICUS II.

[Andronicus, son of Michael VIII. and Theodora, the daughter of Johannes Ducas, was born about the year of Rome 2011 (A. D. 1258). He was declared emperor by his father, 2026 (A. D. 1273), whom he succeeded in 2035 (A. D. 1282). This emperor was dethroned by his grandson, Andronicus III., in 2081 (A. D. 1328), and retiring to private life, died in 2086 (A. D. 1333)].

STYLE:——ANΔPONIK. (*or* ANΔPONIKOC.)——ANΔPONIKOC.
ΔЄCΠOTHC.——ANΔPONIKOC. ΔЄCΠ. . . . ΠAΛ.——ANΔ-
PONIKOC. ЄN. XⲰ. bACIΛ.——ANΔPONIKOC. ЄN. XⲰ.
ΔЄCΠOT. ΠOΛЄⲰs. POMαιων. *(sic).*

Gold medallions (concave) - - - - - - - - - - - - - R 6
Silver, of the usual size - - - - - - - - - - - - - - R 8
Third brass - - - - - - - - - - - - - - - - - - - R 6

GOLD AND SILVER.

1.

ANΔPNICOC. *(sic)* ЄN. XⲰ. ΔЄCΠOT. ΠOΛ. POM. *(sic).* Christ
standing, placing his hand on the head of the emperor, who kneels
before him.—*Rev.* Without legend. The full-faced bust of the
Virgin Mary, with her arms extended, in the midst of the battlements of Constantinople. *(Liebe, Gotha Numaria).* - - - AU

2.

ANΔPNKOC. *(sic)* X̄Ⲱ̄. *(sic) or* ANΔPONIKOC. . . . . ΠOTHC.
. . . . OΛC. . . . ΠΛ. Christ standing, placing his hand on the
head of the emperor, who kneels before him. In the field, ĪC̄. X̄C̄.
and the monogram of Christ.—*Rev.* The Virgin in the midst of the
battlements of Constantinople, as before. - - - - - - AU

3.

ANΔPONIKOC. . — O. AΓ. ΔHMHTPOC. The emperor and Saint
Demetrius, standing.—*Rev.* ĪC̄. X̄C̄. Christ, seated. (See *Ses-*
tini's Lettere, tom. ii.) - - - - - - - - - - - - AU

[ANDRONICUS II., AND HIS SON MICHAEL IX.]

1.

ANΔ. . . . . XAHΛ. Christ, standing; his right hand resting on the
head of the emperor, and his left on that of Michael, his son. In
the field, ĪC̄. X̄C̄.—*Rev.* Without legend. Full-faced bust of the
Virgin, as in the other types, Nos. 1 and 2. - - - - - AU

2.·

ANΔPONIK. *(retrograde)* MXAHΛ. *(sic).* Andronicus and his son
standing, holding between them a labarum.—*Rev.* ANΔPONIKOC.
ΔЄCΠOTHC. A shield, charged with a cross. - *(Eckhel).* AR

THIRD BRASS.

1.

ANΔ. . . . The bust of Andronicus, holding a cross in his right hand, and in his left a globe surmounted by a cross.—*Rev.* KYPIϵ. BOHΘϵI. A shield, charged with a cross. *(Mus. Vindob.).*

2.

ANΔNIKOC. *(sic).* The emperor standing, full-faced, wearing a diadem surmounted by a cross, holding a labarum, and a globe surmounted by a cross.— *Rev.* AΓIOC. ΔHMHTPOC. Saint Demetrius standing, full-faced, with the nimbus encircling the head, holding a spear and a buckler. *(Marchant,* letter x.)

[ANDRONICUS, AND HIS SON MICHAEL IX.]

ANΔPONIK. *(retrograde)* MXΛHΛ. *(sic).* The emperor and his son standing, holding between them the labarum.—*Rev.* ANΔPO-NIKOC. ΔϵCΠOTHC. A shield, charged with a cross. *(Mus. Vindob.).*

MICHAEL IX.

[Michael, the son of Andronicus the Second, and Anna daughter of Stephen King of Hungary, was born in the year of Rome 2030 (A.D. 1277), and in 2048 (A. D. 1295) was associated with his father in the empire. This prince died in 2073 (A.D. 1320)].

STYLE, ASSOCIATED WITH HIS FATHER :——MIXAHΛ.

Gold medallions (concave) - - - - - - - - - - - - -	R 6
Silver, of the usual size - - - - - - - - - - - - -	R 8
Third brass - - - - - - - - - - - - - - - - - -	R 6

(See the coins of his father).

ANDRONICUS III.

[Andronicus, son of Michael IX. and Maria Armenia, was born about the year of Rome 2048 (A.D. 1295). He was associated with his grandfather in 2078 (A. D. 1325), whom he deposed in 2081 (A. D. 1328). Andronicus the Third died in the year of Rome 2094 (A. D. 1341)].

If any coins exist of this prince, they are confounded with those of the second Andronicus.

JOHANNES V.

[Johannes, son of Andronicus III, and Anna of Savoy, was born at Didimotichos in Thrace, in the year of Rome 2085 (A. D. 1332). In 2094 (A. D. 1341) he succeeded to the empire, under the tuition of his mother and the guardianship of Johannes Cantacuzenus, whom he was compelled to receive as his colleague in the empire, in 2100 (A. D. 1347). Cantacuzenus was forced, after some contention, to renounce the throne, in 2108 (A. D. 1355). Johannes being deposed by his son Andronicus, who shut up his father and his brother Manuel in prison, in 2124 (A. D. 1371), was restored to the throne, with the assistance of the Sultan Bajazet, in 2126 (A. D. 1373), and died in the year of Rome 2144 (A. D. 1391)].

No coins are known of Johannes V.

JOHANNES VI.

[Johannes, surnamed Cantacuzenus, was descended from a noble family, and held the office of grand master of the palace under Andronicus III.; and upon the death of that prince, was left guardian of his son Johannes V., in conjunction with the empress Anna, in the year of Rome 2094 (A. D. 1341). A dispute arising between the two guardians, Cantacuzenus caused himself to be proclaimed emperor in the same year, and compelled the young prince to receive him as his colleague in the empire, in 2100 (A. D. 1347). The usurper, however, was forced to relinquish the throne, in the year of Rome 2108 (A. D. 1355), and retired to a monastery, in which he ended his life].

STYLE:——IⲰ. CЄBAϛOC. KAI. MЄΓAC. ΔOMЄCTIKOC.

A medallion in lead, is thus described by Sestini, in his "*Lettere e Dissertazioni Numismatiche*," tomo ii. page 183 :—

O. ΔHMHTPIOC. The bust of St. Demetrius, with the nimbus, holding a spear in his right hand.—*Rev.* + IⲰ. CЄBAϛOC. KAI. MЄΓAC. ΔOMЄCTIKOC. in the field.

The Baron Marchant, in commenting on this coin (or *seal?*), observes that it is not likely that an emperor would use the title of Σεβαστος, in conjunction with the inferior qualification of Δομεστιχος. This writer is of opinion, that Σεβαστος is put for Σεβαστοκρατωρ; and that the coin, or seal, in question, belongs to some prince who was not emperor; perhaps to Johannes Paleologos, brother of Michael VIII.

MATTHAEUS.

[Matthaeus, son of Johannes VI. and Irene, was created emperor by his father, during the contention between the latter and Johannes Paleologos, his colleague, in the year of Rome 2107 (A. D. 1354), and crowned in the following year, after their reconciliation. Upon the abdication of his father, Matthaeus would have maintained his rank by force of arms, but being defeated and made prisoner, he was only restored to liberty upon his agreeing to retire to private life, in 2109 (A. D. 1356). He was allowed, nevertheless, to bear the empty title of *despot*].

No coins are known of this prince.

ANDRONICUS IV.

[Andronicus, surnamed Paleologos, son of Johannes V. and Helena Cantacuzenus, was associated in the empire with his father, as is supposed, after the abdication of Cantacuzenus and his son. This prince deposed his father, whom, with his brother Manuel, he imprisoned, in the year of Rome 2124 (A. D. 1371). His father having been restored to the throne by the Sultan Bajazet, in 2126 (A. D. 1373), Andronicus abdicated in favour of his brother Manuel, and retired into Thrace, where he died].

No coins of this prince are known.

MANUEL II.

[Manuel, son of Andronicus IV., was born in the year of Rome 2101 (A. D. 1348). Declared emperor in 2126 (A. D. 1373), his brother Matthaeus having renounced in his favour. This prince succeeded his father in 2144 (A. D. 1391), and died in 2178 (A. D. 1425)].

No coins of Manuel II. are known.

JOHANNES VII.

[Johannes, son of Andronicus IV. was created emperor by his uncle Manuel, in the year of Rome 2152 (A. D. 1399), but was compelled to abdicate the throne in 2155 (A. D. 1402) by Manuel, who banished him to the Island of Lemnos. He subsequently obtained the sovereignty of Thessalonica. This prince ended his life in a monastery].

No coins are known.

JOHANNES VIII.

[Johannes, son of Manuel II. and Irene, daughter of Constantinus Dragases, was born in the year of Rome 2143 (A. D. 1390); created Augustus in 2172 (A. D. 1419); succeeded his father in 2178 (A. D. 1425), and died in 2201 (A. D. 1448)].

A large gold medallion of this prince has been quoted by old writers, but its authenticity is doubted. It is thus described :—

IꙶẆ. ЄN. XẆ. ΑΥΤΟΚΡΑΤẆΡ. Ο. ΠΑΛΛΙΟΛΟΓΟC. The emperor standing, full-faced, holding a cross in his right hand, and a horn in his left.—*Rev.* IC̅. X̅C̅. The effigy of Christ, seated, holding aloft a cross in the right hand, and in the left, the book of the Evangelists.

This medallion is engraved in *Tanini's Supp. to Banduri.*

CONSTANTINUS XIV.

[Constantinus Paleologos, the fourteenth emperor of that name, was the brother of Johannes VIII. He was born in the year of Rome 2156 (A.D. 1403). He ascended the throne in 2201 (A. D. 1448), after the death of his brother. This prince, during the memorable siege of Constantinople, displayed ability, fortitude, and courage, not unworthy the heroes of ancient Rome. He was killed in the general assault on the city, in the year of Rome 2206 (A. D. 1453)].

The gold medallion described below is given by some writers; but it is not authenticated.

ΚѠΝ⸱ΑΝΤΙΝΟC. ЄΝ. ΧѠ. ΛΥΤΟΚΡΑΤѠΡ. Ο. ΠΑΛΛΙΟΛΟΓΟC.
The emperor standing, full-faced, holding in his right hand a cross, and in his left, a volume.—*Rev.* $\overline{IC}$. $\overline{XC}$. The effigy of Christ, seated; the right hand raised, the left holding the book of the Evangelists. In the field, Φ.

Leaden Seal of Isaacius Angelus; see page 491.

UNCERTAIN COINS.

THIRD BRASS.

1.

Laureated head of Jupiter, to the right.—*Rev.* S. C. An eagle with expanded wings, standing on a thunderbolt.

2.

A bearded head, with the ancient diadem, to the right.—*Rev.* S. C. An eagle, with expanded wings.

3.

A bearded diademed head, to the right.—*Rev.* S. C. An eagle, on a thunderbolt.

4.

The bearded head of the Tiber, to the right, crowned with water weeds. —*Rev.* S. C. Romulus and Remus, suckled by the wolf.

Visconti has supposed this bearded head to be that of Romulus, but Mionnet observes that it is much more likely to be the head of the Tiber.

5.

IMP. III. An eagle with expanded wings, standing on a sceptre.—*Rev.* COS. IIII. A winged thunderbolt.

6.

The diademed head of Juno (or of the younger Faustina?)—*Rev.* S. C. A dove.

7.

The helmed head of Minerva, to the right.—*Rev.* S. C. An owl.

8.

The same head.—*Rev.* S. C. An olive branch.

9.

The same head.—*Rev.* S. C. A cornucopia.

10.

The same head.—*Rev.* S. C. A club.

11.

The same head.—*Rev.* S. C. within a laurel garland.

12.

The same head.—*Rev.* ROMA. across the field.

13.

A bearded helmed head, with coat of mail, to the right.—*Rev.* S. C. A coat of mail.

14.

A bearded, helmed head.—*Rev.* S. C. A trophy.

15.

A bearded, helmed head.—*Rev.* S.C. The Roman eagle, between two standards.

16.

The head of Mercury, with the petasus.—*Rev.* S. C. A caduceus.

17.

A petasus.—*Rev.* S. C. A caduceus.

18.

An infant bust, with a garland of ivy and vine leaves.—*Rev.* S. C. within a garland of ivy and vine leaves.

This bust is thought by some, to be that of Annius Verus. There are several varieties of this coin. On some, the bust, has the chlamys.

19.

An infant head, veiled, and crowned with sea weeds.—*Rev.* S. C. within an olive garland.

20.

A griffin squatting, one foot resting on a wheel.—*Rev.* S. C. A tripod.

21.

A horse, with saddle and bridle, to the right.—*Rev.* A hammer.

22,

A rhinoceros, to the left.—*Rev.* S. C. An olive tree.

23.

A vexillum.—*Rev.* Mars, marching, with a trophy and a spear.

24.

A vexillum.—*Rev.* Minerva standing, an owl on her right hand, and a spear in her left.

25,

A diota.—*Rev.* The modius, holding three ears of corn.

26.

A galley.—*Rev.* D. in the middle of the field.

27.

TR. in monogram.—*Rev.* G. in the middle of the field.

28.

A sceptre, surmounted by a human head.—*Rev.* A. P. P. F, within an oak garland.

29.

Two horse shoes.—*Rev.* TRIVMP. An olive tree. In the field, IO. IO.

APPENDIX.

COMMODUS.

VICT. BRIT. P. M. TR. P. X. IMP. VII. COS. IIII. P. P.   Victory, seated on a heap of bucklers, holding a buckler and a palm-branch.

This coin, engraved at page 323, is omitted in the text. It is not of very uncommon occurrence, but is much valued in this country, especially when fine.

PHILIPPUS THE ELDER.

IMP. M. IVL. PHILIPPVS. AVG.   Radiated head of Philippus, regarding the right.—*Rev.* P. M. TR. P. IIII. COS. II. P. P.   A woman, standing; a caduceus in her right hand, and a cornucopia in her left. - - - - - - - - - - - - - - - - - - AR

This denarius, in *Mr. Brumell's* cabinet, appears to be of good silver: it weighs, though smaller than the usual silver of this emperor, four or five grains more than the usual denarii with the head regarding the left.

GALLIENUS.

The two following types, in third brass, are taken from the catalogue of the *Berne* collection :—

FELICI. AET.   Felicity, leaning on a column, and holding a caduceus.

VIC. GAL. AVG.   Victory, standing, holding a buckler resting on a cippus.

FLORIANUS.

VIRTVS. FLORIANI. AVG.   Laureated bust of Florianus to the left, with javelin and buckler.—*Rev.* VIRTVS. AVG.   The emperor, standing, holding the parazonium and a globe: a captive at his feet.
AR

This coin, of pure silver, is in the collection of the *Berne Museum.* I have followed Mionnet, in asserting that there is no good silver of this period; but the coin in question is almost a proof to the contrary; besides, the very rare denarii of Julianus Tyrannus are of good silver. The quantity of good silver coined at this period may have been small; but it exceeds what may otherwise be considered mere trial pieces.

GALERIUS MAXIMIANUS.

The coin described at page 194, as having brought 8*l.* 8*s.* at the Trattle sale, had not the head of Mars, but the full-length figure of that deity, in the attitude of combat, with shield and spear: in the exergue, SIS. This coin, which was purchased by Mr. Brumell, is probably unique; as is perhaps that with the head of Mars, formerly in the cabinet of the French king.

MAXIMINUS DAZA.

IOVI. CONSERVATORI. AVG.   Jupiter, seated on an eagle with
    expanded wings.   In the exergue, PTR.   - - - - - - AR

SOLI. INVICTO. COMITI.   The Sun, in a quadriga, full-faced.   In the exergue, PTR.

Page 374, Vol. I.   The gold medallions, Nos. 1 and 2, were bought at D'Ennery's sale, for the French cabinet.   They cost together, in one lot, 501 francs.   Mionnet's estimation is far below their real value.

The suite of quinarii, consisting of 218 gold, and 225 silver coins, brought, in one lot, at the sale of D'Ennery's cabinet, 2190 francs; but doubtless many of them were dubious; being in all probability casts from moulds, formed from the brass of the size of the quinarius; indeed, this has been proved in some instances.

Page 222.   The silver of the younger Licinius is extremely base.

Page 253.   *Fine* silver of Constantinus Junior, if any really exists, is of the first rarity.

Page 268.   The silver of the large size, both of Constantinus II. and Constans, is much rarer than that of small size.

Vol. I. page 53.   The Horatia was a spurious coin.

In the *Catalogue d'Ennery* are engraved two medallions, which are not noticed by Mionnet.   Were they discovered to be spurious?   They brought, in one lot, 220 francs.   One was of Caracalla; the other, of Severus Alexander; and both were mounted in an ornamented border. The first bore the figure of Victory, seated on arms, and inscribing on a buckler: before, a trophy, to which are attached two captives: legend— P. M. TR. P. XX. COS. IIII. P. P.: in the exergue, VIC. PART. That of Alexander, bore the figure of Mars, marching, with spoils: legend—P. M. TR. P. VI. COS. II. P. P.

INDEX TO VOL. II.

THE END.